Emotions in Personality and Psychopathology

EMOTIONS, PERSONALITY, AND PSYCHOTHERAPY

Series Editors:
Carroll E. Izard • *University of Delaware, Newark, Delaware*
and
Jerome L. Singer • *Yale University, New Haven, Connecticut*

HUMAN EMOTIONS
Carroll E. Izard

THE PERSONAL EXPERIENCE OF TIME
Bernard S. Gorman and Alden E. Wessman

THE STREAM OF CONSCIOUSNESS: Scientific Investigations into the
Flow of Human Experience
Kenneth S. Pope and Jerome L. Singer, eds.

THE POWER OF HUMAN IMAGINATION: New Methods in Psychotherapy
Jerome L. Singer and Kenneth S. Pope, eds.

EMOTIONS IN PERSONALITY AND PSYCHOPATHOLOGY
Carroll E. Izard, ed.

A Continuation Order Plan is available for this series. A continuation order will bring delivery of each new volume immediately upon publication. Volumes are billed only upon actual shipment. For further information please contact the publisher.

Emotions in Personality and Psychopathology

Edited by
Carroll E. Izard
University of Delaware
Newark, Delaware

Plenum Press · New York and London

Library of Congress Cataloging in Publication Data

Main entry under title:

Emotions in personality and psychopathology.

(Emotions, personality, and psychotherapy)
Bibliography: p.
Includes index.
1. Emotions. 2. Defense mechanisms. 3. Personality. 4. Psychology, Pathological. I.
Izard, Carroll E. [DNLM: 1. Emotions. 2. Personality. 3. Psychotherapy. BF531 E54]
BF531.E52   616.8'9   78-10958
ISBN 0-306-40093-6

© 1979 Plenum Press, New York
A Division of Plenum Publishing Corporation
227 West 17th Street, New York, N.Y. 10011

Printed in the United States of America

Contributors

James R. Averill, University of Massachusetts, Amherst, Massachusetts

Aaron T. Beck, The University of Pennsylvania School of Medicine, Philadelphia, Pennsylvania

Sandra Buechler, University of Delaware, Newark, Delaware

Hope R. Conte, Albert Einstein College of Medicine, Bronx, New York

Hartvig Dahl, Downstate Medical Center, State University of New York, Brooklyn, New York

Thomas Eby, Purdue University, Lafayette, Indiana

Deborah Everhart, University of Wisconsin, Madison, Wisconsin

Ralph V. Exline, University of Delaware, Newark, Delaware

Edward G. Gottheil, Thomas Jefferson University, Philadelphia, Pennsylvania

J. A. Gray, University of Oxford, Oxford, England

Carroll E. Izard, University of Delaware, Newark, Delaware

Henry Kellerman, Postgraduate Center for Mental Health, New York, New York

Maria Kovacs, School of Medicine, University of Pittsburgh, Pittsburgh, Pennsylvania

Howard Leventhal, University of Wisconsin, Madison, Wisconsin

Jacob Levine, West Haven Veterans Administration Hospital, West Haven, Connecticut; and Yale University, New Haven, Connecticut

Helen Block Lewis, Yale University, New Haven, Connecticut

Christina Maslach, University of California, Berkeley, California

Donald L. Mosher, University of Connecticut, Storrs, Connecticut

Alfonso Paredes, University of Oklahoma, Norman, Oklahoma

Paul A. Pilkonis, University of Pittsburgh, Pittsburgh, Pennsylvania

Robert Plutchik, Albert Einstein College of Medicine, Bronx, New York

Jeffrey C. Savitsky, Purdue University, Lafayette, Indiana

Klaus R. Scherer, University of Giessen, Giessen, West Germany

Jerome L. Singer, Yale University, New Haven, Connecticut

Alden E. Wessman, The City College, City University of New York, New York, New York

Richard Winkelmayer, Delaware State Hospital, Wilmington, Delaware

Philip G. Zimbardo, Stanford University, Palo Alto, California

Marvin Zuckerman, University of Delaware, Newark, Delaware

Preface

Significant developments within the past few years have made possible the publication of this rather large volume focusing on specific emotions of human experience, such as interest, joy, anger, distress, fear, shame, shyness, and guilt. The relevant events include new evidence on the relationship of emotions to cognitive processes and to personality traits and defense mechanisms. They also include discoveries relating to the biological foundations of emotions and theory regarding their significance in human evolution. Finally, there have been important findings on the role of emotions and emotion expressions in social relations, pain, grief, and psychopathology. These developments are elaborated in the pages of this volume.

The contributors represent the disciplines of clinical, social, and experimental psychology, psychiatry, and psychoanalysis. The contributions show important common themes that cut across disciplines, but they also reflect some differences that invite further thought and research. Above all, they add to our knowledge of human emotions and to our ability to understand and resolve human problems.

The Department of Psychology of the University of Delaware has provided an excellent intellectual climate for work on a volume that ranges across several specialities and disciplines. Conversations with colleagues in the offices and hallways of Wolf Hall have provided answers to many questions. They also yielded some questions that compelled me to seek greater clarification of an issue.

Our Office Coordinator, Elsie Conte, and the departmental secretarial staff, Judith Fingerle, Mary Jo Todd, Helen Smith, made this book a much happier venture than would have been the case had they not been such an able and congenial group. My secretary, Dawn Downing, has become a genuine expert in the many tasks of manuscript preparation. Her personal interest in her work and her desire for accuracy have made editorial chores much more tolerable and efficient.

CARROLL E. IZARD

Contents

Chapter 7

Chapter 8

PART II
PAIN, ANXIETY, GRIEF, AND DEPRESSION

Chapter 9

Emotion, Pain, and Physical Illness
Howard Leventhal and Deborah Everhart
      (A) Sensory Model of Pain • (B) Sequential Components (Sensation and Emotion)
      Model • (C) A Parallel Processing Model of Pain Distress

Chapter 10

A Neuropsychological Theory of Anxiety
J. A. Gray
      (A) Punishment • (B) Frustrative Nonreward

Chapter 11

Chapter 12

PART III
EMOTION AWARENESS, EXPRESSION, AND AROUSAL

Emotions in Personality and Psychopathology: An Introduction

CARROLL E. IZARD

Speculation and research on the emotions has a long but not consistently venerable history. Many branches of science, as well as religion, philosophy, and law, have some interest in studying and in controlling or regulating these phenomena. In confronting and dealing with the problems of living and adapting to our circumstances, just about everyone is from time to time keenly concerned with the expression, disguise, or suppression of emotions; their effects on our judgment and actions; and their effects, whether expressed or suppressed, on our biological and psychological well-being.

Some poets, playwrights, philosophers, and theologians have through the ages recognized the complexity of emotions and their resistance to being categorized as simply good or bad. Some scientists in the tradition of Darwin and Spencer have held that the emotions do not yield to categorization as good or bad, positive or negative, because they are essentially adaptive, a part of the biopsychological equipment that emerged as a result of the pressures of selection through which our species evolved. This does not mean that the subjective experiences or conscious feelings of the various emotions are equally pleasant/desirable or equally unpleasant/undesirable for the individual human being. What has come to us through evolution has to be evaluated in relation to the species as well as in terms of the individual. The variation in the individual's experience of the pleasantness and tension associated with different emotions, however, guarantees variability of response to the eliciting situations, and a wide repertory of behavioral alternatives is generally adaptive for

CARROLL E. IZARD • University of Delaware, Newark, Delaware.

the individual. Further, one of the functions of an emotion that creates unpleasantness and strong tension is to bring about a change that relieves these feelings or puts them in tolerable perspective.

ISSUES IN THE STUDY OF EMOTIONS

In this volume emotions are discussed in relation to fantasy, conflict, defenses or coping strategies, and psychopathology. In relating emotions to these phenomena, we do not intend to imply that emotions are the roots of psychological disorders or problems. In addition to their role in the problems encountered in adaptation, they have many positive functions. Some of us agree that "the emotions are of quite extraordinary importance in the total economy of living organisms" (Mowrer, O. H. *Learning Theory and Behavior*. New York: John Wiley, 1960, p. 308). They are of primary importance in motivating human behavior, including prosocial activity and creative endeavor, and are perhaps a less likely source of trouble than other personality subsystems.

Some of the contributors to this volume hold that all emotion is a function of cognitive appraisal and consider cognition more basic to motivation, adjustment, and the regulation of behavior than emotion. Their view seems to support the notion that the source of psychological problems and disorders lies more in the cognitive system than in the emotion system. They believe that the emotions are important, though, for a number of reasons and that emotion, once activated, influences cognition and action.

The authors who have contributed to this volume represent the fields of learning theory, personality, social, and clinical psychology, and psychiatry. Each has focused on emotions as they relate to critical problems in their field. The distinction of the contributors and the scope of this volume signify our progress toward a science of the emotions.

This volume does not mark the end of controversies in the field of emotion, however, nor does this book represent a single theory or point of view. On the contrary, an effort was made to represent distinctly different theoretical orientations and different research approaches. I believe the reader will agree that the book has a diversity of ideas and points of view. And I hope that recognition of this heterogeneity will add strength to some common underlying themes so that some unity can be seen in our diversity. The commonly held assumptions of the contributors attest to their belief in the importance of emotions in human affairs and of emotion research in the behavioral sciences.

The field of emotion has suffered from controversy that has resulted in part from efforts to resolve pseudoproblems and answer questions that are put too broadly. The most notorious example of this is the critical and controversial question, "What is an emotion?" which was raised by William

James in 1884, when he published the first statement of his now-famous and often-misunderstood theory. James did not succeed in answering the question to everyone's satisfaction, nor has anyone since James, nor shall we. James's question had beguiling and nonproductive effects, but it may also have inspired some of the advances in the field of emotion that will be reported in this volume.

Although James's question was broadly stated, he addressed himself primarily to the question of mental state or conscious feeling, the subjective experience or phenomenological component of emotion. In this volume there are chapters that are concerned with the various components of emotion: the neurophysiological, the expressive, and the subjective or experiential.

The questions raised by the contributors to this volume are much more specific than James's and the answers inform us and point the way to new avenues of investigation. There are a number of answerable questions that one can expect to explore in the chapters of this volume. How do emotions relate to the fantasy and the imaginative play of children? How do emotions relate to mood and sense of humor? How do emotions relate to personality traits such as sex guilt and sensation seeking and to defense mechanisms such as projection and repression?

How do emotions relate to pain and anxiety? How do emotions relate to grief and depression? How do emotions relate to compulsive disorders and paranoia?

How do expressive behaviors relate to infant development and personality integration? How do facial and vocal expressions of emotion and gaze behavior relate to social behavior and psychopathology? What is the role of undifferentiated arousal and the perception of others' emotion expressions in determining the experiential quality and verbal label of an emotion?

There are eight more general issues in the study of emotions that are touched upon to some extent in one or more of the chapters of this volume. These issues are stated below in declarative form, but they are recognized as assumptions supported by varying amounts of evidence and argument.

1. *Emotions have different components.* An increasing number of theorists and investigators in the field of emotion are recognizing that emotion is a complex concept consisting of different components or aspects, each of which may require different methods of measurement. There is rather general agreement that emotions have a neurophysiological, an expressive, and an experiential or phenomenological component. The neurophysiological–biochemical component is studied by techniques ranging from microelectrode implantations in brain tissue to analysis of the effects of system-specific drugs on learning and performance. The expressive component is studied by micro- and macroanalysis of facial and vocal expressions, and the experiential component is measured by systematic self-report. Electromyographic studies of facial muscles during emotion-eliciting situations have provided additional

evidence on the expressive or neuromuscular component and have furnished concurrent validity for self-report data on subjective experience. Although the components of an emotion normally function as an integrated system, evidence of activity in one component does not always warrant inferences about the involvement of the other components.

2. *There are qualitatively different emotions, each with unique motivational characteristics.* A number of the chapters of this volume are concerned with a specific emotion, and some provide a rather extensive psychology for the emotion under consideration. One of the important implications for recognizing different emotions with different antecedents and consequences is to provide more specific hypotheses and more avenues for research. It also permits us to focus on the importance of each of the emotions, including the positive emotions of interest and joy, which generally have been neglected in psychological literature.

3. *Once activated, a given emotion varies in both intensity and duration.* There are several important reasons for recognizing both the intensity and the temporal dimensions of emotions. An emotion is still considered by many an intense experience of brief duration. Relatively little consideration has been given to the possibility that any particular emotion can linger over indefinite periods of time at varying levels of intensity. Because of this, the scope of the motivational influence of emotions has been greatly underestimated. Equally seriously, the failure to recognize the concept of low-key, enduring emotion has led to the misattribution of behavioral determinants and the crediting of nonemotional phenomena with causing behavior that may have been motivated by low-intensity emotion. I suspect that failure to recognize interest as an emotion, one that is often present without dramatic expressive accompaniments, has led many people to attribute to information or sensory data a motivational function that should have been assigned to interest.

A number of the chapters in Part I demonstrate the importance of the intensity and temporal dimensions of emotion. These are the chapters that discuss moods, traits, and defense mechanisms. Moods are discussed as emotions or emotion–cognition structures of relatively low intensity and relatively long duration. Temporally stable traits and defense mechanisms are shown to be related to specific emotions.

4. *Emotions are in part a function of the individual and not simply of the situation or environment.* All of us agree that human emotions can be triggered by either internal or external events. Most of us think that even when there is an external emotion elicitor, the intensity, duration, and even the quality of the resulting emotion may be a function of the particular individual. The chapters on moods, traits, defense mechanisms, and psychological disorders speak to this issue.

5. *It is heuristic to draw conceptual distinctions between emotion and cognition or between emotion processes and cognitive processes.* One of the

immediate advantages of such conceptual distinctions is to focus on the importance of studying how emotions and cognitions are interrelated. Although all contributors may not agree on this issue, a number of them deal specifically with emotion–cognition interactions. Some see cognitive processes as relatively more important determinants of emotion and behavior, while others explicitly or implicitly see emotion as a more fundamental type of motivation. All seem to agree that there is a kind of interactive net or continuous feedback loop whereby each system can influence the other.

A similar argument can be made for distinguishing between emotion and emotional behavior. If we consider facial and vocal (and sometimes postural and gestural) activity as part of the expressive component of emotion, then what is considered emotional behavior can be seen as a consequence of emotion. The term *emotional behavior*, transferred uncritically from studies of animals where it is most appropriate, may be misleading when used loosely to describe human actions. Describing the functions or dysfunctions of instrumental behavior and relating this behavior to a reliably identified emotion are separate problems. Cursing or striking another person may be termed emotional behavior—or perhaps more precisely, emotion-related or anger-related behavior—but such behavior is also related to cognition, the intention to harm. Further, anger is not always followed by these or any other instrumental behaviors.

6. *Emotions and their effects on cognition and action have important consequences for the individual.* Chapters in Parts I and II show how emotions relate differentially to phenomena ranging from fantasy and imaginative play to severe psychological disorders. One chapter shows how different neurophysiological substrates can be related differentially to separate behavioral systems.

7. *The expressive component of emotion is a significant factor in infant development, social communication, and interpersonal behavior.* Several of the chapters in Part III deal specifically with the social aspect of emotion. The prelingual infant is heavily dependent upon emotion expression as a means of social communication, and expressive behaviors in infancy can be rewarding or disturbing influences on parents. The encoding and decoding of facial and vocal expressions and gaze patterns varies in different types of social relationships and in different types of psychological disorders.

8. *The role of undifferentiated arousal in emotion is neither simple nor completely understood.* Some of the contributors to this volume would argue that undifferentiated arousal is not necessarily involved in emotion at all. Some would argue that the critical type of arousal or activation is emotion-specific, that only activity of the somatic nervous system is part of emotion proper, and that activity of the autonomic nervous system is important in sustaining emotion and emotion-related behavior but not in instigating it. The chapter dealing specifically with this issue shows that undifferentiated arousal

can be not considered a "neutral" physiological component that becomes a particular emotion when cognitive evaluation of contextual information results in an emotion-specific label.

SOME DIFFERENCES AND SIMILARITIES IN CONTRIBUTORS' CONCEPTIONS

While all of us who contributed to this volume agree on some of the characteristics of emotions and believe that common understanding and terminology are important, we recognize certain differences and believe that it is important to make these differences clear and to encourage further study of them. I shall briefly comment on some of the issues on which we differ. Perhaps these are better considered as things on which we have not all agreed, for I daresay there are no issues on which we all hold different opinions.

1. While we all agree that there are different emotions with different antecedents and consequences, we do not all agree on how many there are or whether some are fundamentals or primaries and others secondaries, blends, mixtures, or patterns of fundamentals. The question as to the ultimate list of emotions may be as nonproductive as James's overly general question regarding definition. Other aspects of the issue constitute ever-present problems. For example, are the concepts of anxiety and depression of the same order as the concepts of fear and sadness? Some of us consider anxiety and depression as complex concepts involving a pattern of different emotions, drives, and affective–cognitive structures, while others tend to treat anxiety and depression more as unitary concepts. Some tend to equate anxiety with fear. Others tend to use the terms *anxiety* and *depression* to point to disruptive or chronic problems without concern for precise definition.

2. We do not all agree as to whether cognition is a component of emotion or an intimately interrelated system. While we all agree that cognitive processes can trigger emotion, we do not all agree that cognitive appraisal and evaluation are the only processes that generate emotion. Some would argue that physiological needs can trigger emotion or that one emotion can trigger another one independent of the appraisal or labeling processes. While most of us would probably agree that linear cause–effect logic does not make for a good model of emotion or emotion–behavior relationships and many of us would favor an interactive components or continuous feedback-loop model, we would not agree on the specific components or mechanisms involved in the loop.

3. While most of us agree on the significance of facial and vocal expression, we do not all agree on the precise role of these phenomena in emotion. For example, some consider facial expression an integral component of

emotion, while others see it as an aftereffect, and yet others have simply not addressed the question.

4. While all of us agree that emotions play a substantial role in development and in personal and social adjustment, we do not agree on whether it is more fruitful to look for the source of problems in emotion processes or in cognitive processes. This difference could have significant implications for the assessment and amelioration of mental health problems. It can affect the extent to which we attempt to develop cognitive structures that regulate emotion and the extent to which we seek to activate emotion experiences that regulate cognition. It need not be a devastating problem if we return to our notion of an interactive components or feedback-loop model for explaining emotion–behavior relationships. Working with this model, we can expect cognitive, emotional, and motoric activities to have regulatory effects on each other.

CONCLUDING STATEMENT

Notwithstanding the differences in contributors' conceptions of emotions and emotion–cognition and emotion–behavior relationships, I believe our similarities are sufficient to give the book integrative themes and focus. By way of summary, here are some of the important assumptions we hold in common.

1. There are some distinct and operationally separable emotions or emotion concepts. Thus emotion cannot be described by a single concept, such as arousal or activation.

2. A given emotion has more than one component or aspect. Each emotion has a neurophysiological–biochemical underpinning, a subjective feeling or experiential aspect; and an expressive or signal-sending function that operates internally and externally.

3. Emotions motivate or influence behavior in important ways, and different emotions have different antecedents and consequences. Emotions probably always have some organizing effect on the individual's behavior, but that behavior may be disruptive or adaptive, depending in part upon circumstances and the context.

4. No emotion can be categorically described as good or bad. Interest can be prurient, laughter derisive, fear instructive, shyness attractive.

5. Emotion and cognition are intimately interrelated. Cognitive processes can trigger emotions and play a part in their regulation. Emotion, in turn, can influence perception and cognition.

6. The neurophysiological substrate of emotion cannot be described simply as undifferentiated arousal nor solely as mechanisms and circuits of the autonomic nervous system. There is somatosensory involvement in at least some of the components of emotion.

7. Emotions have an expressive or social aspect, and emotion expression encodes signals that can have subtle and powerful effects on the perceiver. Beginning in infancy, emotion expression influences the development of interpersonal relationships, social affection, and empathy. There are wide individual differences in the expression or encoding of emotions and in the interpretation or decoding of expressions.

8. Emotions have a substantial role in fantasy and imaginative play, in individual development, and in personal and social adjustment. Biological or social conditions or affective–cognitive structures that significantly alter the thresholds for experiencing, expressing, and perceiving emotions can have serious consequences for the individual.

Moods, Traits, and Defense Mechanisms

I

Editor's Introduction

Many of the data for the early and highly influential formulations in personality and psychodynamic psychology came from the study of neurotic and psychotic individuals. The analysis of the conflicts and defenses of these troubled people was almost always cast in terms of negative affects. One longstanding result of this strong precedent has been the neglect of theory and research on positive emotions. Although this volume focuses on conflict and defense, which specifically call for consideration of negative emotions, Singer's chapter demonstrates convincingly that the positive emotions or the cognitive processes with which they are associated must be included in any comprehensive consideration of the adaptive resources of the individual.

The special cognitive processes that have been so well documented and elucidated by Singer and his colleagues are those described by the overlapping terms of *fantasy*, *imagination*, and *make-believe play*. These very terms have an affective connotation for most of us who have engaged in these delightful pastimes, and the emotions that come to mind are interest–excitement and enjoyment–joy. But Singer goes on to demonstrate convincingly that imaginative play is far more than an amusing pastime for the child.

The evidence suggests that fantasy and make-believe play have wide-ranging effects, including the facilitation of language development, cognitive growth, and prosocial behavior. Of equally great import is the evidence suggesting that make-believe play may have an important function in emotion regulation and the control of aggression

It is also clear from Singer's illustrative material that the adaptive functions of fantasy and imagination do not necessarily end with childhood. The ability to enter a world of imagination in a time of crisis can help regulate negative affects and avoid catastrophic reactions. Singer argues cogently that this is not an "escape" from reality but an adaptive use of imagination and fantasy in managing reality. His novel ideas are supported by a considerable body of empirical data and poignant vignettes.

Affect and Imagination in Play and Fantasy

1

JEROME L. SINGER

We often speak of childhood as a period of freely expressive emotionality. Psychologists have, however, only recently begun to study the patterns of emotional response as they emerge naturally in the course of a child's major activity during the preschool years: spontaneous play. Indeed play itself is only now coming under serious scrutiny as the primary "business" of childhood (Bruner, Jolly & Sylva, 1976). While the time available for play and the types of play encouraged or permitted vary considerably from culture to culture, most modern societies make relatively few demands on children's time before school age. The period between 6 months and 6 years is one of amazing cognitive, motor, linguistic, and emotional development, and much of it occurs during some form of play. This chapter is designed to examine a specific type of play in which most children engage at some time during their early years and to look in greater detail at its links with the child's emotional patterns. The type of play on which we will focus can be called *imaginative pretending, make-believe, symbolic,* or *sociodramatic play.* The position we will examine will be whether there are particular qualities of make-believe that are especially linked to positive affective experience, to those inherently positively reinforcing emotions of interest and joy (Tomkins, 1962, 1963). We shall also consider the converse: the possibility that children who have failed through various faulty developmental or socialization opportunities to incorporate imagination as a part of their regular play repertory may be more prone to negative affective experience.

JEROME L. SINGER • Yale University, New Haven, Connecticut. Some of the research described herein by the author was supported by a grant from the RANN program of the National Science Foundation.

I. THE MEANING AND FUNCTIONS OF IMAGINATIVE PLAY

It is generally agreed among observers of early childhood that there are four types of play behavior: sensorimotor play, mastery play, make-believe or symbolic play, and games with rules. Actually, we have as yet no really careful parametric studies that give us a clear notion of the age levels of appearance of all of these types of play, their relative incidence, their likelihood of combination, and under what circumstances they wax or wane. Indeed, the whole field of play behavior still remains relatively wide open to systematic observation and experimentation, although some steps have been taken in recent years (Singer & Singer, 1976a; Weisler & McCall, 1976). Generally speaking, there is agreement that *play* is perhaps best defined as "what children do" when they are not actively involved in direct biological need-reduction or in carrying out required tasks such as household chores or specified schoolwork.

It would appear very likely, therefore, that play behavior must bear a very profound relationship to the learning process, and yet we are only on the threshold of exploring how much learning does occur in the course of the spontaneous play of preschoolers. The animal literature summarized by various contributors to Bruner *et al.*'s (1976) fine compendium of papers points to the extensive role of the rough-and-tumble play of immature organisms as a preparation for later skill acquisition. For humans, imaginative play has a special role, however.

A. Examples of Imaginative Play

Let us take a closer look at some specific instances of play drawn from a rather diverse group of children.

Carew, Chan, and Halfer (1975, pp. 1–2) report an observation of a mother playing with her 26-month-old son, Matthew:

> Matthew ... comes into the kitchen holding a child-sized badminton racket. ... Mother: "Did you get it? Where did it go? Down there?" Matthew: "I got it!" and runs out of the kitchen after an imaginary shuttlecock. ... Matthew swings the racket hitting the imaginary shuttlecock. Mother pretends to toss the shuttlecock back to Matthew. They continue, Matthew and mother taking turns hitting the shuttlecock. The game continues, becoming more sophisticated. Matthew seems to be timing his imaginary shots to follow mother's and looks up at the imaginary "birdie" each time it approaches. Matthew inadvertently drops the racket. Mother: "You lost your racket." Matthew: "Oh I missed." Matthew pretends to serve and mother to return the serve. Matthew retrieves the imaginary shuttlecock from the hallway. They continue. Matthew calls: "Enough, enough." "I want a drink of water." Mother gets a glassful. "Are you thirsty?"; as she holds the imaginary glass for Matthew to drink.

Here is a verbatim account of two boys from lower socioeconomic backgrounds at play in a kindergarten within a high-poverty area:

> Jerry and Michael climb into a "boat" (large cardboard box), don plastic margarine containers with elastic attached (divers' masks) and announce, "We're going swimming." Jerry "dives" into water. Michael throws out a rope, "I'll save you, come back, I'll pick you up." Both "swim" (crawl on the floor) looking for treasure (lunchbox). Jerry puts blocks in the lunchbox for the treasure. "At last we've got the treasure, man!" (Griffing, 1974, p. 261)

Although Piaget (1962) has suggested that "ludic symbolism" or make-believe play is internalized in the form of fantasy and daydreaming by the ages of five or six, I do not believe this is at all the case. Next is an example drawn from an anthropologist's account of play among Alaskan Eskimo children between the ages of 8 and 11:

> The children are playing "Catholic Mass." P. plays the priest wearing a blanket around her shoulders. After having set up a wooden bench to serve as an altar, she orders the others to be seated. Note that although the children normally speak in their native Yupic language, this game is conducted in very formal, monotonous English. The "priest" chants, "Please get the sugar, please get the crackers, please get some Kool-Aid, please get some toilet paper." After each item is collected, it is placed on the bench. The priest mixes the Kool-Aid with sugar and water in a bowl, then gives each child a bite of cracker, then a sip of Kool-aid, wiping off the rim of the bowl with toilet paper after each person has drunk. She next reads the Gospel which goes as follows: "They sat down to eat and drink; then they got up to play." She ends the service by singing "Amazing Grace." (Ager, 1974)

Lest you be left with the impression that Eskimo children, because of their long dark autumns and winters, persist in make-believe play beyond the age of other children, I would like to indulge in a personal anecdote drawn from the life of New York City boys between the ages of 10 and 14. Some friends of mine and I developed a baseball and football league played purely with board games during this age period. We met regularly in one another's home. Each had developed a full baseball or football team, had assigned each player a history, and kept elaborate statistics on his performances in these games. A game usually depended heavily on the roll of the dice, followed by consultation of charts to indicate how many yards were gained, or whether a pass was completed or incomplete. We kept up a steady patter, much as a radio announcer would, describing the player's run, the attempt to stop him, the cheers of the crowd, and so on, until, when the chart was consulted and the outcome known, we would exultantly say, "He's made four yards and a first down: Another great run for Pheneffson!" Despite the fact that chance and the throw of the dice were the major determinants, our "star" players seemed indeed to do better than lesser players in these games.

B. The Role of Make-Believe Play in Early Childhood

Make-believe play in general involves some form of symbolic transformations—the pretense of the 2-year-old that she is "drinking" out of an empty cup or the double transformation of the 2½-year-old that she is "feeding" a plastic "baby" from an empty dish (Fein, 1975). Clearly it involves some degree of imagery—the child building a fort from blocks may easily recognize how little the block structure resembles a fort seen on television or in a picture book, but he or she can use private imagery to make up the difference. Children imagine playmates who are not there; indeed in our most recent research almost two-thirds of 140 3- and 4-year-old children we questioned described such fantasy playmates.

The process of the emergence of make-believe play has just begun to be studied (Singer, 1973; Fein, 1975; Singer & Singer, 1976a). It seems likely that it is an outgrowth of Piaget's (1962) emphasis on assimilation and accommodation as the two basic features of information processing in early childhood. The child seeks to imitate the movements, gestures, and words of adults or to respond to physical objects of the environment and then later seeks to assimilate these new experiences into the already-established memory schema. This *assimilation* calls for a kind of replaying of material and a repetition of words, gestures, and indeed probably of images until they can be matched to early memories or until new structures are formed.

If we focus primarily on the task demands of developing the cognitive and affective systems of the child, we recognize that the child must be prepared with expectations and motor or cognitive "plans" (Miller, Galanter, & Pribram, 1960) to deal with each new setting or demand. In order to do this, it must find a means of transforming externally derived information into a *miniaturized* private representational system, rapidly encoded and decoded as situations demand. We have increasing reason to believe that language encoding and the imagery storage processes are separately organized and processed by the brain (Paivio, 1970; Witelson, 1976) but that both systems ultimately may interact to produce optimal storage (Rohwer, 1967). In imitating language, the child gradually miniaturizes sounds, words, and eventually phrases into a form suitable for efficient storage and retrieval in the long-term system. The same process presumably occurs with the more global material of visual, auditory, or other sensory-modality information, and to the extent that the child rehearses images and verbal labels together, the chances of highly efficient voluntary retrieval of this material is greatly enhanced.

Piaget (1962) in his emphasis on *assimilation* and Tomkins (1970) in the theory of *miniaturization* through repetition are proposing that effective internal representation does depend on some kind of continuing private rehearsal process. I have elsewhere elaborated on these suggestions to propose that make-believe play and pretending in early childhood develop naturally as part of this very process of the child's gaining control over an internal or symbolic representation system (Singer, 1973). Pretending and the profound dimension of "as if" in human experience are intrinsic to the establishment of an efficient set of anticipatory guiding images, verbal labels, and plans with easily spun-out subroutines. Pretending itself depends on the level of the child's cognitive maturation and also on the complexity or "realism" of the structures with which the child is dealing (Fein, 1975).

Although almost all children show some degree of make-believe or fantasy play, the persistence and elaboration of such play in the 3- to 6-year-old period appears to depend upon considerable support and encouragement from adults as well as upon opportunities for practice in privacy (Singer, 1973; Singer, 1976b). Obviously children whose play is more limited to games with rules or to mastery experiences such as climbing, ball playing, or forms of motor exploration also master new schemata and set up coding systems. But there is increasing reason to believe that those children whose play repertory in the preschool period includes a good deal of make-believe and fantasy play have a distinct edge in certain important cognitive areas (Smilansky, 1968). A study by Lewis (1973), for example, found that kindergartners who played more elaborate and extensive sociodramatic or fantasy games showed better performance in picture interpretation tasks, in the amount of language employed, and in organization of language during picture interpretations. In free-association tasks, high-fantasy-play children produced more responses, provided more associations remote from self or the home environment, and showed more use of categorization and associative linkage than of random naming. Lewis found her clearest differences in cognitive organization between the children of high IQ–high sociodramatic play and those with correspondingly high IQ and low levels of fantasy play, thus ruling out sheer intelligence as a factor in the differences. Similar results have been reported recently by Dansky (1976) and in a series of studies summarized by Singer (1977).

Our own current research on 3- and 4-year-olds as well as several earlier studies using observation of free play have consistently found correlations between levels of make-believe and the use of more extended vocabulary (Singer, Caldeira, & Singer, 1977) or the introduction of more complex syntactic structures, such as predicate nominatives, into spontaneous language. In an unpublished report, Corrine Hutt in England also suggests that working-class children whose spontaneous language is characterized by little variation and complexity show an increase in measures such as mean length of utterance and richness of vocabulary when encouraged to engage in make-believe games. The continuing reports by Saltz, Dixon, and Johnson (1976) on urban disadvantaged children trained in thematic play are also corroborative here.

I am suggesting, then, that growing up requires an increasing complexity of vocabulary, and an ability to categorize materials, to retrieve words or images readily, and to generate sets of more remote associations or to recall details of verbally presented situations accurately (Tucker, 1975). Imaginative play provides an arena for rehearsing material, assimilating it to a greater variety of preestablished schemata, and by the very process of scaling it down in the form of toys or small objects standing for large ones (as in blocks for buildings or pencils for airplanes), miniaturizing the material for more effective later retrieval.

C. Affects and Imagination in Early Childhood

Let me briefly talk of the task demands for the growing child in the affective area. There is increasing reason to believe that human beings grow up with a relatively differentiated but circumscribed affect system closely tied to facial representation and to the complexity of and rate of assimilability of information-processing demands (Tomkins, 1962, 1963; Izard, 1977). An important feature of pretend play is that it provides opportunities for expression and control of affect and the representation in miniaturized form of conflictive or frightening scenes or encounters. The child engaged in pretend play of adventurous or hostile encounters gains some sense of competence and power (Sutton-Smith, 1976) or empathy (Gould, 1972; Saltz & Johnson, 1974) and may in effect be establishing better-organized schemata or plans and subroutines for observing others' emotions and expressing or controlling its own. In our own research (to be described in greater detail below), we have regularly observed that children engaged in make-believe play are also "happier" children. That is, when observers rate them for the positive affects of interest and curiosity or for joy and the smiling response, we find consistent positive correlations between imaginativeness of play, positive affect, concentration, elation, and cooperation with peers (Singer & Singer, 1976b).

Important task demands of socialization and moral growth also confront the child. Differentiating aggression or violence from adaptive assertiveness, impulsivity from means–end action, egocentrism from sharing, dependent demanding from cooperating or helping, infantile sexuality from interpersonal intimacy—all these are demands we all must confront in the growth process. Make-believe play, as child psychotherapists have long stressed, is an important arena in which children can express and differentiate issues of this kind. In a sense, the play situation permits the child to examine an array of probabilities or possibilities with impunity and to store these miniaturized new schemata more effectively.

On the basis of her observations of free play in preschoolers, Gould (1972) concluded that children who played more imaginatively also took roles other than self in play and thus developed an empathy for the victims of aggression. They were less likely to be directly aggressive toward others. There is a body of evidence that suggests that by elementary-school age children who show imaginativeness in spontaneous play or in projective test performance are less likely to be overtly aggressive or impulsive and are better able to tolerate delays or are more socially cooperative (Singer & Singer, 1976b). In our current research, as well as in earlier studies (Nahme-Huang, Singer, Singer, & Wheaton, 1977; Singer, Singer, Tower, & Biggs, 1977), we have generally found that imaginative play is also associated with peer-group sharing or cooperation and with somewhat less demandingness or dependency on adults. Rubin, Maioni, and Hornung (1976) also report data suggesting a greater level of social maturity identified with sociodramatic play.

In summary, then, imaginative play can be viewed as a major resource by which children can cope immediately with the cognitive, affective, and social demands of growing up. It is more than a reactive behavior, however, for it provides a practice ground for organizing new schemata and for transforming and storing material for more effective later expression in plans, action, or verbalization. Our own research and the increasing body of studies in this area suggest that play is an active process and one that depends to some degree on reinforcement, modeling, and general encouragement by parental figures (Dennis, 1976; Gershowitz, 1974; Shmukler, 1978; Singer, 1977).

A critical question that remains before us is to identify even more precisely those factors that are particularly conducive to encouraging imaginative play in early childhood so that such play can be effective in helping the child develop further its cognitive, affective, and social skills. Gershowitz (1974) demonstrated that well-trained or empathic adults who offered direction initially to a child and then pulled back were more likely to foster rich imaginative play in the youngsters. Shmukler (1978) has been carrying out an elaborate study of mother–child interaction patterns in relation to make-believe play and imagination with middle-class white parents in South Africa. In a sophisticated Boolean analysis of relevant variables, she finds evidence that a variable reflecting a mother who tells stories to a child, who is accepting of the child's uniqueness, and who shows leadership in stimulating play but then withdraws is the best predictor of imaginativeness.

A recent example of maternal input and its impact on a child's developing imagination can be cited. In an article on new developments in philosophy, Branch (1977) describes the childhood of Sol Kripke, an outstanding young American logician. Kripke's mother used to recite Gilbert and Sullivan passages to him when he was a preschooler. Subsequently intrigued by the wordplay of that delightful material, the boy developed a whole world of gremlins, an absolute monarchy whose king was both the tallest and the shortest character in the realm. He used to delight his younger sisters with running episodes of this fantasy. The progression toward analytic philosophy and the complex wordplay and mathematics of the grownup Sol Kripke's examination of "truth" seems less surprising with such beginnings.

This example calls attention to the close tie between a "playful" mother–child interaction, the reliance on imagery and fantasy, and the positive affects aroused by make-believe. Looking again at the first example of imaginative play above—Matthew, his mother, and the imaginary badminton game—we see all of the cognitive, behavioral, and emotional elements brought together.

II. THEORETICAL RELATIONSHIPS BETWEEN AFFECT AND IMAGINATION

What relationships can we expect to find between pretending or imaginative play and affect? In a sense, because the symbolic or imagery capacities of child and adult permit the human to create a series of alternative environments or contexts to those presented directly to the senses, we should anticipate a full set of affective reactions to imagined situations. Indeed we know that in our dreams we can experience a wide range of emotional responses from terror to joy. Our daydreams, because of their "paler," less hallucinatory quality, evoke less intense emotions perhaps. Yet we know that chance resemblance in a passerby or a snatch of distantly heard music can suddenly generate a vivid waking image of a lost love or dead parent and bring us to tears.

A. Cognitive Assimilation and Differentiated Affects

Tomkins (1962, 1963) has proposed that there may be particular conditions that evoke innately the differential experience and expression of specific emotions. A sudden sharp increase in "density of neural firing" produces the *startle* response or the reaction of *fear* or *terror*. A more moderate gradient of increased density of neural firing, on the other hand, provokes the more positive affects of *surprise* and *interest*—those experiences that motivate the exploratory behavior as essential for learning and adaptation as the flight or defensive reactions generated by fear and terror. Sharp reductions from high levels of density of neural firing or arousal yield the positive affects of *joy* and the *smile* or *laugh*. Persisting very high levels of density of neural firing produce the negative affect of *anger*, while somewhat lower but persisting high levels of such arousal generate *sadness* and *distress* or the *weeping* response.

This position seems to me at least to some extent translatable into information-processing terms. Humans steer themselves through their environment by some degree of anticipatory planning and establishment of expectancy schemata. New experiences are to be matched as quickly as possible to such anticipatory images. If the match is perfect (as is the case when we walk along a familiar street or pace in a familiar room), we are hardly conscious at all of action, environment, or the matching process. Indeed such anticipations permit us to keep cognitive channel space "clear" for the novelties in a situation or for thinking or attending carefully to the conversation of another person.

A loud pistol shot behind us evokes a startle reaction—it could not have been anticipated and therefore cannot almost instantaneously be assimilated into established schemata. The ring of the telephone at midnight or of the doorbell at 5:00 A.M. can produce first a startle and then often a sense of fear since we can scarcely have anticipated such occurrences, nor do we have a reasonably well-established schema to explain them. The ring of the phone at 6:00 P.M. or of the doorbell at 7:00 or 8:00 in the evening is more likely simply to evoke curiosity—we have had an array of differentiated previous experiences that lead us to expect that relatives, neighbors, or friends may call or visit at those times.

Suppose the midnight phone call is just a wrong number. Our first reaction is relief and perhaps even a smile, although if awakened from sleep, we may for some time find it hard to assimilate this unexpected event and experience some anger at the "damned fool" who can't dial right. If the 5:00 A.M. knock on the door is from a stranger who persists in asking for a party with a name unknown to us, we may surely experience anger as we cannot assimilate this new information into any established schema. But if it turns out to be a son returning unexpectedly early on leave from the navy, we can quickly match this information against a host of previous anticipations and experience relief and intense joy.

B. Thought and Affect Regulation

To the extent that in fantasy and imagery we are creating—often without conscious control—sets of alternative environments, we can see how even in thought we can run the gamut of novelty and of its reduction and thus the evocation of specific emotions. Some indications that a trusted wife is unfaithful can recur again and again in thought. The clues (as in Othello's reaction to Cassio's possession of Desdemona's handkerchief) each time call up a fantasy that cannot be assimilated into a previous set of established schemata—the one truly trusted person I've known is playing me false—and the result is anger or sadness and distress produced just by thought.

Thought by its very nature has a certain seemingly random, vague quality compared with immediate experience. Odd juxtapositions of memories occur that can surprise and interest us. Too often the exigencies of daily life necessitate our shifting attention back to the papers on our desks or the dishes in the sink. The writer or the artist or the humorist who is trained to value such novelty and stays with the peculiar combination of schemata indeed may actively play even further with them. Only in our dreams do we usually indulge such novelty longer, and then again we often dismiss that potential resource of creativity too easily.

Our ability to turn thoughts on and off more or less at will gives that medium a special quality as an environment in relation to the evocation of affects. We are rarely likely to be truly startled or even terrified by our thoughts. Indeed we have developed many mechanisms for shifting our attention away from the difficult-to-assimilate in thought and toward the familiar by plodding ahead with our work or by concentrating on the often redundant characteristics of the physical environment. Since the environment provided by thought has a kind of miniaturized quality, it is also more subject to our control; it can be assimilated more easily or manipulated.

A remarkable account of the experience of a kidnapped Italian industrialist (Pepper, 1977) provides a firsthand report of how voluntary thought allowed the victim to sustain some self-control during a terrifying experience. Moments after his capture, blindfolded and handcuffed in the kidnappers' speeding car, Paolo Lazzaroni found himself meditating on the sociological implications of the upsurge of kidnappings in Italy's most prosperous provinces: "Lazzaroni still marvels at how his mind had rambled off on these meditations at that unlikely moment as though to deaden its sense of peril" (Pepper, 1977, p. 43). Notice how shifting the focus to a general issue, one he'd probably discussed with others and read about—his established schema—permitted Lazzaroni some chance to control his terror. Had he kept thinking of the immediate situation, so unexpected and fraught with implications of impending torture, distress for his family, and possible death, he might have lost control and begun to fight in anger or weep in distress at the high level of persisting unassimilable material present in his life.

As his captivity went on, constantly blindfolded, Lazzaroni found a kind of tranquillity by elaborate reminiscences and fantasied trips:

> This time he was back at Caprera, at the sailing school. The harbor has a narrow opening and there was a high wind, making it difficult to get past the rocks. There were many maneuvers to make, using a small two-man Vaurien. He was running with the wind towards the rocks when Bogey's voice brought him back to captivity. (Pepper, 1977, p. 128)

Notice again how the elaborate fantasy reminiscence, while perhaps reflecting some aspect of his current danger, again involved schemata under his control. He knew he would make it to safety. The fantasy was vivid enough to hold his interest, and the situation was one about which he may not have rehearsed so much as to lose its novelty. Yet he did know the outcome and could experience the joy of effective matching. Notice too that he had nicknamed one of his captors Bogey (based on voice resemblance), another means of pretending that maybe this was, after all, a bit like a movie. Lazzaroni is a highly practical, intelligent man as his behavior with his captors revealed during the negotiations for his release. He had not "lost touch with reality" by his shifts into make-believe, but rather he had sustained his affective level at a certain calmness, for had he thought constantly of the very serious dangers facing him, he might have become so anxious that he could not function, might have acted rashly, or might have become physically ill. His finely developed imagination miniaturized events, permitted distance and pacing, and left him ready for effective behavior when it was needed.

C. Fantasy in Child's Play

For the preschool child the world, even if perhaps somewhat better organized than William James's term "booming buzzing confusion" suggests, is full of strange sights, sounds, and smells. Lacking a sufficient range of differentiated schemata with which to match new material, the child can be overwhelmed by complexity and is susceptible to high, persisting levels of arousal that could provoke severe distress. Transforming some of the material into miniature form and playing with it in make-believe terms is one important adaptive possibility for the child. It is impressive indeed how early children (perhaps with adult support or modeling) learn to adopt the "as if" or pretend attitude—the play stance that permits the child to select aspects of the confusing behaviors and verbalizations it experiences and to recast them in small manipulable forms. Indeed this *moderate* novelty holds the child's interest and with repetition is increasingly matched to newly forming and established schemata so that there follows an experience of joy.

The evolutionary origins of this playful stance may already be evident in the "play face" of the primates or the "canid bow" as seen in dogs, wolves, or coyotes, a clear signal of invitation to rough-and-tumble as described by Bekoff (Quanta, 1977, p. 5). In children, playful rough-and-tumble or chasing (Aldis, 1975) is also supplemented by the symbolic games of pretend. These have the special potential advantages of increased miniaturization, practice of vocabulary, development of imagery skills, and usefulness for *self-entertainment* under conditions when children are expected to be "seen and not heard."

As suggested by the reference to the kidnapped industrialist (only one of numerous instances of use by imprisoned individuals of fantasy methods to control terror or to avoid panicky admissions of false guilt, etc.), the resort to make-believe can have a calming effect. It remains for future research to show just how specific are the reductive and simplifying effects of positive imagery and fantasy upon indices of autonomic arousal, for example, blood pressure, heart rate and scalp EMG readings. There are extensive clinical reports that imagery "trips" or fantasies of pleasant nature scenes, etc., do indeed have specific calming effects in psychotherapeutic usage (Singer, 1974, 1978). For our purposes here, it seems possible to hypothesize that children engaged in make-believe play may, on the whole, show a somewhat quieter, more relaxed, and less stressful demeanor. Certainly make-believe games can build to high pitches of excitement, and children engaged in such play may be lively or elated, but rarely do they move out of the game into direct fighting or terror.

In summary, then, the proposition raised is that imaginative play in early childhood is a critical adaptive resource by which children can organize complex experiences into manageable forms. In doing so, they avoid the extreme negative affects of fear–terror, anger, distress, or sadness and maximize the occurrence of the positive affects of interest and joy. If, as Tomkins (1962,

1963) has suggested, our major motives involve maximizing the experience of positive affect, minimizing negative affect, expressing affect, and also controlling it, then the miniature theater of the symbolic system has special advantages for all of us and especially for the child.

III. RESEARCH APPROACHES TO STUDYING IMAGINATION

A. Projective Techniques

Until fairly recently most efforts to study imaginative tendencies in adults and children involved the use of projective techniques, such as the Rorschach inkblots or the Thematic Apperception Test (Singer, 1968; Singer & Brown, 1977). In general (with some methodological qualifications discussed in the above references), the data from these measures support the proposition that adults and children whose responses to projectives reflect more imaginative tendencies are also less likely to be overactive or impulsive in their motor behavior and are less likely to manifest indications of extreme impatience in situations necessitating delay or waiting behavior. Studies of adults characterized by recurrent aggressive behavior (Magargee, 1966; Misch, 1954; Singer, Wilensky, & McCraven, 1956) suggest that they showed less evidence of imaginative patterns (especially human movement responses) in their inkblot responses. Research on adolescents and school-aged children also bears out the link of an absence of imagination as measured by projectives and the tendency for overt violent or grossly antisocial behavior (Goldberg, 1974; Goldfarb, 1949; Spivack & Levine, 1964). A study by Biblow (1973) indicated that 9-year-old boys who showed fewer Rorschach human movement responses were also more likely to erupt into aggressive acts following a frustrating experience than were the children (of comparable intelligence) who showed greater imaginative tendencies.

An intriguing link of imaginativeness to the *control* of affect (in this case a presumably positive response) is reported in an ingenious study by Meltzoff and Litwin (1956). Having demonstrated that a Spike Jones "laughing" record provoked almost universal laughter within a few minutes, they instructed subjects to listen and *not* to laugh. Subjects who showed more Rorschach human movement responses were able to resist laughing more effectively than were listeners whose Rorschachs showed little evidence of imaginative patterns. Further inquiry indicated that many of the successful controllers of affect accomplished this feat not only by muscular control but often by shifting thoughts away from the record toward other fantasies, such as those likely to evoke sorrow. This area of potential systematic links of imagination to the regulation (inhibition or controlled expression) of affects beckons for more research!

B. Observations of Spontaneous Play

A more direct approach to determining imaginative trends in children can be made by observing them systematically in the course of spontaneous play activities or under limited experimental conditions. Singer (1961) found that children aged 6–9 who had reported more tendency toward make-believe and fantasy in their play styles were also better able to sit quietly for a long period of time in a simulated space capsule. An increasing number of studies are examining ongoing play and using recordings of observable behavior and verbalizations during 10-minute periods as a basis for a series of ratings of degrees of *imaginativeness, persistence, positive affects* (interest and joy responses), *overt aggression*, and *cooperation*, as well as specific mood states such as *anger, sadness, elation,* and *fatigue–sluggishness* (Singer, 1973; Singer & Singer, 1976b).

Using some of these methods, Pulaski (1973) found that more imaginative children showed more positive affects when introduced into a playroom in which toys were relatively unstructured and ambiguous in function. They also played more imaginatively with the toys. Franklin (1975) noted that children who played more imaginatively with blocks also evinced more smiling and positive affective responses. A similar link of positive affect to spontaneous imaginative play was reported in the observations of preschoolers described by Singer (1973).

If imaginativeness is estimated by questioning parents or children about the occurrence of imaginary playmates, similar findings emerge. Manosevitz, Prentice, and Wilson (1973) found that parents of preschoolers (from a sample of 222) who had become aware of their children's imaginary companions described the children as showing "happiness and high spirits" while playing with these make-believe companions. A very recent study from our own center (Caldeira, Singer, & Singer, 1978) indicates that those children (from a sample of 141) who had reported having fantasy friends were also rated quite independently as showing more positive affect in the course of spontaneous play in nursery schools and day-care centers. Examples of some very recent independent research studies using comparable observational procedures of preschoolers' ongoing play will be described in more detail below.

C. Intervention Procedures

The past decade has also witnessed the development of training procedures designed to examine whether certain types of exposure to make-believe can increase the level of imaginative play. Marshall and Hahn (1967), Smilansky (1968), Feitelson (1972), Freyberg (1973), Singer and Singer (1976b), and Saltz, Dixon, and Johnson (1976) have all reported the successful use of such training methods under controlled conditions to increase the level of imaginative play in early childhood. Possible implementation of these techniques through systematic exposure to certain television programs has also been explored by Singer and Singer (1976b) and Singer, Singer, Tower, and Biggs (1976).

Generally there have been two types of approaches. Smilansky (1968) made use of more realistic sociodramatic play. Freyberg (1973), Saltz, Dixon, and Johnson (1976), and Singer and Singer (1976a) emphasize make-believe play built around imaginary stories of adventure and exploration. Saltz, Dixon, and Johnson (1976), in the most extensive study yet carried out in this area, seemed to find that the more fanciful thematic-fantasy play training proved most efficacious for the 3- and 4-year-olds.

Singer and Singer (1977) have developed an elaborate series of exercises and techniques for parents or teachers of preschoolers, designed to enhance the development of the child's imaginative resources. More focused methods of talking to oneself and playful self-distraction have been proposed by studies by Mischel and Baker (1975) and more extensively, with somewhat older groups, by Meichenbaum (1975). It would probably be helpful to have some comparative studies of the efficacy of the more general techniques designed to increase the broad-ranging capacity for imaginative play and of techniques, perhaps using systematic reinforcement approaches, that are built around the use of make-believe for specific purposes.

We have as yet relatively few comparative studies of different kinds of approaches to presenting the make-believe materials for children. We do know that direct modeling will work even with 9- and 10-year-old children (Gottlieb, 1973) and with severely emotionally disturbed children (Nahme-Huang, Singer, Singer, & Wheaton, 1977). Most of the methods so far employed have made use of a relative stranger who engaged the children for limited periods of time in a series of make-believe exercises. In the study carried out by Dorothy Singer and myself (Singer & Singer, 1976b), it was apparent that a half hour a day of engaging in a variety of make-believe games with an adult led the children, after two weeks, to manifest significant improvements in make-believe play. Results were less striking when the children were encouraged to watch daily a television show, the *Mister Rogers' Neighborhood* show, in the company of an adult who served as a kind of interpreter for what was happening on the screen. Simply viewing the TV show alone did not have any special effect. By contrast, children in control groups showed a dropping-off in their spontaneous make-believe, whereas those who watched TV with the adult interpreter present showed some increases in spontaneous imaginative play and in positive affects as rated by hypothesis-blind observers. The strongest increases in positive affect and in self-generated make-believe during free-play periods came for those children who had been exposed to the two weeks of a half-hour daily training from the live model employing some of the games and exercises described in Singer and Singer (1977).

It is important to note that both imagination (as evidenced in the children's introduction into play of pretend elements—changes in time, place, and character) and positive affect (based on evidence of smiling and laughing or intense interest) showed increases after the training periods. Although Saltz, Dixon, and Johnson (1976) also reported increases in empathic capacity after thematic fantasy training, their measures did not include specific emotional ratings. Since empathy involves both affective expressive and cognitive components (Feshbach, 1968), we need to separate these in future research to ascertain the specific effects of imaginative training on affective sensitivities.

A more recent study by Singer, Singer, Tower, and Biggs (1977) exposed preschoolers for two weeks to one of three TV-viewing conditions: the *Mister Rogers' Neighborhood* show, *Sesame Street*, or a series of child-oriented animal and nature films not designed psychologically to produce the effects on cognition and imagination that the former two shows should be able to do. Hypothesis-blind observers trained to record all behavior shown by a given child during 10-minute play-sampling periods rated the children prior to and following the viewing periods. The results again indicated that the *Mister Rogers* show, with its emphasis on imagination and on positive reinforcing events, yielded the most clear-cut changes (despite the fact that *Sesame Street* held the children's attention better and evoked more laughter during the viewing itself). Following *Mister Rogers*, the children were more likely to reveal increased imaginativeness in play, positive affect, and more cooperative and helping behavior with peers and adults. Results for *Sesame Street* were more mixed, although generally more positive affective changes emerged than for the control films.

Of particular interest for our purposes is the finding that for the 58 children involved in the study, correlations between imaginativeness of play and the other variables rated showed considerable consistency. During play observed prior to interventions, imaginativeness of spontaneous play correlated $+.70$ with ratings of positive affect, $+.65$ with concentration or persistence, $+.45$ with cooperation with peers, $+.50$ with liveliness, and $+.59$ with elation. Correlations with ratings of fear were $-.51$, sadness $-.40$, and fatigue $-.41$. All rs were significant at $p < .001$. Following the interventions, the correlation between imaginativeness and positive affect was $+.80$ and between imaginativeness and cooperation $+.31$, concentration $+.64$, liveliness $+.62$, and elation $+.60$. The negative association with fear, sadness, and fatigue disappeared, perhaps because of intervention effects.

IV. SOME RECENT RESEARCH FINDINGS WITH PRESCHOOLERS

Two very recent and as yet unpublished studies carried out independently but with nearly identical methodology and rating scales will now be described briefly because they bear on the issue of the relationship between imagination and affect in early childhood. J. Singer and D. Singer are directing a study of about 140 three- and four-year-olds whose play is monitored periodically at nursery school or day-care center while records of their television viewing at home are also maintained. Two independent, hypothesis-blind, trained observers watch each child together for two observation periods a few days apart, and then the child is again observed twice several months later. Data from four pairs of observation periods over a year's time are therefore available. The data to be discussed here reflect only the data based on the first two "probe periods," February and April in 1977.

The sampled observations are rated by the observers after the time period along a series of dimensions that are defined carefully and for which substantial preobservation training reliabilities were obtained. Reliabilities during the actual observations are also ascertained, indicating reasonable consensus between experimenter's definitions and independent "naive" raters. The definitions are designed to minimize "halo" effects. Thus, a child can play imaginatively and show an elaborate make-believe structure without ever smiling or laughing. He or she could also assume make-believe identities and talk to thin air but still appear angry, sluggish, or bored.

In actuality the results consistently show that imaginativeness of play is associated with ratings of positive affect and elation. Table 1 shows the results of a factor analysis for the February and April observation periods separately for boys and girls and then for the sexes together. While about four or five major factors emerged, I am presenting the one relevant to this chapter, the factor of "playfulness" (happy, imaginative, verbal, cooperative).

Notice that positive affect, imagination, interaction cooperation with peers, and liveliness and elation all show by far the most sizable loadings on playfulness, with results especially strong in the February observations and somewhat weaker in the April observations. Note also that language usage also loads here. Differences between the sexes reflect the greater verbal development of 3- and 4-year-old girls and the greater motoric activity of the boys. The combined data, based of course on a more substantial sample, show essentially the same factor emerging.

The emergence of this factor of playfulness is extremely intriguing when one considers that we are talking of 3- and 4-year-olds and are basing data on spontaneous play on two separate days in February and two separate days in April. Considering all of the possible intrusions of "noise" into the system—situational factors interfering with play on a given day, illness, possible variations in observations between different observers or pairs of observers—our data hang together well. Nor does it seem likely that any specific artifact of the rating process alone can account for the emerging cluster since, for example, a verbal child might complain a great deal or a happily smiling child might be absorbed for a full sampling period in simply riding

Table 1. Loadings on "Playfulness" for Selected Variables

Boys (N = 76)		Girls (N = 65)		Combined (N = 141)	
Variable	Loading	Variable	Loading	Variable	Loading
IQ	.226	IQ	.423	IQ	.316
Age	.454	Age	.137	Age	.264
February Ratings					
Imaginativeness of play	.631	Imaginativeness of play	.682	Imaginativeness of play	.627
Positive affect	.740	Positive affect	.807	Positive affect	.825
Concentration	.370	Concentration	.459	Concentration	.468
Interaction with peers	.759	Interaction with peers	.764	Interaction with peers	.769
Cooperation with peers	.613	Cooperation with peers	.677	Cooperation with peers	.677
Fear	−.352	Fear	−.506	Fear	−.399
Fatigue–sluggishness	−.462	Sadness	−.527	Sadness	−.379
Liveliness–activity	.664	Fatigue–sluggishness	−.653	Fatigue–sluggish	−.588
Elation–joy	.685	Lively–active	.746	Lively–active	.717
Number of words	.616	Elation–joy	.749	Elation–joy	.734
Use of future words	.341	Number of utterances	.722	Number of utterances	.604
		Percentage Pronouns	−.401		
April Ratings					
Imaginativeness of play	.541	Imaginativeness	.431	Imaginativeness	.521
Positive affect	.644	Positive affect	.350	Positive affect	.586
Concentration	.530	Interaction with peers	.518	Interaction with peers	.636
Interaction with peers	.625	Cooperation with peers	.415	Cooperation with peers	.534
Cooperation with peers	.467	Sadness	−.333	Fear	−.306
Lively-active	.575	Lively–active	.308	Fatigue–sluggishness	−.346
Elation–joy	.623	Elation–joy	.299	Lively–active	.508
Number of utterances	.421	Number of utterances	.482	Elation–joy	.506
				Number of utterances	.484

a tricycle and demonstrating mastery play with much verbalization such as "Look at me! I'm going fast!" and yet not receive a score for imaginativeness. Two children might cooperate on a form board or on bead stringing and talk to each other a good deal yet receive low scores for imagination and elation. It seems more likely that we are observing a genuine phenomenon, an inherent psychological link between imaginative play, prosocial behaviors, and positive affect.

A stepwise multiple-regression analysis has been carried out with the data using observational ratings, television-viewing patterns, parent interview materials, and test data to determine the optimal predictors of spontaneous imaginative play, positive affect, anger, and overt aggression. The data are too complex to present in detail here, but some highlights will be cited.

What combination of variables best predicts the score that a child will obtain for spontaneous imaginative play? The data, relatively comparable for boys and girls, indicate that the number of utterances a child emits (either in February observations or in April observations), his imaginativeness as reflected in movement responses to inkblots, and the report by parents that he plays with an imaginary companion at home are the best combination of predictors. His use of future verbs during play and his verbal IQ as measured by the Peabody Picture Vocabulary Test are also predictive. Thus, it is not only data obtained during the same observation period that lead to a highly significant multiple R of .75 but information about the child's imaginativeness obtained quite separately from the parent.

If we turn to the prediction of positive affect as evinced during spontaneous play, the results are truly remarkable. For boys the number of times a child speaks (Number of Utterances) during a play period *months later* is a major contributor to the multiple R. The report by parents that the child has an imaginary companion or plays frequently with fantasy companions is the second predictor of positive affect during a given play period, along with the use of future verbs, IQ, inkblot movement responses, etc. The multiple R yielded by these variables is .96, suggesting clearly that imaginative play patterns at home, imagination as measured during inkblot tests weeks before, and the more complex use of language not only at the time of observation but months later can in combination almost perfectly predict whether a child will show surprise, interest, and the smile of joy during a 10-minute observation period. Comparable results emerge for the April observations of positive affect.

It is worth looking at a negative affective response on which data are now available. Anger as rated in this sample is based on facial expressions, scowling, voiced comments of annoyance or resentment, threats, or direct assertions, "I'm mad at you! You're bad!" Clearly a variable of this kind for 3- or 4-year-olds is heavily determined by situational factors, such as the accidental presence in the group of a bullying new child. Nevertheless the data clearly suggest that the best predictors of whether a child will show anger during a 10-minute observational sample turn out to be primarily *home television-viewing patterns* as recorded during two-week log-keeping periods by his or her parents. Thus, the frequent viewing of TV cartoons and action-detective shows and the amount of total viewing by the children are the best predictors of how much anger a child manifests during two 10-minute periods a few days apart during February! It's also worth noting that the tendency to watch the presumably more benign children's shows, especially *Mister Rogers' Neighborhood and Sesame Street,* is linked to a lesser likelihood of manifesting anger. Comparable—indeed even stronger—results obtain for our ratings of overt aggression, defined as direct attacks on other children or property and scored quite independently of anger.

In general, then, our results, as they emerge from a sampling of the play of preschoolers over several months, suggest a close tie between general imaginativeness and positive affect. Specific negative affective reactions, such as flashes of anger or overt aggressive behavior, are not the inverse of positive affect; they seem more closely tied to the kind of programming and the general amount of TV viewing that characterize the child at home.

A very extensive study of play patterns of 114 three- and four-year-old white children in South Africa has been carried out by Shmukler (1977). Her as yet unpublished results are cited here with her permission chiefly for comparison, since she used in one phase of her complex study observational ratings based on the definitions developed in the series of studies by J. and D. Singer cited above. Shmukler also carried out a factor analysis of 10-minute play behavior samples as rated along the dimensions mentioned. She obtained a comparable playfulness factor. Here are the factor loadings on her Factor 1 for comparison with Table 1 above. Note that she did not analyze language patterns or TV viewing at home. Loadings on this factor included imaginativeness of play +.70, positive affect +.78, concentration +.62, interaction with peers +.73, cooperation with peers +.70, sadness −.24, lively +.74, and "happy" (elated) +.77.

Shmukler has carried out extensive analyses of mother–child interaction patterns as they bear on the observed imagination in children's play. Her data suggest that the mother who is accepting of the child, who may stimulate fantasy by storytelling but who then "backs off," giving the child free time, and who has some personal career plus leisure (freedom from housekeeping chores) is most likely to have an imaginative preschool child.

V. SOME IMPLICATIONS FOR THEORY AND RESEARCH

Although evidence is accumulating, it is clear that we are largely at the beginnings of any really intensive or extensive studies of how imagination and emotion interact. In our current research, we are trying to look more carefully at the actual play protocols of children who represent clear-cut instances of high and low imagination or high and low positive affect, etc. What specific types of content may come into play here? Can we pin down more precisely whether imagination stimulates verbal output or vice versa? Can we ascertain whether the general "happiness" of a child is simply the basis of an increased likelihood for make-believe play, or is the imaginative realm itself conducive to the emergence of positive affect? In the present chapter, I've plumped for the latter possibility, but there are certainly other possibilities. Imagination, verbal flexibility, and enjoyment at play may all reflect some other underlying variable. Our results suggest that social class, ethnicity, and IQ (as far as it is measurable in such young children) are implicated but not dominant variables. Clearly we have a long way to go.

It does seem possible to conclude, however, that as early as ages 3 and 4 we can identify children who just seem happier than others and are also more cooperative and helpful with others. Can imagination be the underlying factor? I think it is. The capacity to adopt an *attitude toward the possible*, as Kurt Goldstein called it, may be one of the highest, most liberating of human capacities. Is it an accident that the children who show more joy in their play are also more likely to be using *future verbs* early? By living life not only through immediate response or perception but by reduplicating experience, replaying past material, and trying out alternatives at the level of fantasy, we may be providing ourselves a genuine freedom, a broader perspective, and, indeed, a broader life space on which to play out our term on earth.

REFERENCES

Ager, L. P. Play among Alaskan Eskimos. *Theory into Practice*, 1974, 252–256.

Aldis, O. *Playfighting*. New York: Academic Press, 1975.

Branch, T. New frontiers in American philosophy. *The New York Times Magazine*, August 14, 1977, 12–22.

Bruner, J. S., Jolly, A., & Sylva, K. (Eds.). *Play*. New York: Basic Books, 1976.

Caldeira, J., Singer, J. L., & Singer, D. G. *Imaginary playmates: Some relationships to preschoolers' television-viewing, language and play*. Paper read at Eastern Psychological Association, Washington, D.C., 1978.

Carew, J., Chan, I., & Halfer, C. *Observed intellectual competence and tested intelligence: Their roots in the young child's transactions with his environment*. Paper presented at annual meeting of the Eastern Psychological Association, New York City, 1975.

Dansky, J. L. *Cognitive function of sociodramatic play: A training study*. Unpublished doctoral dissertation, Ohio Dominican College, 1976.

Dennis, L. B. *Individual and familial correlates of children's fantasy play*. Unpublished doctoral dissertation, University of Florida, 1976.

Fein, G. A transformational analysis of pretending. *Developmental Psychology*, 1975, *11*, 291–296.

Feitelson, D. Developing imaginative play in pre-school children as a possible approach to fostering creativity. *Early Child Development and Care*, 1972, *1*, 181–195.

Feshbach, N. Studies of empathic behavior in children. Chapter in B. Maher (Ed.), *Progress in experimental personality research* (Vol. 8). New York: Academic Press, 1968.

Franklin, D. *Block play modeling and its relationship to imaginativeness, impulsivity-reflection and internal-external control.* Unpublished predissertation research, Yale University, 1975.

Freyberg, J. Increasing the imaginative play of urban disadvantaged kindergarten children through systematic training. In J. L. Singer (Ed.), *The child's world of make-believe.* New York: Academic Press, 1973.

Gershowitz, M. *Fantasy behaviors of clinic-referred children in play environments with college undergraduates.* Unpublished doctoral dissertation, Michigan State University, 1974.

Goldberg, L. *Aggression in boys in a clinic population.* Unpublished doctoral dissertation, City University of New York, 1973.

Goldfarb, W. Rorschach test differences between family-reared, institution-reared and schizophrenic children. *American Journal of Orthopsychiatry*, 1949, *19*, 624–633.

Goldstein, K. *Human nature in the light of psychopathology.* Cambridge, Mass.: Harvard University Press, 1940.

Gottlieb, S. Modeling effects upon fantasy. In J. L. Singer (Ed.), *The child's world of make-believe.* New York: Academic Press, 1973.

Gould, R. *Child studies through fantasy.* New York: Quadrangle Books, 1972.

Griffing, P. Sociodramatic play among young black children. *Theory into Practice*, 1974, *13*, 257–264.

Izard, C. E. *Human emotions.* New York: Plenum Press, 1977.

Lewis, R. H. *The relationship of sociodramatic play to various cognitive abilities in kindergarten children.* Unpublished doctoral dissertation, Ohio State University, 1973.

Manosevitz, M., Prentice, N., & Wilson, F. Individual and family correlates of imaginary companions in preschool children. *Developmental Psychology*, 1973, *8*, 72–79.

Marshall, H., & Hahn, S. Experimental modification of dramatic play. *Journal of Personality and Social Psychology*, 1967, *5*, 119–122.

Meichenbaum, D. H. *Cognitive factors in behavior modification: Modifying what clients say to themselves.* Research Report No. 25, University of Waterloo Psychology Department, Waterloo, Ontario, 1975.

Megargee, E. I. Undercontrolled and overcontrolled personality types in extreme antisocial aggression. *Psychological Monographs*, 1966, *80* (Whole No. 611).

Meltzoff, J., & Litwin, D. Affective control and Rorschach Human Movement responses. *Journal of Consulting Psychology*, 1956, *20*, 463–465.

Miller, G., Galanter, E., & Pribram, K. *Plans and the structure of behavior.* New York: Holt, 1960.

Misch, R. C. *The relationship of motoric inhibition to developmental level and ideational functioning: An analysis by means of the Rorschach test.* Unpublished doctoral dissertation, Clark University, 1954.

Mischel, W., & Baker, N. Cognitive appraisals and transformations in delay behavior. *Journal of Personality and Social Behavior*, 1975, *31*, 254–261.

Nahme-Huang, L., Singer, D. G., Singer, J. L., & Wheaton, A. B. Imaginative play and perceptual–motor intervention methods with emotionally-disturbed hospitalized children: An evaluation study. *American Journal of Orthopsychiatry*, 1977, *47*, 238–249.

Paivio, A. On the functional significance of imagery. *Psychological Bulletin*, 1970, *73*, 385–392.

Pepper, C. B. Kidnapped. *New York Times Magazine*, November 20, 1977.

Piaget, J. *Play, dreams and imitation in childhood.* New York: Norton, 1962.

Pulaski, M. Toys and imaginative play. In J. L. Singer, *The child's world of make-believe.* New York: Academic Press, 1973.

Quanta. *The Sciences* (*N.Y. Acad. Sci.*), 1977, *17* (8), p. 5.

Rohwer, W. D., Jr. *Social class differences in the role of linguistic structures and paired associate learning: Elaboration and learning proficiency.* Final Report, Bureau of Research, Office of Education. Berkeley, California: University of California (mimeographed), 1967.

Rubin, K., Maioni, T. & Hornung, M. Free play in middle and lower-class preschoolers: Parten and Piaget revisited. *Child Development,* 1976, *47,* 414–419.

Saltz, E., Dixon, J. and Johnson, J. *Training for thematic play in culturally-disadvantaged children.* Annual report to the Spencer Foundation. Detroit, Wayne State University, 1976.

Shmukler, D. The origins and concomitants of imaginative play in young children. Unpublished doctoral dissertation, University of Witwatersvand, South Africa, 1977.

Singer, D. G., and Singer, J. L. *Partners in play: A step-by-step guide to imaginative play in preschoolers.* New York: Harper and Row, 1977.

Singer, D. G., Singer, J. L., Tower, R. B., and Biggs, A. *Differential effects of television programming on preschoolers' cognition and play.* Paper presented at the annual convention of the American Psychological Association, San Francisco, 1977.

Singer, J. L. Imagination and waiting ability in young children. *Journal of Personality,* 1961, *29,* 396–413.

Singer, J. L. *The child's world of make-believe: Experimental studies of imaginative play.* New York: Academic Press, 1973.

Singer, J. L. *Imagery and daydream methods in psychotherapy and behavior modification.* New York: Academic Press, 1974.

Singer, J. L. Imagination and make-believe play in early childhood: Some educational implications. *Journal of Mental Imagery,*1977, *1,* 127–144

Singer, J. L. The constructive potential of imagery and fantasy processes: Implications for psychotherapy, child development and personal growth, In E. Witenberg (Ed.) *Interpersonal psychoanalysis, New directions.* New York: Gardner Press, 1978.

Singer, J. L., & Brown, S. L. The experience-type: Some behavioral correlates and theoretical implications. In M. A. Rickers-Ovsiankina (Ed.), *Rorschach psychology* (2nd ed.). Huntington, N.Y.: Krieger, 1977.

Singer, J. L., & Singer, D. G. Imaginative play and pretending in early childhood. In A. Davids (Ed.), *Child personality and psychopathology.* New York: Wiley-Interscience, 1976. (a)

Singer, J. L., & Singer, D. G. Can TV stimulate imaginative play? *Journal of Communications,* 1976 *26,* 74–80. (b)

Singer, J. L., Wilensky, H., & McCraven, V. Delaying capacity, fantasy and planning ability: A factorial study of some basic ego functions. *Journal of Consulting Psychology,* 1956, *20,* 375–383.

Smilansky, S. *The effects of sociodramatic play on disadvantaged preschool children.* New York: Wiley, 1968.

Spivak, G., & Levine, M. *Self-regulation and acting-out in normal adolescence.* Progress report for National Institute of Mental Health Grant M-4531. Devon, Pennsylvania: Devereaux Foundation, 1964.

Sutton-Smith, B. The role of play in cognitive development. *Young Children,* 1967, *6,* 202–214.

Tomkins. S. S. *Affect, imagery, consciousness* (Vols. 1 and 2). New York: Springer, 1962, 1963.

Tomkins, S. S. A theory of memory. In J. S. Antrobus (Ed.), *Cognition and affect.* Boston, Massachusetts: Little, Brown, 1970.

Tucker, J. *The role of fantasy in cognitive–affective functioning: Does reality make a difference in remembering?* Unpublished doctoral dissertation, Teachers College, Columbia University, 1975.

Weisler, A., & McCall, R. B. Exploration and play. Resumé and redirection. *American Psychologist,* 1976, *31,* 492–508.

Witelson, S. F. Sex and the single hemisphere: Specialization of the right hemisphere for spatial processing. *Science,* 1976, *193,* 425–427.

Editor's Introduction

2

In a book focusing mostly on emotion-related problems and psychological disorders, a chapter on humor seems a singularly happy choice, but humor, like most emotion-related behaviors, is a complex affair. While the emotion of joy may be the fundamental emotion expressed by laughter, the emotions of anger, contempt, and fear may also be couched in laughter. Levine shows how humor and laughter can both cure and kill. He demonstrates that humor and psychopathology are generally antipodal and that psychiatric patients typically perform poorly on tests of humor appreciation. He shows how people's failure to appreciate a joke or a cartoon can furnish leads as to the nature of their problems, whether they be minor or pathological. He presents evidence for a relationship between certain types of response to humor and specific psychological disorders. He also shows how people can use humor and laughter for amusement or aggression.

This study of laughter and humor demonstrates some important principles of human emotions. It shows how one emotion can amplify, attenuate, or inhibit another and how one emotion expression can be used to disguise other ongoing emotion experiences.

Levine's chapter also illustrates the usefulness of considering the relatively distinct contributors of different personality subsystems to personality functioning. Humor appreciation clearly has an affective and a cognitive aspect, and these two sometimes seem to become dissociated in psychopathology. That is, some people seem to be able to understand humor intellectually without showing any affective response. Others seem to laugh at what they perceive to be a humorous intent without really understanding the joke. Levine also shows that laughter as an expression may become dissociated from the subjective experience of joy and may become painful rather than pleasurable. His review of the work on uncontrollable laughter also has implications for the study of emotion–cognition relationships and the need for a better understanding of the neurophysiological substrates of emotion experience and emotion expression.

Humor and Psychopathology

JACOB LEVINE

In one of Trollope's stories, the doctor proclaims, "The best tonic for all mental ills is laughter." The effectiveness of this prescription in healing all mental ills may be nothing more than a literary hyperbole, but it does express what everyone knows: if one can laugh, enjoy a good joke, and be "in humor," mental distress goes away. A recent account of a remarkable recovery from a painful and usually fatal disease by "laughing it away" has recently received considerable public attention. Paradoxically it makes Trollope's doctor look like a sound prescriber. The dramatic case was described by Adam Smith in his popular book *Powers of Mind* (1975). The patient was a highly respected publisher and writer, Norman Cousins (1976), who confirmed Smith's report in detail in the prestigious *New England Journal of Medicine*. Smith described how Cousins, suffering from the dread crippling disease ankylosing aspondylitis, insisted on leaving the hospital in his crippled state, stopped taking all prescribed medications, and deliberately used laughter "as a positive emotion" to activate his sluggish glands. He borrowed and watched a number of Marx Brothers movies and episodes of *Candid Camera*, laughed, and took big doses of vitamin C. According to his own physician, "Cousins cured himself by his own hand and mind: Notwithstanding the possibility that the recovery was a placebo effect, this exceptional case reminds us of the association of humor and laughter with good mental health."

Despite Cousins's astonishing recovery, growing out of his ideas of the positive effects of humor and laughter upon the body's physiology, no reliable evidence exists to support the notion that humor has any lasting, healing effect upon illness, physical or mental. On the other hand, a considerable amount of evidence does exist that identifies humor and laughter as symptomatic of both

JACOB LEVINE • West Haven Veterans Administration Hospital, West Haven, Connecticut; and Yale University, New Haven, Connecticut.

organic and mental illness. One example is given by the clinical observation that the first clear symptom of certain brain stem tumors is the eruption of uncontrollable laughter. Nevertheless it is in the protean nature of humor that it could well be a symptom and/or a cure of different illnesses.

Ordinarily, humor and mental illness are viewed as antithetical. Mental illness is associated with emotional distress and humor with joyfulness. We know that the ability to enjoy humor is impaired by anxiety and mental anguish. As Freud (1960) and Kris (1940) pointed out, humor cannot overcome strong dysphoric emotions. A man who is very angry, frightened, despairing, or filled with bitter hatred cannot appreciate a good joke. It is the inability to adopt a humorous attitude or orientation toward a comic situation that prevents the anxious or distressed person from enjoying humor. Freud delineated what the adoption of a humorous attitude means.

Clinical observation has shown that psychiatric patients usually reveal some aberration in their humor behavior. But response to humor is not so much pathognomonic of psychopathology as it is a unique expression of the individual that momentarily illuminates his personality. A joke is "one man's meat but another man's poison," or as William Hazlitt put it, "sport to one but death to another." Goethe observed that, "Men show their characters in nothing more clearly than in what they think laughable." Humor appreciation in the form of humor tests has come to be used to diagnose personality as a sensitive mirror of deep-seated personality conflicts. Based upon this common awareness of the extent to which humor is a reflection of the personality, a number of investigators have devised a variety of humor tests that measure an individual's responses to humorous stimuli (Cattell & Luborsky, 1947; O'Connell, 1962; Zigler, Levine, & Gould, 1966). In these humor tests, as in most experimental studies of responses to humor, humor stimuli, in the form of either cartoons or jokes, are presented to subjects, and generally three types of responses are noted: expressions of mirth (smile or laughter), judgments of the relative funniness, and evidence of understanding the humor. Sometimes subjects are asked to create a funny punchline to a cartoon or a joke, and in some clinical studies they are asked to report their favorite joke.

The intent of this chapter is to consider the impact of psychopathology upon humor behavior in its various forms, since, aside from anecdotes and unsystematic observations, we have no reliable evidence that humor has any influence upon psychopathology. We shall first review the observed effects of psychopathology generally upon the cognitive, affective, and behavioral aspects of humor. Early disturbances in laughing and smiling will be considered as symptomatic of infantile interpersonal difficulties that potentially could play a critical role in the developmental process, particularly in the expression of positive affect. Comic behavior in its diverse forms—from tickling and teasing to ridicule, caricature, and satire—is often used as instruments of aggression, sometimes to a pathological degree. The final section will deal with three of the most common forms of psychopathology—organic states, schizophrenia, and depression—as they impact upon humor behavior, often serving as pathognomonic symptoms. In the case of depression, we shall discuss the common observation that humorists, comedians, and others who seek to make people laugh are often depressed individuals.

I. HUMOROUS BEHAVIOR AND ITS PSYCHOPATHOLOGY

A. Early Disturbances of Smiling and Laughing

How humor can be a sign both of good mental health and of mental illness is not so much a contradiction as a reflection of the extraordinary diversity of meanings and purposes that humor can have. It is little wonder that no one has yet been able to come up with an adequate definition of humor. Adult humor is a complex configuration of behavior modalities that was evolved from the elemental responses of infants to specific interpersonal stimuli. The leap is very long from the laughter of the infant at the peek-a-boo of a familiar face to the chuckle of the adult at a witty remark. Although there has been a recent upsurge in interest in children's humor, it is still generally regarded as epiphenomenal to the developmental process. The contributions of laughter and humor to development have not been a serious subject for investigation, perhaps because humor has been viewed as an adult activity. It is probably also a consequence of the fact that humor has always been seen as an incidental and trivial activity, a distraction from serious and purposeful human affairs.

Oddly enough, the best evidence that demonstrates the importance of humor in genetic development is presented by the absence of smiling or laughing by children in situations that normally evoke them. These are the first manifestations of the relation of humor and psychopathology. When infants fail to smile or laugh in appropriate situations, it is evident that these infants are not experiencing the situation as fun or pleasurable but rather as distressing or frightening. Sroufe and Wunsch (1972) noted that infants who were distressed cried in response to stimuli normally evoking laughter. Wolff (1969) observed that distressed infants cried instead of laughed when tickled. A number of clinical studies (Spitz & Wolff, 1946; Bowlby, 1965; Mahler, 1961; Provence & Ritvo, 1961) have considered the fact that institutionalized infants who lacked mothering never smiled or laughed pathognomonic of profound infantile depression. These infants were observed to relapse into a state of unresponsiveness and helplessness and rarely interacted with anyone except by crying. One wonders what the long-term effects are of these early depressed states where the infants cannot learn to use smiling or laughing as so-called social releasers to evoke positive responses in others.

It is reasonable to expect that impairment in the primordial forms of humor, both as responses and as stimuli, are important factors during these critical periods of child development. As basic components in the emergence of the communicative process, these affective responses are likely to have significant effects upon emotional development, particularly the expressions of positive affect. One can assume that these early experiences of interacting with others with positive affect are the basic determinants of what ultimately becomes a sense of humor—or the lack of one. From this point of view, humor is clearly an intrinsic and vital component of the normal growth process.

In a television interview on April 19, 1959, the great Zen master Suzuki was discussing Zen Buddhism. He described how Zen Buddhism began. It was during a lecture by Buddha when he held out a bouquet of flowers that had been handed to him. None of the pupils sitting before Buddha understood what Buddha meant by his holding out the flowers with his outstretched arms—except one old monk. This monk looked up at Buddha and smiled. Buddha smiled back. And that is how Zen Buddhism began. The story may not help very much in the understanding of Zen Buddhism, but it beautifully illustrates the meaningfulness of the simple smile and the mutual understanding that can occur between two people with but a smile. The story points up the interpersonal character of the smile and the immediacy and depth of communication that it can achieve. One point of the fable is that the smile is a gateway to intimate communication. This form of communication is contrasted with language, which, as Koestler (1964) so rightly noted, actually restricts communication. The smile is truly the first emotional and communicative contact between two people.

B. Failures in Humor Appreciation

The appreciation of a joke or a funny cartoon is a real achievement that requires mental effort and emotional elasticity. To "get" the joke is an intellectual accomplishment not unlike the solving of a puzzle or a problem. Sometimes the joke can be understood only if one has the special knowledge about certain critical elements, as in topical jokes. An example of such a joke is given by the remarks of one literary dilettante to another, "Saroyan isn't his real name, you know. It's a pseudonym. Saroyan is nature's spelled backwards." To get this joke, one must first know about Saroyan the writer, and second, one must recognize that the statement "Nature's spelled backwards" is taken from an advertisement for a once-popular laxative called "Serutan." Thus, from the cognitive viewpoint, getting the joke involves both the necessary knowledge and the intellectual capacity to resolve the incongruity.

It is evident that the causes of failure to appreciate or enjoy a particular joke or comic situation are myriad. But before a joke can be enjoyed, it must be understood. Inability to meet that cognitive demand results in failure. The resolution of a joking incongruity is frequently used in intelligence tests like the Stanford–Binet because of the clear-cut cognitive demands that, graded in terms of difficulty, require explaining what's funny in items containing verbal or pictorial absurdities. And yet, failure to understand a joke is not always due to intellectual inadequacy or strangeness of content. A variety of motivational and psychodynamic factors associated with the particular humor content may interfere with the comprehension of the joke. As many of the aphorisms suggest, humorous stimuli can evoke considerable emotional distress and anxiety instead of pleasure. They may lead to the misapprehension or scotomization of essential details as a way of avoiding awareness of the disturbing content. On the other hand, these psychodynamic factors may not interfere with the comprehension of the joke yet still prevent the appreciation of it. It is thus easy to see that because of the manifold bases for the failure of humor to evoke risible responses, it is difficult to differentiate the normal dysphoric responses from those resulting from psychopathological conditions.

These momentary dysfunctional responses to specific humorous stimuli are essentially stress responses indicative of an upsurge of anxiety. It is impressive that ostensibly trivial and innocuous stimuli like jokes can evoke responses expressive either of joyfulness (laughter) or of revulsion. As transient lapses in cognitive and/or affective functioning, they may be viewed generally as reflecting the psychopathology of everyday life. Symptomatic of more serious psychopathology are the various conditions of psychiatric disturbances in which there is a pervasive incapacity to appreciate any forms of humor or to laugh in response to risible stimulation. The person in a depressed state comes immediately to mind as one who is unable to see anything to laugh about. Other pathological conditions associated with anxiety or strong dysphoric states also impair the ability to enjoy humor.

C. The Cognitive Component of the Humor Response

Cognitive functions obviously mediate the humor process. But they also contribute to the experienced pleasure. Freud (1960) observed that one of the two primary sources of pleasure in humor is the exercise of our mental faculties. The more subtle and difficult the point of the joke, the more pleasure do we derive from discovering it. In a study of children between grades 3 and 7, cartoons that approached the upper limit of their ability to comprehend, thereby offering a cognitive challenge, evoked the most laughter (Zigler, Levine, & Gould, 1966). The successful resolution of a humorous incongruity is ego-enhancing and is experienced as an achievement that contributes to a feeling of effectiveness and of mastery. The simplest forms of humor, puns and riddles, which are so much enjoyed by children who have just begun to master language, are the clearest examples of the pleasure obtained by the cognitive mastery of a problem presented in humor. Although puns are considered to be the lowest form of humor, suitable only for children, they really are not. Good puns are still enjoyed by adults. Many puns, like those in which word sounds replace meanings, are understood and enjoyed by children because they make the least cognitive demand but are at the cutting edge of children's intellectual capacities. Because of their simplicity or obviousness they are depreciated by adults. Shakespeare is recognized as the greatest punster in the English language, and his plays abound in puns. One example is given by the dying Mercutio in *Romeo and Juliet*, who declared, "Ask for me tomorrow and you will find me a grave man." An example of a somewhat more simple form of pun is shown by the answer to the question, "Can you give me a sentence with the word *denial?*" Answer, "Cleopatra lived and loved on denial." The effectiveness of this pun is based upon the simplicity of the technique that is so frequently used by children. It focuses attention on the sound of the word *denial* rather than on its meaning. Yet it probably will be understood only by older children. An excellent but more complex pun is "one man's Mede is another man's Persia," which can probably be appreciated only by sophisticated adults.

In the enjoyment of a joke, the pleasure is not so much in getting the point of it as it is in solving a problem. There is the added pleasure in the techniques that create the problem, like incongruity, absurdity, play on words, displacement, condensation, and double entendre. These techniques make up the structure of humor and give it its identity. How these techniques or structural properties of humor give pleasure is still an unresolved problem, despite the fact that they have been a central issue in many theories of humor. Incongruity and its paradoxes, in particular, have been the major focus of many research and theoretical studies as the basic process in humor appreciation. One must remember that though the resolution of an incongruity is a gratifying cognitive achievement, it is not all there is to humor.

Formal structural elements like incongruity, playful absurdity, and double entendre are basic cognitive processes in jokes and getting the point of a joke requires the capacity to meet the intellectual demands it makes. Other cognitive demands of a joke may consist of the specific cultural and social experiences that make up the content. For example, some mentally ill individuals like schizophrenics often lack the social comprehension necessary to grasp what is happening between people in popular cartoons (Senf *et al.*, 1956). But even if the capacity to meet the cognitive demands of a joke are met, other interferences, such as motivational affective conflicts, may prevent full comprehension.

Perhaps the most common mode of cognitive interference is seen in everyday life where relatively normal individuals fail to understand a cartoon or a joke primarily because the thematic features are too full of conflict. The result is that the individual scotomizes an essential element in the cartoon or joke

* bettertowin Than to stand on defeat"

and thereby fails to understand it. In instances where this reaction has been observed, further inquiry reveals a strong negative reaction to the joke. For these individuals, the humor theme is not a joking matter. In other instances, perhaps with greater frequency, individuals may react with less distress over a particular joke or cartoon by mitigating the aggressive or sexual content. This type of response, reflecting a mild perceptual distortion rather than a complete scotomization, usually results in a partial grasp of the joke and does not always lead to a rejection of the joke as unfunny.

Cognitive distortions of a joke or cartoon may also result in an exaggeration of the aggressive or sexual content. These distortions usually can be observed where the conflicted individual is overvigilant or hypersensitive to such intentions. In such instances, the affective reaction tends to be extreme in either direction, that is, either strong approval or disgust. These types of reactions dramatically demonstrate the importance of the joke work that Freud (1960) postulated as characterizing the formal elements of the joke to serve as disguises for the latent and tendentious purposes of the humor.

Despite the absence of any hard evidence (a fact that is true for most of what we "know" about humor), motivational and affective interferences with the comprehension of jokes or cartoons are probably much more common than we assume. As instances of the psychopathology of everyday life, it is not unusual for anyone of us to "overlook" some detail of a joke or cartoon that prevents us from getting the point. We never bother to reflect on the reason for the oversight. But it is a common truism that the best way to kill a joke is to explain it. E. B. White (1935), that great American humorist and essayist, said it best; "Humor can be dissected, as a frog can, but the thing dies in the process and the innards are discouraging to any but the pure scientific mind." His friend and fellow humorist Robert Benchley was more scornful; "There seem to be no lengths to which humorless people will not go to analyze humor."

In one study, when college students were asked to explain the content of aggressive cartoons, they showed a significant drop in their liking for the cartoons (Gollob & Levine, 1967). The failure to understand a joke or a cartoon that is not very subtle is frequently a consequence of an unconscious wish to avoid doing so for emotional reasons (Levine & Redlich, 1955). These reasons may reflect no more serious psychopathology than do the ordinary slips of the tongue or of memory. They occur in persons with high intelligence and achievement. An example of the denial of an essential element in a cartoon is illustrated by the case of a depressed man who had strong guilt feelings about his hostility toward his wife. He looked at a cartoon by Charles Addams in which a placid middle-aged man is depicted raking leaves around a tree to which his wife is tied. The situation clearly suggested that the man was going to ignite the leaves and burn his wife at the stake. The depressed man remarked, "I don't see any particular point to this cartoon. He is raking leaves and she is tied to a tree. He probably just wanted to get her out of the way while he was raking the leaves. I can't see anything particularly funny about it." Asked whether the man appeared to be planning to burn his wife, the man replied with much feeling, "Oh, no, definitely not." He indicated that he disliked this cartoon (Redlich, Levine, & Sohler, 1951). To the same cartoon, a young woman being treated for anxiety neurosis responded, "I don't see anything funny in it. I know what's going to happen. He is going to burn up the man with the leaves." She understood the murderous intent in the cartoon but changed the sex of the victim.

The perceptual distortions and omissions with a consequent misunderstanding caused by a severely disturbing cartoon seem to be all but uncorrectable. For example, a young male who showed no severe disturbance but had anxieties about homosexuality and voyeuristic impulses was shown a cartoon by Peter Arno of a young woman stripped to the waist and sitting before a physician, who looks puzzled. The nipples of her breasts are turned inward in such a way as to give them a cross-eyed look. The doctor says to the girl, "Have you tried an oculist?" The patient reacted to this cartoon with embarrassment and disgust, explaining, "I don't like this . . . it's filthy . . . just sex, just plain dirty. He has got her disrobed . . . it's pure sex. I never did get a kick out of a dirty joke." When the cross-eyed breasts were pointed out to him, he still failed to comprehend and finally refused to look at it. The same cartoon caused a more severe reaction in a paranoid schizophrenic woman. She declared, "The doctor sees spots in front of his eyes and he puts them on her breasts." Her projection served as a defense against the body distortion, which she could not tolerate. Finally, another male patient, only mildly disturbed by anxiety and of superior intelligence, responded to the same cartoon with, "I don't see anything funny in it. The doctor is completely baffled and he asks her to see an eye doctor because she is sort of cross-eyed." This patient had strongly identified himself with women and had many anxieties about his own sexual adequacy. During his wife's pregnancy, he suffered pains in the stomach and nausea. On the night of her delivery, he vomited and was hospitalized.

These examples are presented not as typical instances of everyday psychopathology revealed through humor. They merely illustrate how psychopathology, even circumscribed and not of great magnitude, can impair cognitive function in response to humor. In a recent study, not yet published, some surprising findings suggest the pervasiveness of this cognitive inefficiency without the individuals' being aware of it. A group of 10 Ph.D. psychologists were asked to rate a series of 30 popular and easily understood cartoons for their relative comprehensibility. Following these ratings, the subjects were each asked to explain the joke in each cartoon. Correlations between comprehension scores and difficulty ratings of the cartoons were found not to be significant. These findings suggested that the subjects were not aware of their own comprehension failures and that their judgments of the cartoons' difficulty were unrelated to their own difficulties in getting the joke. A more systematic replication is planned, but the finding, if true, tends to support E. B. White's view that analyzing humor is unpleasant and destructive. We don't want to know why we laugh.

Superior intelligence and sophistication do not protect us from these everyday lapses in cognitive efficiency in responding to humor. An outstanding and sophisticated scientist, chairman of a department in a major university, looked at a cartoon in which an office manager opens the office "suggestions" box. Dropping out of the box he finds a bottle marked "poison." The scientist could not understand the cartoon. When the bottle of poison was finally pointed out to him, he was surprised to see the "poison" label, although it was prominently displayed as the key element of the joke. He finally got the joke that someone had placed the poison there as a suggestion to the boss to take it. Even after he understood the cartoon, the scientist found it unfunny. A little interrogation revealed that the theme of the cartoon touched directly upon a problem that particularly troubled the scientist at that moment. As a new administrator, he was deeply concerned about what his colleagues and students thought of him. He could not confront the problem as something to joke about. By scotomizing the key element, he avoided the confrontation, and he did not appreciate the joke even after he understood it (Levine & Redlich, 1951).

D. The Affective Component

Malcolm Muggeridge, former editor of *Punch*, once remarked, "One thing at any rate I have learned—that what seems uproariously funny to one man can seem devastatingly unfunny to another." That humor can be a power-ful stimulus to emotion is evident. And these emotional reactions can range from one extreme to the other. It is a strange fact that with all the theorizing about humor, few theories have tried to explain the plain fact that humor can be an extremely disturbing stimulus rather than the pleasurable one that it is ostensibly designed to be.

We find not only the idiosyncratic negative responses to specific humor but in many cases of psychopathology an inability to enjoy any kind of humor. Depressives and anxiety-ridden individuals cannot find any humor pleasurable, nor can most schizophrenics. It is safe to say that no form of psychopathology fails to manifest some emotional distortion of the humor response.

Psychiatric patients generally do not enjoy humor. Those forms of humor that they do enjoy are relatively nontendentious, evoking little anxiety in their content. Most people seek humor stimuli that arouse some tension or anxiety, serving as a sort of emotional challenge. We know that the humor stimuli that are most appreciated are those that make a cognitive demand upon the individual (Zigler, Levine, & Gould, 1967). Those jokes or cartoons are preferred that tax the individual's intellectual capacities to the fullest. Analogously, that humor is enjoyed the most that poses the greatest tolerable emotional stress (Levine & Abelson, 1959). For example, most anxious psychiatric patients don't like the cartoons of Charles Addams in contrast to most other people, who find his cartoons with haunted settings and fiendish characters very amusing. People generally like humor that is at least a little bit anxiety-provoking and like least that which tends to be tame and obvious. Thus, it seems that in order to enjoy a particular humorous stimulus, an individual must experience a certain level of anxiety, but a level that he can master. For the mental patient who is already anxious, even the minimal increase in anxiety evoked by humor is not tolerable. It is understandable that the mental patient will dislike a far greater number of humorous stimuli.

The failure of mentally disturbed individuals to experience pleasure is not restricted to humor. It is probably pathognomonic that they show a reduced ability to gain pleasure from anything. Anxious people do not enjoy play, recreation, fantasy, sex, etc. This disability can perhaps be extended to joy, affection, love, and self-esteem. In fact, some theorists and investigators have hypothesized that anhedonia, as a reduction in the capacity of the individual to experience pleasure, is a central symptom of schizophrenia and is genetic in origin (Rado, 1952, 1962; Meehl, 1962; Stein & Wise, 1971; Wise & Stein, 1973; Chapman, 1975). But humor may have a unique relation to mental illness, because of the way humor gives pleasure. Perhaps the most common element in the many theories of humor, going back at least as far as Aristotle, is the momentary sense of superiority when we laugh at something funny as the primary source of pleasure. This feeling of superiority is at the very antipode of most mental disturbances.

The mentally ill are generally in pain, suffering from anxiety and mental anguish. They feel incapable of coping with their problems, and their symptoms reflect their inadequate efforts to deal with their distress. They can not laugh off their suffering, nor can they use humor to experience any joy. These cases of psychopathology are instances of the general fact that humor cannot overcome strong dysphoric affect. Yet, humor is often a great antidote to periodic low feelings and mild annoyances, besides having the ability to elevate the spirits of a group to a high point of conviviality and unity. For those who can respond to humor, it can help significantly as an adaptive process in times of stress. Probably more than anyone, Freud (1928) recognized how humor serves as an adaptive mechanism when he asserted:

> By its repudiation of the possibility of suffering, humor takes its place in the great series of methods devised by the mind of man for evading the compulsion to suffer—a series which begins with neurosis and delusions and includes intoxication, self-induced states of abstraction and ecstasy.

Thus Freud placed humor along with neurosis and psychosis as basic mechanisms of coping with human suffering, but with the essential difference that humor is adaptive and is not pathological.

In contrast to mental illness, humor is not a state of despair or lowered self-esteem. On the contrary, to be "in humor" is to assume an attitude of invulnerability and mastery over whatever fate has in store. This idea did not originate with Freud but has been expressed in many ways. It is said that Aristotle conceived of humor as being due to the "sudden feeling of triumph which comes with the sudden perception of a superiority in us by the comparison with inferiority of others or our own former inferiority". It was restated by Hobbes in 1640 in his famous definition of laughter: "A sudden glory arising from some conception of some eminency in ourselves, by comparison with the infirmity of others, or with our own formerly." These views of humor have most often been classified under theories of humor emphasizing superiority over others, but they fail to recognize the latter part of these statements, which point up the mastery of one's own infirmities. From the psychoanalytic view, the psychogenesis of humor embraces the growing pleasure in the individual's power and mastery of active functions formerly not possible. The earliest stimuli to laughter in the infant appear to be those that evoke certain kinds of motor experiences. According to Jacobson (1946):

> When intense, specially rhythmical stimulation of the whole or a part of the motor system produces a certain or suprising fact or enjoyable experience, which, though first suggesting danger, arouses pleasant anticipation of relief, laughter comes about as a final, intensely pleasurable motor release. The original close relationship between laughter and motor experience paves the way for later stages in the development of laughter from a reaction to complex experiences of bodily mastery, to a victory of the ego over the outer realistic and inner instinctual world.

As children experience the growing mastery of motor and language functions, their humor and laughter express this sense of competence (Jacobson, 1946; Wolfenstein, 1954). Kris (1940) said it most succinctly: "What was feared yesterday is fated to appear funny when seen today."

The humorous attitude is, then, a state of mind. In that state, man reasserts his power and refuses to submit to threat or fear. This is something the mentally ill cannot do. Again, Freud (1928) put it best:

> Humor is not resigned; it is rebellious. It signifies not only the triumph of the ego but also of the pleasure principle, which is able here to assert itself against the unkindness of the real circumstances. These last two features—the rejection of the claims of reality and putting through of the pleasure principle—bring humor near to the regressive or reactionary processes which engage our attention so extensively in psychopathology.

The humorous attitude is thus but one of a number of psychological processes that function as adaptive modes of withdrawal from reality into the world of the imagination. But unlike mental illness, it is a voluntary withdrawal. The ability to withdraw voluntarily from reality is an eagerly pursued state that may be sought in many ways: sports, alcohol, play, literature, drugs, sleep, yoga, movies, television, and humor. Neurotic and psychotic symptoms are also seen as detachments from reality; however, they are not voluntary or adaptive but are pathological. They are maladaptive attempts to cope with conflict and anxiety. They are essentially psychologically defensive flights from threatening or painful reality. They therefore do not function for ego gratification or pleasure.

E. Comic Action and Its Psychopathology

1. Tickling. Tickling is probably the most simple form of acting in humor in order to evoke a risible response. Despite its apparent simplicity, we know little about tickling, even though it is an unlearned response, for very young children respond to tickling by laughter well before they learn to talk. Convincing evidence is now available demonstrating that the higher apes are also responsive to tickling and find it pleasurable. The fact that it is unlearned and that special areas of the body are particularly sensitive to tickling suggests that it is a form of reflex. But one characteristic distinguishes tickling from all other reflexes, and this is its dependence upon a second person. We cannot tickle ourselves, no matter how ticklish we are. Tickling is an interaction between two people in which the relationship is familiar and friendly and surprise enhances the initial response. The great variability of particular areas of ticklishness from individual to individual also is not characteristic of reflexes. The meaning and significance of these features of tickling are not known. It is noteworthy that ticklishness and tickling are associated with childhood and tend to diminish with age.

References to the tickling behavior of primates have been, until recently, casual and incidental to observations of the play of animals (DeVore, 1965). In a recent article in *The New York Times Sunday Magazine* (June 12, 1977) Harold Hayes presented convincing evidence of the wish of a chimpanzee to be tickled. With accompanying photographs, he showed how a female chimpanzee named Lana had been taught to communicate by tapping sentences expressing her wishes on an electronic keyboard. One of the sentences she most frequently used was "Please Tim tickle Lana." For Lana and for a young child to be tickled by a trusted and loved one is fun and much desired.

The few writers who have theorized about tickling have suggested that it is a mild form of aggression (Flugel, 1954; Leuba, 1941). From a phylogenetic viewpoint, tickling may perhaps be related to other forms of aggression characteristic of the play of young animals, such as nipping, biting, and wrestling. Tickling is associated with caressing, stroking, and touching, and its effects have been delineated in man along the pain–pleasure dimension (Kepecs, Robin, & Munro, 1961). In the context of playfulness, continued tickling can be used with increasing aggressiveness to the point of pain. In the social interchange, the metacommunication of tickling is expressive of affection and friendliness. But one must be receptive to the playfulness and humor in tickling. As Eastman (1936), the humorist, noted, "It is unpleasant to be tickled by a stranger, and it is unpleasant to be tickled by a friend when you are 'feeling serious.' It vexes you, and if continued makes you mad."

Another unexplored aspect of tickling is its relation to laughter. It is a familiar fact that when tickling evokes laughter it is involuntary and uncontrollable. Once laughter erupts, continued tickling provokes the laughter unceasingly until the tickled person is helpless to stop. It is no longer pleasurable and becomes painful.

2. Teasing. Teasing is another form of comic action that begins as simple provocative behavior expressed affectionately in a humorous mode. An old German proverb states, "Those who love each other tease each other." It is also another form of joking play that man shares with animals but that later differentiates into a variety of complex modes, particularly with the development of language. In both tickling and teasing, the aggressive component of humor is primary, and as long as it occurs in the context of humor and friendliness, it is tolerated and enjoyed even if it is mildly painful. Sometimes the teasing, like tickling, is carried too far, either intentionally or not, and the humorous set is lost. "I was only kidding" is frequently the apologetic response, and this expression conveys the communication that the inflicted pain was unintentional. In this way, both tickling and teasing illustrate beautifully the manner in which aggression becomes acceptable as humor. The Virginian in Owen Wister's novel said it best when he challenged with drawn gun an insulting remark by a gunfighter with, "When you say that, smile."

In the course of development and socialization, teasing assumes many forms and functions, some of which if carried out outside of the humor context would be seen as grossly pathological. Among many cultures and national groups, teasing has been ritualized into a variety of forms that serve important regulatory functions (Levine, 1961). In some of these instances, these ritualized teasing behaviors release the participants from social, moral, and rational restraints so that they can carry out aggressions and sexual acts that otherwise would be viewed as unacceptable. The sacred clowns of many of our American Indian tribes that are normally very proper and restrained in their conduct, like the Hopi and the Zuni, are privileged in their rituals to make fun of any person or institution and can violate any social taboo, even incest. The grotesque comic antics of these clowns demonstrate the degree to which humor frees an individual or a group from ordinary social restraints.

The ritualization of humor in teasing is not limited to primitive peoples or to aggressive behavior. All cultures indulge in aggressive and sexual teasing in many ritualized forms. We have only to recall the hazing of fraternities and secret societies, the striptease in burlesque shows, and the sexual banter and teasing that takes place in our cocktail bars and taverns to serve as examples of our own form of institutionalized humor. In the so-called joking relationships of many primitive cultures, anthropologists have recognized the functional value of institutional humor in the form of teasing in defining and maintaining certain kinship relationships. Both aggression and sex play significant roles in these joking relationships. Brandt (1948) confirmed the generally held hypothesis that these relationships are expressions of some potential sexual relationships within kinships. Levine (unpublished) has hypothesized that these forms of institutional humor serve an important social function in regulating the sexual and aggressive tensions that normally arise in certain kinship relationships. From this viewpoint, the joking relationships provide extrinsic, social controls for the sexual and aggressive urges that could be expressed only in violation of the culture's taboos.

In the context of humor, taunting and ridicule are treated as a joke, whereas under reality conditions such ridicule could be destructive, even leading to suicide or homicide. Mark Twain observed that nothing can stand up against the assault of laughter.

Throughout the ages and in all cultures, teasing and laughing at others have been the primary paradigm for humor as the basic source of laughter. Plato, Aristotle, Cicero, and Hobbes, as well as modern writers like Bergson, Meredith, and Kronenberger, have based their views of humor on this paradigm. In many times and places, the objects of teasing and ridicule were institutionalized in the persons of clowns, fools, and jesters, who were usually dwarfs or hunchbacks. Such deformed and handicapped individuals were natural objects of derision. A dramatic example of the regulatory function of institutional humor is shown among the Greenland Eskimos, where quarrels are resolved by a duel of aggressive humor. Each contestant, armed only with a drum used as an accompaniment, recites humorous insults and obscene jokes ridiculing his opponent. The duelist who evokes the most laughter from the audience is declared the victor. The loser is profoundly humiliated, often going into exile. These diverse examples demonstrate the recognition by society of the powers of humor in shaping and controlling human relationships.

A number of clinical studies of psychiatric patients who were depressed and anorexic have demonstrated how teasing, caricature, and provoking others to laugh at them were used to gain attention and approval. In their caricatures and impersonations of others, they could also express their aggressive feelings with impunity. We shall discuss later how in an analogous manner some of our most famous humorists and comedians have used their ability to make others laugh as a way of coping with their depression and need for acclaim. For those individuals who strive unceasingly to make others laugh either by making fools of themselves as teasees or by caricaturing others, humor serves not so much to obtain pleasure as it does to relieve anxiety and despair or to release aggressive feelings. But the humor they create and the laughter they provoke in themselves are not pathological. These psychodynamics are well described in the case studies of Jacobson (1946), Reich (1949), Brenman (1952), Sperling (1951), and Story (1976).

The differentiation between the normal and the psychopathological in humor is often unclear, particularly when the psychopathological is seen in the context of the social mores of the cultural group. This relativity is well illustrated by the forms and instances of teasing that are entirely acceptable in one culture but are not in another. Sperling (1953) has presented a number of anthropological examples in which parents are taught deliberately to tease their young children by abruptly withdrawing the breast or otherwise provoking children's rage reactions in order to mold their character. A particularly violent but accepted form of formalized teasing among the poor in the southern states of the United States has frequently been described as "doing the dozens," in which increasingly vicious verbal taunting is used in order to provoke a breakdown in emotional restraint into physical attack. When this happens, the group led by the victorious taunter viciously beats up the loser (Dollard, 1937). The sadistic aspects of many of these teasing games that bait the victims to impotent rage and violence are socially acceptable despite the physical harm. By the social standards of other cultures, these forms of teasing are clearly considered pathological.

II. HUMOR IN SPECIFIC PSYCHOPATHOLOGICAL STATES

A. General Considerations

As a general principle, humor and psychopathology are antipodal. Disturbances in mental functioning sufficient to lead to mental anguish seriously impair the ability to enjoy humor. Even strong emotions like rage, sorrow, or anxiety bar joking. Freud (1960) stressed the fact that the enjoyment of humor can occur only if one is able to experience a sense of mastery or control over anxiety. Without this control there is no joy in the comic, but with it, even death can be laughed at, as evidenced by gallows humor.

Studies that compared psychiatric patients with control subjects have shown that the psychiatric patients, with diverse diagnoses, performed more poorly on humor tests (Redlich, Levine, & Sohler, 1951; Levine & Redlich, 1955). Their humor behavior was clearly impaired not only by the relative absence of mirthful responses but also by their inability to understand the jokes, despite their more than adequate intelligence. Their reactions were often characterized by disturbed affect over the humorous stimuli, and frequently their failures to understand the stimuli were attributable to some scotomization or perceptual distortion of the thematic content, particularly in the direction of overlooking or mitigating the sexual or aggressive content.

Table 1. Mirth Response Spectrum

Patient	Psychiatric Diagnosis	Expressive Behavior	Nega-tive	No Response	Half-Smile	Smile	Chuckle	Chortle or Laugh
1. P. R.	Depression	Inexpressive	0	36	0	0	0	0
2. R. B.	Moderate–severe anxiety reaction	Controlled	0	30	4	2	0	0
3. J. A.	Severe anxiety response with hysterical features	Expressive	0	8	5	12	6	5
4. S. P.	Character disorder, impulse neurosis, kleptomania	Over-expressive	7	4	0	2	3	20
5. W. W.	Paranoid schizo-phrenia	Negativ-istic	21	15	0	0	0	0

Besides the cognitive disturbances shown in their responses to humor, psychiatric patients may also reveal their affective state by their expressive behavior. By way of illustrating the differences in mirth responses given by individual psychiatric patients with differing diagnoses in a mirth response test using a set of 36 popular cartoons, Table 1 was presented by Redlich, Levine, and Sohler (1951).

Without attaching any significance to the spectra of mirth responses in the table, their presentation serves merely to illustrate the aggregate of expressive behavior that reflects not only individual variability but also the emotional states associated with special types of psychopathology. Among other things, these spectra represent many facets of ego functioning and control. It is worth remembering in this context that the expressions of mirth are not fully under ego control. We are all familiar with those embarrassing situations in which the more we strain to suppress our laughter, the less are we able to do so. Conscious effort can only partially control it, particularly in group situations where the laughter is contagious. It is indeed paradoxical that the harder we try to restrain our laughter, the more intense is the impulse to laugh. This commonplace observation is particularly meaningful when we consider those pathological states of involuntary and uncontrollable laughter due to brain damage, where there is complete loss of control of laughter.

Despite the absence of basic research data, there is unquestionably considerable variation in responsiveness and expressiveness to humor from moment to moment. This fact is in no way inconsistent with the great variability of expressiveness across individuals, as was shown by Cupchik and Leventhal (1974), who distinguished between those who are high and low in expressiveness. Shakespeare said it best, as Salarino exclaimed (*Merchant of Venice*, Act I, Scene 1):

> Nature hath fram'd strange fellows in her time:
> Some that will evermore peep through their eyes
> And laugh, like parrots, at a bagpiper;
> And other of such vinegar aspect
> That they'll not show their teeth in way of smile,
> Though Nestor swear the jest be laughable.

B. Organic States—Involuntary Laughter

The search for a specific identifiable center in the brain that controls laughter has a long history. Many of the most eminent neurologists of the 19th and 20th centuries have noted the presence of involuntary and uncontrollable laughter in patients with brain damage. But as a symptom of brain damage, forced laughter has been observed in a variety of diseases and lesions of the brain. Cases have been reported with diffuse brain diseases like Parkinsonism, multiple sclerosis, or double hemiplegia (Wilson, 1923). Though more rarely, cases have also been described with localized lesions in different areas of the brain. To add to the confusion, both cortical and subcortical lesions and even the brain stem have been associated with forced laughter and crying.

In all these diverse instances of pathological laughing, the patient can not restrain himself from laughing; he has to laugh "against his will". Any stimulus can evoke this forced laughter, regardless of its appropriateness. These uncontrolled episodes of laughter, triggered without discrimination of stimuli, do not reflect a joyful state. As Davison and Kelman (1939) pointed out, the forced laughter or crying has nothing to do with the emotional content of the situation, as evidenced by the fact that humorous or sad events can produce either laughing or crying or both. In other instances, patients with brain injuries have been observed to begin to laugh without provocation and were unable to stop (Tissington-Tatlow, 1954).

Gelastic or laughing epilepsy, though rare, is probably the most frequently described form of forced laughter in the clinical literature. Since it was first identified by Trousseau (1873), a sizable number of unusual clinical cases have been reported, such as that by Anderson (1936) in which a woman with pseudobulbar paralysis died laughing as a result of an attack of uncontrollable laughter lasting 1½ hours. In many of the reported cases, the seizures began at an early age, with the youngest beginning soon after birth. According to Lehtinan and Kivalo (1965), gelastic epilepsy is associated with considerable brain damage. During the attacks, patients report neither amusement nor happiness, and this laughter may alternate with crying. Lehtinan and Kivalo (1965) maintain that these laughing fits are distinguished from the other forms of forced laughter, such as in pseudobulbar paralysis, multiple sclerosis, amyotrophic lateral sclerosis, and syphilis, in that the latter are not paroxysmal like the "laughing fits."

Daly and Milder (1957) introduced the term *gelastic epilepsy* to characterize the temporal lobe seizures that are accompanied by laughter. According to them, the laughter in epilepsy is paroxysmal like the other affective states (mostly unpleasant) prodromal to the seizure. This view conflicts with that of other clinicians who maintain that the laughter in epilepsy is not associated with joy or any other specific emotional state (Lehtinan & Kivalo, 1965). Others emphasize the artificiality of the laughter and its unrelatedness to any specific emotion.

The picture emerges from the clinical studies that the laughter due to brain injury is an involuntary spasmodic episode that is evoked by diverse unrelated stimuli. It is not associated with humor as a joyful feeling state in response to visible stimuli. The fact that laughter is not invariably just a response to the stimuli of humor in no way militates against their basic relationship. The fact is that humor, like laughter, is not always expressive of a pleasurable state, for both are employed for purposes other than pleasure. For example, in laughter of derision or contempt or in "laughing things off," laughter is used either to express hostility or to make light of an anxiety-arousing situation. Similar motives can be attributed to the uses of humor. But what seems to be particularly significant about the pathological fits of laughter in the brain-injured is their reflexlike involuntary nature and their intimate association with pathological crying. We must remember that as normal spontaneous responses, both laughter and crying are not altogether voluntary responses. It is often difficult and sometimes impossible to inhibit them. We say we were "overcome by laughter." The pathology then is not in the physical response itself but in the total loss of control of it and its very low threshold in response to diverse stimuli unrelated to their risibility.

The psychopathology of involuntary inappropriate laughter raises the question of what these convulsive episodes with facial, respiratory, and visceral movements contribute to the total emotional state. The absence of any mirthful emotions during these episodes suggests that the emotions normally associated with these movements are not necessarily concomitants of the laughter. The conclusion is supported by the incidence of the reverse pathological condition in those diseases involving the paralysis of the facial muscles such as facial myopathy, myasthenia gravis, paralysis agitans, or postencephalitic Parkinsonian disease. These patients report that they experience the joyfulness and mirthful feeling in response to humor but cannot express it by laughing. Clinicians call this state "inward laughter." The great neurologist S. A. K. Wilson (1923) addressed this problem and stated, "When actors artfully assume the emotional facies of laughter the mere portrayal of an emotion may deceive the audience but never the actor himself." He concluded, "Only when psychical and appropriate visceral components are fused can emotion be felt acutely, and the latter is less significant than the former."

It would appear that the disconnection of the bilateral corticobulbar motor pathways from the cortex releases the motoric expressions of laughing and crying. Lesions in these pathways can occur at any level from the brain stem to the cortex. The cortex then seems to integrate the affective state with motoric expression of that state and also regulates or modulates the response in keeping with the stimulus. Without the regulating influence of the cortex, any arousing stimulus will evoke the responses of laughing or crying, with or without the accompanying affect. Pathological laughter associated with brain damage may then be viewed as the release from central regulation of this form of expressive behavior dissociated from the affective state and having little if any communicative intent. The psychopathology of forced laughter brings home the familiar fact that much laughter has nothing to do with humor.

The breakdown of the response into cognitive and affective components is obviously arbitrary but is useful in separating the effects of pathology. It is particularly helpful in considering the effects of brain damage. In one recent study, Gardner, Ling, Flamm, and Silverman (1975) investigated the degree of impairment of cognitive and affective functions following brain damage upon the humor response, because they recognized that humor involves both functions. They found that humor appreciation was impaired in all the brain-damaged patients they studied, more in severe than in mild aphasics, primarily because of the dependence of humor appreciation on language. Although they could find no significant difference in overall performance between patients with left and right hemisphere lesions, they did find suggestive, specific differences. Left hemisphere patients tended to perform more like normal subjects in their humorous reactions, whereas the right hemisphere patients, although appearing to perform at approximately the same level as the left, tended to react in one extreme direction or the other: either they laughed at all the humor stimuli regardless of their understanding, or else they showed no emotional response even when they understood the cartoons. The authors concluded that the finding is consistent with recent formulations (Geschwind, 1973; Gianotti, 1973; Gardner et al., 1975)

> that the right hemisphere plays an important role in "emotional appropriateness":
> patients with minor hemisphere pathology may well behave in ways less appropriate
> to a given affective situation than those with lesions of comparable size in the
> dominant hemisphere.

The relation of the humor process to brain function, particularly the relative contributions of the two hemispheres, offers interesting possibilities for further exploration of the behavioral components of humor responses. The evidence is still only suggestive, and sharp separations of the function and role of the two hemispheres are not yet firmly established. As Sperry (1966) concluded from his own work, each hemisphere is capable of performing cognitive and affective functions either in synchrony or independent of the other. He reported observing indications of emotional expression originating in the right hemisphere like a broad smile following the successful completion of a task with the left hand in patients with split brains. Despite their overt smiling responses, these subjects were unable to explain verbally the reason for their smiling. The opposite was also observed: patients frowned "at an incorrect verbal response or an inept performance by the right hand when only the minor hemisphere (right) knew the correct answer."

In an interesting study suggesting some differences in schizophrenic and brain damage responsiveness to humor, Brody and Redlich (1952) investigated the effects of frontal lobotomies upon the responses of severe schizophrenics. They administered the mirth response test (MRT) (Redlich, Levine & Sohler, 1951) to nine severe schizophrenics before and after a frontal lobotomy. They found that before lobotomy these patients recognized the cartoons of the MRT as designed to be funny but neither understood them nor enjoyed them. Not only was there a striking absence of pleasurable facial reactions, but there was a high frequency of negative or dysphoric reactions, evidencing strong dislike, disgust, or anxiety, with a tendency to respond in highly personal and even autistic terms. Following the lobotomy, these patients showed a marked increase in the frequency and range of pleasurable facial expression with smiling and laughing. Seven of the nine patients showed a significant increase in comprehension, which seemed to be associated with a marked decrease in autistic thinking. Nevertheless, Brody and Redlich are quick to point out that after lobotomy there was really not a change to a normal sense of humor. Rather, the changes in humor behavior seemed to parallel the clinical changes in the individual; particularly evident was a noticeable decrease in manifest anxiety.

Theoretical formulations about the neurophysiology of laughter, based primarily upon the clinical findings, have been meager. Despite strong evidence of primordial precursors of laughter in the primates, research has been limited to pathological laughter in man. The search for a cortical or subcortical center or even specific neural pathways has led to failure. The findings are well established that the cognitive or intellectual component of the humor response is affected by brain damage. Like all the other measures of intellectual functions involving problem solving and abstraction, the comprehension of humor stimuli has been found to be clearly impaired in individuals with brain injuries (Redlich, Levine, & Sohler, 1951; Levine & Redlich 1955; Ferguson, Schwartz, & Rayport, 1969; Gardner, Ling, Flamm, & Silverman, 1975).

It is noteworthy that involuntary laughter is not always a pathological state, nor does it occur only as a result of brain dysfunction. We all have experienced the embarrassment of not being able to control the impulse of laughter in social situations in which it is inappropriate but something in the situation strikes us alone as funny. In such situations, much to our discomfort, we cannot suppress a laugh or a chuckle or just a smile. Laughter is also an infectious state that may erupt amoung the members of a group and may be beyond voluntary control. The infectiousness of group laughter is another instance of man's inability to maintain complete control of laughter, and probably of any of his affective responses. A dramatic demonstration of this fact was reported in a radio news report (WCBS, Tuesday, August 2, 1977, 11:30 A.M.) in which a group of about 14–17 girls in a country in Africa had to be hospitalized because they were overcome by uncontrollable laughter brought on by contagion and without organic origins. These girls could not stop laughing despite physical isolation.

Bean (1967) describes a report of

> an epidemic of laughing and crying which disorganized community life for six months in an African tribe in Tanganyika. It began in a mission school for girls which was forced to close down when more than half the pupils became affected. Most of those involved were adolescent girls and younger boys. It seemed to spread by example. Laughing and crying lasted for some minutes or a few hours, then things would quiet down only to recur. Restlessness and occasional vomiting were noted. There was nothing abnormal in the physical examination except for the hyperkinetic state and exaggerated tendon jerks. After one or two weeks, the disorder abated. Certain paranoid fears and evidence of hysterical reactions were reported. No example was found among the better educated or more experienced members of the community, regardless of age. (p. 101)

Such dramatic incidents illustrate the fact that laughter by suggestion and contagion can mimic in every respect the forced laughter that occurs as a result of brain damage. They also demonstrate how ego control of suggestibility and affective expression develops with mental and emotional growth.

Wolfenstein (1955) reported the case of a 6-year-old boy who had laughing fits as a substitute for tears in an effort to reverse painful emotions and as a defense against anxiety.

Laughter, then, can erupt involuntarily either by some organic dysfunction or by the contagious laughter of others. Experience teaches us that in neither situation are humor stimuli necessary. On the basis of these data, it is reasonable to speculate that involuntary laughter is probably mediated by specific neurophysiological mechanisms or pathways, and possibly by some subcortical centers yet to be discovered. Cortical control of laughter is only partial, as it is in the case of crying and other expressions of affective states.

C. Humor and Schizophrenia

Perhaps the simplest general statement one can make about the way schizophrenics handle humor is that it mirrors the psychopathology as both a thinking and an affective disorder. Schizophrenics handle humor in a schizophrenic manner. Perhaps even more than in most other patterns of behavior, schizophrenics, when they do respond, often express their responses to humor in bizarre or startling ways. Special terms have been coined to characterize these humor behaviors. Bleuler (1950) coined the terms *parathymia* and *paramimia* (two states that he felt were impossible to differentiate) to describe the inappropriate and bizarre affective behavior often characterized by split expressions of laughter, joy, and sorrow. Redlich, Levine, and Sohler (1951) used the term *parahumor* to describe the strange sense of humor of the schizophrenic, in which the schizophrenic tries to be "in humor" but what emerges are idiosyncratic and loose personal associations with manneristic responses. Levine and Hershkowitz (unpublished) have identified a form of schizophrenic humor that they have labeled *doomsday* or *calamity humor*, in which some patients laugh hilariously at the daily reports of tragic events; the more mayhem the better, and if they don't find any, they make it up.

According to Bleuler (1950), parathymia and paramimia may take several forms. He stated:

> A particularly frequent form of 'parathymia' is represented by unprovoked or inappropriate burst of laughter. The dysfunction of affect may manifest itself in the quantitative relation of the feelings to each other. Thus a patient of Masselon broke out into loud laughter at the news of her brother's death, because she was so pleased at receiving letters with black borders, but the loss of the brother did not seem to arouse any feelings.

In paramimia, there is apparently a dissociation of affective components, which Bleuler attributed to the simultaneous presence of two affects. In an interesting clinical paper, St. John (1968) reported two cases of paramimia in which the patients displayed both sadness and pleasure at the same time. In one case, the patient appeared to be laughing and crying simultaneously: "Her forehead is wrinkled in a worried expression and her eyes are tearful, yet her mouth is set in a caricature of a laugh." In the other case, he reported, the patient's

> facial expression seemed to be split; her eyes, forehead, and body tone seemed to show depression, yet she smiled with her mouth. The smile was warm but exaggerated. When I asked her how she was, she began to cry but said, "I'm fine."

Drawing on the work of Searles (1959, 1965) as well as of Spitz (1963) and Bleuler (1950), St. John postulated that paramimia is a "random unstructured discharge of psychic tension in a patient whose ego is poorly differentiated."

Ordinarily, schizophrenics show little or no responsiveness to comic situations, and yet they are often observed to laugh, giggle, or smile without any apparent reason. This emotional expression seems particularly inappropriate in patients who are mute, withdrawn, and usually unexpressive. Sometimes this laughter becomes highly contagious, and an entire ward can quickly break out in hilarious laughter without apparent cause. The strangeness of the incomprehensible laughter of the schizophrenic is further shown by its interchangeability with crying. The transformation of laughing into crying has frequently been noted and is equally incomprehensible as far as the external provocation is concerned.

Since in these situations the schizophrenic denies feeling happy when he is laughing, the alternation of laughing and crying in schizophrenia suggests either a rapid shift in emotional state or a release of motor expression of affect. In this respect, this interchangeability of laughing and crying is similar to the clinical observations of the pathological laughing and crying in the brain-damaged. It suggests either proximate centers in the brain mediating these two "opposite" emotional states, or similar neurophysiological mechanisms, despite their subjective and expressive differences.

Parahumor, as Redlich, Levine, and Sohler (1951) observed it, reflected the appreciation of humor in a highly personal way and had its own logic. On the rare occasions when there were attempts to be humorous, it was frequently a private joke not understood and therefore viewed as reflecting schizophrenic thinking. An example of the former was given by a schizophrenic patient in response to a cartoon by Steinberg in which a man is portrayed shooting an apple off his own head. The patient laughingly explained the joke by saying, "Why does he have to pop a perfectly good apple? I guess it's a MacIntosh. He ought to eat it." A cartoon by Wiseman shows a man who is so fat that he has to reverse his position on a scale to weigh himself because of his protruding belly. The response was an immediate chuckle by a female schizophrenic who explained, "He's pregnant." In both these instances, the responses indicated a recognition of the humorous intent, an effort to see the humor, and perhaps even an intent to express humor. The responses appeared to reflect personal dynamics.

Two instances of spontaneous parahumor are given in the following incidents. During a patient government meeting on a chronic ward, the president of the patients' government asked, "Does anybody think we need anything?" Mr. H., a relatively silent patient, immediately remarked, "What this ward needs is a trombone." Everyone laughed.

Mr. W., a hostile, negativistic patient, enjoyed rubbing other patients' heads. Though it was looked upon as an expression of affection, it was more likely aggressive teasing in quality. One day he went over and rubbed a particularly uncommunicative patient's head, smiled, and remarked, "You know something? You'll never get out of here because your head is concave."

A chronic and socially withdrawn schizophrenic patient was observed to make strange and incomprehensible requests of a visiting pianist who frequently entertained the patients on the ward (Hershkowitz, 1962). On one occasion, he asked the pianist to play "Mother's Stove." He laughed hilariously when the pianist and the audience appeared to be puzzled by his incomprehensible request. On another occasion, he asked the pianist to play "Money in the Sky" and again laughed when no one understood him. The key to his apparent strange requests was discovered when during the Christmas season he requested the pianist to play "Ring the Gongs." Without understanding him, the pianist began to play "Jingle Bells." It became clear that

"Mother's Stove" meant "Home on the Range," and "Money in the Sky" was a transposition of "Pennies from Heaven." The patient, in making his incomprehensible requests, was teasing or playing a joke on the pianist and the group. He was laughing at them.

The humor of this patient, unique though it was, illustrates a surprising observation in numerous other instances in which chronic schizophrenic patients who are mute, withdrawn, and seemingly out of contact with the environment may reveal a sense of humor and even laughter that is both sensible and appropriate. Understanding it often requires close observation and familiarity. Most of the examples presented have been selected from the data collected in a project involving the continuous naturalistic observations of about 60 chronic schizophrenics aged 25–75 who were hospitalized in closed wards for an average of 14.5 years (Hershkowitz, 1962). The findings from this project clearly show that these patients were not as unaware of their environment as they pretended. Their reactions were hidden and indirect. In the institutional setting, a primary motive of the chronic schizophrenic seems to be making himself invisible, probably because of his social anxiety. His ways of handling his laughter and humor reflects this motive.

The instances of laughter that will be presented will illustrate how chronic schizophrenics used smiling and laughter in essentially three different ways. The first was the direct expression of pleasure, as when the patients got some simple gratification or relief from tension. The receipt of a cigarette or some money was accompanied by a broad smile or a chuckle. G.W., a mute and relatively unresponsive man of 35, often smiled broadly after urinating or receiving a shave. At other times, his smile appeared to express the absence of stress and happiness with himself. If the smile persisted, it became a frozen, masklike facial expression. At one time, G.W.'s feet were treated for sores. Immediately afterward he burst into uproarious laughter and then into a tiny giggle, which seemed to express relief of pain and appreciation of the attention. An example of laughter to express relief of tension was shown by W.W., who was always under great tension, particularly when eating. He refused to sit down and wolfed the food down with both hands. While standing on one foot and gulping the food down rapidly, he smiled occasionally and then laughed to himself, all the time looking around furtively to see if anyone was watching him. He usually finished in just a few minutes and fled.

Another basis for mirth and laughter among institutionalized schizophrenics served as an indirect release of aggression. Humor was obviously the most effective mode of releasing aggressive feelings covertly and with impunity. One safe way of expressing aggression through humor is illustrated by what we have called *doomsday humor*. At least three patients took great delight in combing the daily newspaper for great catastrophes, to which they would respond with hilarious laughter. They would often make up stories, such as 40 thousand whores getting caught by the police, or thousands of people killed in some imaginary disaster. These stories would be reported with great glee.

An example of doomsday humor was given by the running remarks of one patient as he read of a holdup in the newspaper: "Look here. Look, lost two thousand dollars yesterday—guy was stuck up." Patient laughs joyfully. "It's gone, it takes 50 years to get it." Laughter, then he goes on: "Look at this here—crash." Laughs. "Yesterday, murder"—mumbles and laughs, repeating, "Murder." Particularly amusing to some patients is the clumsiness or minor disasters of staff members. When a staff member fell or stumbled, G.W. would burst into much laughter, but he would look self-consciously around to see if it was safe and then would flee the room. Sometimes the humor was directed against the patient himself, in a sort of self-derogating way: V.K. would frequently walk past a group of patients and staff and drop his pants to the floor—he would then burst out into hilarious laughter and run off. He would carry out similar childlike antics, evoking group laughter, including his own, and then he would run away.

A number of patients were observed to use laughter as a way of mastering anxiety. By "laughing it off," patients attempted to cope with social situations that frightened them. A staff member tripped over a stool and dropped his books. G.W. burst out laughing spontaneously but became self-conscious, looked furtively around to see if anyone was paying attention to him, and ran out of the dayroom. The schizophrenic may respond to the attempt of anyone to establish any kind of contact by laughing or by adopting a frozen smile as if to appear friendly. G.W. would giggle and pucker his lips in a half-smile as he approached someone to ask for a cigarette. Before he got a reply, he would begin to laugh as though he were playing a game with you, as though he were not really interested in getting a cigarette. If he received a cigarette, his laughter would change into one of simple pleasure, and he would quickly go to a safe place to smoke his cigarette, chuckling happily.

These examples of the diverse meanings and purposes of laughter, some unrelated to humor, illustrate the nuances of emotional states that the laughter of the schizophrenic can convey. They are obviously little different from the normal meanings of laughter, except that one is impressed with their childlike quality, as well as their apparent spontaneous release character in response to simple gratifications. In this context, Bleuler (1950) emphasized the involuntary nature of some schizophrenic laughter that is unrelated to any experiencing of pleasure. According to him, these patients feel compelled to laugh because of the impending attack of an activated inner "complex." He identified these episodes as unmotivated laughter. An example he gave of the involuntary laughter that some schizophrenics report was given by one patient who, without knowing why, burst out into a paroxysm of laughter that he could not control or stop. He reported that he could not understand it and became frightened by the loss of control. The only apparent explanation that his therapist could provide was that this patient had been building up a tension with homosexuality and feelings of anger that he could not express.

The behavior of W.W. illustrates the interplay between the inner and outer stimuli of his laughter. Typically, his laughter was solitary, for he would stand off by himself, loudly swearing and talking to himself, laughingly abusing somebody with wisecracks and insulting language. He was very self-conscious about this, for when he realized that he was being observed, he would immediately leave the scene or else would start to laugh uproariously. He seemed to be in a state of constant anger and tension, and if one tried to get close to him, he would burst out in an amost demoniacal laughter as if to say, "Get away from me." If one refused to move, he would leave or call the person foul names.

In summary, clinical observations suggest that chronic schizophrenics go to great lengths to appear unreponsive to humor as well as to other social stimuli. They rarely smile or laugh, and when they do, their laughter seems inappropriate and often without apparent joyfulness. Situations that normally evoke laughter, such as clowning of others or comic movies, fail to arouse any expression of mirth. If laughter erupts, these patients become uncomfortable and flee the situation if they can. The freedom to use humor for pleasure or as a social facilitator is not available to the chronic schizophrenic.

D. Humor and Depression

The mental state that most interferes with the ability to enjoy and laugh at humor is depression. In a depressed state of mind, a person cannot experience any pleasure, including humor. Common sense tells us that humor and depression are at the opposite ends of an emotional pole, as they are expressed either by laughing or by crying. Hardly a person has been spared the experience of feeling depressed at some time in his or her life, either as a result of loss, frustration, or disappointment or just because of some internal condition. We do not always know what brings these depressed states on, and we rarely know what ends them. But humor alone cannot overcome depression, especially if it is severe. Many individuals resort to alcohol and drugs to dissolve these low feelings, elevate mood, and reduce the inhibition of pleasure. In these intoxicated states, humor often becomes accessible as a source of pleasure, and spirits may become so high as to require little humor to evoke laughter and gaiety.

Depression is probably the most commonly known mental disorder, and in most instances, it doesn't require any knowledge of psychopathology, or even of the person, to recognize it. Yet little basic knowledge about its etiology, treatment, or course has been available. In the last 10 or more years a great upsurge of research has taken place, especially on the biochemistry and clinical use of antidepressant drugs, which have begun to provide us with new insights into the disorder (see Beck, 1967, for a comprehensive review of the literature), particularly its neurochemical and genetic components. But the new findings and formulations have not as yet given us adequate conceptual models of depression to differentiate the various depressions based upon etiology, symptomatology, and prognosis. Conflicting views about the classification of depression have revolved largely around dichotomies that emphasize different aspects of the disorder. Thus we have dichotomies such as endogenous–exogenous, bipolar–unipolar, psychotic–neurotic, primary–secondary, chronic–acute, good–poor prognosis, and normal–pathological. The bases for these dichotomies are to be found in the observed differences in precipitating factors, severity, periodicity, duration, prognosis, symptom patterns, and responsiveness to drugs. But to date there is no universally accepted classification of the depressions that is capable of accounting for all the variables. And in the meagerness of reliable research findings, there is little that is relevant to the relationship between humor and depression. However, it may be helpful to draw upon the clinical literature on the phenomenology of depression and of humor, particularly in relation to the behavior of some depressive patients in response to humor stimuli.

Beck (1967) defines depression in terms of five basic attributes:

1. A specific alternation in mood: sadness, loneliness, apathy
2. A negative self-concept associated with self-reproaches and self-blame
3. Regressive and self-punitive wishes: desires to escape, hide, or die
4. Vegetative changes: anorexia, insomnia, loss of libido
5. Change in activity level: retardation or agitation

A review of the clinical literature describing the depressive states generally emphasizes feelings of despair, worthlessness, futility, and loss of interest as chief complaints. Other emotional manifestations of depression are self-dislike, loss of gratification and of attachment, crying spells, sinfulness, and loss of mirth response. According to Beck (1967), these negative feelings, especially toward the self, are intensified as the severity of the depression increases. The salient cognitive manifestations of depression are largely in a distorted, unrealistic view of self, inlcuding body image and competence. Beck presents some hypothetical examples to illustrate the

> astonishing contrast between the depressed person's image of himself and the objective facts. A wealthy man moans that he doesn't have the financial resources to feed his children. A widely acclaimed beauty begs for plastic surgery in the belief that she is ugly. An eminent physicist berates himself "for being stupid."

In extremely severe cases these self-derogatory feelings take on delusional form and become associated with feelings of extreme worthlessness and sinfulness, expectations of punishment, and suicidal ideation. The irrationality, intensity and duration of the depressed feeling distinguish pathological depression from the normal periodic feelings of depression common to everyone. However, Beck and others believe that because they are essentially different in character, there is no continuity between the low mood of normal individuals and pathological depressions.

The contrast between the humorous and the depressed states of mind is best reflected by the orientation and attitudes toward the self and the world. The adoption of a humorous attitude represents a shift in internal orientation that views the self as omnipotent and invulnerable, master of any situation no matter how dangerous. In his movies, Charlie Chaplin, seemingly a pitiful weakling, fearlessly faces a car full of thugs or a burly policeman and outwits them all. He walks along the very edge of a 20-story building, always about to fall, but never gets hurt.

Even death is not feared. Gallows humor best shows it. A man approached the gallows with the remark, "This will certainly be a good lesson to me." Or, the prisoner, about to be shot, is offered a last cigarette and refuses with the remark, "No, thank you, I'm trying to give up smoking." It is this humorous attitude that permits us to make light of potentially sad and frightening events, for by the joke techniques everything is reduced to insignificance and becomes the object of amusement.

In contrast, the depressed attitude regards the self as worthless and incompetent. Self-esteem is too low even to accept success, and failure is welcomed as confirmation of incompetence. With such an orientation, it is understandable that humorous situations are not viewed as trivial or amusing but as serious and potentially dangerous. Laughter and mirth are unthinkable. Several clinical examples that were studied with some care may demonstrate the cognitive and affective responses of depressed individuals to humorous stimuli.

The responses of depressives to humorous stimuli generally reveal the basic integrity of their intellectual functions, but they show a profound loss of expressive mirth. The cognitive component, though showing no impairment, does reflect the affective state by the seriousness and circumstantiality of the reactions. Though they understood the cartoons in the mirth response test (Redlich, Levine, & Sohler, 1951), depressed patients took them seriously and were not able to transcend the reality of the comic situations. Responses to the cartoons were typically characterized by remarks such as, "This isn't funny. There is too much disaster around—makes it ridiculous," or "It's unfunny because it's too ridiculous." To a cartoon showing a moustached villain leaving a girl tied to railroad tracks, while two men observing the scene on a bridge just above it remark, "Now there's something you don't see often these days," a depressed physician responded, "The villain has tied the girl to a railroad track. Parody on old movie. Two characters above making the comment. I don't think it's funny. I don't get it. I don't care for the whole thing. I don't want it." Another depressed patient responded to all the cartoons with, "I have no sense of humor. I don't enjoy it—it seems kind of pointless—ludicrous to me." By and large, depressive patients were literal—almost concrete—in their explanations, attending to relatively insignificant details. It was apparent that they could not assume the appropriate set to treat the stimuli as playful fantasy in which they were invited to participate, they could not accept the nonsense, the lack of logic, the violation of natural law and morality. They could not transcend the serious and the real.

Perhaps the most striking aspect of the relation between humor and depression is the prevalence of depression among those who create humor or who act as comedians, that is, those who seek to make others laugh. It is surprising to find that many of our most famous and talented humorists and comedians are depressed or ill-humored people in real life. In a systematic study of 55 of the best-known and best-paid American comedians, Janus (1974) concluded from interviews and psychological testing that most comics are brilliant, angry, suspicious, and depressed people. He also noted that these comics are insecure people who are in perpetual fear of failure.

In a popular article about Bert Lahr in the *Saturday Evening Post* (Zolotow, 1952), where he is characterized as the "melancholy clown," these features of his personality are clearly evident. The writer states that during a period of some three weeks, during which he was with Lahr almost every day,

> He [Lahr] is the most difficult person to draw out that I have ever encountered. He is shy, withdrawn, introverted. During our many hours together there were long gaps of complete silence in which Lahr just stared straight off into space, seemingly detached from everybody and everything around him.

And later,

> It is not merely that Lahr is serious in his private life. A good deal of the time he is enveloped in a state of profound melancholia. As he tortures himself worrying about the horrible things that might happen to him, the fingers of his right hand nervously twist the lower button of his coat. He twists the button until he tears it off. Then he meticulously places it in his change pocket and his wife sews it back on. During the rehearsals, he invariably convinces himself that he is going to be a flop because the material is no good.

This characterization is hardly one to fit a person who by a gesture is able to convulse people into gales of laughter. Yet it seems to fit a large number of those who make others laugh. A profoundly depressed person, W. C. Fields, certainly fits it, for he could not live a day without the effects of large amounts of alcohol. As Maurice Zolotow, the writer of the Lahr story, put it:

> To this day, it is this unsatisfied yearning for love, in the form of an audience's approval, that drives Lahr to work so hard for a big laugh. Abe Burrows remarks, quite keenly, "To Bert, applause is love, applause is his whole life."

Goodman Ace, a famous comic writer, characterized his long-time friend Groucho Marx:

> Groucho is a man driven by strange compulsions. One of these is the need for company. When he comes to New York, which seems to happen all too frequently, he must immediately assault the citadels of his friends: George Kaufman, Sid Perelman, myself. If we resist, he complains that "I'll soon be out of your way, then I won't bother you any more."

Mark Twain revealed his own basic pessimism when he declared "Everything human is pathetic. The secret source of humor itself is not joy but sorrow. There is no humor in heaven."

In his book *The Funny Man*, Steve Allen (1956) pointed out that in Arthur Marx's book *Life with Groucho*, Groucho used jokes as a defense against his social anxiety: "If he was ill at ease in someone's presence he would throw a funny line at him, thus giving himself the mastery of the conversation and the situation."

III. CONCLUSION

In summary, psychological disturbances that are expressed in humor may take many forms and have multiple meanings. They may vary from being pathognomonic of severe psychopathology to momentary lapses expressing the psychopathology of everyday life. Humor performs diverse functions besides those motivated by pleasure seeking. Humor is not only a source of pleasure, for it also serves as a means of affective communication, especially as a self-controlled and acceptable form of aggression. Another prominent function of humor is as a means of coping with anxiety and stress by self-reassurance that one is master of the situation. Because most people with psychological disturbances seem to have diminished motivation for pleasure seeking and laughter, their use of humor for that purpose is greatly diminished. The inability to experience pleasure from humor is generally indicative of psychopathology. In fact, exposure to humorous stimulation by mentally ill patients is often distressing rather than pleasurable. Other evidences of psychopathology can be observed in the cognitive and affective dysfunctions of humor responses. In some instances, psychiatric patients and some comic artists seek to make others laugh as ways of coping with anxiety and depression. Making others laugh and sharing in laughter appear to reduce loneliness and permit a sense of freedom and self-control of angry or aggressive feelings.

REFERENCES

Andersen, C. Crise de rire spasmodique avant décès: Hémorragie thalamique double. *Journal Belge Neurologic Psychiatrica*, 1936, *36*, 223–227.

Bean, W. B. *Rare diseases and lesions; Their contributions to clinical medicine.* Springfield, Ill.: Charles C Thomas, 1967.

Beck, A. *Depression.* New York: Harper & Row, 1967.

Bergson, H. *Laughter: An essay on the meaning of the comic.* New York: MacMillan, 1911.

Bleuler, E. *Dementia praecox or the group of schizophrenias.* New York: International Universities Press, 1950.

Bowlby, J. Grief and mourning in infancy and early childhood. In G. E. Daniels (Ed.), *New perspectives in psychoanalysis.* New York: Grune & Stratton, 1965.

Brenman, M. On teasing and being teased. *Psychoanalytic Quarterly of the Child,* 1952, *7,* 264–285.

Brody, E., & Redlich, F. C. The response to humor as an indication of ego function in schizophrenic patients before and after lobotomy. *Bulletin of the American Psychoanalytic Association,* 1952, *8,* 229–238.

Brown, T. G. Note on the physiology of the basal ganglia and mid-brain of the anthropoid ape, especially in reference to the act of laughter. *Journal of Physiology,* 1915, *49,* 195–202.

Canter, R. C. Importance of pathological laughing and/or crying as a sign of occurrence or recurrence of a tumor lying beneath the brainstem. *Journal of Nervous and Mental Disease,* 1966, *143,* 508–512.

Cattell, R. B., & Luborsky, L. B. Personality factors in response to humor. *Journal of Abnormal Social Psychology,* 1947, *42,* 402–421.

Cohn, R. Forced laughing and crying. *Archives of Neurological Psychiatry,* 1951, *66,* 738–743.

Cousins, N. Anatomy of an illness (as perceived by the patient). *New England Journal of Medicine,* 1976, *295,* 1459–1463.

Cupchik, G., & Leventhal, H. Consistency between expressive behavior and the evaluation of humorous stimuli: The role of sex and self-observation. *Journal of Personality and Social Psychology,* 1974, *30,* 429–442.

Daly, D. D., & Mulder, D. W. Gestatic epilepsy. *Neurology,* Minneapolis, 1957, *7,* 189–192.

Davison, C., & Kelman, H. Laughing and crying. *Archives of Neurological Psychiatry,* 1939, *42,* 595–643.

DeVore, I. (Ed.). *Primate behavior.* Toronto: Holt, 1965.

Dollard, J. The dozens: Dialectic of insult. *American Imago,* 1939, *1,* 3–25.

Druckman, R., & Chao, D. Laughter in epilepsy. *Neurology,* Minneapolis, 1957, *7,* 26–36.

Eastman, M. *Enjoyment of laughter.* New York: Simon & Schuster, 1936.

Eysenck, H. J. The appreciation of humour: An experimental and theoretical study. *British Journal of Psychology,* 1942, *32,* 295–309.

Ferguson, S., Schwartz, M., & Rayport, M. Perception of humor in patients with temporal lobe epilepsy: a cartoon test as an indicator of neuropsychological deficit. *Archives of General Psychiatry,* 1969, *21,* 363–367.

Flugel, J. C. Humor and laughter. In G. Lindzey (Ed.), *Handbook of social psychology,* Vol. 2. Reading, Mass.: Addison-Wesley, 1954, pp. 709–734.

Freud, S. Humour. *International Journal of Psychoanalysis,* 1928, *9,* 1–6.

Freud, S. *Jokes and their relation to the unconscious,* standard edition, Vol. 8. London: Hogarth Press, 1960.

Gainotti, G. Emotional behavior and hemisphere side of lesion. *Cortex,* 1973, *8,* 41–55.

Gardner, H., Ling, P., Flamm, L., & Silverman, J. Comprehension and appreciation of humorous material following brain damage. *Brain,* 1975, *98,* 399–412.

Geschwind, N., & Levitsky, W. Human brain left–right asymmetries in the temporal speech region. *Science,* 1968, *161,* 186–187.

Gollob, H., & Levine, J. Distraction as a factor in the enjoyment of aggressive humor. *Journal of Personality and Social Psychology,* 1967, *5,* 368–372.

Harrow, M., Grinber, R., Holzman, P., & Kayton, L. Anhedonia and schizophrenia. *American Journal of Psychiatry,* 1977, *134,* 794–797.

Herschkowitz, A. Naturalistic observations on chronically hospitalized patients: I. The effects of "strangers." *Journal of Nervous and Mental Disease*, 1962, *135*, 249–264.

Heston, L. The genetics of schizophrenia and schizoid disease. *Science*, 1970, *167*, 149–256.

Janus, S. Comics, brilliant but sad. *The Boston Globe*, Aug. 6, 1974.

Kepecs, J., Robin, M., & Munro, P. Tickle. *Archives of General Psychiatry*, 1961, *5*, 237–245.

Koestler, A. *The act of creation.* New York: MacMillan 1964.

Kris, E. *Psychoanalytic explorations in art.* New York: International Universities Press, 1952.

Lehtinan, L., & Kivalo, A. Laughter epilepsy. *Acta Neurologica Scandinavica*, 1965, *41*, 255–261.

Leubar, C. Tickling and laughter. *Journal of Genetic Psychology*, 1941, *58*, 201–209.

Levine, J., & Abelson, R. Humor as a disturbing stimulus. *Journal of General Psychology*, 1959, *60*, 191–200.

Levine, J., & Redlich, F. Failure to understand humor. *Psychoanalytic Quarterly*, 1955, *24*, 560–572.

Mahler, M. S. On sadness and grief in infancy and childhood: Loss and restoration of the love object. In *Psychoanalytic Quarterly of the Child*, *16*, New York: International Universities Press, 1961.

Meehl, P. Schizotaxia, schizotypy, schizophrenia. *American Psychologist*, 1962, *17*, 827.

Mettler, F. Culture and the structural evolution of the nervous system. In C. Landis (Ed.), *Varieties of psychopathological experience.* New York: Holt, 1964.

O'Connell, W. An item analysis of the wit and humor appreciation test. *Journal of Social Psychology*, 1962, *56*, 271–276.

Provence, S., & Ritvo, S. Effects of deprivation on institutionalized infants: disturbances in development of relationship to inanimate objects. In *Psychoanalytic Quarterly of the Child*, *16*, New York: International Universities Press, 1961.

Redlich, F., Levine, J., & Sohler, T. A mirth response test: Preliminary report on a psychodiagnostic technique utilizing dynamics of humor. *American Journal of Orthopsychiatry*, 1951, *21*, 717–731.

Reich, A. The structure of the grotesque–comic sublimation. *Bulletin of the Menninger Clinic*, 1949, *13*, 152–159.

Rosenthal, D. A program of research on heredity in schizophrenia. *Behavioral Science*, 1971, *16*, 191–201.

Searles, H. Integration and differentiation in schizophrenia. *Journal of Nervous and Mental Disease*, 1959, *129*, 542–550.

Searles, H. *Collected papers on schizophrenia and related subjects.* New York: International Universities Press, 1965.

Senf, R., Huston, P., & Cohen, B. The use of comic cartoons for the study of social comprehension in schizophrenia. *American Journal of Psychiatry*, 1956, *113*, 45–51.

Smith, A. *Powers of mind.* New York: Random House, 1975.

Sperling, S. On the psychodynamics of teasing. *Journal of the American Psychoanalytic Association*, 1953, *1*, 458–483.

Sperry, R. Brain bisection and consciousness. In J. Eccles (Ed.), *Brain and conscious experience*, New York: Springer Verlag, 1966.

Spitz, R. Anxiety in infancy. *International Journal of Psychoanalysis*, 1950, *31*, 138–143.

Spitz, R. Ontogenesis: The proloptic function of emotion. In P. H. Knapp (Ed.), *The expression of emotions.* New York: International University Press, 1963.

Sroufe, L., & Wunsch, J. The development of laughter in the first year of life. *Child Development*, 1972, *43*, 1326–1344.

St. John, R. Smiling in schizophrenia. *Psychoanalytic Quarterly*, 1968, *37*, 103–113.

Story, I. Caricature and impersonating the other: Observations from the psychotherapy of anorexia nervosa. *Psychiatry*, 1976, *39*, 176–188.

Tatlow, W. Laughter in organic cerebral disease. *Canadian Medical Association Journal*, 1954, *70*, 156–158.

Trouseau, A. *Clinique Médicale de l'Hôtel—Dieu de Paris*, 4th ed. Paris, 1973.

White, E. B. *Some remarks on humor in the second tree from the corner*. New York: Harper & Row, 1935.

Wilson, S. Some problems in neurology: II. Pathological laughing and crying. *Journal of Neurological Psychopathology*, 1923, *4*, 299–333.

Wise, C., & Stern, D. Dopamine B hydroxylase deficits in the brains of schizophrenic patients. *Science*, 1973, *181*, 344–347.

Wolfenstein, M. Mad laughter in a six-year-old boy. *Psychoanalytic Quarterly of the Child*, 1955, *10*, 385–394.

Wolff, P. The natural history of crying and other vocalizations in early infancy. In B. M. Foss (Eds.), *Determinants of infant behavior*, Vol. *4*. London: Methuen, 1969.

Zigler, E., Levine, J., & Gould, L. Cognitive processes in the development of children's appreciation of humor. *Child Development*, 1966, *37*, 508–517.

Zolotow, N. Broadway's saddest clown. *Saturday Evening Post*, 1952, *224*, 34–35.

Editor's Introduction

3

Wessman presents a summary of the literature on moods and discusses in detail much of the work that he and his colleagues have been doing in this area for more than a decade. Wessman draws no sharp distinctions between the qualitative characteristics of mood and emotion. In some respects, mood can be considered an emotion of extended duration. Perhaps because of this temporal characteristic, people are often less aware of the causes of mood than they are of a more specific, intense, and temporally restricted emotion experience. Wessman talks about separate and distinct emotions and moods and sees these phenomena as important motivational conditions.

Wessman uses the term *affect* to refer to the subjective component of emotion or mood. His use of the terms *anxiety* and *depression* are generally consistent with the notion that these are complex patterns of affects and affective–cognitive interactions. In fact, Wessman tends to see moods themselves as affective–cognitive interactions. As children learn language, they also learn the vocabulary of emotions and moods, and everyone learns to recognize and talk about his moods and emotions. Wessman points out that our very dependence upon language as an efficient mode of communication, including reporting on our inner experiences, makes the affective and cognitive components of mood intricately interrelated.

Wessman demonstrates some important relationships between mood and personality. Moods influence our ongoing experience and establish our relationship to the world. The author's own longitudinal studies of mood and personality show that a number of measures of mood are significantly related to other personality measures, including projective techniques, and to various aspects of behavior. For example, he has shown that normals characterized by depressed mood show more outer-directed than inner-directed hostility, a reversal of the pattern often found in neurotic and psychotic depressives. Depressed mood in both normal and clinical conditions results in less need-persistence.

Wessman has found a number of interesting distinctions between people characterized by elated mood (happy) and depressed mood (unhappy), on the one hand, and people who are stable in mood or variable in mood on the other. It is possible to see some parallels between his description of stable and variable people and Zuckerman's (Chapter 6) description of low and high sensation seekers.

Moods: Their Personal Dynamics and Significance

3

ALDEN E. WESSMAN

I. INTRODUCTION

Variety and change in emotion and feeling are basic features of human experience. The important events in our lives are registered with a particular affective character as occasions of special joy, sorrow, fear, excitement, or some other distinctive feeling. And in regular day-to-day and even hour-to-hour happenings, we experience the succession of good times and bad—a shifting kaleidoscope of personal emotion. There are periods when the world and we ourselves seem profoundly altered. Everything takes on a different character. Though we may logically say to ourselves that things have not really changed, that these thoughts and feelings will pass in time, we are not really convinced. Such are the moods that occasionally possess us, those pervasive personal feelings that alter profoundly the ways we think and act.

Most of the people we know seem similarly affected. Observing their appearance and actions, we infer their shifting moods. Today our friend is somewhat different from yesterday: we can see that he is unusually troubled, or slightly weary, or bubbling with enthusiasm. In some individuals, these affective alterations are conspicuous and dramatic; in others, they seem such slight perturbations that we may wonder exactly what and how much they do feel. Certain people appear to maintain a very persistent emotional character: we find them generally brusque and irritable, always plaintive and sad, frequently tense and apprehensive, or basically zestful and optimistic. These shifting or persisting emotional characteristics seem basic features of personality intimately related to the ongoing pattern and quality of individual lives.

ALDEN E. WESSMAN • The City College, City University of New York, New York, New York.

The obvious questions arising from such commonplace observations were what led to the investigations of mood and personality to be reported here. It seemed that, if we could systematically study the changing features of people's moods over extended periods and discover how these feelings relate to other aspects of their lives, a richer understanding of human feelings and emotions should result. Before presenting our findings, it will be helpful to consider some of the important theoretical and research contributions that others have made concerning this fascinating topic.

II. THE NATURE AND SIGNIFICANCE OF AFFECT

It must be admitted that basic terminology concerning feelings and emotions is far from fixed and clear. Many terms are imprecise and used with varying meanings both in everyday speech and in more formal academic discourse. In beginning our work, we did not propose or adhere to any strict or new definitions but rather followed general usage (English & English, 1958; Jacobson, 1957; Ruckmick, 1936). We were concerned with conscious (and avowed) personal *feelings* having distinct emotional overtones. Traditionally the subjective aspects of emotion have been designated *affect*. Within the domain of affect, our attention has been directed to *moods*, which have been characterized as shifting yet pervasive emotional feeling states of varying duration—usually not as intense nor as clearly related to a specific provoking object or situation as is the case with a fully developed emotion.

A number of recent contributions (Arnold, 1960, 1970; Izard, 1971; Izard & Tomkins, 1966; Plutchick, 1962; Schachtel, 1959; Tomkins, 1962, 1963) have advanced the understanding of human emotion and indicated the significance of cognitive and affective complexity in accounting for the uniqueness of individual character. It is becoming increasingly clear that differentiated affect plays a critical part in initiating, maintaining, and regulating human action. Personal feelings and emotions instigate, facilitate, sustain, and modify active engagement in an organism oriented toward a complex world that is in some measure its own creation. The cognitive and affective complexity manifest in human beings represents a major evolutionary advance (Schachtel, 1959, pp. 3–77). The individual's relation to the world is in large measure open and developing, regulated only in part by inherited and fixed organization. Active encounter and learning establish complex and changing relations with the natural world and with the shared world of symbolic meanings. The experienced world is made possible by the great advance in human brain structure and function, which allows an enormous increment in the complexity of man's cognitive and affective functioning mediated through imagery, symbols, and language (Cassirer, 1944; Church, 1966; Langer, 1951).

Psychologically, there are an infinite number of aspects of the world potentially significant to the individual and an immense variety of possible ways to relate to them. Each person lives and realizes himself, or fails to, according to the ways he appraises and becomes engaged with his world. The nature of this encounter is in great measure determined by the individual's affective stance and reactions. If fear, anger, sadness, and the other negative affects predominate, he is closed and shut off from growth and self-realization, and instead defensive and security operations constrict his behavior and experience. If joy, zest, active interest, and positive affects predominate, he is more open and better able to proceed along the paths of individual fulfillment and self-realization. Such broad characterizations are too simple, however, and it is necessary to recognize and investigate the personal dynamics of affective complexity and change. No one is constantly and exclusively governed by either a closed defensive stance or an open, growing relation to the world. Within each person are aspects that are closed or open, and he is in continual flux in his affective relations to the world. The study of personality should be concerned with such differences and changes in order to see what feelings generally predominate in the individual and the conditions that cause them to alter. The theoretical and empirical investigation of moods is one avenue for the fuller understanding of such personal affective dynamics.

III. APPROACHES TO THE UNDERSTANDING OF MOODS

The nature of moods and detailed formulations of their features have received various treatments in psychological theory. Some areas of general consensus will be considered first, followed by the particular aspects emphasized in various approaches. Although it would be desirable to fit all these views together and produce a clear, unified formulation, both comprehensive and concise, perhaps no single formula can suffice. Moods are extraordinarily complex phenomena that can be validly investigated and conceptualized in a variety of ways and on different levels. Each approach is a partial revelation, and taken together, they provide a more comprehensive understanding.

The definitions of *mood* in standard psychological dictionaries (Drever, 1952; English & English, 1958; Warren, 1934) customarily indicate its shifting temporal features. *Moods* are generally defined as states of emotional or affective arousal of varying, but not permanent, duration. They are usually seen as milder than full-blown emotions, which are more intense and of shorter duration. Their origins and sources often seem indeterminate and vague, since they frequently are not as clearly related to specific instigating objects and situations as is the case with well-defined emotional episodes. Sometimes they are characterized as emotions in a state of subexcitation or decay. They are also described as predispositions to respond in certain emotional ways and to experience certain kinds of feelings. Elation and depression are usually cited, as well as excitation, interest, irritability, and other familiar examples. Most of these definitions make moods appear rather transient and indefinite, as they often are, and sometimes imply that they are generally matters of no particular importance.

Over 40 years ago, in a detailed analysis of emotion and affective processes, Ruckmick (1936, pp. 72–73) noted that on the subject of mood there was "neither a long literature . . . nor any experimental work of note." Until rather recently, that still was much the case. According to Ruckmick, moods are usually drawn out, lasting for hours or days. However, they share some of the general affective tone and bodily symptoms of emotions. He noted that the source or reasons for the onset and prolongation of a mood are often not evident to the individual possessed by it, but that it does markedly color and pervasively influence the individual's experience and behavior.

When in the mid-1950s we initially searched the psychological literature to discover what theoretical sense had been made of these mysterious comings and goings, we found that with a few notable exceptions, relatively little explicit attention had been paid to them and that the empirical research literature was sparse. In recent years, the situation has altered, and there is a growing body of relevant theory and research. The physiological aspects of mood are not discussed here because of the author's lack of sufficient expertise. But it should be noted that while a great amount has been discovered regarding possible physiological and neurological correlates of affective states, much still remains unclear, speculative, and controversial, so that most well-informed scholars are very cautious and tentative regarding what has been solidly established (Beck, 1967, pp. 125–153, 293–304; Becker, 1974, pp. 177–195; Fawcett, 1975; Mandel & Segal, 1975; Strongman, 1973, pp. 36–65). However, we shall consider the characteristic views of mood held by the other important psychological approaches.

A. Moods as Dimensions of Behavioral Change

Given their emphasis on observable data and operationalism and their strictures against introspection and subjectivity, most behavioristically and empirically oriented psychologists were disposed to ignore moods. Eventually there came to be an acceptance of "verbal behavior" and the admission of "intervening variables" and "hypothetical concepts" as necessary theoretical tools. With this altered climate, mood could finally become a legitimate subject for investigation and theoretical consideration. The focus of the empirically oriented approaches quite understandably has been on mood as measurable behavior. The main programmatic research work in this area has been carried out by Vincent Nowlis and his collaborators and by Raymond B. Cattell and his associates. The results thus far are the substantial beginning of a growing knowledge of the major behavioral variations in varying mood states, with well-replicated delineations of major axes of mood change established through factor-analytic studies of correlated measures.

Nowlis (1965, 1970) described how his mood research began in the early 1950s in attempts to assess the effects of various drugs. Though his initial orientation was behavioristic, Nowlis soon observed that often the most consistent and dramatic effects of drug ingestion were alterations in subjective feelings and moods. To assess these changes, he and his collaborators developed and refined a Mood Adjective Checklist (MACL) for subjects' self-report of how strongly they experienced various feelings. This measure has been used in many subsequent studies by Nowlis and others. The research generally has involved standard R-technique or across-individuals correlational and factor-analytic designs to discover major common factors in reported mood changes. Most of the studies have not been of a long-term, repeated-measures type and have not been concerned with the relationships of mood and personality. Rather, they have sought to discover basic general dimensions of mood change in self-reports and to observe how they are affected by particular experimental conditions.

Combining his results with similar work by others (Clyde, 1960; Lorr, Dalston, & Smith, 1960; McNair & Lorr, 1964), Nowlis reported that 12 basic mood factors have been consistently found. His designation of the 12 factors, with some representative adjectives, was: *aggression* (angry, grouchy, annoyed); *anxiety* (fearful, jittery, tense, nervous); *surgency* (carefree, playful, lively); *elation* (overjoyed, pleased); *concentration* (careful, attentive, serious); *fatigue* (drowsy, tired, weary); *vigor* (active, energetic, peppy); *social affection* (affectionate, warmhearted, friendly); *sadness* (regretful, unhappy, discouraged, blue); *skepticism* (suspicious, dubious); *egotism* (self-centered, boastful); and *nonchalance* (leisurely, quite, placid) (Nowlis, 1965, pp. 360–367; 1970, pp. 271–274).

Nowlis (1970, p. 266) noted that these empirical mood factors appear to be unipolar rather than bipolar, as has often been assumed. He argued that moods thought to be mutually exclusive may in fact vary independently and on occasion may be experienced simultaneously by an individual, such as the happy yet tearful theatergoer, the hostile lover, or the tired but still overactive child. Of course, this general finding may be an artifact of the measurement method employed or of the types of experimental situations. Yet Nowlis's point certainly is well taken in that bipolarity of moods probably should not be assumed automatically (as it shortly will be seen that we did in our scales) but rather should be empirically verified. In any case, it is clear that many aspects of moods that we arrived at and investigated from a more phenomenological and clinically oriented basis also appear consistently in Nowlis's factor-analytic studies.

Emerging more directly out of the psychometric and factor-analytic tradition, another notable example of programmatic empirical investigations of mood is Cattell's series of studies begun in the late 1940s and actively pursued for three decades (Cattell, 1965, pp. 152–157; 1966; 1973, pp. 13–16, 191–229). While his personality trait investigations primarily have used across-individual R-technique correlational methods, Cattell's innovative studies of states and moods have used the much less employed P-technique methods to study variations within individuals over time. As Cattell argues, the latter strategy is particularly suited to revealing the covariance of various physiological, behavioral, and self-report measures in different states and moods. In fact, Cattell was a pioneer in empirically demonstrating the distinctions between trait-and-state conceptions of anxiety and other personality characteristics that have been the focus of much recent theorizing and debate (Mischel, 1968; Spielberger, 1966, pp. 12–19). A further technique employed by Cattell in studying moods is differential R-technique, or dR for short, which measures many individuals on a common set of variables on two occasions sufficiently separated so that everyone may be assumed to have changed his mood somewhat.

According to Cattell (1973, pp. 191–229), such multivariate P-technique and dR-technique studies have consistently shown 9 or 10 state dimensions, possibly a dozen. The clearest of these as measured by self-report questionnaires, and often correlated with objective test and behavioral measures, have been tentatively designated: *anxiety*, *exvia–invia* (i.e. extraversion–introversion), *depression–elation* (with three possible subaspects of general depression—low self-concept, low-energy depression, and anxious-guilty depression), *regression* (or overwroughtness), *high arousal–low activation*, *fatigue–energy* (often related to arousal), *effort stress*, and *guilt*. Cattell's state and mood factors are the distillate of an impressive number of multivariate measurement studies, and though still tentative, they represent a substantial foundation for further empirical research. Again, as with Nowlis's mood factors, they include many of the aspects of moods that we measured in our studies. It should be noted that a number of Cattell's factors appeared to be bipolar, whereas Nowlis's did not. Possibly differences between P and dR techniques account for more mood contrasts' being found in the long-term repeated intraindividual measurement studies (Gorman, 1971, pp. 125–127).

In a more theoretical vein, the major attempts to formulate moods in behavioristic terms (Ryle, 1950; Nowlis, 1965, 1970; Nowlis & Nowlis, 1956), have regarded moods as sets of propensities to act or react for certain periods of time in particular characteristic fashions. Though these views put primary emphasis on overt behavioral manifestations, they argue for the value of verbal reports and avowals as generally valid indicators. Nowlis suggests that "mood may be defined as an intervening variable or predispositional factor that is a source of information, or discriminable stimuli to the organism, about the current functioning of the organism" (Nowlis & Nowlis, 1956, p. 352). Conscious mood is viewed as consisting of the perceptual and cognitive responses to this information. Mood as an intervening variable is regarded as having a direct (unconscious) effect on the probabilities of occurrence of certain responses in certain situations. It is likened to Skinner's (1953) concept of predisposition, a state that changes the probabilities of certain acts in certain situations. Conscious mood, as the response to the cues of the hypothetical mood state, is assumed to supply information about current functioning and to be involved in the self-monitoring and self-regulation of complex behavior. Human beings learn to label or respond verbally to their conscious mood and to discriminate the mood stimuli with adjectives and descriptive phrases. Nowlis holds that such verbal responses give us our best present index of moods and mood changes.

B. Moods as Cognitive–Affective Interactions

In recent years, cognitive approaches have had increasing influence throughout psychology (Neisser, 1967, 1976; Posner, 1973). In the area of emotion, a number of theoretical formulations have emphasized the intimate interrelations of cognition and affect, and particularly the role of cognitive "appraisals" of the personal significance of ongoing events (Arnold, 1970, pp. 169–185; Lazarus, Averill, & Opton, 1970; Leeper, 1970). On the basis of provocative and widely cited experiments, certain theorists have even argued that cognitive–situational interpretations impose upon undifferentiated general physiological arousal the specific and qualitatively differentiated affects experienced by the individual (Mandler, 1975, pp. 65–110; Schachter, 1966). Other theorists, however, look to inherent features in basic emotional response syndromes to account for the differentiated phenomenology characterizing various affects, such as complex physiological patterns (Lacey & Lacey, 1970; Plutchik & Ax, 1967) or facial expressions (Ekman & Friesen, 1975; Ekman, Friesen, & Ellsworth, 1972; Izard, 1971). Despite these differences, all of the contemporary theorists just cited recognize important relationships of cognition and affect.

Turning more directly to cognition and mood, recent contributions include the cognitive interpretations of depression (Beck, 1967, 1976; Becker, 1974, pp. 103–115; Seligman, 1975). Beck analyzed psychogenic affective disorders as primarily thought disorders, holding that "the affective response is determined by the way an individual structures his experience" (1967, p. 287). Such disorders reflect biased personal schemata or selective misinterpretations of reality. In depression, the individual applies very negative evaluative concepts to the world, to himself, and the future. The depressed person sees his environment as a source of defeat, deprivation, or disparagement that imposes a succession of obstacles and burdens. He regards himself as deficient, inadequate, or unworthy—attributing his unpleasant experiences to his physical, mental, or moral defects. Furthermore he anticipates that his current difficulties will continue indefinitely. Beck (1967, pp. 253–274) has analyzed in detail the types of cognitive distortions leading to the affective and motivational symptoms characterizing depressed moods, and he has also discussed (1976, pp. 213–305) the implications of his views for psychotherapeutic treatment.

Similar cognitive accounts have been emphasized in Seligman's (1975, pp. 75–106) "learned helplessness" formulation, which maintains that "the depressed patient believes or has learned that he cannot control those elements of his life that relieve suffering, bring gratification, or provide nurture—in short, he believes that he is helpless" (p. 93). However, Seligman argues that depression is concurrently a cognitive and an affective disorder. Cognitions of helplessness lower mood, and lowered mood increases susceptibility to cognitions of helplessness. This insidious vicious circle, consistently observed in clinical cases, is one of the reasons Seligman holds that a cognition–emotion distinction is untenable. The two are inseparable: one does not feel depressed without depressing thoughts, and one does not have depressing thoughts without feeling depressed.

In considering the relations of cognition to affect and mood, we also should recognize the role of verbal labels and formulations in structuring and interpreting experience. Though much emotional behavior and communication is clearly nonverbal (Weitz, 1974), when we wish to think or communicate about emotion we regularly resort to words and language in order to formulate and express our observations. There is a distinct possibility that many affective states or feelings that we regard as basic are more the product of shared linguistic conventions and distinctions rather than discrete fundamental response patterns. For example, the Japanese language recognizes certain "basic" and culturally important emotions that have no exact equivalents in European languages (Lazarus *et al.*, 1970, pp. 215–217). Our formulated self-aware experience is necessarily conceptualized through the available words. The increasing recognition in social psychology of the importance of labeling and attribution processes in interpreting behavior and causality is clearly relevant (Jones, Kanouse, Kelley, Nisbett, Valins & Weiner, 1972). While the naive conviction may be that private subjective experiences are immediately and directly known, it must be acknowledged that most discussion and thinking about ourselves and our experience use concepts and interpretations shaped by the norms of our linguistic culture and our social judgment processes.

Recognition and verbal expression of feelings, moods, and emotions are shaped by previous training, both informal and formal, in the use of language as an effective means of communication. Emotion words must be learned, and every normal child in some degree comes to recognize and talk about his own and other individuals' feelings and emotions (Izard, 1971, pp. 317–349). Some people, like Henry James or sensitive clinicians, develop remarkable acumen and subtlety in recognizing and expressing fine nuances of feeling. Others, especially the inarticulate products of too many modern schools, are sadly deficient in such skills, not able to communicate much regarding their own feelings and even less prepared to appreciate those of someone else. Fortunately, as Davitz (1969) has shown, at least for educated individuals from similar backgrounds, there is fairly high consensus regarding many features that seem to define or describe a variety of feelings and emotions.

An area of considerable research activity concerns the relationships of cognition and personality (Warr, 1970). Characteristic ways of perceiving and thinking, termed *cognitive styles*, show important individual differences that are associated with many other features of personality and behavior. Witkin's (1965) studies of field dependence–independence or global versus articulated cognitive style have found it related to body image, sense of identity, defensive style, and types of psychopathological disturbance. Some of our findings (Gorman & Wessman, 1974) regarding how cognitive styles relate to personal mood characteristics will be presented later. For all the reasons discussed above, there is ample reason to hold that the features of affect and cognition are deeply interwined. It seems incorrect to divorce reason and feeling as Western philosophical tradition generally has done; rather, the challenge is to understand better how cognitive and affective complexity are united in ongoing personal functioning.

C. Moods as Subjective Experience

The phenomenological and existential approaches are concerned with a full account of the experiential features of mood. A phenomenological investigation attempts to address itself to the rich primary content of experience and ultimately to understand its signification or personal meaning. There have been a number of such studies of the nature and significance of various emotions and affects (Buytendijk, 1950; Spiegelberg, 1960). We will indicate briefly what both the theoretical, philosophical formulations of existentialism and the more clinical and descriptive accounts of phenomenology have to say about mood.

In one of the major theoretical formulations of existential philosophy, Martin Heidegger (1962) had as a central concern the analysis and understanding of moods. He emphasized the particular significance of moods and states of mind as revelations of the fundamental situation of the human being. Heidegger stated that "a mood makes manifest how one is and how one is faring" (1962, pp. 172–176). Mood is a primary disclosure of "being-in-the-world," indicating the significance of the individual's total condition. The quality and implications of one's personal engagement with life are revealed by mood. Heidegger argued that at every moment existence or *Dasein*, in its current state of mind, admits of certain possibilities—its "potentiality-for-being," which may or may not be realized. Thus mood discloses what is and what may be. Heidegger saw the "projection" into the future as a crucial feature. Such significance is not something trivially or artificially attached to the present moment but rather the totality of personal involvement—past, present, and future. Heidegger's abstruse formulations of various moods are necessary reading for any serious student of the subject. A less difficult account of existential analyses of anxiety, guilt, and other moods is found in May, Angel, and Ellenberger (1958, especially pp. 50–55), and the contributions of the school as a whole are presented in various introductory surveys (Hall & Lindzey, 1970, pp. 552–581; May, 1961; Ruitenbeek, 1962).

The necessity for detailed phenomenological studies of subjective experience has been argued from Husserl on (Spiegelberg, 1960; van Kaam, 1969, pp. 241–340). However, the primary origin of psychiatric and clinical phenomenology was increasing interest in the bizarre feelings and ideas of patients in various psychopathological conditions. The early studies were primarily detailed descriptive accounts of the subjective worlds of particular patients. Eventually the general characteristics of major syndromes became established, and the basic categories or dimensions of experience, particularly temporality and spatiality, were studied in detail (Ellenberger, 1958). For example, the studies by Minkowski (1958), Straus (1966), and others of depressed patients showed how the experience of time was slowed or arrested in such cases. One of the main features of depression is the sluggish flow of time. The future appears inaccessible or blocked. In such monotony, there is no reaching ahead and personal impetus disappears. Space, too, is altered and may appear bleak and empty, or dark and constricted. Some very impressive contributions to the understanding of psychopathology have resulted from these phenomenological studies.

Normal moods, as well as pathological moods, should be subjected eventually to the same kind of descriptive analysis. An individual's mood at a particular moment establishes the nature of his relationships with the world. In one mood, he perceives and is different things than when he is in another mood. Our own research on the subjective experience of time (Gorman & Wessman, 1977; Wessman, 1973; Wessman & Ricks, 1966, pp. 117–122) has attempted to clarify some major aspects of the phenomenology of temporal experience and to investigate their relations to personality, affect, and mood. It seems that a full phenomenology and realization of the existential significance of moods is a most promising development and is part of a necessary rapprochement of various traditions in psychology.

D. Moods as Psychodynamic Changes

Most psychotherapists and personality theorists have attempted to account for human behavior in terms of hypothetical structures of personality and their dynamics (Hall & Lindzey, 1970; Murray & Kluckhohn, 1953). The main edifice, subject to frequent remodeling, is psychoanalysis. It is fair to say that over the years no other theoretical approach has been as penetrating in its scrutiny of the personal dynamics of affect and mood. Early in his career Freud recognized emotional conflict as critical for understanding neurosis. And anxiety has remained a central focus in psychodynamic theory (May, 1950). Later Freud (1953) and Abraham (1954a,b) made fundamental contributions to the understanding of depression. Though there are serious biases and limitations in the classical approach and even in the later formulations of "ego psychology" (Erikson, 1959, 1963; Hartmann, 1964), psycho-analytic theory remains an essential foundation for understanding many features of affect and their possible sources (Fenichel, 1945).

Edith Jacobson's (1957) paper is probably the best contemporary psychoanalytic account of moods. She discussed in detail the pervasive aspects of mood as influencing for a period a person's entire behavior and experience, the variety of moods, the general polarity and duality of mood axes, the nature of experienced changes in the self and object world, and much else of interest. Her main concern was with the "economic function" of moods as a basic and primitive aspect of general psychological functioning in all individuals. Jacobson characterized moods as "barometers of the ego state" (p. 75). Less clearly focused toward particular objects than affects, moods are more pervasive and may dominate many aspects of ego functioning. Jacobson summarized her view in the following way:

> Moods are ego states characterized by generalized discharge modifications which temporarily influence the qualities of all feeling, thoughts, and actions. They are evoked by intense experiences which cause high energetic tensions leading to an overflow and spreading of energy throughout the ego by virtue of cathetic shifts. . . . [M]oods transfer the qualities of the provocative experience to all objects and experiences; thus, they impart a special coloring to the whole world and, hence, also to the self. Since they permit gradual, repetitive discharge with reality testing on many objects, they must be regarded as a primitive economic modality of the ego. (1957, p. 86)

Jacobson maintained that distinctions between normal and pathological moods can be made only in terms of the individual's total psychodynamic functioning, particularly . the adequacy of reality testing. Without such knowledge, it is often impossible to distinguish, from the phenomenological point of view alone, between normal mood deviations and those arising from pathological conflicts. Inasmuch as moods involve generalized transference phenomena, they may lead to temporary impairment of critical judgment and discrimination regarding the self and object world. To the degree that moods, normal or pathological, color or overstate certain aspects of reality and blot out or understate differing aspects, they involve mechanisms of denial and distortion. Jacobson held that a mood is within the normal range as long as reality is not greatly distorted, the experienced affect is appropriate to its source, and eventual recovery may be anticipated. However, while the individual is in a particular mood, his views of himself and the significant objects in his world are much altered.

Shortly we will report some of our attempts (Wessman & Ricks, 1966, pp. 33–54; Wessman, Ricks, & Tyl, 1960) to test in normal mood swings certain features of the classical psychoanalytic theory of depression, particularly the hypotheses of a marked drop in self-esteem and of aggression directed inward. The psychoanalytic formulations of affect that have emerged from intensive clinical studies of psychopathology are a rich source of hypotheses for empirical investigation of normal mood fluctuations.

E. Some Shared Perspectives and Their Implications

By now it is evident that even though the terminology, theories, and data of the various views of mood show important differences, there are many areas of basic agreement. All hold that in some degree all human beings show variation both in manifest behavior and in how they regard themselves and their world. These objective and subjective changes follow certain basic patterns characteristic of the specific type of experienced affect. Although each person's moods and affective organization undoubtedly are unique, there nevertheless would appear to be considerable general similarity in the major dimensions of mood swings and their psychodynamic significance. The pattern and quality of recurrent moods seems to be a basic feature of the individual's emotional life that significantly reflects and influences his ongoing activities and relationships. All these considerations argue that the systematic study of personal mood characteristics should prove a rewarding area for personality research. Our studies have attempted to substantiate these views.

IV. AIMS AND METHODS IN STUDIES OF MOOD AND PERSONALITY

Over the past 20 years, some of my colleagues and I have been engaged in extended studies of normal mood variability using repeated nightly self-reports on a set of mood scales. The original studies developed from an interest in personal characteristics related to happiness and unhappiness (Wessman, 1956) and took shape in a series of investigations carried out at the Harvard

Psychological Clinic (Wessman & Ricks, 1966; Wessman, Ricks, & Tyl, 1960). There has been further work (Gorman & Wessman, 1974; Gorman, Wessman, & Ricks, 1975; Wessman, 1973). In addition, a number of other investigators have used our methods and addressed themselves to similar or related questions that will be discussed later in the relevant contexts when presenting our findings.

A. The Setting of Our Initial Studies

Our initial work was done as part of a five-year personality assessment research project directed by Henry A. Murray. We studied a small group of Harvard undergraduates for three years using the intensive case study and clinical assessment methods that Murray so creatively employed throughout his research (Hall & Lindzey, 1970, pp. 160–208; Murray, 1938). This meant that we had an unusually rich body of personality assessment data to relate to our mood measures. Each subject wrote his autobiography and philosophy of life, took standardized personality inventories (MMPI, 16PF, etc.) and projective tests (TAT, Rorschach, etc.), and participated in a variety of interviews and experimental situations. The interested reader is referred to our book (Wessman & Ricks, 1966) for full details, including four representative case histories of the happiest and unhappiest and the most and least moody subjects. Here we will simply summarize our methods and findings and the results of subsequent research.

B. Research Aims and Strategies

We aimed to contribute to the understanding of moods in everyday life. As far as possible, we wanted to study the diversity, complexity, and richness of normal human affect and to discover the nature of its sources and its relations to personality. This is a large order for any investigation, and capable of only limited realization, but it was the grand intent.

A promising strategy appeared to be the gathering of regular reports on moods and affective experiences over an extended period of time from our small group of thoroughly studied individuals. Through repeated affective reports, we felt that we could study personal dynamics and change and derive measures that represented the features of individual affective experience. The group studied intensively was small enough for us to know each individual in depth yet large enough and sufficiently diverse in personality to provide reasonable expectation of some general significance in the findings. We wanted to study both the unique mood patterns and affective dynamics of particular individuals and the more general features characteristic of the group as a whole.

One of our emphases was an enthusiastic acceptance of subjectivity and feeling as primary data for psychological study. In part, our work was an attempt to remedy the paucity of methods for the study of personal affect and mood.

Also we were oriented toward emotional change and dynamics. We felt that the use of repeated affective reports over extended periods has great potential value. Temporal change in psychological reports and measurements should not be dismissed as mere error or an unfortunate nuisance but rather should be systematically utilized to discover meaningful general and individual dynamic regularities.

When we began our work in the late 1950s, there had been very little empirical investigation of mood fluctuations in normal subjects over extended periods. The only prior long-term studies we could discover were those of Flugel (1925), Hersey (1932), and Johnson (1937). The only instruments we found for the measurement of moods were the Hildreth (1946) Feeling and Attitude Scales and an early version of the Nowlis (1965) Mood Adjective Checklist, neither of which had been used in long-term studies. Taking the past work and the general clinical literature into account, we decided to construct our own instrument on an *a priori* basis.

C. The Personal Feeling Scales (PFS)

Our aim was to provide subjects with a comprehensive set of scales suitable for repeated self-reports of affect over an extended period. Ideally, we wanted the mood scales to have a number of characteristics. They should facilitate the report or "measurement" of a *variety of feelings* because mood is not a unitary phenomenon but has a number of aspects. It was desirable to keep each scale as *unidimensional* as possible, so that it measured just one specific type of feeling. On each dimension, we wished to *encompass a wide and graduated range of feelings*, so that either the slight aura or the great perturbation could be represented appropriately. We decided that each bipolar scale should contain 10 descriptive statements ranging from extreme feelings at one end of the continuum, through more neutral feelings, to extreme contrasting statements at the opposite end. Through the use of appropriate descriptive statements, we tried to approximate *equal subjective gradations* in a stepwise progression to provide some degree both of *cross-subject comparability of responses* and of *cross-scale comparability in extremeness of items*. We did not employ the refined empirical techniques of scale construction, which though scientifically desirable are very time-consuming and would have deflected us from our pressing research interests. However, we did put much effort and pretesting into the developmental work, and the indications are that the scales have worked well in the initial and subsequent studies.

Table 1. Content of Personal Feeling Scales

    I. Fullness versus emptiness of life (how emotionally satisfying, abundant, or empty your life felt today)

    II. Receptivity toward and stimulation by the world (how interested and responsive you felt to what was going on around you)

    III. Social respect versus social contempt (how you felt other people regarded you, or felt about you, today)

    IV. Personal freedom versus external constraint (how much you felt you were free or not free to do as you wanted)

    V. Harmony versus anger (how well you got along with, or how angry you felt toward, other people)

    VI. Own sociability versus withdrawal (how socially outgoing or withdrawn you felt today)

    VII. Companionship versus being isolated (the extent to which you felt emotionally accepted by, or isolated from, other people)

    VIII. Love and sex (the extent to which you felt loving and tender, or sexually frustrated and unloving)

    IX. Present work (how satisfied or dissatisfied you were with your work)

    X. Thought processes (how readily your ideas came and how valuable they seemed)

    XI. Tranquility versus anxiety (how calm or troubled you felt)

    XII. Impulse expression versus self-restraint (how expressive and impulsive, or internally restrained and controlled, you felt)

    XIII. Personal moral judgment (how self-approving, or how guilty, you felt)

    XIV. Self-confidence versus feeling of inadequacy (how self-assured and adequate, or helpless and inadequate, you felt)

    XV. Energy versus fatigue (how energetic, or tired and weary, you felt)

    XVI. Elation versus depression (how elated or depressed, happy or unhappy, you felt today)

Eventually we arrived at a set of 16 Personal Feeling Scales (PFS), which were to be used for nightly self-reports by subjects of (1) their "average" feeling for the day; (2) the "highest" they had felt; and (3) the "lowest" they had felt. The highs or lows might be only fleeting but were to represent the extremes the subjects had experienced during that day. The titles of the 16 scales and the nature of the self-ratings the subject was asked to make are presented in Table I.

The scale most used in our data analysis was the last scale, elation–depression. Its form was:

XVI.   Elation versus depression (how elated or depressed, happy or unhappy, you felt today.)

       (10) Complete elation. Rapturous joy and soaring ecstasy.

        (9) Very elated and in very high spirits. Tremendous delight and buoyancy.

        (8) Elated and in high spirits.

        (7) Feeling very good and cheerful.

        (6) Feeling pretty good, "OK."

        (5) Feeling a little bit low. Just so-so.

(4) Spirits low and somewhat "blue."

(3) Depressed and feeling very low. Definitely "blue."

(2) Tremendously depressed. Feeling terrible, miserable, "just awful."

(1) Utter depression and gloom. Completely down. All is black and leaden.

Each week the subjects were provided with a set of seven sheets titled "Daily Record of Personal Feelings," upon which they were to report nightly their "highest," "average," and "lowest" on each of the 16 scales, and to make additional ratings on physical health and pressure of academic work. Also there were requests for information concerning hours of sleep the previous night; use of medicines, drugs, or alcohol; and any detailed personal comments or observations that the subjects might care to make regarding how they felt and the reasons why.

We first tried out our research techniques in a six-week mood study with a group of Radcliffe students and obtained interesting results (Wessman, Ricks, & Tyl, 1960). We then used the same methods in a six-week study with the Harvard students participating in the three-year clinical assessment study (Wessman & Ricks, 1966). The presentation here reviews the major areas of research concern and the main findings and indicates the results of subsequent studies following up aspects of the initial work.

V. CHANGES IN NORMAL ELATION AND DEPRESSION

The literature of clinical psychology, psychiatry, and psychoanalysis is very detailed concerning the psychodynamics of extreme depression and elation (Arieti, 1959, pp. 419–454; Becker, 1974; Fenichel, 1945, pp. 390–411; Medelson, 1974; White & Watt, 1973, pp. 479–506). We wished to see whether the dynamic changes postulated to occur in severe affective psychopathology would also characterize the milder elations and depressions of our normal subjects. Clinical theories of depressed mood emphasize the critical role of changes in self-esteem and in hostility.

A. Changes in Self and Ideal Concepts

According to the clinical literature, a basic feature distinguishing elation from depression is variation in self-esteem. Elation is characterized by a rise in self-esteem, depression by a fall. In depression, it appears that one judges oneself against an ideal standard and feels deficient; in elation, one's self-concept seems more closely to approximate one's personal ideal. The major change in the self-concept would appear to be that it becomes much less "favorable" or "good" in depression. These hypotheses were tested intraindividually by comparable Q-sort self- and ideal-descriptions obtained from our subjects both in depression and in elation. The hypotheses were significantly confirmed. The results held both for the 14 Radcliffe subjects on whom we originally tried out the mood study techniques and for the 17 Harvard students in the main study. The data from these normal subjects supported the view that depression is marked by an increase in unfavorable attitudes regarding the self and by a marked discrepancy between one's self and one's personal ideal. In short, the loss of self-esteem generally noted in most accounts of depression was found.

Not all hypotheses were confirmed, however. We had anticipated that possibly the ideal self-description might be more "good" and therefore more demanding in depression. Instead most subjects had relatively stable personal ideals that did not change markedly with alterations in mood. Perhaps only in severe pathological depressions does the ideal become more demanding. In any case, the other results indicated that even if the ideal did not become more demanding, the depressed self was clearly regarded as deficient compared to the ideal.

There were many significant content shifts in the Q-sorts. For both groups of students, the most consistent general changes in self-descriptions with depression were marked feelings of social withdrawal accompanied by increased self-preoccupation. Major dissatisfactions in depression focused on deficiencies in the areas of intellectual achievements and lack of progress toward important life goals.

The men's Q-sort had been constructed with Erikson's (1959, 1963) psychosocial stages in mind. These young men apparently felt most short of their ideals, in both elation and depression, regarding characteristics associated with the *latency* ("industry versus inferiority") and *adolescence* ("identity versus role diffusion") stages. Even in elation, they felt significantly below their ideals, which upheld excellence in work and productive accomplishments. And they regarded themselves as not realizing their ideals of knowing who they were and what they wanted from life. These felt shortcomings were even more strongly experienced in depression. The most important further lapse from their ideals involved items indicating failures in the developmental concerns of *young adulthood* ("intimacy versus isolation"). They added to their previous self-reproaches the sense that they were far too lonely, remote, and self-preoccupied.

The changes in self-concept just cited were general ones characterizing the group as a whole. It should be noted, however, that each person's self-concept and ideal was unique and that the mood-related changes were sometimes quite idiosyncratic. Later we shall consider evidence that the self and ideal concepts of happy or unhappy and of stable or variable people may differ considerably. For example, the ideals of men whose moods were stable emphasized steadiness and independent character, whereas the ideals of men whose moods were more variable emphasized spontaneity and creativity.

B. Changes in Hostility and Responses to Frustration

Again based on the clinical literature, we tested the hypotheses that in depression people would be (1) less extrapunitive and more intropunitive and (2) less need-persistent and more obstacle-dominated and ego-defensive. These types of reaction were defined in terms of projective responses to the frustrating situations depicted in the Rosenzweig picture-frustration test (1947) taken by the subjects when they were elated and when they were depressed. The findings were not clear-cut. Contrary to expectations, subjects were more extrapunitive and less intropunitive in depression (trend for Harvard students, significant for Radcliffe and for both groups combined). However, conforming to our expectations, subjects were less need-persistent in depression (same pattern of results).

The findings contradicted the generally held notion that in depression aggression becomes directed inward. This may be true for severe neurotic and psychotic cases (melancholia) but may not be typical of the milder depressions of normal individuals. Although most psychoanalytic writers have stressed the role of ambivalence and inwardly directed aggression in depression (Rosenfeld, 1959, p. 15), a few have argued that it has been overemphasized and hold that basic depression, a simple fall in self-esteem without marked inward aggression, should by recognized (Bibring, 1953; Cohen *et al.*, 1954; Jacobson, 1957). Additional studies using the PFS to investigate "the continuity hypothesis" regarding the relationship of normal and pathological moods and the role of aggression in depression have been undertaken (Becker & Nichols, 1964; Blatt, Dafflitti, & Quinlan, 1976; Laxner, 1964; Schless, Mendels, Kipperman, & Cochrane, 1974). Such studies have been reviewed in the light of other work (Becker, 1974, pp. 142–153; Gershon, Grower, & Kerman, 1968; Miller & McManus, 1976), and the evidence strongly suggests that the classical psychodynamic formulation of inwardly directed aggression as the primary basis for depression needs considerable revision. Izard (1972, pp. 255–282) has found distress to be the central component in depression, with anger and other affects as further interacting features in various complex patterns.

The decreased need-persistent responses we found in depression indicated that in such moods subjects gave fewer responses directed toward amelioration or improvement of frustrating situations. This was congruent with formulations that analyze depression as perserveration in helplessness and distress by an individual fixated on his own entanglements and discomforts in the face of frustrations (Bull and Strongin, 1956; Lichtenberg, 1957; Seligman, 1975).

VI. LEVEL AND VARIABILITY OF ELATION–DEPRESSION REPORTS OVER EXTENDED PERIODS

Only a few prior investigations of moods in normal people had used repeated self-reports over extended periods (Flugel, 1925; Hersey, 1932; Johnson, 1937). These studies had indicated a predominance of pleasurable or elated moods over unpleasurable or depressed moods. Flugel reported that the more variable people appeared to be less happy. Hersey and Johnson noted varying degrees of periodicity or rhythmic tendencies in individual records. The findings from our initial six-week mood studies and subsequent investigations agreed with the previous work in some respects and disagreed in others.

A. Hedonic Level and Variability

The overall balance of elation–depression can be regarded as an important measure of one's relative *happiness-unhappiness* or general *hedonic level* (Murray, 1938, pp. 90–93; Murray, 1951, pp. 455–457; Murray and Kluck-hohn, 1953, pp. 17–18; Wessman, 1956). In both the Radcliffe and Harvard groups, the overall mean of the daily "average" on the PFS elation–depression scale for the six-week period was close to "6, Feeling pretty good, OK." Individual mean scores ranged from "5, Feeling a little bit low, just so-so" throughout the period, to slightly higher than "7, Feeling very good and cheerful." The great majority of subjects averaged slightly on the elated side throughout the period.

These findings were consistent both with the earlier mood studies and with a large body of studies and surveys concerned with avowals of "average level of happiness" (Arkoff, 1975; Wessman, 1956; Wilson, 1967) that have generally found most subjects reporting overall mood levels on the mildly happy side. The validity of such avowals is problematic. However, for the Harvard students and in later studies, the reported individual hedonic levels have appeared consistent with other information and only slightly affected by social desirability and other response sets (Gorman, Wessman, & Ricks, 1975).

The standard deviation of the daily "average" reported on elation–depression provided a measure of *day-to-day variation* in average hedonic level. Individuals varied greatly in this regard. Some stayed practically constant from day-to-day; others were markedly "up" or "down" on different days.

Another measure of hedonic variability is the mean range between the "highest" and the "lowest" values reported each day on the elation–depression scale. This "mean daily range" is a measure of *within-day variation*, the customary spread between the most elated and the most depressed points in a single day. Here again there were great differences among subjects: some customarily spanned only one scale position in a day, while others spanned five. Most spanned two or three scale positions on the average.

These measures of day-to-day and within-day variability were moderately related, at least for the men (Radcliffe .34, not significant; Harvard .56, $p <$ .05). The men whose average hedonic level fluctuated a great deal from day-to-day tended also to show a great deal of hedonic variation within single days. This evidence, plus the consistent pattern in the correlates of the variability measures with other clinical data, led us to conclude that variability of hedonic level, both within days and across days, is a general characterological trait. A number of subsequent investigations have studied mood variability and its correlates using the PFS over extended periods (Becker & Nichols, 1964; Clum & Clum, 1973a,b; Frank, 1968; Fried, 1968; Gorman, 1971; Gorman & Wessman, 1974). The findings have demonstrated the value of mood variability measures in personality research.

B. Independence of Hedonic Level and Variability

Our data did not support Flugel's (1925) inference that those who "experience the most extreme degrees of feeling are on the whole less happy than those whose feelings are usually less intense." In neither group were the correlations significant between hedonic level and the measures of its variability.

Among our subjects, we found individuals who were relatively happy and stable, happy and variable, unhappy and stable, and unhappy and variable, with most, of course, intermediate on these aspects. The absence, at least in our two groups of subjects, of a significant correlation between average hedonic level and its variability indicated that the two were independent and could be considered separately, anticipating the findings that they were related to rather different aspects of personality. All of the later studies using the PFS have generally sustained that conclusion.

C. Absence of Regularity and Rhythm in Normal Mood Records

Conceptions of mood fluctuation often assume marked regularity and periodicity, and some investigators report such rhythms in long-term studies (Hersey, 1932). Careful plotting and inspection of our subjects' individual six-week records showed no such patterning. Almost without exception, the records were quite irregular from day to day, with no periodicity. Possibly periodic functions might have become evident over a longer observation time.

Johnson (1937) found no apparent relationship of mood and menstrual cycle; however, others occasionally report such findings (Bardwick, 1971, pp. 21–33). For the Radcliffe women, the two days prior to the onset of menstruation were *generally* marked by a distinct lowering of hedonic level, but this did not greatly alter the otherwise marked irregularity of their mood fluctuations. In later studies, we have sometimes found and other times not found a relationship between menstruation and lowered moods, such as depression, anxiety, and irritability. We now believe that the moods of the majority of women are rather little affected but that for a relatively small number it does make a difference. Also the particular group of women and their attitudes regarding menstruation are probably important. For obvious reasons some women in fact may be happy when their period does arrive! Although there may be physiological rhythms and cycles influencing moods (Luce, 1973), the great irregularity we have consistently observed in most records suggests that the often unpredictable events of everyday living are probably of much greater significance as determinants of mood. The subject's diaries clearly indicated the considerable impact of ongoing events in lowering and raising moods.

D. Elation–Depression as a Major Dimension of Mood

To see how subjects' relative standing on elation–depression related to their relative standing on the other affects, we correlated across subjects and factor-analyzed their mean six-week scores on each of the PFS scales. The major factor was a pervasive overall level of "good mood–bad mood" that tended to hold across subjects for most of the scales. Thus an individual who was regularly high (or low) on elation–depression relative to his fellows would tend to be similarly high (or low) on the other affects. Relative elation–depression appeared to be a major representative mood axis on which subjects could be meaningfully compared.

Similar correlation and factor analysis of the affective-scale standard deviations also found one major factor. Thus it appeared that there was a general dimension of variability–stability holding for all the affective scales and in terms of which all our subjects could be compared. The standard deviation of the daily "average" on elation–depression appeared to be an appropriate index for this general trait of mood variability.

VII. INDIVIDUAL PATTERNS OF AFFECTIVE COVARIATION

Individual configurations of affective change were separately factor-analyzed and interpreted for each individual's six-week mood records (Wessman & Ricks, 1966, pp. 71–89). The information gained through P-technique was very revealing. For each person, it provided an "affective map" showing the main vectors of his mood changes. Clinical knowledge often corroborated many of the factors. This technique can have considerable usefulness in personality study. Such individual affective analysis—in conjunction with physiological, behavioral, and environmental measures—has potential for research into the nature of affective dynamics.

The number of factors produced by an individual, a possible index of affective complexity, was inversely related to mood variability. That is, the more stable men showed a greater complexity and differentiation in their affective life. The more variable men were prone to global swings of affect organized around overall elation–depression. In this first investigation, it appeared that stable men made fine distinctions in their affects, while moody men did not. Subsequent studies (Frank, 1968; Gorman, 1971; Wessman & Gorman, 1974) have attempted to relate various measures of *mood differentiation* to field articulation and other cognitive styles. Unfortunately the findings have not been as clear-cut as hoped, but general *mood variability* was related to cognitive style, as we shall see.

Another general finding from the P-technique factor analyses of individual mood records was that the happier men seemed more influenced throughout the day by their good experiences, while the less happy appeared more influenced by their bad experiences. Peaks of good mood were maximized and sustained by the happy men, while the peaks were more transitory in their effect on the less happy. Also the individual's customary level of happiness and its variability appeared related to particular components of his mood changes. The *happy* men seemed most influenced by their energy and involvement in the world. The *unhappy* men seemed most influenced by feelings of sociability–withdrawal and personal moral judgment. The *variable* men were particularly influenced by their feelings of the fullness or emptiness of life and self-confidence. The *stable* men were much more influenced by their relative feelings of energy and of harmony versus anger.

The individual patterns of affective organization and change indicated that discussions of "happiness" and "unhappiness" have much to gain by taking account of the different sources and content of moods in the stable and the variable, the happy and the unhappy.

VIII. PERSONALITY CHARACTERISTICS OF THE HAPPY AND THE UNHAPPY

How do happy and unhappy people differ and why? We were in an advantageous position to find some answers with access to the rich data accruing from three years' intensive personality study of the men. To do so, we correlated 365 test scores and clinical ratings with the mean daily "average" report on elation–depression from the six-week mood study. We also made detailed case studies of all subjects, with particular attention given those whose mood data was of greatest interest, including the most and least happy individuals (Ricks & Wessman, 1966; Wessman & Ricks, 1966, pp. 90–173). The major conclusions will be reviewed.

The first concern was the validity of the mean score on elation–depression as a measure of relative happiness–unhappiness. It correlated very highly (.71) with a prior composite clinical rank order of subjects' relative happiness–unhappiness made by six staff psychologists after two years' assessment of the men. It correlated − .83 with the "depression scale" of the MMPI taken two years earlier. All evidence indicated that the mean daily average on elation–depression was an excellent indicator of relative hedonic level.

From the mass of clinical data, consistent patterns emerged. A variety of characteristics indicating overall goodness–badness of psychological functioning and general adjustment–maladjustment were significantly related to degree of happiness. The happy men were optimistic and possessed self-esteem and confidence. They were successful and satisfied in interpersonal relations. They showed ego strength and gratifying sense of identity. There was excellent organization and purpose in their lives, together with the necessary mastery of themselves and interpersonal situations to attain their goals.

On the other hand, the less happy men were more pessimistic in their expectations and lower in self-esteem and self-confidence. They were more unsuccessful and dissatisfied in their interpersonal relations, with much evidence of isolation, anxiety, and guilt. They showed poorer ego integration and an unsatisfying sense of ego identity. They were dissatisfied and felt inferior in their academic performance (which did tend to be somewhat lower). They lacked a personal sense of temporal continuity and purpose (Wessman, 1973) and were less successful in attaining the necessary organization and mastery to achieve goals.

The intensive case studies indicated that no single developmental crisis or trauma could account for the origins of unhappiness; rather, the sources were in the cumulative series of the individual's life experiences. In various ways, self-esteem and self-acceptance seemed to have been impaired for the less happy men, hampering their potential for interpersonal intimacy and satisfying commitment. There seemed to have been a series of relatively unfavorable outcomes at the major psychosocial developmental crises (Erikson, 1963), which left the unhappy individual more prone to self-limitation and subsequent frustration in the fact of later challenges.

Again no one source could account for the greater success of the happier men, typically well-adjusted social extraverts who found genuine satisfaction in their personal relations and work. These men were not of a single pattern either, but by and large they came from warm and supportive home environments conducive to growth and gradual assumption of responsibilities. Though there were exceptions, developmental transitions were relatively smooth and residual conflicts seemed subdued. Important needs had not become overly compounded by distressing and disturbing affect. Their childhood experiences apparently established a solid sense of competence from repeated rewarding transactions with their environments. They were able to make positive identifications with respected and approachable models that encouraged the establishment and growth of a worthwhile sense of self. Begun in the family, this continuing process was furthered as they moved out into the world. While most conspicuous in the area of work and close personal relationships, their growth toward full and satisfying adulthood was evident in most areas.

For a long period, psychological investigation of the nature of happiness was neglected (Wessman, 1956). In recent years, much interesting work has been done and ably reviewed (Arkoff, 1975; Wilson, 1967). Most of the findings are in accord with the favorable picture we found. Lest the reader conclude that this is an unqualified ode to joy, our position should be made clear. We believe it desirable that people be happy—happiness is superior to misery. But happiness is not the only value in life and "good adjustment" can sometimes be constricting. There often was much to admire and respect in the lives of some of the more complicated and less happy men.

IX. PERSONALITY CHARACTERISTICS OF THE STABLE AND THE VARIABLE IN MOOD

Using the same data and case study methods, we attempted to penetrate the mysteries of mood variability (Wessman & Ricks, 1966, pp. 174–241). It will be recalled that *day-to-day variability* and *within-day variability* were correlated. Thus an individual who reported great swings within the day was also very likely to report considerable shifts in his average mood from day to day. The two aspects also showed similar relationships with the other personality measures. In view of these findings, it was appropriate to consider together people who were stable or varied in both regards. (However, the magnitude of correlations was customarily greater for the mean daily range.) The personality characteristics about to be described thus related to general variability in many aspects of mood.

Variability in the avowal of moods was clearly related to low degrees of denial and repression. A number of test scores and clinical ranks showed the variable men more willing to admit feelings, while the stable men were more likely to repress, conceal, or deny them. Thus, in general, negative affects were more openly avowed by the variable men and also found expression in TAT stories. But their positive affects also were more powerfully experienced and expressed.

The mood diaries of variable men were colorful. While the stable men appeared calm, modest, and somewhat lethargic, the moody men were lively in their reports and their actual behavior. Highly involved with others, energetic and subjective, with tension spilling over into conflict, with fantasy enriching life but at times overembellishing it, they moved from deep troughs of despair to soaring peaks of joy.

In Q-sort self-descriptions, in both elation and depression, the steady men presented themselves as independent, serious, quiet, and reserved, with pride in their standards and character. The moodier men, whose self-concepts varied more in the contrasting states, generally presented themselves as open, out-going, and productive. While the personal ideals of the two groups were rather similar, the stable men seemed to put greater value on work where clear consensual standards applied, whereas the variable men put more value on originality and inventiveness. The self and ideal descriptions, supported by our clinical impressions, suggested that mood stability is related to personal accommodation to the constraints of the environment. Variability provides a range of alternate responses, thus avoiding rigidity and allowing more resourceful openness to change. Consistency, on the other hand, increases efficiency in relatively unchanging situations, since invariant actions are performed with little effort (Fiske, 1955, 1961). Our findings on the personality correlates of mood variability support Fiske's formulation. The stable men appeared to subject inner pressures to the demand of steadiness in confronting the environment with emotional stability and "character." The moody men were more liable to inner turmoil but were rewarded with a more intense inner life and greater responsiveness and originality.

These conclusions were sustained by the other psychological test data. The stable men were more tightly organized and controlled. They were generally objective, cautious, "rational," and little given to imagination. The variable men were more impulsive, carried along by their whims and enthusiasms with little critical control. A number of tests supported these findings, but the dif-ferences were strikingly manifest in their Rorschach performances. Moody men showed high productivity, with a rich intermixture of color, shading, and the less-developed movement responses, a richness of response often achieved at the expense of integration and control.

The stable men could be viewed, then, as relatively closed systems, with their characteristics well established and their social roles selected and organized. The variable men, on the other hand, were more open to both internal stimulation and the social environment, and later research has indeed found them more field-dependent (Gorman & Wessman, 1974). In Cattell's (1950, 1957) language, and on his test, the stable men were more sizothymic or reserved, and the variable were more cyclothymic or open. In terms of the Freudian psychodynamic scheme of development, the stable men tended toward more controlled "anal" character structures, the variable men toward character structures that were more "phallic and urethral" (Murray, 1955). The variable people seemed to be seeking self-actualization and peak experiences (Gorman & Wessman, 1974; Maslow, 1954, 1962). Their goals were not stable habits and routines but initiative, drive to achieve, and desire to change themselves and the world and to be recognized for doing it. Their preferences among various metaphors for time, for instance, were for images like "a soaring bird," "ceaseless effort," "unappeasable ambition," and "the thrust of forward purpose." Like Icarus, they break the bounds of ordinary experience, and if they at times fall into the sea of gloom, they also fly high into the thin air and bright sunshine of peak experiences.

In short, both steady and moody people have characteristic strengths and limitations. Probably a moderate degree of affective variability is easiest to live with, but fortunately the world has need as well for individuals of solid character and those with lively passions.

X. CONCLUSION

Extended mood-measurement studies employing the PFS techniques have been carried out in many areas of research in addition to those already cited. They include investigations of moods of black and white college students (Carter, 1973) and lesbian women (Greene, 1976); of psychotherapists' and patients' mood interactions (Gurman, 1972, 1973); of defense mechanisms and mood characteristics (Clum & Clum, 1973a, 1973b); and of affective responses to menstrual cycles (May, 1976), cardiac surgery (Kimball, Quinlan, Osborne, & Woodward, 1973; Quinlan, Kimball, & Osborne, 1974), and drugs (Stephens, Schaffer, & Brown, 1974). In all these studies, repeated mood measures have proved a useful tool.

At the beginning of this chapter, it was noted how in recent years there has been heightened interest in emotion and affect by psychologists representing many different research approaches and theoretical backgrounds. What has already been accomplished represents substantial progress toward fuller understanding of the range of emotion, and new contributions may be anticipated. In this advance, further studies of mood can play an important role by revealing both general and unique dynamic patterns in emotional experience. The character and quality of human life are revealed by our varied and changing moods.

REFERENCES

Abraham, K. Notes on the psychoanalytical investigation and treatment of manic-depressive insanity and allied conditions (1911). In *Selected papers of Karl Abraham*. New York: Basic Books, 1954. (a)

Abraham, K. A short study of the development of the libido viewed in the light of mental disorders (1924). In *Selected papers of Karl Abraham*. New York: Basic Books, 1954. (b)

Arieti, S. Manic–depressive psychosis. In S. Arieti (Ed.), *American handbook of psychiatry*, Vol. 1. New York: Basic Books, 1959.

Arkoff, A. The state of happiness. In A. Arkoff (Ed.), *Psychology and personal growth*. Boston: Allyn and Bacon, 1975.

Arnold, M. B. *Emotion and personality*, 2 vols. New York: Columbia University Press, 1960.

Arnold, M. B. *Feelings and emotions*. New York: Academic Press, 1970.

Bardwick, J. M. *The psychology of women*. New York: Harper and Row, 1971.

Beck, A. T. *Depression: Clinical, experimental and theoretical aspects*. New York: Hoeber Medical Division, Harper and Row, 1967.

Beck, A. T. *Cognitive therapy and the emotional disorders.* New York: International Universities Press, 1976.

Becker, J. *Depression: Theory and research.* Washington, D.C.: V. H. Winston (Wiley), 1974.

Becker, J., & Nichols, C. H. Communality of manic depressive and "mild" cyclothymic characteristics. *Journal of Abnormal and Social Psychology,* 1964, *69,* 531–538.

Bibring, E. The mechanism of depression. In P. Greenacre (Ed.), *Affective disorders.* New York: International Universities Press, 1953.

Blatt, S. J., Dafflitti, J. P., & Quinlan, D. M. Experiences of depression in normal young adults. *Journal of Abnormal Psychology,* 1976, *85,* 383–389.

Bull, N., & Strongin, E. The complex of frustration: a new interpretation. *Journal of Nervous and Mental Disease,* 1956, *123,* 531–535.

Buytendijk, F. J. J. The phenomenological approach to the problem of feelings and emotions. In M. L. Reymert (Ed.), *Feelings and emotions.* New York: McGraw-Hill, 1950.

Carter, A. An investigation into the moods of black and white college students (doctoral dissertation, Columbia University, 1973). *Dissertation Abstracts International,* 1974, *35,* 1041-B (University Microfilms No. 74-17, 848).

Cassirer, E. *An essay on man.* Garden City, N.Y.: Doubleday Anchor Books, 1944.

Cattell, R. B. *The sixteen personality factor questionnaire.* Champaign, Ill.: Institute for Personality and Ability Testing, 1950.

Cattell, R. B. *Personality and motivation structure and measurement.* Yonkers, N.Y.: World Book, 1957.

Cattell, R. B. *The scientific analysis of personality,* Baltimore: Penguin Books, 1965.

Cattell, R. B. Anxiety and motivation: Theory and crucial experiments. In C. D. Spielberger (Ed.), *Anxiety and behavior.* New York: Academic Press, 1966.

Cattell, R. B. *Personality and mood by questionnaire.* San Francisco: Jossey-Bass, 1973.

Church, J. *Language and the discovery of reality.* New York: Vintage Books, Random House, 1966.

Clum, G. A., & Clum, J. Choice of defense mechanisms and their relationship to mood level. *Psychological Reports,* 1973, *32,* 507–510. (a)

Clum, G. A., & Clum, J. Mood variability and defense mechanism preference. *Psychological Reports,* 1973, *32,* 910. (b)

Clyde, D. Self-ratings. In L. Uhr and J. G. Miller (Eds.), *Drugs and behavior.* New York: Wiley, 1960.

Cohen, M. B., Baker, G., Cohen, R. A., Fromm-Reichmann, F., & Weigert, E. V. An intensive study of twelve cases of manic-depressive psychosis. *Psychiatry,* 1954, *17,* 103–107.

Davitz, J. R. *The language of emotion.* New York: Academic Press, 1969.

Drever, J. *A dictionary of psychology.* Hammondsworth, England: Penguin Books, 1952.

Ekman, P., & Friesen, W. V. *Unmasking the face: A guide to recognizing emotions from facial cues.* Englewood, N.J.: Prentice-Hall, 1975.

Ekman, P., Friesen, W. V., & Ellsworth, P. *Emotion in the human face.* New York: Pergamon Press, 1972.

Ellenberger, H. F. A clinical introduction to psychiatric phenomenology and existential analysis. In R. May, E. Angel, & H. F. Ellenberger (Eds.), *Existence.* New York: Basic Books, 1958.

English, H. B., & English, A. C. *A comprehensive dictionary of psychological and psychoanalytic terms.* New York: Longmans, Green, 1958.

Erikson, E. H. Identity and the life cycle. *Psychological Issues,* 1959, *1,* No. 1.

Erikson, E. H. *Childhood and society* (2nd ed.). New York: Norton, 1963.

Fawcett, J. Biological and neuropharmacological research in the affective disorders. In E. J. Anthony & T. Benedek (Eds.), *Depression and human existence.* Boston: Little, Brown, 1975.

Fenichel, O. *The psychoanalytic theory of neurosis.* New York: Norton, 1945.

Fiske, D. W. The inherent variability of behavior. In D. W. Fiske & S. R. Maddi (Eds.), *Functions of varied experience.* Homewood, Ill.: Dorsey Press, 1961.

Fiske, D. W., & Rice, L. Intra-individual response variability, *Psychological Bulletin*, 1955, *52*, 217–250.

Flugel, J. C. A quantitative study of feeling and emotion in everyday life. *British Journal of Psychology*, 1925, *15*, 318–355.

Frank, K. A. Mood differentiation and psychological differentiation: Some relations between mood variations and Witkin's research (doctoral dissertation, Columbia University, 1967). *Dissertations Abstracts* 1968, *28*, 5203B (University Microfilms No. 68-8583).

Freud, S. Mourning and melancholia (1917). In S. Freud, *Collected papers*, Vol. 4. London: Hogarth Press, 1953.

Fried, K. W. Measure for measure: Test variability as a function of trait, method and person (doctoral dissertation, Columbia University, 1968). *Dissertation Abstracts International*, 1969, *30*, 2418B (University Microfilms No. 69-17, 584).

Gershon, E. S., Crower, M., & Kerman, G. L. Hostility and depression. *Psychiatry*, 1968, 31, 224–235.

Gorman, B. S. A multivariate study of the relationships of cognitive control and cognitive style principles to reported daily mood experiences (doctoral dissertation, City University of New York, 1971). *Dissertation Abstracts*, 1972, *32*, 4211B (University Microfilms, No. 72-5071).

Gorman, B. S., & Wessman, A. E. The relationships of cognitive styles and moods. *Journal of Clinical Psychology*, 1974, *30*, 18–25.

Gorman, B. S., & Wessman, A. E. (Eds.), *The personal experience of time*. New York: Plenum, 1977.

Gorman, B. S., Wessman, A. E., & Ricks, D. F. Social desirability and self-report of moods: a rejoinder. *Perceptual and Motor Skills*, 1975, *40*, 272–274.

Greene, D. M. Women loving women: An exploration into feelings and life experiences (doctoral dissertation, City University of New York, 1976). *Dissertation Abstracts International* 1977, *37*, 3608B (University Microfilms No. 76-30, 267).

Gurman, A. S. Therapists' mood patterns and therapeutic facilitativeness. *Journal of Counseling Psychology*, 1972 *19*, 169–170.

Gurman, A. S. Effects of therapist and patient mood on the therapeutic functioning of high- and low-facilitative therapists. *Journal of Consulting and Clinical Psychology*, 1973, *40*, 48–58.

Hall, C. S., & Lindzey, G. *Theories of personality* (2nd ed.). New York: Wiley, 1970.

Hartmann, H. *Essays on ego psychology*. New York: International Universities Press, 1964.

Heidegger, M. *Being and time* (1927). New York: Harper and Row, 1962.

Hersey, R. B. *Workers' emotions in shop and home: A study of individual workers from the psychological and physiological standpoint*. Philadelphia: University of Pennsylvania Press, 1932.

Hildreth, H. M. A battery of feeling and attitude scales for clinical use. *Journal of Clinical Psychology*, 1942, *2*, 214–221.

Izard, C. E. *The face of emotion*. New York: Appleton-Century-Crofts, 1971.

Izard, C. E. *Patterns of emotions: A new analysis of anxiety and depression*. New York: Academic Press, 1972.

Izard, C. E., & Tomkins, S. S. Affect and behavior: Anxiety as a negative affect. In C. D. Spielberger (Ed.), *Anxiety and behavior*. New York: Academic Press, 1966.

Jacobson, E. Normal and pathological moods: Their nature and functions. *The Psychoanalytic Study of the Child*, 1957, *12*, 73–113.

Johnson, W. B. Euphoric and depressed moods in normal subjects. *Journal of Character and Personality*, 1937, *6*, 79–98, 188–202.

Jones, E. E., Kanouse, D. E., Kelley, H. H., Nisbett, R. E., Valins, S., & Weiner, B. *Attribution: Perceiving the causes of behavior*. Morristown, N.J.: General Learning Press, 1972.

Kimball, C. P., Quinlan, D. Osborne, F., & Woodward, B. Experience of cardiac surgery: 5. Psychological patterns and prediction of outcome. *Psychotherapy and psychosomatics*, 1973, *22*, 310.

Lacey, J. I., & Lacey, B. C. Some autonomic–central nervous system interrelationships. In P. Black (Ed.), *Physiological correlates of emotion*. New York: Academic Press, 1970.

Langer, S. K. *Philosophy in a new key*. New York: Mentor, New American Library, 1951.

Laxner, R. M. Relation of real self-rating to mood and blame and their interaction in depression. *Journal of Consulting Psychology*, 1964, *28*, 538–546.

Lazarus, R. S., Averill, J. R., & Opton, E. M., Jr. Towards a cognitive theory of emotion, In M. B. Arnold (Ed.), *Feelings and emotions*. New York: Academic Press, 1970.

Leeper, R. W. The motivational and perceptual properties of emotions as indicating their fundamental character and role. In M. B. Arnold (Ed.), *Feeling and emotions*. New York: Academic Press, 1970.

Lichtenberg, P. A. A definition and analysis of depression. *Archives of Neurology and Psychiatry*, 1957, *77*, 519–527.

Lorr, M., Daston, P., & Smith, I. R. An analysis of mood states. *Educational and Psychological Measurements*, 1967, *27*, 89–96.

Luce, G. G. *Body time: Physiological rhythms and social stress*. New York: Bantam Books, 1973.

Mandell, A. J., & Segal, D. S. Neurochemical aspects of adaptive regulation in depression: Failure and treatment. In E. J. Anthony & T. Benedek (Eds.), *Depression and human existence*. Boston: Little, Brown, 1975.

Mandler, G. *Mind and emotion*. New York: Wiley, 1975.

Maslow, A. H. *Motivation and personality*. New York: Harper, 1954.

Maslow, A. H. *Toward a psychology of being*. Princeton, N.J.: Van Nostrand, 1962.

May, R. *The meaning of anxiety*. New York: Ronald Press, 1950.

May, R. (Ed.), *Existential psychology*. New York: Random House, 1961.

May, R., Angel, E., & Ellenberger, H. F. (Eds.). *Existence: A new dimension in psychiatry and psychology*. New York: Basic Books, 1958.

May, R. R. Mood shifts and menstrual cycle. *Journal of Psychosomatic Research*, 1976, *20*, 125–130.

McNair, D. M., & Lorr, M. An analysis of mood in neurotics. *Journal of Abnormal and Social Psychology*, 1964, *69*, 620–627.

Mendelson, M. *Psychoanalytic concepts of depression* (2nd ed.). Flushing, N.Y.: Spectrum, (Wiley), 1974.

Miller, H. L., & McManus, B. Effects of depression and target status on aggressive responding. *Psychological Reports*, 1976, *38*, 75–81.

Minkowski, E. Findings in a case of schizophrenic depression (1923). In R. May, E. Angel, & H. F. Ellenberger (Eds.), *Existence*. New York: Basic Books, 1958.

Mischel, W. *Personality and assessment*. New York: Wiley, 1968.

Murray, H. A. *Explorations in personality*. New York: Oxford University Press, 1938.

Murray, H. A. Toward a classification of interactions. In T. Parsons & E. A. Shils (Eds.), *Toward a general theory of action*. Cambridge, Mass.: Harvard University Press, 1951.

Murray, H. A. American Icarus. In A. Burton & R. E. Harris (Eds.), *Clinical studies of personality*, Vol. 2. New York: Harper, 1955.

Murray, H. A., & Kluckhohn, C. Outline of a conception of personality. In C. Kluckhohn, H. A. Murray, & D. M. Schneider (Eds.), *Personality in nature, society and culture* (2nd ed.). New York: Knopf, 1953.

Neisser, U. *Cognitive psychology*. New York: Appleton-Century-Crofts, 1967.

Neisser, U. *Cognition and reality*. San Francisco: Freeman, 1976.

Nowlis, V. Research with the Mood Adjective Checklist. In S. S. Tomkins and C. E. Izard (Eds.), *Affect, cognition and personality*. New York: Springer, 1965.

Nowlis, V. Mood: Behavior and experience. In M. B. Arnold (Ed.), *Feelings and emotions*. New York: Academic Press, 1970.

Nowlis, V., & Nowlis, H. H. The description and analysis of mood. *Annals of the New York Academy of Science*, 1956, *65*. 345–355.

Plutchik, R. *The emotions: Facts, theories, and a new model*. New York: Random House, 1962.

Plutchik, R., & Ax, A. F. A critique of "Determinants of emotional state" by Schachter and Singer (1962). *Psychophysiology*, 1967, *4*, 79–82.

Posner, M. I. *Cognition: An introduction*. Glenview, Ill.: Scott, Foresman, 1973.

Quinlan, D. M., Kimball, C. P., & Osborne, F. Experience of open-heart surgery: 4. Assessment of disorientation and dysphoria following cardiac surgery. *Archives of General Psychiatry*, 1974, *31*, 241–244.

Ricks, D. F., & Wessman, A. E. Winn: A case study of a happy man. *Journal of Humanistic Psychology*, 1966, *6*, 2–16.

Rosenfeld, A. An investigation into the psychoanalytic theory of depression. *International Journal of Psychoanalysis*, 1959, *40*, 1–25.

Rosenzweig, S., Fleming, E. E., & Clarke, H. J. Revised scoring manual for the Rosenzweig Picture-Frustration Study. *Journal of Psychology*, 1947, *24*, 165–208.

Ruckmick, C. A. *The psychology of feeling and emotion*. New York: McGraw-Hill, 1936.

Ruitenbeek, H. M. *Psychoanalysis and existential philosophy*. New York: Dutton, 1962.

Ryle, G. *The concept of mind*. London: Hutchinson, 1950.

Schachtel, E. G. *Metamorphosis: On the development of affect, perception, attention and memory*. New York: Basic Books, 1959.

Schachter, S. The interaction of cognitive and physiological determininants of emotional state. In C. D. Spielberger (Ed.), *Anxiety and behavior*. New York: Academic Press, 1966.

Schless, A. P., Mendels, J., Kipperman, A., & Cochrane, C. Depression and hostility. *Journal of Nervous and Mental Disease*, 1974, *159*, 91–100.

Seligman, M. E. P. *Helplessness: On depression, development, and death*. San Francisco: Freeman, 1975.

Skinner, B. F. *Science and human behavior*. New York: Macmillan, 1953.

Spiegelberg, H. *The phenomenological movement: An historical introduction* (2 vols.). The Hague, Netherlands: Martinus Nijhoff, 1960.

Speilberger, C. D. Theory and research on anxiety. In C. D. Spielberger (Ed.), *Anxiety and behavior*, New York: Academic Press, 1966.

Stevens, J. H., Schaffer, J. W., & Brown, C. C. Controlled comparison of effects of diphenylhydantoin and placebo on mood and psychomotor functioning in normal volunteers. *Journal of Clinical Pharmacology*, 1974, *14*, 543–551.

Straus, E. W. *Phenomenological psychology*. New York: Basic Books, 1966.

Strongman, K. T. *The psychology of emotion*. London: Wiley, 1973.

Tomkins, S. S. *Affect, imagery, consciousness* (2 vols.). New York: Springer, 1962, 1963.

van Kaam, A. *Existential foundations of psychology*. Garden City, N.Y.: Doubleday Image Books, 1966.

Warr, P. B. (Ed.). *Thought and personality*. Baltimore: Penguin Books, 1970.

Warren, H. C. *Dictionary of psychology*. Boston: Houghton Mifflin, 1934.

Weitz, S. (Ed.). *Nonverbal communication*. New York: Oxford University Press, 1974.

Wessman, A. E. A psychological inquiry into satisfactions and happiness (Doctoral dissertation, Princeton University, 1956). *Dissertation Abstracts* 1957, *17*, 1384–1385. University Microfilms 57-2228).

Wessman, A. E. Personality and the subjective experience of time. *Journal of Personality Assessment*, 1973, *37*, 103–114.

Wessman, A. E., & Ricks, D. F. *Mood and personality*. New York: Holt, Rinehart and Winston, 1966.

Wessman, A. E., Ricks, D. F., & Tyl, M. M. Characteristics and concomitants of mood fluctuation in college women. *Journal of Abnormal and Social Psychology*, 1960, *60*, 117–126.

White, R. W., & Watt, N. F. *The abnormal personality* (4th ed.). New York: Ronald Press, 1973.

Wilson, W. Correlates of avowed happiness. *Psychological Bulletin*, 1967, *67*, 294–306.

Witkin, H. A. Psychological differentiation and forms of pathology. *Journal of Abnormal Psychology*, 1965, *70*, 317–336.

Editor's Introduction

4

Mosher presents a comprehensive review of the literature on the objective measurement of guilt. Much of this work has been done by Mosher and his colleagues, and their work has culminated not only in the successful measurement of guilt but in well-differentiated and relatively independent scales for measuring sex-guilt, hostility-guilt, and moral-guilt. By beginning his project on the measurement of guilt with an incomplete-sentences test, Mosher anchored his test items in the language and phenomenology of a broad sample of individuals.

Most of Mosher's work has been devoted to the study of the personality disposition of guilt, although he recognizes the usefulness of the concept of state guilt. He presents a substantial body of evidence to support his assumption that guilt as a personality disposition predicts behavior in situations of conscience. For example, in a study of prison inmates, sex-guilt correlated highly significantly with sexual crimes, hostility-guilt with violent crimes, and moral-guilt with the total number of crimes. In laboratory studies, Mosher and his colleagues have found that people low on hostility-guilt express more aggression toward a frustrating experimenter than do people high on hostility-guilt. A number of other laboratory and field studies show that the personality disposition to guilt inhibits sexual and aggressive behavior.

Mosher argues for the appropriateness of the term *disposition* in preference to *trait*. His treatment of the concept of "personality disposition of guilt" suggests that he conceives it as an interaction of cognition and emotion or as an affective–cognitive structure. Thus the tendency to experience guilt as an affective state is determined by the kinds of cognition that the individual has previously linked to feelings of guilt. Although Mosher notes some of the limitations of his approach to the study of guilt, his work is an outstanding example of what can be done to develop measures of a single emotion and to enrich scientific and professional endeavors in the field of emotions in general.

The Meaning and Measurement of Guilt

4

DONALD L. MOSHER

I. INTRODUCTION

A. A Construct Validational Approach

The chapter reviews selectively the research supporting the construct validity of a set of self-report inventories that were developed to measure the personality disposition of guilt. In focusing on guilt as a personality disposition, a psychologist studies how a person perceives and responds to a class of situations that have a moral dimension in which the self and the behavior of the self are compared to a set of standards for moral conduct. It is assumed that humans exhibit a patterned consistency of behavior through time and across situations, that the pattern has become organized as a function of that person's history in similar past situations, and that such a dispositional pattern can be measured in the present from self-reports sampling a variety of perceptions and responses in the relevant domain.

The person's score on a measure of guilt serves as a simple, additive index of his proneness to experience feelings of guilt for violating or anticipating the violation of a moral standard. The anticipation of guilt may serve a warning function and lead to the inhibition of unacceptable behavior, or the person may proceed in spite of the warning voice of conscience and later experience feelings of guilt.

The validation of a measure of a personality dimension such as guilt entails more than the correlation of the test scores with some single and sovereign criterion of guilt. There is no single criterion that can be universally accepted as encompassing the meaning of the concept of guilt. The meaning of

DONALD L. MOSHER • University of Connecticut, Storrs, Connecticut.

guilt as a psychological concept is a function of its theoretical relationships to other constructs and to its operational referents. A measure of guilt proposes a set of operations suitable for ordering individuals along a dimension of proneness or liability to guilt inhibition or feelings on the basis of their responses to an item domain specified as relevant by the theory of guilt. The validity of the measure of guilt increases when it is employed as the operational definition of the construct of guilt, and a hypothesis stemming from the relevant theory of guilt is confirmed by experimental data. As favorable experimental evidence is gathered, confidence increases in the theory of guilt generating the hypotheses tested, in the usefulness of the concept of guilt, and in the validity of the measure of guilt. This approach, emphasizing the importance of the nomological net or pattern of theoretical relationships in generating operational definitions as well as in suggesting hypotheses of investigation, has been called *construct validation* by Cronbach and Meehl (1955).

B. The Meaning of Guilt

In psychoanalytic theory, the concept of guilt is usually used as a descriptor of an affective experience of self-blame and self-remorse, but the concept of guilt is also used to describe inferred motives for defense and as an unconsciously operative motive for self-punishment. Fenichel (1945) distinguished the guilt feeling proper from the warning function of conscience that serves to inhibit immoral action. The concept of guilt is related to a wide range of phenomena as an important explanatory concept and enters into theoretical accounts of various forms of psychopathology, including depressive and obsessional reactions. Failure to internalize standards of moral conduct or defensive processes that neutralize the warning function of conscience are prominent in accounts of delinquent and criminal behavior. The construct of guilt is a major component of intrapsychic conflict over sexual and aggressive actions and fantasies. The clinical theory of psychoanalysis, in contrast to the metapsychological theory of psychoanalysis, guided the inclusion of referents in the measures of guilt and specified many of the hypotheses that have been tested.

In understanding the research to be reviewed, it is important to remember that the Mosher inventories were designed to measure the personality disposition of guilt rather than the affective state of guilt. The disposition of guilt is a more inclusive construct than the affective state of guilt. The disposition of guilt is defined as a generalized expectancy for self-mediated punishment for violating or anticipating violating internalized standards of moral behavior and is thus a cognitive predisposition rather than an affective state. The inhibition of morally unacceptable behavior when violations are anticipated and the occurrence of self-punishing behavior for moral violation as experienced in guilt feelings and regrets are the principal domains to be reviewed in this chapter.

Some psychologists might use the terms *trait guilt* and *state guilt* to refer to the personality disposition of guilt and affective state of guilt, respectively. Here, the concept of *disposition* was preferred to that of *trait* for two reasons. First, too often traits are regarded as *pansituational*, as if the specific situation were an unimportant determinant of personality; yet, personality is the interaction of the person and the situation. A disposition is *transituational* and is engaged by the person as a function of his appraisal of relevant cues in a specific situation. The personality disposition of guilt is regnant in situations providing cues relevant to the potential violation of an internalized moral standard. Second, the state and trait distinction has been associated in past practice with inadequate measuring operations for a trait. The usual procedure has been to develop a state measure of an affect by asking for a report of present feelings in a situation expected to engender affects. Investigators have then asked subjects to indicate on the same measuring device how they feel "in general" as a trait measure. It is not useful to think of guilt feelings in general, as if the person with trait guilt feels guilty everywhere over everything. Guilt feeling is a response to a specific moral violation in a specific situation. A more inclusive set of referents and a different method of measurement are required to measure adequately any general characteristic of a person. The disposition of guilt must be more adequately assessed before attempting to predict the inhibition of immoral behavior or the occurrence of guilt feeling.

C. The Measurement of Guilt

The Mosher Incomplete Sentences Test (MIST) was developed in a doctoral dissertation (Mosher, 1961) to provide a reliable, quantitative instrument suitable for research that would also be acceptable for clinical use. From a large pool of potential stems, pilot investigations led to the selection of sets of stems to be scored for sex-guilt, hostility-guilt, and morality-conscience. The scoring manual that accompanied the MIST provided both scoring principles and weighted sample completions. For example, completions indicative of the disposition of guilt included admissions of feeling guilty, ashamed, disgusted, sinful, and revolted by sexual or aggressive actions or fantasies; attitudes that immoral acts were abnormal, insane, self-destructive, or detrimental to society; and self-reports that judged the self to be evil, unworthy of forgiveness, desiring self-punishment or practicing ascetic denial, confessing, and engaging in acts of contrition, undoing, and restitution. The absence of proneness to guilt was inferred from completions that denied feelings of guilt, that indicated that sexual and aggressive needs were fulfilled with pleasure, that stated that traditionally disapproved acts were normal and desirable, and that planned means of avoiding detection or punishment when disapproved acts were contemplated. Interscorer reliability for the MIST yielded coefficients in the .90s, but coefficients of equivalence and stability were only marginally adequate.

Since the original research with the MIST had been encouraging, a decision was made to construct true–false and forced-choice versions of the guilt inventories for males and females to improve the psychometric properties. The MIST scoring manual had contained different scoring examples for men and women, some of which were sex specific (e.g., *"Prostitution . . .* is not a career that I would choose"). Item pools of 500–800 items drawn from the MIST scoring examples were administered to approximately 100 men and women undergraduates at the Ohio State University. An internal-consistency item analysis and social desirability ratings were used to select items for the inventories. Item weights from the MIST scoring manual were retained. Some sample items from the true–false inventory are:

Prostitution makes me sick when I think about it. (SG +2)
After an outburst of anger I feel much better. (HG −2)
I punish myself when I make mistakes. (MC +1)

Some sample items from the forced-choice inventory are:

If in the future I committed adultery . . .
A. I hope I would be punished very deeply. (SG +2)
B. I hope I enjoy it. (SG −2)
After a childhood fight, I felt . . .
A. Like I was a hero. (HG −2)
B. As if I had done wrong. (HG +2)
A guilty conscience . . .
A. Does not bother me too much. (MC −2)
B. Is worse than a sickness to me. (MC +2)

The three measures of the three aspects of guilt were administered to samples of 95 men (Mosher, 1966a) and 62 women (Mosher, 1968), and the resulting intercorrelations were cast into separate multitrait–multimethod matrices (Campbell & Fiske, 1959). The matrix is a device for examining convergent and discriminant validity. Correlations between the same aspect of guilt as measured by different methods (sentence completion, true–false, forced choice) were higher than correlations between different aspects of guilt measured in the same way or between different aspects of guilt measured by different methods. These matrices, plus a factor analysis of the female matrix, generally supported the usefulness of distinguishing between sex-guilt, hostility-guilt, and morality-conscience as discriminable aspects of the concept of guilt. There is a bandwidth-fidelity tradeoff, so that increasing accuracy of prediction can be obtained by narrowing the domain to be predicted. The Mosher inventories are additive scales in which responses to diverse items are summed and used as an index of guilt to predict to a broad range of situations relevant to guilt. That domain is narrowed by using sex-guilt items to predict to sexual situations and hostility-guilt to predict to aggressive situations; however, items can be devised that predict more accurately to even smaller subdomains of guilt. For example, a measure of guilt over masturbation predicts masturbatory behavior better than sex-guilt (Abramson & Mosher, 1975; Mosher & Abramson, 1977). The inclusion in the matrices of measures of anxiety, social desirability, and favorable impression response sets added further evidence supporting the discriminant validity of these measures of guilt. Campbell and Fiske's (1959) definitions of reliability and validity are as follows:

> Reliability is the agreement between two efforts to measure the same trait through maximally similar methods. Validity is represented in the agreement between two attempts to measure the same trait through maximally different methods. (p. 83)

According to these definitions, the foregoing studies were closer to the reliability end of the continuum than to the validity end. However, they did demonstrate sound psychometric foundations for the true–false and forced-choice inventories of guilt.

II. EVIDENCE OF CONSTRUCT VALIDITY

Space limitations require a selective review of the rapidly mounting empirical literature that provides evidence of the construct validity of the Mosher guilt inventories. The relation of the disposition of guilt to behavioral inhibition as measured by self-reports and in the laboratory, the relation of guilt to moral judgment, and the relation of guilt to guilty affect and physiological indices of emotion were selected for review.

Such a selective review omits a considerable amount of evidence pertinent to construct validation. As a guide for the interested reader, some of the omitted research will be briefly cited. The measures of guilt discriminated first offenders from recidivists at the Ohio Penitentiary (Mosher & Mosher, 1966), delinquent boys from matched controls (Ruma, 1967), and incarcerated homosexual inserters from homosexual insertees (Oliver & Mosher, 1968). Evidence of convergent and discriminant validity was provided in studies correlating the Mosher measures of guilt with a number of other personality inventories (Abramson, Mosher, Abramson, & Wochowski, 1977; Dubeck, Schuck, & Cymbalisty, 1971; Galbraith, 1969; Mortimer, 1966; J. Mosher, 1975; Nicholas, 1965; O'Grady & Janda, in press; Oliver & Mosher, 1968; Persons, 1970; Schill, Evans, & McGovern, in press; Schill & Schneider, 1970a,b; Schwartz, 1973a). The relation of attitude measures or demographic variables to guilt was examined in several investigations (Abramson & Mosher, 1975; Bradbury, 1967; Mendelsohn, 1970; J. Mosher, 1975; C. Proenza, 1968; Ray & Walker, 1973). Hostility-guilt has been related to defensive processes (Schill, Rader, Evans, & Segall, in press). The influence of guilt on the appreciation of cartoon humor has received attention (Lamb, 1968; McSweeney, 1974; Schwartz, 1972). Guilt has been related to thematic fantasy (James & Mosher, 1967; Janda, 1975; Selvey, 1970), fantasies told to explicitly sexual films (Abramson & Mosher, in press; Kier, 1972), and both sexual daydreams and induced sexual fantasies (Carlson & Coleman, 1977). The effects of guilt as disposition on operant verbal conditioning (Mosher, 1966b), perception (Proenza, 1966), short-term memory (Greenberg, 1968; Lanzafame, 1970), part–whole learning (Kelly, 1972), and the retention of birth control information (Abramson, 1976, in press; Schwartz, 1973b) have been studied. Two studies have examined the influence of guilt on performance in the Valin's (1966) paradigm using false–heart-rate feedback (Botto, Galbraith, & Stern, 1974; Hawkins & Janda, in press). The sex-guilt of the interviewer or psychotherapist has been related to self-disclosure and avoidance of sexual content (Persons & Marks, 1970; Vroubel, 1976). Women disposed to guilt over sex were more punitive and condemning of women who admit having premarital sex (Corey, 1970; Mendelsohn, 1970). A series of investigations related guilt to person perception (Janda, 1975; Janda, O'Grady, & Barnhart, in press; Wheaton, 1972). These investigations have extended considerably the realm of phenomena to be predicted by a construct such as guilt beyond the areas selected for review.

A. Guilt and Behavioral Inhibition

Guilt as a disposition is intended to predict behavior in moral situations, and the data have indicated that subjects disposed to guilt do, indeed, report engaging in less immoral behavior. Ruma (1967) found that forced-choice, hostility-guilt, and morality-conscience were negatively correlated ($r = -.45$) with the Arnold (1965) Scale of Delinquent Behavior, which is based on self-reports of assault, theft, and vandalism, and that guilt was negatively correlated ($r = -.41$) with staff ratings based on nominations of which boys lie, cheat, steal, and argue. Heyman (1969) correlated the true–false hostility-guilt inventory with subtests of a modified version of the Kulik, Stein, and Sarbin (1968) checklist of antisocial behaviors in a sample of 197 delinquent males. Hostility guilt was moderately negatively correlated with the delinquent role subtest ($r = -.46$), the assaultive behavior subtest ($r = -.45$), and a newly devised aggressive behavior subtest ($r = -.43$). Persons (1970b) interviewed 75 anonymous inmates of a maximum security reformatory for habitual and serious offenders about crimes they had committed in the past, often undetected and unpunished. The number of sex crimes, violent crimes, and the total of all crimes were correlated with the forced-choice guilt subscales. Sex guilt was the best predictor of the number of sexual crimes ($r = -.65$), hostility guilt of violent crimes ($r = .65$), and the total of all crimes was predicted equally well by morality conscience ($r = -.62$) and hostility guilt ($r = -.64$).

Schill and Althoff (1975) studied the relationship of forced-choice morality-conscience to drug experience, knowledge, and attitudes in a sample of male and female undergraduates. High-morality-conscience subjects had more critical attitudes toward five classes of drugs: marijuana, hallucinogens, stimulants, depressants, and opiates. Low-guilt subjects had used a significantly greater variety of drugs and had used significantly more of all the drug classes except for the almost-never-used class of opiates. Both high- and low-morality-conscience subjects had the same factual knowledge of drugs, but the less guilty group knew more drug subculture slang and operating procedures.

In a study of 70 polydrug users in three drug-free addiction-treatment programs, drug users who preferred sedatives (i.e., barbiturates and/or heroin) scored significantly higher on forced-choice sex-guilt than drug users who preferred stimulants (i.e., amphetamines and/or cocaine). The data were consistent with the authors' (Ungerer, Harford, Brown, & Kleeber, 1976) view that sedative preference may involve using drugs to lessen the effects of expected punishment or to reduce the frequency of punished behavior. In other words, sedative preference is compatible with more guilty subjects' needs to inhibit sexual and aggressive expression to avoid guilt-induced self-punishment.

The most frequently replicated finding in the sex-guilt literature has been the negative correlation with anonymous self-reports of level of sex experience. Mosher and Cross (1971) reported negative correlations of $-.60$ and $-.61$ between sex-guilt and the cumulative level of sex experience in a University of Connecticut sample of male and female undergraduates. Somewhat smaller negative correlations between sex-guilt and the Brady–Levitt sexual experiences (1965) measure have been found consistently in subsequent studies (Abramson & Mosher, 1975; D'Augelli & Cross, 1975; Kier, 1972; Mosher, 1973; Nichols, 1970). Langston (1973, 1975) correlated Bentler's (1968a,b) Heterosexual Behavior Assessment with sex-guilt in a sample of 76 male and 166 female undergraduates in Houston, Texas. His correlations of $-.43$ and $-.56$ for males and females, respectively, and his item-by-item comparison with the Mosher and Cross results were supportive of the usefulness of sex-guilt as a predictor of sexual behavior. In addition, sex-guilt has been negatively correlated with single questionnaire items that inquired about sexual behavior, for example, frequency of sexual intercourse (Love, Sloan, & Schmidt, 1976; Mosher, 1973) and number of past sexual partners (Mosher, 1973). Two of these studies (Mosher, 1973; Mosher & Cross, 1971) have inquired about the factors that prevented the person from more freely expressing his or her sexuality; high-guilt subjects should have inhibited their behavior for moral reasons, and both men ($r = .37$) and women ($r = .49$) reported that they did. Anticipation of guilt feeling was another reason offered by high-guilt subjects for inhibiting their sexual expression.

Undergraduate males who scored higher on sex-guilt reported that they were less likely to attempt sexual behavior with their dates, to believe that exploitative tactics were justified, and to have employed exploitative tactics with their dates than lower-scoring males (Mosher, 1971b).

B. Behavioral Inhibition in the Laboratory

When the self-reports òf behavioral inhibition coincide with observations of behavioral inhibition in the laboratory, then confidence in both sets of data is increased. For example, college men scoring higher on sex-guilt reported having seen (Mosher, 1973) and purchased (Love *et al.*, 1976) less pornography than their low-guilt peers. Schill and Chapin (1972) brought males into the laboratory and unobtrusively observed whether they chose to read erotic rather than nonerotic magazines while waiting for the experiment to begin. Males who chose to read the erotic magazines scored lower on sex-guilt. Love *et al.* (1976) brought males to the laboratory to view pornographic slides that had been rated previously for the degree of obscenity. Supporting Amoroso, Brown, Pruesse, Ware, and Pilkey (1970), they found that unobtrusively measured viewing time increased as a linear function of obscenity ratings for their total sample. While low sex-guilt males showed the linear increase of viewing time with increasing obscenity, this was not the case for moderate and high sex-guilt males. Moderate sex-guilt subjects increased viewing time from the slightly to moderately obscene slides, but limited the time they spent viewing the highly obscene slides. High sex-guilt males spent less time viewing the slides and showed no increase in viewing time as a function of the increasing obscenity of the slides.

In the first study of sex-guilt using the MIST, Mosher (1961, 1965) investigated the interaction of fear and guilt in inhibiting the reporting by males of tabooed words in a perceptual-defense type of task. Males with low sex-guilt were responsive to cues about external censure, while males with high sex-guilt seemed insensitive to such cues. Ridley (1976), using the same task, found that women with high sex-guilt took longer to report tabooed words, but there was no interaction between guilt and expectancy for censure. The "differential sensitivity" hypothesis has generated several studies with mixed results (Fricke, 1974; Galbraith & Mosher, 1968; Hayward, 1970; Janda, 1975; Janda & O'Grady, 1976; Janda *et al.*, 1976; Ridley, 1976; Schill & Chapin, 1972; Wheaton, 1972). One conclusion that can be drawn is that low-guilt subjects are even less inhibited in making responses in situations where there is a reduced possibility of external censure. It remains possible that high-guilt males are less sensitive than low-guilt males to external cues relevant to possible censure, but the "differential sensitivity" hypothesis requires more precise conceptual specification to reduce inappropriate applications.

The most frequently used laboratory paradigm in studies of sex-guilt has been the double entendre word-association procedure (Galbraith, 1968a). Subjects who scored higher on sex-guilt gave fewer sexual associations to such words as *lay, snatch, and rubber* (Fricke, 1974; Galbraith, 1968b; Galbraith, Hahn, & Lieberman, 1968; Galbraith & Mosher, 1968; Janda & O'Grady, 1976; Janda *et al.*, 1976; Ridley, 1976; Schill, 1972a; Smith, 1977). Sexual stimulation prior to the task increased the number of sexual associations given by males with low sex-guilt (Galbraith, 1968b; Galbraith & Mosher, 1968). Low-guilt males were influenced by cues related to external approval or disapproval, while high-guilt males continued to make few sexual responses regardless of external cues (Galbraith & Mosher, 1968). Subjects with high sex-guilt who were in a sexual stimulation condition recalled associations more poorly, particularly with neutral stimulus words, than subjects with low sex-guilt in a sexual stimulation condition, while the reverse was true in a control condition (Galbraith & Mosher, 1970). Males with low sex-guilt gave more sexual associations to male than to female experimenters, while high-guilt males were less variable in their associative responding across experimenters (Fricke, 1974). Low sex-guilt males gave more sexual associations when tested by an approachable female experimenter, while the approachability of the female examiner led to no differences in high-guilt males or in female subjects. While high sex-guilt males reported less awareness of the sexual implications of the double entendre words (Galbraith & Mosher, 1968), Schwartz (1975) demonstrated that response inhibition rather than differential knowledge of sexual meanings accounted for the data. Schwartz used repeated administrations of the word association task with instructions to give a new association on each trial, to discover that high sex-guilt subjects produced sexual associations later in their responses hierarchy than low sex-guilt subjects. In two studies of response modality that permitted the subjects (1) to respond orally or to write their response or (2) to anonymously tape-record their response with either the examiner present or absent, Janda and O'Grady (1976) found high-guilt females gave more sexual responses in the written or experimenter-absent conditions. The authors argue that the results were consistent with an interpretation of guilt as preservation of self-esteem rather than the interpretation of guilt as conditioned avoidance of anxiety.

An interesting case study in scientific progress is contained in Galbraith's efforts to understand response latencies in the double entendre word-association procedure. Carl Jung (1906) had used delayed reaction times as one indicator of a complex. It seemed reasonable to expect that sex-guilt might be related to delayed reaction times in the double entendre task, yet Galbraith found none. Pursuing the issue, Galbraith and Sturke (1974) studied free-associative response latencies to ascending and descending lists of words scaled for sexual meaning; highly sexual word-stimuli produced longer response latencies than words scaled as having less sexual meaning. Contrary to expectations derived from both the social desirability hypothesis (Cramer, 1968; Geer & Mollenauer, 1964) and the conditioned-avoidance hypothesis (Cramer, 1968; Pollio & Lore, 1965), males with high sex-guilt tended to have *shorter* response latencies to highly sexual words. Galbraith correctly perceived the outcome to be a function of differential encoding of the stimulus words. High-guilt subjects encoded the words asexually and low-guilt subjects encoded them sexually. Using a restricted association procedure in which women were required to give either sexual or asexual associations on cue, Kerr and Galbraith (1975) demonstrated that sexual responses were accompanied by longer latencies than asexual responses. Women with high sex-guilt had the longest latencies to sexual responses but did not differ from low sex-guilt women on latencies to nonsexual responses. These results were replicated in college men (Galbraith & Wynkoop, 1976).

The relation of hostility guilt to the inhibition of aggression in the laboratory has been investigated by a variety of approaches. When delinquents actively entered into a competition to assemble a formboard to win a prize of a pack of cigarettes and were permitted to distract, criticize, or derogate their opponent, delinquents with low hostility-guilt expressed more retaliatory verbal aggression (Mosher, Mortimer, & Grebel, 1968). Females with low hostility-guilt expressed more aggression, as measured by a questionnaire, toward a frustrating experimenter than did high-guilt women (Schill, 1972b); Hardy (1973) failed to replicate this result with males, but he cautioned that his procedure used fewer insulting remarks and elicited less aggression on his questionnaire than had been reported previously. Groh (1976) reported both angered and nonangered males with high hostility-guilt administered less intense electric shocks but in another study, high-guilt males administered less intense electric shocks when they had not been provoked by a confederate, and there was no difference between the guilt groups in choice of electric shock levels after they were subjected to insults from a confederate (Schallow, 1972). Hayward (1970) reported that low-guilt subjects used longer durations of electric shock, but the number of electric shocks was not always related to guilt as he had expected. Low-guilt subjects did, as expected, give fewer electric shocks when they knew their victim would have an opportunity to retaliate, while high-guilt subjects did not differ in their expression of aggression as a function of fear of reprisal. Females with high hostility-guilt were more responsive to social reinforcement from the experimenter in both decreasing and increasing their level of operant aggression on a Buss Aggression Machine (Carver, 1968). Research in this area has encountered several problems: (1) deceptions are probably differentially effective; (2) instigations to aggression are not uniformly effective, and reports of anger are not always obtained; (3) there is insufficient concern with specifying the nature of the moral violation that would engender guilty inhibition or guilty emotion; and (4) administering electric shocks is not typically in a person's repertoire of aggressive acts.

Taken as a whole, these laboratory investigations indicated that the disposition of guilt inhibits sex-related and aggressive behaviors. The observations in the laboratory of guilt-induced inhibition of morally unacceptable behavior mutually strengthens the value of the evidence obtained from the inverse relationships between guilt and sexual, delinquent, aggressive, and drug-related behaviors reported by both students and prisoners. The data would provide even stronger conceptual support if investigators would ascertain from the participants that the inhibited behaviors were morally unacceptable or that anticipating such acts produced guilt feeling. Striking evidence was available of the greater influence of situational cues on low-guilt persons as predicted by social learning theory (Mosher, 1965). People who were high on guilt inhibited immoral behavior regardless of situational cues related to the probability of punishment in the situation, although high sex-guilt men who were sexually stimulated did recall fewer associations in the double entendre task. However, there were a series of interactions that revealed the importance of situational cues in determining the behavior of low-guilt individuals. Low-guilt students were more sexual or aggressive when sexually stimulated, when few situational cues for censure were present, when fear of reprisal was low, when with same-sexed experimenters, when the experimenter was playing an approachable role, when the experimenter was absent from the room, and when they were permitted to write rather than having to verbalize their responses. High-guilt participants chose nonsexual responses unless they were required to give a sexual association in the double entendre task. Individuals with high sex-guilt were able to respond with a required sexual association, but only after significantly longer latencies suggestive of conflict. The Mosher guilt inventories provided a generally adequate measurement of the disposition of guilt in its function as an inhibitor of morally unacceptable behavior in the laboratory.

C. Guilt and Moral Judgment

The studies of moral judgment and guilt bring together two streams of thought originating in the work of Piaget and Freud. Lawrence Kohlberg's (1976) cognitive-developmental approach to moral reasoning considers the structural changes in the person's logic–value system to represent an invariant universal developmental sequence. The achievement of higher levels of moral judgment represents a genuine moral achievement. The moral reasoning underlying a decision to have or not to have premarital sexual intercourse takes precedence over the issues of predicting the inhibition of premarital sex or the experience of guilt emotion for having sex. While guilt as a personality disposition is also a form of cognitive disposition, the emphasis is not developmental, nor does the presence or absence of a disposition to guilt provide an adequate criterion for judging moral character. The two approaches to the realm of moral reasoning and behavior are not competitors and can provide complementary avenues of approach to certain problem areas.

In a study of the relationships of guilt and moral judgment in delinquent boys, Ruma and Mosher (1967) interviewed the boys about their feelings following the transgression that led to their incarceration. The interviews were scored by a content system based on (1) the absence of emotional disturbance,

(2) an external focus on fear of punishment, and (3) an internal focus on negative self-judgments due to the violation of moral standards. In addition, a global clinical rating of guilt emotion was made from the tape recordings of the transgression interview. The content analysis of internalization and the ratings of guilt emotion were significantly correlated with both Kohlberg's moral judgment stage ($r = .47$ and $r = .43$) and the Mosher Forced-Choice Guilt Inventory ($r = .31$ and $r = .53$, respectively). The stage of moral development and guilt was significantly correlated ($r = .55$) as well.

Ruma (1967) continued this research in her study of 30 delinquents and 30 matched controls. The delinquents scored significantly lower on guilt and reported more delinquent behaviors than the controls but did not differ from the controls on stage of moral judgment. Guilt was negatively correlated with self-reported delinquent behavior and staff rating of moral behavior. The Kohlberg moral dilemmas were not correlated with these measures, but the stage of moral reasoning as scored from specifically devised moral dilemmas relevant to the current life situation of the boys was significantly correlated with both boys' ($r = .29$) ($r = .39$) ratings of moral behavior. Stage of moral judgment and guilt were not significantly correlated in this sample.

The relationship of guilt and moral judgment to the premarital sex experience of 119 undergraduate females was investigated by D'Augelli and Cross (1975). Women were classified into five sex-experience categories—(1) neckers, (2) light petters, (3) heavy petters, (4) technical virgins, and (5) nonvirgins—and into six sexual-expression categories based on their sexual philosophies and experiences: (1) inexperienced virgins, (2) adamant virgins, (3) potential nonvirgins, (4) engaged nonvirgins, (5) liberated nonvirgins, and (6) confused nonvirgins. Significant differences in the sex-guilt of the subjects were obtained using the above classification of sex experience and sexual expression, and the means for sex-guilt, in both cases, were linearly ordered as above from highest to lowest sex-guilt. Women who were modally oriented at the law-and-order stage on Kohlberg's moral dilemmas had significantly less sex experience and scored higher on sex-guilt than women who were modally oriented at the personal-concordance or social-contract stages. In a second study of the moral reasoning and guilt in 76 unmarried couples, men and women who were at the law-and-order stage of moral reasoning were higher on sex-guilt than those classed at other stages. An ordered stepwise multiple-regression analysis predicting conjoint sexual experience of the couple using male and female guilt, stage, and relationship predictors yielded a multiple R of .51. Male sex-guilt ($r = -.38$) made the largest contribution, followed by male law-and-order stage ($r = .29$) and female sex-guilt ($r = -.34$). In the couples, if the male was oriented at the law-and-order stage, then it was unlikely for the couple to report having had intercourse. However, if the woman was oriented at the law-and order stage and the male was at another stage, intercourse was a more likely occurrence. Guilt appeared to be an important mediator, since the sex-guilt of both men and women was contributing to sexual decision making.

These studies suggested that high scorers on the Mosher guilt inventories were modally oriented at the law-and-order stage. Delinquents who oriented predominantly at preconventional and conventional levels might show a positive correlation with guilt. In college students who mainly oriented at personal-concordance, law-and-order, and social-contract stages, the relationship was curvilinear, with greatest guilt associated with the law-and-order stage and less mean guilt at the personal-concordance stage and even lower guilt scores at the social-contract stage. This finding implies that the guilt inventories are measuring a predisposition to inhibit behavior that violates traditional law-and-order standards of morality or to experience guilt feelings for violating such traditional moral standards.

D. Guilt as Personality Disposition and as Affect

Okel and Mosher (1968) performed the first laboratory experiment to induce guilty emotion as a function of a disposition to guilt over aggressive behavior. Undergraduate males partitioned at the median on hostility-guilt derogated the performance of a stranger who became increasingly distressed and disorganized. By having the subjects voluntarily choose to aggress, by making the aggressive behavior manifestly unfair and inappropriate, and by providing ample cues of distress in the victim as a function of hostile attack, it was assumed that standards of proper conduct relevant to aggressive behavior were violated. Males who were predisposed to guilt over aggressive behavior reported significant increases in guilt emotion on a mood adjective checklist, and a postaggression interview revealed that the subjects felt bad, believed that the aggressive behavior was wrong morally, and believed that they would not have done it if they had known the stranger would become so upset. Cogan (1969), using similar procedures, found that males with high hostility-guilt reported more guilt emotion but not more shame, anxiety, depression, etc., after an unfair and pain-inducing aggressive attack. Lawner (1968) studied the relation of hostility-guilt to overt verbal hostility, changes in mood, and expiatory behavior. Hostility-guilt was unrelated to level of hostility and mood changes, but over a third of his subjects were considered suspicious of the deceptions involved and consequently were less hostile and experienced less negative affects. Subjects with high hostility-guilt believed that their attacks were not morally justified and wanted to explain their behavior to the victim or to reduce the level of their hostile attacks. Schallow (1972) reported that high-guilt males who had been insulted and had retaliated by shocking the insulter subsequently reported more feeling of guilt and complied with requests to volunteer for altruistic efforts.

Mosher and Greenberg (1969) studied undergraduate women's reactions to reading erotic literature. Women who scored high on sex-guilt reported feeling guilty following the reading of an erotic literary passage. Subjects were given free choice in participating, and the authors speculated that either this behavioral choice or the subject's involvement in the fantasy while reading or their awareness of experiencing sexual arousal might have violated a moral standard related to sex. In a study that surreptitiously observed the time spent in viewing erotic magazines in a waiting room, Schill and Chapin (1972) had found that men who chose to read erotic magazines scored lower on sex-guilt. When they compared the six high sex-guilt men who had not inhibited reading the erotic magazines with the eight high sex-guilt men who had inhibited their erotic interest, the high sex-guilt readers reported feeling more guilty on an affect adjective measure of guilt than the high sex-guilt nonreaders.

Mosher (1971a, 1973) studied the relation of sex-guilt to the affective reactions to viewing explicitly heterosexual films in 194 male and 183 female undergraduates. After viewing the film, subjects with high sex-guilt reported feeling more guilty, ashamed, embarrassed, and depressed than low sex-guilt subjects. High sex-guilt men reported more feelings of guilt and internal unrest in the 24 hours following the viewing of the film than in the preceding day. Mosher and Abramson (1977) studied the affective reactions of 96 male and 102 female undergraduates to viewing films of masturbation. Subjects who were higher on sex-guilt experienced more affective guilt, disgust, anger, and shame after viewing the films than did their counterparts who were less disposed to guilt over sex. Ray and Walker (1973) showed four sexual slides for 20-second periods and failed to find differences in the affective state of guilt as a function of the disposition of sex-guilt. It may be that briefly viewing slides in an experiment does not involve the subjects in a violation of their moral standards since they have less time to become engaged in sexual fantasy or to notice their own sexual arousal.

Most studies thus far have examined the reactions of college students to pornography, but there are different responses in older, married male subjects as a function of sex-guilt. Mosher (1970) made a *post facto* comparison of the reactions of single men and women undergraduates to explicitly sexual films to the reactions of 32 married couples. Single men, single women, and married women who scored higher on sex-guilt responded with less favorable reactions to the explicitly sexual films. However, married men with high sex-guilt responded more favorably to the films than did the low sex-guilt married men. The high sex-guilt married men enjoyed the films more and found them less disgusting, and they reported feeling more impulsive, pepped up, and peaceful and less guilty, ashamed, repelled, bored, and depressed while viewing the films than did their low sex-guilt married counterparts. This pattern represented a clear reversal of the pattern for single males, single females, and married females. A possible explanation for these results was suggested by additional correlational data. The high sex-guilt married men were less satisfied with their sex lives. They were older when they began to have intercourse, reported being fellated less often, and had less experience with wife swapping. The wives of the high sex-guilt males reported that they were less satisfied with their sex lives and had orgasms less frequently than did the wives of the married men who were less disposed to guilt over sex. The high sex-guilt married men who had less sexual variety and satisfaction in their marriages also reported that they had masturbated more frequently over the past six months.

Polsky (1967) has applied Kingsley Davis's argument about prostitution to pornography. Polsky argued that pornography provides an outlet for impersonal, nonmarital sex by masturbatory, imagined intercourse with a fantasy object. Citing Kinsey, Polsky indicated that masturbating to pornography was largely a phenomenon of the better-educated classes, such as the present sample. The variety of acts and partners that were not present in the marriage was present in the pornographic films enjoyed by the high sex-guilt married men. Perhaps the pornography and masturbation provided a pleasant, fantasy-based, sexual outlet for the high sex-guilt married men, who experienced less satisfaction and variety in their marital sex.

Several studies have attempted to relate sex-guilt to guilt emotion in the word association paradigm. Janda and Magri (1975) first reported that women with high sex-guilt reported higher guilt scores on the Otterbacher and Munz (1973) state measure of guilt following free association in the double entendre paradigm. Janda and O'Grady (1976) failed to replicate this result in two samples of undergraduate women. Of course, these inconsistencies are not surprising, since the Galbraith studies on stimulus encoding indicated that the functional stimulus is unknown, and all three studies found that subjects with high sex-guilt were giving fewer sexual associations to the double entendre words. Janda, Magri, and Barnhart (1977) then used a procedure requiring sexual association to be given to the double entendre words. This has the advantage of producing sexual responses, but it may or may not violate moral standards to give sexual responses following experimental instructions. Janda *et al.* (1977) also administered the Otterbacher and Munz (1973) measure of trait guilt, which was not correlated with the Mosher sex-guilt subscale. Mosher guilt, but not trait guilt, was related to word association responses in the usual fashion. The trait guilt measure was related to state guilt, but the Mosher guilt scale was not. However, the trait and state guilt measures devised by Otterbacher and Munz consist of the same 11 adjective items, ranging from *innocent* to *unforgivable* and differ only in instructions to check the adjective that applies generally (trait) and at a specific moment in time (state). These studies, then, are difficult to interpret on several grounds: (1) no clear conceptual distinction is offered between dispositional and trait guilt; (2) the trait guilt measure has little evidence supporting its construct validity; (3) it is unclear what moral violation is occurring, particularly when high-guilt subjects are not producing sexual associations; and (4) the relation between trait and state guilt may be an artifact of a response set due to similarity in format.

E. Guilt and Physiological Indices of Arousal

Gambaro and Rabin (1969) studied the diastolic blood-pressure responses in male undergraduates following direct and displaced aggression subsequent to anger arousal as a function of hostility guilt as measured by the MIST. Following a frustration condition that led to self-reported increases in anger, subjects were allowed to aggress against the frustrater, a nonfrustrater, or no one. Diastolic blood pressure increased following frustration. Subjects with both high and low hostility-guilt had significant decreases in diastolic blood pressure after directly aggressing against the frustrater. When subjects displaced their aggression against a nonfrustrating person, low hostility-guilt males had a significant decrease in diastolic blood pressure, comparable to that of the direct aggression group, while high hostility-guilt males showed a nonsignificant rise in mean diastolic blood pressure. The no-aggression group showed very small decreases in diastolic blood pressure with the passage of time. It appeared that low-guilt subjects could displace aggression and reduce diastolic blood pressure, but displaced aggression apparently violated the moral standard of high hostility-guilt men, whose diastolic blood pressure remained elevated.

Schill (1972b) studied the aggression and blood pressure response in females partitioned on the forced-choice hostility-guilt inventory. Women were assigned to frustration or nonfrustration conditions. Frustrated women and subjects with low hostility-guilt were more hostile toward the frustrater as measured by a rating questionnaire. Diastolic blood pressure was elevated for the women in the frustration condition. Following aggression, there was a significant decrease in diastolic blood pressure for subjects as a function of conditions and guilt. The low hostility-guilt women had a significantly greater decrease in diastolic blood pressure following aggression than high-guilt subjects. A subanalysis selected 14 subjects who had expressed above-average aggression against the frustrator; only 1 of the 6 high-guilt aggressive subjects had a decrease in diastolic blood pressure, while 7 of 8 low-guilt subjects decreased their level of diastolic blood pressure following aggression.

Meyer (1968) studied chronic high blood pressure in 68 inmates of a state prison as a function of inhibiting aggression. All of the inmates were incarcerated for a crime involving direct physical aggression. Inmates were categorized into expressive and inhibited aggression groups based on their behavior pattern during the preceding 18 months of incarceration. The group who had inhibited their aggression while in the institution had significantly higher diastolic blood pressure. Within the group of inmates who continued to express aggression while in prison, the men who scored higher on hostility guilt as measured by the MIST had significantly higher chronic diastolic blood pressure levels than men with low hostility-guilt.

Ray and Thompson (1974) investigated the autonomic correlates of female responses to erotic visual stimuli as a function of sex guilt. The women exhibited a significant increase in galvanic skin response when viewing two sexual stimuli in comparison to a dating stimulus. With the use of two heart-rate measures, the level of sex-guilt interacted significantly with the stimuli. Females low in sex-guilt exhibited a significant cardiac deceleration during a 30-second presentation of a slide depicting coitus. Subjects high in sex-guilt on a true–false form had a nonsignificant cardiac acceleration to the coital slide. The authors interpreted the data as partially supporting their hypotheses formulated by combining Mosher's (1965) theory of sex-guilt and Lacey's (1959, 1967) theory of cardiac acceleration and deceleration.

Pagano and Kirschner (1978) studied the relation of sex-guilt (on a forced-choice form) in 36 male undergraduates to urinary acid phosphatase output. Barclay (1970, 1971; Barclay & Little, 1972) had shown urinary acid phosphatase levels to be positively correlated with sexual arousal in males. Two urine samples were collected and analyzed, providing a basal measure and a measure following 30 minutes of exposure to erotic slide stimuli. Sex-guilt was significantly negatively correlated ($r = -.44$) with basal acid phosphatase. A regression analysis performed to determine the influence of sex-guilt on postarousal acid phosphatase level independent of basal level yielded a significant beta coefficient of .32. Sex-guilt was also positively correlated ($r = .41$) with negative affective reactions to viewing the erotic stimuli.

These results created further complications in specifying the exact relation of sex-guilt to sexual arousal. When affect adjective checklists or rating scale measures of subjective sexual arousal have been employed, sex-guilt has not inhibited reported arousal to erotic literature or visual material (Bahm, 1972; Mosher, 1971a, 1973; Mosher & Abramson, 1977; Mosher & Greenberg, 1969; Ray & Walker 1973). Self-reports of physiological changes were negatively related to sex-guilt when these reports were placed in an ordinal scale (Mosher & Abramson, 1977). Women reported more sexual arousal to films of masturbation on the affect adjective measure of sexual arousal than men, but no sex differences were present on ratings and physiological self-reports of subjective sexual arousal (Mosher & Abramson, 1977). Further research needs to employ a multimethod approach including both physiological and subjective measures of sexual arousal while systematically varying the nature of sexual stimuli presented to persons varying in their disposition to sex guilt.

III. PROGRESS AND PROSPECT

A. Successful Construct Validation

This review of research has provided strong evidence of the construct validity of the Mosher guilt inventories. Careful construction of forced-choice and true–false inventories led to reliable measures of discriminable aspects of guilt adequately controlled for social desirability. The measures of guilt diverge from measures of anxiety or general neuroticism while converging, in the form of moderate negative correlations, with measures of theoretically parallel constructs such as sexual interest, agression, and psychopathy. The data revealed that the guilt measures successfully predicted to a wide range of psychological phenomena believed to be associated with the disposition of guilt. Correlations with self-reports of delinquent or sexual behavior were unusually large for a personality inventory. The inhibition of sex-related behavior in the laboratory as a function of sex-guilt was demonstrated repeatedly. The prediction of laboratory aggression was less consistent, perhaps because there is less consensus on traditional moral standards for aggression. When it comes to sex, the traditional standards are that, outside of marriage, you don't do it, you don't talk about it, and you don't see it everywhere. While there are some universal moral standards for aggression, such as not hurting the young or the weak, the norms concerning retaliation or being aggressive upon the request of an authority figure are simply less clear and universal. The data revealed that the person who uses traditional, law-and-order moral reasoning scores high on guilt, and that a person must anticipate violating a traditional moral standard before the disposition to guilt is engaged in ways that inhibit immoral action. If the people actually transgress a moral standard, then the data indicate that those individuals who are disposed to guilt indeed do experience guilt emotion and other negative affects.

Many of the studies that have been done were empirical demonstrations of the existence of relations expected to be present if the inventories were a valid index of the disposition to guilt. Some findings have emerged that are nonobvious yet intuitively plausible. Examples are: (1) the differential sensitivity hypothesis, which is based on as yet inconclusive evidence suggesting that guilty men are less aware of situational cues pertinent to possible external censure or disapproval; (2) the enjoyment of pornography by married men with high sex-guilt who were less satisfied with their marital sex life and masturbated more frequently; and (4) the importance of considering stimulus encoding to understand response latencies in the double entendre word-association task.

B. Limitations of the Inventories and the Construct Validational Approach

One limitation of trait approaches is an excessive reliance on self-report inventories. The approach is dimensional rather than morphogenic (Allport, 1962) and leads to correlational studies or experiments that partition individuals at some point along the relevant dimension. This strategy can be both restrictive in scope and limited by the adequacy of the self-report measure. The chapter by Lewis can serve as an antidote to an overly constricted view of the phenomenon of guilt by providing a clinical–phenomenological perspective. The limitations of the Mosher guilt inventories include the following shortcomings: (1) although they were additive scales, they contained a limited sample of the domain of guilt that can be both more inclusive and more specific; (2) the inventories sampled behavior, attitudes, and emotions that increased bandwidth at the expense of fidelity; (3) the disposition was not always carefully differentiated from other constructs, such as shame; (4) separate inventories for men and women were probably not necessary and created difficulties in comparing the sexes; (5) there is no evidence that the item weights increased prediction over the simpler procedure of counting the number of guilt items endorsed; (6) the means of the sex-guilt subscale have declined over the last 10 years, truncating the range; and (7) the inventories measured the disposition to guilt in relation to traditional moral standards and did not represent concerns with existential guilt, pathological guilt, positive conscience, and principled morality.

A second limitation often attributed to trait approaches is an overemphasis on the person at the expense of consideration of the situation. The present author's indebtedness to social learning theory (Mosher, 1965; Rotter, 1954) precluded such one-sidedness, and situational variables were viewed as providing both the context that engaged the disposition to guilt and cues concerning the expectation of punishment that can also serve to inhibit unacceptable behavior.

A more pertinent limitation of the use of the construct validational approach is that the investigations have concentrated on the construct of guilt disposition, but the nomological net contains many related constructs that must be adequately measured and understood as well. The accumulating data, then, are organized to demonstrate the empirical usefulness of a measure of a construct rather than focusing on broader theoretical delineation and extension.

C. Future Research on Guilt

Although the number of problems and approaches to understanding guilt are far too numerous to explicate here, the following represents a small sample of needed developments: (1) the development of miniature theories of a sub-domain of guilt (e.g., guilt over masturbation, confessional behavior, self-punishment) that includes a measure of guilt as a disposition as one construct among other equally important constructs; (2) more precise theoretical specifi-cation of when guilt as a disposition leads to inhibition and when it fails to inhibit but produces guilt emotion; (3) the development of measures of other emotions, such as shame or disgust, as dispositions and as emotion states; and (4) the development of research programs that relate guilt to defensive processes and psychoneuroses.

REFERENCES

Abramson, P. R. Implications of ipsative measurement for inferences concerning cross-situational consistency in the study of human sexual behavior. Unpublished doctoral dissertation, University of Connecticut, 1976.

Abramson, P. R. Input modality, sex guilt, and retention of sexual information. In press.

Abramson, P. R., & Mosher, D. L. Development of a measure of negative attitudes toward masturbation. *Journal of Consulting and Clinical Psychology*, 1975, *43*, 485–490.

Abramson, P. R., & Mosher, D. L. An empirical investigation of experimentally induced mastur-batory fantasies. *Archives of Sexual Behavior*, in press.

Abramson, P. R. Mosher, D. L., Abramson, L. M., & Wochowski, B. Personality correlates of the Mosher guilt scales. *Journal of Personality Assessment*, 1977, *41*, 375–382.

Allport, G. W. The general and the unique in psychological sciences. *Journal of Personality*, 1962, *30*, 405–422.

Amoroso, D. M., Brown, M., Pruesse, M., Ware, E. E., and Pilkey, D. W. An investigation of behavioral, psychological, and physiological reactions to pornographic stimuli. *Technical Reports of the Commission on Obscenity and Pornography* (Vol. 8). Washington, D.C.: U.S. Government Printing Office, 1970.

Arnold, W. R. Continuities in research: Scaling delinquent behavior. *Social Problems*, 1965, 59–66.

Bahm, R. M. The influence of non-sexual cues, sexual explicitness and sex guilt on female's erotic response to literature. Unpublished doctoral dissertation, University of Massachusetts, 1972.

Barclay, A. Urinary acid phosphatase secretions in sexually aroused males. *Journal of Experi-mental Research in Personality*, 1970, *4*, 233–238.

Barclay, A. Information as a defensive control of sexual arousal. *Journal of Personality and Social Psychology*, 1971, *4*, 233–238.

Barclay, A., & Little, M. Urinary acid phosphatase secretion under different arousal conditions. *Psychophysiology*, 1972, *9*, 69–77.

Bentler, P. M. Heterosexual behavior assessment: I. Males. *Behavior Research and Therapy*, 1968, *6*, 21–25. (a)

Bentler, P. M. Heterosexual behavior assessment: II. Females. *Behavior Research and Therapy*, 1968, *6*, 27–30. (b)

Botto, R. W., Galbraith, G. G., & Stern, R. M. Effects of false heart rate feedback and sex-guilt upon attitudes toward sexual stimuli. *Psychological Reports*, 1974, *35*, 267–274.

Bradbury, B. R. A study of guilt and anxiety as related to certain psychological and sociological variables. Unpublished doctoral dissertation, North Texas State University, 1967.

Brady, J. P., & Levitt, E. E. The scalability of sexual experiences. *Psychological Record*, 1965, *15*, 377–384.

Campbell, D. T., & Fiske, D. W. Convergent and discriminant validation by the multitrait-multimethod matrix. *Psychological Bulletin*, 1959, *56*, 81–105.

Carlson, E. R., & Coleman, C. E. H. Experiential and motivational determinants of the richness of an induced sexual fantasy. *Journal of Personality*, 1977, *45*, 528–542.

Carver, J. B. Modifiability of aggression under two verbal reinforcement contingencies as a function of generalized expectancy for guilt. Unpublished doctoral dissertation, Emory University, 1968.

Cogan, J. M. Internal versus external control, the attributes of responsibility and guilt over aggressive behavior. Unpublished master's thesis, University of Connecticut, 1969.

Corey, S. L. Sex guilt and punishment of sexual behavior of others. Unpublished master's thesis. University of Connecticut, 1970.

Cramer, P. *Word association*. New York: Academic Press, 1968.

Cronbach, L. J., & Meehl, P. E. Construct validity in psychological tests. *Psychological Bulletin*, 1955, *52*, 281–302.

D'Augelli, J. F., & Cross, H. J. Relationship of sex guilt and moral reasoning to premarital sex in college women and in couples. *Journal of Consulting and Clinical Psychology*, 1975, *43*, 40–47.

Dubeck, J. A., Schuck, S. Z., & Cymbalisty, B. Y. Falsification of the forced-choice guilt inventory. *Journal of Consulting and Clinical Psychology*, 1971, *36*, 296.

Fenichel, O. *The psychoanalytic theory of neuroses*. New York: Norton, 1945.

Fricke, L. Associative sexual responses and corresponding response latencies to a presentation of double-entendre words in relation to sex-guilt and sex of experimenter. Unpublished doctoral dissertation, Washington State University, 1974.

Galbraith, G. G. Effects of sexual arousal and guilt upon free associative sexual responses. *Journal of Consulting and Clinical Psychology*, 1968 *32*, 707–711. (a)

Galbraith, G. G. Reliability of free associative sexual responses. *Journal of Consulting and Clinical Psychology*, 1968, *32*, 622. (b)

Galbraith, G. G. The Mosher Sex-Guilt Scale and the Thorne Sex Inventory: Intercorrelations. *Journal of Clinical Psychology*, 1969, *25*, 292–294.

Galbraith, G. G., Hahn, K., & Lieberman, H. Personality correlates of free-associative sex resonses to double-entendre words. *Journal of Consulting and Clinical Psychology*, 1968, *32*, 193–197.

Galbraith, G. G., & Mosher, D. L. Associative sexual responses in relation to sexual arousal, guilt, and external approval contingencies. *Journal of Personality and Social Psychology*, 1968, *10*.142–147.

Galbraith, G. G., & Mosher, D. L. Effects of sex guilt and sexual stimulation on the recall of word associations. *Journal of Consulting and Clinical Psychology*, 1970, *34*, 67–71.

Galbraith, G. G., & Sturke, R. W. Effects of stimulus sexuality, order of presentation, and sex guilt on free associative latencies. *Journal of Consulting and Clinical Psychology*, 1974, *42*, 828–832.

Galbraith, G. G., & Wynkoop, R. H. Latencies of restricted associations to double entendre sexual words as a function of personality variables. Psychological Reports, 1976, *43*, 1187–1197.

Gambaro, S., & Rabin, A. I. Diastolic blood pressure responses following direct and displaced aggression after anger arousal in high- and low-guilt subjects. *Journal of Personality and Social Psychology*, 1969, *12*, 87–94.

Geer, J. H., & Mollenauer, S. O. Meaning class and affective class in word associations. *Psychological Reports*, 1964, *15*, 900.

Greenberg, I. R. Influence of sex-guilt upon the retention of sexual and nonsexual words. Unpublished master's thesis, Ohio State University, 1968.

Groh, R. Infant stimuli as aggression inhibiting cues. Unpublished doctoral dissertation, University of Connecticut, 1976.

Hardy, S. L. The relationship of hostility guilt, need for approval, and assault to the expression of aggression under arbitrary and nonarbitrary frustration. Unpublished doctoral dissertation, Southern Illinois University, 1973.

Hawkins, D. L. & Janda, L. H. The effects of guilt and false heartrate feedback upon associative sexual responses. *Journal of Personality Assessment,* in press.

Hayward, G. W. Expressed aggression as a function of guilt level under varying conditions of legitimacy and external threat. Unpublished doctoral dissertation, University of Texas, 1970.

Heyman, D. S. The effect of film-mediated aggression on subsequent aggressive behavior. Unpublished doctoral dissertation, University of Connecticut, 1969.

James, P. B., & Mosher, D. L. Thematic aggression, hostility guilt, and aggressive behavior. *Journal of Projective Techniques and Personality Assessment,* 1967, *31,* 61–67.

Janda, L. H. Effects of guilt, approachability of examiner, and stimulus relevance upon sexual responses to thematic apperception stimuli. *Journal of Consulting and Clinical Psychology,* 1975, *43,* 369–374.

Janda, L. H., & Magri, M. B. Relation between affective and dispositional guilt. *Journal of Consulting and Clinical Psychology,* 1975, *43,* 116.

Janda, L. H., Magri, M. B., & Barnhart, S. A. Affective guilt states in women and the perceived guilt index. *Journal of Personality Assessment,* 1977, *41,* 79–84.

Janda, L. H., & O'Grady, K. E. Effects of guilt and response modality upon associative sexual responses. *Journal of Research in Personality,* 1976, *10,* 457–462.

Janda, L. H., O'Grady, K. E. & Barnhart, S. A. Effects of guilt, physical attractiveness and sexual attitude upon person perception, in press.

Janda, L. H., Witt, C. G., & Manahan, C. The effects of guilt and approachability of examiner upon associative responses. *Journal of Consulting and Clinical Psychology,* 1976, *44,* 986–990.

Jung, C. G. The reaction-time ratio in the association experiment. In *Collected Works of C. G. Jung,* Vol. 2. Princeton, N.J.: Princeton University Press, 1906.

Kelly, F. S. The effects of sex guilt on part–whole free-call learning of sexual and neutral words. Unpublished doctoral dissertation, University of Connecticut, 1972.

Kerr, B. J., & Galbraith, G. G. Latencies of sexual and asexual responses to double-entendre words as a function of sex-guilt and social desirability in college females. *Psychological Reports,* 1975, *37,* 991–997.

Kier, R. G. Sex, individual differences, and film effects on responses to sexual films. Unpublished doctoral dissertation, University of Connecticut, 1972.

Kohlberg, L. Moral stages and moralization: The cognitive-developmental approach. In T. Lickona (Ed.), *Moral development and behavior.* New York: Holt, Rinehart, and Winston, 1976.

Kulik, J., Stein, K., & Sarbin, T. Dimensions and patterns of adolescent anti-social behavior. *Journal of Consulting and Clinical Psychology,* 1968, *32,* 375–382.

Lacey. J. I. Psychophysiological approaches to the evaluation of psychotherapeutic process and outcome. In E. A. Rubinstein & M. B. Parloff (Eds.), *Conference on Research in Psychotherapy, Proceedings.* Washington, D.C.: APA, 1959. Pp. 106–208.

Lacey, J. I. Somatic response patterning and stress: Some revisions of activation theory. In M. H. Appley & R. H. Trumbull (Eds.), *Psychological stress: Issues in research.* New York: Appleton-Century-Crofts, 1967, pp. 14–42.

Lamb, C. W. Personality correlates of humor enjoyment following motivational arousal. *Journal of Personality and Social Psychology,* 1968, *9,* 237–241.

Langston, R. D. Sex guilt and sex behavior in college students. *Journal of Personality Assessment,* 1973, *37,* 467–472.

Langston, R. D. Stereotyped sex role behavior and sex guilt. *Journal of Personality Assessment.* 1975, *39,* 77–81.

Lanzafame, L. J. Influence of sex-guilt and cue upon the retention of neutral and double-entendre sexual words. Unpublished master's thesis, University of Connecticut, 1970.

Lawner, P. Hostility-guilt and its relationship to overt verbal hostility, changes in mood, and expiatory behavior. Unpublished doctoral dissertation, University of Connecticut, 1968.

Love, R. E., Sloan, L. R. & Schmidt, M. J. Viewing pornography and sex guilt: The priggish, the prudent, and the profligate. *Journal of Consulting and Clinical Psychology*, 1976, *44*, 624–629.

McSweeney, J. A. The effect of varying degrees of arousal on appreciation of aggression relevant humor. Unpublished master's thesis, Northern Illinois University, 1974.

Mendelsohn, M. J. Sex-guilt and role-played moral reactions. Unpublished master's thesis. University of Connecticut, 1970.

Meyer, R. G. Chronic high blood pressure, essential hypertension, and the inhibition of aggression. *Proceedings*, 76th Annual Convention, APA, 1968. Pp. 535–536.

Mortimer, R. L. Verbal aggression in adolescent delinquents as a function of hostility-guilt and verbal attack by competitors. Unpublished doctoral dissertation, Ohio State University, 1966.

Mosher, D. L. The development and validation of s sentence completion measure of guilt. Unpublished doctoral dissertation, Ohio State University, 1961.

Mosher, D. L. Interaction of fear and guilt in inhibiting unacceptable behavior. *Journal of Consulting Psychology*, 1965, *29*, 161–167.

Mosher, D. L. The development and multi-trait-multi-method matrix analysis of three measures of three aspects of guilt. *Journal of Consulting Psychology*, 1966, *30*, 25–29. (a)

Mosher, D. L. Differential influence of guilt on the verbal operant conditioning of hostile and "superego" verbs. *Journal of Consulting Psychology*, 1966, *30*, 280. (b)

Mosher, D. L. Measurement of guilt in females by self-report inventories. *Journal of Consulting and Clinical Psychology*, 1968, *32*. 690–695.

Mosher, D. L. Sex guilt and reactions to pornographic films. Paper presented at symposium of the Commission on Obscenity and Pornography, APA Convention, Miami Beach, 1970.

Mosher, D. L. Psychological reactions to pornographic films. In *Technical Report of the Commission on Obscenity and Pornography*. Vol. 8: *Erotica and social behavior*. Washington, D.C.: U.S. Government Printing Office, 1971. (a)

Mosher, D. L. Sex callousness toward women. In *Technical Report of the Commission on Obscenity and Pornography*, Vol. 8: *Erotica and social behavior*. Washington, D.C.: U.S. Government Printing Office, 1971. (b)

Mosher, D. L. Sex differences, sex experience, sex guilt, and explicitly sexual films. *Journal of Social Issues*, 1973, *29*, 95–112.

Mosher, D. L., & Abramson, P. R. Subjective sexual arousal to films of masturbation. *Journal of Consulting and Clinical Psychology*, 1977, *45*, 796–807.

Mosher, D. L., & Cross, H. J. Sex guilt and premarital sexual experiences of college students. *Journal of Consulting Psychology*, 1971, *36*, 22–32.

Mosher, D. L., & Greenberg, I. Females' affective responses to reading erotic literature. *Journal of Consulting and Clinical Psychology*, 1969, *33*, 472–477.

Mosher, D. L., Mortimer, R. L., & Grebel, M. G. Verbal aggressive behavior in delinquent boys. *Journal of Abnormal Psychology*, 1968, *73*, 454–460.

Mosher, D. L., & Mosher, J. B. Guilt in prisoners. *Journal of Clinical Psychology*, 1966, *23*, 171–173.

Mosher, J. B. Deviance, growth motivation, and attraction to marital alternatives. Unpublished doctoral dissertation, University of Connecticut, 1975.

Nicholas, D. J. Guilt as related to self-concept and personality adjustment. Unpublished doctoral dissertation, North Texas State University, 1965.

Nichols, M. F. The relation of parental childrearing attitudes to the sexual behavior and attitudes of women. Unpublished master's thesis, University of Connecticut, 1970.

O'Grady, K., & Janda, L. Psychometric correlates of the Mosher Forced-Choice Guilt Inventory. *Journal of Consulting and Clinical Psychology*, in press.

O'Grady, K., Janda, L., & Gillen, H. A multidimensional scaling analysis of sex guilt. *Mutivariate Behavioral Research*, in press.

Okel, E., & Mosher, D. L. Changes in affective states as a function of guilt over aggressive behavior. *Journal of Consulting and Clinical Psychology*, 1968, *32*, 265–270.

Oliver, W. A., & Mosher, D. L. Psychopathology and guilt in heterosexual and subgroups of homosexual reformatory inmates. *Journal of Abnormal Psychology*, 1968, *73*, 323–329.

Otterbacher, J. R., & Munz, D. C. State–trait measure of experiential guilt. *Journal of Consulting and Clinical Psychology*, 1973, *40*, 115–121.

Pagano, M., & Kirschner, N. M. Sex guilt sexual arousal, and urinary acid phosphatase output. *Journal of Research in Personality*, 1978, *12*, 68–75.

Persons, R. W. Intermittent reinforcement, guilt, and crime. *Psychological Reports*, 1970, *26*, 421–422. (a)

Persons, R. W. The Mosher Guilt Scale: Theoretical formulation, research review and normative data. *Journal of Projective Techniques and Personality Assessment*, 1970, *34*, 266–270. (b)

Persons, R. W., & Marks, P. A. Self-disclosure with recidivists: Optimum interviewer-interviewee matching. *Journal of Abnormal Psychology*, 1970, *76*, 387–391.

Pollio, H. R., & Lore, R. K. The effect of semantically congruent context on word association behavior. *Journal of Psychology*, 1965, *61*, 17–26.

Polsky, N. On the sociology of pornography. In *Hustlers, beats and others*. Chicago: Aldine, 1967.

Proenza, C. L. A Cross-cultural and intracultural investigation of guilt, *machismo*, and sex role. Unpublished master's thesis, University of the Americas, 1968.

Proenza, L. M. Differential "response-strategies" to sexual words as a function of sex-guilt. Unpublished master's thesis, Ohio State University, 1966.

Ray, R. E., & Thompson, W. D. Autonomic correlates of female guilt responses to erotic visual stimuli. *Psychological Reports*, 1974, *34*, 1299–1306.

Ray, R. E., & Walker, C. E. Biographical and self-report correlates of female guilt responses to visual stimuli. *Journal of Consulting and Clinical Psychology*, 1973, *41*, 93–96.

Ridley, C. K. Inhibitory aspects of sex guilt, social censure, and need for approval. Unpublished doctoral dissertation, University of Manitoba, 1976.

Rotter, J. B. *Social learning and clinical psychology*. New York: Prentice-Hall, 1954.

Ruma, E. H. Conscience development in delinquents and non-delinquents: The relationship between moral judgment, guilt, and behavior. Unpublished doctoral dissertation, Ohio State University, 1967.

Ruma, E. H., & Mosher, D. L. Relationship between moral judgment and guilt in delinquent boys. *Journal of Abnormal Psychology*, 1967, *72*, 122–127.

Schallow, J. R. Direct and displaced aggression, transgression compliance, and liking for one's victim in high- and low-guilt subjects. Unpublished doctoral dissertation, University of Texas, 1972.

Schill, T. R. Aggression and blood pressure responses of high and low guilt subjects following frustration. *Journal of Consulting and Clinical Psychology*, 1972, *38*, 461. (a)

Schill, T. R. Need for approval, guilt, and sexual stimulation and their relationship to sexual responsibility. *Journal of Consulting and Clinical Psychology*, 1972, *38*, 31–35. (b)

Schill, T. R., & Althoff, M. Drug experiences, knowledge, and attitudes of high and low guilty individuals. *Journal of Consulting and Clinical Psychology*, 1975, *43*, 106–107.

Schill, T., & Chapin, J. Sex guilt and males' preference for reading erotic magazines. *Journal of Consulting and Clinical Psychology*, 1972, *39*, 516.

Schill, T., Evans, R., & McGovern, T. Child-rearing attitudes of subjects varying in guilt. *Journal of Clinical Psychology*, in press.

Schill, T., Rader, G., Evans, R., & Segall, S. Defense preference of high and low-hostility guilt subjects. *Journal of Consulting and Clinical Psychology*, in press.

Schill, T., & Schneider, L. Guilt and self-report of hostility. *Psychological Reports*, 1970, *27*, 713–714. (a)

Schill, T., & Schneider, L. Relationships between hostility guilt and several measures of hostility. *Psychological Reports*, 1970, *27*, 967–970. (b)

Schwartz, S. The effects of arousal on appreciation for varying degrees of sex relevant humor. *Journal of Research in Personality*, 1972, *6*, 241–247.

Schwartz, S. Effects of sex guilt and sexual arousal on the retention of birth control information. *Journal of Consulting and Clinical Psychology*, 1973, *41*, 61–64. (a)

Schwartz, S. Multimethod analysis of three measures of six common personality traits. *Journal of Assessment (Personality)*, 1973, *37*, 559–567. (b)

Schwartz, S. Effects of sex guilt on word association responses to double-entendre sexual words. *Journal of Consulting and Clinical Psychology*. 1975, *43*, 100.

Selvey, C. L. Concerns about death in relation to sex, dependency, guilt about hostility, and feelings of powerlessness. Unpublished doctoral dissertation, Columbia University, 1970

Smith, T. The development of measures of individual differences in shame and guilt. Unpublished master's thesis, University of Connecticut, 1977.

Ungerer, J. C., Harford R. J., Brown, F. L., Jr., and Kleeber, H. D. Sex guilt and preferences for illegal drugs. *Journal of Clinical Psychology*, 1976, *32*, 891–895.

Valins, S. Cognitive effects of false heart-rate feedback. *Journal of Personality and Social Psychology*, 1966, *4*, 406–408.

Vroubel, I. R., An analogue study of the relationship between therapist sex-guilt and responses to patients. Unpublished doctoral dissertation, Arizona State University, 1976.

Wheaton, C. H. Implicit personality theory: Relationships with sex-guilt. Unpublished doctoral dissertation, Arizona State University, 1972.

Editor's Introduction

Pilkonis and Zimbardo provide us with a rich array of new information on the emotion of shyness. Their empirical data improve our conceptualization of shyness and our understanding of its antecedents and its consequences for the individual and his or her social surround.

Pilkonis and Zimbardo have shown how shyness can cause the bashful child or the awkward adolescent to avoid people and shrink away from life, and they show how shyness can have psychopathological consequences. They see shyness as a multidimensional concept, at least in terms of the social and behavioral context in which it can appear. They see shyness as including or closely related to a variety of social anxieties, with anxiety defined largely in terms of the emotion of fear. One might raise the question as to whether shyness can be adequately defined in terms of another emotion (anxiety or fear in a social context), but Pilkonis and Zimbardo make their conception clear and show that shyness has important implications for developing and maintaining adaptive and satisfying interpersonal relationships. The findings from the authors' work with the Stanford Shyness Survey will be an eye-opener for some and perhaps a reassurance for those who have at one time counted themselves among the dispositionally shy.

In their consideration of shyness and psychopathology, the authors show how shyness can contribute to alcoholism, irrational violence, and sexual dysfunction. In the concluding section of the chapter, the authors draw on their conceptual and empirical analysis of fear in a discussion of therapeutic techniques for treating shyness. This discussion is enriched by experience at their own shyness center.

The Personal and Social Dynamics of Shyness

5

PAUL A. PILKONIS and PHILIP G. ZIMBARDO

We began our systematic study of the causes, correlates, and consequences of shyness five years ago, utilizing a multimethod approach that included extensive survey analyses, intensive interviews, field observations, laboratory experiments, and therapeutic interactions. Although we have learned much from our investigations, shyness still remains a fuzzy concept that defies simple definition. *Shyness* evokes a rich and varied set of associations; it is the bashful child, the awkward adolescent, the timid adult. Shyness is a "people phobia," a social anxiety elicited by the apprehension that one's behavior or self is being evaluated by others—negatively. Shyness to Bertrand Russell is "the malady of the introvert, who, with the manifold spectacle of the world spread before him, turns away and gazes only upon the emptiness within." To author Pablo Neruda, "Shyness is a shrinking back from life." But it can also be thought of as modest reserve, a diffident social manner that we find appealing in certain of our acquaintances and some celebrities. However, it is the darker side of shyness that is more common, incapacitating the person and inhibiting a wide range of social as well as academic and vocational behaviors. It is not too dramatic to use the metaphor of the silent, self-imposed prison of shyness when a shy person relates:

> I have so much of what is supposed to make life good—a husband who loves me, two bright, promising children, a home in the country. I should be happy, but I'm

PAUL A. PILKONIS • University of Pittsburgh, Pittsburgh, Pennsylvania. PHILIP G. ZIMBARDO • Stanford University, Palo Alto, California. Much of the research reported in this paper and the preparation of this manuscript were funded by a grant to Philip G. Zimbardo from the National Institute of Mental Health (MH-27543) and funds from the Boys Town Center for the Study of Youth Development at Stanford University. However, the opinions expressed or the policies advocated herein do not necessarily reflect those of the funding agencies.

nearly always miserable. I hide. I cower. I'm afraid of people. In a word, I'm shy. My profession (nursing) terrifies me. I avoid unpleasant confrontations at all costs. Sometimes I'm "depressed" (or self-indulgent) to the point of immobilizing myself altogether. And I'm tired of it. Somewhere in me I know there is the capacity to be free, to laugh, to love (maybe even myself), to be committed to ideals and to the people in my life who matter. . . . But, because I sometimes get a glimpse of a stronger, more joyful me, I know I can change if I can just find the key. (Personal communication, May, 1977)

Although initially it was scientific curiosity that fueled our search to understand this curiously complex phenomenon of shyness, it has become our concern to "help find the key" to unlock the prison of shyness that motivates much of our current work. Accordingly, in this chapter, we will consider treatment implications for shyness that grow out of our understanding of the personal and social dynamics of shyness. After a summary of basic findings about the general nature of shyness, we will focus upon two primary shy reactions: the publicly shy introvert and the privately shy extrovert. Then we will turn to examine some of the more pathological consequences of the experience of shyness: sexual dysfunction; recruitment into alcoholism; extremely assaultive, violent reactions; and the passive conformity that may eventuate in submission to political authority. Although shyness is experienced at a personal level and is the product of individual transactions, it is nevertheless symptomatic of basic cultural programming. Thus we examined cross-cultural data from nearly 5,000 respondents in eight different cultures to discover how shyness is promoted and sustained in some societies and suppressed in others. Such an analysis calls attention to the need for a public health model of treatment for shyness-generating societies as well as therapy for people who find their shyness an undesirable problem they feel helpless to change by themselves.

I. THE PHENOMENON OF SHYNESS

Shyness is a multidimensional concept, and as the term is commonly used, it can include a variety of social anxieties: performance difficulties in large group settings, public-speaking anxieties, lack of assertiveness, and anxieties about informal social contacts with members of both the same and the opposite sex. Our interest has been primarily in the last category, and we define shyness as a tendency to avoid social situations, to fail to participate appropriately in social encounters, and to feel anxious, distressed, and burdened during interpersonal interactions. Shyness therefore includes cognitive, affective, physiological, and behavioral components that are elicited by certain types of people and social situations. In some cases, phobic avoidance develops as the anxiety-controlling response style. But for many, it is difficult to avoid people altogether. For them, shyness may be handled by the "safe" strategy of keeping a low profile of virtual nonperformance; no eye contact, no talking, no initiating action, thus no behavior emitted to be evaluated by others. Still others have learned to cope publicly with their shyness by developing the requisite social skills; however, they still experience the internal discomfort of the attendant anxiety. It has been a question of considerable interest to us whether the various public and private components of shy reactions vary in significance in different types of shy people. If so, then interventions designed to modify shyness must be tailored to such differential weighting schemes; for example, they must be focused on skills training for the publicly shy with inadequate or inappropriate behavior repertoires, and on esteem building for the privately shy who know what to do but still do not feel comfortable in certain social settings. We are optimistic about the efficacy of therapeutic interventions to overcome the adverse consequences of shyness, because believing shyness to be a learned response style to social stimuli, we think it can be "unlearned."

Indeed, the contrary notion that shyness is an inherited trait not amenable to "reeducation" (advanced by Cattell, 1973) probably accounts for the noticeable absence of prior research on this quite fascinating psychological experience. Psychologists seem loath to study innately fixed responses or traits that are not readily modifiable through their planned interventions. In her provocative essay in this volume, Helen Block Lewis shows us how "shame" has been a neglected construct; so too, we argue, has "shyness"—both of them, as we shall see later, share other attributes in common.

Despite the lack of a body of research on shyness *per se*, related aspects of the construct have been addressed from many different theoretical perspectives. The psychometric approach to this presumed "trait" is typified in the work of Comrey (1970) and Cattell (1973). In the latter's typology, shyness is designated as H⁻, *threctia*; a high susceptibility to threat due to the more sensitive, easily aroused nervous system of the shy. In a similar personality-trait vein, Eysenck and Eysenck (1969) describe introversion–extraversion as a critical, second-order factor in their conception of personality structure. From a psychoanalytic orientation (Kaplan, 1972), shyness originates in the preoccupation of the ego with itself, in the form of narcissism. Beneath their modest, unassuming exteriors, shy psychoanalytic patients are hypothesized to be full of unexpressed grandiose fantasies and hostility.

The social anxiety at the core of the experience of shyness has been the focus of considerable interest by researchers utilizing a social-learning-model approach. Three aspects of social anxiety have been addressed by these behaviorally oriented investigators: (1) the development of conditioned anxiety to social stimuli (Bandura, 1969); (2) the role of social skills deficits in generating anticipatory performance anxiety (Curran, 1977); and (3) the impact of dysfunctional cognitive processes and faulty attributional analyses in intensifying the experienced anxiety (Clark & Arkowitz, 1975). Despite the likely interaction of these aspects of social anxiety, they have unfortunately been studied in isolation. It is easy to imagine a sequence in which failures, embarrassments, and other aversive social interactions (experienced either directly or vicariously) generate conditioned anxiety to previously neutral social stimuli. Such anxiety may then motivate a variety of avoidance behaviors that, though decreasing anxiety, also prevent the learning of appropriate social skills or disrupt previously learned behaviors. In addition, such anxiety may create serious cognitive consequences, producing expectations of failure in social situations, excessive sensitivity to negative evaluations from others, and a chronic tendency to evaluate oneself negatively. In part, such cognitions may be realistic if important skills deficits do exist, but they probably also include exaggerated and unrealistic ideational components fostered by heightened self-consciousness. These dysfunctional cognitions may in turn elevate the original anxiety and further encourage avoidance in an escalating negative-loop cycle.

Regardless of the perspective one brings to the problem, it is clear that shyness has important implications for adequate social adjustment. Personal isolation, deficient social skills, and other aspects of shyness have traditionally been seen as both causes and concomitants of psychological difficulties (e.g., Sullivan, 1947). Argyle and his colleagues (Argyle, Trower, & Bryant, 1974; Bryant, Trower, Yardley, Urbieta, & Letemendia, 1976), in assessments of various psychiatric patients, have substantiated these clinical impressions with results suggesting that a "relatively high proportion of patients, one in six on the most conservative estimate, and probably over one in four, were judged by psychologists and psychiatrists to be socially inadequate" (Bryant et al., 1976, p. 101). Other investigators have established links between social anxiety and the development of specific behavioral and affective problems, for example, alcoholism (Kraft, 1971). Among "nonclinical" populations, the prevalence of social anxiety is also substantial. A variety of surveys with college students have shown, for example, that social anxiety and interpersonal difficulties are common among late adolescents and young adults in university settings (Borkovec, Stone, O'Brien, & Kaloupek, 1974; Bryant & Trower, 1974; Martinson & Zerface, 1970).

Shyness, to the extent that it encourages social isolation and personal withdrawal, has at least three negative consequences. First, it drastically reduces the rewards available from one of the most potent reinforcers in the environment, other people. By avoiding the anxiety associated with social encounters, shy people also eliminate the potential rewards that such encounters can provide. A lack of adequate social reinforcement may play a critical role in the development of subsequent difficulties, such as depression (cf. Lewinsohn, 1974). Second, shyness limits the general availability of the social support provided by significant others. As a result, shy people may be more vulnerable to life stresses ordinarily mitigated by the advice and encouragement of relatives, friends, and acquaintances. Third, shyness, by limiting interaction, deprives isolated people of valuable social comparison information. Excessively harsh self-evaluations (and other cognitive aspects of anxiety states) arise in part from ignorance about the commonness of such social anxiety and also from a lack of realistic standards against which to judge one's social behavior. Autistic thinking, not bound to the constraints of consensual validation, thus becomes a likely and extreme consequence of this phobic avoidance of social situations. Paradoxically, it is only because the shy are so concerned about others that many organize their lives around avoiding their evaluation, while also shunning desired intimate association with other people.

II. STANFORD SHYNESS SURVEY

The pervasive difficulties that shyness creates were made most apparent to us by many of our own students who complained of problems in interpersonal relationships, of loneliness, and even of failures to achieve academically because of their reluctance to approach faculty members for help or to participate in classroom discussions. Our informal observations were consistent with those of counselors in the student health service at Stanford University, who find that a major presenting problem for psychiatric treatment is that of difficulty in social adjustment, "making friends," and overcoming social anxieties.

In order to investigate the various meanings, manifestations, and consequences of shyness in a more systematic way, we constructed the Stanford Shyness Survey (Zimbardo, Pilkonis, & Norwood, 1974) and administered it to a sample of 817 high school and college students in northern California. The survey contains a variety of items designed to elicit a thorough self-report about a respondent's shyness (its extent, its variability, its severity in comparison to that of one's peers, etc.), and it includes checklists of the elicitors, correlates, and consequences, both positive and negative, of shyness that respondents can specify as relevant for themselves.

The results of the original survey made two facts apparent. First, the prevalence of self-reported shyness is impressively large: 42% of the respondents described themselves as "shy persons" in an important dispositional sense; that is, they felt that their shyness was a significant part of their personalities. Second, shyness is perceived as a negative attribute, with few of the more positive connotations of modesty and diffidence that the term can sometimes imply. Of the persons who characterized themselves as currently shy, 79% said that they did not like their shyness, and 63% endorsed an even stronger statement, saying that it posed a real "problem" for them. Such results have been replicated in a half-dozen independent samples. Our current sample of students from throughout the United States numbers 2,482 persons, and as each new subsample has been added, the proportion of shy persons has remained close to 40%, with the large majority of these people describing their shyness as "problematic." Men reported themselves as shy at least as often as women—laying to rest the myth of shyness as a woman's problem. While this figure of four in ten people likely to label themselves as currently shy was surprisingly high to us, it pales before the statistic of 80% of the population who report having suffered from shyness at some point in their lives. Curiously, a study by a team of market researchers of the worst fears of 3,000 U.S. inhabitants revealed that the number one human fear was "speaking before a group" (Wallace *et al.* 1977). And the percentage who gave that fear as their most serious was 41%. It far exceeded even sickness and death!

In our operational terms, you are shy if you say you are. However, to further assess the validity of these self-reports and to explore the convergent and discriminant relationships between shyness and some related constructs, a subsample (N = 263 male and female undergraduates at Stanford University) was also administered a battery of questionnaires that included the Self-Monitoring Scale (Snyder, 1974); the Self-Consciousness Scale (Fenigstein, Scheier, & Buss, 1975), which contains subscales for public self-consciousness (concern about oneself as a social object), private self-consciousness (sensitivity to inner thoughts and feelings), and social anxiety (distress in the presence of others); and the Eysenck Personality Inventory (Eysenck & Eysenck, 1968), which yields scores for neuroticism and extraversion. These students were also asked to rate themselves on a 7-point scale of introversion–extraversion, where these terms were defined on the basis on one's usual focus of attention, regardless of the anxiety or behavior associated with this perspective. An introvert was defined as "one whose thoughts and interests are primarily directed inward," while an extravert was specified as "one primarily interested in others or in the environment."

The results (Pilkonis, 1977b) demonstrated that individuals who labeled themselves as "shy persons" were less extraverted (on both the 7-point self-report and the Eysenck scale), less capable of monitoring their social behavior, and more socially anxious than their not-shy peers. In addition, shy respondents were significantly more neurotic as measured by the Eysenck Personality Inventory, reinforcing the contention that self-ascribed shyness is a valid indicator of poorer personal adjustment among a late adolescent sample. In several studies, we have also found the expected high negative correlation with self-esteem—in some as high as $r = -.62$.

Some interesting sex differences also appeared. Women described themselves as more outwardly oriented in general than men on the 7-point, introversion–extraversion rating, and the predicted intercorrelations among the measures tended to be weaker with women than with men. Across both sexes, a 7-point rating of the extent of one's shyness was positively correlated with the independent scale of social anxiety ($r = .67$), while significant negative correlations were found between the shyness self-report and the measures of extraversion (introversion–extraversion, $r = -.38$; Eysenck extraversion, $r = -.43$).

However, only in males did several of the other expected relationships obtain. In men, the shyness scale was correlated positively with public self-consciousness ($r = .27$) and neuroticism ($r = .39$) and negatively with self-monitoring ($r = -.25$). Similarly, only in men was public self-consciousness associated with social anxiety ($r = .26$). A closer examination of the public self-consciousness scores showed that the male groups lay at the extremes (shy males were most self-conscious and not-shy males were least self-conscious), while the two female groups were identical and fell in the middle. The pattern suggests that public self-consciousness does not play as large a role in the development of social anxiety among women. Perhaps women are more uniformly socialized to be publicly self-conscious, and for that reason, their public self-awareness is a less likely predictor of shyness.

The lack of any relationship between neuroticism and shyness in women is perhaps most easily understood if one assumes that shyness is a more "acceptable" characteristic for women. Interestingly, in women, neuroticism was most highly correlated with private self-consciousness ($r = .47$). The females who were the most introspective tended to be the least well adjusted according to the Eysenck scale.

In general, then, the validity of our simple, direct self-reports of shyness was substantiated by their relationships with other independently validated and more complex measures of extraversion, neuroticism, self-monitoring, self-consciousness, and social anxiety.

The most direct test of the validity of our shyness self-reports came from observing the behavior patterns of shy and not-shy males and females in experimentally manipulated laboratory settings (Pilkonis, 1977a). Verbal and nonverbal reactions were recorded and systematically analyzed for differences between these groups when behaving in structured and unstructured environments. A structured experimental episode consisted of giving a brief speech from prepared materials before a TV camera. The unstructured episode placed the subject alone in a room where he or she was free to interact with a person (confederate) of the opposite sex.

Three interesting results were obtained. First, shy individuals differed significantly from the not-shy in verbal behavior during the opposite-sex interaction; shy people spoke less frequently, spoke for a smaller percentage of the time, allowed more silences to develop, and broke fewer of the silences that did occur (silence was defined as any pause in the conversation of greater than 10 seconds). Shy subjects also reported less pleasant affect after both the interaction and the speech, supporting the contention that the emotional experience of shy individuals is less positive than that of not-shy persons in social situations. In addition, shy and not-shy individuals were reliably distinguished by observers' global ratings of shyness, friendliness, assertiveness, and relaxation during the experimental session. These basic differences are important to document because of the reported lack of success in isolating behavioral differences among those who vary in self-reported anxiety (cf. Arkowitz, Lichtenstein, McGovern, & Hines, 1975; Borkovec *et al.*, 1974).

The second finding of note was that despite these general differences, several interactions between sex and shyness and between situational variations and shyness also appeared. Therefore, it seems that any investigation of the ways in which individual differences emerge in social contexts must include a fine-grained analysis of both person factors and situation factors. Shyness was less relevant, for example, in the structured atmosphere of preparing and delivering the speech than in the unstructured interpersonal encounter, where more pronounced shy–not-shy differences appeared. This finding suggests that shyness is less of a problem in those contexts where influences such as task demands and role requirements remove the ambiguity present in "unfocused" interpersonal encounters (cf. McGovern, 1976). We will discuss later how such a finding generated an analysis of the shy as a "silent majority," who in seeking to escape from the uncertainties freedom poses, may come to support the political status quo and even dictatorships.

The distinctive response styles of shy men and women were apparent in the unstructured setting where they interacted with a member of the opposite sex. Social anxiety was a sharper discriminator of males than females in the opposite-sex episode, at least for the *active* indicators of willingness to interact (i.e., talking and looking). There was a suggestion in the data, however, that female anxieties were expressed in more *reactive* modes (i.e., nodding and smiling), presumably because the normative female role in the interaction was a less assertive one. Among men, social anxiety created a reluctance to talk, look, or make eye contact with a partner of the opposite sex; among women, shyness created a need to be pleasing that was expressed through excessive nodding and smiling. Again, the meaning and manifestations of shyness seem to vary between the sexes.

We will suspend discussion of the third finding of interest until we distinguish between public and private varieties of shyness in a later section. The differences found between males and females on some of the self-report measures suggest that the antecedents of shyness and its implications for personal adjustment may vary between the sexes. Males may experience the anxiety of shyness whenever they are expected to initiate interaction, because traditional masculine roles demand such assertion. Females, on the other hand, are more often evaluated than acting as evaluators, thereby increasing their anxiety about being found unworthy and rejected.

III. SITUATIONS AND ATTRIBUTIONS

> I consider myself to be shy. I wasn't until I was in the seventh grade when a teacher said I was "quiet." From that time on, I have felt I am below average in my conversational ability. I now have a fear of rejection.

This description by a middle-aged person forces us to consider a different dimension of shyness, that of the attributional process underlying acceptance of the "shy" self-description. It may be that for some people the shyness label precedes and then creates experiences of shyness. This seems to occur in cases where the label is imposed by significant others, when, in fact, the individual was listening quietly, was inattentive through boredom or distraction, or was nonresponsive for other reasons.

Only a small percentage of all our respondents reported being shy in all situations, with virtually everyone, all the time. For the majority of shy people, "it depends" on the circumstances. Of the shy, 51% are so only on selected but important occasions, as opposed to being shy about half the time (44% reporting) or always (the remaining 5%). What is important is that despite the situation-specific quality of their shyness, the majority nevertheless persist in applying a chronic, negative trait label to themselves. In the more intensively studied sample of 263 subjects, the variability of their experienced shyness was rated as "varying to a large degree" (a mean of 5 on a 7-point scale). But variations aside, the label remains consistently applied. Of course, it may be that whenever it occurs, shyness poses serious problems for the shy person. But locating the source of the problem within oneself rather than identifying its situational determinants has several obvious consequences. If the locus of the problem is perceived as internal, then it is carried like a disease, from place to place. "My shyness comes out when I have to give a speech, go on a blind date, or confront authority," says the dispositionally shy person. The shy "know" they are shy because of the vivid experience of physiological arousal (blushing, racing pulses, hearts pounding, heavy breathing, maybe perspiration, and butterflies in the stomach). Then too, there are the unpleasant, discomforting affect, the uncomplimentary cognitions, and the awkward or inadequate overt behaviors. Together they ought to be certain evidence that latent shyness is manifest. But our research indicates that very different others also experience the same kinds of symptoms elicited by the same kinds of people and social situations. They are those who said they are "not-shy" but nevertheless feel shy sometimes. The difference between the dispositionally shy and these situationally shy people is primarily a difference in labeling and the tendency to blame oneself for one's social anxiety or to look to the external situation for the causes of one's distress. The quality of the reactions are comparable, and the difference is one of quantity: more situations trigger the shyness, and there are more manifestations of shyness to attend to for the dispositionally shy. They see their shyness reaction as providing subjective information about their inadequacy. In contrast, the situationally shy infer a quite different conclusion from their shyness reaction; it offers objective information about the aversiveness of the eliciting situation: "Blind dates are a drag," or "Giving public speeches makes me feel anxious." The corollary is the assumption of the normativeness of such reactions: "Don't they make everyone feel that way?" Unfortunately, attributing a negative "trait" to oneself (as opposed to using more situationally testable explanations to account for anxiety) exacerbates the difficulties that shyness creates. Such labeling may encourage avoidance, fears about future encounters, self-fulfilling prophecies about one's social inadequacy, and pessimism about the possibility of personal change. Interventions to lessen anxiety will require encouraging shy persons to use less global and less negative self-descriptions while also becoming more aware of the situational determinants of their behavior. Future research should be directed toward establishing antecedents of this tendency toward ascription of chronic trait labels versus transient state descriptions. Such differences may prove important in the decision to label oneself *bad, stupid, ugly, incorrigible*, or *mad*.

Other misattributions and self–other discrepancies in perceptions also emerged from our research. Attractive shy people were typically judged to be "reserved," "aloof," "condescending," or even "rejecting" by opposite-sex peers. Such evaluations stem from the mistaken belief that with "everything going for them," failure to get involved with others was motivated by a purposeful lack of desire to do so. Thus, the attractive shy, and those in positions of some authority and power, suffer doubly the slings and the arrows of their outrageous misfortune.

Another type of discrepancy noted was for sizable groups of respondents to describe themselves as "shy, but extraverted" or to say, "I'm shy, but my acquaintances don't recognize it." In the original survey sample, a fourth of the shy respondents rated themselves on the extraverted half of the introversion–extraversion scale. Many of these persons may be individuals whose attention is directed outward but whose anxiety prevents them from being friendly; however, some of them are probably people who are, in fact, outgoing but whose public behavior does not express something that they feel privately is important about themselves, perhaps increasing their sense of isolation as a result. They may experience uncomfortable degrees of arousal when interacting in social situations, feel dissatisfied with the amount of effort that sociability demands, or make unflattering comparisons between themselves and others who appear to "perform" more easily in public, even if their social behavior is not deficient.

IV. PUBLIC VERSUS PRIVATE SHYNESS

These kinds of "contradictory" results raised the question posed earlier in this essay: Are there differences among shy people in the importance they attach to different aspects of their experience, particularly in the weight they assign to internal versus external events? Shyness contains, after all, both important public and private components. It is often accompanied privately by physiological arousal, subjective discomfort, and fear of negative evaluation, while publicly it entails much awkwardness and failure to respond in socially appropriate ways. First, these are things that different actors, in labeling themselves shy, may weight differently, depending on whether they focus on internal feelings or worry more about public behavior. Second, these are things to which actors and observers have different access and which they may perceive differently, leading to misattributions with important social psychological consequences. If, for example, we draw the wrong conclusion and assume that those around us are aloof or arrogant or snobbish, then our behavior toward them will be very different than if we see them as being shy or ill at ease. Also, if a kind of differential weighting occurs, then efforts to change an individual's shyness must be sensitive to both phenomenology and behavior, attempting not just to enhance social skills, but attending also to the role of affect and arousal as well as the evaluation and labeling of internal experience.

Such reflections link our work conceptually with a growing body of literature in social psychology that bears on the issues of internal–external orientation and sources of bias in the perception one has of one's own behavior as well as judgments of others (cf. Bem, 1967; Ross, 1977). We were therefore led to the use of a cluster analysis in the attempt to create a typology of different kinds of shy people, one that we hoped would be interpretable within our developing "public–private" framework.

Earlier inventories of social anxiety (e.g., Dixon, deMonchaux, & Sandler, 1957; Watson & Friend, 1969) have been composed primarily of items from five major categories, designed to tap (1) internal discomfort in social situations (e.g., emotional upset and physiological arousal); (2) fear of negative evaluation; (3) avoidance of social situations; (4) failures to respond appropriately in social situations (e.g., a reluctance to talk, an avoidance of eye contact), and (5) awkward behaviors arising from attempts to respond (e.g., an inability to be fluent or articulate, physical clumsiness). The first two categories focus on private events, while the last three are concerned with public behavior (or the lack of behavior). We assumed that all shy people experience both public and private components of shyness to some degree, but it seemed possible that different types of shy people would vary in the significance they attached either to privately experienced anxiety and cognitions or to publicly manifested behavior. Having made this *a priori* distinction, we asked a sample of 100 shy people to rank-order the importance of these aspects of their experience of shyness. The correlation between the rankings of any two individuals provided a measure of similarity between those individuals, and the similarity coefficients constituted the data for the cluster analysis (Johnson, 1967).

Four clusters, capturing 93 of the 100 subjects, were interpretable within the solution generated. The *n*s for each cluster and the mean ratings of each of the five aspects of shyness within the clusters are included in Table 1.

Table 1. *Mean Ratings of Five Aspects of Shyness within Clusters*[a]

	Cluster			
	1	2	3	4
	Avoidance and failure	Performance deficits	Subjective discomfort	Fear and behavioral deficits
Aspects of shyness	(*n* = 7)	(*n* = 37)	(*n* = 27)	(*n* = 22)
Internal discomfort	(4)[b] 2.14[c]	(3) 3.30	(1) 4.30	(4) 2.36
Fear of negative evaluation	(5) 1.43	(4) 2.16	(2) 4.07	(1) 4.82
Avoidance of social situations	(1) 4.57	(5) 1.30	(5) 1.52	(5) 1.55
Failure to respond	(2) 4.43	(2) 4.03	(3) 3.26	(2) 3.45
Awkward behavior	(3) 2.43	(1) 4.22	(4) 1.85	(3) 2.82

[a] Adapted from Pilkonis (1977b).
[b] Rank orderings of the means are given in parentheses.
[c] Range = 1 "least important" to 5 "most important."

The first cluster was the smallest (*n* = 7), but it was quite homogeneous (mean intracluster similarity correlation = .77) and consisted of those people who *avoided social situations and failed to respond* appropriately while in them. Avoidance is probably the most extreme of the aspects ranked, and the size of the cluster suggested that only a small percentage of our student respondents were attempting to eliminate all interaction with others. In addition, a college campus, with its variety of group settings (dormitories, dining halls, classrooms), makes it virtually impossible to completely avoid interacting with others. Whether shy avoiders constitute a larger proportion of all shy people in the géneral population is a difficult question to assess because such people would rarely be captured by traditional surveys or voluntary requests for research participation.

The second cluster was the largest (*n* = 37, mean intracluster correlation = .62) and was composed of people who emphasized *performance deficits* (both awkward behavior and failures to respond) in describing their shyness. Members of this cluster focused on public behavior in labeling themselves shy.

At the other extreme, *subjective discomfort* (internal arousal and fear of negative evaluation) was the major complaint of individuals in the third cluster (*n* = 27, mean intracluster correlation = .64). These persons focused on the private aspects of shyness.

Members of the fourth cluster (*n* = 22, mean intracluster correlation = .61) were a particular mix of the latter two types, pointing to both *fear of negative evaluation and behavioral deficits* in calling themselves shy.

The third and fourth clusters were more similar than the second and fourth, however, and when combined, they formed a larger group that was still reasonably homogeneous (mean intracluster correlation = .50). By disregarding the first cluster (which seems least relevant for the present population), the solution could therefore be reduced to two primary types: persons who are *publicly* shy (Cluster 2) and focus on behavioral deficits, and persons who are privately shy (Clusters 3 and 4) and focus on internal arousal and anxiety. There were no sex differences in frequency of membership in specific clusters or in the larger public–private clusters.

This contrast between public and private, between behavior and phenomenology, is a distinction that seems justified by the present cluster analysis and makes intuitive sense. But was there any additional evidence for its validity? Yes, as one would expect, members of the private cluster were significantly more self-conscious than their outwardly oriented peers (on the Fenigstein *et al.*, 1975, measure of public self-consciousness).

A second difference between the public and private clusters was also important. Although publicly and privately shy people rated the extent of their shyness as similar, individuals in the public cluster tended to say that their shyness was more of a "problem." This is somewhat surprising, since the phenomenology of subjects in the private cluster seemed to be more aversive. They complained of greater self-consciousness, and their shyness would appear to be more affectively laden as a result. However, it was publicly shy persons who reported that they had more difficulty coping with social anxiety. Behavioral deficits, rather than internal experience, carried more weight in decisions about how much of a problem shyness posed. For they not only suffered in silence, they were penalized for the behavioral failures. Compared to the publicly shy, their private counterparts are better off. They have learned to conceal their anxiety, to contain it within while carrying out necessary social rituals, vocational roles, and academic functions. Surprisingly, successful conduct of these role behaviors often does not have a spread of generalization to reduce future evaluation apprehension. We have observed this pattern in many shy celebrities, performers in the public limelight whose public role effectiveness is kept isolated from their "real" private selves, which remain insecure despite the acclaim and the applause.

This public–private distinction between shy subgroups was apparent in the phase of our experimental setting in which subjects had to prepare and deliver a formal speech. The other task, the informal social interaction, did not generate measurable differences in the performance of these groups. Asking the publicly shy, who generally focus on the inadequacy of their behavior, to concentrate on this public performance only served to aggravate their behavioral difficulties. They showed more speech anxiety and less satisfaction with their speeches, which were rated by judges as having less stylistic appeal than those of the privately shy. The demand to focus outward on a structured, clearly defined task seemed to distract the privately shy from their self-consciousness and their excessive monitoring of internal events.

Future research (by Pilkonis) will systematically examine individual differences in focus of attention and sensitivity to internal versus external events.

Table 2. Differences in Attentional Styles

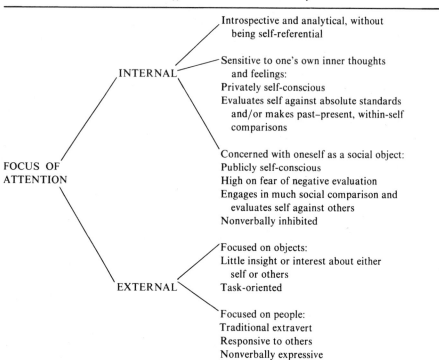

INTERNAL
- Introspective and analytical, without being self-referential
- Sensitive to one's own inner thoughts and feelings:
  Privately self-conscious
  Evaluates self against absolute standards and/or makes past–present, within-self comparisons
- Concerned with oneself as a social object:
  Publicly self-conscious
  High on fear of negative evaluation
  Engages in much social comparison and evaluates self against others
  Nonverbally inhibited

FOCUS OF ATTENTION

EXTERNAL
- Focused on objects:
  Little insight or interest about either self or others
  Task-oriented
- Focused on people:
  Traditional extravert
  Responsive to others
  Nonverbally expressive

This program of research will relate such differences to other dimensions of mood, cognition, and behavior in shy and not-shy people who vary in level of public and private self-consciousness. Exploration of the cognitive characteristics associated with internal–external attentional styles will proceed from the kind of distinctions outlined in Table 2.

In a series of recently completed studies on self-attentional processes and shyness, both memory and persuasibility were shown to be affected by manipulating the subject's evaluative focus. Recall for the content of a speech was most impaired when shy subjects experienced greatest discomfort in a condition where they were the object of evaluation ($r = -.70$ between arousal and recall). For the not-shy in the same condition, the relationship was weakly positive ($r = .27$). No memory differences were found in other conditions where the evaluation was less focused on the subject's performance and more on the communicator of the speech (Hatvany & Zimbardo, 1977). This laboratory finding underscores the personal experience of a shy executive who told us:

> One of the key things about shyness, as I have found, is that the worst effects of shyness cause a person to be so self-preoccupied that, truly, he simply misses what is

going on, doesn't hear or see. For instance, I often find myself unable to follow what's going on in a conversation because I've been so nervously conscious of myself.

When the not-shy are the focus of evaluation, they generally react appropriately to the demands of the situation. They do so by concentrating most on the dimensions of the task performance on which the evaluation will be based. In constrast, being made aware that their behavior is under evaluation, the shy more typically respond inappropriately, either by not identifying the key elements of the task or by focusing excessively on internal processes. It has been our working assumption that attentional and retrieval mechanisms are affected by psychological processes such as evaluation anxieties. This negative affect, intensified among the shy, redirects part of the learner's focus away from the selection of and attention to the central task-relevant stimuli and toward the self-monitoring of subjective states. Given both the limited information-processing capacity of the individual and a task load above a given difficulty level, performance decrements should occur. Where they do not, and the duration of the task is extended in time, we would expect to find evidence of the buildup of residual stress in the individual. The dual tasks of external vigilance and self-monitoring place a heavy burden on the shy person, one likely to be reflected in greater fatigue and other symptoms of stress. Such an effect should be more pronounced among the privately shy than among the publicly shy because of their greater willingness to accept performance demands that the publicly shy avoid or circumvent in subtle ways. Current research is being addressed to these issues.

For the present, it is important to restate that the deleterious impact of shyness extends beyond social settings to academic and vocational ones. The recall deficits in the study by Hatvany and Zimbardo (1977) were found among very bright, generally successful Stanford University undergraduates. The more severely shy may never even make it to college or top positions of business or leadership. A variety of findings support this conclusion (reported in Zimbardo, 1977). Observations we have made in elementary-school classrooms reveal that shy children are less likely than their not-shy peers to ask the teacher for help with assignments they find difficult. The not-shys more often ask for, and typically get, the teacher's counsel—and go on to succeed on the task. Similarly, among a large sample of naval personnel, the shy reported being less able than not-shys to ask their supervisor for help with a personal problem. Shy junior-high-school girls described themselves as less intelligent than not-shy peers or shy males. The inhibiting influences of shyness extend to failures to initiate action, to control interactions, to influence the direction of conversations, and to recall the names of "contacts" or other vital business information. Thus the effect not only lowers job satisfaction but induces feelings of frustration about being passed over by management and not having one's contributions appreciated. These findings obtained from sales and supervisory personnel in a large corporation become more serious when viewed in conjunction with the results of a long-term survey of factors that predict to success among graduates of business schools. "Verbal fluency" is the single best predictor of the likelihood that an M.B.A. will become successful in the business world (Harrell & Harrell, 1975). And of course verbal fluency is hardly the shy person's long suit.

Under what circumstances, if any, might shy people perform up to their level of ability, and perhaps even be superior to their not-shy peers? We would suggest that the following conditions would lead to optimal task performance of the shys: specific, explicit directions to attend to the external task demands, a highly structured setting, clear criteria for evaluating appropriate responding, unambiguous and reasonable standards for achieving success, and little free time available to engage in non-task-relevant thoughts. Not only should such conditions facilitate ideal performance of the shy, but in addition, they ought to result in lowered anxiety in ordinarily arousing situations. This anxiety reduction is a consequence of the redirection of attention away from self and toward the external world.

This issue of biased attentional focus created by the shy person's socially oriented anxiety extends beyond matters of recall of information to those of persuasibility and conformity. In Janis's (1955) studies of the personality correlates of persuasibility, he predicts that:

> Persons who are exceptionally lacking in a sense of personal adequacy are excessively fearful of social disapproval and therefore are strongly motivated to conform with the demands or suggestions of others.... a high degree of socially oriented anxiety (shyness, fear of being criticized, low self-confidence in relationships with other people, etc.) gives rise to high persuasibility. (p. 663)

A recent thesis by Souza e Silva (1977) offers strong confirmation of Janis's analysis. When subjects were exposed to a persuasive communication and expected to express their opinion on the issue in a social and evaluative setting, shys were strongly influenced, and not-shys rejected the message. Not-shys seemed to be more selective and rationally objective in basing their final opinion on an evaluation of the content of the speech and the speaker's characteristics. By contrast, shy individuals were more affected by their emotional discomfort and the anticipated public expression of their opinion. Only for the shy was there a significant negative correlation between discomfort and persuasion, and the absence of a correlation between speech or speaker evaluation and acceptance of the message. Further, these effects occurred only in the public evaluation treatment, no differences in persuasibility being found in nonevaluative situations.

In a followup study, when the status of the speaker was more clearly that of a familiar, credible expert, the not-shy subjects were as persuaded by his message as the shy. However, the underlying mechanisms for this comparable degree of persuasion still appear to be different. For the shys, acceptance of the speech depended on their evaluation of the speaker as competent, an acceptance of his power role that minimized counterarguing. For the not-shys, acceptance of the message depended on feeling comfortable that the speaker was an informational rather than a propaganda source. The more comfortable they felt, the more they attended to the "lecture," and the greater impact it had on them.

A final interesting result emerged from this investigation of shyness, recall, and persuasibility that points up the bidirectionality of human consciousness. In experimental treatments where the shy subjects attended most closely to the speech and recalled most, they felt most comfortable. It is as if their attention outward on the demands of the task distracted them from preoccupation with internal feelings of evaluative anxiety. This happens when the task is perceived as one of their ability to learn a given set of material. Quite the opposite occurred when shy subjects believed that the evaluative dimension was their social performance (discussion of their opinion). Under these conditions, shy subjects recalled less of the specific information in the speech than the not-shy. These data accord well with the two-factor process postulated by Leibling and Shaver (1973) between evaluative self-awareness and performance. When evaluative instructions maintain anxiety at a high level, then chronically anxious subjects perform poorly due to greater self-centered attention. However, under lower evaluation circumstances, the higher state of self-awareness of the shy should lead to increased motivation to do well and to enhanced task performance. Thus, the considerable impact of shyness on attentional focus, recall, and persuasibility may be overcome when the task is highly structured and the evaluative demands for performance are specific to the task at hand and do not generalize to a broader evaluation of the social–personal competence of the shy individual.

In another study relating shyness to conformity (Maslach & Solomon, 1977), the shy conformed more to the expressed opinions of their peers than did not-shy subjects. These opinions centered on a case study of a mentally disturbed patient. In addition to their greater peer-group conformity, the shys displayed a constellation of reactions that could be characterized as "dehumanizing" this person in distress and using dispositional labels rather than situational analysis to understand the causes of her problem and to recommend treatment. Thus, compared to not-shy subjects, shys were less willing to work with the patient as a paraprofessional; were more likely to recommend hospitalization than therapy; rated her as more passive and abnormal; made fewer sympathetic statements and more dehumanizing ones about the patient; used more categorical labels to describe her; and perceived her as more mentally ill.

These disturbing findings imply that the tendency toward self-labeling and self-denigration of the shy is generalized to other victims in distress.

V. SHYNESS AND ASSORTED PATHOLOGIES

In this section, we shall briefly examine some of the more devastating effects of shyness on our lives. In its extreme forms, shyness is implicated in a variety of pathological reactions. Fear of negative evaluation by others may develop into paranoid reactions. Phobic avoidance of other people may lead to the kind of isolated existence that is the breeding ground of depression, autistic thinking, suicide, and other abnormal behaviors. Four other pathological consequences of severe shyness that have captured our interest are its relationship to political and social control, alcoholism, sexual dysfunction, and irrational violence.

A. Political and Social Control

Extending our previous discussion of persuasion to a macro-level of analysis leads to speculation about the role of shyness as a mechanism of social control. The shy fear authorities, taking public stands, confrontations, and having to be assertive and generally do not stand up for their rights. It is from such a foundation of submissiveness that oppressive forms of social and political control ultimately derive their power. Totalitarian governments, according to Erich Fromm's brilliant thesis *Escape from Freedom* (1941), flourish when their citizens can be induced to trade their freedom for security. From our observations, it is not much of an overgeneralization to state that "shyness abhors freedom." We have seen that shy people avoid or perform most poorly and are made most anxious by precisely those situations that have minimal structure—the novel ones, unfamiliar ones, personal ones, ambiguous ones where there is most freedom to act, to initiate, to decide, to take responsibility. The shy fare better playing follow-the-leader than being the opposition. In this way the passive conformity of the shys might be exploited to lend legitimacy to the status quo, to established authorities, and to dictators who promise an illusion of security to replace the burdens of freedom.

B. Alcoholism

Recruitment into alcoholism involves a complex set of variables, one of which we believe to be shyness. "It is dramatically evident," according to a

Department of Health, Education, and Welfare report on alcohol and health (1971), "that alcohol-related problems go hand in hand with other forms of unhappiness." Shyness can generate considerable unhappiness when one is expected to entertain colleagues or neighbors and is frightened of people. It can cause much discomfort when one is desperate to make intimate contact with others at work, at a party, or at a bar and fears rejection. "And so they start to drink to loosen themselves up," says David Helms of the Washingtonian Center, Boston (personal communication, 1977). A former alcoholic told us: "the alcoholic who is shy has a desperate need to fit in, to belong, in his social group.... With a drink in my hand, I believed I was a more interesting person, a more scintillating conversationalist." And another alcoholic directs us back to our earlier discussions of the egocentric preoccupation of the shy with her statement:

> Everyone I met in Alcoholics Anonymous was pathologically shy. When I think of why, I am struck by the reason for my own alcoholism being that drinking "turns off" the ever present monitor. Overdrinking turns it too far off into social irresponsibility, but I suspect that alcoholics do drink to begin with because they are so shy.

Conformity also comes into play in the process of giving in to social pressures by peers to drink (or take drugs). Shy teenagers are especially vulnerable to these pressures to "be one of the boys," "be part of the group," "not to stand out," or "not to be noticed as different." We would not be surprised, then, to discover that shy youngsters are overrepresented in the growing population of teenage alcoholics. Another aspect of this problem is the reluctance of the shy to seek and ask directly for help. To do so requires at least minimal social skills, an act of assertion, and the readiness to admit to being "a deviant with a problem." So once addicted, or on the way, it should be more difficult for the shy than the not-shy to break out of the destructive cycle by utilizing available therapeutic resources.

C. Irrational Violence: Sudden Murderers

One of the most frightening aspects of alcoholism is its association with violence, either indirectly through automobile homicides or directly via assault, battery, and murder. But what is the connection between the passive, overcontrolled, mild-mannered, shy young man and violence? While shy people tend to avoid aggressive encounters, we have discovered that they often harbor considerable repressed anger. In some cases, they have not learned the verbal skills required to direct their anger at the appropriate source in a way that yields the desired change in the situation and a measure of personal satisfaction. In other cases, they know what to do, but are unwilling to enter into a confrontation. It is just easier for many shy people to be unwillingly cooperative and compliant than to assert their rights.

In our shyness center, shy clients often report being "bored" by dinner conversations or class discussions where they know as much as or more than those in the spotlight but feel unable to contribute. They are not only trapped in the situation but realize that others are probably judging their limited participation as a lack of information, intelligence, or interest. With only slight probing, their "boredom" gives way to rather strong expressions of anger: anger at the pomposity of the others and their false appraisal of the shy person's assets, and finally inward anger for feeling helpless to alter the situation.

But some shy people do take action. Unfortunately, it comes too late and with too much violence. The result of this sudden thawing of years of frozen violence can be of murderous proportions.

An instance of the type is Fred Cowan, who was described by relatives and acquaintances (he had no friends) as "a nice quiet man," "a gentle man who loved children," "a real pussycat." A co-worker said of this man, who had received A grades in courtesy, cooperation, and religion, "he never talked to anybody and was someone you could push around." On Valentine's Day, 1977, Fred Cowan had had enough; without apparent provocation, he shot to death four of his co-workers, two policemen, and himself.

To discover whether such an incident is truly indicative of a relationship between shyness, impulse control, and sudden violence, Lee, Zimbardo, and Bertholf (1977), surveyed two groups of California prisoners. All 19 had been sentenced for homicide, but 9 of them had been charged with prior acts of violence as well, while for the other 10, this murder was their first violent act (of record). A comparison group of inmates convicted of lesser crimes was also surveyed. Each man completed the Stanford Shyness Survey and selected subscales of the Minnesota Multiphasic Personality Inventory and the Bem Sex Role Inventory.

The findings strongly support the contention that shyness is implicated in sudden violence. With the 25% of the comparison group who reported being dispositionally shy are contrasted a mere 11% of the habitually violent murderers and a startling 80% of the sudden murderers. These shy sudden murderers also reveal a greater degree of ego overcontrol than their more frequently hostile cohorts, who tend toward undercontrol of their impulses (cf. Megargee, 1966; Megargee & Mendelsohn, 1962). Of greater surprise was the third finding, which revealed that the majority (70%) of the shy sudden murderers described themselves with feminine adjectives, while more of the habitually violent (78%) selected more "macho" self-descriptions.

These gentle, kind, nurturant, supportive, shy, overcontrolled, sudden murderers obviously needed to learn how to express their resentment, vent frustrations, and make appropriate requests for help, for promotion, and for redress of grievances. The teaching of these skills may not have been forthcoming because parents, teachers, and other agents of social control prefer "manageable" children and compliant adults. Training in assertion skills is clearly called for with such people before they explode, and even after they do so the first time—to prevent the lightning fury from striking twice (cf. Bower & Bower, 1976).

D. Sexual Dysfunction

Close behind "strangers," but ahead of "authorities" as shyness elicitors are "members of the opposite sex." Fully 60% of the shy college students we've surveyed are sexually shy in this way. Simply being alone in a dyad with someone of different sex is sufficient to arouse the syndrome of reactions characteristic of shyness. Sexual encounters represent a source of terror for many shy people, for reasons that by now should be apparent. It is a personal, intimate situation full of ambiguity, without explicit guidelines, clear criteria, or performance standards. It involves a complex interaction where sharing is vital and a host of skills are called into play—but usually with little opportunity for practice or even vicarious learning through modeling. Finally, there is the vulnerability of being naked, stripped of one's outer defenses.

A survey we conducted of 100 shy and 160 not-shy college students offered solid evidence of the different reactions of these groups to the sexual relationship. Shys have less sexual experience of all types than not-shys, and the difference between these groups increases as the sexual behavior is more intimate and taboo. Moreover, even when they have had intercourse (37% shy to 62% not-shy), shys report more negative reactions to the experience.

These reactions are often ones of embarrassment and awkwardness, of feeling ridiculous and not in control, of not knowing what to do when or how to interpret the subtle cues from one's partner. It is at this point that "shyness" and "shame" appear to merge. In Helen Block Lewis's cogent analysis (1978), shame "is the self's vicarious experience of the other's negative evaluation." It involves a self-consciousness, a self-imagining, and an intensification of feedback from all perceptual modalities. We would maintain that shyness is the more chronic state that predisposes an individual to shame reactions across a wider variety of situations in response to more minimal shame-inducing cues. Since so much of sex is cognitive, excessive thoughts about one's performance, about being evaluated and measuring up, and about one's discomfort all combine to inhibit the natural flow of sexuality. Impotence and frigidity would seem to be the unfortunate consequences of this narcissistic involvement with oneself.

For some shy males, one way to cope with the threats posed by the intimacy of a sexual relationship is to depersonalize sex. The purchase of sex through prostitution enables the buyer to render the seller an object or a product. Shy males should be more likely, then, to seek the services of prostitutes than not-shy males, to get sex without intimacy and without concern for meaningful social-emotional feedback (and thus potential negative self-evaluation). Our interviews with 20 prostitutes in San Francisco provide some validation of this line of reasoning. These women estimated that on the average, 60% of their customers were "shy" men who were reluctant to initiate the contact, were passive and submissive during the sex act, and were eager to have the women direct the activity. They often reported feeling embarrassed and ashamed of themselves during sex episodes with their wives and fearful of being labeled "pervert" for desiring anything that is not "standard operating procedure." For other shy men, even the physical closeness of a sexual being that they have purchased is too threatening. For them, the next level of impersonality is more appropriate: pornographic movies and perhaps plastic, inflatable sexual partners—who offer no negative evaluations.

VI. SHYNESS ACROSS CULTURES

Not only is the experience of shyness common among Americans, it appears to be quite prevalent (perhaps universal) across many cultures. Table 3

Table 3. Cross-Cultural Comparisons of Shyness (Ages 18–21, Unless Noted Otherwise)

	Prevalence of shyness (now)	Ever shy (now and/or past)	Never shy	Shy men (of total men)	Shy women (of total women)	Shyness is a personal problem
	Percent					
2482 American students	42	73	7	44	39	60
123 Oriental Americans	48	88	0	50	44	59
136 Hawaiian Orientals	44	89	2	47	42	61
28 Hawaiian Hawaiians	60	85	7	75	39	68
291 Taiwanese	55	84	0.4	59	51	58
305 Japanese	60	82	2	60	43	75
84 Germans	50	92	1	45	55	91
167 Students from India	47	66	10	46	52	82
307 Mexicans	39	81	3	30	56	75
231 Israelis	31	70	10	28	43	42
152 Jewish Americans	24	70	2	30	16	68
163 Obesity clinic clients[a]	40	68	7	33	40	73
540 Navy personnel[b]	33	68	9	33	33	46
	39	75	4	40	33	44

[a] This is a sample obtained at a clinic for obese individuals; average age is 35.

[b] This is a sample from the U.S. Navy. The top line describes the overall sample, with an average age of 26. The bottom line describes a subgroup of 18- to 21-year-olds.

offers a comparison across a number of different cultural groups of the prevalence of shyness (now and ever), separately for men and women, and a measure of whether shyness is considered to be a personal problem. (For a fuller analysis of this cross-cultural data, the reader is referred to Zimbardo, 1977, and Zimbardo, Pilkonis, & Zoppel, 1977).

What is apparent from these data is the overall relatively high frequency of shyness, and particularly its status as a "personal problem." Second, beyond these cross-cultural consistencies are certain notable variations. For example, shyness is higher in the Oriental cultures of Japan and Taiwan and lower in Israel than it is in the United States. Observations of children in mainland China by a team of psychologists (reported by Kessen, 1975) and a Chinese-speaking member of our research team point to a low level of shyness in the People's Republic of China.

The value of such cross-cultural data is to alert us to the social programming of shyness. The traditional personality-trait approach locates shyness in an individual, while our therapeutic recommendations are likewise designed to change something about that individual. By putting the shy person in his or her cultural context, we are sensitized to the social values, norms, codes of etiquette and protocol that form the foundation of the experience of shyness. Shyness is more than an intrapsychic phenomenon; it is an interpersonal one and ultimately a social-cultural transaction.

Shyness is engendered in societies that promote a cult of the ego (introspection and self-consciousness); emphasize individual rather than communal goals; overvalue competition, with failure a source of personal shame and where success is underplayed by modesty training; make love and respect of children contingent upon fluctuating, vague, and critical standards of performance; and provide little room for expression of emotions and sharing of intimate feelings.

VII. TREATMENT IMPLICATIONS

On the basis of our research findings and an initial evaluation of our shyness center effectiveness (conducted in collaboration with Margaret Marnell and Rochelle Kramer), we are in a position to offer some recommendations for treatment of the shy. First, we reiterate our optimism about reducing the impact of shyness, perhaps even overcoming it, by identifying the elicitors of the social anxiety and the types of reactions they generate. With this information, one can then determine whether the central problem is in the area of specific social-skills deficits or a generally inappropriate response style, or whether it lies in the area of low self-esteem and self-confidence.

A small-group therapeutic setting enables the shy person to learn to relate to others (of both sexes) in a supportive, nonevaluative atmosphere. Co-therapists model appropriate interpersonal behaviors, while clients practice these skills with immediate videotaped feedback. It is essential for clients to keep charts, diaries, or journals of their shyness experiences, of times when they behaved inappropriately, were put down, or were inhibited from taking a desired action. This information is not only important for developing a baseline against which to evaluate change but as an estimate of the extent of avoidance of shyness-inducing situations and stress-coping styles. To promote the generalization of in-session changes in responding to the client's own life setting, we strongly encourage "homework" exercises that take place in the person's life space. Saying hello to strangers, asking for information or advice, calling for a date, asking a question in class, and "doing three scary things" are the kind of *in vivo* behaviors that bridge the gap between safe therapy setting and dangerous real-world setting.

Social-skills training often requires learning quite basic aspects of human interaction, such as smiling, nodding approval, being a responsive listener, making eye contact, and starting and ending conversations, as well as effectively interrupting. Such skill rehabilitation is becoming widespread for those with dating inhibitions (Curran, 1977; Glasgow & Arkowitz, 1975; Twentyman & McFall, 1975), those with aggressive behavior (Frederiksen, Jenkins, Foy, & Eisler. 1976), and a variety of psychiatric patients (Hersen & Bellack, 1976).

Beyond getting the specific nuts and bolts of social interaction, shy people need assistance in developing more adequate general response styles. They must be encouraged and instructed in ways to "restructure" the ambiguous social encounters that arouse anxiety largely because of their formlessness. Thus a powerful therapeutic technique may be to provide shy people strategies for "restructuring" social situations in those cases where task demands, role constraints, or situational pressures are absent and cannot distract them from their anxiety. Not all encounters can have obvious, task-oriented purposes, but perhaps shy people could be taught to provide their own "agenda" in such cases. For example, in informal situations with a new person, one such goal might be to get to know as much as possible about the person with whom one is interacting. For some everyday encounters, demanding explicit "purposes" may be unrealistic or farfetched. In these cases, simple attempts to initiate and direct conversations by asking questions, raising new topics, and breaking pauses may be a suitable way of lessening ambiguity. Research has shown that the person who asks questions is likely to be perceived as smarter than the one cast in the role of answerer (Ross, Amabile, & Steinmetz, 1977). In a quiz-show format, one subject was randomly assigned to pose 10 hard questions to the other "contestant." Despite the arbitrary assignment to ask or to have to answer these difficult questions, all parties involved rated the quiz-show master as smarter than the contestant. The implication of this research is to learn to take control of the domain of the conversation, to ask the first question, not wait passively to answer someone else's questions. If one controls the substance and flow of conversation, then one need not feel uncertain or defensive about what is likely to occur. Shy people, of course, balk at taking such initiatives on their own, and adequate social-skills training must provide both the techniques and the motivation to overcome this reluctance.

Ideally this kind of social-skills training should encourage a general "problem-solving" attitude toward feared social encounters rather than a set of highly specific skills relevant to only a single context. The technique appropriate for all difficult encounters is to decide on a "purpose" that one hopes to achieve and then to map out the steps required to reach it. After practicing with one or two specific problems, shy people would hopefully feel more competent, not only in those contexts but also in applying their "problem-solving" skills to new areas. Different kinds of therapeutic interventions may be necessary for the publicly and privately shy. Publicly shy people, who are concerned primarily with behavioral difficulties, would presumably benefit most directly from social-skills training. Privately shy people, who focus on the quality of internal events, may require interventions aimed at changing their experience and their evaluation of their experience, as well as their behavior. While they would also benefit from skills training, additional techniques seem relevant for them. For example, relaxation training might be useful for lessening both actual and imagined arousal, and cognitive behavior modification techniques might be helpful in lessening excessive self-consciousness and altering negative self-evaluations. Esteem building would concentrate on stopping negative self-references, while increasing the frequency of self-praise. It would also involve cataloging one's assets and seeking settings where they would be most valued. These are but a few of the steps in a program to increase the sense of self-efficacy of the shy person.

But beyond helping the shy with their personal problem, treatment must also take into consideration social and cultural values that might be subject to modification. This approach involves a "revolutionary" program to reduce competitive striving, excessively critical evaluations of others, and overemphasis on the ego and the self to the exclusion of group goals and communal objectives. It also entails encouraging greater trust in the relationship of children to parents and other authorities; the open sharing of feelings, especially of inadequacy and about failure; and the modeling of tenderness and loving human relationships.

Shyness, from our data, is an insidious personal liability that is reaching the proportions of a social disease epidemic. While helping the shy learn new ways to relate to others and to appreciate themselves better, we must also look to basic strains in our socialization practices that foster chronic shyness in the next generation for the sake of having children who are seen and not heard, compliant pupils who don't make trouble, and submissive citizens who are never management problems.

In helping others overcome their shyness, we acknowledge the need to penetrate the isolation of solitary existence with the touch of humanity that gives it meaning and purpose beyond narcissistic survival. Theologian Martin Buber puts it this way:

> Man wishes to be confirmed in his being by man, and wishes to have a presence in the being of the other—secretly and bashfully he watches for a "Yes" which allows him to be and which can come to him only from one human person to another.

REFERENCES

Argyle, M., Trower, P. E., & Bryant, B. M. Explorations in the treatment of personality disorders and neuroses by social skills training. *British Journal of Medical Psychology*, 1974, *47*, 63–72.

Arkowitz, H., Lichtenstein, E., McGovern, K., & Hines, P. The behavioral assessment of social competence in males. *Behavior Therapy*, 1975, *6*, 3–13.

Bandura, A. *Principles of behavior modification*. New York: Holt, Rinehart, and Winston, 1969.

Bem, D. J. Self-perception: An alternative interpretation of cognitive dissonance phenomena. *Psychological Review*, 1967, *74*, 183–200.

Borkovec, T. D., Stone, N. M., O'Brien, G. T., & Kaloupek, D. G. Identification and measurement of a clinically relevant target behavior for analogue outcome research. *Behavior Therapy*, 1974, *5*, 503–513.

Bower, S. A., & Bower, G. H. *Asserting yourself: A practical guide for positive change*. Reading, Mass.: Addison-Wesley, 1976.

Bryant, B. M., & Trower, P. E. Social difficulty in a student sample. *British Journal of Educational Psychology*, 1974, *44*, 13–21.

Bryant, B., Trower, P., Yardley, K., Urbieta, H., & Letemendia, F. J. J. A survey of social inadequacy among psychiatric outpatients. *Psychological Medicine*, 1976, *6*, 101–112.

Cattell, R. B. *Personality and mood by questionnaire*. San Francisco: Jossey-Bass, 1973.

Clark, J. V., & Arkowitz, H. Social anxiety and self-evaluation of interpersonal performance. *Psychological Reports*, 1975, *36*, 211–221.

Comrey, A. L. *Manual for the Comrey personality scales*. San Diego: Educational and Industrial Testing Service, 1970.

Curran, J. P. Skills training as an approach to the treatment of heterosexual-social anxiety: A review. *Psychological Bulletin*, 1977, *84*, 140–157.

Dixon, J. J., deMonchaux, C., & Sandler, J. Patterns of anxiety: An analysis of social anxieties. *British Journal of Medical Psychology*, 1957, *30*, 102–112.

Eysenck, H. J., & Eysenck, S. B. G. *Manual for the Eysenck personality inventory*. San Diego: Educational and Industrial Testing Service, 1968.

Eysenck, H. J., & Eysenck, S. B. G. *Personality structure and measurement*. San Diego: Robert Knapp, 1969.

Fenigstein, A., Scheier, M. G., & Buss, A. H. Public and private self-consciousness: Assessment and theory. *Journal of Consulting and Clinical Psychology*, 1975, *43*, 522–527.

First Special Report to the U.S. Congress on Alcohol and Health from the Secretary of H.E.W. (Dec. 1971), DHEW Pub. No. HSM 72-9099, United States Government Printing Office, p.v.

Frederiksen, L. W., Jenkins, J. O., Foy, D. W., & Eisler, R. M. Social-skills training to modify abusive verbal outbursts in adults. *Journal of Applied Behavior Analysis*, 1976, *9*, 117–125.

Fromm, E. *Escape from freedom*. New York: Farrar and Rinehard, 1941.

Glasgow, R. E., & Arkowitz, H. The behavioral assessment of male and female social competence in dyadic heterosexual interactions. *Behavior Therapy*, 1975, *6*, 488–498.

Harrell, T. W., & Harrell, M. S. A scale for high earners. Stanford School of Business, Office of Naval Research Technical Report No. 7, July, 1975.

Hatvany, N., & Zimbardo, P. G. Shyness, arousal and memory: The path from discomfort to distraction to recall deficits. Unpublished manuscript, Stanford University, 1977.

Hersen, M., & Bellack, A. S. Social skills training for chronic psychiatric patients: Rationale, research findings, and future directions. *Comprehensive Psychiatry*, 1976, *17*, 559–580.

Janis, I. Anxiety indices related to susceptibility to persuasion. *Journal of Abnormal and Social Psychology*, 1955, *51*, 663–667.

Johnson, S. C. Hierarchical clustering schemes. *Psychometrika*, 1967, *32*, 241–254.

Kaplan, D. M. On shyness. *International Journal of Psycho-Analysis*, 1972, *53*, 439–453.

Kessen, W. *Childhood in China*. New Haven: Yale University Press, 1975.

Kraft, T. Social anxiety model of alcoholism. *Perceptual and Motor Skills*, 1971, *33*, 797–798.

Lee, M., Zimbardo, P. G., & Bertholf, M. J. Shy murderers. *Psychology Today*, November, 1977, pp. 68–70, 76, 148.

Leibling, B. A., & Shaver, P. Evaluation, self-awareness, and task performance. *Journal of Experimental Social Psychology*, 1973, *9*, 297–306.

Lewinsohn, P. M. A behavioral approach to depression. In R. M. Friedman & M. M. Katz (Eds.), *The psychology of depression: Contemporary theory and research*. New York: Wiley, 1974.

Lewis, H. B. Shame and depression. In C. E. Izard (Ed.), *Emotions in personality and psychopathology*. New York: Plenum, 1978.

Martinson, W. D., & Zerface, J. P. Comparison of individual counseling and a social program with non-daters. *Journal of Counseling Psychology*, 1970, *17*, 36–40.

Maslach, C., & Solomon, T. Pressures toward dehumanization from within and without. University of California, Berkeley. Unpublished manuscript, 1977.

McGovern, L. P. Dispositional social anxiety and helping behavior under three conditions of threat. *Journal of Personality*, 1976, *44*, 84–97.

Megargee, E. Undercontrolled and overcontrolled personality types in extreme anti-social aggression. *Psychological Monographs*, 1966, No. 11, whole issue.

Megargee, E., & Mendelsohn, G. A cross validation of twelve MMPI indices of hostility and control. *Journal of Abnormal and Social Psychology*, 1962, *65*, 431–438.

Pilkonis, P. A. The behavioral consequences of shyness. *Journal of Personality*, 1977, *45*, 596–611.(a)

Pilkonis, P. A. Shyness, public and private, and its relationship to other measures of social behavior. *Journal of Personality*, 1977, *45*, 585–595.(b)

Ross, L. The intuitive psychologist and his shortcomings: Distortions in the attribution process. In L. Berkowitz (Ed.), *Advances in Experimental Social Psychology*, Vol. 10. New York: Academic Press, 1977, pp. 173–220.

Ross, L., Amabile, T., & Steinmetz, J. Social roles, social control, and biases in social perception processes. *Journal of Personality and Social Psychology*, 1977, *35*, 485–494.

Snyder, M. Self-monitoring of expressive behavior. *Journal of Personality and Social Psychology*, 1974, *30*, 526–537.

Souza e Silva, M. C. Social and cognitive dynamics of shyness. Master's thesis, Stanford University, 1977.

Sullivan, H. S. *Conceptions of modern psychiatry*. Washington: W. A. White Foundation, 1947.

Twentyman, C. T., & McFall, R. M. Behavioral training of social skills in shy males. *Journal of Consulting and Clinical Psychology*, 1975, *43*, 384–395.

Wallace, I., Wallechinsky, D., & Wallace, A. *The People's Almanac presents the Book of Lists*. New York: Morrow, 1977.

Watson, D., & Friend, R. Measurement of social-evaluative anxiety. *Journal of Consulting and Clinical Psychology*, 1969, *33*, 448–457.

Zimbardo, P. G. *Shyness: What it is, What to do about it.* Reading, Mass.: Addison-Wesley, 1977.

Zimbardo, P. G., Pilkonis, P. A., & Norwood, R. M. The silent prison of shyness. Office of Naval Research Technical Report No. Z-17. Stanford, Calif.: Stanford University, November 1974.

Zimbardo, P. G., Pilkonis, P. A., & Zoppel, C. A cross-cultural analysis of the emic and etic of shyness. Unpublished manuscript. Stanford University, 1977.

Editor's Introduction

6

Zuckerman has pursued the conceptualization and measurement of sensation seeking with such success that it is beginning to take its place alongside such long-established concepts as introversion and extraversion. Zuckerman conceives sensation seeking as a motive that can be measured as both trait and state.

Sensation seeking is defined in part by emotion concepts, by emotion-related behavior (e.g., emotionally expressive actions in social situations), and by some of the same dimensions that are used to describe emotions (e.g., impulsiveness).

Sensation seeking is measured by terms that relate either to the positive emotions of interest–excitement (e.g., *curious*) or to joy (e.g., *elated–pleased*) or to both (e.g., *enthusiastic, adventurous, playful*). However, the question of how discrete positive emotions relate to sensation seeking in specific situations has not been pursued.

In relating anxiety to sensation seeking, Zuckerman conceives of anxiety as equivalent to fear, and when he speaks of different types of anxiety (general, specific, trait, state), the construct is anchored by the particular instrument used to measure it. General anxiety—as measured by the Spielberger–Gorsuch–Lushene State–Trait Anxiety Scale, whose content relates to several different emotions (Izard, 1972)—is unrelated to sensation seeking. However, anxiety operationally defined as fear, as on the sensation-seeking and anxiety state tests, is complexly related to sensation seeking, and the relationships fit well into Zuckerman's conceptual framework.

Zuckerman and his colleagues have shown that sensation seeking is significantly related to a number of psychodiagnostic indicators and more characteristic of some psychological disorders than others. For example, the research shows that primary psychopaths are higher in sensation seeking then acting-out neurotic types. Zuckerman has also found that high sensation seekers are more prone to experiment with drugs, that manics may be extremely high in sensation seeking and schizophrenics low, and that sensation seeking successfully predicts some specific phobias.

Sensation Seeking and Risk Taking

6

MARVIN ZUCKERMAN

I. THEORETICAL BACKGROUND

A. Theoretical Links with Psychopathology

When I first conceptualized the sensation-seeking trait in the early 1960s (Zuckerman, Kolin, Price, & Zoob, 1964), I did not conceive of it as a trait embodying psychopathology, not even at the extremes. What we were trying to do was to take the constructs optimal level of stimulation (OLS) and optimal level of arousal (OLA) and make them operational as personality dimensions. The research was a relatively minor part of a larger effort aimed at defining the situational and person variables in sensory deprivation and how they interacted. The OLS construct, which has been around a long time (Wundt, 1873), has been translated into an OLA construct by Berlyne (1960), Hebb (1955), Malmo (1959), and Schlosberg (1954). Lindsley (1957, 1961) described how the OLA might be based on a feedback control system involving the sensory receptors, the reticular activating system (RAS), and the cortex. In a paper given in 1964 (Zuckerman, 1964), I suggested that individual differences in this neurophysiological mechanism might account for differences in response to sensory deprivation, and this idea was later made the central construct in a theory of sensory deprivation (Zuckerman, 1969). Schultz (1965) also postulated a homeostatic drive that he called "sensoristasis," based on the functioning of the RAS.

While we were pursuing our hypothesis in sensory deprivation experiments, with mixed results, the OLS and OLA constructs were being incor-

---

MARVIN ZUCKERMAN • University of Delaware, Newark, Delaware.

porated in other theories of personality and psychopathology. Eysenck (1963, 1967) proposed that because the introvert has a higher level of cortical arousal and the extravert a lower level, the extravert has a higher OLS and should therefore function and feel better at higher levels of stimulation; the converse should be true for the introvert. Eysenck has mustered various evidence from drug experiments and correlations with experience to substantiate this theory.

The input-dysfunction theory of schizophrenia (McGhee & Chapman, 1961; Payne, Matussek, & George, 1959; Venables, 1964) postulated a disorder of the selective and inhibitory functions of attention that might make complex or high levels of stimulation overarousing to the schizophrenic. By implication, this theory also points to the RAS, since this system is centrally involved in the inhibitory and selective function through descending connections extending as far as the receptors themselves (Lindsley, 1961).

Quay (1965) used the OLA construct to explain sociopathic behavior, suggesting that because sociopaths are underaroused and/or underarousable, they require more intense or varied stimuli to feel good and seek such stimulation in antisocial behavior. Quay's theory can be extended to the use of illegal drugs, particularly stimulants, where the desired change in arousal is sought through chemical rather than behavioral means. However, here we run into the problem of the use of CNS-suppressant drugs, such as opiates and heroin, where the drug effect would not fulfill the function of increasing arousal.

Mania is another area of psychopathology where the sensation-seeking construct is relevant. The relevance of the construct for this area was not seen initially but emerged in an interesting inductive cumulation of relationships with trait tests of psychopathology and common physiological correlates. If I had thought originally about possible psychopathological correlates of sensation seeking, the clinical description of the manic, as given here, would have struck me as a caricature of the description of the normal sensation-seeker: "These episodes are characterized by excessive elation, irritability, talkativeness, flight of ideas and acceleration of speech" (APA DSM II, 1968, p. 36).

The Diagnostic and Statistical Manual also describes a cyclothymic personality: The "periods of elation may be marked by ambition, warmth, enthusiasm, optimism, and high energy" (p. 42).

These two descriptions may represent sections of an underlying continuum of states whose frequency defines a trait. Mania may be the extreme of this continuum. The normal sensation-seeker may be characterized as a person with a high frequency of such states but without the qualitative delusional or quantitative overactivity of the manic.

B. Development of the Sensation Seeking Scales (SSS)

The SSS was developed through a series of forms aimed at measuring the most basic and reliable dimensions of the construct. The first finished form (II, Zuckerman et al., 1964) contained a general scale composed of diverse items loading highest on the first large factor discovered in the experimental form, I. The same general factor was found in a subsequent analysis, and the general scale based on this factor was kept in the next form (IV, Zuckerman, 1971) to provide a marker for previous studies done with form II. Rotation yielded four factors, three of which were reliably similar in males and females. A recent study (Zuckerman, Eysenck, & Eysenck, 1978) showed that the same four factors were reliably identified in English males and females. On the basis of the four-factor analyses, a new form (V) has been constructed that contains 10 items representing each factor and yields a total score on all 40 items that is better balanced for the factors than was the old general scale.

The four factors on which the SSS subscales are based are described as follows:

1. Thrill and Adventure Seeking (TAS) consists of items expressing desires to engage in sports or other activities involving some danger, risk, or personal challenge, such as mountain climbing, parachute jumping, scuba diving, and speeding in a car.

2. Experience Seeking (ES) contains items describing the desire to seek new experiences through the mind and senses, by living in a nonconforming life-style with unconventional friends, and through travel.

3. Disinhibition (Dis) was named for the items describing the need to disinhibit behavior in the social sphere by drinking, partying, and seeking variety in sexual partners. As with other scales, most of the items express the preference for or desire to engage in certain kinds of behavior, or the values compatible with such behavior, rather than a description of actual experience.

4. Boredom Susceptibility (BS) items indicate an aversion to repetitive experience of any kind, routine work, or even dull or predictable people. There are also items indicating restlessness when things are unchanging.

C. Sensation Seeking as an Emotional State

Sensation seeking was initially conceptualized as the level of arousal that was optimal for a given individual. This concept, based on a single-factor arousal theory, ignored the fact that the same level of arousal might be positive or negative, depending on the appraisal of the situation, or the possibility that there might be more than one type of emotional arousal at the level of the biological mechanisms. If there was only one type of arousal, then there should be a rather high negative correlation between the traits of sensation seeking and anxiety since anxiety would only reflect the level of arousal at which hedonic tone shifted from positive to negative. This expectation was not confirmed at the trait level, although there is evidence of interaction between states of sensation seeking and anxiety.

The fact that two traits may not show a relationship does not tell us what happens to the states that are relevant to the traits. A person scoring high on an anxiety trait scale, for instance, may or may not react with indications of a high anxiety state in a given situation. Much depends on the nature of the situation and the specificity of the trait measure. A considerable amount of research has been done on the trait–state relationships of anxiety (Spielberger, Gorsuch, & Lushene, 1970; Zuckerman, 1960; Zuckerman & Lubin, 1965). Only recently have attempts been made to apply the trait–state approach to other kinds of personality constructs (Patrick & Zuckerman, 1977; Patrick, Zuckerman, & Masterson, 1974; Zuckerman, 1976a).

Apart from the question of what the basic kinds of emotional arousal are or how many kinds of basic emotions may be identified, it may be postulated that each kind of personality trait has a particular kind of emotional arousal associated with it, the arousal being a mixture of broad physiological arousal patterns and more specific cognitive labeling of these patterns. The trait may be conceptualized as the frequency with which these states occur and the variety of situations in which they are elicited.

Neary (1975) developed a state measure of sensation seeking as described in Zuckerman (1976b). The state measure of sensation seeking is combined with a state measure of anxiety (which is essentially a shortened version of the Zuckerman, 1960, Affect Adjective Check List) in the same test. This instrument has enabled us to look at the interactions of the states of anxiety and sensation seeking in actual and hypothetical situations. The results, which will be discussed in more detail in a later section, show that the two states interact in different ways as a function of the degree of appraised risk in situations. The distinction between these two kinds of state arousal is crucial to an understanding of how psychopathology affects behavior.

D. Risk

The construct of risk is important to our understanding of many kinds of psychopathology. Risk is partly a function of the objective situation and partly a function of the individual's appraisal of the situation. Freud's (1926) distinction between neurotic anxiety and reality anxiety, for instance, seems to refer to how much the individual's appraisal of the riskiness of a situation is consensually normative and how much is due to internal factors causing an idiosyncratic type of appraisal. (In some cases anxiety may occur when there is no change in the external situation but when past or future situations are symbolically construed.) Phobias, as an example, are defined as anxiety reactions related to stimuli or situations that are not appraised as risky by most persons.

The appraisal of the situation is central to the anxiety theories of Lazarus (1972) and Spielberger (1966), both of which suggest that a cognitive appraisal precedes and governs the emotional reaction to situations. This assumption is basic in cognitive approaches to behavior modification such as those of Ellis

(1973) and Meichenbaum (1974). One characteristic that seems to govern the behavior of manics, psychopaths, drug abusers, and normal sensation-seekers is their engaging in behavior that others regard as quite risky and refrain from. Questions that must be answered are whether the difference in risk takers and avoiders is due to differences in appraisal of risk, in tolerance for the higher levels of arousal produced by such situations, or in the quality of arousal produced by such situations. We must also consider the possibility that all or some combination of these factors explains risk-taking behavior. My recent work, which will be described in this chapter, addresses these questions.

To summarize my conception of sensation seeking and anxiety states and traits:

Sensation seeking and anxiety represent two phenomenally distinct types of affect associated with approach and inhibition (or avoidance) responses, respectively. Both affects are associated with physiological arousal of the cortex. People may be characterized by consistent individual differences in the frequency with which either of the two states are aroused or the variety of situations that will elicit the states. The traits of sensation seeking and anxiety are not correlated. Under certain conditions, such as those where risk is appraised to be high, there may be a negative relationship between the two states, that is, high anxiety associated with low sensation-seeking.

According to the theory I propose, appraisal of a real or imagined situation as risky will elicit an anxiety state that varies in direct proportion to the appraised risk. However the situation may also contain elements of novelty and the promise of new experience that elicit a sensation-seeking state. The state scale, developed by Neary, was developed to measure sensation seeking and anxiety states at a given time in response to either real or imagined situations. The research that will be discussed examined the relationships between sensation-seeking trait, appraised risk, and sensation-seeking and anxiety states.

E. Sensation Seeking in Normals

Much of the research using the SS scales on normals has been summarized in previous papers (Zuckerman, 1974, 1976b, 1978a, and in press) and will not be extensively discussed in this one. Correlations between the SSS and other trait tests have revealed that sensation seeking is related to the impulsive, but not the sociable, aspects of extraversion. Sensation seeking also correlates with a nonconforming autonomy and a need for change that, in its extreme, resembles psychopathy. Sensation seekers tend to be impulsive and emotionally expressive in social interactions. Sensation seeking is unrelated to scales of neuroticism or social anxiety. However, one of the SS subscales, Thrill and Adventure Seeking (TAS), does seem to be inversely related to specific fears of physical harm, and all of the scales show negative relationships with harm avoidance as a trait. A study by Mellstrom, Cicala, and Zuckerman (1976), which will be discussed in a later section, showed that the TAS scale was highly predictive of fearless responses to phobic types of situations.

In the realm of experience, sensation seeking has been found to be associated with sexual, drug, alcohol, and smoking experience; voluntarily engaging in risky activities such as skydiving; choice of risky occupations; and volunteering for unusual kinds of experiments, such as experiments on sensory deprivation, hypnosis, and drugs. Most of these activities have been evaluated as entailing moderate to high degrees of risk by undergraduate subjects. Except for drug experience, none of these activities is illegal but represents socially acceptable ways of increasing arousal through exciting experiences.

Conversely, when high sensation-seekers are put into unchanging situations with little external stimulation, such as meditation or social isolation, they typically exhibit restlessness and intolerance for the situations.

F. Development of State Scales for Sensation Seeking

Neary (1975) developed state scales for sensation seeking and anxiety using empirical and factor-analytic methods to select items. The details of the scale development can be found in chapters by Zuckerman (1976b, 1978). He gave the two scales in nonarousing neutral classroom situations and in two experimental situations. The same subjects were tested in all situations. The experimental situations consisted of (1) being asked to take an experimental drug (a placebo) that might produce some "unusual effects"; and (2) waiting to participate in a group hypnosis experiment for which they had not specifically volunteered.

Trait sensation-seeking correlated with the SS state in baseline and drug situations but not in the hypnosis situation. The two states correlated minimally in the baseline condition, but the negative correlations increased and became significant as the situation became more risky, going from the baseline to the hypnosis to the drug situations. In other words, the interaction between sensation-seeking and anxiety states seems to be minimal in low-risk situations but increases as the situation becomes more risky and presumably elicits more arousal.

Sensation-seeking states assessed just prior to the experimental conditions predicted the reactions of consenting to take the drug in that situation and of hypnotizability in the hypnosis situation. The last finding is significant in view of the fact that trait sensation-seeking could not predict hypnotizability in this study, as well as in the last study (Zuckerman, Bone, Neary, Mangelsdorf, & Brustman, 1972).

The decision to take the unknown drug in an experiment was predicted by both the state of sensation seeking (positive correlation) and the state of anxiety (negative correlation), but only the SS state predicted hypnotizability; this difference may be due to the fact that the drug experiment elicited higher levels of anxiety than the hypnosis experiment or the baseline conditions.

On the basis of this study, a two-factor theory was formulated (Zuckerman, 1976b) relating the behavior in novel or risky situations to the interactions of the two states elicited by such situations. The model in Figure 1 suggests that novelty and risk appraisal vary together up to a certain point, beyond which increased novelty does not necessarily generate increased risk appraisal. Anxiety state is hypothesized to vary directly with risk appraisal, but the relation between sensation-seeking state and risk is assumed to be curvilinear, in the manner of the optimal-level-of-arousal curves. The decreasing sensation-seeking state in high-risk situations was observed in this experiment as well as in one by Patrick *et al.* (1974), where the need change scale of the Gough–Heilbrun Adjective Check List (ACL) decreased on examination days in a classroom situation.

The interaction of the two states is presumed to determine behavior in situations: when the SS state arousal is higher, persons should enter into the situation, and when the anxiety state is higher, they should withdraw or avoid the situation. On first exposure to a novel situation, the sensation-seeking trait could be related to either or both types of state arousal, and the curves for high

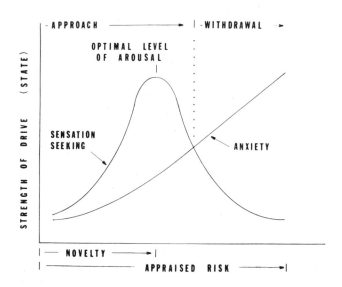

Figure 1. Sensation-seeking and anxiety states as determinants of behavior in novel situations: a model. (From M. Zuckerman, 1976. Permission of Hemisphere Publishing Co.)

and low sensation-seekers should differ. The anxiety curve should be lower or displaced to the high end for high sensation-seekers, and their sensation-seeking curve should be higher and should decrease only in the riskiest situations, compared to the curve for low sensation-seekers. The next set of studies to be described attempted to provide an initial test of these trait–state hypotheses using hypothetical situations varying along the risk appraisal dimension.

G. The Relation between Novelty and Risk

Novelty may be linked with risk taking and anxiety since novel situations often produce states of perceptual and cognitive incongruency that some theorists (e.g., McReynolds, 1976) see as factors in producing anxiety. An experience once related to me illustrates this point. A couple living on Long Island were invited to a party given by some casual friends. They arrived to be greeted by their hostess, who was totally nude. She invited them in, politely offering them hangers for their clothes. Glancing over her shoulder, they saw a living room full of persons of both sexes drinking, smoking, and engaged in earnest conversation, all totally nude. With some embarrassment and confusion, they apologized and left. The incongruency of the novel situation could not be assimilated into their system of cognitive structures and summoned up risk potentials that they were not prepared to cope with. As they were only moderate-range sensation-seekers, their anxiety state was considerably stronger than their sensation-seeking state, and an avoidance response was inevitable.

But not all novel situations are necessarily appraised as risky. If they were, most persons would rarely do anything new. In order to assess the relationship between novelty of situation and risk appraisal, 116 situations were devised using the items of the SSS as points of departure but also including some commonplace situations (such as going to a movie) and some highly improbable ones (taking a trip to the moon). The subjects were 31 students of both sexes in a psychology class. Since this was only a pilot study to select items for subsequent forms of the Situation Inventory, we did not make an attempt to get larger numbers of subjects.

Each subject was asked to make two ratings of the 116 situation items:

1. Risk was defined as risk of physical harm or injury; mental harm, such as shame, guilt, embarrassment, or humiliation; and/or punishment or loss of something valuable. The ratings were made on a scale of 1 to 9 going from "no risk at all" to "very great risk."

2. A rating of experience was defined by how many times the subject had been in the situations described or in very similar situations. The ratings went

from 1 to 9, or "have never been in the situation" to "have been in the situation 8 times or more."

Mean ratings for the total group were obtained for each of the two scales for each of the 116 items. The two sets of mean ratings were correlated over the items, and a scatter plot was constructed to examine the relationship between novelty–experience and risk appraisal.

The correlation between novelty (as the reverse of experience) and risk appraisal was .56, which is highly significant. However, in looking at the scatter plot, it became clear that the correlation was produced entirely by the relationship at the low novelty end, where there were no situations that persons had experienced more than four times that they considered moderately risky or greater. Among the very novel situations, an equal number were appraised as low and high risk. Being in a psychology experiment in a dark room and seeing a flying saucer in the sky were examples of novel low-risk situations; taking heroin and being involved in a battle were examples of novel high-risk situations.

The fact that no situations were found in the low-novel, high-risk quadrant does not mean that such situations do not exist. Conceivably, unavoidable but frequently experienced unpleasant situations, such as examinations and trips to the dentist, might fall at the moderate-risk level. It may be that most persons do not voluntarily expose themselves to situations that they regard as highly risky with any great frequency. Another explanation may be that frequent exposure reduces the risk appraisal of most situations.

Whatever the explanation, I decided to pursue the study of risk appraisal by selecting only the situation items at the novel end of the scale, where there was no confounding of novelty with risk appraisal and I could examine the influence of risk appraisal independent of novelty and experience. These are situations with which most of our college freshman and sophomores have had little or no experience.

H. Relationships between Risk Appraisal, Sensation-Seeking Trait, and Eysenck Dimensions

The next question concerned the relationship between sensation-seeking trait and risk appraisal. Do high sensation-seekers engage in activities seen as risky by most persons, because they appraise the situations as less risky? Eysenck's dimensions are also relevant to the question of risk appraisal since he conceives of extraverts as risk takers and introverts as risk avoiders. His dimension of neuroticism is also relevant since it correlates highly with trait anxiety. Are highly anxious or neurotic persons likely to appraise situations as more risky than low neurotic ones? The newly added dimension of psychoticism is also relevant, since persons high on this dimension might be assumed to have highly deviant appraisals of situations in general and risk appraisal in particular.

Fifty situations were chosen for the next form of the Situation Inventory, using situations where the mean experience rating was less than 2. The three types of risk, used in the overall definition in the prior form, were assigned separate ratings in the second form in order to see if subjects differed on the separate types of risk and if the different types of risk related differently to the SS subscales. TAS, for instance, might relate more to appraisal of physical risk than other kinds, while disinhibition might relate more to mental harm and punishment risks. The subjects were asked to make three ratings for each of 50 situations: physical-harm risk, mental-harm risk, and punishment or loss risk.

The subjects for this study were 96 males and 114 females from introductory psychology classes, primarily freshmen and sophomores, 17–20 years of age. They were given the SSS form V and the Eysenck and Eysenck (1975) Personality Questionnaire (EPQ) in class. At a later time, they were given form II of the Situation Inventory, on which they were asked to rate the three kinds of risk for the 50 situations. Separate risk-appraisal scores were obtained for each subject for each of the three types of risk by totaling their ratings across situations, and a total risk score was obtained by totaling the three specific risk scores. The correlations between the SSS and EPQ scores and the four risk scores were computed for males and females separately. The results are shown in Table 1.

The three risk scores—physical, mental, and punishment—are highly intercorrelated: the rs in males were .80, .77, and .74, and in females, .78, .61, .62. The results suggest that there is a general risk-appraisal tendency that is

Table 1. Correlations[a] between Risk Appraisal, SSS and EPQ

		Physical risk		Mental risk		Punishment risk		Total risk	
		(Male	Female)	(Male	Female)	(Male	Female)	(Male	Female)
SSS	TAS	-35^b	-40^b	-35^b	-36^b	-23^c	-27^b	-33^b	-39^b
	ES	-29^b	-27^b	-31^b	-34^b	-28^b	-18^c	-32^b	-30^b
	Dis	-23^c	-23^b	-33^b	-17^c	-13	-10	-25^c	-18^c
	BS	-16	-23^b	-16	-21^c	-14	-23^b	-17	-26^b
	Total	-40^b	-40^b	-45^b	-38^b	-30^b	-27^b	-42^b	-40^b
EPQ	Extravert	10	-04	00	-04	11	03	07	-02
	Neurotic	15	06	10	16^c	12	-02	13	08
	Psychotic	-05	06	-18	-01	05	00	-03	02
	Lie	11	14	27^b	14	11	28^b	18	21^c

[a] Decimals omitted.
[b] $p < .01$.
[c] $p < .05$.

reflected in the total score summing the three kinds of risk. However, some of the specific situations do elicit primarily one kind of risk in contrast to the others. The generality of risk appraisal tendency refers to subjects, not situations.

The total score on the SSS V correlated $-.42$ with total risk appraisal in males and $-.40$ in females. Both total risk and the three risk subscales correlated significantly with all of the SSS subscales—except Boredom Susceptibility (BS) in males—and with all of the subscales in females, the exceptions to this generalization are the insignificant correlations between punishment risk and disinhibition. The expected patterning of the correlations among the subscales of the risk and SS scales was not seen.

There was little correlation between the scales of the EPQ and the risk appraisal scales; only three of the 32 correlations were significant, and two of these were with the Lie scale, for which no predictions had been made. Most of the correlations were close to zero.

The significant correlations between sensation seeking and risk appraisal indicate that high sensation-seekers do tend to appraise novel situations as less risky than lows for all types of risk. This is not a surprising finding, but it was not inevitable. The high sensation-seeker might conceivably appraise risk like the low but might accept the higher risk in some new situations.

In view of Eysenck's (1967) theory, it is surprising that none of his dimensions is related to risk appraisal. The low correlations even rule out the possibility that risk appraisal is determined by an interaction of two dimensions such as extraversion and neuroticism. If there were an interaction, we would see low correlations with two or three of the dimensions, which might achieve significance in a multiple regression; instead we have essentially zero correlations with all dimensions.

The fact that risk appraisal is related to sensation-seeking trait posed difficulties in proceeding to the next stage of examining the relationships with sensation-seeking and anxiety states, since the same situations would tend to have different appraisals of risk for high- and low-trait sensation-seekers, and it is the risk appraisal that constitutes our independent dimension. In order to work with the dimension of risk appraisal, I had to find a subset of situations where there were no correlations between risk ratings and SSS trait scores. Another desideratum was that males and females have equivalent risk appraisal levels in order to combine the two sex groups in future analyses.

In examining the correlations between the risk ratings for each of the 50 situations and the SSS scores, a subset of situations in a common content area was found where SS trait and risk appraisal were not confounded. Five situations dealing with travel that met the criteria and covered a range of risk are given in Table 2 with the mean risk values and correlations with total SSS scores. The risk value used for these situations is physical-harm risk, since it was the primary type elicited by the travel situations.

Table 2. Mean Risk Ratings of Situations and Correlations with SSSV-Total

Travel situations	Mean risk rating		rs with SSS	
	Male	Female	Male	Female
Europe	1.5	1.7	−.15	.08
USA	2.1	2.4	−.09	−.03
Asia	3.1	3.0	−.07	−.11
Antarctica	5.2	4.9	−.03	−.09
Moon	5.4	5.9	−.13	−.10
Psychology experiment situations				
Social psychology experiments	2.1	2.1	−.13	−.26[a]
Hypnosis	3.7	4.1	−.15	−.37[a]
Taking drug	7.4	7.6	−.12	−.21[b]

[a] $p < .01$.
[b] $p < .05$.

Another small group of psychology experiment situations only partially met the criteria, since the risk ratings did not correlate significantly with SSS scores in males but did for females. The situations with the mean ratings on mental-harm risk and correlations are also given in Table 2. It was decided to analyze these situations as well in the next study, since we could look at the male and female results separately. These situations are also valuable because they can be studied as actual experimental as well as hypothetical situations.

1. Summary. Sensation seeking is negatively related to risk appraisal; that is, high sensation-seekers tend to evaluate many kinds of situations as less risky than lows. This conclusion holds for the three kinds of risk—physical, mental, and punishment harm—as well as for all of the SSS subscales with the exception of Boredom Susceptibility. The Eysenck dimensions of extraversion, neuroticism, and psychoticism are not related to risk appraisal. Two subsets of situations were found, one dealing with travel and another with psychology experiments, where correlations with the sensation-seeking trait were nonsignificant for males. These were useful for the next phase of the study: relating the situational dimension of risk to sensation-seeking and anxiety state responses.

I. State Responses to Hypothetical Situations

The travel and psychological experiment situations from form II of the Situation Inventory were included in a new form (III). This form called for anxiety (A) and sensation-seeking (SS) state responses to the situations, in place of the risk appraisal reactions called for in the last form. The A and SS scales consisted of abbreviated versions of the two state scales developed by Neary (1975). Using the factor loadings on the two state scales as the primary criterion for selection, 6 of the original 15 adjectives from each of the two scales were chosen for inclusion in the abbreviated form of the Sensation Seeking and Anxiety State Test (SSAST). Subjects were presented with each situation and asked to imagine themselves in the situation and describe how they thought they would respond by rating reactions on the 12 adjectives (1–5 scale).

A sample situation is given below:

A. You are about to start traveling in Asia. How would you feel? Rate 1 to 5 on scale for:

1. Frightened	7. Shaky
2. Elated	8. Worried
3. Pleased	9. Tense
4. Nervous	10. Playful
5. Enthusiastic	11. Panicky
6. Adventurous	12. Curious

Items 1, 4, 7, 8, 9, and 11 comprise the abbreviated A scale, and items 2, 3, 5, 6, 10, and 12 make up the SS scale. The last situation in the inventory was an attempt to determine the A and SS states in the current test situation. At the time the subjects finished the inventory, they were waiting for a second group experiment but had not been informed of the nature of the second study.

The subjects were 60 males and 111 females from the upper and lower 10% of the range of scores on the SSS V total. The SSS V had been previously administered to the three large sections of students taking introductory psychology. The students scoring at the extremes on the SSS were contacted by mail and asked to serve in a further study to fulfill a requirement of the course. They were assembled in large groups of about 100 subjects to take the Situation Inventory III.

The results were analyzed for each of the two sets of situations for A and SS scores, using an analysis of variance; the between-group factors consisted of trait sensation-seeking (high versus low) and sex of subject (male versus female), and the within-group factor consisted of the situations in each set.

Situations were a highly significant ($p < .001$) source of variance in all analyses. The A and SS scores for all subjects are plotted as a function of situations for the travel and the psychological experiment subsets in Figure 2.

Since our travel situations were selected from the highly novel end of the ratings of the first Situation Inventory, they did not include very-low-risk, familiar situations such as going down to Main Street in Newark, Delaware. Presuming that such a situation would elicit little or no state A or SS, the lines of the graph are extended to the expected ratings for zero risk. The statistical

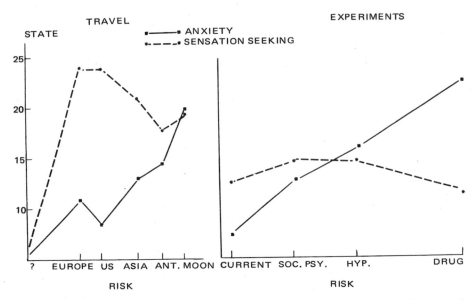

Figure 2. Anxiety and sensation-seeking state scores in response to hypothetical situations of increasing risk.

analyses, however, were done only on the five identified situations: travel in Europe, in the USA, in Asia, in Antarctica, and to the moon. For the psychology experiments, the current state was put at the low end of the risk dimension since it was obtained in an innocuous large-group situation, and three other situations ranging along the risk dimension included being in a social psychology experiment, in a hypnosis experiment, and in a drug experiment where they would be asked to take an unknown drug. The situations are ranged along the abscissa in rough proportion to their rated risk values in the second study using the most relevant risk dimension for each of the subsets (physical risk for travel, mental-harm risk for experiments).

Within the travel situations sampled, sensation-seeking trait decreased with increased risk of situation in a linear fashion, with a slight reversal between the last two situations; and anxiety increased directly with risk, with a slight reversal between the first two situations. If we accept the hypothesis that a very familiar travel situation of zero risk would elicit no state A or SS, then the curve for A would be linear and the curve for SS would be curvilinear as postulated in the model pictured in Figure 1. The fact that the curves do not cross as they do in Figure 1 may be a function of the lack of equivalance in the two unstandardized state scales or the range of risk in the sampled situations. What was not anticipated in the model was the fast rise of SS state in a minimal-risk situation. The results for the experiment situations conform more directly to the model, with a straight linear increase in A state and a curvilinear increase and decrease of SS state, with the two curves crossing.

SS trait was a significant source of variance for both A and SS states in both sets of situations; sex was a significant source of variance for the A state, but not for the SS state, in both sets of situations. The interactions f SS trait and situations, and sex and situations were significant for both A and SS states in both sets of situations. The SS trait and situation interactions are shown in Figures 3 to 5.

Figure 3 shows the interactions for the A and SS states in the travel situations. Overall, high-SS trait subjects reported *less* A state than lows but the differences between highs and lows were not significant for the low-risk situations (Europe and USA) and were significant for the high-risk situations (Asia, Antarctica, and the moon).

Overall, the high-SS trait subjects had *higher* SS states, and the differences were significant for all situations, but the differences got larger as the risk value of the situations increased, producing the interaction effect.

Figure 4 shows the interactions for the A and SS states in the psychology experiment situations, including the current one placed at the low-risk end. Again, the high-SS trait subjects showed *less* A state and *greater* SS state than the lows in these situations. For both A and SS states, the differences between high and low SS trait subjects were not significant in the current low-risk situation, but the differences became larger and more significant (from .05 to .001 levels) with increasing riskiness of the situations (from a social psychology to a drug-taking experiment).

A significant triple interaction justifies breaking down the results further, looking at males and females separately, and the results for males are shown in

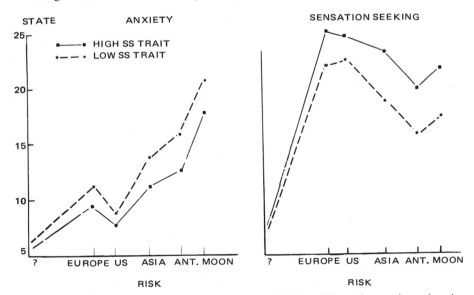

Figure 3. Anxiety and sensation-seeking state scores of high- and low-trait sensation-seekers in response to hypothetical travel situations of increasing risk.

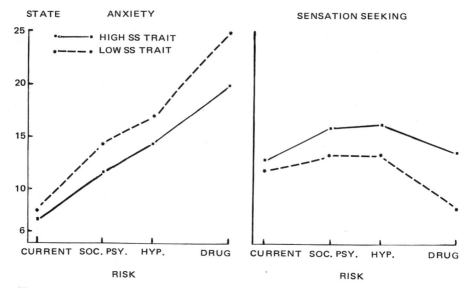

Figure 4. Anxiety and sensation-seeking state scores of high- and low-trait sensation-seekers in response to hypothetical psychological experiments of increasing risk.

Figure 5. While both high- and low-trait SS females showed a significant decrease in SS state for the high-risk drug experiment, the high-SS trait males had no decrease in SS state and only a minimal and insignificant increase in A state going from the hypnosis to the drug situation. The results for males are particularly significant in view of the fact that risk appraisal was not correlated

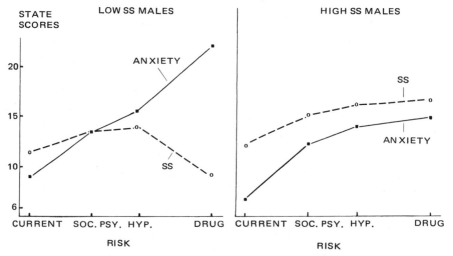

Figure 5. Anxiety and sensation-seeking state scores of high- and low-trait male sensation-seekers in response to hypothetical psychological experiments of increasing risk.

with SS trait for this set of situations in the prior study (see Table 2), whereas they were correlated for females.

1. Summary. The findings from these studies of reactions to hypothesized situations are summarized below:

1. High sensation-seekers appraise many situations as less risky than do lows.

2. When risk appraisal of high and low sensation-seekers is equivalent, highs report a reaction of less anxiety and more positive affect, or sensation-seeking state arousal.

3. The differences between high and low sensation-seekers on A and SS states are less in low-risk than in high-risk situations.

4. For high sensation-seekers, particularly the male highs, there is little increase in anxiety and little drop in sensation seeking in response to high-risk situations in terms of the model proposed. This means that they would be more prone to enter into such high-risk situations since sensation-seeking state would tend to remain stronger than anxiety state in contrast to the lows, where the rise in anxiety state and drop in sensation-seeking state should produce withdrawal or avoidance.

The data from the psychology experiments are quite compatible with the findings of significant correlations between SS trait scores and the willingness to be in hypnosis and drug experiments (Bone, Cowling, & Choban, 1974; Zuckerman, Schultz, & Hopkins, 1967) and the correlations between the SSS and experimentation with drugs in college students (Segal & Singer, 1976; Zuckerman et al., 1972). Neary's (1975) study showed that when subjects were actually offered the opportunity to take an unknown drug in an experimental context, A state increased more in high-SS trait subjects than in lows, and both the SS and A states interacted to affect their decisions as to whether or not they would take the drug. Although the SSS trait measure correlated with these states in the situation, it could not be used to predict the decision directly.

The results support a two-factor theory of sensation-seeking behavior. Persons high on this trait judge many novel situations as less risky than do lows. In the actual presence of high-risk situations, they respond with less anxiety and more of the surgency–elation affect (or joy–interest or positive affect) typical of the SS state. This combination of states is likely to result in behavioral choices to approach or enter into such risky situations. If the consequences of the interaction are rewarding in providing a pleasurably arousing experience with no pain or punishment, the risk appraisal will probably be lowered, increasing the probabilities of seeking out the situation again.

II. SENSATION SEEKING AND PSYCHOPATHOLOGY

Most of the work on sensation seeking in abnormal groups has been done with prisoners, delinquents, sociopaths, and drug offenders. Quay's (1965)

Table 3. Correlations[a] between the General SS Scale and the MMPI

	College[b] (Male	Female)	Psychiatric offenders—males[c]	Felons[d] (Male	Female)	Psychiatric patients (mostly schizophrenic)[e] males
n's	60	82	83	42	65	78
MMPI						
Hs	06	18	05	−30[f]	00	−09
D	−06	06	−18	−18	00	−30[g]
Hy	03	16	−04	−26	01	−08
Pd	10	32[g]	25[f]	−08	11	11
Mf	−10	04	10	−07	16	13
Pa	16	19	27[f]	−26	14	08
Pt	20	10	14	−26	05	−02
Sc	22	24[f]	22[f]	−04	13	07
Ma	30[f]	41[g]	47[g]	47[g]	40[g]	44[g]
Si	−10	−14	−01	−12	07	−25[f]

[a] Decimals omitted.
[b] From Zuckerman et al. (1972).
[c] From Blackburn (1969).
[d] From Thorne (1971).
[e] From Daitzman & Tumilty (1974).
[f] $p < .05$.
[g] $p < .01$.

hypothesis linking psychopathy to sensation seeking probably accounts for this concentration. However, there are theories and some cogent data suggesting a link between sensation seeking and mania, schizophrenia, and phobic neurosis.

Table 3 shows the correlations between the Minnesota Multiphasic Personality Inventory (MMPI) scales and the General SSS in four studies, one using college males (Zuckerman et al., 1972), two using criminal offenders (Blackburn, 1969; Thorne, 1971), and one using psychiatric patients, primarily schizophrenic (Daitzman & Tumilty, 1974). In every one of these samples, the general sensation-seeking tendency correlated significantly with the Hypomania (Ma) scale. Significant correlations with the Psychopathic Deviate (Pd) scale were found in only two samples, although it correlated more highly with the Experience Seeking and Disinhibition subscales in the college population.

A. Psychopathic Personality and Delinquency

Although Blackburn (1969) and Hare (1978) found no relationship between the SSS and clinical diagnoses and ratings of psychopathy, two studies have found that when primary psychopaths are diagnosed from test criteria aimed at separating the primary and secondary types, the primary types do score higher on some of the SS scales than other groups of prisoners.

Emmons and Web (1974) separated a group of prison inmates who peaked on the MMPI Psychopathic Deviate scale and divided them into two groups: (1) a group who scored low on the Total Anxiety Reactivity score of Lykken's (1968) Activity Preference Questionnaire; (2) a group who scored high on this anxiety scale. The first group were defined as primary psychopaths (P) and the second group as secondary (S) or acting-out neurotic types. Both of these groups were compared to other normal prison inmates (NP) on the SSS IV.

Table 4 shows the means of the three groups on the SSS IV; the significant differences are indicated by the subscripts. The primary (P) psychopaths were significantly higher than the secondary types (S) and the normal prisoners (NP) on the Disinhibition (Dis), Experience Seeking (ES), and Boredom Susceptibility (BS) scales. The three groups did not differ on the General or Thrill and Adventure Seeking (TAS) scales.

In a similar kind of study, Blackburn (1978) classified psychiatric offenders as primary and secondary psychopaths and nonpsychopaths on the basis on MMPI scores. The MMPI criteria were based on a prior cluster analysis of offenders' MMPIs. Psychopaths were diagnosed as those with a peak on the Psychopathic Deviate scale and a high score on an Impulsivity scale. The primary psychopaths were those scoring above the mean on a Sociability scale, and the secondary psychopaths were defined as those below the mean on sociability. The two psychopathic groups differed from the nonpsychopathic group in being less socialized and more impulsive, aggressive, and assaultive. The psychopathic groups differed from each other in that the secondary group was also more socially withdrawn, anxious, and introverted than the primary group.

The means of the three groups on the SSS are shown in Table 4. The primary psychopath (P) group was significantly higher than the secondary group (S) on the Thrill and Adventure Seeking and Disinhibition scales and

Table 4. Comparisons between Primary (P) and Secondary (S) Psychopathic and Nonpsychopathic (NP) Prisoners on the SSS IV

	Emmons & Webb (1974)				Blackburn (1978)			
	P	S	NP	F	P	S	NP	F
	20	20	20	df = 2/57	12	13	20	df = 2/42
SSS								
Gen	12.0^a	9.7^a	9.6^a	2.53	11.2^a	8.8^a	6.0^b	6.16^d
TAS	10.4^a	9.6^a	9.1^a		9.9^a	6.5^b	5.5^b	5.60^d
ES	9.6^a	6.8^b	7.2^b	4.98^d	9.1^a	6.5^a	4.5^b	7.32^d
Dis	8.7^a	5.7^b	5.2^b	7.83^d	8.1^a	5.5^b	3.0^c	14.69^d
BS	7.1^a	4.0^b	5.2^b	7.16^d	6.9^a	5.9^a	3.8^b	6.97^d

a,b,c Means with the same subscript are not significantly different.
d $p < .01$.

was significantly higher than the normal, or nonpsychopathic, prisoner group (NP) on all of the scales. The secondary psychopathic group was significantly higher than the normal prisoner group on the Disinhibition and the Boredom Susceptibility scales.

Although the two studies used somewhat different types of test criteria in defining the primary and secondary psychopath groups, there is some consistency in the results. In general, the primary psychopaths were higher in sensation seeking than the other two groups. The Disinhibition scale, in particular, showed this difference most clearly in both studies. Zuckerman (1978b) has suggested that the Disinhibition scale is the one linked more closely with psychopathy.

A surprising finding in Blackburn's study was that the primary psychopaths showed evidence of higher initial physiological arousal on both EEG and skin conductance indices. Hare's (1978) studies have suggested that psychopaths have lower basal arousal than nonpsychopaths. However, the primary psychopaths showed signs of more rapid cortical dearousal but slower skin conductance habituation to the stimuli.

The data do not support the view of the psychopath as an underaroused person who seeks intense and varied stimulation in order to raise his level of arousal to a normal optimum. However, psychophysiological studies of sensation seeking (Neary & Zuckerman, 1976) have not found any differences in basal levels of arousal using the SSS to define the criterion groups from college populations. What did distinguish the high and low sensation-seekers in the latter study was the stronger electrodermal (skin conductance) response of high sensation-seekers to stimuli when they were novel. Highs and lows did not differ in response to nonnovel or repeated stimuli, but whenever a new stimulus was presented, the highs showed a stronger response. These data were interpreted as evidence of a hyperarousability to novelty, which might set a high optimal level for subsequent stimuli in the high sensation-seeker.

In Blackburn's (1978) study there were no differences between the groups in skin-conductance, heart-rate, or blood-pressure responses to simple novel stimuli. Some previous studies (Borkovek, 1970; Hare, 1968) have actually found a hypoarousability of the psychopath in response to such stimuli. The Neary and Zuckerman (1976) data seem to reveal a psychophysiological characteristic of the high sensation-seeker that is not found in the psychopath. Behaviorally the characteristic of strong orienting reflexes is associated with alertness, interest, and freedom from distracting states of anxiety (Neary & Zuckerman, 1976). Perhaps the psychopath is more selective than normal sensation-seekers and might show a strong orienting reflex if the stimuli were more relevant for his reward system.

Thorne (1971) compared groups of felons, younger delinquents, and mentally ill patients. In view of the previously discussed findings, one would not expect to find a difference between an unselected group of delinquents or criminals and other groups, since any unselected group of criminals would contain both primary and secondary psychopaths as well as nonpsychopathic types. After age adjustments to his data, Thorne found that female felons and delinquents were higher than mentally ill females, but the differences for males were not significant.

Farley and Farley (1972) found that the SSS was related to behavioral differences within groups of incarcerated female delinquents. The high scorers on the General SSS made more escape attempts, were punished more often for disobeying supervisors, and engaged in fighting more than lows. Farley (1973) found similar results for male delinquents. Much of the behavior of sensation-seeking delinquents may be viewed as attempts to raise their levels of arousal and an intolerance for unstimulating or unchanging environments.

B. Drug Abusers

Zuckerman (1972) has suggested that drug use is one expression of the sensation-seeking trait. There is ample evidence from studies of college students (Segal, 1976; Zuckerman, 1972; Zuckerman et al., 1972) that the tendency to experiment with varied drugs—particularly marihuana, hashish, amphetamines, cocaine, and LSD and other hallucinogens—is a characteristic of high sensation-seekers in college. Drug use did not correlate only with the Experience Seeking scale (which contains two items on drugs) in these studies; it also correlated with other scales that have no specific content relevant to drug use. In the large-scale studies of Segal and Singer (Segal, 1976), the correlations between the SSS and drug use were just as high without the SSS drug items as with them.

In this section, I will discuss studies dealing with drug users defined as a clinical group. Most of these subjects were from therapeutic groups consisting of persons who have been arrested in connection with drug abuse or related offenses. They were mostly a noncollege population from lower socioeconomic groups and were somewhat older than the college groups. For these reasons, their mean scores cannot be compared with college norms but must be compared within their own populations.

Kilpatrick et al. (1976) compared groups from a representative sample of young male consecutive admissions to a Veterans Administration Hospital. The subjects were hospitalized on medical, surgical, psychiatric, and substance-abuse wards of the hospital. On the basis of information from individual interviews regarding personal drug and alcohol use, they were divided into the four categories shown in Table 5. The regular drug users reported addiction to heroin or barbiturates or a pattern of consistent polydrug use. Of the 25, 17 were polydrug users. The "problem drinker group" is labeled "alcoholic" in Table 5 because the criteria the authors used are those conventionally used for

Table 5. Comparisons of Drug Users, Alcoholics, Nonusers

	Kilpatrick et al. (1976)					Platt (1975)		
	Drug	Alcohol	Occasional	Nonusers	F	Heroin	Nonaddicts	F
n	25	28	109	54		27	20	
Gen	13.4^a	9.8^b	9.5^b	7.6^c	12.32^e	10.0	8.3	5.94^d
TAS	10.3^a	7.5^b	8.0^b	6.8^c	6.16^e	9.5	8.9	2.67
ES	11.7^a	7.7^b	7.2^b	4.9^c	22.21^e	8.0	6.2	5.83^d
Dis	8.8^a	6.6^b	5.8^b	4.2^c	16.89^e	6.6	6.1	1.53
BS	8.0^a	7.6^a	5.8^b	4.2^c	16.37^e	6.4	5.7	2.20

a,b,c Means with the same subscript are not significantly different.
d $p < .02$
e $p < .01$.

the diagnosis of acute alcoholism. The third category is occasional users and includes those who reported use of drugs or alcohol that was not extensive or associated with medical, legal, social, or occupational problems. This was the modal group in the population. The fourth group, called *nonusers*, reported no use of drugs or alcohol. The mean ages of the groups ranged from 27 to 29 years of age, with no significant differences among groups.

As seen in Table 5, comparisons between the groups yielded significant F values for all of the SSS IV scales. The drug abusers scored significantly higher than the alcoholics on all of the scales except Boredom Susceptibility (BS). The alcoholics did not score significantly higher than the occasional users, except on the BS scale. The occasional users scored significantly higher than the nonusers (who were abnormally low) on all of the SS scales.

Similarly to the results with college students, drug abuse in this population seemed to be associated with a high level of a general sensation-seeking trait. In contrast, alcoholics differed from the modal, nonuser group only on Boredom Susceptibility. The nonuser group was characterized by a low general level of sensation seeking on all scales.

Platt (1975) compared groups of heroin addicts and nonaddicts from a group of consecutive admissions to a youth correctional center. The groups were of average intelligence and in their teens. Their mean SSS scores are shown in Table 5.

The heroin addicts, who constituted about 65% of this population, scored significantly higher on the General and Experience Seeking scales. They were also higher on the other scales, but not significantly so. The fact that a group composed specifically of heroin addicts scored higher than nonaddicts on the SSS is interesting but posed some difficulty for an optimal level of arousal theory. Since heroin is a physiological depressant, its most extended effect is a low level of arousal ("nodding"), although there is a high "rush" experienced at the time of injection. This latter effect tends to habituate in experienced users; since the addicts in this study were still quite young, they might still have been enjoying the stimulant effects of heroin.

Several studies have explored the relationship between sensation seeking and the preferred type of drug within populations of drug abusers. Murtaugh (1971) compared three groups from a prison population: (1) those with a history of depressant drug (heroin and other opiates) use; (2) those with a history of stimulant (amphetamine, cocaine, and LSD) use; (3) a nonuser group who used nothing but alcohol or marijuana. All groups were matched for age, education, and IQ, and all but four subjects were black. They were tested on the SSS II General scale. The heroin users scored significantly *lower* than the nonuser group, and the stimulant users scored significantly *higher* than the nonusers. These results are what would be expected, on the assumption that a drug abuser who has a preferred drug will choose that drug for its effects on arousal, low sensation-seekers preferring depressant drugs and highs preferring stimulant and psychedelic drugs. However, judging from Platt's findings, only the higher sensation-seekers will take the risks associated with the use of any drug.

Another study by Skolnick (1977) compared groups of hard (heroin and opiate) users with a group of soft (amphetamine, hallucinogen, barbiturate) drug users. Part of his sample came from persons admitted to two therapeutic communities for hard and soft drug abusers, and part came from a prison population. The latter group was classified, by the use of drug history, into hard- and soft-drug users. Table 6 shows that the soft-drug users are significantly higher than hard-drug users on the General and Boredom Susceptibility scales of the SSS IV. The finding on the General scale supports Murtaugh's finding, since the hard-drug user was a depressant user and the soft-drug user was primarily a stimulant or polydrug user, although in this case there was no nonuser sample to compare with the two drug groups.

Table 6. Comparisons of Different Types of Drug Users

	Skolnick (1977)			Carrol & Zuckerman (1977)					
	Hard drugs	Soft drugs	F	High depressant	Low depressant	t	High hallucinogen	Low hallucinogen	t
n	52	44		40	40		40	40	
Gen	10.4	12.2	3.76[a]	11.1	11.8	0.9	12.1	10.7	1.7
TAS	8.7	9.8	2.32	9.5	10.0	0.8	10.3	9.3	1.4
ES	9.1	10.5	2.06	9.5	11.0	2.2[a]	11.1	9.3	2.8[b]
Dis	6.8	6.7	.05	7.0	7.4	0.7	7.7	6.6	2.0[a]
BS	6.2	6.8	3.37[a]	7.3	7.5	0.3	7.8	7.0	1.8

[a] $p < .05$.
[b] $p < .01$.

A study by Carrol and Zuckerman (1977) defined three types of drug use—depressant, stimulant, and hallucinogenic—on a scale derived from the drug history. In the published study, correlations are presented between the SSS scales and the scales for the three drug types, partialling out the effects of age, race, and IQ. Low but significant correlations were found between the Disinhibition scale and the Stimulant and Hallucinogen experience scales. A negative correlation was found between the Experience Seeking scale and experience with depressant drugs. Table 6 shows the differences between groups formed on the basis of median splits on two of the drug experience scales. These *F*s are not controlled for the variables partialled in the correlations. No differences were found on the stimulant experience scale, so it is not shown in the table. When the group is divided on the basis of experience with depressant drugs (mostly heroin), the high users score significantly *lower* than the low users on the Experience Seeking scale. When the group is divided on the basis of experience with hallucinogens, the high users score significantly *higher* on the Experience Seeking and Disinhibition scales.

On the basis of all of these studies, a theory of drug abuse may be formulated. The initial tendency to experiment with drugs of any type other than alcohol seems to be characteristic of high sensation-seekers. At this point, the sensation seeker is looking for a new experience and may be less concerned with the effects of particular drugs. After experimenting, the very-high sensation-seekers continue to use a variety of drugs, looking for new and varied experiences or develop a preference for the more stimulating drugs like amphetamine, which produce direct CNS activation and euphoria, or psychedelic drugs, which produce new and varied perceptual and emotional experiences. The relatively lower sensation-seekers fix upon drugs that produce low arousal levels and keep them "cool" emotionally. This is not to deny the importance of social factors in drug experimentation and choice but to call attention to what seems to be an important and often overlooked personality factor.

It should also be emphasized that a high proportion of drug abusers are also psychopathic personalities. After treatment in a therapeutic community, about two-thirds of the MMPI profiles of the former drug abusers show the classical "4-9" psychopathic pattern (Zuckerman, Sola, Masterson, & Angelone, 1975). Sensation seeking is relevant to both patterns, and drug use is one form that "pathological sensation-seeking" may take.

C. Mania

Although no studies have been done giving the SSS to a sample of clinical manics, there are a considerable number of data suggesting that mania may represent an extreme of the genotype underlying sensation seeking, or the failure of a homeostatic feedback system that is neurophysiological and/or biochemical and on which the sensation seeker has a high set-point. As I have noted early, the most characteristic MMPI correlate of the SSS in normals, prisoners, and clinical patients is the Hypomania scale. This suggests that the high sensation-seeker may have a cyclothymic personality, although the lack of correlation with depression suggests that he may swing between high and normal rather than high and low.

Buchsbaum and Pfefferbaum (1971) developed a measure of cortical reactivity based on changes in the amplitude of the averaged evoked response (AER) to stimuli varying in intensity. The slope of the relationship between stimulus intensity and the AER is used to define the "augmenting–reducing" continuum. High augmenters show a positive slope, while reducers have a zero or negative slope, showing little increase of AER with increasing intensity of stimulation, and often a marked reducing of response at the highest intensities. Reducing seems to represent some kind of feedback inhibitory control in the CNS that protects the cortex from overexcitation from stimulation.

Buchsbaum, Landau, Murphy, and Goodwin (1973) have shown that augmenting is a characteristic of bipolar (manic–depressive, cyclic type) patients as opposed to unipolar (depressive psychosis) types of patients. Lithium, used to smooth out the manic's mood swings, also tends to change augmenting to reducing patterns (Buchsbaum, Goodwin, Murphy, & Borge, 1971). The augmenting characteristic of untreated (with lithium) manic–depressives appears to be a trait rather than a state, for it remains stable even when they are not in the manic condition.

Buchsbaum (1971) first suggested that the augmenting–reducing characteristics of normals might be related to the sensation-seeking trait. His results in a pilot study were positive, but not significant. Zuckerman, Murtaugh, and Siegel (1974) tested the hypothesis that high sensation-seekers were augmenters and lows were reducers by correlating the SSS with the AER–stimulus intensity slope in 49 college students. The stimuli were flashing lights of different intensities. The augmenting measure correlated positively with all of the scales, but an outstanding significant correlation of .59 ($p < .00005$) was found with the Disinhibition scale. Comparing the amplitudes of the AER of high- and low-scoring subjects on Disinhibition, it was found that their AER did not differ at the lowest stimulus intensity, but the slope difference was primarily produced by the marked augmenting of the high sensation-seekers at the highest stimulus intensity and the marked reduction in the low sensation-seekers at that intensity. The pattern of correlation of the augmenting measure with the SS scales was the same as that of the SS scales with the MMPI Hypomania scale.

While the findings of the Disinhibition–augmenting correlation using visual stimuli has not yet been replicated, Coursey, Buchsbaum, and Frankel (1975) found significant correlations between the General SS scale and augmenting to auditory stimuli.

Another area of convergence between sensation seeking and manic tendencies has emerged in studies of the enzyme monoamine oxidase (MAO). Oxidative deamination by MAO represents a major degradative metabolic pathway for various biogenic amines, such as norepinephrine, serotonin, and dopamine. High levels of MAO in the brain would deplete these neurotransmitters and presumably reduce the excitability of the pathways and structures where such depletion occurred. Drugs that inhibit MAO were among the first antidepressant drugs, and they seem to have the behavioral effect of increasing activity in depressed patients. Murphy and Weiss (1972) found that a group of bipolar manic–depressive patients had significantly reduced platelet MAO levels compared to both controls and unipolar depressed patients. The unipolar depressives did not have levels of MAO that differed from normal controls. Among the affective disorders, a reduced MAO level appears to be characteristic of the cyclic manic–depressive type.

Murphy and his co-workers have been interested in the relation between MAO levels and personality in normals. Murphy, Belmaker, Buchsbaum, Wyatt, Martin, and Ciaranello (1977) correlated platelet MAO with the SSS IV in 30 male and 65 female college students. Significant negative correlations were found between MAO and the General ($r = -.45$), Disinhibition ($r = -.51$), and Boredom Susceptibility ($r = -.34$) scales of the SSS, but the correlations in females were not significant. In a subsequent study, Schooler, Zahn, Murphy, and Buchsbaum (1978) correlated platelet MAO and the SSS in 46 male and 47 female college students. Significant negative correlations of MAO were found with the General SS scale in both males ($r = -.52$) and females ($r = -.43$) and with the Experience Seeking scale in males ($r = -.43$) and females ($r = -.42$). The other SS scales correlated significantly with MAO in the combined group of males and females.

1. Summary. All of these data make it appear that augmenting of the AER at high stimulus intensities and low MAO levels are characteristic of both bipolar manic–depressives in the clinical population and high sensation-seekers in the normal population. The high sensation-seekers also tend to have high scores on the Hypomania scale of the MMPI. While all of these data are correlational and many of the connecting links (such as the relation between MAO, the neurotransmitters, and augmenting) are missing, the total pattern suggests that a common physiological substrate may underlie both manic–depressive psychoses and sensation seeking. In this respect, it is interesting to note that both augmenting (Buchsbaum, 1974) and platelet MAO (Murphy, Belmaker, & Wyatt, 1974) are reliable individual traits that show strong heritability patterns in twin studies. Some major questions that emerge from these studies are (1) Does MAO play a role in the augmenting–reducing mechanism? (2) Is MAO part of the genotype underlying both sensation seeking and bipolar manic–depressive psychosis? (3) What is the role of neural states and traits?

D. Schizophrenia

Many theories of schizophrenia have postulated some kind of input dysfunction (Venables, 1964) characterized by a failure of filter mechanisms, so that the schizophrenic is bombarded with sensory stimuli with no ability to focus attention or separate foreground from background. Some of the subjective reports collected by McGhie and Chapman (1961) suggest an increase in the perceived intensity of visual and auditory stimuli in schizophrenia. Buchsbaum (1975) has theorized that reducing (of cortical response) may be a system that is overactive in some schizophrenics as a protection against sensory overload. All of these theories lead to the prediction that the schizophrenic is a low sensation-seeker. However, there are many varieties of schizophrenia. The low sensation seeking hypothesis would seem to apply most to the withdrawn, catatonic type whose behavior seems to have stimulus reduction as its aim. Grandiose, overactive schizoaffective or paranoid types might be expected to be high or moderate sensation seekers.

Brownfield (1966) compared alcoholic, schizophrenic, and other patients with normals on the SSS and found the clinical groups to be lower on a total item score than normals but not different from each other. Differences in age and education were not controlled in this study, and the normals were younger than the patients.

Kish (1970) compared groups of male chronic schizophrenics, general psychiatric patients, and normal hospital attendants. His groups did not differ in age or education. The schizophrenics scored significantly lower on the SSS II General scale than the normal controls, the alcoholics, and the general psychiatric group. The latter three groups did not differ significantly among themselves. The schizophrenics were subdivided on the basis of their scores on the SSS. Those schizophrenics scoring in the upper quartile were compared with the group in the lower quartile on their behavior ratings on six factors of a rating schedule. The group differed on one factor, Behavior Retardation; the low scorers were more behaviorally retarded than the highs. Kish summarized his results:

> The lowered SSS score appears to reflect the apathy of the schizophrenics as a group. Individually, the SSS appears to measure a trait related to alertness and interest in the environment, which is reflected in degree of ward activity. (p. 173)

Tumilty and Daitzman (1977) compared a group of older ($\overline{X}$ age = 52) chronic schizophrenics with a group of medical patients matched for age, education, and intelligence ($\overline{X}$ IQ = 106). The mean of the medical patients (8.17) on the General SSS was significantly ($p < .01$) higher than the mean of the schizophrenics (4.65).

Landau, Buchsbaum, and Carpenter (1975) applied the AER augmenting-reducing method (described previously in the section on mania) to groups of schizophrenics. As a group, schizophrenics were reducers on the first component of the AER, on which bipolar manic–depressives showed an extreme augmenting pattern. The schizophrenics showed lower mean amplitudes across intensities and no increase in amplitude with increasing intensity of stimulation. Their reducing was greater than that seen in normals as well as in bipolar patients. The most extreme reducing was seen early in hospitalization, with some shift toward augmenting later in hospitalization. Those who improved during hospitalization had shown a marded reducing pattern when they came in; all of the patients who worsened or were unchanged during hospitalization were augmenters.

The data tend to support the idea that reducing serves a protective function in schizophrenics, protecting them from sensory overload. Schizophrenics in which this function is lacking (augmenters) tend to worsen or not to improve during hospitalization. The finding that schizophrenics, as a group, are reducers is consistent with the finding that they score low on the SSS.

Low platelet MAO levels have been found in chronic hospitalized schizophrenics (Murphy & Wyatt, 1972) but not in acute schizophrenics (Carpenter, Murphy, & Wyatt, 1975), where levels were the same as in normals. The low MAO schizophrenics tended to have more severely impaired reality testing and more paranoid and grandiose delusions. On the basis of these data, we might hypothesize that a schizophrenic who is a high sensation-seeker, in contrast to the generally low level of the group, would also have a poorer prognosis. Both the AER and MAO studies suggest a protective function of AER reducing and high MAO levels in early schizophrenics.

E. Phobias

In many trait correlation studies, the SSS has shown little or no relationship with the dimensions of neuroticism or general anxiety. However, the study of Mellstrom, Cicala, and Zuckerman (1976) suggests that low sensation-seeking trait may predispose one toward phobias. Subjects in this study were unselected college students who were exposed, on different occasions, to three situations that are phobic for some persons: being asked to approach and pick up a snake; being asked to look down from an open balcony 16 stories high; and remaining alone in a totally dark room. Besides the general and specific measures of anxiety used to predict behavior in these situations, the authors used the Thrill and Adventure Seeking (TAS) subscale of the SSS. The TAS correlated negatively and significantly with almost all of the self-report, observer-rating, and behavioral indices of fear in all three situations: low sensation-seekers reported and demonstrated more fear than highs. The TAS correlated more highly and consistently with fear reactions than the general anxiety or neuroticism trait tests, and in the darkness situation, the SS subscale accounted for a significant portion of the variance, independent of the contribution of the specific fear of darkness itself.

The surprising predictive power of the SS–TAS was not confined to the snake or heights situations, where there were tangible threats of physical harm, but was even higher in the darkness exposure situation. Why should low sensation-seekers be more susceptible to phobic situations? The data from our earlier studies indicate that they tend to appraise novel situations as more risky and to react with more state anxiety than the high sensation-seekers. Under conditions where they are compelled to remain in a situation that has elicited fear (e.g., being caught in a stalled elevator or in a room during a power failure), they would easily develop a conditioned fear response to the generalized situation. The low sensation-seeker avoids the novel and prefers routine. We might also expect some obsessive–compulsive tendencies in the low sensation-seeker, but there is as yet no evidence to substantiate this hypothesis.

III. A BIOLOGICAL THEORY OF SENSATION SEEKING

Kish (1973) suggested that the Montgomery (1955) two-process theory might be applicable to sensation seeking. This theory proposes that both fear and exploratory tendencies are aroused by novel stimuli, creating an approach–avoidance conflict in the organism. Individual differences in sensation seeking are seen as resulting from variations in the characteristic strengths of the two component states involved in the conflict.

Previously (Zuckerman, 1974), I had questioned this theory on the basis of lack of an inverse relationship between sensation seeking and anxiety at the trait level. The subsequent research described in a previous paper (Zuckerman, 1976b), as well as this one, has demonstrated that sensation-seeking and anxiety states do interact at high levels of arousal and that the nature of the interaction depends upon trait levels of sensation seeking and degree of appraised risk in the situations. High sensation-seekers react with less anxiety and more sensation-seeking affect than lows, particularly to situations of high risk.

Gray's (1973) theory suggests sites for these two types of affect in the limbic system. What follows is an adaptation of his theory, combined with the biochemical theory of Stein (1974), extended to encompass the physiological data on sensation seeking. However, the biochemical bases of these systems are based on Stein's (1974) theory, which is at variance with Gray's on the role of norepinephrine. The theory will be stated in the declarative mode for simplicity of expression rather than absolute confidence.

The tendency to explore novel or risky situations is based on reactivity in the septal-lateral hypothalamic-medial forebrain bundle circuit, described by Olds and Olds (1965) as the "positive reinforcement" area. Gray (1973) suggested that this area is associated with "high susceptibility to signals of reward," approach behavior, and the trait of "impulsivity" in humans.

Sensation seeking is not an inappropriate term to use for the behavior controlled by this system, considering the insatiable responding of animals to the production of stimulation in these structures. Stein (1974) has suggested that norepinephrine and dopamine are the neurotransmitters that govern the rewarding characteristics of stimulation of these pathways. Gray disagrees with this view of norepinephrine as the primary mediator of reward. Gray discusses some of the issues in his chapter in this book. The theory I propose accepts Gray's structural distinctions and Stein's biochemical ones.

Anxiety, or fearfulness, is based on the sensitivity of the orbital-frontal septal hippocampal circuits discussed by Gray in this volume. The primary effect of activation in this "stop system" is inhibition of ongoing behavior. Stein suggests that serotonin is the primary transmitter in this system. The two systems provide two kinds of neural reaction that may be differentially experienced as positive or negative affect, or sensation seeking and anxiety states. There is neurophysiological evidence that the two systems interact; stimulation in the negative reinforcement area blocks response in the positive reinforcement area, but the converse influence is not found (Olds & Olds, 1965). This finding suggests a basis for the reduction of sensation-seeking states in most persons when anxiety is elevated by risky situations.

Novel stimuli reach the cortex directly through the thalamocortical system and stimulate general cortical arousal through the ARAS; the influx of information and arousal facilitates the appraisal process. Gray suggests that the hippocampus is also involved in the process of comparing stimuli in terms of past effects.

Situations that are appraised as risky activate both the approach (A) and inhibition (I) systems that produce differential patterns of reaction, related to the orienting (OR) or defensive physiological patterns. While the amount of general, tonic cortical arousal is similar in high and low sensation-seekers, the "A"-type reaction is stronger and the "I" reaction is weaker in the high sensation-seekers. This would explain the stronger OR in the high sensation-seekers in response to novel stimuli, as well as their tendency to approach such stimuli.

"A"-type reaction is characterized by the release of norepinephrine at hypothalamic and other limbic sites and dopamine in the striatum; norepinephrine sensitizes the reward mechanisms and dopamine mobilizes and facilitates approach responses (Stein, 1974). "I"-type reaction is characterized by the release of serotonin, which depresses behavioral activity (Barchas & Usdin, 1973). The relative balance between neurotransmitters and neuroregulators, such as MAO, determines the influence of the limbic systems on the cortex. Given a balance favorable to accumulation of transmitters, the cortex is able to respond to highly novel or intense stimuli and process such stimuli. High levels of neuroregulators, which deplete transmitters intraneuronally or inhibit their reuptake, or block receptor neurons, produce reduced cortical reactivity to high intensities of stimulation or novel stimulation. Low levels of such neuroregulators result in the accumulation of high levels of neuro-transmitters, particularly norepinephrine and dopamine.

At high levels of sensation-seeking state, produced by an excess of transmitters at the synapses of reward systems, persons will be receptive to the arousal produced by high-risk situations and may engage in manic or psychopathic behavior. When levels of transmitters in the reward systems are low, behavior is likely to be depressed, phobic, or schizoid and characterized by avoidance of or withdrawal from high-risk situations. The lack of natural protective neural inhibition produced by an excess of neurotransmitters may lead to behavioral attempts to reduce the intensity of stimulation through alcohol and depressant drug use or social withdrawal. Alternation of the chemical balance may produce bipolar manic–depressive behavior. This kind of breakdown of homeostatic control may be produced by another genetic factor other than the one producing sensation seeking.

This biological theory, described in more detail in Zuckerman (in press), sees a continuum from the risk-taking behavior of normal sensation-seekers to that of impulsive psychopaths, drug abusers, and manics and points toward new areas of research such as:

1. The relation between sensation-seeking trait and state and brain levels of norepinephrine and dopamine.
2. The effects of norepinephrine, dopamine, serotonin, and MAO on coritcal reactivity (augmenting–reducing) to novel or intense stimuli, activity, and exploration of novel environments. This kind of research could best be done on animals, where the relevant biochemicals can be directly delivered to the postulated brain sites of their influence or can be chemically blocked or depleted.

In the office of Hans Eysenck, there is a sign hanging on the wall that reads, "A theory is a policy not a creed." A change in theory is risky, but that is what sensation seeking is about.

REFERENCES

American Psychiatric Association. *Diagnostic and Statistical Manual*, 2nd ed. (DSM-II). Washington, D.C.: APA, 1968.

Barchas, J. & Usdin, E. *Serotonin and behavior*. New York: Academic Press, 1973.

Berlyne, D. E. *Conflict, arousal, and curiosity*. New York: McGraw-Hill, 1960.

Blackburn, R. Sensation seeking, impulsivity, and psychopathic personality. *Journal of Consulting and Clinical Psychology*, 1969, *33*, 571–574.

Blackburn, R. Psychopathy, arousal, and the need for stimulation. In R. D. Hare & D. Schalling (Eds.), *Psychopathic behavior*. New York: Wiley, 1978.

Bone, R. N., Cowling, L. W., & Choban, M. C. Sensation seeking and volunteering for experiments. Unpublished data from personal communication, 1974.

Borkovec, T. D. Autonomic reactivity to sensory stimulation in psychopathic, neurotic, and normal juvenile delinquents. *Journal of Consulting and Clinical Psychology*, 1970, *35*, 217–222.

Brownfield, C. A. Optimal stimulation levels of normal and disturbed subjects in sensory deprivation. *Psychologia*, 1966, *9*, 27–38.

Buchsbaum, M. Neural events and the psychophysical law. *Science*, 1971, *172*, 502.

Buchsbaum, M. Average evoked response and stimulus intensity in identical and fraternal twins. *Physiological Psychology*, 1974, *2*, 365–370.

Buchsbaum, M. Average evoked response augmenting/reducing in schizophrenia and affective disorders. In D. X. Freedman (Ed.), *Biology of the major psychoses*. New York: Raven Press, 1975.

Buchsbaum, M., Goodwin, F., Murphy, D., & Borge, AER in affective disorders. *American Journal of Psychiatry*, 1971, 128, 51–57.

Buchsbaum, M., Landau, S., Murphy, D., & Goodwin, F. Average evoked response in bipolar and unipolar affective disorders: Relationship to sex, age of onset, and monoamine oxidase. *Biological Psychiatry*, 1973, *7*, 199–212.

Buchsbaum, M., & Pfefferbaum, A. Individual differences in stimulus intensity response. *Psychophysiology*, 1971, *8*, 600–611.

Carpenter, W. T., Murphy, D. L., & Wyatt, R. J. Platelet monoamine oxidase activity in acute schizophrenia. *American Journal of Psychiatry*, 1975, *132*, 438–441.

Carrol, E. N., & Zuckerman, M. Psychopathology and sensation seeking in 'downers,' 'speeders,' and 'trippers': A study of the relationship between personality and drug choice. *International Journal of Addictions*, 1977, *12*, 591–601.

Coursey, R. D., Buchsbaum, M., & Frankel, B. L. Personality measures and evoked responses in chronic insomniacs. *Journal of Abnormal Psychology*, 1975, *84*, 239–249.

Daitzman, R. & Tumilty, T. N. Support for an activation–regulation deficit in schizophrenia. Implications for treatment. *Newsletter for Research in Mental Health and Behavioral Science*, 1974, *16*, 31–35.

Ellis, A. *Humanistic psychotherapy: The rational emotive approach*. New York: Julian Press, 1973.

Emmons, T. D. & Webb, W. W. Subjective correlates of emotional responsivity and stimulation seeking in psychopaths, normals, and acting-out neurotics. *Journal of Consulting and Clinical Psychology*, 1974, *42*, 620–625.

Eysenck, H. J. *Experiments with drugs*. New York: Pergamon Press, 1963.

Eysenck, H. J. *The biological basis of personality*. Springfield, Ill.: Thomas, 1967.

Eysenck, H. J., & Eysenck, S. B. G. *Manual of the Eysenck Personality Questionnaire*. London: Hodder and Stoughton, 1975.

Farley, F. H. Personal communication, 1973.

Farley, F. H., & Farley, S. V. Stimulus-seeking motivation and delinquent behavior among institutionalized delinquent girls. *Journal of Consulting and Clinical Psychology*, 1972, *39*, 140–147.

Freud, S. *The problem of anxiety*. New York: Norton, 1936.

Gray, J. A. Causal theories of personality and how to test them. In J. R. Royce (Ed.), *Multivariate analysis and psychological theory*. New York: Academic Press, 1973.

Hare, R. D. Psychopathy, autonomic functioning, and the orienting response. *Journal of Abnormal Psychology*, Monograph Supplement, 1968, *73* (3, Part 2), 1–24.

Hare, R. D. Electrodermal and cardiovascular correlates of psychopathy. In R. D. Hare & D. Schalling (Eds.), *Psychopathic behavior*. New York: Wiley, 1978

Hebb, D. O. Drives and the CNS (conceptual nervous system). *Psychological Review*, 1955, *62*, 243–254.

Kilpatrick, D. G., Sutker, P. B., & Smith, A. D. Deviant drug and alcohol use: The role of anxiety, sensation seeking and other personality variables. In M. Zuckerman & C. D. Spielberger (Eds.), *Emotions and anxiety: New concepts, methods and applications*. Hillsdale, N.J.: Erlbaum, 1976.

Kish, G. B. Reduced cognitive innovation and stimulus-seeking in chronic schizophrenia. *Journal of Clinical Psychology*, 1970. *26*, 170–174.

Kish, G. B. A developmental and motivational analysis of stimulus-seeking. Paper presented at symposium, "The sensation-seeking motive," at 81st meeting of the American Psychological Association, Montreal, August 1973.

Landau, S. G., Buchsbaum, M. S., & Carpenter, W. Schizophrenia and stimulus intensity control. *Archives of General Psychiatry*, 1975, *32*, 1239–1245.

Lindsley, D. B. Psychophysiology and motivation. In M. R. Jones (Ed.), *Nebraska symposium on motivation*. Lincoln, Neb.: University of Nebraska Press, 1957.

Lindsley, D. B. Common factors in sensory deprivation, sensory distortion, and sensory overload. In P. Solomon *et al.* (Eds.) *Sensory deprivation*. Cambridge, Mass.: Harvard University Press, 1961.

Lykken, D. T. Manual for the Activity Preference Questionnaire (APQ). Report No. PR-68-3 from the Research Laboratories, Dept. of Psychiatry, University of Minnesota, 1968.

Malmo, R. B. Activation: A neuropsychological dimension. *Psychological Review*, 1959, *66*, 367–386.

McGhie, A., & Chapman, J. Disorders of attention and perception in early schizophrenia. *British Journal of Medical Psychology*, 1961, *34*, 103–117.

McReynolds, P. Assimilation and anxiety. In M. Zuckerman & C. D. Spielberger (Eds.), *Emotions and anxiety: New concepts, methods, and applications*. Hillsdale, N.J.: Erlbaum, 1976.

Meichenbaum, D. H. *Cognitive behavior modification*. Morristown, N.J.: General Learning, 1974.

Mellstrom, M., Cicala, G. A., & Zuckerman, M. General versus specific trait anxiety measures in the prediction of fear of snakes, heights, and darkness. *Journal of Consulting and Clinical Psychology*, 1976, *44*, 83–91.

Montgomery, K. C. The relation between fear induced by novel stimulation and exploratory behavior. *Journal of Comparative and Physiological Psychology*, 1955, *48*, 254–260.

Murphy, D. L., Belmaker, R. H., Buchsbaum, M., Wyatt, R. J., Martin, N. F., & Ciaranello, R. Biogenic amine-related enzymes and personality variations in normals. *Psychological Medicine*, 1977, *7*, 149–157.

Murphy, D. L., Belmaker, R., & Wyatt, R. J. Monoamine oxidase in schizophrenia and other behavioral disorders. *Journal of Psychiatric Research*, 1974, *11*, 221–247.

Murphy, D. L., & Weiss, R. Reduced monoamine oxidase activity in blood platelets from bipolar depressed patients. *American Journal of Psychiatry*, 1972, *128*, 1351–1357.

Murphy, D. L., & Wyatt, R. J. Reduced monoamine oxidase activity in blood platelets from schizophrenic patients. *Nature*, 1972, *238*, 225–226.

Murtaugh, T. L. Perceptual isolation, drug addiction, and adaptation phenomena. Unpublished Master's thesis, Temple University, 1971.

Neary, R. S. The development and validation of a state measure of sensation seeking. Unpublished doctoral dissertation, University of Delaware, 1975.

Neary, R. S., & Zuckerman, M. Sensation seeking, trait and state anxiety, and the electrodermal orienting reflex. *Psychophysiology*, 1976, *13*, 205–211.

Olds, J., & Olds, M. E. Drives, rewards, and the brain. In F. Barron *et al.* (Eds.), *New directions in psychology II*. New York: Holt, Rinehart, & Winston, 1965.

Patrick, A. W., & Zuckerman, M. An application of the state–trait concept to the need for achievement. *Journal of Research in Personality*, 1977, *11*, 459–465.

Patrick, A. W., Zuckerman, M., & Masterson, F. A. An extension of the trait–state distinction from affects to motive measures. *Psychological Reports*, 1974, *34*, 1251–1258.

Payne, R. W., Matussek, P., & George, E. I. An experimental study of schizophrenic thought disorder. *Journal of Mental Science*, 1959, *105*, 627–652.

Platt, J. J. "Addiction-proneness" and personality in heroin addicts. *Journal of Abnormal Psychology*, 1975, *84*, 303–306.

Quay, H. C. Psychopathic personality as pathological stimulation seeking. *American Journal of Psychiatry*, 1965, *122*, 180–183.

Schlosberg, H. Three dimensions of emotion. *Psychological Review*, 1954, *61*, 81–88.

Schooler, C., Zahn, T. P., Murphy, D. L., & Buchsbaum, M. Psychological correlates of monoamine oxidase activity in normals. *Journal of Nervous and Mental Diseases*, 1978, *166*, 177–186.

Schultz, D. P. *Sensory restriction: Effects on behavior*. New York: Academic Press, 1965.

Segal, B. Personality factors related to drug and alcohol use. In D. J. Letteri (Ed.), *Predicting adolescent drug abuse: A review of issues, methods, and correlates*. Washington, D.C.: U.S. Government Printing Office, National Institute on Drug Abuse. Research Issues II. DHEW Publication No. (ADM) 72-299, 1976.

Skolnick, N. J. Personality change in chronic drug abusers: A comparison of treatment and no-treatment groups. Unpublished master's thesis. University of Delaware, 1977.

Spielberger, C. D. Theory and research on anxiety. In C. D. Spielberger (Ed.), *Anxiety and behavior*. New York: Academic Press, 1966.

Spielberger, C. D., Gorsuch, R. L., & Lushene, R. E. *The state–trait anxiety inventory (STAI) test manual for form X*. Palo Alto, Calif.: Consulting Psychologists Press, 1970.

Stein, L. Norepinephrine reward pathways: Role in self-stimulation, memory consolidation, and schizophrenia. *Nebraska Symposium on Motivation*. Lincoln: University of Nebraska Press, 1974.

Thorne, G. L. Sensation-seeking scale with deviant populations. *Journal of Consulting and Clinical Psychology*, 1971, *37*, 106–110.

Tumilty, T. N., & Daitzman, R. Locus of control and sensation seeking among schizophrenics: Extensions and replications. Unpublished manuscript, 1977.

Venables, P. H. Input dysfunction in schizophrenia. In B. A. Maher (Ed.), *Progress in experimental personality research*, Vol. 1. New York: Academic Press, 1964.

Wundt, W. M. *Grundzuge der physiologischen psychologie*. Leipsig: Engleman, 1873.

Zuckerman, M. The development of an affect adjective check list for the measurement of anxiety. *Journal of Consulting Psychology*, 1960, *24*, 457–462.

Zuckerman, M. Toward isolating the sources of stress in perceptual isolation. Paper presented in symposium, "Sensory deprivation research: Where do we go from here?" at meeting of American Psychological Association, Los Angeles, September, 1964.

Zuckerman, M. Theoretical formulations: I. In J. P. Zubek (Ed.), *Sensory deprivation: Fifteen years of research*. New York: Appleton-Century-Crofts, 1969.

Zuckerman, M. Dimensions of sensation seeking. *Journal of Consulting and Clinical Psychology*, 1971, *36*, 45–52.

Zuckerman, M. Drug usage as one manifestation of a "sensation-seeking" trait. In W. Keup (Ed.), *Drug abuse, current concepts and research*. Springfield, Ill.: Charles C Thomas, 1972.

Zuckerman, M. The sensation-seeking motive. In B. A. Maher (Ed.), *Progress in experimental personality research*, Vol. 7. New York: Academic Press, 1974.

Zuckerman, M. General and situation-specific traits and states: New approaches to assessment of anxiety and other constructs. In M. Zuckerman & C. D. Spielberger (Eds.), *Emotions and anxiety: New concepts, methods, and applications*. Hillsdale, N.J.: Erlbaum, 1976. (a)

Zuckerman, M. Sensation seeking and anxiety, traits and states, as determinants of behavior in novel situations. In I. G. Sarason & C. D. Spielberger (Eds.), *Stress and anxiety*, Vol. 3. Washington, D.C.: Hemisphere, 1976. (b)

Zuckerman, M. Sensation seeking. In H. London & J. Exner (Eds.), *Dimensions of personality*. New York: Wiley, 1978. (a)

Zuckerman, M. Sensation seeking and psychopathy. In R. D. Hare & D. Schalling (Eds.), *Psychopathic behavior*. New York: Wiley, 1978. (b)

Zuckerman, M. *Sensation seeking: Beyond the optimal level of arousal.* Hillsdale, N.J.: Erlbaum, in press.

Zuckerman, M., Bone, R. N., Neary, R., Mangelsdorf, D., & Brustman, B. What is the sensation seeker? Personality trait and experience correlates of the Sensation Seeking Scales. *Journal of Consulting and Clinical Psychology,* 1972, *39,* 308–321.

Zuckerman, M., Eysenck, S. B. G., & Eysenck, H. J. Sensation seeking in England and America: Cross-cultural, age, and sex comparisons. *Journal of Consulting and Clinical Psychology,* 1978, *46,* 139–149.

Zuckerman, M., Kolin, E. A., Price, L., & Zoob, I. Development of a Sensation Seeking Scale. *Journal of Consulting Psychology,* 1964, *28,* 477–482.

Zuckerman, M., & Lubin, B. *Manual for the Multiple Affect Adjective Check List.* San Diego, Calif.: Educational and Industrial Testing Service, 1965.

Zuckerman, M., Murtaugh, T., & Siegel, J. Sensation seeking and cortical augmenting-reducing. *Psychophysiology,* 1974, *11,* 535–542.

Zuckerman, M., Schultz, D. P., & Hopkins, T. R. Sensation seeking and volunteering for sensory deprivation and hypnosis experiments. *Journal of Consulting Psychology,* 1967, *31,* 358–363.

Zuckerman, M., Sola, S., Masterson, J., & Angelone, J. F. MMPI patterns in drug abusers before and after treatment in therapeutic communities. *Journal of Consulting and Clinical Psychology,* 1975, *43,* 286–296.

Editor's Introduction

Dahl's chapter reflects both his psychoanalytic training and his work as a research psychoanalyst, but his theory is distinctly different from current psychoanalytic conceptions of affects and motives. It has elements in common with contemporary emotion theories (e.g., emotions are fundamental human motivations), but there are elements distinct from all of them. To his identification with psychoanalysis and his knowledge of psychological theories of emotion he adds an evolutionary perspective.

He classifies emotions in terms of three dimensions: IT–ME, to–from (passive–active), and attraction–repulsion (positive–negative). He notes the similarity of these to Freud's three polarities: subject–object (or ego–world), pleasure–unpleasure, and active–passive. His three dimensions yield eight categories of emotion. Each of these emotions can be examined with respect to its object, self (me emotion) or not-self (it emotions); its motivational direction (to–from the object); and its affective quality (positive–negative). He views the initial and inevitable experience of novelty by the infant as inherently satisfying. The satisfying experience associated with novelty has elements in common with the emotions of interest and enjoyment (Singer, Chapter 1) and the positive affective component of sensation seeking (Zuckerman, Chapter 6).

Dahl, who uses the terms *emotions*, *affects*, and *feelings* more or less interchangeably, holds that there are three components of emotion: (1) a distinct perception (subjective experience or felt emotion); (2) a typical species-specific expression (facial and/or postural); and (3) an implicit wish and implied action (motive). The first two of these are among the components several of us attribute to the emotions. Some might consider the "implied action tendency" to be part of the subjective or experiential component, but the implicit-wish aspect of Dahl's third component is a distinctive feature of his theory. For the IT emotions, the implicit wish is for satisfaction, which is essentially appetitive in nature. This thesis leads Dahl to the bold and provocative conclusion that getting rid of an anger-producing situation is to anger as eating is to hunger or as orgasm is to sexual excitement.

Dahl sees the ME emotions as a system of internal or intrapsychic messages and signals, giving information about the status of the satisfaction or nonsatisfaction of one's appetites and wishes.

Dahl discusses a number of social and clinical implications of his theory. He maintains that there is a discrepancy between "the large amount clinicians 'know' about emotions and the confused place that emotions hold in our theories of personality and of behavior." He points out, for example, that clinicians already understand that the three components of an emotion can have different clinical characteristics and that a patient may repress one or all or any combination of them.

The Appetite Hypothesis of Emotions:

A NEW PSYCHOANALYTIC MODEL OF MOTIVATION

7

HARTVIG DAHL

I. INTRODUCTION

So much has been written and thought and felt about emotions that one has to be a little presumptuous to offer yet another hypothesis or model. Nearly every component of the model that I shall outline here has already been proposed in some form or other. Sometimes I have merely made explicit what has been vague or implicit, but I have also put the pieces together in an unfamiliar pattern. Although my own specific conceptual debts are extensive and will be made clear as I proceed, all have been incurred in the service of my commitment to psychoanalysis as a discipline of both *causal* and *becausal* explanations.[1]

I have felt encouraged to continue because, as Holt (1976) wrote:

> Its theory of motivation is at once the glory of psychoanalysis and its shame. What is loosely known as the theory of instincts includes both a number of Freud's most important and lasting insights and some of his most regrettable theoretical failings. It badly needs fundamental revision; but the process must be both radical and conservative—what is not good must be extirpated at the root, but what is good must be retained. (p. 158)

Holt went on to extirpate drives and retain wishes in his suggestions for a new model. Others, such as Bowlby (1969, 1973), Brenner (1974a,b, 1975), and

[1] By *becausal* I mean explanation in terms of "reasons."

HARTVIG DAHL • Downstate Medical Center, State University of New York, Brooklyn, New York.

Rubinstein (1974, 1977), have also proposed fresh and novel views of emotions and motivations. My own ideas have been developing for a dozen years, but it seems clear that others are hot on the trail along converging courses. I cannot now go into the detailed comparisons of these other views with my own, but I shall have occasion to refer briefly to each.

I shall begin the outline of the theoretical model with a three-dimensional classification scheme that defines eight major categories of emotions. Next, since the appetite hypothesis rests fundamentally on a particular definition of a wish, I shall present this definition in some detail. I shall then compare the essential properties of emotions and appetites and conclude that our emotions about objects are much like appetites and that our emotions without objects are feedback messages about the status of our appetites and wishes. Finally, after discussion of some clinical and social implications of the model, I shall indulge myself in a brief excursion into phylogenetic speculation.

In what follows, I take certain matters for granted. First, although I say nothing about an explicitly neurophysiological model, I assume that the brain is sufficient unto its emotional tasks. I must leave to others the exploration of how (see Arnold, 1960b, 1970; Pribram & Melges, 1969; Pribram, 1976).If I correctly understand Nauta's (1975) reviews of the limbic system and its connections, there is nothing inconsistent with the *appetite hypothesis* and much that is suggestively supportive of it. Second, I assume that the many bodily manifestations of emotion play their role in preparation for and participation in emotional behavior. But I also agree with Bindra (1969) that there is no *necessary* "physiological core . . . no distinctive autonomic or postural reaction" that sufficiently defines an emotion. Third, my perspective is evolutionary. Man was not constructed *de novo*, and he is not alone among animals in showing emotional behavior. Darwin's (1872) great contribution, standing long after his discredited Lamarckian explanations of the inheritance of behaviors, was his demonstration of the continuity of emotional expression in animals and man.

II. CLASSIFICATION

The classification of emotions that I shall describe in this section is a modified adaptation of de Rivera's (1962) "decision" theory of emotions. My choice of this particular classificatory scheme is based partly on my own aesthetic attraction to abstract *n*-dimensional conceptual spaces. But I will not further justify the choice, because I prefer to let its consequences speak for themselves. de Rivera postulated that a person encountering (or fantasying) an object arrives at an "end-decision" about how to relate to the object by making separate decisions on six orthogonal dimensions. Five of these dimensions consisted of two states (binary) and one of three states (ternary). Independent decisions on each of these dimensions yield 96 $(3 \cdot 2^5)$ intersections, each uniquely defining a single emotion.

Although I was intrigued by this attempt to account for so many different emotions, it also seemed that three of the dimensions were, in some hard-to-define way, more "basic" than the others. These three were called *subject–object*, *attraction–repulsion*, and *extensor–contractor*.[2] In a pilot study, Barry Stengel and I presented judges with de Rivera's description of each dimension separately and asked them to assign emotion words to one of the two polarities. Partly as a result of our judges' difficulties with the extensor–contractor dimension, I decided to redefine it as to–from. But my substitution of to–from was additionally determined by a notable correspondence with three dimensions that Freud (1915) proposed when he wrote:

> Perhaps we shall come to a better understanding of the several opposites of loving if we reflect that our mental life as a whole is governed by *three polarities*, the antitheses
>   Subject (ego)—Object (external world),
>   Pleasure—Unpleasure, and
>   Active—Passive.
> The antithesis ego–non-ego (external), i.e., subject–object, . . . remains, above all, sovereign in our intellectual activity and creates for research the basic situation which no efforts can alter. The polarity of pleasure–unpleasure is attached to a scale of feelings, whose paramount importance in determining our actions . . . has already been emphasized. The antithesis active–passive must not be confused with the antithesis ego-subject–external world-object. The relation of the ego to the external world is passive in so far as it *receives* stimuli *from* it and active when it *reacts to* these. (pp. 133–134) (latter italics added)

The correspondence between pleasure–unpleasure and attraction–repulsion posed no special problems and it seemed to me that Freud's definition of *active* and *passive* was really a directional idea corresponding to to–from. Stengel and I, using revised operational definitions of the three dimensions subject–object, attraction–repulsion, and to–from, had a new group of judges complete the classification of 371 emotion words (Dahl & Stengel, 1978).

The results, while differing in certain details from de Rivera's own earlier classification data, convinced me of the compelling quality of the eight categories produced by the three dimensions illustrated in decision tree form in Figure 1. Note that the subject–object dimension has been renamed *IT–ME*. A decision on this dimension produces two major categories of emotions: the IT emotions, in which there is an explicit object (with oneself as subject), and the ME emotions, in which one has no explicit object, that is, when one is oneself the implicit object. Separate decisions on each of the other two dimensions determine the particular emotion category. Thus, for example, an attraction to an object (ATTRACTION TO IT) yields an emotion such as love, and a

---

[2] De Rivera (1977) later revised his theory, changed two of the three major dimensions, reduced the total number to five, and transformed the theory into a thoroughly phenomenological theory of the interrelationships among emotions.

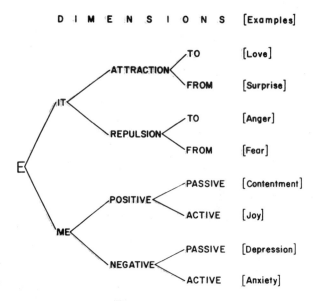

Figure 1. A three-dimensional classificatory tree. An emotion (E)
is defined by concurrent, independent decisions on each of the
hypothesized dimensions. The left–right sequence shown here is
arbitrary and corresponds to the one used by judges to classify
emotion words (de Rivera, 1962; Dahl & Stengel, 1978).

repulsion from an object (REPULSION FROM IT) would produce some sort
of fear.

For the ME emotions the *attraction–repulsion* demension is named
positive–negative, and the *to–from* becomes *passive–active*, but the underlying
concepts of the dimensions are assumed to remain unchanged.[3] Thus contentment is an example of a POSITIVE PASSIVE ME pattern of decision, and
anxiety is the result of NEGATIVE ACTIVE ME choices. It is further postulated that these hypothesized choices, though they are clearly "cognitive
appraisals" in Arnold's (1960a) sense, are largely unconscious. Only the result
of these decisions becomes conscious in the form of a distinctive perceptual
experience for each discriminable emotion. Of course there is nothing to
prevent a person from making preformed judgments about whole classes of
objects and thus being disposed to make particular decisions on the basis of the
class to which an object belongs rather than on the basis of a object's individual characteristics and behavior.

From the beginning of my work with de Rivera's "decision theory," I
understood his use of the term *end decision* to mean essentially what I meant

---

[3] The rationale for these terminology changes is complex and involves assumptions about the
nature of internalization processes (e.g., identification) that I cannot pursue here.

by a *wish*. So for me the dimensions provided, in effect, a fundamental classificatory scheme for wishes. Our next step, therefore, is to define what I mean by a wish, and in the course of that, it will also be necessary to redefine *pleasure* and *unpleasure*.

III. DEFINITION OF A WISH

In order to define a wish we will find it useful to go back 75 years to the seventh chapter of *The Interpretation of Dreams* (Freud, 1900). Here Freud eloquently described three basic concepts: (1) an experience of satisfaction, (2) perceptual identity, and (3) the definition of the wish in terms of these two concepts. Let me quote what has become a classic passage:

> The exigencies of life confront . . . [the baby] first in the form of the major somatic needs. The excitations produced by internal needs seek discharge in movement, which may be described as an "internal change" or an "expression of emotion." A hungry baby screams or kicks helplessly. But the situation remains unaltered, for the excitation arising from an internal need is not due to a force producing a *momentary* impact but to one which is in continuous operation. A change can only come about if in some way or other (in the case of the baby, through outside help) an "experience of satisfaction" can be achieved which puts an end to the internal stimulus. An essential component of this experience of satisfaction is a particular perception (that of nourishment, in our example) the mnemic image of which remains associated thenceforward with the memory trace of the excitation produced by the need. As a result of the link that has thus been established, next time this need arises a psychical impulse will at once emerge which will seek to re-cathect the mnemic image of the perception and to re-evoke the perception itself, that is to say, to re-establish the situation of the original satisfaction. An impulse of this kind is what we call a wish; the reappearance of the perception is the fulfillment of the wish. (pp. 565–566)

Freud then went on to imagine that there may have been a time when the reactivation of the perceptions of the need led to hallucinating the previous experience of satisfaction:

> A current of this kind . . . starting from unpleasure and aiming at pleasure, we have termed a "wish"; and we have asserted that only a wish is able to set the apparatus in motion. . . . The first wishing seems to have been a hallucinatory cathecting of the memory of satisfaction. (p. 598)

The boldness of this proposition seemed to have troubled even Freud, for he wrote in 1917 of the "*Fiktion*" of the hallucinatory gratification. He did not know that there even then existed startling evidence of its validity from a natural experiment (Dahl, 1965) that had already occurred. I refer to Helen Keller's (1908) report of the nature of her mental life before she had learned language. Referring to this time of "nothingness," she wrote:

> When I wanted anything I liked—ice cream, for instance, of which I was very fond—I had a delicious taste on my tongue (which, by the way, I never have now),

and in my hand I felt the turning of the freezer. I made the sign, and my mother
knew I wanted ice cream. (p. 115)

She quite literally hallucinated a previous experience of satisfaction[4]!

Whether or not one wants to take seriously the suggestion that the infant
really hallucinates in the beginning,[5] the model nonetheless offers a remarkably
useful definition of a wish: an attempt to achieve "perceptual identity" with a
previous "experience of satisfaction." If we start with this definition, it then
becomes possible to define pleasure and unpleasure in a way that is quite different from two common erroneous views. One of these is the misconceived
notion of "pleasure centers" in the brain that add some abstract quality called
pleasure to other ongoing cognitive and affective processes, a view that has
resulted from misinterpretations of experiments on intracranial self-stimulation (see Deutsch & Deutsch, 1966, Chapter 4, for a review). The other is the
early Freudian misconception of pleasure as a discharge of some energic
quantity and of unpleasure as a buildup of a similar quantity.

Instead I propose to redefine *pleasure as satisfaction of a wish* and
unpleasure as nonsatisfaction of a wish. Klein (1967) implied just this redefini-
tion when he wrote, "For Freud, pleasure (satisfaction) and unpleasure
(nonsatisfaction)— *affective qualities*—were much more important and closer
to central events of motivational sequence than rises or falls in tension" (p.
96). Freud (1924) himself understood that pleasure and unpleasure could not
be simply correlated with increases or decreases of a quantity but must depend
on some "qualitative" factors that, if they could be understood, would imply
an important advance in the psychology of motivation.[6]

The key to understanding the nature of the "qualitative" factors is to
realize that they include far more than the mere "affective qualities" of
pleasure and unpleasure. If we examine our "experiences of satisfaction," we
can easily recognize many specific sensory qualities (unique for each sensory
system) besides pleasure. In his peremptory ideation model, Klein (1967) specifically ascribed informational properties to such sensory qualities and postulated that appropriate sensations could "switch off" (i.e., satisfy) internal need
states. He defined pleasure as "switch-off" (or its anticipation) and unpleasure
as the absence of "switch-off" (or its anticipation).

It follows then that "perceptual identity" must be achieved by reinstating
(in some manner) specific sensory experiences similar to those of a previous
experience. Deutsch and Deutsch (1966) offer an evolutionary explanation of
why certain experiences are satisfying:

[4] Today we would probably describe this as a sensorimotor schema.

[5] Basch (1976), for example, flatly asserts that the hallucinatory model is impossible and incorrectly (in my judgment) uses Piaget to support his contention.

[6] For an extended and careful review of Freud's writings distinguishing pleasure and unpleasure as
principles of mental functioning from the affective qualities of pleasure and unpleasure, see Schur
(1966, pp. 125–193).

The most plausible way of interpreting experimental evidence on reward agrees well with common sense and introspection. It is the taste of water, the feeling of satiety, the sensations from the genitalia that an animal finds rewarding. The connection of these sensations with need reduction is not one which is made by each individual animal. Such a connection between reward and physiological deficit has been made by the process of natural selection. Only those animals which have found certain sensations rewarding have survived. Learning with physiological need reduction as reward has already occurred in the species; the individual need not recapitulate it. (pp. 143–144)

Which is to say that the capacity to find pleasure in the sensory experiences that also serve physiological needs has been wired in by evolution. Tomkins (1970) dramatically imagined what might happen if we were built differently:

Let us suppose that the hunger drive were "rewired" to be localized in the urethra, and the sex drive localized in the palm of the hand. For sexual satisfaction, the individual would first open and close his hand and then reach for a wide variety of "objects" as possible satisfiers, cupping and rubbing his hand until orgasm. When he became hungry he might first release the urethra and urinate to relieve his hunger. If this did not relieve it, he might use his hands to find objects which could be put inside the urethra, depending on just how we had rewired the apparatus. (p. 104)

Although such behavior would have negative survival value, people nonetheless often rewire themselves symbolically, and it would not surprise me in the least to find somebody with a classic conversion symptom of urethral discomfort when he was hungry! Certainly it is within the symbolic capability of the human being. Nonetheless there remains the core truth that there are quite specific perceptual requirements for the experiences of satisfaction capable of fulfilling the wishes that we have traditionally termed *somatic drives*.

Let us leave aside the obvious question of how we come to have the first experiences of satisfaction and instead ask how we would behave if we really take our new definition of a wish seriously. Remember, we have postulated that we only wish for repetitions of previous satisfactions. If this were the whole story, we should expect ourselves to behave in a very restricted and stereotyped manner, simply doing the same old things over and over. Thus far, there is nothing in the definition of a wish that would permit us to increase the range and variability of our experiences of satisfaction. In short, the definition does not appear to account for our exploratory, curious behavior. Thus the fact of our curiosity is a serious embarrassment unless we can explain the fact that we regularly search for novel perceptual experiences when our definition leads us to suppose that all we search for is identity—the opposite of novelty! And I do not want to seek refuge, as Rapaport (1960b) did, by simply asserting that curiosity is a cause of behavior, not a motive. So we shall have to look for another path out of this dilemma.

Suppose we view the experience of novelty as a derivative of the orienting response, whose defining feature is that of attending to a novel stimulus. Is it possible that we could discover a tendency to achieve "perceptual identity" in curiosity behavior and thus save our definition? In other words, could the attribute of novelty as such have the properties of a perception, of an experience of satisfaction? If so, then we might be inclined to attribute to novelty the same status we attribute to perceptions such as taste and smell and touch, which phylogeny has guaranteed that the organism finds pleasurable.[7] If novelty qua novelty were the object of a wish—that is, the object of a search for "perceptual identity"—then we would have to grant it the same primal motivating status granted by other experiences of satisfaction that evolution has associated with the regulation of bodily needs. Is there any such evidence?

Peter Wolff (1966) has presented data on human neonates that is relevant to this question. He reported that "in the first seven days smiling is observed only during irregular sleep and drowsiness, and never during regular sleep or when the infant is alert, fussy, or crying" (p. 77). This suggests that there is a wired-in program for the motor expression of smiling. He went on to describe smiling in somewhat older infants:

> Since smiling is not only a spontaneous discharge but also the response to particular qualities of stimulation, it is possible to identify the common elements in an array of physically unrelated stimulus conditions all evoking the smile, and by a method of "stimulus equivalence" . . . to penetrate beyond physical properties of the stimulus to arrive at its "meaning" for the organism. . . . The element common to these diverse conditions for smiling is mild surprise, while more intense surprise evokes a startle. Although the event that will surprise the baby changes with time, the fact of surprise and its close functional relation to both smiling and startling remain constant. (p. 77)

I assume that the "mild surprise" was in response to novel stimuli. Thus, if we accept that the property shared (the "identity" if you will) by the stimulus conditions that evoked smiling is novelty, and if we accept a smile as an indicator of an experience of satisfaction, then we have solved our problem. What is perceptually identical is the property of unexpectedness, which is the defining characteristic of novelty.

We have now conserved our basic definition. It remains possible to maintain the position that we start with an experience of satisfaction (again leaving aside how it was first experienced) and to postulate a disposition to repeat the experience of satisfaction—in other words, we assume an attempt to achieve perceptual identity with the previous experience. But now we have a much more interesting creature, one with built-in opposing tendencies. On the one hand, it will tend to repeat the same old experiences of satisfaction, but on the other hand, it will also tend to enlarge its repertoire of experiences, including

---

[7] Clearly this view requires something more than a simple template model of perception and memory. Instead what is required are processes that construct our perceptions and memories (Jerison, 1976). Rubinstein (1974) has presented a fascinating model of feature analyzers and classificatory processes that could do the job.

experiences of satisfaction. And we know that in fact this is what happens. We develop the capacity to enlarge and refine our sensual appetites. Whereas once we were content with the taste of milk alone, we can indeed acquire an appetite for such odd tastes as a dry martini with onion.

Two problems remain with the definition of a wish in terms of perceptual indentity and experience of satisfaction. Let us deal with perceptual identity first. Clearly the matter is not so simple as is implied by the term. It is possible that in early childhood, as has been asserted, dreams are mostly direct wish-fulfillments, that is, in the form of perceptual identities.[8] Obviously this state does not long persist, and fulfillment must soon be provided by various symbolic equivalents of perceptual identity. Indeed the fundamental question is most readily posed in regard to dreams. If we consider a nocturnal orgasm with dream imagery of an exciting sexual partner to be an instance of the achievement of perceptual identity in a hallucinatory manner, then the question is: Do other dreams from which we infer comparable wishes fulfill the requirement of perceptual identity, and if so, how? It is a critical question that, until recently, I thought could not be studied experimentally. But Premack (1975) has invented an ingenious method of quantifying the effects of symbolic behavior on appetitive behavior and vice versa. It offers (in principle, if not yet in practice) hope that one day we may be able to study systematically the functional relationships between perceptual experiences and their symbolic equivalents. In any case, the need to take symbolic expression into account leads to this revised definition of a wish: an attempt to achieve perceptual identity and/or symbolic equivalence with a previous experience of satisfaction.

The other fundamental question is: What are the basic experiences of satisfaction? And how can we determine what they are? The definition of a wish that I have proposed works quite well with the relationships between what we have called physiological needs and the sensual and sexual appetites. But there are experiences that the definition cannot thus far readily illuminate, experiences that we all know personally and that clinicians know professionally, namely, emotions, affects, feelings—terms that for the time being I will use loosely and to some extent interchangeably. So now we must turn our attention to some of the characteristics of emotions.

IV. THREE COMPONENTS OF EMOTIONS

I assume that the experience of an emotion is the ultimate way we have of knowing its uniqueness. Hence the perceptual quality of an emotion is one of its defining properties. This is not to say of course that one cannot imagine

[8] Helen Keller (1908) reported a number of undisguised wish-fulfillment dreams, which she recalled from the early years before Anne Sullivan taught her sign language.

unconscious emotions (of which more later), but that concept would make no sense whatever if we did not first have an *a priori* set of defining characteristics that include a typical conscious experience for each discriminable emotion. Leeper (1965, 1970) maintains that emotions *are* perceptual processes and has defined emotions as "long sustained perceptions of the more enduring and significant aspects of . . . situations" (1970, p. 156). He includes both motivation and cognitive appraisals in perceptual processes—a conceptual strategy with problems of its own.

The motivational properties of emotions are widely accepted, even if there is little agreement on the nature of these motivations. Uniquely among experimentalists, Bindra (1969) has called for a unified interpretation of "emotional and motivational" phenomena, which he conceptualizes as central motive states (CMS):

> The CMS is not a drive, but a neural functional change that occurs through an interaction of physiological state and incentive stimuli; thus hunger drive is merely a physiological state, but when it interacts with appropriate incentive stimuli (e.g., smell and sight of food) a CMS is created. The central motive state consists of neural changes that favor *selective attention* to a certain class of incentive stimuli and also creates a *response bias* in favor of a certain class of species-typical actions. (p. 1081)

Although the terms in which it is couched are different, this view is in principle not incompatible with the one I shall offer.

The expressive and communicative properties of emotions are fundamental. Darwin (1872) was enormously impressed by the "intimate relation which exists between almost all the emotions and their outward manifestations" (p. 366). He described the stereotyped expressive behaviors of a wide variety of mammals and people in a variety of emotional situations, and he was deeply committed to tracing the evolution of expressions from lower mammals to man. Scott (1958) wrote:

> Many mammals, like the dog and wolf, have a variety of postures and behavioral patterns which stimulate other members of the same species, but most of these seem to convey only *simple information* about the *emotional* state of the animal. For example, when a dog holds its tail very erect and wags it slowly, it is a sign of a dominant attitude. When two strange males approach each other in this fashion, a fight frequently follows. A crouching posture with the tail held low and wagging rapidly is associated with subordination. (p. 196) (italics added)

Bindra (1969), along similar lines, stated:

> Most mammals appear capable of recognizing emotions in others, for they adjust their own actions to the expected actions of others. Postural reactions and facial expressions may serve as a basis for predicting what another animal is likely to do . . . the recognition of emotion is [not] an idle activity, devoid of any adaptive significance. . . . On the contrary, recognition by one animal of another's emotion means . . . that the former animal has made some assessment of the type of behavior the other animal is likely to display. (p. 1079)

Although Darwin (1872) gathered a great deal of anecdotal information on the facial expressions shared by people of all races, it remained for Izard (1971) and Ekman (1973) to document the fact thoroughly. Numerous studies of literate and preliterate cultures make clear that in human beings, there is some small set of emotions (perhaps six to nine) in which the same facial expressions are associated with the same emotional situations regardless of culture or language. We may conclude that species-specific expressive and communicative emotional behavior is the rule. It is also possible to trace the evolution of these expressions from lower animals through primates to man (Andrew, 1963; Chevalier-Skolnikoff, 1973).

It is implicit in what I have said thus far about emotions that I have considered only emotions that take objects (the IT emotions of Figure 1). In terms of the three components that I have outlined, I shall tentatively suggest that an emotion is an intergrated unit (a package, if you will) of experience consisting of (1) a distinctive *perception*; (2) an *implicit wish* and *implied action* (motive); and (3) a typical *expression* (facial and/or postural) that is species-specific (and in man also culturally adapted). But a mere listing of components is of limited interest and I have not made clear what I mean by an *implicit wish*. In order to say something about the relationships among these components and to explain the meaning of *implicit wish*, we need some additional conceptual tools that we shall find by examining the characteristics of appetites.

V. GENERAL CHARACTERISTICS OF APPETITES

Let us begin with a passage from Lorenz (1965):

> It is highly characteristic of the ontogeny of behavior in higher animals that a phylogenetically adapted motor pattern makes its first appearance in tolerably complete, or at least clearly recognizable, form but in a biologically inadequate situation. . . . In his classic paper on appetites and aversions, Craig . . . has demonstrated in a masterly fashion that the phylogenetically adapted mechanism of the consummatory act itself is so constructed as to impart to the subject the "knowledge" of the environmental situation in which to discharge the motor pattern in question. (p. 63) The information concerning the biologically "right" environmental situation is, in this case, not only contained in the organization of receptor patterns alone but also essentially in the fixed motor pattern itself which produces the reinforcing reafferences only if very definite environmental conditions are fulfilled. (p. 65)

Such learning takes place in the context of *appetitive* behavior. What Lorenz emphasizes is the teaching function of phylogentically adapted motor patterns. This teaching function is accomplished by the afferent feedback that terminates a consummatory act:

> The teaching function of the consummatory act is based partly on phylogenetically acquired information contained in the motor pattern itself and partly on that

contained in the receptor organization of the releasing mechanism but mainly on the interaction of both, that is to say, on the reafference which the organism produces for itself by performing the consummatory act in the adequate consummatory situation. (p. 88)

Using the model of infant feeding, we can say that the infant's consummatory act of sucking teaches it that the incoming fluid satisfies its appetites of hunger and thirst because that is the way the infant is built.

The structural components of an appetite appear to be (1) a perception (e.g., of thirst); (2) a wish to achieve perceptual identity with the previous experience of satisfaction (e.g., the taste of water); and (3) a consummatory act (e.g., drinking water). The formal similarity to the components of IT emotions is interesting. But of greater interest is the fact that we normally take quite for granted that our perception of an appetite—thirst, for example—implies a wish to drink. When we feel hungry or when we smell delicious food, we speak of our wish to eat. In other words, we know intuitively and intimately that the perception either of an appetite or of the objects that satisfy it means that we wish for specific experiences of satisfaction.

Now if emotions with objects were like appetites, then we might understand that the perception of an emotion is comparable to the perception of an

ATTRACTION TO IT [Touch and hold it] Loving, Tender, Compassionate	REPULSION TO IT [Get rid of it] Angry, Contemptuous, Indignant
ATTRACTION FROM IT [Explore it] Fascinated, Amused, Surprised	REPULSION FROM IT [Escape from it] Frightened, Horrified, Startled
POSITIVE PASSIVE ME [Mission Accomplished (Chein) Gratification (Pribram & Melges)] Contented, Secure, Relaxed —[Pleasure - Satisfaction]— POSITIVE ACTIVE ME [Mission Going Well (Chein) Satisfaction (Pribram & Melges)] Energetic, Elated, Vigorous	NEGATIVE PASSIVE ME [Mission Failed (Chein) Dissatisfaction (Pribram & Melges)] Depressed, Helpless, Lonely —[Unpleasure - Nonsatisfaction]— NEGATIVE ACTIVE ME [Mission Not Going Well (Chein) Distress (Pribram & Melges)] Anxious, Distressed, Tense

Figure 2. These eight (2^3) generic emotion categories result from the intersection of three orthogonal dimensions adapted from de Rivera (1962). Each category is illustrated by three typical emotion words. The IT emotions are appetites whose satisfaction requires appropriate consummatory acts, such as the examples in brackets. The ME emotions are messages (examples in brackets) about the status of satisfaction or nonsatisfaction of appetites and other wishes.

appetite. We would also expect to find a consummatory act and we would expect to be able to infer an implicit wish. Thus, if anger were an appetite, then repulsion of the object of anger would be its consummation, and it would be easy to infer the wish to carry out some aggressive act. Similarly, if fear were an appetite, then escape would be its consummation. If surprise were an appetite, curious attention would be its consummation. And if tenderness were an appetite, the implicit wish would be tender touching and holding, and carrying out that wish would be its consummation.

Before we continue along this line, let us examine some further properties of appetites. Rapaport (1960b, pp. 187–188) gave four defining characteristics of "appetitiveness": (1) *peremptoriness*, defined as the amount of delay possible before performing the consummatory act; (2) a *cyclic character* of the peremptoriness; (3) *selectiveness* of object, meaning that there are objects "which are the specific necessary conditions" for the satisfaction of the appetite; and (4) *displaceablity* of object, meaning that in the absence of the selected object a substitute may suffice. The presence of a cyclic character betrays Rapaport's attribution of appetitiveness to "instinctual drives" and their somatic (physiological) sources. The first, third, and fourth defining characteristics clearly apply as well to emotions as appetites as to other appetites. That emotions *may* be cyclic is clear, but that they *need* be is doubtful.[9] To these characteristics we may add two additional features of appetitive behavior: (1) a tendency to *self-stimulation* of appetites when appropriate consummatory acts can be carried out, and (2) a tendency to *expansion* of range and *refinement* of discrimination of the experiences that will satisfy the appetite—in other words, a tendency to acquire new "tastes."

✔What seems essential for our immediate purposes is that one satisfies an emotional appetite by performing an appropriate consummatory act in a suitable environment. Thus escape from a fear-producing situation is to fear as eating is to hunger. Getting rid of an anger-producing situation is to anger as drinking is to thirst. And tender touching is to feeling tender as orgasm is to sexual excitement.

VI. EMOTIONS AS APPETITES AND MESSAGES

Figure 2 illustrates the eight categories defined by the three classificatory dimensions. The top four boxes contain the generic name of each IT emotion

---

[9] Tomkins (1970, pp. 104–105), who also sees emotions as primary *human* motives, specifically denies the rhythmic character of emotions. Two other of his four essential characteristics seem to be roughly equivalent to displaceability ("generality of object") and peremptoriness ("generality of intensity"). The fourth, that affects may be "invested in other affects, combine with other affects, intensify or modulate them, and suppress or reduce them," is a nice illustration of a reified concept taking on an affective life of its own! A full exposition of the differences in my views and his will have to await a later occasion.

(e.g., ATTRACTION TO IT), an example of an appropriate consummatory act, and typical emotion words empirically obtained (Dahl & Stengel, 1978).

Much more can be said about the concept of IT emotions as appetites with appropriate consummatory acts. For one thing, it can be seen that it is not necessary to speak of "negative wishes" (Holt, 1976) when referring to fear. According to this model, fear is as much an appetite as thirst or hunger or sexual desire, and it requires a specific consummatory act of escape (or some symbolic equivalent) to satisfy it. From the tendency to self-stimulation of appetites it follows that we should expect to see animals and people put themselves in real or imagined danger situations where they experience fear that they can readily escape either by exercising their own motor or intellectual skills or by returning to reality, as, for example, by leaving a horror movie. And indeed we do see such behavior. We see it in the mock fighting and flight of dogs at play. We see it in children and adults alike, courting dangerous situations and consummating their intensely aroused fear with obvious excitement and delight. The classic hide-and-seek games of children can be understood as a playful self-stimulation of an appetite and its appropriate consummatory acts, though the games are commonly interpreted as attempts to achieve mastery over the fear of separation. Certainly we do try to achieve mastery and control over the circumstances of our appetites. We especially try to guarantee their satisfaction. But I think mastery is usually a precondition for self-stimulative behaviors rather than an explanation of them. I think the evidence will show that normally we stimulate our own appetites only when we are in a position to assure their satisfaction.[10]

What I have said about fear should apply equally to anger, love, and surprise. Who, for example, has not nursed and savored an old grudge or imagined the pleasure of destroying the reputation of someone he holds in contempt? Who has not stimulated his or her own loving feeling by fantasies of a tender encounter? And who has not planned a vacation to strange and exotic places in anticipation of satisfying his or her thirst for novelty? Surely no one will have the least trouble recalling examples of his or her own.

So far, I have postulated that the concept *appetite* applies to the IT emotions, and I have asserted that each separate emotion would have corresponding appropriate consummatory acts. But the question arises: How do we fit the previous definitions of pleasure as satisfaction and unpleasure as nonsatisfaction of wishes (e.g., appetites) into this model? The answer lies in the nature of the ME emotions. It is tempting, because in some way it would be simpler, to extend the view of the emotion as appetite and consummatory act to the ME emotions. In one specific sense, which I will mention later, this does seem to be the case, but in general the view I propose is that the ME "feelings" seem to

---

[10] Of course, there are repetitious attempts at mastery accompanied by intense and unsatisfied fear, as in certain traumatic neuroses. But clinically we have little difficulty distinguishing these failures of mastery from playful appetite arousal.

have the specific function of information feedback systems associated with our other wishes. In Pribram's (1970) view they are "monitors" of how matters are going for us. In Chein's (1972) view they are comments or information about how our enterprises are working out. Pribram and Melges (1969) in their psychophysiological theory of emotions use terms compatible with this idea.

In the lower half of Figure 2, I have given the generic name of the category, examples of the messages (in brackets), and three typical affect words. The POSITIVE ME feelings are by definition pleasurable and convey the generic message of satisfaction. In the language of wishes, the POSITIVE PASSIVE ME feelings convey the message that our wishes (e.g., appetites) have been satisfied, and the POSITIVE ACTIVE ME feelings convey the message that our wishes are being satisfied and that we anticipate further satisfaction. Notice the implied distinction between the *message* (e.g., wishes are being satisfied) and the *signal* that carries it (e.g., the pleasurable affect of hopefulness).[11]

Since by definition these feelings are pleasurable and since we clearly wish to repeat experiences of satisfaction, we must ask why the POSITIVE ME feelings do not qualify as appetites. The answer lies in the fact that we cannot specify a generic consummatory act that would produce satisfaction, and this violates the requirement for specificity of object, which we have accepted as a defining property of appetitiveness. It is in the nature of the ME feelings that they must be produced derivatively, that is, in the course of attempting to satisfy some other wishes and appetites. It is clear that we wish for positive feelings, but we cannot say that we have an appetite for them. Nonetheless, under certain circumstances, POSITIVE ME feelings acquire *specific* appetitive properties. Certain chemicals can produce false feedback information in the form of feelings of contentment or elation, for example. In effect, the messages of these chemically produced feelings is the message of satisfaction. Once an addiction to such a chemical is established, then the POSITIVE ME feelings are produced following the consummatory act of ingestion or injection of the specific object, the drug of addiction.[12]

NEGATIVE ME feelings are by definition unpleasurable and convey the generic messages of unsatisfaction. NEGATIVE ACTIVE ME feelings such as anxiety carry the message that certain of one's wishes (conscious or unconscious) are not being satisfied or are not likely to be satisfied. The message of

[11] In other words, the distinction between a signal affect and what it signals. The distinction is necessary to understand clinical observations that lead us to infer defensive processes applied to the signal, the message, or both.

[12] Lorenz (1965, p. 17) noted that even phylogenetically adapted teaching mechanisms "can miscarry, that is, a mechanism which acts on the generally reliable 'hypothesis' that a situation affording relief of tension is also one desirable in the interest of survival. As is to be expected, the mechanism also responds to all drugs causing relief of tension and thus conditions men ... to become alcoholics and ... addicts." I overlook the imprecision of the term *relief of tension*. I prefer the false feedback formulation.

NEGATIVE PASSIVE ME feelings such as depression is that certain of one's wishes cannot be or have not been satisfied and/or must be abandoned. It goes without saying that these messages pertain to the status of wishes that include one's sensual appetites as well as one's emotional appetites toward objects (the IT emotions). The message of unpleasure is that one is unsatisfied, commonly because the object is not available or perhaps because of the universal dilemma where the satisfaction of one wish precludes the satisfaction of another. This is the fundamental occasion for a defensive process to be invoked. One tries to get rid of the signal or the message or both by playing defensive tricks on oneself. Thus I agree with Brenner (1975) that both of the generic NEGATIVE ME feelings of *anxiety* and *depression* are commonly (though not, of course, necessarily) occasions for defensive operations.

Now we are in a position to explain why appetites such as fear and anger are so often regarded as negative emotions. It is because there are so many occasions when the "exigencies of life," to use Freud's (1900) carefully imprecise phrase, prevent the carrying out of the consummatory acts necessary to satisfy these appetites. The infant or young child is often unable to escape the situation that, for example, arouses his fears of separation from his mother. Nor can the child who is already afraid of losing his mother very easily get rid of her to satisfy his anger at her for leaving in the first place. These are fundamental dilemmas of childhood, as Bowlby (1973) has beautifully captured in his evocative descriptions of the "anxious attachment" of children who have suffered excessive separation or the threat of it. Thus it is no problem to see how anger and fear so often come to be regarded as aversive. In the language of the present model, the child would suffer unpleasure in the form of anxiety as it is losing hope and would suffer depression when it has lost hope of satisfaction. What is aversive is not fear or anger, but the inability to satisfy them.

VII. SOME CLINICAL IMPLICATIONS

Now, just to whet our appetites so to speak, let me touch on a few areas where the appetite hypothesis might inform our understanding of what we observe. Clinical applications come to mind, but I warn the reader now that I have no immediately startling revelations. The reason lies in the discrepancy between the large amount clinicians "know" about emotions and the confused place emotions have in our theories. Psychoanalysis and psychotherapists of all persuasions know that emotions are profoundly motivating. When clinicians write case reports or vignettes, they almost invariably lapse into the language of emotions. They know that a patient may not experience the perception of anger, for example, yet he may exhibit compelling evidence of his wishes to be rid of some objects. They know that the classical hysteric perceives and expresses his emotions but is often extraordinarily naive about the wishes (the appetites) implicit in them, whereas the classical obsessional neither feels nor satisfactorily expresses the very emotional appetites whose implicit wishes he may discuss at length. Thus the clinician already understands that the three components of an IT emotion (an emotion with an object)—perception, wish, and consummation—can have different clinical fates. A patient may repress (for example) one or all or any combination of these components.

What the clinician may not have understood, however, are the quite close parallels with other appetites. For example, a man may experience no sensual sexual pleasure and/or he may have no interest in any sexual objects and/or he may be impotent when attempting consummation. In other words, he may invoke defenses against the perception, the wish, or the consummation necessary for satisfaction. If we systematically look at all the IT emotions, we are likely to find clinical phenomena that closely parallel much of what we know about the fate of sexual appetites.

This model also highlights the unavoidable fact of ambivalence. It does so because of the nature of its definitions of pleasure and unpleasure as satisfaction and nonsatisfaction. It is inevitable that in the course of our development, we must confront the unpleasure of nonsatisfaction of some wishes whose satisfaction is incompatible with others (as I have already illustrated). But this is hardly a revelation to any clinician who already understands that one of the central problems of growing up is to achieve delay of gratification, to achieve some mastery over the circumstances of the satisfaction of one's appetites. However, I have suggested one area of clarification in making a clear distinction between behavior aimed at achieving mastery (including, if necessary, renunciation) and self-stimulation of appetites when mastery already obtained permits satisfaction.

The model also makes apparent the necessity for "emotional" insight. We speak of emotional insight to imply insight into our predominant unconsious wishes along with full recognition of the pertinent emotions (see Brenner, 1974b). The present model implies that this must necessarily be so since many of our most important unconscious wishes involve emotional appetites. If we do not experience the emotions, we have simply not perceived the wishes in the primary way that such wishes are apprehended, a pretty good indication of successful resistance.

But there is another more significant consequence of this model. It lies in our ability to posit explicitly that the emotional appetites are as profoundly important to our development and survival as our more traditional appetites of thirst and hunger and sexual excitement, and that the vicissitudes of emotional appetites are distinguishable from the vicissitudes of our somatic appetites. All the emotions in man do not manifest themselves at birth. Some developmental unfolding, which includes interaction with the environment (learning), is required. Bridges (1932) and Emde, Gaensbauer, and Harmon (1976) have studied the sequences of emergence of different emotions in the first months of life. The feeding model as our fundamental metaphor for experiences of satisfaction is particularly misleading when it comes to understanding emotional development in the infant because feeding behavior does indeed have the characteristics of an appetite. But it is hard to speak of the infant's having an appetite for love, and it is the emergence of just such an appetite that we need to understand.

The infant, by expressing its phylogenetically adapted motor patterns of crying and smiling, communicates its needs to be held, to be touched, to be fondled, in short, to get the cues whose message is mother's love, affection, and tenderness for her infant. The mother, by caring for her infant, consummates her emotional appetite of love, and the infant gets ME messages of contentment and security. We know for a fact that such messages are vital to the infant's survival. I recommend Spitz's (1965) chapters on "Psychotoxic Disturbances," "Emotional Deficiency Diseases of Childhood," and "The Effects of Object Loss" to the reader who needs to refresh his memory on the devastating consequences of the separation of an infant from its mother when its somatic requirements are adequately met, and on the pathological consequences of deprivation of love and tenderness, and the equally pathological effects of a mother's chronic anger, resentment, and fears. Truly an infant does not live by milk alone, no matter how much satisfaction it may get from nursing. Deprived of the natural cues that mean that it is tenderly loved, it has little chance of developing into a loving adult and a 30 to 40% chance of not surviving its second year (Spitz, 1965, pp. 277–281).

It seems clear that certain POSITIVE ME emotions are vital to life, emotions that the infant can get only by being the object of someone else's appetite of love. Our intuition tells us this and Bowlby's (1973) descriptions of "anxious attachment"—the clinging of a child insufficiently loved—poignantly confirm what our model predicts. There is no consummatory act that the child can perform to satisfy his wish to be loved. What the child can do, and does, is to communicate his distress and his wishes to be loved, but he can only get satisfaction if others take him as the object of their appetites of love—a necessary precondition for him to develop his own appetite of love.

Some of these results are implied by the way de Rivera's (1962, 1977) theories define the IT–ME dimension. The theories postulate that specific ME emotions can occur as transformations of corresponding IT emotions. I have summarized (Dahl, 1977) the implicit conditions under which such transformations can occur: (1) when one is the recipient of someone else's IT emotion (appetite); (2) when one projects one's own emotional appetite onto someone else and perceives that appetite directed back toward oneself; and (3) when one internalizes an object to whom one ascribes an emotional appetite directed to oneself. Thus *love* transforms to *security; contempt* to *shame; fear* to *anxiety;* and *anger* to *depression.* Thus to be loved transforms to feeling secure. And to identify with someone who loves us is to create in ourselves an enduring disposition to feeling secure.

Many years ago, I was struck by an odd passage that Anne Sullivan had written recounting her experiences as Helen Keller's (1902) teacher. After some vigorous battles, Miss Sullivan had expressed her delight in having "tamed the wild creature." And at the end of a letter to a friend, she announced her triumph that Helen was learning "the only two essential things I can teach her, obedience and love" (p. 248). It was easy for me to understand the lesson of obedience, for I was preoccupied at that time with Rapaport's (1960a) systematization of Freud's theory, a model that postulated the need for delay. And delay is intimately associated with a capacity for obedience. But I had really not understood the lesson of love.

What could Anne Sullivan's love teach Hellen Keller? Now we can say that it would convey a message of assurance and certainty, of security and trust, faith that her teacher would remain and that her needs and wishes would continue to be satisfied; in short, the fundamental message that the world is a dependable, secure place. This is what Erikson's (1950) concept of basic trust is all about. The role of internalization appears to be to reduce uncertainty and to regularize expectations, both prerequisites for mastery. This transforming effect of internalization applies whether the emotion is one of anger and fear or of love and fascination. The practical outcomes are quite different, but the function of internalization seems comparable. In a profound sense, then, the enduring ME emotions that result from such internalization processes must carry the powerful imprint and the record of the history of our former experiences as objects of others' emotional appetites toward us.

VIII. SOME SOCIAL IMPLICATIONS

The appetite hypothesis of emotions has other important implications for a theory of object relations and therefore for theories of social organization. What gives emotional appetites their central importance is that the typical and primary objects necessary to provide appropriate experiences of satisfaction are other members of one's own species. By comparison, it is much easier to satisfy one's appetites for food and water and even sexual pleasure than it is to satisfy one's emotional appetites. This is true because the appropriate objects of one's emotional appetites are other people's personalities and *their* emotional appetites. We can buy food, drink, and sex, but we can't buy love.[13] It is the inherent complexity of integrating one's own emotional appetites with those of others in order to achieve reciprocal satisfactions that provides the most difficult problems of adaptation.

Many years ago, English and Pearson (1945) wrote a textbook of psychiatry entitled *Emotional Problems of Living*. It was an apt title; every clinician understands its referents. But emotional problems, although clinically

---

[13] Of course we can buy the unearned devotion of a dog!

pervasive, have been conceptual foundlings with no clear theoretical home of their own. They have had to share quarters with "instinctual drives." I believe that the concepts of *libido* and *aggression* are theoretically inelegant not so much because they are energic concepts but rather because they confuse on the one hand erotic appetites with the emotional appetite of love and on the other aggressive behavior with the emotional appetites of anger and hate.

I want to draw attention to just two of the many problems connected with these con-fusions[14] of two separable concepts into one. One problem with the con-fusion of emotions with "instinctual drives" is that it becomes very awkward to account for such facts as Spitz (1965, pp. 199–292) summarized. Drive theory cannot really explain, without adding "object relations" concepts, why it is that a child, adequately fed in a foundling home or nursery but cared for by many different mothering figures, does not automatically adopt the feeding person as the consummatory object of its affection. But even if we introduce object relations concepts, we have not solved our theoretical problems because the widely recognized and vitally important emotional components of object relations have no consistent and general theoretical elaboration (see Bowlby, 1973; Castelnuovo-Tedesco, 1974).

A second problem with the libido concept lies in one of its ultimate derivations, namely, the ideal character type of the monogamous heterosexual genital character. It appears to be a reasonable deduction from the libido concept that the most advanced and mature adaptation one can make would involve the maximum satisfaction of one's appetites, both somatic and emotional, with one permanent heterosexual object. It takes only minimal knowledge of present and past societies to realize how rarely such adaptations are achieved. There is something deficient in a model that postulates such a rarely attained state as its norm and implicitly regards variations from it as in some degree pathological.

One merit of the appetite hypothesis model, which allows for emotions as appetites with independent status, is that it intrinsically permits a much wider range of effective social adaptations to be accepted as "normal." And it further permits us to examine the adaptations themselves for the criteria of what is and what isn't effective or what the norms are rather than predetermining the criteria by derivation from a theoretical concept such as libido. It allows us to look for the criteria in what *is* rather than in what ought to be.

IX. PHYLOGENETIC SPECULATIONS

That emotions and their expressions in animals and man are the result of complex phylogenetic adaptations to a variety of natural selection pressures is

[14] I hyphenate to emphasize both *confusion* and *fusion of*, in the sense that psychoanalysts sometimes speak of the fusion of libidinal and aggressive drives or of the fusion of drive components.

widely accepted (Darwin, 1872; Plutchik, 1962; Hamburg, 1963; Andrew, 1963; Izard, 1971; Chevalier-Skolnikoff, 1973; Ekman, 1973). Interest has been directed toward tracing the evolution of patterns of motor expressions, toward postulating the survival value of particular emotions, and toward the communicative functions of emotions, especially those involved in maintaining and regulating social bonds among animals.

Jerison (1976), while considering the evolution of language, wrote, "If there were selection pressures toward the development of language specifically for communication, we would expect the evolutionary response to be the development of 'prewired' language systems" (p. 101). Such a language would have a vocabulary of phylogenetically adapted motor patterns who expression and recognition would be common to all members of the species. In fact, these are precisely the properties of emotional expression that force us to accept the language function of emotions. I agree with Bindra (1969) that communication and recognition of intentions must be important functions of this language.

Now I want to speculate in response to a question that is rarely asked: Why is it that we experience an emotion in the form of a particular distinctive perception? Given our classification model, why wouldn't we arrive at decisions by making intellectual appraisals on each dimension and act accordingly, without any unique perceptual experience? To ask the question this way is almost to answer it. We can easily imagine people making just such judgments because they have a flexible and plastic symbolic language system that, in Jerison's (1976) words, helps to construct "worlds in which sensory information from various modalities is integrated as information about objects in space and time" (p. 101). But our basic emotion language evolved before symbolic language. And for the animal without symbolic language, perception is the primary means of "knowing."

Lorenz (1965) described the way in which adaptively useful information can be genetically preserved by the

> interaction of the species with its environment during evolution. By mutation and selection, a method analogous to learning by trial and success (not by error!) and also analogous to induction devoid of any deductive procedure, the species gathers information and stores it, coded in the form [of] chain molecules, in its genome. (p. 103)

I am suggesting that among the mechanisms that succeeded were those that allowed the perceptual system to encode in a single "chunk"—a gestalt, if you will—the distinctive perceptual quality of a particular emotion and that this coding occurred in response to a wide range of elementary natural cues in the environment, including especially those cues offered by the behaviors of other members of the same species. Such a coding process would be an early "'intelligence' system in which varied patterns of stimuli are transformed into invariant objects" (Jerison, 1976, p. 99).

We can imagine two quite different sorts of selection pressures relevant to emotions. One would tend to select for some particular emotional behavior trait, for example, aggressivity or timidity or curiosity. One sees artificial pressure of this sort, for example, in the breeding of dogs. But another kind of pressure would select on the grounds of maximum variability and discriminability, that is, for greater range and appropriateness of emotional behavior. It seems clear that the second type of pressure has become increasingly dominant in mammals, reaching its maximum in primates and man.

Bindra (1969) suggested that

> the phenomenon of recognizing or classifying emotions, in others as well as in oneself, is one of multi-dimensional categorizing, the judgment being of the same type as that involved in categorizing a girl as nice, a day as fine, and a wine as great. (p. 1079)

I believe, as Freud (1915) and de Rivera (1962) did, that the three classificatory dimensions that I have used do indeed produce fundamental categories of mental life.

Now we can answer our question as to why we *perceive* some basic set of emotions, each uniquely. We can claim that evolution has made the equivalent of the choices on each polarity and packaged the perceptual code for it! Furthermore we can readily attribute unique advantages to those of our mammalian ancestors whose increased cortical capacity was used to construct such codes. Powerful survival advantages would accrue to those specimens who best "knew" (perceived) when to be attracted (ATTRACTION) or when to be repulsed (REPULSION), when to approach (TO) or when to withdraw (FROM), and when to relate to an object (IT) or when to attend to its own internal evaluative messages (ME).

X. CONCLUSION

The *appetite hypothesis* offers a unified motivational model that permits us to see a wide range of seemingly disparate motivated behavior as having certain essential features in common. Its basic terms either are susceptible to operational definition and/or empirical determination or else make clear where the gaps in our knowledge lie. For example, "experiences of satisfaction" can in principle be empirically determined. "Perceptual identity," on the other hand, raises certain problems because of the necessity to postulate "symbolic equivalents." Here our model exposes our ignorance and makes clear our need for new experimental methods (e.g., Premack, 1975) to study the functional relationships between perceptions (especially those involved in appetitive behavior) and their symbolic equivalents. Despite the ambiguity arising from "perceptual identity," the concept of *wish* offers important advantages over the concept of *drives*. Holt (1976) has persuasively argued the case for wishes. In my view, a decisive advantage rests in the need to postulate a wisher, a doer.

The appetite hypothesis alone has already led to the nonobvious deduction that fear is appetitive. The entire model promises to provide a theoretical framework for reformulating object relations theories, which until now have depended heavily on the dynamic motivational attributes of emotions but have lacked a coherent theory of emotions. It permits us to explain a wide range of angry, hostile behavior, not as a function of aggressive drives but rather as the operation of a special class of wishes with the properties of appetites.

Moreover, since the terms of this model so strongly emphasize the basic, conflicting nature of appetites, particularly those we experience as emotions, it requires us to focus on the central problem of adaptation as the resolution of competing appetites. In a profound sense, the task of growing up is the task of establishing workable priorities among one's appetites. And *workable* implies a control system (what we traditionally call *ego*) sufficient to the job of making the required compromises and renunciations. What makes the appetite hypothesis of emotions especially appealing in this regard is that it permits explicit weighting of degrees of commitment not only to the traditional appetites for sensory experiences but also to the newly recognized emotional appetites for people.

Finally, this new motivational model, if we take it seriously, will require us to reexamine the data of child development, of animal observation and experimentation, and of the ego's mechanisms of adaptation. Because its terms are explicit and in principle operationally definable, the model's central strength lies in the possibility of either confirming or refuting deductions derived from it. Insofar as the model represents a novel view of the emotional world, it may itself give rise to further novelty. Let us end on a note of anticipation, awaiting further surprises, whetting our curiosity in preparation for a feast of new knowledge!

REFERENCES

Andrew, R. J. Evolution of facial expressions. *Science*, 1963. *142*, 1034–1041.

Arnold, M. B. *Emotion and personality, Vol. I: Psychological aspects*. New York: Columbia University Press, 1960. (a)

Arnold, M. B. *Emotion and personality, Vol. II: Neurological and physiological aspects*. New York: Columbia University Press, 1960. (b)

Arnold, M. B. Perennial problems in the field of emotion. In M. B. Arnold (Ed.), *Feelings and emotions, the Loyola Symposium*. New York: Academic Press, 1970.

Basch, M. F. Theory formation in Chapter VII: A critique. *Journal of the American Psychoanalytic Association*, 1976, *24*, 61–100.

Bindra, D. A unified interpretation of emotions and motivations. *Annals of the New York Academy of Sciences*, 1969, *159*, 1071–1083.

Bowley, J. *Attachment and loss, Vol. I: Attachment*. New York: Basic Books, 1969.

Bowlby, J. *Attachment and loss, Vol. II: Separation*. New York: Basic Books, 1973.

Brenner, C. Depression, anxiety and affect theory. *International Journal of Psychoanalysis*, 1974, *55*, 25–32. (a)

Brenner, C. On the nature and development of affects: A unified theory. *The Psychoanalytic Quarterly*, 1974, *43*, 532–556. (b)

Brenner, C. Affects and psychic conflict. *The Psychoanalytic Quarterly*, 1975, *44*, 5–28.

Bridges, K. M. B. Emotional development in early infancy. *Child Development*, 1932, *3*, 324–341.

Castelnuovo-Tedesco, P. Toward a theory of affects. *Journal of the American Psychoanalytic Association*, 1974, *22*, 612–625.

Chein, I. *The science of behavior and the image of man*. New York: Basic Books, 1972.

Chevalier-Skolnikoff, S. Facial expression of emotion in nonhuman primates. In P. Ekman (Ed.), *Darwin and facial expression, a century of research in review*. New York: Academic Press, 1973.

Dahl, H. Observations on a "natural experiment": Helen Keller. *Journal of the American Psychoanalytic Association*, 1965, *13*, 533–550.

Dahl, H. Considerations for a theory of emotions. In J. de Rivera, A structural theory of emotions. *Psychological Issues*, Monograph 40, 1977.

Dahl, H., & Stengel, B. A classification of emotion words: A modification and partial test of de Rivera's decision theory of emotions. *Psychoanalysis and Contemporary Thought*, 1978, *1*, 269–312.

Darwin, C. *The expression of the emotions in man and animals*. London: John Murray, 1872.

de Rivera, J. A decision theory of emotions (doctoral dissertation, Stanford University, 1961). *Dissertation Abstracts International*, 1962. (University Microfilm No. 62-2356.)

de Rivera, J. A structural theory of emotions. *Psychological Issues*, Monograph 40, 1977.

Deutsch, J. A., & Deutsch, D. *Physiological psychology*. Homewood, Ill.: Dorsey Press, 1966.

Ekman, P. *Darwin and facial expression, a century of research in review*. New York: Academic Press, 1973.

Emde, R. N., Gaensbauer, T. J., & Harmon, R. J. Emotional expression in infancy: A behavioral study. *Psychological Issues*, Monograph 37, 1976.

English. O. S., & Pearson. G. H. *Emotional problems of living*. New York: Norton, 1945.

Erikson, E. H. *Childhood and society*. New York: Norton, 1950.

Freud, S. (1900) The interpretation of dreams. *Standard Edition*, Vol. 5. London: Hogarth Press, 1953.

Freud, S. (1915) Instincts and their vicissitudes. *Standard Edition*, Vol. 14. London: Hogarth Press, 1957.

Freud, S. (1917) A metapsychological supplement to the theory of dreams. *Standard Edition*, Vol. 14. London: Hogarth Press, 1957.

Freud, S. (1924) The economic problem of masochism. *Standard Edition*, Vol. 19. London: Hogarth Press, 1961.

Hamburg, D. A. Emotions in the perspective of human evolution. In P. Knapp (Ed.), *Expression of the emotions in man*. New York: International Universities Press, 1963.

Holt, R. R. Drive or wish? A reconsideration of the psychoanalytic theory of motivation. *Psychological Issues*, Monograph 36, 1976.

Izard, C. E. *The face of emotion*. New York: Appleton-Century-Crofts, 1971.

Jerison, H. J. Paleoneurology and the evolution of mind. *Scientific American*, 1976, *234*, 90–101.

Keller, H. (1902) *The story of my life*. New York: Doubleday, 1954.

Keller, H. *The world I live in*. New York: Century, 1908.

Klein, G. S. Peremptory ideation: Structure and force in motivated ideas. In R. R. Holt (Ed.), *Motives and thought: Psychoanalytic essays in honor of David Rapaport*. New York: International Universities Press, 1967.

Leeper, R. W. Some needed developments in the motivational theory of emotions. In D. Levine (Ed.), *Nebraska Symposium on Motivation*, Vol. 13. Lincoln: University of Nebraska Press, 1965.

Leeper, R. W. The motivational and perceptual properties of emotions as indicating their fundamental character and role. In M. B. Arnold (Ed.), *Feelings and emotions, the Loyola Symposium*. New York: Academic Press, 1970.

Lorenz, K. *Evolution and modification of behavior.* Chicago: University of Chicago Press, 1965.

Nauta, W. J. H. The Limbic system of the mammaliam brain: An anatomical survey. Thomas William Salmon Lectures, New York Academy of Medicine, December 4, 1975.

Plutchik, R. *The emotions: facts, theories and a new model.* New York: Random House, 1962.

Premack, D. Symbols inside and outside of language. In J. G. Kavanagh & J. E. Cutting (Eds.), *The role of speech in language.* Cambridge, Mass.: MIT Press, 1975.

Pribram, K. H. Feelings as monitors. In M. B. Arnold (Ed.), *Feelings and emotions, the Loyola Symposium.* New York: Academic Press, 1970.

Pribram, K. H. Self-consciousness and intentionality. In G. E. Schwartz & D. Shapiro (Eds.), *Consciousness and self-regulation advances in research.* New York: Plenum, 1976.

Pribram, K. H., & Melges, F. T. Psychophysiological basis of emotion. In P. V. Vinken & G. W. Bruyn (Eds.), *Handbook of clinical neurology.* Amsterdam: North-Holland, 1969.

Rapaport, D. *The structure of psychoanalytic theory, a systematizing attempt.* New York: International Universities Press, 1960. (a)

Rapaport, D. On the psychoanalytic theory of motivation, In M. Jones (Ed.), *Nebraska Symposium on Motivation,* Vol. 8. Lincoln: University of Nebraska Press, 1960. (b)

Rubinstein, B. B. On the role of classificatory processes in mental functioning: Aspects of a psychoanalytic theoretical model. In L. Goldberger & V. Rosen (Eds.), *Psychoanalysis and contemporary science,* Vol. 3. New York: International Universities Press, 1974.

Rubinstein, B. B. Hope, fear, wish, expectation, and fantasy: A semantic–phenomenological and extraclinical theoretical study. In T. Shapiro (Ed.), *Psychoanalysis and contemporary science,* Vol. 5. New York: International Universities Press, 1977.

Schur, M. *The id and the regulatory principles of mental functioning.* New York: International Universities Press, 1966.

Scott, J. P. *Animal behavior.* Chicago: University of Chicago Press, 1958.

Spitz, R. A. *The first year of life, a psychoanalytic study of normal and deviant development of object relations.* New York: International Universities Press, 1965.

Tomkins, S. S. Affect as the primary motivational system. In M. B. Arnold (Ed.), *Feelings and emotions, the Loyola Symposium.* New York: Academic Press, 1970.

Wolff, P. H. *The causes, controls, and organization of behavior in the neonate.* New York: International Universities Press, 1966.

Editor's Introduction

8

The authors began their work with the assumption that defense mechanisms are related to emotion in a dynamic and regulatory fashion, and that ego defenses are interrelated and have implications for adaptation in both an evolutionary and an ontogenetic perspective. Based on their review of the literature on ego defenses and their own theoretical considerations, they conclude that (1) there is overlap among defenses as traditionally defined; (2) some defenses are polar opposites; and (3) some are more primitive than others. The authors develop a model for interrelating defense mechanisms, emotions, and diagnostic concepts. They postulate four pairs of basic bipolar emotions: fear–anger, joy–sadness, acceptance–disgust, and expectancy–surprise. These bipolar emotions vary in the degree to which they are similar to each other. They are considered basic because they are rooted in our biological-evolutionary history and were selected through evolution because of their adaptive functions.

Plutchik's previous theory and research had described emotions in terms of a subjective, a biological, and a trait language. These are briefly reviewed in the present paper. Central to the present chapter, however, is the work of the present authors in adding two additional languages relating to the emotions: defense mechanisms and diagnostic concepts. They hold that the personality traits most characteristic of an individual will lead him to rely on particular defense mechanisms and that each major diagnostic concept is associated with one dominant defense mechanism.

On the assumption that most people can report their own feelings and describe their own behavior as it relates to their defense mechanisms, the authors developed a self-report measure (the Life Style Index) to show the degree to which individuals use particular defenses. Beginning with a large number of items representing most of the ego defense mechanisms defined in the literature, they used both empirical and conceptual analysis to reduce the list to eight basic defenses, which relate to the eight basic emotions.

Research with the Life Style Index has differentiated between normals and diagnostic groups and between individuals with different dominant traits. For example, the authors show that schizophrenics use virtually all of the ego defense mechanisms more than do normals, and that highly anxious people use regression, compensation, projection, and displacement, whereas people high in self-esteem tend to use these defenses minimally. Their theoretical model is supported by their initial research endeavors and is well depicted in their illustrations. The model predicts, for example, that the basic emotion of anger is regulated by the defense mechanism of displacement and tends to result in a passive–aggressive personality of the aggressive type, whereas the basic emotion of fear relates to the defense mechanism of repression and tends to result in the passive–aggressive personality of the passive type. The model thus presents a new way of integrating practical clinical problems with theoretical concepts.

A Structural Theory of Ego Defenses and Emotions

8

ROBERT PLUTCHIK, HENRY KELLERMAN, and
HOPE R. CONTE

The concept of ego defenses is among the more important contributions of
psychoanalysis to personality theory and to the theory of psychological adaptations. Recently, Vaillant (1971) has suggested that the theory of ego mechanisms
of defense may also contribute to a theory of diagnosis and prognosis.

From a psychoanalytic point of view, ego mechanisms of defense are
mental processes that attempt to resolve conflicts among drive states, affects,
and external reality. According to Vaillant (1971), they moderate levels of
emotion produced by stress, they help keep awareness of certain drives at a
minimal level, they provide time to help an individual deal with life traumas,
and they help deal with unresolvable loss. However, despite their obvious
importance, there have been few attempts made to provide a theoretical framework for understanding: (1) the relations among specific defenses; (2) the relations between specific defenses and specific emotions; and (3) the adaptive
implications of these relations.

I. DEFINING AND MEASURING EGO DEFENSES

In addition to these issues, it is important to emphasize that the concept
of defenses is a broad one and is not limited in applicability to adult human
beings. Psychoanalysts have written about defenses in relation to both children

ROBERT PLUTCHIK • Albert Einstein College of Medicine, Bronx, New York. HENRY
KELLERMAN • Postgraduate Center for Mental Health, New York, New York. HOPE R.
CONTE • Albert Einstein College of Medicine, Bronx, New York.

and infants (Chess, 1964; 1966), and ethologists have demonstrated the operation of certain defense mechanisms—for example, displacement and regression—in lower animals (Goodall, 1967; Lorenz, 1966). These observations imply a need to put the concept of defenses in a broad evolutionary framework. In light of these issues, the present chapter proposes a structural model for describing ego defenses and their relations to affect states and diagnostic constructs, provides an evolutionary framework for this structure, and describes the development of a paper-and-pencil test for the measurement of the domain of defense mechanisms.

A. Variations in the Concept of Ego Defenses

Despite the wide acceptance of the concept of defense mechanisms, and despite their extensive usage in clinical contexts, there are two pressing needs. One is for the development of an integrated, consistent model of the defenses, and the other is for the development of a reliable and valid method for measuring the extent to which individuals use the different defenses.

There are several reasons for claiming that a coherent model of defenses is needed. For one thing, there is little agreement among clinicians on just how many defenses there are. For example, Anna Freud's original monograph (1937) described over 15 defenses. Coleman (1956), author of a textbook on abnormal psychology, listed 17 ego defense mechanisms. In the Psychiatric Glossary published by the American Psychiatric Association in 1975 (Frazier, 1975), 23 ego defenses are listed. In Vaillant's glossary of defenses (1971), 18 are defined.

Although a number of different names have been given to defenses, many writers of psychiatric textbooks have pointed out the extensive overlap of meanings that exist. For example, English and Finch (1964) point out that it is not always easy to distinguish between the various mechanisms of defense, and that there are no distinct boundaries limiting one from the other. They note that some defenses are related quite closely to each other, such as reaction formation and undoing, or denial and projection. Noyes and Kolb (1963), authors of a major textbook of psychiatry, point out that projection is, in many respects, a form of identification. Freedman, Kaplan, and Sadock (1975) argue that although the term *introjection* has been applied to the symbolic taking into oneself of other individuals, it has been discarded as unsatisfactory by many analysts. In a similar vein, Arieti (1974) notes that *isolation* and *splitting* are two names for the same concept. To emphasize the point being made, Noyes and Kolb (1963) claim that conversion should not be considered a defense mechanism because it is a process in which repression, identification, displacement, and denial are involved.

Bellak, Hurvich, and Gediman (1973) point out that the psychoanalytic literature uses the terms *internalization, identification, introjection,* and *incorporation* interchangeably and inconsistently. And Vaillant (1971) states that the term *intellectualization* includes the concepts of *isolation, rationalization, ritual, undoing,* and *magical thinking.*

These various citations were made to emphasize the point that clinicians do not agree on the total number of defenses, nor on their degree of overlap, nor even on their explicit definitions in some cases. It is thus evident that an integrating model of the defenses would be useful.

To complicate matters further, some authors distinguish between primary and secondary defenses (White, 1948). According to White, rationalization, isolation, and undoing are all forms of the secondary defense of intellectualization. The primary defensive processes are denial and repression, and the secondary ones are projection, reaction formation, displacement, and intellectualization.

White (1948) apparently is referring to a distinction that other authors have described as degree of primitiveness. For example, Arieti (1974) describes denial as very primitive, while Ewalt and Farnsworth (1963) describe repression as basic to all other defense mechanisms and as usually the first to be utilized. In contrast to White, English and Finch (1964) describe both introjection and projection as among the most primitive types of mechanisms, while Ewalt and Farnsworth (1963) consider regression a very primitive type of defense. Semrad (1967) has proposed that the most regressed schizophrenics tend to use denial and projection as defenses, but that recovery is associated with the use of hypochondriasis, ritual, and somatization. Most recently, Vaillant (1976) has classified defenses into four levels representing their relative degrees of theoretical maturity. The most primitive ("narcissistic") defenses are denial, projection, and distortion. The "immature" defenses typical of character disorders include fantasy, hypochondriasis, acting out, and passive–aggressive behavior. "Neurotic" defenses include intellectualization, repression, displacement, reaction formation, and dissociation. At the top of this theoretical hierarchy are the "mature" defenses of sublimation, suppression, altruism, anticipation, and humor.

Finally, the literature hints at the notion of polarity in relation to ego defenses. For example, Arieti (1974) considers reaction formation the replacement of an unacceptable drive derivative by its opposite. Both Chapman (1967) and English and Finch (1969) point out that introjection and incorporation are the opposite of projection. The literature thus implies at least three concepts in relation to defenses. One is that defenses overlap and vary in their degree of similarity to one another. The second is that some defenses at least are polar opposites. The third point frequently made is that some defenses are more primitive than others. From an analogue point of view, the first two implications can be topographically represented in a circular schematic diagram. This concept will be systematically explored later in the paper.

B. Attempts to Measure Defense Mechanisms

In the past decade, a modest literature has evolved that is concerned with the problem of measuring the presence and extent of defensive functioning in an individual. Some of these techniques of measurement depend upon self-reports. Others require the judgments of an interviewer (Ablon, Carson, & Goodwin, 1974; Froese, Vasquez, Cassem, & Hackett, 1974; Haan, 1965; Hackett & Cassem, 1974; Semrad, Grinspoon, & Feinberg, 1973). However, only those in the self-report format will be considered in the present review.

Of the 10 or so self-report measures of defense mechanisms in existence, all but a few are limited to only a few defenses (usually one or two). The defenses most frequently studied include denial, rationalization, and projection (Gleser & Ihilevich, 1960; Little & Fisher, 1958; Kreitler & Kreitler, 1972; Sarason, Ganzer & Singer, 1972; Sweney & May, 1970). Several of the scales are simply a rearrangement of items from the Minnesota Multiphasic Personality Inventory—MMPI (Byrne, 1961; Little & Fisher, 1956; Millimet, 1970; Sarason, 1958). In almost half of the published papers, references to internal reliability are absent, and in some, no reference is made to validity issues. Those tests that do report validity data usually refer either to correlations with MMPI scales or other tests or to correlations with clinical judgments. A number of the validity studies have attempted to discriminate between groups.

What all these defense mechanism tests have in common is a lack of a theoretical framework. In most cases there is a narrow preoccupation with one or two defenses. No attempt is made to embed the choices in a model that implies certain relations among defenses and that helps answer the question of which are primary and which secondary, and in general, how many there are.

C. Development of an Initial Model

It is evident that defense mechanisms relate to affective states and diagnostic concepts. For example, the relation of the ego defense mechanism of displacement to the clinical state of anger or aggression is seen throughout the social-psychological literature on scapegoating and in the psychoanalytic literature on passive–aggressive behavior (Kellerman, 1977). Similarly, the ego defense of repression is generally seen in its extreme form among clinical patients who are passive personalities. Such individuals generally seek secure, nonthreatening environments and tend to become acutely anxious and fearful when their security is threatened.

Another example of the relations among ego defenses, affective states, and diagnostic concepts is the relation between the defense of projection and the paranoid personality. Persons who are paranoid tend to be highly critical and rejecting. The use of projection becomes an attempt to see the world as a threatening environment in order to justify excessively rejecting, critical attitudes. Such persons frequently experience disgust toward others, which causes them to act in a rejecting manner.

Still another example of the relations among defense mechanisms and clinical and affective states is the relation between the defense of denial and the hysterical personality pattern. The chief characteristic of the hysteric personality is high suggestibility. The defense of denial is used by the hysteric to avoid having any critical attitudes at all and to assume a generally accepting stance towards the environment. The high suggestibility reflects an overuse of the feeling of acceptance.

These examples support the notion that defense mechanisms and affect states are related to one another. They also support the idea that personality traits and diagnostic labels are related to defenses. In addition, the previous discussion has suggested that defenses have at least three defining characteristics: (1) they vary in degree of similarity to one another; (2) they can be conceptualized in terms of polarities; and (3) they vary in degree of primitiveness (developmentally).

These descriptions of ego defenses are remarkably like the descriptions used to characterize emotions. Plutchik, (1962, 1970) has shown that emotions vary in their degree of similarity to one another, that they show the property of polarity, and that they vary in degree of intensity. In addition, he has shown that the domains of personality and diagnosis (Kellerman & Plutchik, 1968; Plutchick, 1967; Schaefer & Plutchik, 1966) are intimately related to the domain of emotion.

The many interrelations that have been mentioned can be conceptualized in terms of a particular model of emotions that has been fully described elsewhere (Plutchik, 1962). In brief, the model postulates that there are four pairs of basic bipolar emotions that vary in degree of similarity to one another. Since emotions are identifiable in lower animals as well as in humans (as Darwin and the ethologists have shown), the concept of basic emotions must have some relevance to broad phylogenetic issues.

The connection between emotions and evolution is based upon the fact that all organisms, in order to survive, must deal adequately with certain common problems. These problems are created by the nature of the environment, which in certain ways is similar for all animals. In order to survive, any organism must take in nourishment and eliminate waste products. It must distinguish between prey and predator, between a potential mate and a potential enemy. It must explore its environment and orient its sense organs appropriately as it takes in information about the beneficial and harmful aspects of its immediate world. And in organisms that are relatively helpless at birth and for a while thereafter, there must be ways of indicating the need for care and nurturance. The mechanisms by which these functions are carried out vary widely throughout the animal kingdom, but the basic prototypic functions remain invariant. These basic functions of protection, destruction, reproduction, reintegration, incorporation, rejection, exploration, and orientation define the basic emotional reaction patterns.

However, although emotions can be described in functional terms, they can also be described by the use of other appropriate languages. There is, for example, a subjective language of emotion, a behavioral language, a trait language, and a diagnostic language. Table 1 illustrates three of these languages. The layman tends to think of emotions in terms of subjective feeling states, but it is evident that feelings are neither reliable enough nor general enough to serve as a general basis for a theory of emotion. The other languages illustrated in Table 1 are just as valid ways of representing the theoretical states we call *emotions*.

It is also important to emphasize the fact that the relations between emotions (or behaviors, or traits) can be schematically represented by means of a circle. On the circle, fear is opposite anger, joy is opposite sadness, acceptance is opposite disgust, and expectancy is opposite surprise. Comparable circles can be drawn for both the behavioral and the trait descriptions.

In our attempt to carry these ideas further, it appeared possible to add two more languages to the lists shown in Table 1. These might be called the *diagnostic language* and the *ego defense language*. (see Table 2). Some evidence exists for a connection between diagnoses and affects (Schaefer & Plutchik, 1966; Plutchik, 1967; Plutchik & Platman, 1972), but the proposed connection between ego defenses, diagnoses, and affects is hypothetical. The remainder of this paper will help support this particular theoretical model.

Table 1. Three Languages That May Be Used to Describe Emotional States

Subjective language	Behavioral language	Trait language
Fearful	Escaping	Timid
Angry	Attacking	Aggressive
Joyful	Cooperating; mating	Sociable
Sad	Crying for help	Gloomy
Accepting	Affiliating; grooming	Trusting
Disgusted	Rejecting; vomiting	Distrustful
Anticipating	Exploring; mapping	Controlled
Surprised	Losing control; disorienting	Dyscontrolled

Table 2. *Hypothesized Relations among Traits, Diagnoses, and Ego Defenses*

Trait language	Diagnostic language	Ego defense language
Timid	Passive–aggressive passive type	Repression
Aggressive	Passive–Aggressive aggressive type	Displacement
Sociable	Manic state	Reaction formation
Gloomy	Depression	Compensation
Trusting	Hysteria	Denial
Distrustful	Paranoid state	Projection
Controlled	Obsessive–compulsive	Intellectualization
Dyscontrolled	Psychopathic state	Regression

There are a number of implications of the preliminary model of affects and ego defenses that is presented here. For one thing, it implies that persons with strong characteristic personality traits probably tend to rely on certain particular ego defenses as ways of coping with life stresses. For example, a very controlled person probably would tend to use intellectualization as a major coping mechanism. Second, the model implies that each major diagnostic entity describing personality disorders is associated with a dominant ego defense; the most obvious example of this is the fact that paranoid states are associated with projection. Third, the model implies that there is a small number of basic ego defenses and that the various lists that have been proposed by different writers reflect either overlapping ideas (different names for the same thing) or combinations of the basic defenses. This might be illustrated by the notion that isolation, rationalization, and undoing all represent variations on the defense of intellectualization and constitute an obsessional defense syndrome. Finally, the model suggests that there are some explicit polarities among the ego defenses. Specifically, it implies that repression and displacement are bipolar; that reaction formation and compensation are bipolar; that projection and denial are bipolar; and that intellectualization and regression are bipolar. Evidence for these relations will be presented later.

D. Constructing an Ego Defense Scale: Rationale

The model that has been outlined above implies that any measure of ego defenses should relate to affect states and diagnostic concepts. But how can such measures be obtained? With few exceptions, previous attempts to measure defenses have relied upon MMPI items, with little attention being paid to the theoretical (in contrast to the purely empirical) relevance of the items. In addition, since few defenses have been studied in the past, it seemed necessary to begin anew and attempt to construct a self-report test of ego defenses that measured a wide variety of defenses and that could be fully evaluated from a psychometric point of view.

A paper-and-pencil self-report test was decided on in contrast to the use of a projective instrument, primarily because all projective measures currently in use provide somewhat global measures of certain defenses, but none provide a specific index for each defense; for example, the defense of denial may be seen in figure drawings by the absence of the pupils in the eyes or by the usual "smile of denial" on the face. However, that same figure drawing may not be able to reveal any extensive information regarding the degree to which denial is being used. Also, indices of other defenses may not be apparent. Similarly, although the Rorschach may be able to reveal information regarding defenses, it cannot systematically evaluate the entire spectrum of ego defenses. Finally, none of the tests currently available, projective or otherwise, have made any attempt to relate the domain of defense mechanisms in terms of similarity and polarity, nor have they embedded them in any larger context as the present chapter proposes to do.

An important methodological issue arises in this connection. Since defense mechanisms are considered unconscious processes, how can a self-report instrument be used to measure them? There are two general answers. First, although it is true that defense mechanisms may develop ontogenetically in an unconscious fashion, this does not mean that their use must remain unconscious. Many individuals, either through psychotherapy or through other life experiences, learn to identify their own typical defense styles. Second, most individuals can report their own feelings and can describe behavior that reflects their own ego defenses, even though they cannot interpret the dynamic meanings of such behavior. For these reasons, it was felt that a self-report instrument was potentially feasible and could be a valid measure of a person's defenses.

It might be noted, parenthetically, that a number of writers have distinguished between ego defenses and coping behaviors. There is a tendency to describe ego defenses in such perjorative terms as *rigid*, *maladaptive*, and *distorting* (Alker, 1968) and to lump them with such other modes of control as tranquilizers, alcohol, and sleeping pills (Lazarus, 1975). In contrast, coping mechanisms include such things as empathy, concentration, logic, intellectuality, and objectivity (Alker, 1968). In Haan's (1965) test for ego functioning, all the defense scales were based on MMPI items, while all the coping scales were based on California Personality Inventory items. The present chapter is not concerned with this distinction. The model deals only with ego defense mechanisms.

The method we have adopted to increase our understanding of defenses combines theoretical considerations and empirical procedures. It attempts to integrate psychoanalytic insights about the nature of defense mechanisms with psychometric techniques of test construction. In addition, it draws on theoretical models of emotions and diagnoses to provide a meaningful context. The final outcome of the series of studies to be described is both a general model of defenses and a practical paper-and-pencil test that can be used to identify the degree to which individuals rely on the various defenses proposed as basic.

II. STUDY I: DEVELOPMENT OF A PRELIMINARY SELF-REPORT DEFENSE MECHANISMS TEST[1]

In order to identify the conceptual domain of defense mechanisms, a number of different sources were examined, which included both psychoanalytic writings and general psychiatric and psychological sources (Arieti, 1974; Chapman, 1967; Coleman, 1956; English & Finch, 1964; Ewalt & Farnsworth, 1963; Fenichel, 1948; Freedman, Kaplan & Sadock, 1975; Gilbert, 1970; Gregory, 1968; Lazarus, 1966; Noyes & Kolb, 1963; O'Kelly, 1949; Reich, 1945; White, 1948). From these various sources, 16 defense mechanisms were indentified as constituting the domain of ego defenses. General definitions for each defense mechanism were synthesized from the various sources. These definitions are listed in Table 3. Each definition was used to define a general universe of content for each defense.

A. Method

The procedure used to develop test items was to construct statements of the type that a person might use if he was consciously or unconsciously expressing a particular defense. For example, the statement "If I am angry at my boss, I will probably take it out on someone else" reflects the defense of displacement. Similarly, the statement "I always see the bright side of things" reflects denial. As an example of the fact that a person may be aware of his own behavior without knowing the defensive implications of it, the following type of item was included to indicate the defenses of repression: "I never remember my dreams."

Items were constructed to sample each of the 16 ego defense mechanisms. A total of 224 items comprised the initial test, called the Life Style Index. The number of items per defense scale varied from 11 to 16. Seventy undergraduate students ranging in age from 18 to 29 years were asked to respond to each item as "Usually true" or "Usually not true" for them.

[1] The authors would like to thank Inez Jerrett for her valuable assistance in connection with the analysis of the data in the studies reported here.

Table 3. Synthesized Definitions of 16 Ego Defense Mechanisms

Acting out   Reduction of the anxiety aroused by forbidden impulses by permitting their direct or indirect expression, without the development of guilt.

Compensation   Intensive attempt to correct or find a suitable substitute for a real or imagined physical or psychological inadequacy.

Denial   Lack of awareness of certain events, experiences, or feelings that would be painful to acknowledge.

Displacement   Discharge of pent-up emotions, usually of anger, on objects, animals, or people perceived as less dangerous by the individual than those that originally aroused the emotions.

Fantasy   Retreat into imagination in order to escape realistic problems or to avoid conflicts.

Identification   Unconscious modeling of attitudes and behaviors after another person as a way of increasing feelings of self-worth or coping with possible separation or loss.

Intellectualization   Unconscious control of emotions and impulses by excessive dependence on rational interpretations of situations.

Introjection   Incorporation of values, standards, or traits of other people in order to prevent conflicts with, or threats from, these people.

Isolation   Recollection of emotionally traumatic experiences or situations, without the anxiety originally associated with them.

Projection   Unconscious rejection of one's emotionally unacceptable thoughts, traits, or wishes, and the attribution of them to other people.

Rationalization   Use of plausible reasons to justify actions caused by repressed, unacceptable feelings.

Reaction formation   Prevention of the expression of unacceptable desires, particularly sexual or aggressive, by developing or exaggerating opposite attitudes and behaviors.

Regression   Retreat under stress to earlier or more immature patterns of behavior and gratification.

Repression   Exclusion from consciousness of an idea and its associated emotions, or an experience and its associated emotions.

Sublimation   Gratification of a repressed instinct or unacceptable feeling, particularly sexual or aggressive, by socially acceptable alternatives.

Undoing   Behavior or thoughts designed to cancel out a previous act or thought that has much anxiety or guilt attached to it.

B. Results

Two types of item analysis were employed to determine which items were best able to discriminate among individuals. In the first analysis, the percentage of "Usually true" responses was tabulated. Items for which "Usually true" responses were less that 10% or over 90% were eliminated. In addition, after the elimination of these items, each person was given a total score on each group of items representing each of the defense mechanisms. For each item representing a given defense mechanism, the 25% of the group who were high scorers on total score were compared with the 25% of the group who were low scorers on total score for that scale.

Comparisons were then made on the basis of the percentage of high scorers who responded "True" to a given item minus the percentage of low scorers who responded "True." Those items for which there was not at least a

20% difference between the high and low scorers were eliminated from each defense mechanism scale. These procedures resulted in a reduction of the original test from 224 items to the 184 items considered to be the most discriminating. Each individual scale now contained from 8 to 15 items. This test, which we called the Life Style Index, now appeared ready as the basis for further studies.[2]

III. STUDY II: CLINICIANS' CONCEPTIONS OF EGO DEFENSES IN RELATION TO DIAGNOSES

Clinicians agree that patients given different diagnostic labels tend to use psychological defenses to different extents and in somewhat different ways. For example, paranoid patients are believed to use the defense of projection predominantly. Obsessive–compulsive patients are believed to use intellectualization to a greater degree than, for example, hysterics. Although these are generally accepted clinical impressions, there are very few empirical data that deal directly with this issue. In view of these observations, it was decided to employ the new Life Style Index to determine the extent to which different clinicians agreed on the defense mechanisms typically used by patients in a number of diagnostic categories.

A. Method

Eight diagnostic labels were selected from the nonpsychotic personality disorders listed in DSM II (1968). They were as follows: paranoid; obsessive–compulsive; passive–aggressive (passive); passive–aggressive (aggressive); cyclothymic (depressed); cyclothymic (manic); hysteric; and psychopathic. To these was added one additional label: well-adjusted. Thirty-six experienced clinicians completed the Life Style Index for the nine diagnoses, four clinicians per diagnosis. Of these, 75% had either a Ph.D. or an M.D. degree, and 26% had either an M.A. or an M.S.W. The average length of clinical experience for the entire group was 14 years. The clinicians were given the following instructions:

> The following pages contain a number of statements that describe things people sometimes feel or do. We would like you to respond to each statement in the way that describes patients in a certain diagnostic category. The diagnostic category we are interested in is:
>
> *(one of the diagnostic categories)*
>
> Please try to imagine what a *typical* patient is like who might be given this characterological diagnosis. Then respond to all the statements in the way that would

---

[2] Copies of the Life Style Index may be obtained from the senior author.

characterize this person. If you think that a statement is true or usually true for this person, circle "T" on the separate answer sheet. If you think the statement is false or usually false for this person, circle "F" on the answer sheet.

It is important to emphasize that the clinicians were describing a general type of patient and were not rating specific individuals. Therefore, to some extent the descriptions reflect theoretical expectations as well as practical experiences.

The intraclass correlation (Guilford, 1965) was used to determine the degree to which judges agreed with one another on the extent to which each defense mechanism is used by patients in each of the diagnostic categories. The intraclass correlation (r_{kk}) indicates the reliability of the averaged ratings of four judges rating the use of a given defense mechanism—for example, denial—by different categories of patients.

B. Results

All but three of the intraclass correlations for each of the 16 defense mechanisms were over $+.71$. With the two exceptions of compensation and identification, all the coefficients were significant, with many at well beyond the .001 level. It thus appears that experienced clinicians have a well-defined conception of the way in which these defense mechanisms are used by different types of patients. This agreement among clinicians may reflect a common core of training or may be a true reflection of the way that patients given different diagnoses actually use defense mechanisms.

IV. STUDY III: A FACTOR ANALYSIS OF CORRELATIONS AMONG DEFENSE MECHANISM SCALES

As previously mentioned, it is generally agreed that there is some degree of overlap in meaning among the ego defenses. In order to get information about this overlap of meaning among the defense mechanism scales, an inter-correlation matrix was constructed. It was based on the data of the 184-item revised version of the original 224-item Life Style Index completed by the 70 college students (Study I). This 16 × 16 intercorrelation matrix was then factor-analyzed with a varimax rotation of a principal-components solution (Kaiser, 1958).

A. Results

The first three factors accounted for approximately 50% of the variance. Eleven of the scales loaded moderately to heavily on the first factor, while two scales, denial and sublimation, loaded heavily on the second factor. Two scales, acting-out and intellectualization, loaded oppositely on the third factor.

The way in which the defenses appear to cluster, with the vast majority loading on the first factor, is only suggestive since the size of the sample is somewhat small for the number of variables involved. One important conclusion that can be drawn from these data is that most defense mechanisms tend to have a lot in common. Such a finding is consistent with psychoanalytic observations that imply that anxiety is a common ingredient of all defenses inasmuch as the initial development of any defense is an attempt to cope with the anxiety produced by a threatening or conflictive situation. In addition, all defenses have in common a self-protective function. This point is discussed in the context of group theory by Kellerman and Plutchik (1977).

B. Discussion

Given these findings, it seemed reasonable to try to reduce the number of ego defenses to a smaller number. However, rather than use a purely empirical approach to the problem of grouping, we considered both psychoanalytic theory and the emotion theory outlined earlier. On this basis, eight ego defense scales were constructed as a first approximation to an adequate taxonomy for defense mechanisms. Four of the original scales were unchanged. Four new scales resulted from the regrouping of items. The new repression scale contained items from the previous repression, isolation and introjection scales. The new compensation scale consisted of items from the previous compensation, identification, and fantasy scales. The new regression scale was composed of items from the previous regression and acting-out scales. Finally, the new intellectualization scale added items representing rationalization, undoing, and sublimation. A number of ambiguous items were dropped, producing a new version of the Life Style Index that contained 138 items. The number of items in any individual scale ranged from 10 to 26.

V. STUDY IV: CLINICIANS' RATINGS OF THE APPROPRIATENESS OF ITEMS

After the items of the Life Style Index had been constructed, pretested, and shortened, the extent to which other clinicians would agree that the items appropriately sampled the various defenses was evaluated. For this purpose the following procedure was developed.

A. Method

The items of each scale of the questionnaire were typed on separate sheets of paper. At the top of each list, the following question was asked: "How well does a 'Yes' response to each of the following items reflect the operation of the defense mechanism listed at the top of the page?" A 4-point rating scale, ranging from "Not at all" to "Very well," was provided beside each item. Scores for each item could range from 0 to 3. A special category titled "Not sure" was also available to the raters.

Some scales were completed by 3 clinicians and some by 4 clinicians. The total number of clinicians involved was 17. They represented the disciplines of psychiatry, psychology, and social work and had an average of 13 years of experience. The mean rating for each item of each scale was obtained, and for each scale, the items were ranked on the basis of these means.

The eight ego defense scales represented by these items in fact included several that were clusters or combinations of ego defenses. For example, the scale "intellectualization" actually included items reflecting the defenses of sublimation, undoing, and rationalization. Similarly, "compensation" included items representative of identification and fantasy. The combinations of scales are shown in Table 4. Examples of the highest ranked items for each scale are also presented. These items all received a mean rating of 3.0 or nearly 3.0.

In all cases the clinicians could agree on a few items as clearly indicative of a defense mechanism. However, in some cases, there was considerably more

Table 4. Items Ranking Highest on Relevancy for the Eight Ego Defense Scales

Compensation, Identification, Fantasy
1. I daydream a lot.
2. When someone says I am not able to do something, then I really want to do it just to show him he was wrong.

Denial
1. I'm not prejudiced against anyone.
2. I never feel disgusted.

Displacement
1. If someone bothers me, I don't tell it to him, but I tend to complain to someone else.
2. When I get angry, I sometimes go out and watch a movie with lots of violence in it.

Intellectualization, Sublimation, Undoing, Rationalization
1. I'm not afraid of getting old because it happens to everybody.
2. I usually put things off because I think I'll be in a better frame of mind to do them later.

Projection
1. If I'm not careful, people will take advantage of me.
2. I find fault with my friends.

Reaction Formation
1. It is always important for me to be neatly and cleanly dressed.
2. Pornography is disgusting.

Regression, Acting Out
1. I get irritable when I don't get attention.
2. Sometimes I act childishly.

Repression, Isolation, Introjection
1. I never remember my dreams.
2. I've never had a major crisis in my life.

disagreement on the appropriateness of an item for a given scale. To illustrate this point, the item "I am generally careful and watchful" was considered by the clinicians to reflect the mechanism of projection only slightly or they were "Not sure." Similarly, the clinicians did not consider the item "I try very hard not to be nasty to anyone" as being particularly appropriate to the defense of intellectualization.

In addition, it was evident that the items for certain scales were considered more appropriate than were those for other scales. For example, the scales designed to measure projection and intellectualization seemed to have the most disagreement concerning the appropriateness of items. In contrast, the items on the scales for repression and for regression (acting out) showed good agreement as to their relevance for these scales. These findings permitted a refinement and selection of items in order to represent most adequately the different ego defenses.

VI. STUDY V: RATINGS OF DEVELOPMENTAL LEVEL OF EGO DEFENSES

The clinical literature implies that the different defense mechanisms represent in some way different levels of development or different levels of primitiveness. This is reflected in part by the difference between primary-process and secondary-process activity and by the correlation of specific defenses with particular psychosexual stages. With these considerations in mind, it was decided to try to determine the level of ego development reflected by each defense in the judgment of experienced clinicians. In order to accomplish this, six psychiatrists with an average of 12 years of clinical experience were asked to rank a list of the eight defense mechanisms in an order that represented the level of development of each ego defense.

A. Results

The relative ranking of these defenses in terms of level of ego development was obtained by averaging the ranks given by each of the psychiatrists and is given in the following list: denial; regression; projection; displacement; repression; reaction formation; intellectualization; and compensation. The psychiatrists appeared to be in a good agreement that denial, regression, and projection are very primitive defenses and that intellectualization and compensation are not primitive but represent higher levels of development. The degree of agreement among the psychiatrists is reflected by a Kendall Coefficient of Concordance of .71 (Siegal, 1956), which is significant at the .01 level.

B. Discussion

These findings are partly consistent with the theoretical statements of psychoanalysts. White (1948), for example, described denial and repression as primary defenses, while he considered all the other defenses on the list secondary ones. Consistent with the present findings is the statement by Ewalt and Farnsworth (1963) that regression is a very primitive defense. Similarly, English and Finch (1964) considered projection a primitive defense, as did the psychiatrists questioned in the present study.

The most detailed attempt to order ego defenses in terms of levels of maturity has been made by Vaillant (1971, 1976). He considers denial and projection the most primitive (or "narcissistic") defenses, a finding entirely consistent with the judgments of the psychiatrists making the evaluations here. Intellectualization and reaction formation are considered relatively nonprimitive by the present psychiatrists. This is also consistent with Vaillant's conceptualization, which consider these ego defenses "neurotic" defenses, representing the third level of maturity.

It thus seems reasonable to conclude that there is good agreement among experienced clinicians as to the estimated degree of primitiveness of the various defenses. This may reflect a common background of training, or it may reflect a gradual refinement of the meanings of these terms during the course of the past few decades. The development of ego psychology within the psychoanalytic movement has brought more attention to the defenses as basic adaptive tools, with a consequent increase in the clarity and usage of these concepts. Despite this increased attention, there is still a need for a satisfactory theoretical framework for relating defenses to one another and to affective states and diagnostic constructs.

VII. STUDY VI: A COMPARISON OF SCHIZOPHRENICS AND NORMALS ON THE LIFE STYLE INDEX

In an effort to determine the usefulness of the Life Style Index and to obtain one measure of its validity, it was decided to investigate whether the scales could discriminate between a normal population and a schizophrenic population. The hypothesis was made that schizophrenic patients would be more likely to use the defense mechanisms, and particularly the more primitive ones, to a greater extent than would a normal comparison group. This hypothesis is consistent with psychoanalytic theory as well as with the findings of Vaillant (1971, 1975, 1976). It is also likely that some defenses—for example, projection—would be used much more by psychiatric patients and that other defenses—for example, intellectualization—would be used relatively more frequently by normal individuals. In other words, the relative extent to which defenses are used may be quite different in normal and abnormal populations.

A. Method

With these considerations in mind, 29 schizophrenic patients in a State hospital were administered the Life Style Index. Approximately one-half of these patients were diagnosed as paranoid schizophrenics, while the remainder had other schizophrenic diagnoses. Of the sample, 19 were males with a mean age of 32 years (SD = 11.50), and 10 were female with a mean age of 36 years (SD = 15.50). The average scores on the scales for this group of patients were compared with the average scores of the 70 college students, whose mean age was 26 years (SD = 6.00). The students were significantly younger than the patients (t = 3.62, $p <$ .01). However, there was no significant difference in the proportion of males and females in the two samples.

B. Results

Table 5 presents the mean scores of the schizophrenic subjects and the college students on each of eight defense mechanisms. Since each scale has a different number of items, they are therefore also presented in the form of percentage of total possible score for each scale.

The mean defense-mechanism scores for the two groups were compared by t tests. The results show highly significant differences for all but one of the defenses, namely, regression. For all other scales, the schizophrenic subjects scored significantly higher than the college students, and even though the difference in scores for regression did not reach significance, the schizophrenic patients also scored higher on this defense.

These results indicate that the extent to which defenses are used is different in normals and schizophrenics. Schizophrenic patients use defenses of all

Table 5. Mean and Percentage Scores for Each Defense Mechanism: Schizophrenics Compared with College Students

Defense mechanism	College students means	College students percentages	Schizophrenics means	Schizophrenics percentages	t
Reaction formation	2.26	18.8	6.41	53.4	7.57[a]
Repression	4.24	21.2	8.17	40.8	5.28[a]
Intellectualization	9.56	36.8	14.10	54.2	4.56[a]
Compensation	8.71	34.8	11.11	44.4	3.36[b]
Projection	5.26	47.8	6.76	61.4	2.89[b]
Denial	3.04	27.6	4.55	41.4	2.69[b]
Displacement	2.19	21.9	3.21	32.1	1.98[c]
Regression	6.93	30.1	8.24	35.8	1.42

[a] $p <$ .001.
[b] $p <$ .01.
[c] $p <$ .05.

types much more frequently than do normal college students. This finding confirms one of the original hypotheses and is consistent with the reports of Vaillant. It also provides a measure of discriminant validity for the scales of the Life Style Index.

VIII. STUDY VII: EGO DEFENSES IN RELATION TO SELF-ESTEEM AND ANXIETY

The marked differences between a normal and a schizophrenic group observed in Study VI suggests another hypothesis. Since it seems reasonable to assume that schizophrenic patients have low self-esteem, it also seems plausible that even among normal persons, those with low self-esteem will be more likely to use ego defenses than will those with high self-esteem. The following study was conducted in order to test this hypothesis. In addition, it was hypothesized that high levels of anxiety would increase the probability of the use of ego defenses. To test this hypothesis, all subjects were given the short form of the Taylor Manifest Anxiety Scale.

The Life Style Index was completed by 58 persons, 37 women and 21 men. The mean age of the women was 24.2 years (SD = 7.7) and that of the men was 24.9 (SD = 5.3). All the subjects either had some college training or were college graduates. They were asked to complete the Life Style Index along with a self-esteem scale. This latter scale is based on the Tennessee Self Concept Scale (Fitts, 1965), on which there are extensive published validity data. The spilt-half reliability of the self-esteem scale used in the present study is +.85. In addition, all subjects completed the brief (20 items) version of the Taylor Manifest Anxiety Scale that has been developed by Bendig (1956). This self-report scale, the MAS, is answered in a true–false format and has a reported reliability of +.75. The items cover such areas as working under a great deal of tension, inability to concentrate, extreme sensitivity and self-consciousness, lack of self-confidence, and being easily upset.

A. Results

Table 6 summarizes the major findings of this study. The mean scores for each scale for a group of "normal" subjects are presented along with the internal split-half reliability of each scale. Correlations of each scale with the self-esteem scale and with the Manifest Anxiety Scale are also given.

The means for the ego defense scales are quite close to those of 70 college students who were compared with the schizophrenic patients in Study VI and thus provide a cross-validation of the test. The internal reliabilities as estimated by split-half correlations are significant in all cases except one, but they

Table 6. Correlations of Ego Defenses with Self-Esteem and Anxiety

Ego Defense	Mean	Standard deviation	Split-half reliability	Correlation with SES	Correlation with MAS
Denial	2.98	1.80	.52	.23	−.35[a]
Repression	4.07	2.65	.55	−.25	.23
Regression	6.52	3.08	.51	−.52[a]	.48[a]
Compensation	9.19	3.13	.58	.28[b]	.40[b]
Projection	6.36	2.21	.61	−.31[b]	.57[a]
Displacement	1.72	1.39	.16	−.22	.34[b]
Intellectualization	9.71	3.53	.73	−.40[a]	.42[a]
Reaction formation	2.76	2.17	.75	.09	.35[a]

[a] $p < .01$.
[b] $p < .05$.

tend to be a little lower than is usually considered desirable for personality test scales. In part, this may reflect the fact that some of the scales are composed of items representing several clusters of items (for example, the intellectualization scale includes items for rationalization, undoing, and sublimation). In addition, each ego defense is probably multidimensional, so that the moderate degrees of internal reliability that were found may result from the low intercorrelations among the items of each particular scale.

The Pearson product-moment correlations of the ego defenses with the self-esteem scale is negative in all cases where there is a significant correlation. In other words, the greater the self-esteem of a person, the less are his scores on regression, compensation, projection, and intellectualization.

Essentially the opposite holds true with regard to the anxiety scale. The greater the anxiety score, the greater the tendency to use regression, compensation, projection, displacement, intellectualization, and reaction formation. The only puzzling exception is the one negative correlation with denial. This may be interpreted as indicating that people who show strong denial may be avoiding recognition of their own anxiety. These results thus provide additional evidence of the construct validity of the scales.

IX. STUDY VIII: SIMILARITY RATINGS OF DEFENSE MECHANISMS: A DIRECT ESTIMATION METHOD

In other sections of this chapter, it was hypothesized that defense mechanisms vary in their degree of similarity to one another and that they may be bipolar as well. To the extent that such relations in fact exist among the ego defenses, to that extent can they be represented schematically or topologically by means of a circle. In order to subject this hypothesis to an empirical test, two independent procedures were used. The first was based on a method described more fully by Conte (1975).

A. Method

Of the 16 defenses, 3 were chosen as "reference" terms, and all other defenses were compared directly to these for degree of similarity. These ratings were made on an 11-point scale ranging from −5 ("opposite") through various degrees of dissimilarity to 0 ("no relation") to various degrees of similarity up to +5 ("the same").

Nine clinicians—five psychologists and four psychiatrists—were asked to rate for similarity each of the 16 defenses against each of the 3 defenses chosen as reference terms. The clinicians were provided by the authors with definitions of each of the ego defenses (see Table 3).

Mean ratings were obtained for each defense relative to each of the three reference terms. These three means were converted to angular positions on a circle by means of an equation that was based on the assumption that "opposition" corresponded to 180° and that "no relation" corresponded to 90°. These angular positions were then translated into angular placements relative to one of the reference terms and averaged. Finally, a first approximation to the similarity and polarity relations among the defenses was determined by plotting their empirical angular locations on a circle.

B. Results

Examination of Figure 1 shows that the ego defenses are distributed around a circle. This distribution is an empirical finding and is in no way a necessary outcome of the technique used. These results suggest that a circle is at least a rough approximation of the similarity and polarity relations among ego defenses.

From this point of view, it is instructive to examine the circle for possible groupings of similar defenses. One such grouping is seen in the cluster of sublimation, rationalization, intellectualization, and isolation, which may be considered a syndrome of obsessional defense. Another way of looking at the circle is in terms of polarities. From this point of view, the displacement–projection cluster is opposite the fantasy–introjection cluster, and reaction formation and regression are both opposite sublimation and rationalization. These polarities appear to reflect differences in a number of implicit characteristics of the ego defenses. For example, displacement–projection is outward, labile, and action-oriented, while fantasy–introjection is inward, controlled, and passive. Regression suggests a primitivization of feelings or behavior,

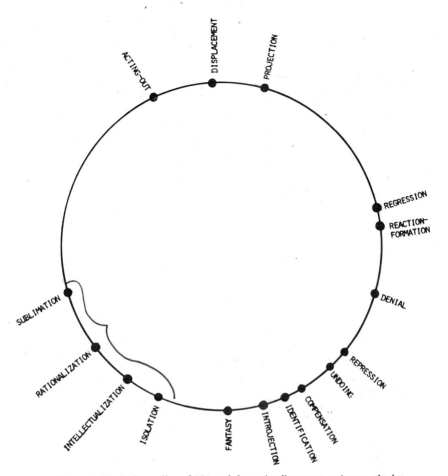

Figure 1. Similarity scaling of 16 ego defenses by direct comparison method.

while its opposite (sublimation and rationalization) suggests intellectual control.

These findings suggest that experienced clinicians do in fact see ego defenses varying in similarity to one another, a fact that is consistent with the relations among personality traits (Conte, 1975) as well as emotions (Plutchik, 1970). This empirical circular structure of ego defenses lends support to the model that is being presented, which assumes that ego defenses are derivatives of particular emotions. The details of this model are examined in a later section.

An important question left unanswered by Study VIII concerns the subjective basis for the similarity judgments made about defenses. In order to examine this question in some detail, Study IX was carried out.

X. STUDY IX: SIMILARITY RATINGS OF DEFENSE MECHANISMS: A SEMANTIC DIFFERENTIAL COMPARISON

When two items or categories are compared for degree of similarity, there may be many different criteria that the judges can use. In order to determine which criteria are in fact used, a modified semantic differential technique has been found to be helpful (Conte, 1975).

A. Method

Twenty semantic differential scales were selected as a basis for describing the connotations of each defense mechanism. These scales sampled each of the dimensions isolated by Osgood (1967) as characteristic of language; namely, activity, potency, and evaluation.

The judges were to rate the degree of connotative relevance of each of the semantic differential terms for describing each defense mechanism. For example, the judges were asked to rate the relevance of words such as *active*, *unpleasant*, *sad*, or *effective* for describing rationalization, displacement, etc. A unipolar 5-point scale of relevance was used for the ratings. Six clinicians provided the ratings for all 16 defense mechanisms using the 20 semantic differential terms.

A mean profile for each defense resulted. The profiles were intercorrelated by the use of Pearson product-moment correlations to form a correlation matrix composed of all possible pairs of defense profiles. The correlation matrix was then factor-analyzed by the method of principal components, and five factors were extracted and rotated, The first three factors accounted for 74% of the variance.

B. Results

The ego defenses appear to load heavily on the first two majors factors. When the data are plotted, acting out, projection, and displacement are very close, as we found in Study VII using the method of direct estimation. Identification and introjection are also found close together, as was discovered in Study VII. However, the data do not form a circular pattern, or circumplex. It appears that at least three factors are necessary to account for an appreciable portion of the variance when using this method.

Differences in results between the direct estimation method and the semantic differential profile method for measuring similarity of concepts may be due to a number of possibilities. In one case, similarity of defenses is a direct judgment, while in the second case, it reflects an inference based upon a complex statistical procedure. A second possibility is that several of the semantic differential terms may not be appropriate for making judgments about ego defenses. For example, the word *hard* was apparently interpreted by some judges as meaning "difficult," while others interpreted it as connotating the opposite of *soft*. A third possibility is that the judges had difficulty applying the semantic differential terms to the very abstract concepts represented by ego defenses. A fourth possibility is that ego defenses are such complex concepts that they may not be adequately representable by two dimensions, which is a requirement for a circular configuration.

XI. A THEORETICAL MODEL FOR DEFENSE MECHANISMS

The studies that have been described have had several purposes. First, they provide a description of the development of a new test designed to measure ego defense mechanisms through the use of self-reports. Several of the studies have described the item selection and analysis procedures. Others have evaluated the discriminative and construct validities of the scales. The result of these studies is to provide a basis for claiming that the Life Style Index is a first approximation to a reliable and valid self-report test of ego defenses.

A second purpose of the studies was to examine the hypothesis of a circular structure as an appropriate analogue model for the relations among ego defenses. The results of these studies partially confirm the existence of both a similarity and a polarity structure. These findings, on the psychometric properties of the scales and on the topological relations among the scales, provide a guide for the development of a theoretical model of ego defenses in relation to affects. The present section attempts to elaborate such a model.

It seems evident that although there are many words that have been used by different authors to label defenses, these terms do not describe independent and totally different concepts. The factor-analytic study (III) has demonstrated the overlap of scales designed to measure defenses.

Based on the material presented at the beginning of this chapter, and based on the results of the studies, we propose five postulates designed to provide a theoretical model of defenses:

Postulate 1: Specific defenses are designed to manage specific emotions.

Postulate 2: There are eight basic defense mechanisms that have evolved to deal with the eight basic emotions.

Postulate 3: The eight basic defense mechanisms show the properties of both polarity and similarity.

Postulate 4: Major diagnostic personality types are derived from particular defensive styles.

Postulate 5: An individual may utilize any combination of the defense mechanisms.

In the process of growing up, each individual faces a large variety of situations that trigger emotional states such as anger, fear, disgust, resentment, and sadness. Quite often, the expression of the emotional state creates a further conflict and additional danger. For example, attacking a larger, older person can lead to destructive retaliation; criticizing one's parents can lead to hostile rebukes or threats of loss. The result is that the child develops defensive strategies that represent indirect ways of dealing with emotional conflicts.

However, the specific defensive strategies one develops depend on the specific emotions involved in the conflict. For example, one way to deal with anger aimed at a stronger adversary is to displace the anger to a weaker scapegoat. Displacement, therefore, represents a coping strategy or defense mechanism designed to deal with conflicts over the emotion of anger. In a similar way, projection is a defense designed to deal with the feeling of self-rejection. A person who blames himself, feels guilty, and is disgusted with himself may deal with this conflict by attributing the disgust or blame to others who he believes are rejecting him. We conclude that specific defenses are designed to manage specific emotions (Postulate 1).

In order to decide how many defense mechanisms there are, we must therefore attempt to relate them to emotions. Although there are many emotion terms in our language, it is possible to demonstrate that they can all be conceptualized as mixtures of one or more of eight primary emotions (Plutchik, 1962, 1970; Plutchik & Kellerman, 1974). These eight emotions can be described in terms of different languages; for example, a subjective language, a behavioral language, a functional language, or a trait language, as has been discussed earlier. We propose that the eight defense mechanisms that deal with these emotions are displacement, projection, compensation, regression, repression, denial, reaction formation, and intellectualization (Postulate 2).

In order to make clearer the choice of these particular eight defenses as basic, we present Table 7. In it are listed 16 defense mechanisms. These are arranged to show which defenses are grouped under each of the eight major categories. For example, regression is postulated to include the defenses of fantasy and acting out. Intellectualization includes the defenses of rationalization, undoing, and sublimation.

Also included in Table 7 is a brief mnemonic or image designed to capture of essence of each defense. For example, the image for displacement is "Attack something that represents it." The image for projection is "Blame it"; for identification, "Be like it," etc. The word *it* means, in each case, the stimulus (an event, a person, or an impluse) that triggers each particular emotion. For example, in the case of displacement, the "it" refers to the person who initially triggered the emotion of anger. In denial, the "it" refers to some person or event that might be disappointing to an individual. In undoing, the "it" is something to which a commitment has been made.

One of the important characteristics of defenses that has received scant attention is the fact that they vary in their degree of similarity to one another.

Table 7. A Schema for Describing Primary and Secondary Defense Mechanisms

Major defense mechanisms	Characterization
• Displacement	"Attack something that represents it"
• Projection	"Blame it"
• Compensation	"Try to regain it"
Identification	"Be like it" (so it can't be lost)
• Regression	"Cry for it"
Fantasy	"Daydream about it"
Acting out	"Do something"
• Repression	"Don't remember it"
Introjection	"Don't admit where you got it"
Isolation	"Don't feel it"
• Denial	"Don't see it"
• Reaction formation	"Reverse it"
• Intellectualization	"Redefine it" "Recategorize it"
Rationalization	"Make an excuse for it"
Undoing	"Take it back" ("Cancel it out")
Sublimation	"Transform it"

Thus, as has been shown, displacement and projection are more similar to one another than they are to denial. Similarly, denial and repression are more similar to one another than they are to intellectualization. These similarities are evident if we consider the two similarity scaling studies.

We therefore assume that the implicit similarity structure of defenses can be described by means of a hypothetical circular model. This is shown in Figure 2. It can be seen that denial and projection are opposites, displacement and repression are opposites, reaction formation and compensation are opposites, and intellectualization is the opposite of regression (Postulate 3). The application of these ideas in a group-therapy context may be found in Kellerman and Plutchik (1977).

The opposition of these various defenses may be seen in some of the examples given earlier; for instance, in the discussion of paranoia and hysteria and their respective defenses of projection and denial, or in the opposition of passive and aggressive and their respective defenses of repression and displacement. The same kind of opposition may be seen between intellectualization and regression. Intellectualization implies control or a nonmotoric transformation of an impulse, and aggression implies a lessening of control and a tendency toward a motoric expression of an impulse. Reaction formation is opposite to compensation in that compensation implies an attempt to overcome the effects of a real or a perceived loss (or lack), and reaction formation is an attempt to reduce the threat of a (sexual) gain.

One implication of this circular model of defenses is that the diagnostic labels implied by ego defense styles may also have a circular structure. This is also illustrated in Figure 2. As confirmation of this circular diagnostic model,

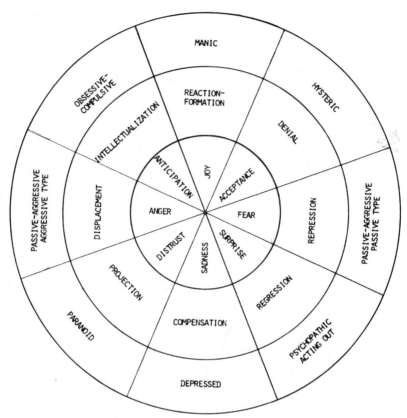

Figure 2. Theoretical model relating emotions, ego defenses, and diagnostic categories.

Schaefer and Plutchik (1966) and Plutchik and Platman (1977) have empirically demonstrated circular models for the nonpsychotic personality types listed in DSM II (1968) (Postulate 4).

Finally, it is evident that the vicissitudes of life lead to complex mixtures of emotional conflicts for each unique individual, and therefore they must also lead to complex blendings of ego defenses to deal with them (Postulate 5).

XII. CONCLUSION

This chapter has attempted to present a new model of the nature of ego defense mechanisms. It has examined the conflicting and ambiguous statements and definitions that have previously been offered about ego defenses and has proposed a simplification in terms of the concepts of similarity, polarity, and developmental level. These notions lead to the hypothesis of a circular topographic analogue structure for representing ego defenses. In addition, an attempt is made to relate ego defenses to affect states and diagnostic concepts, so that a broad phylogenetic underpinning for the ego defenses is provided.

The model provides the basis for the development of a self-report test designed to measure basic ego defenses. A summary follows of a series of nine studies that are designed to explicate the properties of the test and to demonstrate empirically its reliability and validity. Several studies of the similarity structure of ego defenses then provide empirical support for the theoretical model that is presented.

We believe that the theory that appears in this chapter contributes to a clarification of the concept of ego defenses. However, it also contributes to our understanding of personality as well as the nature of the diagnoses of psychopathology. Of equal importance is the fact that ego defenses can be incorporated within a general theory of organism–environment interactions that is applicable to both persons and lower animals.

REFERENCES

Ablon, S. L., Carlson, G. A. & Goodwin, F. K. Ego defense patterns in manic–depressive illness. *American Journal of Psychiatry*, 1974, *131*, 803–807.

Alker, H. A. Coping, defense and socially desirable responses. *Psychological Reports*, 1968, *22*, 985–988.

Arieti, S. (Ed.). *American handbook of psychiatry*. New York: Basic Books, 1974.

Bellak, L., Hurvich, M., & Gediman, H. K. *Ego functions in schizophrenics, neurotics, and normals*. New York: Wiley, 1973.

Bendig, A. W. The development of a short form of the Manifest Anxiety Scale. *Journal of Consulting Psychology*, 1956, *20*, 384–387.

Byrne, D. The repression–sensitization scale: Rationale, reliability, and validity. *Journal of Personality*, 1961, *29*, 334–349.

Chapman, A. H. *Textbook of clinical psychiatry: An interpersonal approach*. Philadelphia: Lippincott, 1967.

Chess, S. *An introduction to child psychiatry*. New York: Grune & Stratton, 1964.

Chess, S. Psychiatry of the first three years of life. In S. Arieti (Ed.), *American handbook of psychiatry*. New York: Basic Books, 1966.

Coleman, J. C. *Abnormal psychology and modern life*. New York: Scott, Foresman & Company, 1956.

Conte, H. R. A circumplex model for personality traits (doctoral dissertation, New York University, 1975). (University Microfilms No 7601731.)

DSM-II *Diagnostic and statistical manual of mental disorders* (2nd ed.). Washington, D.C.: American Psychiatric Association, 1968.

English, O. S., & Finch, S. M. *Introduction to psychiatry*. New York: Norton, 1964.

Ewalt, J. R. & Farnsworth, D. L. *Textbook of psychiatry*. New York: McGraw-Hill, 1963.

Fenichel, O. *The psychoanalytic theory of neurosis*. London: Routledge and Kegan Paul, 1946.

Fitts, W. H. *The Tennessee Self Concept Scale*. Nashville: Counselor Recordings & Tests, 1965.

Frazier, S. H. *A psychiatric glossary*. Washington, D.C.: American Psychiatric Association, 1975.

Freedman, A. M., Kaplan, H. I., & Sadock, B, J. (Eds.), *Comprehensive textbook of psychiatry*, Vol. 2. Baltimore: Williams & Wilkins, 1975.

Freud, A. *Ego and the mechanisms of defense.* London: Hogarth, 1937.

Froese, A., Vasquez, E., Cassem, N. H., & Hackett, T. P. Validation of anxiety, depression and denial scales in a coronary care unit. *Journal of Psychosomatic Research,* 1974, *18,* 137–141.

Gilbert, G. M. *Personality dynamics: A biosocial approach.* New York: Harper & Row, 1970.

Gleser, G. C., & Ihilevich, D. An objective instrument for measuring defense mechanisms. *Journal of Consulting and Clinical Psychology,* 1969, *33,* 51–60.

Goodall, J. Mother–offspring relationships in the free ranging chimpanzees. In D. Morris (Ed.), *Primate ethology.* Chicago: Aldine, 1967.

Gregory, I. *Fundamentals of psychiatry.* Philadelphia: Saunders, 1968.

Guilford, J. P. *Fundamental statistics in psychology and education.* New York: McGraw-Hill, 1965.

Haan, N. Coping and defense mechanisms related to personality inventories. *Journal of Consulting Psychology,* 1965, *29,* 373–378.

Hackett, T. P., & Cassem, N. H. Development of a quantitative rating scale to assess denial. *Journal of Psychosomatic Research,* 1974, *18,* 93–100.

Kellerman, H. Hate. In B. B. Wolman (Ed.), *International encyclopedia of neurology, psychiatry, psychoanalysis and psychology.* New York: Van Nostrand Reinhold, 1977.

Kellerman, H., & Plutchik, R. Emotion–trait interrelations and the measurement of personality. *Psychological Reports,* 1968, *23,* 1107–1114.

Kellerman, H., & Plutchik, R. The meaning of tension in group psychotherapy. In L. R. Wolberg, M. L. Aronson, & A. R. Wolberg (Eds.), *Group psychotherapy 1977: An overview.* New York: Stratton Intercontinental Medical Book Corp., 1977.

Kreitler, H., & Kreitler, S. The cognitive determinants of defensive behavior. *British Journal of Social and Clinical Psychology,* 1972, *11* 359–273.

Lazarus, R. S. *Psychological stress and the coping process.* New York: McGraw-Hill, 1966.

Lazarus, R. S. Psychological stress and coping in adaptation and illness. In *Proceedings of the National Heart and Lung Institute Working Conference on Health Behavior.* DHEW Publ. No. (NIH) 76-868, May, 1975.

Little, K. B., & Fisher, J. Two new experimental scales of the MMPI. *Journal of Consulting Psychology,* 1958, *22,* 305–306.

Lorenz, K. *On aggression.* New York: Harcourt Brace, 1966.

Millimet, C. R. Manifest anxiety–defensiveness scale: First factor of the MMPI revisited. *Psychological Reports,* 1970 *27,* 603–616.

Noyes, A. P., & Kolb, L. C. *Modern clinical psychiatry.* Philadelphia: Saunders, 1963.

O'Kelly, L. I. *Introduction to psychopathology.* New York: Prentice-Hall, 1949.

Osgood, C. E., Suci, G. J., & Tannenbaum, P. H. *The measurement of meaning.* 8th printing. Urbana: University of Illinois Press, 1971.

Plutchik, R. *The emotions: facts, theories, and a new model.* New York: Random House, 1962.

Plutchik, R. The affective differential: Emotion profiles implied by diagnostic concepts. *Psychological Reports,* 1967, *20,* 19–25.

Plutchik, R. Emotions, evolution and adaptive processes. In M. Arnold (Ed.), *Feelings and emotions: The Loyola Symposium.* New York: Academic Press, 1970.

Plutchik, R., & Kellerman, H. *Manual for the Emotions Profile Index.* Los Angeles: Western Psychological Services, 1974.

Plutchik, R., & Platman, S. R. Personality connotations of psychiatric diagnoses. *Journal of Nervous and Mental Disease,* 1977, *165,* 418–422.

Reich, W. *Character analysis* (3rd ed.). New York: Farrar, Straus, 1963.

Sarason, I. G. Interrelationships among individual difference variables, behavior in psychotherapy, and verbal conditioning. *Journal of Abnormal and Social Psychology,* 1958, *56,* 339–344.

Sarason, I. G., Ganzer, N. J., & Singer, M. Effects of modeled self-disclosure on the verbal behavior of persons differing in defensiveness. *Journal of Consulting and Clinical Psychology,* 1972, *39,* 483–490.

Schaefer, E. S., & Plutchik, R. Interrelationships of emotions, traits, and diagnostic constructs. *Psychological Reports*, 1966, *18*, 399–410.

Semrad, E. The organization of ego defenses and object loss. In D. M. Moriarity (Ed.), *The loss of loved ones*. Springfield, Ill.: Charles C Thomas, 1967.

Semrad, E. V., Grinspoon, L., & Feinberg, S. E. Development of an Ego Profile Scale. *Archives of General Psychiatry*, 1973, *28*, 70–77.

Siegel, S. *Nonparametric statistics for the behavioral sciences*. New York: McGraw-Hill, 1956.

Sweney, A. B., & May, J. M. *The defense mechanism index: Handbook and interpretation manual*. Kansas: Test Systems, 1970.

Vaillant, G. E. Theoretical hierarchy of adaptive ego mechanisms. *Archives of General Psychiatry*, 1971, *24*, 107–118.

Vaillant, G. E. Natural history of male psychological health: III. Empirical dimensions of mental health. *Archives of General Psychiatry*, 1975, *32*, 420–426.

Vaillant, G. E. Natural history of male psychological health: The relation of choice of ego mechanism of defense to adult adjustment. *Archives of General Psychiatry*, 1976, *33*, 535–545.

White, R. W. *The abnormal personality: A textbook*. New York: Ronald Press, 1948.

Pain, Anxiety, Grief, and Depression

II

Editor's Introduction

9

Leventhal and Everhart make it quite clear that pain and the emotions associated with it play a significant part in the development and well-being of the physical and social self. Their emphasis is on the contribution of emotions to the subjective experience of pain, and the explanatory model that has been developed by Leventhal and his colleagues pushes back the frontier of research on pain and pain–emotion–cognition interactions.

Leventhal and Everhart provide a critical review of two earlier models of pain. They show that the sensory model, which defines pain as a sensory experience resulting from particular types and intensities of physical energy, has led to a number of false but commonly held assumptions about the sources and meanings of pain. They note, for example, that this model falsely predicts that injury always leads to pain and that the magnitude of the injury is directly related to the magnitude of the pain.

They describe the sequential components model in terms of the formula, pain = sensation + emotion. In this framework, the emotion, typically fear, is somehow added to the sensory information resulting from the injury. Investigators following this model recognize the power of emotion in influencing subjective experience and hence they emphasize the treatment of the emotion component as a method of alleviating the pain. Leventhal and Everhart discuss the question of the relative contribution of the sensory data from tissue injury and the emotion component and find the sequential components model inadequate for resolving this issue.

In order to resolve the problems inherent in the earlier theories of pain, the authors propose a parallel processing model in which the sensory-informational data from tissue damage are processed simultaneously or in parallel with the emotional component. The end result of this parallel processing of data from the pain and emotion systems is a pain–distress (or pain–emotion) experience in which there is integration of the sensory information about the noxious stimulus with emotion responses. According to this model, one neural pathway handles the sensory data from the noxious stimulus or injury and provides information about the location, duration, intensity, and other attributes of the stimulus. The second pathway generates the emotion experience, and the integration of the data from the two pathways produces pain–distress or the pain–emotion experience. The interaction of the two components takes place very early in the signal conduction sequence, but the interaction may be inhibited or altered by attentional processes.

The integration of the sensory data of tissue damage (pain information) with emotion requires what the authors term "schematic processing." Through experience, each individual develops affective–cognitive structures or schemata that represent the informational and pain–emotion aspects of earlier experiences. What we experience in a given noxious stimulus-situation is determined in part by the schema we have for that situation. The authors illustrate schematic processing in a detailed discussion of phantom limb pain. This discussion enables them to point up the various important functions of schemata, including the way in which they facilitate adaptation to noxious, threatening situations. The authors review a number of empirical studies from their own and other laboratories that support their parallel-processing model of the pain–emotion experience.

Emotion, Pain, and Physical Illness

9

HOWARD LEVENTHAL and DEBORAH EVERHART

Physical illness and pain are integral to human existence; "There has never been a culture which has not concerned itself with disease" (Baken, 1968 p. 3). Whiting and Child (1953) were able to use "customs relating to illness and the threat of death" as indices of normative personality characteristics in their classic cross-cultural study of the relationship of child-training practices to personality as "sickness and death occur in all societies, and customs relating to them have grown up everywhere." Freud (1962a,b) emphasized the importance of pain and illness to the development of the ego. He suggested that the ego was first and foremost a body ego (Freud, 1962a; see also Schilder, 1950) and regarded pain produced by illness as an important source of libidinal excitation for the cathexis of body imagery. Recent, cognitively oriented writings on personality, such as Epstein's (1973) and Lifton's (1976), have also stressed the central role of images and concepts of pain and death in the processes of self-definition.

Involvement with illness, pain, and death is not confined to a few intellectual theoreticians. The average person is also concerned with the experience of illness, pain, and death and seeks knowledge regarding the control of these experiences. The magnitude of this concern is attested to by the proliferation of popular books on death and dying (e.g., Becker, 1973), health columns in daily newspapers, articles and columns in mass-circulation magazines such as *Redbook* and *Reader's Digest*, and "health" spots interspersed in radio and television broadcasts. Perhaps the single best testament to the average citizen's view of the importance of controlling pain and ill-

HOWARD LEVENTHAL and DEBORAH EVERHART • University of Wisconsin, Madison, Wisconsin. Research supported by grants from the National Science Foundation (SOC 75–02482) and the Robert Woods Johnson Foundation.

ness is the rapid growth in the size and cost of the health care system. In 1950 the national health bill was $450 million; in 1977 a single corporation, General Motors, will pay $1 billion for health insurance (Marshall, 1977). The rising costs of medical care are due to a number of crucial factors, but the public, the users of the system, are accomplices to the resultant increases. Few people are willing to tolerate pain when they feel pain can be controlled, and few people are willing to leave illnesses untreated when they feel treatment can be beneficial—all want the best doctors and the best medicines. In summary, pain and illness play a key role in both the elaboration and the maintenance of the physical and social self and as a result, they contribute greatly to the proliferation of institutional structures for protecting the ego by coping with pain and illness.

I. THE ROLE OF EMOTION IN PAIN AND ILLNESS

The central role of pain and illness in human motivation suggests that pain and illness provoke powerful emotional forces that sustain involvement in health topics. Emotion contributes to the seeking of medical care and contributes to the generation of illness. Our chapter will focus, however, on the contribution of emotion to the subjective experience of pain. We will examine the contribution of emotion to pain from the point of view of a particular theory of emotion (Leventhal, 1974, 1977, in press) that is representative of a set of theories that can be called *expressive–motor* or *attitude theories*, whose antecedents lie in the writings of Darwin (1872), Bull (1962), and Dewey (1894) and the recent writings of Tomkins (1962), Izard (1971), Ekman, Friesen, and Ellsworth (1972), and Ekman and Friesen (1971). The bulk of the chapter will elaborate on the theory and apply it to pain experience.

II. MODELS OF PAIN AND EMOTION

Before beginning a technical discussion of the way in which emotion relates to pain, we will present a case example to help clarify the way emotion appears to be involved in pain reactions.

A case example: A young, pregnant woman has been lying in bed in a labor room for 6 hours. About 3 hours ago her contractions became more distinct and noticeable, and both her enthusiasm and apprehension rose. Her husband, who had been with her until then, left for 2 hours. While he was gone, she became increasingly concerned that her first baby might be too large to deliver or that she might not be strong enough to push him clear. She hurt all over, felt severe pain with each contraction, writhed, gripped the bedpost, and cried out during each contraction. She seriously doubted that she could take more pain and became frightened about further pain from the episiotomy and delivery, and as she became more upset, she asked for pain medication and began to cry quietly. Her husband returned about an hour before delivery and she calmed considerably. She remained reasonably calm and controlled as the contractions became stronger, though she still clutched vigorously at the bed railing. But she was hopeful that she would soon be able to rest and enjoy the sight of her new infant.

Two salient factors stand out in the case example. First, the level of distress and emotional activation become more severe over time; indeed, there seems to be a fairly direct linkage between overt expression and inner feelings of distress (Leventhal & Sharpe, 1965). A second factor is the marked increase and then decrease in emotional expressiveness and reported distress with the leaving and return of the patient's husband. The presence of a person who is loved and trusted appears to have a marked impact on the intensity of the various responses indicating pain and emotional distress. Had we observed a sample of mothers in what appears to be more-or-less the same situation, we would have been impressed by the very large individual differences in the various indicators of pain and distress. The behavior of the mother described was toward the "high" end of the scale, which should not be very surprising as her labor was longer and appeared to be more distress-inducing than typically found for mothers having their first baby. But one can observe mothers whose expressions of distress are still more intense and who can be quieted only if heavily sedated. On the other hand, there are mothers who endure the stresses of labor with little or no observable reaction. It is not clear whether they can simply tolerate high levels of pain or whether they have higher pain thresholds and do not notice their contractions. As all mothers, regardless of their overt distress, match the contractions and sensations in the second stage of labor, when the cervix is fully (10 cm) dilated, to the intensity of heat of a lamp that will burn the skin (Javert & Hardy, 1950) the differences among the mothers seem to be related to emotional reactions rather than to variations in sensory pain experience.

Our example illustrates the relationship of emotion to pain experience. But what mechanisms are involved in this relationship? We will explore the question of mechanism by examining the way in which emotion is integrated into the subjective experience of pain. To better illustrate some of the subtleties and problems involved in depicting such a mechanism, we will review three different theories of the pain mechanism: (1) the *sensory model* of pain; (2) the *sequential component* theory of pain; and (3) the current authors' "processing model" of pain. The first two models are elaborated to provide a contrast to and to deepen our understanding of the third. We will also attempt to show that these models are the basis of many erroneous commonsense beliefs about pain, and we will suggest that the faults of common sense reflect faults in the underlying models.

A. Sensory Model of Pain

In textbooks of medicine and medical physiology (Guyton, 1971; Mountcastel, 1968), pain is treated as a sensory system, as an experience generated by particular types and intensities of physical energy (tearing of tissues, excessive heat or cold, pressure, etc.) acting on specialized receptors (usually free nerve endings), which then transmit signals through spinal pathways to "pain centers" in the brain. Thus, as with any sense, pain begins with specialized receptors responsive to particular cortical "pain" centers (see Figure 1).

Treating pain as a sensory system leads to a number of expectations, such as the following: The same stimuli will elicit pain for different persons; the threshold for pain, while different for different people, will cluster over a narrow range of stimulus values; the consciousness of pain is similar in different persons; and the experience of pain typically precedes subsequent emotional reactions. These assumptions are embedded in the substantial body of work on the psychophysics of pain: "Since pain is an aesthetic experience its perceptual component can be studied only in conscious man, its presence is best established through reports given by trained subjects" (Hardy, Wolff, & Goodell, 1952). If the goal is to define sufficient or necessary stimuli and to specify thresholds for different types of sensations (e.g., burning and pricking, etc.), and given that people's responses are similar, it may indeed be wise to use practiced subjects.

Underlying the sensory model of pain is the fundamental assumption that pain and illness are caused by agents that impinge upon us from without, causing breakdowns in an otherwise normal system. The alternative assumption—that endogenous factors and the normal operation of the system itself may produce pain and disease—is essentially alien to the sensory model and to most medical models of illness.

The linkage of pain with external intrusions is seen in two hypotheses derived from the sensory model. The first is the assumption of a direct physical to physiological linkage in pain mechanisms, and the second is that of a direct

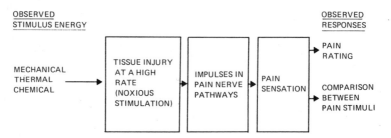

Figure 1. The sensory model of pain (adapted from Hardy, Wolff, & Goodell, 1952, p. 53).

physiological to psychological linkage in pain experience (Melzack, 1973; Melzack & Wall, 1965, 1970). The assumption of a physical to physiological linkage requires that a particular stimulus or class of stimuli (pressure, electrical shock) reliably give rise to physiological activity in a receptor or neural conducting unit and that the receptor and conducting unit be relatively unresponsive to other forms of stimulation. The first assumption is the less troublesome of the two as it can be tested by presenting a stimulus to a receptor and recording the receptor (or nerve) response. The difficulty is that complex stimulus patterns and complex neural interactions may underlie what appears to be a simple stimulus–response connection. But this first assumption can still be tested, and it makes no assumptions about the end product of experience.

The second, the physiological to psychological assumption, is the source of great difficulty as it suggests that activity in a particular receptor or particular neural pathway is necessary and (possibly) sufficient for a subjective pain experience. This assumption is what leads us to incorrectly label stimuli, receptors, and pathways as "pain" stimuli, "pain" receptors, and "pain" pathways. Melzack and Wall (1970) state:

> To call a receptor a *pain* receptor . . . is a psychological assumption . . . and the stimulation of the receptor must always elicit pain and only the sensation of pain. The facts of physiological specialization provide the power of specificity theory; its psychological assumption is its weakness.

In short, while neurophysiological research does indeed suggest that

> a small number of specialized fibers may exist that respond only to intense stimulation, . . . this does not mean that they are "pain fibers"—that they must always produce pain, and only pain when they are stimulated. (Melzack & Wall, 1970).

Melzack and Wall are warning us against the expectation of a tight or near-perfect correlation between particular physical stimuli and pain and of a tight or near-perfect correlation between activity in particular neural pathways and pain.

A number of important commonsense beliefs are based on the sensory view of pain; two of these are the *magnitude* rule and the *pain–injury* rule. Imagine someone sitting in a dentist's chair to have a cavity repaired. The dentist's drill whirls, cuts quickly through the enamel, and then into the rotted area of the tooth. The heat and vibration are considerable, but several rapid strokes of the drill remove the rot and the tooth is filled.

Now imagine a soldier trudging through the battlefield. A shell landmine explodes nearby and his leg is practically ripped off; the bone is completely shattered, pieces of skin and flesh are hanging down, and he drops to the ground. He is carried by stretcher to an operating tent and a surgeon examines and pokes in the deep flesh, looks at the exposed bone, touches it with a sterile probe, and talks to the soldier about the impending operation.

If you imagined each scene vividly, we would guess that your distress was substantially greater for the second than the first. If so, you implicitly assumed that the *magnitude* of injury is related to the *magnitude* of pain. This is the *magnitude* rule. But is it true? Among the men he observed from the battle fields in Italy during World War II, Beecher (1946) reports that roughly 57.8% of those who were wounded reported either *no* or *slight* pain and only 23.7% reported severe pain. The percentage reporting pain did vary by type of injury and was highest for abdominal injuries, where 48% of the wounded reported pain. The failure to report pain did not reflect inhibition of reporting or lack of pain sensitivity, as the men complained about pain from simple inoculations even though they did not request pain medication for their extensive wounds. We would guess that close to 100% of them would complain of pain had they been the dental patient in our first example.

Chaves and Barber (1975) give another example of the magnitude rule in their description of the awed reactions of observers watching surgery done under hypnosis. They suggest that observers are overly impressed by the effectiveness of hypnosis because they expect surgical pain to be exceptionally severe because surgery causes deep and extensive penetrations of the body. As they point out, however, most pain receptors are located near the body surface, and visceral and other internal structures are less sensitive than the surface.

The second false assumption based on the sensory-theory view of pain that we wish to examine is the tendency to believe that the presence of pain is a sign of injury, that is, to reason from consequents (Merskey, 1968; Walters, 1961). We all know it is illogical to reason from the consequent, that is, to assume the truth of a premise because we have evidence as to the truth of a conclusion. Thus, even though injury can lead to pain, I cannot conclude that I am injured if I feel pain. The second assumption does not follow logically from the first, and more importantly, we feel pain in the absence of a noxious stimulus or an injury. We suspect that most people would consider it more likely they are injured when they feel pain than they will feel pain when injured. The ease with which we can think so incorrectly could in part be accounted for by the fact that our language tends to fix this type of error into our daily thought. For example, the dictionary defines *hurt* as follows: "To afflict with body pain; to do physical or material harm" (Webster's Unabridged, 1966). The same term is used to describe the antecedent and the consequent.

Of course, the assumption, "pain means injury," may be due to more than a language bias. It may also be due to the bias or tendency of the human mind to leap rapidly from a concrete sensory experience to an abstract generalization (I feel pain; pain means injury), and to move cautiously from an abstract generalization to a specific experience (Injury sometimes gives rise to pain; if I feel pain, I may or may not be injured).

In summary, many commonsense beliefs about pain are based on sensory-model assumptions, that is, that a specific stimulus excites specific pain receptors and that the experience of pain, its presence and magnitude, is a direct indicator of the presence and the magnitude of the eliciting stimulus. Unfortunately for the sensory model, the major "puzzle of pain" (Melzack, 1973) is the poor correspondence between physical stimuli and pain experiences. If pain is a sensory system, is it not puzzling that drilling a tooth and receiving an injection may elicit more intense pain than a major leg wound?

The specificity theorist has two responses to the above argument. The first is that the distribution and action of pain receptors is not fully known. Anomalies such as the greater pain from superficial surface wounds than from deep wounds may be a function of receptor distribution and different ways of stimulating receptors in different locations; for example, to excite sparsely distributed visceral pain receptors may require a different form of mechanical action (stretching) than to excite the more numerous surface receptors (cutting). But this argument does not easily handle dramatic observations such as the cultural practices of *couvade* and the *lack* of the pain response observed in religious ceremonies performed in India. In *couvade* the husband goes to bed and writhes in pain while his wife continues working and, when ready, delivers herself of her child (Trethowan & Conlon, 1965). In the religious ceremonies of southern India, a person is exalted when he is lifted aloft on ropes so he can bless the multitudes below; the ropes are tied to steel hooks that have been inserted beneath the large muscle groups in his back (Kosambi, 1967). Yet he can smile benignly at the throng while performing his solemn duties. Because the many differences in pain response cannot be accounted for by the hypothesis of varying receptor distribution, sensory theorists have been forced to a second option, which is to adopt Beecher's (1959) suggestion that pain is made up of two components: a sensory component and an emotion, reaction component.

B. Sequential Components (Sensation and Emotion) Model

Beecher (1959; 1965) has posited that an emotional or reactive component is added to the primary sensory component of pain once the primary sensation becomes sufficiently strong. As with the sensory model, we will also stereotype and simplify this position to demark it better from the processing model to be presented next. Figure 2 presents a picture of this type of additive model. First, the physical stimulus initiates activity in the sensory-perceptual pain system, which gives rise to pain experience. The pain experience and associated memories then give rise to an affective response, usually thought of as a *fear* reaction, which is a key part of the overtly expressed and overtly visible pain reaction. The degree of separation between these components is exemplified by Beecher's (1946) discussion of pain from combat wounds; he suggests that the sensation component be treated with analgesics or opiates such as morphine,

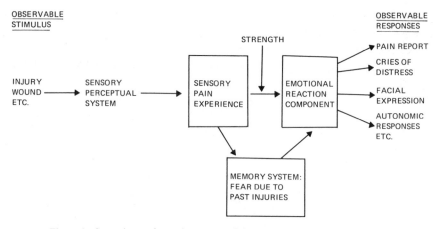

Figure 2. Sensation and emotion: sequential components in pain experience.

while the reaction component is treated with emotion-reducing agents such as barbiturates.

Studies illustrating the contribution of emotion to pain tend to pay less attention to the specific stimuli and specialized pain receptors that make up the sensory system for pain and focus instead on variables such as personality factors, set, etc., that affect the intensity of the emotional or reactive response to pain. Read (1959) has suggested that many of the intense pain reactions during childbirth reflect emotional factors and believes that preparation can reduce fear and lead to a nonpainful labor experience. Javert and Hardy (1950) attributed the substantial individual differences they observed in mothers' reactions to childbirth to differences in the strength of the mother's emotional response. It seemed reasonable to attribute the individual differences in pain to the "reaction or emotional response component" because differences in the mothers' pain–distress reactions were unrelated to the mothers' judgments of the strength of the pain stimuli.

If the individual differences in overt distress behaviors are due entirely to differences in the mothers' emotional response component while the sensation component remains constant, we confront a key theoretical question as to whether "real *pain*" actually varies across persons. This question is extremely difficult to answer. If we argue that "real pain" is constant, we are suggesting that we can equate the sensory pain for women manifesting quite different levels of overt distress and that overt distress is independent of "real pain." So extreme an interpretation seems unreasonable, given the data from a study by Leventhal and Sharp (1965), which investigated the relationship between facial expressions of emotional distress and stimulus strength during delivery and found that forehead and brow contractions, which are assumed to indicate emotional distress (Coleman, 1949; Ekman & Friesen, 1971; Hanawalt, 1944;

Izard, 1971), increased linearly with cervical dilation during labor. Thus distress does not seem to be a factor that is simply added on by the individual personality, *independent of the stimulus.*

In spite of the shortcomings of the sequential-component model, such as its failure to address the question of the degree to which distress and sensation pain are separate or integral factors, the model has provided a framework for viewing a wide range of experimental findings, such as the following:

1. Females tend to show lower pain tolerance than males (Notermans & Tophoff, 1975), which can be attributed either to a greater tendency to respond emotionally (Cupchik & Leventhal, 1974) or to a greater willingness to express and/or report on internal emotional states (Jourard & Lasakow, 1958).

2. Athletes have a higher pain tolerance than nonathletes, and the highest tolerance can be found among participants in contact rather than noncontact sports (Ryan & Kovacic, 1975).

3. Subjects report reductions in pain generated by 0°C ice water by thinking of the water as cool and refreshing on a hot day (Spanos, Horton & Chaves, 1975).

4. Anesthesia instructions will sharply increase pain tolerance when combined with white noise (Melzack, Weisz, & Sprague, 1963) or when given along with a hypnotic suggestion (Hilgard, 1973, 1971, 1969; Hilgard & Hilgard, 1975; Zimbardo, Rapaport, & Baron, 1969; Zimbardo, Cohen, Weisenberg, Dworkin, & Firestone, 1969).

The model does not, however, provide a detailed explanation of the mechanism underlying these effects and therefore makes few suggestions as to why results vary from study to study; for example, anesthesia instructions worked only when combined with hypnotic instructions or white noise in the studies just listed, yet alone they were found to be sufficient for pain reduction in studies by Barber and Hahn (1962) and Spanos, Barber, and Lang (1975).

In summary, there is a large body of evidence suggesting that many factors, including both individual differences and situational variations, appear to influence emotional responsiveness and the strength of pain reactions. It seems reasonable to conclude, therefore, that these factors are operating on an emotional distress mechanism. The question, however, is whether it is adequate to conceptualize this mechanism as something that simply adds the emotional reaction on to the sensory experience of pain.

One set of studies that seems relevant to determination of the adequacy of the sequential model of pain is Clark's (1969) application of signal detection analysis to pain threshold measurement. Clark suggests that each pain threshold measurement consists of two parts: (1) a sensory informational part and (2) a decision criteria or reaction component. Using signal detection procedures and analysis, Clark has found that differences in thresholds between different age, sex, and instruction groups reflect differences in the criterion or emotional reaction component and not differences and/or changes in the sensory or informational component of pain (Clark & Mehl, 1973; Clark & Goodman, 1974). Thus, there seems to be an informational and a decision component for how much pain one is willing to tolerate as well as for when one is first able to detect it.

At first glance, Clark's analysis and findings appear to support the sequential pain model, that is, that pain involves two stages with an initial sensory stage followed by a second, emotional response stage. On closer reflection, his findings make clear an ambiguity that may be fatal to the model. The signal detection analysis argues and demonstrates that the first and second stages are independent and uncorrelated. But the sequential model appears to suggest that the second, emotional reaction component of pain varies with the strength of the earlier, sensory component and implies, therefore, a relationship between the two. This hypothesis, with supporting data using the traditional method of limits, has been advanced by Gelfand (1964), Gelfand, Ullman, and Krasner (1963), and Wolf, Krasnegor, and Farr (1965); they suggested that individual differences in emotional reactions would make a stronger contribution to variance in the threshold for how much pain subjects would tolerate (when the sensory component is very powerful) than to variance in the sensory threshold, the point at which pain is initially detected.

How can we resolve the contradiction between the findings of signal detection theorists, which argue for the independence of the emotional and the sensory components, and the results of the other investigators, which point to a dependence between the two. One resolution is to argue that the signal detection analysis offers the most accurate picture of the threshold process (see Green & Swets, 1966; Massaro, 1975; Swets, 1961) and that the sequential model is likely to be wrong. This conclusion would also be consistent with earlier data showing that the same factors affect emotional reactions at both pain and tolerance thresholds (Clark & Bindra, 1956). A second resolution would be to argue that the procedures used in the signal detection experiment, which presents a large number of stimuli in series and asks the subject to focus on the sensory components rather than seeing how much pain he can tolerate, cause an artificial separation of sensation and emotion, and that under real-life conditions involving clinical pain, sensation and emotional reaction components are integral and correlated (Garner, 1974). But even if this alternative is true, it will not save the sequential model, as the model lacks the constructs needed to deal with the possibility that subjects treat sensory pain and distress as a common or integral event under some conditions and as separable events under other conditions. To make matters yet more complex, recent findings (Clark, 1976) from signal detection experiments suggest that psychological factors can produce changes in the sensation component. In summary, we clearly need a pain mechanism more complex than that offered by the sequential model if we accept that the emotional reaction component contributes equally to both pain and tolerance thresholds, that psychological factors can produce changes in both criterion and sensory pain, and that subjects may respond to an amalgam of sensory pain and distress under some but not all conditions.

C. A Parallel Processing Model of Pain Distress

1. Resolving the Pain—Distress Problem. Fortunately, the issues mentioned above can be resolved by a parallel processing model which differs in several critical ways from the sequential model of pain (see Figure 3). First, it arranges the informational and distress-emotional components in parallel rather than in sequence (Leventhal, 1970). Thus, the information about the stimulus, its location, its sensory properties of coldness or hotness, its pricking or numbness, etc., are processed at the same time that the feelings of distress or suffering is processed. In this arrangement, the emotional distress response is not dependent upon the conscious experience of pain; it is produced rapidly and virtually simultaneously with the pain experience (see Hilgard & Hilgard, 1975, p. 20).

The second important feature of the model is that it posits that most of the processing of pain and distress goes on preconsciously. This statement has two important implications. First, it is a way of saying that the stimulus is encoded in peripheral receptors and conducted to the central nervous system, where it is elaborated upon in different ways before becoming part of our perceptual worlds. Second, it points to a separation between *perception* and *focal awareness*! *Perception* refers to all the stimulus material that has been processed and can gain access to focal awareness; it is all of the material to which one *can* attend (Neisser, 1967; Posner, 1973). *Focal awareness* involves the material to which one does attend. Finally, the parallel processing model includes attentional devices (filters) or channels to bring material from perception to focal awareness (Broadbent, 1977; Kahneman, 1973). The notion of attentional channels provides a means of accounting for the influence of situational conditions on the separation or integration of sensory pain and emotional distress. For example, the instructions used in the signal detection experiment encourage the subjects to separate the sensory information and emotional reaction components and to attend and respond only to the stimulus information. The instructions are as follows: "We wish to determine your ability to feel warmth, heat and faint pain" (Clark & Goodman, 1974, p. 366). "Remember, we do not want to see how much pain you can stand; rather, we want to know how good you are at detecting the presence of a just noticeable amount of pain" (Clark & Mehl, 1971, p. 204). The situation, therefore, is highly controlled, and the subject is told to pay close attention to the sensations and not to "see how much pain [he] can stand." Focusing on the informational component should make it less susceptible to the influence of the reaction component, as the two are no longer blended in the subject's pain experience.

2. Elaboration of the Processing Steps. If pain–distress is the end product of a temporal processing sequence and an integration of information about the noxious stimulus with emotional reactions, we need to spell out the details of the mechanisms that produce this pain–distress experience.

Figure 3 was the starting point for our model. As with the *sensory* and *sequential components* model, Figure 3 showed that a number of mechanisms intervene between the stimulus input and the conscious experience of pain–distress. The first step is an encoding stage involving the conversion of the noxious stimulus into neural activity. The second step involves the elaboration of the encoded stimulus by motor reactions and memory systems. Following that, the elaborated signal is available to perception. The fourth step involves the attentive selection and amplification of the signal, after which it appears in focal awareness.

The processing model departs from the sensory and sequential components model in several important ways. The most obvious, as we have already suggested, is the postulation of two separate and parallel pathways for the development of pain experience: one is a sensory-perceptual or informational path that creates the individual's experience of the location, duration, intensity, and attributes of the stimulus; the second is an emotion path that generates the perceptual experience of distress. Figure 4 provides a more detailed picture of the above mechanisms and indicates three important features absent in Figure 3. First, it suggests that parallel processing begins at the very outset, that is, with encoding of the noxious stimulus. Second, it suggests that elaboration of the informational and emotional inputs is generated by a hierarchically arranged set of processing mechanisms, that is, several mechanisms arranged in a nested order. Third, it suggests that a number of specific interactions take place between these parallel systems. We shall discuss each of these issues.

a. Sensory Encoding and Its Interactions. The separation of informational and pain–emotion processing appears virtually with the onset of stimulus encoding because of receptor specialization; different receptors are reactive to different properties of the stimulus. For example, if the noxious stimulus is a bath of circulating 0°C ice water, coldness, touch, and other sensations will be encoded by different receptors than those encoding bright pain and dull pain, as the skin is endowed with separate receptors for *cold, touch, pressure,* and *bright prickly pain* or *dull pain* (Melzack, 1973; Mountcastel, 1968). We have italicized the features listed to emphasize that action in these receptors is not yet the experience of coldness, touch, pressure, and bright or dull pain; these terms are psychological. But at the level of physical-physiological description, it does seem that different properties of the stimulus are related to action in different receptors and neural paths.

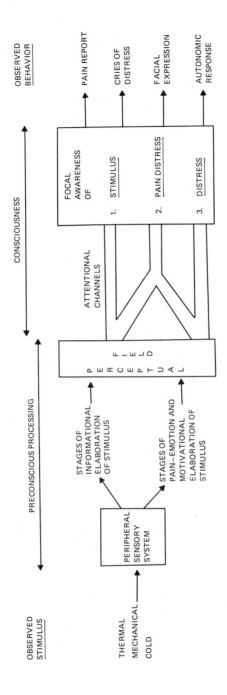

Figure 3. Parallel processing of information, pain, and distress.

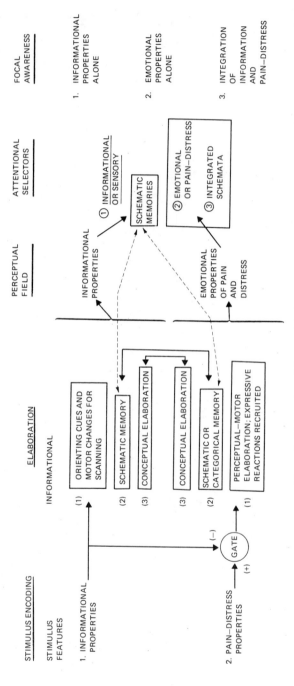

Figure 4. Elaboration of the parallel processing model.

These two major paths interact with one another very early in the signal conduction sequence; the interaction is described by Melzack and Wall's (1965, 1970) gate theory of pain (see Figure 4). The gate theory states that pain experience depends on the transmission of signals from a T-cell system for further processing as pain distress. The T-cell system lies in the dorsal root of the spinal cord. Three factors seem to affect the degree to which the T-cell system will send signals upward for pain distress processing:

1. The T-cell system is stimulated to fire by small A-delta and very small, unmyelinated C fibers, called *pain* fibers by Casey (1973), which run from the site of stimulation to the dorsal horn of the spinal cord. As a stimulus becomes stronger, it will activate more of these small fibers.

2. The T-cell system is inhibited by activity in A-alpha fibers, as these large fibers stimulate the substantia gelatinosa (which inhibits T-cell firing) as well as conducting signals to the brain and to the T cells in the dorsal horn of the spinal cord. Because the larger informational fibers conduct more rapidly, they are able to inhibit T-cell activity even when the noxious stimulus is rather strong. For example, Melzack, Wall, and Weisz (1963) and Higgins, Tursky, and Schwartz (1971) have demonstrated that an informational input, such as a vibratory input, will block the pain experience from a noxious stimulus such as a shock or a slap if the vibration is applied immediately before the noxious event.

3. Finally, Melzack (1973) hypothesizes that activity in higher centers of the brain, can stimulate reticular system activity, which then sends signals to the cord to inhibit T-cell firing.

b. Hierarchical Elaboration. The peripheral sensory structures and the gate system are the initial step in the production of pain–distress perception and pain–distress awareness. One cannot draw a sharp line, however, between the end of the encoding phase and the beginning of the next steps in the construction of the pain–distress experience. But from the gate upward, the informational and emotional systems appear to take different, though interacting, paths, with each becoming more complex and the processing of inputs becoming deeper over time. The following three hierarchical mechanisms seem to be involved in the further processing of the pain signals after they leave the gate system: (1) *perceptual-motor* processing; (2) *schematic* or categorical processing; and (3) *conceptual* processing.

Perceptual–motor processing is the initial level of processing in the elaboration of emotion and is a level of structuring that is automatic and to a great extent innate (see Figure 4). Perceptual-motor processing gives rise to a perceptual signal that is recognizable as an emotional response. The second, schematic, stage of processing combines or integrates the perceptual-motor signals with schemata or categories that have been built up by the activation and storage in memory of past emotional activity. And finally, there is a higher order, conceptual, processing where the activity at the perceptual-motor and schematic levels contacts conceptual systems whose symbols represent the more concrete informational and emotional schemata that record past episodes of pain–distress experience. Conceptualized in this way, all three of these systems are simultaneously active and enrich and add to the pain–distress experience.

Perceptual-motor processing must be considered separately in the informational and the pain–emotion systems. In the information system, it generates the outputs that make up the perception of the fundamental sensory attributes or properties of the noxious stimulus. For example, if the noxious stimulus is ice water, perceptual-motor processing generates the experiences of the touch and pressure of the cold water on the skin, the coldness, the location and duration of the stimulus, the overall felt intensity of the features, and so forth. This type of information about the concrete features of a noxious stimulus that is involved in perceptual-motor processing has been termed *sensation information* (Johnson, 1973; Johnson & Leventhal, 1974; Johnson, Morrisey, & Leventhal, 1973; Leventhal, 1975).

The perceptual-motor elaboration in the emotional distress system seems to have two components: (1) a component of bright, pricking pain, which is often followed by numbness, which may reflect adaptation or habituation, and (2) a component consisting of generalized arousal and a specific response of emotional distress. One might argue that the first component, that of bright pricking pain, belongs with the informational part of the system. We prefer to discuss it within the context of emotional elaboration partly because of neural evidence that shows that the pathways that eventuate in these pain experiences are part of the emotional system; they exit from the dorsal horn region, presumably from the T-cell system, and ascend in the ventral-lateral spinal pathways along with the other fibers that eventuate in general arousal and specific emotions, such as distress. But unlike the other fibers in the ventral-lateral pathway, which eventuate in emotional responses, these bright pain-carrying fibers go fairly directly to higher centers in the thalamus and cortex (Casey, 1973) to be further processed and integrated in memory systems. In the experiments discussed briefly later on, all of the sensory experiences—coldness, intensity, duration, bright and pricking sensations, and numbness—are grouped under the informational systems and labeled as *sensation information*.

The second aspect of perceptual-motor processing appears to correspond to what Casey (1973) diagrams as the paramedial branch of the ventral-lateral pathway. The paramedial branch connects to structures such as the reticular system, the hypothalamus, and the midpart of the thalamus and to a set of structures called the *medial forebrain bundle*. It is likely that generalized arousal occurs through activity in the reticular system, which is known to activate and possibly to inhibit the cortex, and by the hypothalamus, which can alter a variety of internal autonomic functions (Melzack, 1973).

Finally, both the hypothalamus and the medial forebrain structures are likely to be involved in the production of central and peripheral *motor* activity that makes up the expressive motor reactions associated with specific emotional states. Taken together we have arousal and the expressive reaction that make up intense emotional distress.

In summary, the neurological evidence suggests that three types of pathways generate the perceptual experience of pain. The first appears to be purely informational, dealing with features such as location, sensory attributes, and so on. The second and third appear to create pain distress; the second generates a somewhat informationlike bright, pricking pain, and the third most clearly emotional-motivational path seems to generate a generalized arousal state and a specific emotional response, such as distress. This third system is the one altered by various pain-killing drugs, such as opiates (Snyder, 1977). It is posited that these three pathways represent the structures involved in the perceptual motor processing of pain. However, it is clear that we can deal only in relatively trivial ways with the relationship between perception of the features of a noxious stimulus and perceptions of pain and emotion if we keep our discussion at the level of perceptual-motor processing. The integration of information, bright pain, and emotion requires that we define and elaborate *schematic* processing, the next level of pain–emotion processing.

Once an individual is no longer naive regarding pain, a noxious stimulus will retrieve and be integrated with the schematic memory of earlier pain experiences. To be very specific, we are arguing that the individual forms a schema, or categorical structure, that represents the informational and pain–emotion aspects of these experiences. This schema includes a representation of the visual, auditory, and somesthetic events associated with the stimulus and also includes both a representation of bright, pricking pain and a representation of the various emotional reactions (experienced, expressive, and autonomic) that accompanied the painful episode.

The level of processing under discussion could be discussed in terms of a conditioning paradigm (Geer, 1968). We prefer to talk about the process in terms of schemata, or categorical information, as do Izard (1971) and Tomkins (1962), in order to emphasize the following four factors:

1. The schemata for emotion episodes integrate or join together a wide range of stimuli and responses.

2. Each of the stimulus and response elements joined in the schemata can evoke the others. Indeed, it is very likely that the components function in an additive manner, with each component increasing the total strength of the emotional response (see Bowlby, 1973; Cupchik & Leventhal, 1974; Leventhal & Cupchik, 1976).

3. The schemata of codes can be thought of as prototypes or abstractions (Posner, 1973; Posner & Keele, 1968). Although they are relatively concrete in nature, they are not simply photographic representations of a simple pain epi-

sode. Also, they are not highly abstract, flexible memories such as those involved in the conceptual system that produces speech. Rather, they are more like image memories, or plastic representations, to use a Freudian term (Freud, 1900, 1958).

4. Emotional schemata can form (and change) by internal, feedback pressures, for example, phantasies feeding on emotion and being enriched by emotion without direct external support. It is this internal process that seems to be involved in the formation of emotional schemata, such as the acquisition of phobias in the absence of direct injury or external conditioning (e.g., Bandura & Menlove, 1968; Bronson, 1968).

The nature of schemata can be illustrated by phobias and by phantom limb pain. Phobic reactions appear to involve image–affect complexes that have powerful controlling effects over behavior. The treatment or removal of these phobic systems can proceed in a variety of ways, such as desensitization or modeling, that aim to separate the various aspects of fear emotion, both autonomic and subjective, from the images of the threatening object. In both cases, this entails an altering of the same underlying schematic system.

Phantom limb pain is the continuing experience of the sensory features of a part of the body that occurs with fairly high frequency following its surgical removal (Hoffman, 1954; Melzack, 1971; Simmel, 1962). Phantoms occur only when there is a sudden loss and are not observed following gradual loss or deterioration, as in leprosy (Simmel, 1962). They have been reported for paraplegics when the neural connection between the amputated limb and the brain has been severed days or weeks before surgery (Li & Elvidge, 1951). Observations of this sort suggest that phantoms and phantom pain cannot be readily explained by hypotheses arguing that phantoms are based on continuing stimulation of remaining peripheral nerve roots (Morgenstern, 1970).

Many phantoms are extremely painful. Indeed, the pain and distress can be so severe that the victim is driven to spinal cord surgery. But even drastic surgical intervention may not bring relief. That surgery should fail to bring relief is not surprising; the expectation that it will is based on a sensory pain model that argues that cutting the sensory pathways will eliminate the pain experience. But there is substantial evidence that the phantom and the pain are centrally coded memory structures. For example, pain is far more likely in a phantom if there was pain prior to surgery (Simmel, 1962). Second, the appearance and severity of pain is closely related to its emotional significance. For example, Henderson and Smyth (1948) report a case of a soldier who experienced phantom pain of an ankle sprain and not of the wound leading to amputation as he attributed his injury and amputation to the sprain; Parkes (1973) found more phantom pain in those persons who unexpectedly lost their jobs postsurgically than in those whose jobs proved secure; and Kolb (1950) reports that discussion of life crises with amputees produced recurrence of severe phantom pain.

If the schemata underlying phantom pain are similar to the schemata underlying other types of emotional behavior, it should be possible to treat them with similar methods (e.g., Fordyce, 1976; Meichenbaum & Turk, 1976). Supporting this suggestion is a case reported by McKechnie (1975) in which relaxation exercise was used to remove a pain that had appeared and endured for 9½ years after the fitting of an artificial limb, even though the injury occurred 13 months before the fitting. The patient imagined clenching and then relaxing the phantom fist and then did the same for the limb. These exercises were performed during therapy sessions and at home and provided relief for up to an hour. A 6-month followup showed that the posttreatment benefits of relaxation training were still detectable.

It would be wrong to conclude from the above discussion that pain schemata are responsible only for unusual phenomena such as phantom pain, as we believe thay play a significant role in many everyday pain experiences. For example, pain schemata may be responsible for so-called psychogenic regional pain, or pain experienced in a part of the body in the absence of identifiable pathology (Walters, 1961). Psychogenic regional pain is a common experience, and many persons experiencing such pain are subjected to unnecessary surgeries. A study of pathology reports in England showed that for certain population groups (e.g., females between 18 and 35 years of age), unnecessary surgery occurred in 60% of the cases with abdominal pain (Ingram, Evans, & Oppenheim, 1965). Being male or a younger or older female reduced the likelihood of unnecessary surgeries, but the proportion of needless cutting was still substantial.

Pain schemata may produce phantom pain that is unrecognized as such in a multitude of everyday settings. For example, when drinking very cold water, the senior author frequently experiences severe pain in one particular tooth. What is unusual about this is that the tooth that hurts has been completely devoid of neural connections for over 13 years. The noxious, cold stimulation seems to reactivate a pain schema that was formed by the pain experienced during the death of the nerve and the root canal work. A study conducted by Hutchins and Reynold (in Nathan, 1962) found evidence for such memory pain; they used a mild electrical probe to stimulate the nasal mucosa of patients who had been treated (drilling, etc.) for tooth decay a week earlier and found that the patients had been treated while under nitrous oxide. However, it did not occur if novacaine was used during the initial treatment. The nitrous oxide blocks consciousness of pain but does not block the conduction of signals and the formation of traces (schemata) in the central nervous system; novacaine, on the other hand, blocks neural conduction and prevents the formation of the schemata.

To this point we have discussed schemata as memory factors. If we look again at Figure 3, we can see that perhaps the most important role schemata play in pain–distress processing is their function as attention selectors. Schemata are integrated with perceptual-motor processes and amplify and organize perceptual materials, and by doing this they encourage or influence selective attention and determine which material enters focal awareness. Thus, schemata determine the form of a particular perceptual product and whether we attend to it. Thus, they can alter the organization of focal attention so that it includes awareness of distress, or awareness of an integration of *stimulus–pain–distress*, with no particular element standing out from the rest.

Schemata have other functions as well. First, they change the individual's sensitivity to particular classes of stimuli, as stimuli with features matching those of the events originally integrated into the schemata will rearouse the entire schematic complex. Second, schemata can bind different emotional reactions to the informational component of pain. Distress is the affective reaction most likely to accompany the pain experience; fear seems the second most likely. But pain can be linked to depression, guilt, shame and anger. On rare occasions pleasure and sexual arousal can be integrated into schemata involving noxious stimulation. What are the conditions that permit such a wide range of emotions to be grouped with pain? First, it is likely that the characteristics of the noxious stimulus itself may alter the emotion generated by the perceptual-motor mechanisms, and variation in what is elicited by perceptual-motor processing will alter what is available for schema formation. For example, Tomkins (1962) hypothesizes that constant high levels of stimulation provoke distress, while constant very high levels of stimulation provoke anger. Startle and fear, on the other hand, are stimulated by intense stimuli that increase rapidly in strength. If noxious stimuli meet these criteria, they are likely to elicit different emotions from different schemata.

The presence of other persons and their expressive cues provide the second and perhaps the most important source of stimulation for emotional reactions, which can then be integrated with pain experiences elicited in that social context. For example, a parent wagging a finger and saying "but boys don't cry" can elicit powerful shame responses, which are integrated with the noxious event that initially elicited distress and crying.

A third function of schemata is the summation and integration of different inputs. For example, a mild noxious stimulus is likely to add to and increase the total level of pain experienced by an individual suffering with a severe injury. The minor noxious stimulus intensifies both the expressive motor and the arousal reactions that are part of the pain–distress schemata activated by the major injury and adds to the total level of pain and suffering.

A fourth, critical function of schemata is to facilitate adaptation to noxious, threatening situations. This is achieved by the tendency of schemata to expand and include additional motor response components when they are repeatedly activated. The motoric expansion will include a wide range of autonomic and instrumental behaviors that were not necessarily a part of the initial perceptual-motor response pattern responsible for the formation of the earliest schemata.

All of the points discussed emphasize the integrative function of schemata; they play a critical role in melding and uniting a diverse set of behavioral reactions. The consequences of these integrative processes could be spelled out virtually indefinitely. But there are two that merit specific comment. First, schemata are critical in the selective blending of primary (innate) perceptual-motor emotional reactions for the formation of new emotional experiences. Given the sensitivity of emotional processing to interpersonal stimuli, and the likelihood that the individual will experience pain in a diverse range of interpersonal situations, each person's schematic system for pain is likely to be complex and to have unique subjective features.

Second, the integrative function of schemata and their tendency to incorporate additional motor elements suggests that we have presented a far too limited view of schematic processes. We have discussed pain–emotion schemata as active at a given instant in time and as determining the quality of the pain experience to a specific noxious stimulus. But the important painful episodes of life extend over time; pain from systemic disease, surgical pain, pain from accidental injuries, etc., last for hours and days in contrast to the punctate onset and rapid termination of typical laboratory pain. And these extended episodes incorporate a variety of contextual stimuli generated by other people's activites in reacting to one's pain. The notion of schemata must be expanded in order to capture the temporal and social extensions that occur in real-life pain experience. The concept of scripts as used by sociologists (Gagnon & Simon, 1973) seems to encompass these extensions of schemata over time and interpersonal context.

A more precise explication of the nature of the temporal-social factors coded in a script seems to be warranted. Time *per se*, in hours, minutes, or seconds, is not the temporal variable; the temporal variable that is coded in a script is a series of interactive expectations. Thus a script represents a code of a sequence of one's own reactions (e.g., of one's subjective, overt expressive, autonomic, and instrumental acts) and a code of a sequence of the replies expected from others (e.g., of their feelings, overt expressive reactions, and instrumental acts). Thus a scripted interaction is not a stimulus–response sequence where the behavior of Person A stimulates the response of Person B, with B's response then serving to elicit further behaviors from A, etc. In a scripted interaction the other's response or reply is already expected; thus the other's response is not so much an external stimulus that elicits a new reaction by the actor as an event that confirms (or disconfirms) the expectations in the actor's script. When the reply disconfirms the script, it will lead to heightened awareness and arousal, new emotional reactions, and searching for new responses.

An important consequence of the building of expectations of replies and responses to them in a common script is that individuals often fail to detect disconfirmation. Thus the neutral behavior of an observer may seem to confirm scripted expectations. When noxious stimulation elicits shame and distress, one is likely to expect that an observer is appraising one's toughness in response to a noxious stimulus. Indeed the mere presence of another is likely to confirm this expectation, and an observer would have to provide exceptionally strong and clear disconfirmation in order to alter the incorrect expectations.

Finally, scripts make up what the sociologist refers to as *roles*. For example, Parsons (1951) uses the concept of *sick role* to encompass a variety of interactive scripts or mutually supportive expectations that guide behavior while being cared for, being exempted from responsibilities, and taking on the responsibility of getting well. We have chosen to describe the temporally extended, interpersonal, affective interchanges as scripts to emphasize their self-contained or centrally programmed nature. We do not necessarily mean to imply that scripts possess the dramaturgic characteristics ascribed to them by many sociologists (e.g., Goffman, 1959).

Two series of investigations provide evidence that is compatible with the schematic integration hypothesis. The first is a line of research conducted by Hilgard and his collaborators, and the second is a series of studies by the senior author and his associates on the effects of sensation information and attention on pain–distress experience.

Hilgard (1973, 1971, 1969) and his associates (Hilgard, Cooper, Lenox, Morgan, & Voevodsky, 1967; Hilgard & Hilgard, 1975; Lenox, 1970; Sachs, 1970) have conducted a large number of studies using hypnosis as a means of reducing pain–distress. Several of the investigations (e.g., Lenox, 1970; Hilgard, Morgan, & Macdonald, 1975) show that subjects report very low levels of pain–distress if given anesthesia instructions under hypnosis.

An examination of his data led Hilgard (1973) to postulate a dissocation theory of hypnotic pain reduction. The essential idea is that a division occurs in the mind so that the conscious part experiences and verbally reports very little pain, while the preconscious or preattentive component of the mind continues to process (and presumably to "feel") a higher level of pain–distress. Thus, the pain–distress experience is dissociated or segregated from awareness.

But this is only part of the phenomenon. In addition to segregating pain–distress from awareness, hypnotically induced anesthesia instructions appear to divide or dissociate the informational and emotional components of pain. The data suggest that the emotional, distress-suffering component of pain is suppressed or eliminated, so that the preattentive process includes only the informational part of the pain experience.

A fascinating experiment by Hilgard, Morgan, and Macdonald (1975) provides empirical support for the above analysis. Subjects in this study were trained to adopt hypnotic sets and were given anesthesia instruction while exposed to ice water pain for 45 seconds. An additional component of the procedure was to train the subjects to use a pair of keys to automatically (without attending to it) tap out ratings of pain on a 100-point scale. Practice in key tapping was given for several sessions so the response would be completely automatic and not require attention. The goal was to allow the preattentive component of the mind to report pain–distress by automatic key tapping while allowing pain–distress ratings from the conscious part of the mind by traditional verbal report.

The results are exceptionally interesting. Taking the verbal reports at face value, the 20 subjects in the study reported very low levels of pain–distress under hypnotic analgesia; pain–distress was greatly attenuated at a conscious level. The results for automatic tapping, presumably reflecting preconscious "experience," showed substantially higher reports of pain–distress, though these reports were still far lower than those given by the same subjects when they immersed their hands in ice water without hypnotic anesthesia instructions. Elaborate interviewing both during and after the experiment provided a rather interesting clue as to why the preattentive (automatically reported) distress was lower than that reported in the normal control state and greater than that reported by the conscious mind under hypnotic analgesia. These interviews involved automatic talking; that is, the subjects were trained to talk automatically when signaled by the experimenter's touch on their shoulders. These reports of their preattentive feelings suggested that the preattentive experience included the sensory component of pain but *did not include distress or suffering.*

The data reported support several aspects of our processing model. First, there is a strong suggestion that the noxious stimulus can be processed or integrated with pain–distress schemata *or* with "informational" schemata in the preattentive sphere, even though the preattentive experience frequently excludes the emotional distress or suffering component. The distinction between pain and suffering was also found in earlier data by Knox, Morgan, and Hilgard (1974). Second, the substantially lower levels of pain found with pain reports from verbal, conscious reporting suggest that integration of the noxious cues into a nonemotional schema is critical for the further minimization of pain in consciousness by hypnotic analgesia. Once the noxious input is schematized as a set of sensory features or sensory pain in the preattentive sphere, it may be easier to block it from awareness by reinterpreting the meaning of the features or ignoring them completely by focusing on other mental contents. It may be impossible to ignore them for long periods of time, however, when they are amalgamated with a strong emotion such as pain–distress.

Finally, hypnosis may introduce other phenomena, such as highly motivated distraction, that could reduce distress without any change in the schematization of the noxious input. This possibility should not be ignored, as many of the studies reported by Hilgard and his co-workers use relatively short exposures to noxious stimulation. For example, in the Hilgard, Morgan, and Macdonald (1975) study, the subject's hand was immersed in ice water for only

45 seconds. Highly motivated distraction may be effective in distress reduction for relatively short periods of time.

The second line of studies providing evidence for schematic integration are on the effects of sensation information and attention on pain distress. Jean Johnson (1973) conducted the first of a series of studies on the effects of sensation information on the reduction of distress. She reasoned that a subject who is prepared for and has accurate expectations about sensory features will process them as information, but if he is unprepared for the sensory cues, they will arouse surprise and be processed as emotional reactions. The formulation is consistent with "our" general frame of reference (Leventhal, 1970) that noxious or threatening stimuli can be processed either as objective information or as affective reactions, with one or the other mode of processing being dominant, depending on the individual's readiness for the stimulus inputs.

Johnson (1973) exposed subjects to ischemic pain by having them squeeze a hand dynamometer to 20-lbs pressure while their circulation was cut off by an inflated blood pressure cuff. One group was told the various sensations they would experience, such as aching, pins and needles, numbness, change in skin color, etc., and the other was told about the procedures to be used by the experimenter. The subjects made separate ratings of the strength of the stimulus sensations and the strength of their distress. The subjects prepared with sensation information reported substantially less distress than the control subjects told about the procedure; the groups did not differ significantly in their ratings of strength of sensations.

Johnson ran two additional studies to see if the group differences could be attributed to distraction or to differences in prestress expectations about the harmfulness of the procedure. The first study showed that the sensation-prepared groups reported less distress regardless of distraction, and the second study found no differences in prestress beliefs or expectations between subjects given sensation instructions and subjects given procedural information.

At an empirical level, Johnson's studies lent strong support to the hypothesis that accurate sensation information will reduce distress on contact with a stressor. But the interpretation emphasized the accuracy of the expectations rather than processing by sensory as opposed to pain–distress schemata. If accuracy is the key factor in distress reduction, then the more accurate information a subject is given about the stimulus, the less distress he should experience. For example, if we describe the sensations produced by a stimulus and then tell our subject that the stimulus will be painful, another accurate bit of information, his distress should be lower than with sensation information alone. Epstein (1973), however, compared three groups—one forewarned that the stimulus would be very painful, one that it would be moderately painful, and one that it would be slightly painful—and found that subjects given the strong pain warning showed an exaggerated (stronger) response on the first of the shock trials; warnings of pain created anticipatory fear and did not reduce distress, even if the warning was disconfirmed by a less severe shock than expected (Janis, 1958).

How then will pain warnings interact with sensation information? The accuracy hypothesis suggests that pain warnings will increase the distress reduction achieved with sensation information. On the other hand, the schematic integration hypothesis of the processing model just presented suggests that the word *pain* will strengthen pain–distress schemata, lead to their integration with the stimulus input, and block distress reduction by sensation information. With sensation information alone, however, the inputs will be coded in informational terms, that is, as a set of features, and not in a pain–distress schema.

To test this hypothesis, Brown, Engquist, and Leventhal (1977) had subjects judge both strength of sensations and distress while their hand was immersed in 2°C ice water. One group of subjects received information on the sensations of the cold pressor stimulus (coldness, aching, tightness of the skin across the hand, pins and needles sensations, numbness, etc.) and were also told that the cold water would be painful; another sensation group did not receive the pain warning. An additional pair of groups were instructed about the procedure, and one of these did receive and the other did not receive the pain warning. The accuracy hypothesis predicts that sensation-informed groups will be less distressed than the procedurally informed groups and that the group given sensation information and a pain warning will be least distressed, as it has the greatest amount of accurate information about the cold pressor stimulus. The processing hypothesis, on the other hand, predicts that the sensation information will reduce distress by integrating the noxious input with schemata of the stimulus features, but that the pain warning will strengthen emotionally relevant pain–distress schemata for the integration of the noxious information. Thus subjects given the pain warning will show no distress reduction due to preparation with sensation information.

The results clearly supported the second processing interpretation, as the subjects given sensation information with no pain warning were less distressed and showed higher hand temperatures; these differences became most pronounced during the latter half of the 6-minute immersion. The remaining groups—the group sensation-informed with pain warning and the two procedurally informed groups—were virtually indistinguishable.

The Brown, Engquist, and Leventhal study strongly suggests that distress reduction depends on the *way* the input is processed and not merely on the accuracy of the subject's expectations. Further evidence for this processing hypothesis is provided by Shacham and Leventhal (1978). They argue that coding the stimulus in terms of its particular sensory features requires monitoring the site of impact during the early part of exposure, that is, before the stimulus has been processed as pain–distress. In their first investigation, they compared two groups of subjects: one that was instructed to pay attention to and monitor the various sensations and experiences produced in their hand by the cold pressor stimulus, and the other an uninstructed control. The second study made a more precise comparison between attention to hand and distraction. It used four groups: one that attended to the site of impact for the entire 5-minute period of immersion; a second that was distracted by a series of color slides for the entire period; a third that attended to the hand for the first half and watched slides for the second half; and a fourth that watched slides for the first half and attended to the hand for the second half.

In both studies, subjects in the attention or monitoring condition reported substantially less distress than subjects in the distraction control condition (either with or without slides). The additional critical finding was that the group that monitored their hand for the first half and saw slides for the second half of the period reported the same distress level as subjects who monitored their hand for the entire 5 minutes; attention at the early part of noxious stimulation is most critical for distress reduction. This finding is of special significance as it fits the suggestions made by Epstein (1973) and by Groves and Thompson (1970) that habituation or decreased responding occurs more rapidly for stimuli that are increasing in strength (the early part of cold pressor), and that little habituation occurs if the stimulus is strong when first attended to; i.e., there was no habituation in the group that monitored only during the second half of immersion.

The results obtained so far support the hypothesis that sensation information and attention lead to an alternative way of processing the stimulus, which eventuates in distress reduction. Our interpretation of the effect is that these variables integrate the stimulus input with schemata of sensations only, rather than with schemata of sensations and distress. Certain features of the data, however, are not fully congruent with this interpretation. The most important of these is that distress reports increased over the first 1½–2½ minutes and reached a common peak in all groups; differences did not appear until *later* in the exposure period. This pattern is clearly inconsistent with a simple "demand" interpretation and somewhat inconsistent with our expectations, as one might expect an immediate difference in the level of reported distress if the input were integrated with a sensory schema lacking a distress component from the outset. Instead, the distress seems to drop out of the response pattern, with the process leading to its disappearance beginning immediately upon exposure; for example, in the second Shacham and Leventhal study, attention during the first half of exposure led to distress reduction in the second half.

Four important questions can be raised about the findings. First, are they reliable? Second, do they imply that sensory information and monitoring produce a durable or lasting reduction in distress? Third, does this pattern of distress reduction differ from that for other psychological techniques of distress reduction? Fourth, does the idea of schematic processing provide an adequate account of the data?

Two recent studies provide evidence regarding these questions. In the first, Shacham (1977) compared three groups of subjects: in one group subjects were asked to generate an image of their immersed hand (look at it, close your eyes, and generate an image of it and the sensations); in a second group, subjects were asked to imagine that it was a hot, uncomfortable day and that the hand was immersed in a bath of cool, pleasant water; and a third, control, group went through the cold pressor treatment. On the first (*treatment*) trial, subjects in each group performed as instructed; on the second (*test*) trial, they reexposed themselves to the cold water without engaging in any particular mental activity. The results showed that the effects of monitoring, or imaging, were quite different from those of positive suggestion; the latter produced the lowest distress ratings on the *treatment* trial, while the treatments were actively applied. But positive suggestion had absolutely no effects on the second (*test*) trial. By contrast, subjects who imaged or monitored the hand reported less distress than *control* or *positive suggestion* subjects on the second (*test*) trial. A serious limitation of the finding is that subjects were selected for high and low scores on an imagery test, and as expected, only good imagers showed the effects.

The second study by Leventhal, Ahles, and Rutter (1977) randomly assigned male subjects to a *sensation verbalization* condition in which subjects talked about the sensations they felt while immersed in ice water; a *control* condition, where they talked about courses and teachers they had in high school and college; and an *expressive verbalization* condition, where they were encouraged to and let themselves make expressive sounds of distress (moan and groan) while exposed to the cold water.

On the first *treatment* trial, when the subjects engaged in verbalization, subjects who were verbalizing sensations reported less distress than control subjects, and subjects who were making expressive sounds reported more distress than control subjects; these differences were most noticeable during the last half of the immersion period. On the second *test* trial, where subjects were passive, prior expressive verbalization had no effect on reported distress; this manipulation and that of thinking pleasant thoughts affect distress only when actively applied. But subjects who had previously verbalized sensations continued to report substantially lower levels of distress than subjects in either the control or the expressive sounds group. The effects of sensation verbalization carried over to the second *test* exposure.

Both studies provide further evidence for the reliablity of distress reduction through sensation information and monitoring. More important, they show that these variables produce a durable and lasting measure of distress reduction and that the pattern of effects, particularly its durability, differentiates sensation information and monitoring from other distress-reducing procedures such as thinking positive thoughts. Thinking positive thoughts and moaning and groaning produced effects that were similar in that they both were restricted to the treatment trial; they did not last and carry over to the test trial. But, can our notion of schematic processing account for the differences between these treatment conditions?

In our judgment, the temporary effects of positive thinking and expressive sounds reflect both schematic and perceptual-motor processes; by following instructions, the subject decreases or increases the availability of pain–distress schemata and strengthens or weakens perceptual-motor processes. The more durable effects of sensation instructions and self-monitoring appear to reflect a more permanent modification in the pain–distress schema leading to a neutral (sensory pain only) schema that no longer stimultes perceptual-motor distress reactions. A strong possibility is that sensation information and self-monitoring encourage the buildup of an active inhibition of distress. Indeed, it is possible that the sensations themselves become conditioned stimuli for an inhibitory process (see Stein, 1966; Siegal, 1975, 1977).

The final level of processing involves the individual's conceptualization of his pain distress experiences, which include the situations that he sees as causes of pain–distress and the various beliefs he holds about the consequences of pain–distress experiences. This level of processing includes beliefs such as the *magnitude* rule, the *pain–injury* rule, the belief that distraction is an effective way of eliminating distress, or the belief that pain–distress is visible in facial expressions. These beliefs are important because they can affect the individual's social behavior and his reaction to various expressive and verbal replies to his pain–distress experience.

Two examples are worth mentioning. The first concerns the distraction belief and the hypothesis that subjects hold about distraction's being an effective way of minimizing distress. We suspect that this belief comes from two kinds of self-observation: the observation that acute, sudden pain (e.g., puncture with needles) can be minimized by distraction, and the observation that the anxiety in lengthy, anticipatory periods, which is often as uncomfortable and distressful as the impact of the noxious stimulus itself, can also be reduced by distraction. The distraction rule was expressed by subjects in several of our studies. For example, in the Shacham–Leventhal (1978) studies subjects who saw slides thought it helped them tolerate and reduce their distress, but the experimental data showed that the slides had no effect at all. Since distraction is probably effective in some settings, it is probably incorrect to assert that the *distraction* belief is a wrong hypothesis. The issue is that it seems to be incorrect for inescapable pain, and people do not necessarily discriminate between situations were distraction will or will not be effective.

The second example concerns the belief that subjective *feelings show* in outer expression. A study by Reinhardt (1974) found very high correlations between the level of subjective distress reported during exposure to the cold pressor and the belief that the distress showed in the sufferer's facial expression—a correlation of about .60 between the two variables. There are two interesting aspects to this correlation. First, the correlations were of the same magnitude in experimental conditions where the experimenter commented upon the subject's expression (i.e., indicated he could tell that the subject was distressed) and conditions where no comment was made on the subject's expression. Second, there was *no* relationship between an observer's ratings of the subject's overt expression and either of the two self-ratings—reports of distress during the cold pressor and reports that distress showed.

The data suggest that many people do not accuarately monitor their overt expressive behavior, which should not be surprising as the behavior is not directly observable. But people do believe that their expressive behavior is present and visible, and the belief that feelings show may influence real-life interchanges. For example, a woman may regard a man as cold and unconcerned if he fails to be attentive to and to notice her distress, even though her overt expression may not correspond to her subjective feelings.

In summary, conceptual processing involves the activation of beliefs about pain–distress. These beliefs will contribute to the pain–distress experience by leading to subsequent behaviors (e.g., reactions to others, shifts in attention), which may then alter perceptual-motor and schematic processing. We have assigned relatively few functions to this level of processing, as we do not feel that it is well understood. We may be in error in suggesting that conceptual beliefs of the sort discussed are inaccurate, as we have not cataloged this system and know little of its extent and structure. These beliefs may exist in different arrangements or may be used in different sequences by different people, and some of these patterns may facilitate adaptation to pain–distress, while others may not. In short, we have much to learn in this area.

III. APPLICATIONS TO DISTRESS REDUCTION DURING MEDICAL TREATMENT

In this section we wish to review a number of studies illustrating the application of sensation information and monitoring to the reduction of distress in real-life treatment settings. The first investigations were conducted at the University of Wisconsin on distress reduction during the endoscopic examination (Johnson & Leventhal, 1974; Johnson, Morrissey, & Leventhal, 1973), a diagnostic procedure in which the patient swallows a fiber optic tube about the thickness of a thimble and retains this tube for a 20- to 30-minute period while the doctors peer through the view finder of a reflex camera and observe and photograph portions of the stomach lining. The procedure is uncomfortable and is accompanied by noxious experience ranging from throat swabbing and injections with a local anesthetic before the tube is swallowed to the actual swallowing and retaining of the tube in one's mouth and gullet while one's stomach is inflated with air to assist observation. In our studies some patients were told about the actual sensations (numbness of throat, gagging, full stomach, etc.) that they would experience with each procedure, and in one experiment half of the sensation-prepared subjects were told about and given the opportunity to rehearse a few coping reactions: mouth breathing and swallowing. Sensation information alone substantially reduced gagging and helped maintain stable heart rates. Coping or action instructions added to this beneficial effect: 50% fewer patients gagged in swallowing the tube in the group given both types of information than in an uninformed control group.

Johnson and her associates at Wayne State University (Johnson, Kirchoff, & Endress, 1975) have given children sensation information to reduce distress and resistance to treatment during a procedure for cast removal. The children who listened to a brief tape recording that included the sound of the saw and a description of the sensation (e.g., vibration, heat, flying chalk powder) showed minimal distress and resistance during the procedure. Subjects who were given a description of the procedure did no better than uninformed controls.

In an extremely important recent study of 81 cholecystectomy patients, Johnson, Rice, Fuller, and Endress (1977) found that patients given sensation information in a 7-minute tape-recorded message that described post-surgical sensations in the incision (tenderness, pulling, pressure, smarting or burning, sensitivity), the sensations from medications (sleepiness, light-headedness, and relaxation), and step-by-step instructions on deep breathing, coughing, leg exercises, etc., not only reported less postoperative fear but required an average of .7 of a day hospitalization and were out of their homes three days sooner than uninformed patients. Patients given procedural information alone or behavioral instructions alone were somewhat better off than uninformed patients, but not as well off as patients in the sensation-informed groups. The reliability of these findings are seen in a study by Wilson (1977), he obtained nearly identical reductions in the length of hospitalization for 37 hysterectomy and 35 cholecystectomy patients. Wilson also found interesting interactions of individual difference factors with sensation information. The importance of these findings for reductions in the cost of hospitalization and savings in productive days of work cannot be ignored.

Further evidence for the generality of the effect is seen in an investigation of women's reactions during a pelvic and breast examination; Fuller, Endress, and Johnson (1977) found fewer overt signs of distress and a smaller increase in pulse rate during the examination for women who listened to a 6-minute message describing the subjective sensations that typically accompany this examination. Women given relaxation instructions fared no better than women given sensation information. Women given both sensation information and relaxation instructions tended to do best.

Finally, in a recent use of attentional sets in the medical setting, Leventhal, Booth, Shacham, and Leventhal (1977) compared the postdelivery mood reports of two groups of women: one instructed to monitor and pay close attention to their sensations and to use them to guide their breathing and pushing, and a group that received equal amounts of personal contact and were told to follow the instructions about breathing and pushing without the instruction to monitor contractions. All 49 women in the study became increasingly distressed as labor progressed, but the attention-instructed group reported being less anxious, angry, and upset during the second stage of labor when the mother was pushing and expelling the fetus. These effects held regardless of the mother's prior participation in childbirth training classes.

The field experiments provide interesting evidence for the value of sensation information and important data on the interaction of this information with behavioral instruction for controlling the noxious situation. In general, sensation information appears to facilitate some form of habituation or inhibition of distress to continuous stimulation. Second, it is clear that additional gains in distress reduction occur when sensation information is combined with action instructions, detailed information, and practice in the steps needed for behavioral adaptation to the stressor setting. Sensation information and attention provide an alternative way of schematizing the stressor, which facilitates distress reduction, and the decline in distress allows the individual to perform additional responses to control the stressful setting. If these behaviors alter the stressor itself, as is probably the case in the pushing in childbirth and/or practice in swallowing the endoscopic tube, the acts will produce further reductions in distress. On the other hand, if the behaviors are themselves a source of noxious stimulation, like postsurgical exercise, or only partially effective in altering the sensory impact of the noxious stimulus, as in relaxation during a pelvic examination, further decrements in distress from performing the behavioral program may be relatively small or nonexistent.

The field studies also support the hypothesis that the patient's conceptual understanding of pain–distress need not correspond to the "facts." Thus patients may be enthusiastic and claim benefit from tactics such as relaxation and not from sensation information (Fuller, Endress, and Johnson, 1977). They may resist tactics such as self-monitoring and show no resistance to but rather a preference for distraction (Booth, Leventhal, Shacham, & Leventhal, 1977) even though relaxation and distraction are relatively ineffective for distress reduction. Indeed, resistance to self-monitoring was so strong in our study of labor that it required several modifications of our instructions before mothers would follow them, and several that did expressed surprise that monitoring was beneficial.

IV. CONCLUSION

The multilevel processing model offers both an integrative frame of reference and an analytic tool for pursuing research in a variety of areas. Detailed investigation is needed of what we have called the *perceptual-motor mechanism*, or the primary source of emotional experience. Better understanding of this mechanism should make possible still more effective means of distress reduction. The concept of schematic processing appears to be a powerful analytic tool and will be a still more robust heuristic as we more clearly define the components of schemata and their interdependencies. For example, the concept has given rise to research on the cerebral lateralization of schemata used in emotional processing, and studies have shown that right-hemispheric structures may be better suited to the schematic processing of emotion (Safer & Leventhal, 1977). It is hoped that studies of this sort will deepen our insight into the nature of emotional schemata. The specification of emotional scripts will represent yet another step toward classification of the model (see Lang, 1978).

The investigations described here also make clear the need for differentiating between schematic and conceptual cognitive mediators. Whether these terms mark a simple qualitative dichotomy or define the ends of a continuum of controllable (conceptual-verbal) *versus* automatic and less controllable cognitive events is unclear. It is conceivable that a common memory structure underlies both systems and that the differences exist because of separate retrieval mechanisms. At present, however, we favor the former hypothesis of two relatively independent types of cognitive codes.

One of the most important aspects of our theoretical model is its applicability to real-life settings. The consistent findings in various field studies suggests that the model presented here can be useful for the exploration of ways of reducing human distress and suffering. Of equal importance to us, as investigators, is that field studies seem to provide even more consistent findings and a potentially better way of enriching theory than do laboratory experiments. This should not surprise us, as pain in the laboratory is nearly always artificial and subject to varied sets and interpretations that may minimize the activation of emotion and maximize an analytic, schoolroom set that substantially alters the organization and integration of sensory and emotional factors. The separate attention to cues required for critical judgment is undoubtedly not conducive to pain–distress schematization. That the results may reduce unavoidable pain and suffering in a variety of treatment settings and may provide insight into the control of coping patterns inimical to health is an important bonus that can enrich our lives as investigators.

REFERENCES

Bakan, D. *Disease pain and sacrifice*. Chicago: University of Chicago Press, 1968.
Bandura, A., & Menlove, F. Factors determining vicarious extinction of avoidance behavior through symbolic modeling. *Journal of Personality and Social Psychology*, 1968, *8*, 99–108.
Barber, T. X., & Hahn, K. W., Jr. Physiological and subjective responses to pain producing

stimulation under hypnotically-suggested and waking-imagined "analgesia." *Journal of Abnormal and Social Psychology*, 1962, *65*, 411–418.

Becker, E. *The denial of death*. New York: The Free Press, 1973.

Beecher, H. K. Pain in men wounded in battle. *Annals of Surgery*, 1946, *123*, 96–105.

Beecher, H. K. *Measurement of subjective responses*. New York: Oxford University Press, 1959.

Beecher, H. K. Quantification of the subjective pain experience. In P. H. Hoch & J. Zubin (Eds.), *Psychopathology of perception*. New York: Grune & Stratton, Inc., 1965, pp. 111–128.

Bowlby, J. *Separation: Anxiety and anger*. New York: Basic Books, 1973.

Broadbent, D. E. The hidden preattentive process. *American Psychologist*, 1977, *32*, 109–118.

Bronson, G. W. The development of fear in man and other animals. *Child Development*, 1968, *39*, 409–431.

Brown, D., Engquist, G., & Leventhal, H. The effects of information on sensations, arousal, procedure, and painfulness on cold pressor distress. Unpublished manuscript, University of Wisconsin, Madison, 1977.

Bull, N. *The body and its mind*. New York: Las Americas Pub. Co., 1962.

Casey, K. L. Pain: A current view of neural mechanisms. *American Scientist*, 1973, *61*, 194–200.

Chaves, J. F., & Barber, T. X. Hypnotism and surgical pain. In M. Weisenberg (Ed.), *Pain: Clinical and experimental perspectives*. Saint Louis: Mosby, 1975.

Clark, J. W., & Bindra, D. Individual differences in pain thresholds. *Canadian Journal of Psychology*, 1956, *10*, 69–76.

Clark, W. C. Sensory-decision theory analysis of the placebo effect on the criterion for pain and thermal sensitivity (d'). *Journal of Abnormal Psychology*, 1969, *74*, 363–371.

Clark, W. C. Signal detection theory and pain. Paper presented at the American Psychological Association, Washington, D.C., 1976.

Clark, W. C., & Goodman, J. S. Effects of suggestion on d' and C_x for pain detection and pain tolerance. *Journal of Abnormal Psychology*, 1974, *83*, 364–373.

Clark, W. C., & Mehl, L. Thermal pain: A sensory decision theory analysis of the effect of age and sex on d' various response criteria, and 50% pain threshold. *Journal of Abnormal Psychology*, 1971, *78*,(2), 202–212.

Clark, W. C., & Mehl, L. Signal detection theory procedures are not equivalent when thermal stimuli are judged. *Journal of Experimental Psychology*, 1973, *97*, 148–153.

Coleman, J. C. Facial expressions of emotions. *Psychological Monograph*, 1949, pp. 1–296.

Cupchik, G. C., & Leventhal, H. Consistency between expressive behavior and the evaluation of humorous stimuli: The role of sex and self-observation. *Journal of Personality and Social Psychology*, 1974, *30*, 429–442.

Darwin, C. *The expression of the emotions in man and animals*. Chicago: The University of Chicago Press, 1965. (Originally published 1872.)

Dewey, J. The theory of emotion: (1) Emotional attitudes. *Psychological Review*, 1894, *1*, 553–569.

Ekman, P., & Friesen, W. V. Constants across culture in the face and emotion. *Journal of Personality and Social Psychology*, 1971, *17*, 124–129.

Ekman, P., Friesen, W. V., & Ellsworth, P. *Emotion in the human face*. New York: Pergamon Press, 1972.

Epstein, S. Expectancy and magnitude of reaction to a noxious UCS. *Psychophysiology*, 1973, *10*, 100–107. (a)

Epstein, S. The self-concept revisited: The theory of a theory. *American Psychologist*, 1973, *28*, 404–416. (b)

Fordyce, W. Behavioral concepts in chronic pain and illness. In P. O. Davidson (Ed.), *The behavioral management of anxiety, depression, and pain*. New York: Brunner/Mazel, 1976.

Freud, S. *The interpretation of dreams*. New York: Basic Books, 1958. (Originally published, 1900.)

Freud, S. *The ego and the id*. London: The Hogarth Press, 1962. (a)

Freud, S. *Three essays on the theory of sexuality*. London: The Hogarth Press, 1962. (b)

Fuller, S. S., Endress, M. P., & Johnson, J. E. Control and coping with an aversive health examination. Paper presented at the American Psychological Association, San Francisco, California, 1977.

Gagnon, J. H., & Simon, W. *Sexual conduct: The social sources of human sexuality*. Chicago: Aldine, 1973.

Garner, W. R. *The processing of information and structure*. Potomac, Md.: Lawrence Erlbaum, 1974.

Geer, J. H. A test of the classical conditioning model of emotion: The use of non-painful aversive stimuli as unconditioned stimuli in a conditioning procedure. *Journal of Personality and Social Psychology*, 1968, *10*, 148–156.

Gelfand, S. The relationship of experimental pain tolerance to pain threshold. *Canadian Journal of Psychology*, 1964, *18*, 36–42.

Gelfand, S., Ullmann, L. P., & Krasner, L. The placebo response: An experimental approach. *Journal of Nervous and Mental Diseases*, 1963, *136*, 378–387.

Goffman, E. *The presentation of self in everyday life*. New York: Doubleday, 1959.

Graham, D. T. Psychosomatic medicine. In N. S. Greenfield & R. A. Sternbach (Eds.), *Handbook of psychophysiology*. New York: Holt, Rinehart & Winston, Inc., 1972.

Green, D. M., & Swets, J. A. *Signal detection theory and psychophysics*. New York: Wiley, 1966.

Groves, P. M., & Thompson, R. F. Habituation: A dual-process theory. *Psychological Review*, 1970, *77*, 419–450.

Guyton, A. C. *Basic human physiology: Normal function and mechanism of disease*. Philadelphia: Saunders, 1971.

Guyton, A. C., Coleman, T. G., Cowley, A. W., Scheel, K. W., Manning, R. D., Jr., & Norman, R. A., Jr. Arterial pressure regulation. *American Journal of Medicine*, 1972, *52*, 584–594.

Hanawalt, N. G. The role of the upper and the lower parts of the face as the basis for judging facial expression: II. In posed expressions and "candid camera" pictures. *Journal of General Psychology*, 1944, *31*, 23–36.

Hardy, J. D., Wolff, H. G., & Goodell, H. *Pain sensations and reactions*. Baltimore: Williams & Wilkins, 1952.

Henderson, W. R., & Smyth, G. E. Phantom limbs. *Journal of Neurology, Neurosurgery, and Psychiatry*, 1948, *11*, 88–112.

Higgins, J. D., Tursky, B., & Schwartz, G. E. Shock-elicited pain and its reduction by concurrent tactile stimulation. *Science*, 1971, *172*, 866–867.

Hilgard, E. R. Pain as a puzzle for psychology and physiology. *American Psychologist*, 1969, *24*, 103–113.

Hilgard, E. R. Hypnotic phenomena: The struggle for scientific acceptance. *American Scientist*, 1971, *59*, 567–577.

Hilgard, E. R. A neodissociation interpretation of pain reduction in hypnosis. *Psychological Review*, 1973, *80*, 396–411.

Hilgard, E. R., Cooper, L. M., Lenox, J., Morgan, A. H., & Voevodsky, J. The use of pain-state reports in the study of hypnotic analgesia to the pain of ice water. *The Journal of Nervous and Mental Disease*, 1967, *144*, 506–513.

Hilgard, E. R., & Hilgard, J. R. *Hypnosis in the relief of pain*. Los Altos, Calif.: William Kaufmann, 1975.

Hilgard, E., Morgan, A., & Macdonald, H. Pain and dissociation in the cold pressor test: A study of hypnotic analgesia with "hidden reports" through automatic key pressing and automatic talking. *Journal of Abnormal Psychology*, 1975, *84*, 280–289.

Hoffman, J. Pantom limb syndrome. *Journal of Nervous and Mental Disorders*, 1954, *119*, 261–270.

Ingram, P. W., Evans, G., & Oppenheim, A. N. Right illiac fossa pain in young women. *British Medical Journal*, 1965, *2*, 149–151.

Izard, C. E. *The face of emotion*. New York: Appleton-Century-Crofts, 1971.

Janis, I. *Psychological stress.* New York: Wiley, 1958

Javert, C. T., & Hardy, J. D. Measurement of pain intensity in labor and its physiologic, neurologic, and pharmacologic implications. *American Journal of Obstetrics and Gynecology,* 1950, *60,* 552–563.

Johnson, J. E. Effects of accurate expectations about sensations on the sensory and distress components of pain. *Journal of Personality and Social Psychology,* 1973, *27,* 261–275.

Johnson, J. E., Kirchoff, K. T., & Endres, M. P. Deferring children's distress behavior during orthopedic cast removal. *Nursing Research,* 1975, *75,* 404–410.

Johnson, J. E., & Leventhal, H. Effects of accurate expectations and behavioral instructions on reactions during a noxious medical examination. *Journal of Personality and Social Psychology,* 1974, *29,* 710–718.

Johnson, J. E., Morrissey, J. F., & Leventhal, H. Psychological preparation for an endoscopic examination. *Gastrointestinal Endoscopy,* 1973, *19,* 180–182.

Johnson, J. E., Rice, V. H., Fuller, S. S., & Endress, M. P. Sensory information, behavioral instruction, and recovery from surgery. Paper presented at the American Psychological Association, San Francisco, California, 1977.

Jourard, S. M., & Lasakow, P. Some factors in self-disclosure. *Journal of Abnormal and Social Psychology,* 1958, *56,* 91–98.

Kahneman, D. *Attention and effort.* Englewood Cliffs, N.J.: Prentice-Hall, 1973.

Knox, V. J., Morgan, A. H., & Hilgard, E. R. Pain and suffering in ischemia: The paradox of hypnotically suggested anasthesia as contradicted by response from the "hidden observer," *Archives of General Psychiatry,* 1974, *30,* 840–847.

Kolb, L. C. Psychiatric aspects of treatment for intractable pain in the phantom limb. *Major Clinics of North America,* 1950, *34,* 1029.

Kosambi, D. D. Living prehistory in India. *Scientific American,* 1967, *216,* 105.

Lang, P. Imagery in therapy: An information processing analysis of fear. *Behavior Therapy,* 1977, *8,* 862–886.

Lenox, J. R. Effect of hypnotic analgesia on verbal report and cardiovascular responses to ischemic pain. *Journal of Abnormal Pscyhology,* 1970, *75,* 199–206.

Leventhal, H. Findings and theory in the study of fear communications. In L. Berkowitz (Ed.), *Advances in experimental social psychology.* New York: Academic Press, 1970.

Leventhal, H. Emotions: A basic problem for social psychology. In C. Nemeth (Ed.), *Social psychology.* Chicago: Rand McNally, 1974.

Leventhal, H. The consequences of depersonalization during illness and treatment. In J. Howard & A. Strauss (Eds.), *Humanizing health care.* New York: Wiley, 1975.

Leventhal, H. Perceptual-motor theory of emotion. Unpublished manuscript, University of Wisconsin, Madison, 1977.

Leventhal, H. A processing model of emotion: Applications to the study of pain and humor. In P. Pliner (Ed.), *Erindale Symposium on Emotion.* Elmsford, New York: Pergamon Press, in press.

Leventhal, H., & Cupchik, G. A process model of humor judgment. *Journal of Communication,* 1976, *26,* 190–204.

Leventhal, H., & Sharp, E. Facial expressions as indicators of distress. In S. S. Tomkins & C. E. Izard (Eds.), *Affect, cognition, and personality.* New York: Springer, 1965.

Leventhal, H., Ahles, T., & Rutter, M. The effects of verbalizing sensations and expressive sounds on the lateralized experience of pain and distress. Unpublished manuscript, University of Wisconsin, Madison, 1977. (a)

Leventhal, H., Booth, C. A., Shacham, S., & Leventhal, E. A. Attention, coping, and the control of distress in childbirth. Unpublished manuscript, University of Wisconsin, Madison, 1977. (b)

Li, C. L., & Elvidge, A. R. Observation on phantom limb in a paraplegic patient. *Journal of Neurosurgery,* 1951, *8,* 524–526.

Lifton, R. J. *The life of the self.* New York, N.Y.: Simon & Schuster, 1976.

Marshall, E. What's bad for General Motors. *The New Republic*, 1977, *176*, 22–23.

Massaro, D. W. *Experimental psychology and information processing*. Chicago: Rand McNally, 1975.

McKechnie, R. J. Relief from phantom limb pain by relaxation exercises. *Journal of Behavior Therapy and Experimental Psychiatry*, 1975, *6*, 262–263.

Meichenbaum, D., & Turk, D. The cognitive–behavioral management of anxiety, anger and pain. In P. O. Davidson (Ed.), *The behavioral management of anxiety, depression, and pain*. New York: Brunner Mazel, 1976.

Melzack, R. Phantom limb pain: Implications for treatment of pathological pain. *Anaesthesiology*, 1971, *35*, 409–419.

Melzack, R. *The puzzle of pain*. New York: Basic Books, 1973.

Melzack, R., & Wall, P. D. Pain mechanisms: A new theory. *Science*, 1965, *150*, 971–979.

Melzack, R., & Wall, P. D. Psychophysiology of pain. *The International Anesthesia Clinics*, 1970, *8*, 3–34.

Melzack, R., Wall, P. D., & Weisz, A. Z. Masking and metacontrast phenomena in the skin sensory system. *Experimental Neurology*, 1963, *8*, 35–46.

Melzack, R., Weisz, A. Z., & Sprague, L. T. Strategies for controlling pain: Contributions of auditory stimulation and suggestion. *Experimental Neurology*, 1963, *8*, 239–247.

Merskey, H. Psychological aspects of pain. *Postgraduate Medical Journal*, 1968, *44*, 297–306.

Morgenstern, F. S. Chronic pain. In O. U. Hill (Ed.), *Modern trends in psychosomatic medicine*. New York: Appleton-Century-Crofts, 1970.

Mountcastle, U. B. Pain and temperature sensibilities. In U. B. Mountcastle (Ed.), *Medical physiology*, Vol 2. St. Louis: Mosby, 1968.

Nathan, P. W. Pain traces left in the central nervous system. In C. A. Keele and R. Smith (Eds.), *The assessment of pain in man and animals*. Edinburgh: E. and S. Livingston, Ltd., 1962.

Neisser, U. *Cognitive psychology*. New York: Appleton, 1967.

Notermans, S. L. H., & Tophoff, M. M. W. A. Sex differences in pain tolerance and pain apperception. In M. Weisenberg (Ed.), *Pain: Clinical and experimental perspectives*. St. Louis: Mosby, 1975.

Parkes, C. M. Factors determining the persistence of phantom pain in the amputee. *Journal of Psychosomatic Research*, 1973, *17*, 97–108.

Parsons, T. Illness and the role of the physician: A sociological perspective. *American Journal of Orthopsychiatry*, 1951, *21*, 452–460.

Posner, M. I. *Cognition: An introduction*. Glenview, Illinois: Scott, Foresman, 1973.

Posner, M. I., & Keele, S. W. On the genesis of abstract ideas. *Journal of Experimental Psychology*, 1968, *77*, 353–363.

Read, G. D. *Childbirth without fear*. New York: Harper & Row, 1959.

Reinhardt, L. C. Attributions to self and other: Integration of internal and social stimuli in the cold pressor. Unpublished master's thesis, University of Wisconsin, Madison, 1974.

Ryan, E. D., & Kovacic, C. R. Pain tolerance and athletic participation. In M. Weisenberg (Ed.), *Pain: Clinical and experimental perspectives*. St. Louis: Mosby, 1975.

Sachs, L. B. Comparison of hypnotic analgesia and hypnotic relaxation during stimulation by a continuous pain source. *Journal of Abnormal Psychology*, 1970, *76*, 206–210.

Safer, M. A., & Leventhal, H. Ear differences in evaluating emotional tones of voice and verbal content. *Journal of Experimental Psychology: Human Perception and Performance*, 1977, *3*, 75–82.

Schilder, P. *The image and appearance of the human body*. New York: Wiley, 1950.

Shacham, S. Imagery and suggestion in pain reduction. Unpublished manuscript, University of Wisconsin, Madison, 1977.

Shacham, S., & Leventhal, H. Attention and the control of distress during cold pressor impact. Unpublished manuscript, University of Wisconsin, Madison, 1978.

Siegal, S. Evidence from rats that morphine tolerance is a learned response. *Journal of Comparative and Physiological Psychology*, 1975, *89*, 498–506.

Siegal, S. Morphine tolerance acquisition as an associative process. *Journal of Experimental Psychology; Animal Behavior Processes*, 1977, *3*, 1–13.

Simmel, M. L. The reality of phantom sensations. *Social Research*, 1962, *29*, 337–356.

Snyder, S. H. Opiate receptors and internal opiates. *Scientific American*, 1977, *236*, 44–56.

Spanos, N. P., Barber, T. X., & Lang, P. Cognition and self-control: Cognitive control of painful sensory input. In H. London & R. E. Nisbett (Eds.), *Thought and feeling*. Chicago: Aldine, 1974.

Spanos, N. P., Horton, C., & Chaves, J. F. The effects of two cognitive strategies on pain threshold. *Journal of Abnormal Psychology*, 1975, *84*, 677–681.

Stein, L. Habituation and stimulus novelty: A model based on classical conditioning. *Psychological Review*, 1966, *73*, 352–356.

Swets, J. A. Is there a sensory threshold? *Science*, 1961, *134*, 168–178.

Tomkins, S. S. *Affect, imagery and consciousness*, Vol. 1. New York: Springer, 1962.

Trethowan, W. H., & Conlon, M. F. The couvade syndrome. *British Journal of Psychiatry*, 1965, *3*, 57–66.

Walters, A. Psychogenic regional pain. *Brain*, 1961, *84*, 1–18.

Webster's Third New International Dictionary. Springfield, Mass.: G. & C. Merriam Co., 1966.

Whiting, J. W. M., & Child, I. L. *Child training and personality*. New Haven, Conn: Yale University Press, 1953.

Wilson, J. F. Coping styles influencing the effectiveness of preoperative intervention procedures. Paper presented at the American Psychological Association, San Francisco, California, 1977.

Wolff, B. B., Krasnegor, N. A., & Farr, R. S. Effect of suggestion upon experimental pain response parameters. *Perceptual and Motor Skills*, 1965, *21*, 675–683.

Zimbardo, P. G., Cohen, A., Weisenberg, M., Dworkin, L., & Firestone, I. The control of experimental pain. In P. G. Zimbardo (Eds.), *The cognitive control of motivation*. Glenview, Ill.: Scott, Foresman, 1969.

Zimbardo, P. C., Rapaport, C., & Baron, J. Pain control by hypnotic induction of motvational states. In P. G. Zimbardo (Ed.), *The cognitive control of motivation*. Glenview, Ill.: Scott, Foresman, 1969.

Editor's Introduction   **10**

Gray makes it quite clear that readers should be prepared for a novel conception of anxiety that will strike some as paradoxical. He maintains that the two major components of anxiety are conditioned fear and conditioned or anticipatory frustration. It is his data-supported argument that these two phenomena can be viewed as separate states or as a single state (anxiety) that will create a paradox for some readers. Gray resolves the paradox by demonstrating the functional equivalence of conditioned fear and conditioned frustration in animals.

The evidence supporting Gray's conception of anxiety is rooted in experimental learning theory and neurophysiology. The data come largely from studies of the effects of antianxiety drugs on the behavior of rats under well-specified and highly controlled conditions. Gray's development of the learning-theory background and his tracing of the neurophysiological routes and biochemical processes of drugs provide exciting reading for the serious student of emotions.

Some of the concepts and principles elaborated by Gray are held in common with other contributors. He believes that an emotion state may set the stage for learning by providing discriminative stimuli. He is clearly supportive of the notion that emotions play an important role in learning and behavior.

Gray's inclusion of both conditioned fear and conditioned frustration as components of anxiety has an analogue in clinical theory, if we assume conditioned frustration to be an antecedent or a concomitant of anger. Some clinicians have speculated that fear and anger play a part in the dynamics of the anxiety neurotic. But this analogy may be inappropriate, because Gray assumes that aggressive behavior results from unconditioned punishment or frustrative nonreward and is coordinate with the "fight/flight system," while conditioned frustration and conditioned fear are functionally equivalent components of anxiety, which is coordinate with the behavioral inhibition system. Those who are inclined to question the functional equivalency of conditioned fear and conditioned frustration are invited to examine the detailed data and arguments that Gray presents here.

Those who are unfamiliar with current learning-theory research and Gray's earlier contributions may find helpful the following summary of some key concepts. Unconditioned fear is elicited by unconditioned punishment (e.g., pain). Unconditioned fear is functionally equivalent to unconditioned frustration, which is elicited by nonreward. Either unconditioned fear or unconditioned frustration may lead to escape or aggressive behavior. Such behaviors characterize the fight/flight system.

Conditioned fear is elicited by secondary punishing stimuli or by stimuli that signal punishment by virtue of their association with primary punishment, such as pain. Conditioned fear is functionally equivalent to conditioned or anticipatory frustration, which is elicited by secondary frustrative stimuli, stimuli that signal frustrative nonreward. Conditioned fear or conditioned frustration may lead to the inhibition of ongoing behavior or, in the extreme, freezing. These are some of the characteristics of the behavioral inhibition system, the central theme of Gray's chapter.

The reader will find Gray's conception of novelty and its functions different from that of other contributors (e.g., Singer, Chapter 1; Zuckerman, Chapter 6). Most of us probably would agree with Gray that novelty changes ongoing behavior. However, while Gray sees novelty as having an inhibitory effect and thus as being a determinant of or a contributor to anxiety, others see novelty as having the capacity to elicit interest, surprise, the orienting reflex, fear, behavioral inhibition, or some combination of these. Perhaps the difference here can be explained in part by considering the degree to which the novel stimuli are discrepant from existing schemata or by considering a broader interpretation of behavioral inhibition and anxiety. Gray's definition of the behavioral inhibition system includes phenomena like attention focusing and switching that others might attribute to other systems or concepts. It should also be borne in mind that, in Gray's formulation, novelty's contribution to anxiety and the behavioral inhibition system is adaptive in increasing attention to environmental stimuli.

Gray's data and those of others lead him to conclude that antianxiety drugs alter behavior by acting on the septum and the hippocampus, structures included in Papez's emotion circuit and MacLean's limbic system. he examines the function of the septohippocampal system in relation to anxiety and learning in considerable detail. He also reviews several studies that support his premise that the effects of antianxiety drugs are mediated by the dorsal ascending noradrenergic bundle, which provides inputs to the septohippocampal system. Although the exact neural pathways and biochemical substrates of anxiety, fear, or any other emotion have yet to be determined, Gray's research is likely to elicit interest in further investigations in this area.

A Neuropsychological Theory of Anxiety

10

J. A. GRAY

This chapter presents a theory of anxiety that has much in common with a number of earlier approaches to the psychology of emotion (especially with the work of O. H. Mowrer, 1960) but that is in its details relatively novel. The major premise which underlies its development is that one can describe the psychological state which constitutes anxiety by studying the behavioral effects of drugs that reduce anxiety, and that by studying the physiological route by which antianxiety drugs produce their behavioral effects, one can discover the physiological substrate of anxiety.

This premise can be taken in a stronger and a weaker form. In its strong form (which can hardly be true), it would claim that the antianxiety drugs reduce all aspects of anxiety and only anxiety. In its weak form, it would claim that these drugs reduce at least some aspects of anxiety (hence their clinical usefulness) but not necessarily all of them or only anxiety. In spite of the implausibility of the strong form of our major premise, the arguments pursued here will, with minor exception, assume its truth. In this way, it will be possible to develop a relatively strong theory with comparative clarity. It can then be left to future research (assuming that the general approach is found sufficiently convincing to warrant it) to determine the extent to which "anxiety" as described here overlaps with "anxiety" as it emerges in the theory and research of other workers (e.g., Izard, 1972). The cautious reader is therefore advised to continue to put quotation marks around "anxiety" after we have dropped them, or perhaps to think of the emotional state that is described in this

J. A. GRAY • University of Oxford, Oxford, England. The experimental work reported in this chapter was supported by the U.K. Medical Research Council. During the time of writing the author held a Social Science Research Fellowship from the Nuffield Foundation.

chapter as the F state (after two of its major components, fear and conditioned frustration) rather than anxiety.

Our major premise is itself embedded in the conceptual framework provided by learning theory. Since this theory is based almost entirely on experimental work with animals, some may wish to label what follows a rat's eye view of the emotions (and perhaps read no further in consequence). However, the drugs whose behavioral and physiological effects we shall consider—the benzodiazepines (e.g., Librium, Valium), the barbiturates (e.g., sodium amytal), and alcohol—derive their validity for our arguments from their clinical effects in human beings. Thus the fact that (as we shall see) the conceptual framework of learning theory provides a comfortable and well-illuminated niche for the behavioral effects of these drugs is strong support for the view that animal learning theory is relevant to people, and in particular to their emotions.

I. LEARNING THEORY BACKGROUND

If we are to make efficient use of this framework, some preliminaries are in order concerning the treatment accorded the emotions within learning theory. As discussed elsewhere (Gray, 1972a, 1975), the most common strategy (e.g., Spence, 1956; Mowrer, 1960; Amsel, 1962; Plutchik, 1962; Millenson, 1967; Weiskrantz, 1968) is to treat the emotions as states elicited by instrumentally reinforcing stimuli or by stimuli that have been associated with such reinforcing stimuli. Although the details differ from author to author, this strategy usually forms part of a version of "two-process theory," according to which goal-directed behavior is the outcome of an interaction between two fundamental learning processes, one being classical conditioning (Pavlov, 1927), the other instrumental or operant conditioning (Skinner, 1938). The particular version of two-process theory in which it is proposed here to embed the emotions is one I have recently spelled out in some detail (Gray, 1975). The description given of it here can therefore be brief.

For our present purposes, the most important feature of this version of two-process theory is that the instrumental learning component is further subdivided into two varieties, one concerned wtih maximizing reward, the other with minimizing punishment. The classical component is concerned with learning the associative relationships between discrete stimulus events (i.e., it is stimulus–stimulus, or S–S, learning); the instrumental conditioning component is concerned with the establishment of behavior patterns that affect the organism's exposure to stimulus events (i.e., it is response–stimulus, or R–S, learning). If responses followed by a particular stimulus consequently increase in their probability of recurrence, the particular stimulus is a reward, or positive reinforcer. If responses followed by a particular stimulus consequently decrease in their probability of recurrence, the particular stimulus is a punishment, or negative reinforcer.

Further postulates of the present version of two-process theory concern "frustrative nonreward" (Amsel, 1962) and "relieving nonpunishment." Frustrative nonreward is the omission of reward after a particular response, given that reward has previously followed the same or similar responses and/or that reward is predicted to occur by stimuli to which the animal is currently exposed. Frustrative nonreward is held to have effects on behavior that are in certain respects identical to those produced by punishment, and there is much evidence to support this hypothesis (Wagner, 1966; Gray, 1975). Relieving nonpunishment is the omission of punishment after a particular response, given that punishment has previously followed the same or similar responses and/or that punishment is predicted to occur by stimuli to which the animal is currently exposed. Nonpunishment is held by the theory to have effects on behavior that are in certain respects identical to those produced by reward. In addition, the termination of reward is thought to be an operation with the same behavioral effects as frustrative nonreward, and the termination of punishment an operation with the same behavioral effects as relieving nonpunishment.

The various behavioral paradigms that result from presenting, terminating, or omitting reward or punishment and the terminology applied to them are set out in Table 1.

In the analysis so far it is supposed that, for a given animal species, there exist simuli that may act without prior learning as rewards and other stimuli that may act without prior learning as punishments. These stimuli[1] may act as "unconditioned stimuli" (UCS: Pavlov, 1927) in a classical conditioning paradigm or as positive or negative reinforcers, as defined above, in an instrumental conditioning paradigm. As UCSs they may therefore elicit unconditioned responses, or UCRs, while as reinforcing stimuli they may alter the probability of responses on which they are contingent. However, if the UCS in a classical conditioning paradigm is provided by a reinforcing stimulus (reward or punishment), classical conditioning may confer on initially neutral stimuli rewarding (appetitive) or punishing (aversive) properties, respectively.

These secondary or conditioned appetitive or aversive properties fall into two general classes: reinforcing and motivational. The reinforcing property corresponds to the reinforcing property of the UCS with which the conditioned stimulus (CS) has been paired. Thus a secondary rewarding stimulus increases the probability of recurrence of the responses that it follows, and a secondary punishing stimulus (often called a *warning signal*) decreases the probability of the responses that it follows. The motivational properties of secondary reward-

---

[1] Such stimuli are sometimes termed, in the ethological phrase, *innate releasers*. The stimulus most often used in this capacity in animal experiments on punishment is electric shock, which presumably acts by stimulating pain fibers. Other stimuli, however, may also act in the same capacity (though they have been subjected to much less experimental analysis). In an earlier analysis (Gray, 1971b), I concluded that such stimuli are usually either intense or novel, but that in addition there are a number of particular stimuli that are either connected with "special evolutionary dangers" (e.g., snakes) or arise during social interaction (e.g. bared teeth).

Table 1. Instrumental Reinforcing Procedures with Unconditioned Reinforcing Events (from Gray, 1975)[a]

Procedure	Outcome	
	$p(R)\uparrow$	$p(R)\downarrow$
Presentation	Rew [approach]	Pun [passive avoidance]
Termination	Pun! [escape]	Rew! [time-out]
Omission	Pun [active avoidance]	Rew [extinction]

[a] The abbreviations and symbols are as defined by the intersection of row (procedure) and column (outcome). $p(R)\uparrow$: outcome is an increase in the probability of the response on which the reinforcing event is made contingent. $p(R)\downarrow$: outcome is a decrease in the probability of this response. Dots and dashes indicate those procedures-plus-outcomes that define a stimulus as an S^{k+} or an S^{R-}, respectively. Bracketed phrases refer to typical learning situations in which the various reinforcing procedures are employed. Rew: reward; Pun: Punishment; !: termination; —: omission.

ing and punishing stimuli correspond to (though they are not identical with) the eliciting properties of the UCS (reward or punishment) from which they have been derived. These motivational properties are still very much the subject of empirical research, and their exact nature is not entirely clear. Most of the relevant experimental studies have been carried out by presenting secondary rewarding or punishing stimuli to an animal engaged in instrumentally rewarded behavior or "active avoidance" behavior (i.e., behavior followed by omission of punishment) and observing the elicited changes in response rate or response vigor. The best-established result of such experiments is that a secondary punishing stimulus reduces the rate of performance of a rewarded operant. This phenomenon, known variously as the *conditioned emotional response* or *conditioned suppression*, was originally demonstrated by Estes and Skinner (1941), and it has subsequently been much used in drug research.

The UCS that confers secondary appetitive or aversive properties on a CS need not be a simple primary reward or punishment; it may be a complex event such as frustrative nonreward or relieving nonpunishment. In consequence of pairing with the former of these events a stimulus acquires secondary aversive properties as a conditioned frustrative stimulus; in consequence of pairing with the latter, it acquires secondary appetitive properties as a conditioned relieving stimulus (often called a *safety signal*). Responses followed by conditioned frustrative stimuli, other things being equal, are likely to decline in probability of recurrence; responses followed by conditioned relieving stimuli are likely to increase in probability of recurrence. With regard to the motivational properties of these types of stimuli, there are indications that those possessed by conditioned frustrative stimuli resemble those of secondary punishing stimuli, and those possessed by conditioned relieving stimuli resemble those of secondary rewarding stimuli.

If this description has inevitably been overcondensed, I hope that it has nonetheless served to introduce the reader to the main lines of division that can be used to fractionate the behavioral effects of the antianxiety drugs. As already indicated, the emotions are usually treated wtihin learning theory as states elicited by unconditioned instrumentally reinforcing stimuli or by stimuli that have been associated (by classical conditioning) with such unconditioned reinforcing stimuli. The most convenient way, therefore, to consider the behavioral effects of the antianxiety drugs is with reference to the kinds of unconditioned or conditioned reinforcers by which the relevant behavior is elicited, reinforced, or motivated. I have recently reviewed a very large number of drug studies along these lines (Gray, 1977); I shall summarize here the conclusions of that review.

II. THE BEHAVIORAL EFFECTS OF ANTIANXIETY DRUGS

None of the antianxiety drugs has any consistent effects on rewarded behavior of a kind that can be interpreted as an alteration in basic reward processes, whether conditioned or unconditioned. Studies of the effects of the antianxiety drugs on electrical self-stimulation of the brain confirm this conclusion. It is consistently found that response rates are increased on certain kinds of intermittent schedule in the Skinner box. However, the most likely explanation for these effects is that they are connected to the changes produced by the drugs in responses to frustrative nonreward (see below).

A. Punishment

All the antianxiety drugs reduce the behavioral effects of punishment, provided behavior prior to the delivery of the punishment is measured. This behavior normally, of course, consists in the suppression of the punished response (passive avoidance). Under the influence of the antianxiety drugs, such passive avoidance behavior is impaired; that is, the punished response is emitted with a higher probability than in undrugged animals. This effect (which has been known since Jules Masserman's and Neal Miller's work in the 1940s) is found in a wide range of situations and with a wide range of different specific drugs in the barbiturate and benzodiazepine classes. It might be due to a reduction in the felt intensity of the punishment (usually an electric shock), that is, to an analgesic effect. However, this explanation can be ruled out by a number of lines of evidence.

First, there is no evidence of any general reduction by the antianxiety drugs in responses directly elicited by unconditioned aversive stimuli (e.g., flinching, jumping, squealing, or unconditioned escape). The one example of such an effect is the frequently reported reduction produced by the benzodiazepines in aggressive responses elicited by aversive stimuli. However, there are also many reports of failures to reduce aggressive responses with the benzodiazepines and several reports of an actual facilitation of aggression. Facilitation has also been reported after the administration of barbiturates and alcohol.

Second, when shock is used as the reinforcer in learning paradigms other than passive avoidance, impairments are not produced by the antianxiety drugs. Thus, escape learning (in which the learned response terminates shock) and one-way active avoidance (in which a unidirectional locomotor response is followed by the omission of shock) are not changed in any consistent or specific manner by these drugs. There are, moreover, two situations in which the drugs actually improve active avoidance. The first is two-way active avoidance, most commonly studied in the Miller–Mowrer shuttlebox. This situation necessarily involves a conflict between active and passive avoidance, since the animal can avoid shock only by reentering a compartment in which it has previously been shocked and from which it has just fled.

The improvement produced by the antianxiety drugs in shuttlebox avoidance is thus probably due to a reduction in the passive avoidance of this compartment. Improvement is also seen after administration of the antianxiety drugs in nonspatial active avoidance (e.g., in the Skinner box), in which the avoidance response leaves the animal in the same place. It is known that rats trapped in an inescapable dangerous place have a strong tendency to freeze (Bolles, 1971), and the improvement produced by the antianxiety drugs in bar-press avoidance is probably due to a reduction in this tendency. The exact relationship between freezing (in which all active responses are suppressed) and passive avoidance (in which one specific response is suppressed) is not clear. But it is probable that the two are closely connected and that the antianxiety drugs impair passive avoidance—and improve both shuttlebox and bar-press avoidance—as a result of a single underlying change.

Third, there are no consistent changes produced by the antianxiety drugs in classically conditioned fear (i.e., with no response–punishment contingency).

The one exception to this generalization in the existing data (which, however, leave much to be desired) consists in a number of reports that the benzodiazepines reduce conditioned suppression. In this paradigm, a CS is paired with shock and presented to the animal while it is performing a rewarded operant, typically bar pressing; the term *conditioned suppression* refers to the reduction in performance of the operant that is produced by such as CS. A conditioned-suppression experiment may be conducted in two ways. In an *on-the-baseline* procedure, the CS–shock pairings are carried out while the animal is performing the rewarded operant. The benzodiazepines reduce conditioned suppression when this paradigm is used. In an off-the-baseline procedure, the classical conditioning of CS and shcok is carried out in a separate environment, and the CS alone is presented while the animal performs the rewarded operant. Under these conditions, neither the benzodiazepines nor other antianxiety drugs consistently alter conditioned suppression. Thus, it is unlikely that the alteration in passive avoidance produced by the antianxiety drugs is due to any impairment in the classical conditioning of fear.

Several conclusions can be drawn from the pattern of findings described in the preceding paragraphs.

First, the behavioral effects of the antianxiety drugs in experiments using aversive stimuli are not due to analgesia.

Second, drug-produced impairments in such experiments are virtually limited to the passive avoidance paradigm. The antianxiety drugs rather specifically impair the animal's ability to withold responses in anticipation of punishment. They do not impair the ability actively to make responses that are followed by the termination or omission of punishment, nor do they reduce responses elicited by the punishing stimulus. Where they produce other behavioral changes, these are often secondary to the reduction in passive avoidance. This applies to the improvement in two-way active avoidance and in bar-press avoidance; it may also apply to the facilitation of aggression (via a reduction in the passive avoidance of the opponent—a phenomenon well known in human beings under the title of "Dutch courage").

Third, the pattern of change produced by the antianxiety drugs suggests that they reduce the behavioral effects of stimuli that warn of punishment (secondary punishing stimuli) but not those of the unconditioned punishing stimuli themselves. Passive avoidance necessarily occurs in advance of contact with the punishment and is presumably under the control of secondary punishing stimuli that have been associated with the primary punishment. Responses elicited by punishment, on the other hand, are unaltered by the drugs. This generalization depends, however, on the assumption that active avoidance (unimpaired by the drugs) is not principally controlled by secondary punishing stimuli, in opposition to the well-known theory proposed in the late 1940s by Neal Miller (1948) and O. H. Mowrer (1947). I have discussed this issue elsewhere (Gray, 1975) and, in common with a number of other writers (e.g.,

Bolles, 1972), concluded that active avoidance is to a large extent reinforced by the attainment of stimuli associated with nonpunishment (safety signals) rather than with the termination of secondary punishing stimuli. The latter, however, are undoubtedly involved in active avoidance, if only to establish the dangerous environment in contrast to one that is safe. Thus the view that antianxiety drugs affect responses to conditioned punishing stimuli implies that the role of these stimuli in active avoidance learning is a relatively weak one. An alternative possibility is that the antianxiety drugs block specifically the *inhibition* of responses produced by secondary punishing stimuli (and thus passive but not active avoidance). But, as we shall now see, there is evidence against this point of view from experiments on the effects of these drugs on responses to nonreward.

B. Frustrative Nonreward

We have so far considered four of the six reinforcement paradigms shown in Table 1. The antianxiety drugs do not affect the acquisition or performance of new responses in three of these paradigms: presentation of reward, termination of punishment (escape), or omission of punishment (active avoidance). In contrast, they reduce the suppression of established responses in the fourth paradigm, punishment. Of the remaining two paradigms, there are no relevant data on termination of reward. We consider now the final paradigm: the omission of reward, or frustrative nonreward.

Much the greatest volume of experimental work on frustrative nonreward has been concerned with the barbiturates, especially sodium amobarbital. However, such data as exist for the benzodiazepines and alcohol are consistent with the reported barbiturate effects. These may be summarized simply: across a wide range of conditions, these drugs antagonize the behavioral effects of nonreward, whether this takes the form of total omission of reward or of reduction in the magnitude of reward. As in the case of punishment, the suppression of responses that occurs in the undrugged animal before the point of reinforcement is reduced under the drug. In the simplest case (extinction following continuous reinforcement), this is seen as an increase in resistance to extinction.

Also as in the case of punishment, there is evidence that responses *elicited* by frustrative nonreward are unchanged by antianxiety drugs. The clearest instance of this lack of effect is the Amsel and Roussel (1952) double-runway situation, in which nonreward in the first of two goal boxes causes animals to run faster in the second of the two sequential alleys. This phenomenon (called the *frustration effect*, or FE) may reflect an increase in arousal or excitement due to frustrative nonreward, or it may be an escape response elicited by the aversive properties known to accrue to stimuli associated with nonreward (Gray, 1975). Either way, it is clearly unaffected by sodium amobarbital (there are five negative reports), although this drug reliably decreases the behavioral effects of *anticipated* nonreward under a wide range of conditions.

The effects of the antianxiety drugs on responses to nonreward, as so far described, are consistent with the hypothesis, considered above in connection with passive and active avoidance, that these drugs block specifically the *inhibition* of responses. Thus they impair extinction (in which a previously rewarded response is suppressed) but not the FE (in which, after nonreward, animals run faster). This hypothesis is ruled out, however, by experiments on the partial reinforcement-acquisition effect (PRAE: Goodrich, 1959; Haggard, 1959). This consists in the fact that, if rats are run in the straight alley with reward on a random 50% of trials (partial reinforcement, PRF), they run at asymptote faster than rats given continuous reinforcement (CRF), that is, reward on every trial. Amsel (1962) has analyzed this phenomenon as demonstrating the increased arousal ("drive") produced by anticipation of nonreward in the PRF group, and there is indeed clear evidence of such changes in arousal in response to both conditioned frustrative and conditioned punishing stimuli (Gray, 1975). Here, then, is a phenomenon in which there is an increase in performance (as with the FE), but in anticipation of nonreward rather than elicited by it. Thus, if the antianxiety drugs only block inhibitory changes, they should not alter the PRAE. If, on the other hand, they generally reverse any behavioral changes produced by conditioned frustrative stimuli, they should reduce the PRAE. There are several experiments that support the latter prediction: the increased running speed of PRF animals is reduced by sodium amobarbital (Wagner, 1963; Gray, 1969; Capaldi & Sparling, 1971), alcohol (Nelson & Wollen, 1965) and chlordiazepoxide (Iwahara, Iwasaki, Nagamura, & Masuyama, 1966).

The impairment produced by the antianxiety drugs in the control of behavior by conditioned frustrative stimuli probably underlies a number of other behavioral changes seen with these drugs.

Among these are changes in response rates on various free-operant schedules of reinforcement. There are no effects of the antianxiety drugs on response rates under CRF or variable interval (VI) schedules; but rates are reliably increased under fixed interval (FI), fixed ratio (FR), and differential reinforcement of low-rate (DRL) schedules. The latter three schedules have in common that there is an event that signals that, for a period of time, the animal's responses will go unreinforced (i.e., an event that can serve as a conditioned frustrative stimulus). On the FI and FR schedules, that event is the delivery of reward; on the DRL schedule, it is either the animal's previous response or the delivery of reward. Neither the CRF nor the VI schedules, in contrast, contain any reliable signals of nonreward. Thus, the most parsimonious explanation of the effects of the antianxiety drugs on responding on the FI, FR, and DRL schedules (given the other known effects of these drugs) is that they reduce the inhibitory effects of the conditioned frustrative stimuli constituted by reward delivery and/or the last response. (There is much evidence that reward and other reinforcers may possess cue properties of this kind: Mackintosh, 1974.) On this hypothesis, one would expect that the effect of the antianxiety drugs would be particularly pronounced at the point at which the inhibitory effects of the conditioned frustrative stimuli are greatest. On the FI schedule, for example, this is just after the delivery of reward. Consistent with this prediction, the rate-increasing effects of these drugs is greatest early on during the fixed interval, terminal rates not being affected.

A second kind of behavior in which the effects of the antianxiety drugs on responses to nonreward may be seen is that of discrimination learning. This may be divided into two fundamental varieties. In a simultaneous discrimination, the animal is faced with a choice between the correct and the incorrect stimuli; in a successive discrimination, the two stimuli are presented separately and the animal shows that it has learned the discrimination by responding in the presence of the correct stimulus and withholding its response in the presence of the incorrect one. It is possible to solve a simultaneous discrimination simply by learning to approach the correct stimulus. In a successive discrimination, however, it is also necessary to respond appropriately to the incorrect stimulus. Thus one would expect the antianxiety drugs to impair successive discriminations (by disinhibiting responses to the incorrect stimulus); and this indeed is the result obtained. There has been very little work using these drugs in simultaneous discriminations, but there is no evidence of any effect of the drugs in this kind of task.

Let us try to summarize the behavioral effects of the antianxiety drugs, as these have been seen in animal experiments. These drugs have no effect on basic reward processes, either when conventional reinforcers or when electrical self-stimulation of the brain is used. The behavioral effects of punishment, in contrast, are reduced, but only if (1) the measured response occurs in anticipation of punishment (responses elicited by the punishing stimulus are unaffected), and (2) a true punishment paradigm is used (i.e., the aversive stimulus is made contingent upon the animal's response). Neither escape learning nor active avoidance is directly affected by the antianxiety drugs; in cases where active avoidance is in conflict with passive avoidance (e.g., in the shuttlebox), active avoidance may apparently be improved. Finally, the antianxiety drugs antagonize the behavioral effects of anticipated nonreward across a wide variety of conditions, while not altering responses elicited by nonreward. In consequence, response rates are increased on certain operant schedules (FI, FR, DRL), and successive (but not simultaneous) discriminations are impaired. It is important to note that the alterations produced by the antianxiety drugs include a reduction not only in the inhibition of punishment or nonrewarded responses but also in the increased behavioral vigor or arousal seen under the same conditions.

III. THE PSYCHOLOGY OF ANXIETY

It appears from the findings discussed in the previous section that there is an important similarity between nonreward and punishment: responses controlled by stimuli that predict that imminent occurrence of these events are impaired by the antianxiety drugs; responses elicited by them are unchanged. This similarity in drug sensitivity is paralleled by a large number of purely behavioral similarities between punishment and nonreward (Wagner, 1966; Gray, 1975). In terms of the emotions, these similarities may be expressed as two functional equivalences: (1) between unconditioned fear and unconditioned frustration, elicited by punishment and nonreward, respectively; and (2) between conditioned fear and conditioned frustration, elicited by secondary punishing and secondary frustrative stimuli, respectively. It seems, furthermore, that the two emotional states joined together in (1) are different from the two joined together in (2). We have already seen that they differ in their response to drugs, the conditioned emotional states being sensitive to the antianxiety drugs, the unconditioned states not being sensitive. Behaviorally, there is again a parallel to this difference in drug sensitivity. Whereas the chief behavioral signs produced by unconditioned punishment and nonreward are increases in locomotor activity, attempts at escape, and aggressive behavior, what is observed in an animal anticipating punishment or nonreward is quite different: inhibition of ongoing behavior, taking the form of freezing in extreme instances (Gray, 1975).

These various lines of argument have led to the hypothesis that there are two independent systems: one a *fight/flight system* that is responsive to unconditioned punishment and nonreward, and the other a *behavioral inhibition system* that is responsive to stimuli that are associated with these aversive events (Gray, 1972a). It is the latter system that is the theme of this chapter. Since activity in the behavioral inhibition system appears to be selectively antagonized by the antianxiety drugs, it is a reasonable hypothesis that such activity underlies the emotion of anxiety. Viewed in this way, *anxiety* is synonymous with "conditioned fear plus conditioned frustration."

It might be objected to this hypothesis that since we are able correctly to apply the words *fear* and *frustration* to the separate states to which they each apply, they cannot possibly refer to the same state. But this objection would be misplaced. The theory advanced here is a theory about the emotions, not about the words used to describe the emotions. As Schachter (Schachter & Singer, 1962) has shown, in labeling one's own emotional state one takes account not only of the internal nature of that state, as it is available to introspection, but also of the situation that has given rise to that state. This, indeed, is also what we do when we label emotions in others, whether they are members of our own species or of a different one. The words *fear* and *frustration* are used systematically differently when experimental psychologists talk about rats, but this is because they take account of the operation (punishment or the omission of reward) to which they have exposed their subjects. These different uses do not render meaningless the hypothesis that the rat enters the same emotional state, reagrdless of the particular reinforcing event (punishment or nonreward), to which it has been exposed. In the same way, there is no difficulty in supposing that the emotional state produced by signals of punishment (fear) is the same as that produced by signals of omission of reward (anticipatory frustration) in man, even though (since one knows the events that have given rise to the emotional state) both the experiencing subject and an observer of the subject will use different words to label this state, depending on those events.

From now on, therefore, we shall use the word *anxiety* to mean that emotional state to which secondary punishing and secondary frustrative stimuli (but not unconditioned punishment or frustrative nonreward) give rise, and we shall use the term *behavioral inhibition system* to mean that system, activity in which produces the emotion of anxiety. *Ex hypothesi*, the behavioral inhibition system is activated by secondary punishing and frustrative stimuli, and its activity is reduced by the antianxiety drugs.

So far, in our treatment of the behavioral inhibition system, we have considered only stimuli with clear-cut reinforcing effects as defined by Table 1. There is some reason, however, to add to the list of adequate stimuli for anxiety one further event that does not figure in that table, namely, novelty. As pointed out elsewhere (Gray, 1975), novel stimuli share with conditioned aversive stimuli the properties of inhibiting ongoing behavior (originally described by Pavlov as "external inhibition") and of increasing the level of arousal (Sokolov, 1960). The major effect of novel stimuli—almost their defining characteristic—is, however, that they attract attention to themselves and also increase attention to other features of the environment in which they occur (the phenomenon of dishabituation: Sokolov, 1960). But the same appears to be true of conditioned frustrative stimuli (Sutherland, 1966; McFarland, 1966).

There are also indications that the antianxiety drugs reduce attention to environmental change, whether under conditions of novelty alone or under conditions involving frustrative nonreward. For example, Ison, Glass, and Bohmer (1966) found that sodium amobarbital reduced the tendency of rats to enter the changed arm of a T maze. Also in the T maze, a number of experiments have shown a reduction in spontaneous alternation after injection of an antianxiety drug; that is, whereas the undrugged rat tends to alternate his choices of arm, the drugged rat tends to repeat his first choice. In a more complex experiment involving nonreward, McGonigle, McFarland, and Collier (1967) showed that sodium amobarbital reduced the attention paid by an animal to a second stimulus dimension added after a first one had been learned on a PRF schedule in a simultaneous discrimination.

There is a case, therefore, for the addition of novelty to the list of adequate stimuli for anxiety. No doubt, however, the degree of novelty must rise beyond some threshold if it is to provoke emotional reactions (surprise or apprehension). Furthermore, since novel stimuli also evoke approach behavior, such emotional reactions are unlikely ever to be unmixed. There is also a case for adding to the list of outputs of the behavioral inhibition system one of switching attention, especially to novel features of the environment.

Adopting these additions, we may summarize the key features of the theory of anxiety proposed here as follows:

1. Anxiety is a central state consisting of activity in a hypothetical behavioral inhibition system.
2. The adequate stimuli for activating this system are secondary punishing stimuli, secondary frustrative stimuli, and novel stimuli.
3. The behavioral effects of activity in this system are inhibition of ongoing behavior, increased arousal, and increased attention to environmental stimuli, especially novel ones.
4. The function of activity in this system is to suppress existing but maladaptive behavior patterns while scanning the environment for possible alternative behavior patterns.

No evidence is offered in support of the last of these postulates; it is put forward simply as a reasonable interpretation of the remaining properties attributed to the behavioral inhibition system.

IV. THE SEPTOHIPPOCAMPAL SYSTEM

If the behavioral inhibition system exists, it must be in the brain. A first clue as to *where* comes from the behavioral effects of lesions to the brain. If the antianxiety drugs act by impairing the function of a particular brain region, then destruction of that region should produce effects on behavior similar to those produced by these drugs. On the basis of this argument, I suggested (Gray, 1970) two particular brain structures as likely candidates for the site of action of the antianxiety drugs: the septal area and the hippocampus.

These structures are very closely interrelated, both anatomically and physiologically (Figure 1). The hippocampus displays a characteristic pattern of rhythmic slow electrical activity ranging from about 4 to 12 Hz (the hippocampal theta rhythm) under most conditions in which the animals is behaviorally active. The functional significance of this rhythm is still a matter of considerable dispute (e.g., Vanderwolf, Kramis, Gillespie, & Bland, 1975; Landfield, 1976; Gray, 1977), but it is well established that it is controlled physiologically by pacemaker cells located in the medial septal area (Stumpf, 1965). Fibers from the medial septal area innervate the hippocampus diffusely after traveling in the fimbria and the fornix (Meibach & Siegel, 1977). Conversely, the major direct subcortical projection of the hippocampus is to the lateral septal area via the fimbria (Raisman, Cowan & Powell, 1966; De France, 1976). Thus lesions of the anterior septal region (containing the medial and lateral septal areas) destroy both a major input to the hippocampus and a major output from it, as well as radically altering hippocampal electrical

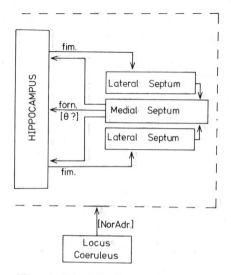

Figure 1. Schematic diagram of the septohippocampal system; forn.: fornix; fim.: fimbria;
NorAdr.: the noradrenergic input to the
septohippocampal system from the locus
coeruleus.

activity by permanently abolishing the theta rhythm (Stumpf, 1965; Gray, 1971a).

We have recently completed an exhaustive review of the very large number of reports of the behavioral effects of septal and hippocampal lesions (Gray & McNaughton, in preparation). The major conclusions from this review are set out in Table 2, which also permits the reader to compare the septal and hippocampal syndromes with the syndrome produced by the antianxiety drugs. Two key findings emerge: (1) in the great majority of behavioral paradigms for which data are available on both lesions, their effects are strikingly similar; (2) whenever the effects of the two lesions are similar and corresponding drug data are available, the direction of the behavioral change produced by the lesions is the same as that produced by the antianxiety drugs. Let us consider some examples of these generalizations.

There are no consistent effects of either septal or hippocampal lesions on rewarded behavior. There is some indication that septal lesions increase the incentive effects of reward, in that they increase response rate in the Skinner box on a CRF schedule. But these lesions do not affect running speed on a CRF schedule in the alley, and hippocampal lesions do not increase performance on CRF schedules in either situation (which is also the case for the antianxiety drugs).

Turning to passive avoidance experiments, both septal and hippocampal lesions, like the antianxiety drugs, clearly release responses that have been suppressed by the threat of punishment. In this respect, our review of the literature (Gray & McNaughton, in preparation) supports the earlier reviews by Douglas (1967) and Altman, Brunner, and Bayer (1973) on the hippocampus, and by McCleary (1966) and Lubar and Numan (1973) on the septal area, rather than the criticisms of these reviews advance by Nadel, O'Keefe, and Black (1975) and Caplan (1973). But it will be recalled that the antianxiety drugs, while they antagonize the behavioral suppression produced by response-contingent punishment, do not generally alter classically conditioned measures of fear (e.g., off-the-baseline conditioned suppression). The same negative seems to apply also to septal and hippocampal lesions. The only apparent exception to this rule is that conditioned freezing is reduced by septal lesions, but this seems to be a change specific to motor responses, since similar changes are seen in experimental situations that do not involve conditioned fear stimuli. Thus, like the antianxiety drugs, septal and hippocampal lesions specifically impair the animal's ability to withhold responses on which punishment is made contingent.

Table 2. Similarities between Behavioral Effects of Antianxiety Drugs, Septal Lesions, and Hippocampal Lesions[a]

	Effects of		
Type of Task	Antianxiety Drugs	Septal Lesions	Hippocampal Lesions
Food and water intake	+	+	0
Rewarded running, CRF	0	0	0
Rewarded bar-pressing, CRF	0	+	0
Passive avoidance	−	−	−
Motor reactions to shock	?	+	+
Aggressive reactions to shock	?	+	−
Aversive classical conditioning	0	0	0
Escape from shock	0	0	0
1-way active avoidance	0	−	0
2-way active avoidance	+	+	+
Bar-press active avoidance	+	+	+
Extinction	−	−	−
Rewarded bar-pressing, FI or DRL	+	+	+
Simultaneous discrimination	0	0	0
Successive discrimination	−	−	−
Double-runaway FE	0	0	0
Spontaneous alternation	−	−	−

[a] −: performance is generally reported to be impaired; 0: the literature fails to reveal any consistent changes; +: performance is generally reported to be enhanced; ?: insufficient data.

In experiments in which the event contingent upon a response is shock termination or shock omission, the effects of septal and hippocampal lesions are, with one exception, concordant. Both lesions leave learned escape unaltered and improve two-way active avoidance and nonspatial (bar-press) avoidance—which, as we know, is the pattern of change also seen after administration of the antianxiety drugs. One-way active avoidance, however, is unaffected by hippocampal lesions (as also by the antianxiety drugs) but impaired by septal lesions. This pattern of results could be explained if the effect of septal lesions on one-way active avoidance were due to the disruption of septal connections with structures other than the hippocampus. Evidence that this is in fact so is presented by Grossman (1976), who has implicated the septal projection to the habenular nuclei (via the stria medullaris) in this effect.

A rather mixed picture emerges when we consider the effects of septal and hippocampal lesions on unconditioned responses elicited by aversive stimuli. Neither lesion alters thresholds for responses to electric shock; thus, like the antianxiety drugs, they do not have any general analgesic effects. Both lesions increase the intensity of locomotor response (e.g., jumping) elicited by shock; there are insufficient data to judge the effects of the antianxiety drugs on such responses. A clear discrepancy between the effects of the two lesions emerges, however, when we look at aggressive responses to shock. These are increased by septal but reduced by hippocampal lesions. Interestingly, aggressive behavior is also the major point of discrepancy between the behavioral effects of the different classes of antianxiety drugs (Gray, 1977): the benzodiazepines sometimes reduce and sometimes increase aggressive behavior, whereas only facilitatory effects have been clearly seen after the barbiturates and alcohol.

Turning next to experiments using nonreward, we find that (like the antianxiety drugs) both lesions increase resistance to extinction after reward on CRF schedule and impair successive discriminations (by increasing the emission of responses in the presence of the negative cue), while not affecting simultaneous discriminations. Both lesions impair the reversal of simultaneous discriminations (in which it is, of course, necessary to inhibit the old positive response); the one relevant drug experiment (Caul, 1967) found the same result. Neither lesion alters the double-runway FE, and both lesions increase response rates on FI, FR, and DRL schedules. All these effects are, again, like those of the antianxiety drugs.

It is clear, then, that the behavioral effects of septal lesions resemble those of hippocampal lesions in the great majority of cases (Table 2). It is reasonable to suppose that those effects that are common to the two lesions reflect the functions of an integrated septohippocampal system (SHS), as indicated in Figure 1, whereas those that differ in the two syndromes are a consequence either of disruption of other septal or hippocampal connections (as we saw in the example of one-way active avoidance: Grossman, 1976) or of damage to adjacent structures as well as to the septum and hippocampus. Thus the fact that, whenever the two lesions produce the same behavioral change, this change is also produced by the antianxiety drugs supports the hypothesis that these drugs act in some way on the SHS. Furthermore, since the drugs do not appear to produce behavioral effects additional to those they share with septal and hippocampal lesions (with the exception of the sedation, anesthesia, and motor incoordination produced only at higher doses than those considered here), it is possible that *all* of the relevant behavioral effects of the antianxiety drugs are due to an action on the SHS. Thus these data allow one to propose the hypothesis (Gray, 1970) that the antianxiety drugs reduce anxiety by altering the activity of the SHS.

The research that my collaborators and I have been pursuing over the last seven years has been directed to gaining an understanding of the nature of the action of the antianxiety drugs on the SHS. In the remainder of this chapter, I shall outline this research and the conclusions we have been able to draw from it.

V. THE PARTIAL REINFORCEMENT EXTINCTION EFFECT

Many of the experiments that I shall describe have been concerned with the partial reinforcement extinction effect (PREE). As is well known (Mackintosh, 1974), animals reinforced on a PRF schedule subsequently display greater resistance to extinction than animals trained for an equal number of trials on CRF. As argued by Amsel (1962) in his application of frustration theory to this phenomenon, it may be considered a consequence of the fact that PRF animals develop tolerance for the aversive effects of frustrative nonreward. There is a great deal of evidence that frustrative nonreward, and conditioned stimuli associated with this event, *are* aversive (Gray, 1975). There is also evidence that nonreward, like other stressful stimuli (e.g., cold, electric shock), activates the pituitary–adrenal system, as shown by a rise in corticosterone levels in blood (Levine, Goldman, & Coover, 1972; Valero & Gray, unpublished data). Thus extinction of previously rewarded responses may be regarded as a model of stress-produced behavior and the PREE as a model of behavioral tolerance to stress.

There is evidence, furthermore, that the tolerance to frustrative nonreward that is developed by a PRF schedule can transfer to tolerance for electric shock (Brown & Wagner, 1964). These authors also showed that tolerance to electric shock, produced by a counterconditioning schedule of shock paired with food reward, can transfer to tolerance for nonreward, as indicated by an increased resistance to extinction. Since other workers (Weiss, Glazer, Pohorecky, Brick, & Miller, 1975) have shown that a similar cross-tolerance may be demonstrated between electric shock and cold stress, it is possible that a common physiological change underlies, at least in part, tolerance for all forms of stress, irrespective of the particular stressor used. If that is correct, the PREE may perhaps serve as an index of that general physiological change.

It has the very great advantage over other similar behavioral measures that it has been the subject of a substantial research effort. In consequence, we know a great deal about the behavioral factors that affect its magnitude, and we have a good theoretical understanding of how these factors work (Mackintosh, 1974).

It seems, in fact, that there is not one kind of PREE, but two. The first kind, which owes its elucidation to the extensive theoretical and experimental work of E. J. Capaldi (1967), is due to the counterconditioning of the immediate aftereffects of nonreward (or, in later writings by Capaldi, the "memory" of nonreward), so that they become discriminative stimuli for the performance of the instrumental rewarded response. This form of counterconditioning is particularly prominent with short intertrial intervals (ITI) and a small number of trials (Mackintosh, 1974). The second kind of PREE appears to work according to Amsel's (1962) analysis: the animal develops a conditioned frustration response, and it is the cues from this internal state that become counterconditioned as discriminative stimuli for the continued performance of the rewarded instrumental response. This form of counterconditioning is favored by long ITIs and many trials (Mackintosh, 1974). (For these purposes a "short ITI" lasts up to 20 minutes, and a "long ITI" is 24 hours; intermediate values have not been the subject of much research.)

For our present purposes, the most important difference between the two forms of PREE and the theoretical analyses to which they have each been subjected is that the first kind depends on responses (aftereffects) elicited by unconditioned nonreward, and the second depends on responses (conditioned frustration) elicited by conditioned frustrative stimuli. In view of what has been said earlier in this chapter, therefore, we would expect the former not to be influenced by antianxiety drugs but the latter to be impaired by them (since these agents impair responses to conditioned but not unconditioned aversive stimuli). Existing data for the most part bear out this analysis.

When a short ITI (1.5 minutes) and few trials (6) are used, sodium amobarbital has no effect on the PREE (Ziff & Capaldi, 1971). If the ITI remains relatively short (4–5 minutes) but the number of trials is increased to 40, there is an attenuation of the PREE when this drug is administered during acquisition only (placebo injections being given during extinction) (Ison & Pennes, 1969). If the same design is used, but the number of trials is increased to 64, the PREE can be abolished (Gray, 1969). If the ITI is lengthened to 24 hours, it is possible to abolish the PREE with sodium amobarbital even if only 7 trials are run during acquisition, and this is also the outcome with 21 acquisition trials (Feldon, Guillamon, Gray, de Wit, & McNaughton, in press). The same effect can be obtained using chlordiazepoxide and a 24-hour ITI (Feldon & Gray, unpublished).

Under conditions, then, in which the PREE depends principally not on the aftereffects elicited by nonreward but upon some form of conditioned response established on the basis of these aftereffects as UCS, the antianxiety drugs

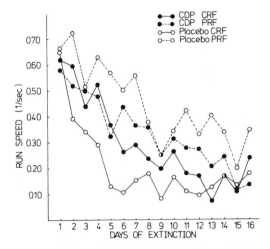

Figure 2. Course of extinction, at one trial per day in a
straight alley, in groups of rats given continous reinforcement (CRF) or partial reinforcement (PRF) during
training, and chlordiazepoxide (CDP; 5 mg/kg) or
placebo throughout training and extinction. Data kindly
supplied by J. Feldon.

block the PREE. This effect bears two diametrically opposed interpretations.
The first is that the drug interferes with the counterconditioning process by
which tolerance to the aversive effects of nonreward develops. The second is
that it blocks the behavioral effects of nonreward so that there is nothing to
which tolerance can be developed. Other effects of the antianxiety drugs in the
same or similar situations make it clear that the latter interpretation is the correct one. Thus, in the same alley situation in which the PREE is blocked,
sodium amobarbital or chlordiazepoxide administered during extinction after
CRF training increases resistance to extinction, an effect that is consistent with
a general reduction in the behavioral effects of nonreward, but not with disruption of counterconditioning (Figure 2). But, as we shall see, there are other
interventions which appear to disrupt counter-conditioning directly.

VI. THE SEPTOHIPPOCAMPAL SYSTEM AND THE PARTIAL REINFORCEMENT EXTINCTION EFFECT

As we have seen, there is good reason to suppose that the antianxiety
drugs alter behavior by way of an action on the SHS. Given the control that
the septal area exerts over the hippocampal theta rhythm (Stumpf, 1965), a
natural first hypothesis is that the antianxiety drugs in some way impair this
control, and this was indeed the hypothesis I proposed in 1970. In its crudest
form, this hypothesis would hold that (1) the hippocampus cannot perform its

behavioral functions properly without a theta rhythm; (2) septal lesions have effects like those of hippocampal lesions because they eliminate the theta rhythm; and (3) the antianxiety drugs also eliminate the theta rhythm. This hypothesis is not tenable. To begin with, the antianxiety drugs do not eliminate the theta rhythm (though, as we shall see, they do have other effects on this pattern of electrical activity). In addition, the theta rhythm accompanies not only forms of behavior that are disrupted by septal and hippocampal lesions and the antianxiety drugs, but also forms that are not. Thus, if the theta rhythm plays any role in mediating the behavioral effects of the antianxiety drugs, it must be a more subtle one.

A first hint as to what this role might be came from the observation (Gray & Ball, 1970) that the frequency of the theta rhythm recorded from a free-moving rat in a simple alley task varies predictably, depending on its behavior and on what is happening to it. In particular, we observed a frequency of approximately 6–7 Hz when the animal was rewarded and in the process of consuming the reward (water) in the goal box; a frequency of about 9–10 Hz when a well-trained rat was running down the alley towards the goal box; and an intermediate frequency when the animal entered a goal box in which it expected to find water and was instead exposed to frustrative nonreward. The mean theta frequency under the latter conditions was found to be 7.7 Hz, a value later confirmed by Kimsey, Dyer, and Petri (1974). A similar value has been reported by Kurtz (1975) when sexual behavior is nonrewarded. Theta frequencies at around 7.7 Hz are also seen when rats explore a novel environment for the first time (Gray & Ball, 1970).

Since the antianxiety drugs attenuate the behavioral effects of nonreward and of novelty, but not those of reward, these data considerably limit the scope of any hypothesis purporting to relate these drug effects to the theta rhythm. They imply that any alteration produced by these drugs in septal control of theta is restricted to frequencies lying close to 7.7 Hz. I therefore proposed a *frequency-specific* hypothesis of the functional significance of theta and of the effects on theta of the antianxiety drugs (Gray, 1970). According to this hypothesis, theta consists of three functionally distinct frequency bands: a low-frequency band (less than about 7 Hz in the rat) is related to fixed action patterns, including consummatory behavior; a middle-frequency band (centered on 7.7 Hz) is related to the activity of the behavioral inhibition system as described in this chapter; and a high-frequency band (above about 8.5 Hz) is related to the performance of goal-directed behavior (rewarded or active avoidance). The antianxiety drugs, on this hypothesis, alter septal control of theta only in the middle-frequency band.

This, then, is the hypothesis that has guided our research in the last few years. Had we known at the time we proposed it of the extensive work of Vanderwolf and his associates (e.g., Vanderwolf *et al.*, 1975) showing a close positive correlation between theta frequency and the intensity of motor behavior, we would probably have disregarded our own findings as being merely a consequence of the degree to which the animal was moving under our different conditions of observation: little when consuming a reward, perhaps more after nonreward, and obviously a great deal when running down the alley. Fortunately, we did not know of this work and instead conceived the idea that there is something special about theta frequencies close to 7.7 Hz—in particular, that such frequencies are related to the behavior patterns that antianxiety drugs impair. Testing this hypothesis has produced a number of findings that fit rather well with it and has led us to a number of new ideas concerning the action of the antianxiety drugs and the organization of the SHS.

We have tested our frequency-specific hypothesis of the significance of the theta rhythm in a number of ways. First, it was reasoned that, if a theta frequency of 7.7 Hz is functionally part of a brain system that mediates responses to nonreward, then artificially inducing such a theta frequency (which may be done by stimulating the medial septal area at the required frequency through permanently implanted electrodes) should strengthen or mimic the behavioral effects of nonreward. This deduction was confirmed by experiments in which theta-driving at 7.7 Hz during extinction after CRF increased the speed of extinction, while theta-driving at this frequency during acquisition on a random 50% of trials (the animal being rewarded with water on every trial) produced a "pseudo-PREE" (i.e., greater resistance to extinction than that shown by an unstimulated control group, neither group being stimulated during extinction) (Gray, 1972b). Using different techniques, Glazer (1974) has produced a similar pseudo-PREE by experimentally inducing 7.7 Hz theta. Coversely, it was reasoned that blocking the normal 7.7 Hz response to nonreward (which can be done by means of high-frequency stimulation of the medial septal area) ought to reduce resistance to extinction in animals trained on a PRF schedule, and this deduction was also confirmed (Gray, Araujo-Silva, & Quintao, 1972).

A further way of testing our hypothesis was by lesioning the septal area or hippocampus and observing behavior that had so far not been investigated after such lesions but that was known to be affected by antianxiety drugs. The PREE is one such phenomenon. It was known that septal and hippocampal lesions increase resistance to extinction after CRF (as of course do the antianxiety drugs). But it is clear from Figure 2 that the antianxiety drugs also reduce resistance to extinction after PRF training (Gray, 1969). Could this effect also be found after septal or hippocampal lesions?

In a first experiment on the effects of septal lesions on the PREE, Gray, Quintao, and Araujo-Silva (1972) showed that this effect could indeed by obtained: resistance to extinction was increased by these lesions after CRF training but decreased after PRF training. A subsequent experiment by Henke (1974) confirmed this. In a further investigation of these effects Feldon, Rawlins, and I (unpublished) have been looking at lesions confined to the medial or lateral septal areas, respectively. This work has been carefully controlled electrophysiologically, a medial septal lesion being defined as one that virtually abolishes theta but is otherwise as small as possible, a lateral septal lesion as one that does not alter theta but is otherwise as large as possible. Our results (Figure 3) show clearly that, at a 24-hour ITI, the increased resistance to extinction seen after CRF training in septal animals is due to *medial* septal

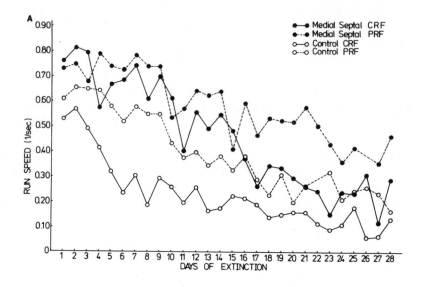

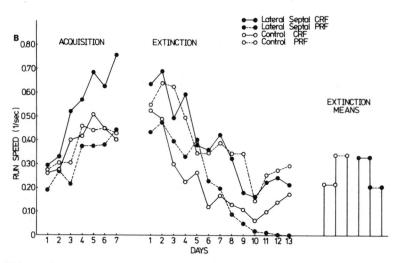

Figure 3. Effects of medial septal lesions (A) and lateral septal lesions (B) on the partial reinforcement extinction effect in the alley at one trial per day. CRF: continuous reinforcement. PRF: partial reinforcement. Data kindly supplied by J. Feldon.

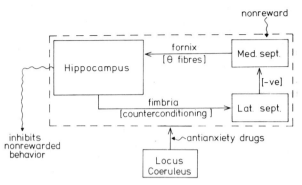

Figure 4. A model for the role of the septohippocampal system in counterconditioning. For explanation, see text.

damage, but the decreased resistance to extinction after PRF training (and the consequent abolition of the PREE) is due to *lateral* septal damage.

We have tried to relate this double dissociation between the behavioral effects of medial and lateral septal lesions to the organization of the SHS by way of the hypothesis shown in Figure 4. According to this hypothesis, the medial septal area is the recipient of information, conveyed via an unknown route by secondary frustrative stimuli, concerning the imminence of non-reward. This information is conveyed to the hippocampus by way of the theta-producing fibers that travel in the dorsal fornix (Myhrer, 1975). The hippocampus has the job of inhibiting the nonrewarded behavior (by an unknown route) while determining the best behavioral strategy in the changed circumstances. (This period of behavioral inhibition and uncertainty is subjectively experienced as anxiety.) Under conditions in which the best strategy is in fact to continue with the original behavior (as on a PRF schedule), the hippocampus sends a message (perhaps via the fimbria) to the lateral septal area which, in turn, via septal interneurons (DeFrance, 1976), inhibits or otherwise alters the medial input to the hippocampus. The operation of this hippocampo-septal pathway underlies the phenomenon of counterconditioning. We are at present testing this hypothesis. It may easily be generalized from nonreward to punishment and novelty, and we plan also to extend our experiments to deal with these kinds of stimuli.

The findings that Figure 4 attempts to integrate pose new questions about the site of action of the antianxiety drugs. It is clear that they exclude both the medial and the lateral septal regions as *unique* sites of action, since lesions to each of these areas produce only part of the antianxiety syndrome. It is possible that the drugs act on both regions, increasing resistance to extinction via the medial septal area and blocking counterconditioning via the lateral septal area. But this hypothesis lacks parsimony. It also treats the blocking of the PREE by the antianxiety drugs, not as a secondary consequence of the general attenuation produced by these agents in the behavioral effects of aversive stimuli, but as a direct interference with the process of counterconditioning. While this view appears to be correct with regard to lesions of the lateral septal area, it is somewhat counterintuitive to suppose that antianxiety drugs make it harder to learn to tolerate stress, though this possibility should not be dismissed out of hand. A more attractive hypothesis, which avoids these problems, is that the the drugs act directly on the hippocampus. Another possibility is that the antianxiety drugs act upon some set of inputs to the SHS that initiate the processes illustrated in Figure 4. This latter possibility is made particularly plausible and more concrete by the data discussed in the following section.

VII. THE DORSAL ASCENDING NORADRENERGIC BUNDLE

It will be recalled that our observations of changes in the hippocampal theta frequency in the alley (Gray & Ball, 1970) showed that consummatory behavior was associated with theta frequencies in the range 6–7 Hz, exploratory behavior and reactions to nonreward with frequencies in the range 7–8.5 Hz (with a mean response to nonreward of 7.7 Hz), and locomotor approach behavior with frequencies in the range 8.5–10.0 Hz. From these observations it was proposed that antianxiety drugs should alter septal control of theta only in the middle frequency band, since it is only this band that is associated with behavior that the drugs impair. One way of testing this hypothesis is to measure the current threshold for eliciting theta by septal stimulation (theta-driving) as a function of stimulation (and therefore theta) frequency, and then to look at the effect on the obtained function of the antianxiety drugs. If the frequency-specific hypothesis is along the right lines, we would expect the threshold for theta-driving to be particularly raised at a frequency of about 7.7 Hz after the administration of antianxiety drugs.

It should be noted that, in the undrugged free-moving male rat, there is a characteristic relation between theta-driving threshold and septal stimulation frequency: over the range 6–10 Hz, there is a minimum threshold located precisely at 7.7 Hz (i.e., at an interpulse interval of 130 msec) (Gray & Ball, 1970; James, McNaughton, Rawlins, Feldon, & Gray, 1977). It is intriguing that this minimum in the theta-driving curve is at the same frequency that is seen in response to frustrative nonreward. As predicted by the frequency-specific hypothesis, a representative barbiturate (sodium amobarbital), several benzodiazepines (chlordiazepoxide, diazepam, nitrazepam), and alcohol all selectively raise the theta-driving threshold at 7.7 Hz and eliminate the minimum threshold found at this frequency in the undrugged rat (Gray & Ball, 1970; Gray, McNaughton, James & Kelly, 1975; Nettleton, personal communication: Figure 5).

These results offer striking support for the frequency-specific hypothesis, and we therefore tried to establish their neuropharmacological basis. To this end, we attempted to mimic the characteristic effect on the theta-driving curve of antianxiety drugs by using other agents with better-understood effects on putative neurotransmitters (Gray *et al.*, 1975; McNaughton, James, Stewart, Gray, Valero, and Drewnowski, 1977). We found that we were unable to produce this effect by altering cholinergic, serotonergic, or dopaminergic transmission. Selective blockade of noradrenergic function, however, gave an effect that was highly similar to that of the antianxiety drugs (Figure 5).

These results prompted us to look for the neural substrate of the effects we had obtained by the pharmacological blockade of noradrenergic function. The natural candidate is the dorsal ascending noradrenergic bundle (DANB) (Ungerstedt, 1971). This bundle originates in the locus coeruleus in the brain stem and innervates the whole of the forebrain, including the hippocampus and the septal area (Figure 6). In order to ascertain whether it was involved in the effects shown in Figure 5, we used a local injection of a neurotoxin, 6-hydroxydopamine (6-OHDA: Ungerstedt, 1968), which is specific to noradrenergic and dopaminergic neurons. Injection of this poison into the DANB produced a virtually total loss of noradrenaline in the hippocampus, with no change in dopamine levels and no evidence of involvement of the other major noradrenergic projection, the ventral bundle (Gray *et al.*, 1975). In animals treated in this way there was no sign of a minimum threshold at 7.7 Hz in the theta-driving curve (Gray *et al.*, 1975: Figure 5).

These results suggest that the antianxiety drugs exert their characteristic effects on the theta-driving curve by an action on the DANB. Independent evidence for this locus of action had earlier been obtained by Corrodi, Fuxe, Lidbrink, and Olson (1971) and Lidbrink, Corrodi, Fuxe, and Olson (1972). These workers showed that stress increases forebrain noradrenaline turnover and that this increase is antagonized by barbiturates, benzodiazepines, and alcohol. A further implication of this hypothesis is that the *behavioral* effects of the antianxiety drugs might also be mediated by an action on the DANB (Gray *et al.*, 1975). It follows from this hypothesis that destruction of the DANB by injection of 6-OHDA ought to reproduce the behavioral effects of these drugs. For example, in a situation involving both reward and nonreward, the behavioral effects of nonreward should be reduced after such a lesion, but those of reward should be unaltered.

Notice that this hypothesis runs directly counter to the most accepted contemporary view of the function of the DANB, namely, that this pathway mediates the behavioral effects of reward. The latter hypothesis is based on studies of electrical self-stimulation of the brain (Stein, 1964; Rolls, 1975) and on experiments using electrolytic lesions of the locus coeruleus (Anlezark, Crow, & Greenway, 1973). The locus coeruleus is a very small structure, however, and electrolytic lesions are bound to damage other areas. Furthermore, destruction of the locus coeruleus also interrupts the noradrenergic innervation of the cerebellum, which also has its origin in this nucleus. Thus the use of stereotaxic injections of 6-OHDA is to be preferred as a technique for investigating this problem.

When natural reward (as distinct from brain stimulation reward) is used, it is clear that the reward hypothesis of the functions of the DANB is not substantiated: after virtually complete destruction of the DANB with 6-

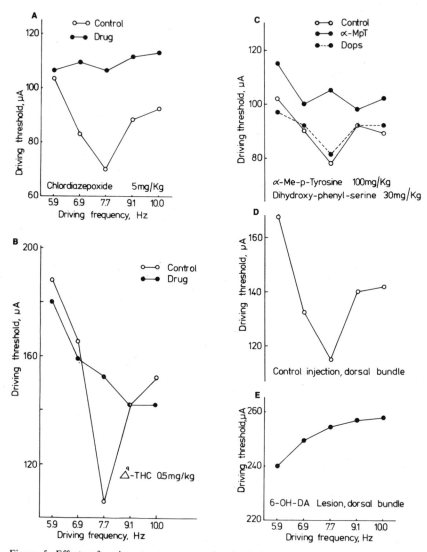

Figure 5. Effects of various treatments on thresholds for septal driving of hippocampal theta rhythm as a function of stimulation frequency in the free-moving male rat.

NORADRENALINE

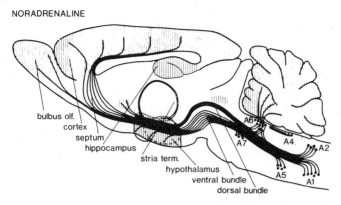

Figure 6. Sagittal projection of the ascending NA pathways. The descending pathways are not included. The stripes indicate the major nerve terminal areas.

OHDA, animals run just as well as controls for food rewards in the alley (Mason & Iversen, 1975; Owen, Boarder, Gray, & Fillenz, unpublished), and they press bars just as well in the Skinner box (Msason & Iversen, 1977). The nonreward hypothesis, in contrast, fares very well. Mason and Iversen (1975) showed that resistance to extinction after CRF in the alley is increased by DANB lesions, and Owen et al. (unpublished) not only replicated this effect but also showed that resistance to extinction after PRF is decreased and the PREE abolished (Figure 7). Thus, in the alley PREE situation, the DANB

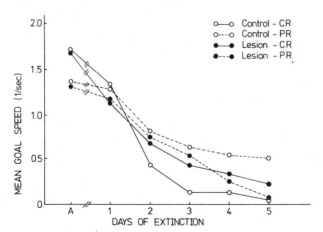

Figure 7. Course of extinction, at 10 trials per day, in the alley as a function of continuous reinforcement (CR) or partial reinforcement (PR) during training and 6-hydroxydopamine (lesion) or control injections into the dorsal noradrenergic bundle. The point marked A on the abscissa is the last day of acquisition. Data kindly supplied by Mrs. S. Owen.

lesion mimics very well the behavioral effects of the injection of antianxiety drugs (e.g., Gray, 1969; and see Figure 2).

These findings support the hypothesis that the behavioral effects of the antianxiety drugs are mediated by an action on the DANB. If so, we may make use of the premise with which this chapter opened: if the antianxiety effects of these drugs are produced by impairing activity in the DANB, then activity in the DANB forms part of the neural substrate of anxiety. From this argument we may deduce that individuals who are particularly susceptible to anxiety should have much activity in the DANB and that those resistant to anxiety should have little such activity.

This prediction is, of course, difficult to test in man. However, we have recently commenced testing it in rats selectively bred to be high or low on a trait of fearfulness (the Maudsley reactive, MR, and nonreactive, MNR, strains, respectively: Broadhurst, 1960, 1975). We have not so far directly investigated the function of the DANB in these animals. But we have measured the theta-driving curve in them, with encouraging results. Male MR rats resemble unselected rats, including the Wistar strains from which they were derived, in displaying a 7.7-Hz minimum in the theta-driving curve; male MNR rats lack this minimum (Drewett, Gray, James, McNaughton, Valero, & Dudderidge, 1977). We may deduce from this finding that the response to selective breeding for low fearfulness in the MNR strain has included a reduction in the activity of the DANB. We hope soon to investigate this deduction directly.

VIII. CONCLUSION

Let us attempt to integrate the findings discussed in the previous two sections. As shown in Figure 4, it is possible to account for most of these findings if we assume that the primary action of the antianxiety drugs is at the level of the DANB (though it should be noted that we have no knowledge of the way in which these drugs act on this pathway, nor whether they do so directly or by way of some further, "more primary" structure). In this way these drugs alter the noradrenergic input to the SHS, removing the selective facilitation that this input confers on theta rhythms in the 7.7-Hz band. The target areas within the SHS whose input is thus altered may consist of the septal area (both medial and lateral), the hippocampal formation, or both (Figure 1). The system made up of the DANB and the SHS has the task of inhibiting ongoing behavior upon the receipt of information about secondary punishing, secondary frustrative, or novel stimuli (though most of our data concern frustration only). This function involves the medial but not the lateral septal nucleus. The DANB–SHS system also has the job of deciding whether, in the light of the changed circumstances signaled via the medial septal area, the behavior pattern that was originally in progress should be permanently abandoned (passive avoidance, extinction) or persisted in (PREE, persistence in the face of stress). The latter outcome involves counterconditioning (the development of tolerance for stress), which may depend on signals from the hippocampus traveling in the fimbria to the lateral septal area.

This, then, is our model of anxiety. At the psychological level, it is an internal state entered upon receipt of stimuli associated with punishment or frustrative nonreward or novel stimuli; its behavioral effects consist of the inhibition of ongoing behavior, heightened arousal, and heightened attention to environmental stimuli, especially novel ones; and its function is to enable the organism to decide whether or not the changed circumstances require an alteration of existing behavior patterns. At the physiological level, it consists of activity in the DANB–SHS system (Figures 1 and 4) as discussed above. There is much that has been left out of this account. At the psychological level, we have ignored the stimuli that occur during social interaction and that appear to be of great importance for anxiety (Gray, 1971b, 1976). At the physiological level, we have ignored the probable role played by the serotonergic mechanisms that also innervate the SHS (Stein, Wise, & Berger, 1973; Gray, 1976), and we have left out recent evidence that the process of developing tolerance for stress may include changes in the DANB. But, hopefully, enough has been said to convince the reader of the value of the general approach to anxiety of which this chapter is a brief token.

ACKNOWLEDGMENTS

My thanks are due to all my colleagues for allowing me to refer to their as yet unpublished data, and especially to Nicholas Rawlins, Joram Feldon, and Susan Owen.

REFERENCES

Altman, J., Brunner, R. L., & Bayer, S. A. The hippocampus and behavioural maturation. *Behavioural Biology*, 1973, *8*, 557–596.

Amsel, A. Frustrative nonreward in partial reinforcement and discrimination learning: Some recent history and a theoretical extension. *Psychological Review*, 1962, *69*, 306–328.

Amsel, A., & Roussel, J. Motivational properties of frustration: I. Effect on a running response of the addition of frustration to the motivational complex. *Journal of Experimental Psychology*, 1952, *43*, 363–368.

Anlezark, G. M., Crow, T. J., & Greenway, H. P. Impaired learning and decreased cortical norepinephrine after bilateral locus coeruleus lesions. *Science*, 1973, *181*, 682–684.

Bolles, R. C. Species-specific defence reactions. In F. R. Brush (Ed.), *Aversive conditioning and learning*. New York, London: Academic Press, 1971.

Bolles, R. C. The avoidance learning problem. In G. H. Bower (Ed.), *Learning and motivation*, Vol. 6. London, New York: Academic Press, 1972.

Broadhurst, P. L. Applications of biometrical genetics to the inheritance of behaviour. In H. J. Eysenck (Ed.), *Psychogenetics and psychopharmacology*, Vol. 1. London: Routledge and Kegan Paul, 1960.

Broadhurst, P. L. The Maudsley reactive and nonreactive strains of rats: A survey. *Behaviour Genetics*, 1975, *5*, 299–319.

Brown, R. T., & Wagner, A. R. Resistance to punishment and extinction following training with shock or non-reinforcement. *Journal of Experimental Psychology*, 1964, *68*, 503–507.

Capaldi, E. J. A sequential hypothesis of instrumental learning. In K. W. Spence & J. T. Spence (Eds.), *The psychology of learning and motivation*, Vol. 1. New York, London: Academic Press, 1967.

Capaldi, E. J., & Sparling, D. L. Amobarbital and the partial reinforcement effect in rats: Isolating frustrative control over instrumental responding. *Journal of Comparative and Physiological Psychology*, 1971, *74*, 467–477.

Caplan, M. An anlysis of the effects of septal lesions on negatively reinforced behavior. *Behavioral Biology*, 1973, *9*, 129–167.

Caul, W. F. Effects of amobarbital on discrimination acquisition and reversal. *Psychopharmacologia*, 1967, *11*, 414–421.

Corrodi, H., Fuxe, K., Lidbrink, P., & Olson, L. Minor tranquilizers, stress and central catecholamine neurons. *Brain Research*, 1971, *29*, 1–16.

DeFrance, J. D. A functional analysis of the septal nuclei. In J. D. DeFrance (Ed.), *The septal nuclei*. New York: Plenum Press, 1976.

Douglas, R. J. The hippocampus and behaviour. *Psychological Bulletin*, 1967, *67*, 416–442.

Drewett, R. F., Gray, J. A., James, D. T. D., McNaughton, N., Valero, I., & Dudderidge, H. J. Sex and strain differences in septal driving of hippocampal theta rhythm as a function of frequency: Effects of gonadectomy and gonadal hormones. *Neuroscience*, 1977, *2*, 1033–1041.

Estes, W. K., & Skinner, B. F. Some quantitative properties of anxiety. *Journal of Experimental Psychology*, 1941, *29*, 390–400.

Feldon, J., Guillamon, A., Gray, J. A., de Wit, H., & McNaughton, N. Sodium amylobarbitone and responses to nonreward. *Quarterly Journal of Experimental Psychology*, in press.

Glazer, H. I. Instrumental conditioning of hippocampal theta and subsequent response persistence. *Journal of Comparative and Physiological Psychology*, 1974, *86*, 267–273.

Goodrich, K. P. Performance in different segments of an instrumental response chain as a function of reinforcement shedule. *Journal of Experimental Psychology*, 1959, *57*, 57–63.

Gray, J. A. Sodium amobarbital and effects of frustrative nonreward. *Journal of Comparative and Physiological Psychology*, 1969, *69*, 55–64.

Gray, J. A. Sodium amobarbital, the hippocampal theta rhythm and the partial reinforcement extinction effect. *Psychological Review*, 1970, *77*, 465–480.

Gray, J. A. Medial septal lesions, hippocampal theta rhythm and the control of vibrissal movement in the freely moving rat. *Electroencephalography and Clinical Neurophysiology*, 1971, *30*, 189–197. (a)

Gray, J. A. *The psychology of fear and stress*. London: Weidenfeld and Nicolson: New York: McGraw-Hill, 1971. (b)

Gray, J. A. The structure of the emotions and the limbic system: a theoretical model. In R. Porter & J. Knight (Eds.), *Physiology, emotion and psychosomatic illness*. (Ciba Foundation Symposium, 8). Amsterdam: Associated Scientific Publishers, 1972. (a)

Gray, J. A. Effects of septal driving of the hippocampal theta rhythm on resistance to extinction. *Physiology and Behavior*, 1972, *8*, 481–490. (b)

Gray, J. A. *Elements of a two-process theory of learning*. London: Academic Press, 1975.

Gray, J. A. The behavioural inhibition system: A possible substrate for anxiety. In M. P. Feldman & A. Broadhurst (Eds.), *Theoretical and experimental bases of the behaviour therapies*. London: Wiley, 1976.

Gray, J. A. Drug effects on fear and frustration: Possible limbic site of action of minor tranquilizers. In L. Iversen, S. Iversen, & S. Snyder (Eds.), *Handbook of psychopharmacology*, Vol. 8. New York: Plenum Press, 1977, pp. 433–529.

Gray, J. A., Araujo-Silva, M. T., & Quintao, L. Resistance to extiction after partial reinforcement training with blocking of the hippocampal theta rhythm by septal stimulation. *Physiology and Behavior*, 1972, *8*, 497–502.

Gray, J. A., & Ball, G. G. Frequency-specific relation between hippocampal theta rhythm, behavior, and amobarbital action. *Science*, 1970, *168*, 1246–1248.

Gray, J. A., McNaughton, N., James, D. T. D., & Kelly, P. H. Effects of minor tranquillizers on hippocampal theta rhythm mimicked by depletion of forebrain noradrenaline. *Nature*, 1975, *258*, 424–425.

Gray, J. A., Quintao, L., & Araujo-Silva, M. T. The partial reinforcement extinction effect in rats with medial septal lesions. *Physiology and Behavior*, 1972, *8*, 491–496.

Grossman, S. P. Behavioral function of the septum: A re-analysis. In J. F. DeFrance (Ed.), *The septal nuclei*. New York: Plenum Press, 1976.

Haggard, D. F. Acquisition of a simple running response as a function of partial and continuous schedules of reinforcement. *Psychological Reports*, 1959, *9*, 11–18.

Henke, P. G. Persistence of runway performance after septal lesions in rats. *Journal of Comparative and Physiological Psychology*, 1974, *86*, 760–767.

Ison, J. R., Glass, D. H., & Bohmer, H. M. Effects of sodium amytal on the approach to stimulus change. *Proceedings of the American Psychological Association*. 1966, *2*, 5–6.

Ison, J. R., & Pennes, E. S. Interaction of amobarbital sodium and reinforcement schedule in determining resistance to extinction of an instrumental running response. *Journal of Comparative and Physiological Psychology*, 1969, *68*, 215–219.

Iwahara, S., Iwasaki, T., Nagamura, N., & Masuyama, E. Effect of chlordiazepoxide upon partially-reinforced behavior of rats in the straight runway. *Japanese Psychological Research*, 1966, *8*, 131–135.

Izard, C. E. *Patterns of emotions: A new analysis of anxiety and depression*. New York: Academic Press, 1972.

James, D. T. D., McNaughton, N., Rawlins, J. N. P., Feldon, J., & Gray, J. A. Septal driving of hippocampal theta rhythm as a function of frequency in the free-moving male rat. *Neuroscience*, 1977, *2*, 1007–1017.

Kimsey, R. A., Dyer, R. S., & Petri, H. L. Relationship between hippocampal EEG, novelty and frustration in the rat. *Behavioral Biology*, 1974, *11*, 561–568.

Kurtz, R. G. Hippocampal and cortical activity during sexual behavior in the female rat. *Journal of Comparative and Physiological Psychology*, 1975, *89*, 158–169.

Landfield, P. W. Synchronous EEG rhythms: Their nature and their possible functions in memory, information transmission and behavior. In W. H. Gispen (Ed.), *Molecular and functional neurobiology*. Amsterdam: Elsevier, 1976.

Levine, S., Goldman, L., & Coover, G. D. Expectancy and the pituitary–adrenal system. In R. Porter & J. Knight (Eds.), *Physiology, emotion and psychosomatic illness*. Amsterdam: Associated Scientific Publishers, 1972.

Lidbrink, P., Corrodi, H., Fuxe, K., & Olson, L. Barbiturates and meprobamate: Decreases in catecholamine turnover of central dopamine and noradrenaline neuronal systems and the influence of immobilization stress. *Brain Research*, 1972, *45*, 507–524.

Lubar, J. F., & Numan, R. Behavioral and physiological studies of septal functions and related medial cortical structures. *Behavioral Biology*, 1973, *8*, 1–25.

Mackintosh, N. J. *The psychology of animal learning*. London: Academic Press, 1974.

Mason, S. T., & Iversen, S. D. Learning in the absence of forebrain noradrenaline. *Nature*, 1975, *258*, 422–424.

Mason, S. T., & Iversen, S. D. Effects of selective forebrain noradrenaline loss on behavioral inhibition in the rat. *Journal of Comparative and Physiological Psychology*, 1977, *91*, 165–173.

McCleary, R. A. Response-modulating functions of the limbic system: initiation and suppression. In E. Stellar & J. M. Sprague (Eds.), *Progress in physiological psychology*, Vol. 1. New York: Academic Press, 1966.

McFarland, D. J. The role of attention in the disinhibition of displacement activities. *Quarterly Journal of Experimental Psychology*, 1966, *18*, 19–30.

McGonigle, B., McFarland, D. J., & Collier, P. Rapid extinction following drug-inhibited incidental learning. *Nature*, 1967, *214*, 531–532.

McNaughton, N., James, D. T. D., Stewart, J., Gray, J. A., Valero, I., & Drewnowski, A. Septal driving of hippocampal theta rhythm as a function of frequency in the male rat: drug effects. *Neuroscience*, 1977, *2*, 1019–1027.

Meibach, R. C., & Siegel, A. Efferent connections of the septal area in the rat: An analysis utilizing retrograde and anterograde transport methods. *Brain Research*, 1977, *119*, 1–20.

Millenson, J. R. *Principles of behavioral analysis*. New York: Macmillan, 1967.

Miller, N. E. Studies of fear as an acquirable drive: I. Fear as motivation and fear-reduction as reinforcement in the learning of new responses. *Journal of Experimental Psychology*, 1948, *38*, 89–101.

Mowrer, O. H. On the dual nature of learning: A re-interpretation of "conditioning" and "problem-solving." *Harvard Educational Review*, 1947, *17*, 102–148.

Mowrer, O. H. *Learning theory and behavior*. New York: Wiley, 1960.

Myhrer, T. Normal jump avoidance performance in rats with the hippocampal theta rhythm selectively disrupted. *Behavioral Biology*, 1975, *14*, 489–498.

Nadel, L., O'Keefe, J., & Black, A. A critique of Altman, Brunner and Bayer's response–inhibition model of hippocampal function. *Behavioral Biology*, 1975, *14*, 151–162.

Nelson, P. B., & Wollen, K. A. Effects of ethanol and partial reinforcement upon runway acquisition. *Psychonomic Science*, 1965, *3*, 135–136.

Pavlov, I. P. *Conditioned reflexes* (translated by G. V. Anrep). London: Oxford University Press, 1927.

Plutchik, R. *The emotions: Facts, theories and a new model*. New York: Random House, 1962.

Raisman, G., Cowan, W. M., & Powell, T. P. S. An experimental analysis of the efferent projections of the hippocampus. *Brain*, 1966, *89*, 83–108.

Rolls, E. T. *The brain and reward*. Oxford: Pergamon Press, 1975.

Schachter, S., & Singer, J. E. Cognitive, social and physiological determinants of emotional state. *Psychological Review*, 1962, *69*, 379–399.

Skinner, B. F. *The behavior of organisms*. New York: Appleton-Century, 1938.

Sokolov, Ye. N. Neuronal models and the orienting reflex. In M. A. B. Brazier (Ed.), *The central nervous system and behaviour*, 3rd Conference. New York: Josiah Macy Jr. Foundation, 1960.

Spence, K. W. *Behavior theory and conditioning*. New Haven, Conn.: Yale University Press, 1956.

Stein, L. Reciprocal action of reward and punishment mechanisms. In R. G. Heath (Ed.), *The role of pleasure in behavior*. New York: Harper & Row, 1964.

Stein, L., Wise, C. D., & Berger, B. D. Anti-anxiety action of benzodiazepines: Decrease in activity of serotonin neurons in the punishment system. In S. Garattini, E. Mussini, & L. O. Randall (Eds.), *The benzodiazepines*. New York: Raven Press, 1973.

Stumpf, Ch. Drug action on the electrical activity of the hippocampus. *International Review of Neurobiology*, 1965, *8*, 77–138.

Sutherland, N. S. Partial reinforcement and breadth of learning. *Quarterly Journal of Experimental Psychology*, 1966, *18*, 289–301.

Ungerstedt, U. 6-Hydroxydopamine induced degeneration of central monoamine neurons. *European Journal of Pharmacology*, 1968, *5*, 107–110.

Ungerstedt, U. Stereotaxic mapping of the monoamine pathways in the rat brain. *Acta Physiologica Scandinavica*, 1971, *82* (Suppl. 367), 1–48.

Vanderwolf, C. H., Kramis, R., Gillespie, L. A. & Bland, B. H. Hippocampal rhythmical slow activity and neocortical low voltage fast activity: relations to behavior. In R. L. Isaacson & K. H. Pribram (Eds.), *The hippocampus*, Vol. 2. New York: Plenum, 1975, pp. 101–128.

Wagner, A. R. Sodium amytal and partially reinforced runway performance. *Journal of Experimental Psychology*, 1963, *65*, 474–477.

Wagner, A. R. Frustration and punishment. In R. M. Haber (Ed.), *Current research on motivation*. New York: Holt, Rinehart and Winston, 1966.

Weiskrantz, L. Emotion. In L. Weiskrantz (Ed.), *Analysis of behavioral change*. New York: Harper & Row, 1968.

Weiss, J. M., Glazer, H. I., Pohorecky, L. A., Brick, J., & Miller, N. E. Effects of chronic exposure to stressors on avoidance–escape behavior and on brain norepinephrine. *Psychosomatic Medicine*, 1975, *37*, 522–534.

Ziff, P. R., & Capaldi, E. J. Amytal and the small trial partial reinforcement effect: Stimulus properties of early trial nonrewards. *Journal of Experimental Pscychology*, 1971, *87*, 263–269.

Editor's Introduction

11

Grief, like other important human problems such as death, was seriously neglected in psychological theory and research for a very long time. One reason for the new place achieved by grief in our field is the stimulating contributions of Averill. In this chapter, he elaborates his conception of grief and discusses its determinants and functions at the biological, psychological, and social levels.

While Averill has made some useful distinctions between grief and mourning, he observes that in reality one without the other is an abstraction. He views grief not as a unitary emotion experience but as a complex syndrome or system of behavior, including stages of protest and yearning, disorganization and despair, and attachment and reorganization. It is clear from this analysis that Averill includes emotion experience, affective-cognitive structures, and emotion-related behavior in his conception of grief. His conception of grief suggests that it can include emotion experiences of sadness, anger, and depression and their cognitive and behavioral concomitants.

Averill makes a strong case for the interspecies continuity of grief and for its universality among human beings. The arguments are developed in an evolutionary-biological perspective. He shows that grief serves a number of biologically adaptive functions. His most incisive argument is that grief is part of the mortar of the social life and social attachment that clearly enhances chances for survival.

Averill discusses the strenghts and weaknesses of the psychological concepts of extinction, learned helplessness, and interruption of behavior in explaining the symptoms of grief. His conclusion is that each concept can add to our understanding of grief but that none of them is completely adequate—grief is more than the anxiety of interruption or a generalized sense of helplessness.

In discussing the psychological functions of grief, Averill points out that selfish, secondary gains are maladaptive in the long run but that grief can facilitate psychological development, reorganization, and personal growth. He shows how the social functions of grief and mourning help meet the needs of society by increasing the sense of community and collective responsibility and how they help the individual articulate grief.

Averill notes that bereavement is a period that is associated with increased susceptibility to somatic and psychological disorders. A wide range of problems can occur, and some of these require extended therapy. He concludes, however, that it is neither possible not desirable to eliminate grief as a human experience.

The Functions of Grief

11

JAMES R. AVERILL

Until about 1960, the emotion of grief was almost totally neglected in American psychology. The reasons for this neglect were undoubtedly multiple. On a broad cultural level, there was a general aversion to topics related to death, just as there were taboos related to sex. In commenting on this aversion, Gorer (1965) spoke of the "pornography of death"—death, grief and mourning were apt subjects for black humor, euphemisms, and even morbid curiosity, but they were not fit topics for polite discussion (especially in front of children). But the neglect of grief as a substantive area of inquiry was not due simply to broad cultural prejudices. Psychological theory, too, discouraged interest in an emotion such as grief. During the 1940s and 1950s, emotions were often treated as intervening "drive" variables; for example, fear was postulated as the drive behind avoidance behavior, anger as the drive behind aggression, and so forth. For more physiologically oriented psychologists, this same theme took the form of "activation" theory; that is, emotions (drives) are states of high arousal mediated by the reticular activating system (Lindsley, 1951) or by mass activation of the sympathetic nervous system (Cannon, 1929; Duffy, 1962). Within this drive/activation scheme there was little place for an emotion like grief, which is characterized by neither fight nor flight but, rather, by a profound depression and inhibition of activity.

During the early 1960s the situation began to change. Cultural mores lost some of their puritanical flavor, and both sex and death became acceptable areas for discussion and research. American psychology, too, underwent a rather profound change. The grand theories (such as those by Hull and Tolman), which only a few years before ruled supreme, now appeared like

JAMES R. AVERILL • University of Massachusetts, Amherst, Massachusetts. Preparation of this chapter was supported, in part, by a grant (MH 22299) from the National Institute of Mental Health.

intellectual dinosaurs. And with their demise, the attention of psychologists turned toward the development of minitheories that, although limited in scope, were more faithful to the phenomena being investigated.

With the above changes in cultural and scientific orientation, some of the general obstacles to the study of grief were removed. Meanwhile, Lindemann's (1944) classic study of the families of victims who died in the Coconut Grove fire provided the first detailed description of grief as a definite syndrome. About the same time, it was becoming evident that bereavement can be an important etiological factor in a wide range of somatic and psychological disorders (e.g., Bowlby, 1951; Clarke, 1961; Dennehy, 1966; Engel, 1961; Parkes, 1965; Schmale, 1958; Shoor & Speed, 1963; Spitz, 1946). Finally, these early trends were brought together and given further impetus by the seminal theoretical work of Bowlby (1960, 1961, 1963), about which we shall have more to say shortly.

As a result of the above factors, interest in grief and related issues has increased tremendously. Numerous books—popular as well as scientific—are now published on the topic each year; a journal, *Omega*, has been established for the publication of original research on death and bereavement; a Foundation of Thanatology has been formed; and international reputations have been made by specialists in the treatment of bereavement disorders. It is as though psychologists and psychiatrists suddenly discovered a fertile field of inquiry that, having lain fallow for many years, is now yielding a rich crop.

The purpose of the present chapter is twofold: first, to examine the biological, psychological, and sociocultural determinants of grief; and, second, to explore the possible functions of grief on each of these levels of analysis. This dual purpose dictates the organization of the chapter, which is divided into four section. The first section distinguishes grief from closely related syndromes—for example, mourning and depression—and it outlines the major symptoms of grief, from the initial protest against loss to the establishment of new object relations. The remaining three sections of the chapter consider the mechanisms that might account for the symptoms of grief, and the possible functional significance these mechanisms might have for the species, for the individual, and for society. The nature of the argument and the extent of the empirical evidence vary, of course, depending upon the type of mechanism being considered. Some parts of the chapter are therefore more speculative than others. This is particularly true with regard to the possible functions of grief. Functional explanations are notoriously difficult to prove and—in the view of some—are therefore scientifically untrustworthy. Nevertheless, it is sometimes important to ask not only about mechanisms but also about reasons. This is especially true in a case such as grief, because of its potential for psychopathology. The grieving individual is inevitably led to ask the reasons for his or her suffering, and the absence of answers may lead to feelings of hostility, guilt, and/or helplessness that further exacerbate the condition. Hopefully, the following discussion will demonstrate that some tentative answers can be offered not only for the "how" but also for the "why" of grief.

I. THE NATURE OF GRIEF

Let us begin with a few definitions. *Bereavement* refers to the real or symbolic loss of some significant object, particularly a loved one (spouse, parent, child, etc.). Bereavement typically results in a complex series of responses, of which two aspects may be distinguished: *grief* and *mourning*. In an earlier paper (Averill, 1968), I made a rather sharp distinction between these two aspects of bereavement behavior, defining *grief* as a set of stereotyped physiological and psychological reactions of biological origin and *mourning* as a conventional pattern of response dictated by the mores and customs of society. However, for reasons that have been discussed in detail elsewhere (Averill, 1974, 1976), such a sharp distinction between the biological and the sociocultural determinants of grief no longer seems warranted. It is true that mourning, at least in its ritual aspects, may be exhibited for social reasons with little or no affective accompaniment. And, conversely, grief may be experienced under conditions where no set mourning practices are prescribed. But mourning without grief and grief without mourning are abstractions that seldom occur in practice. At best, they can be taken to represent the extremes of a continuum. Any actual episode of grief will contain socially determined elements, as well as elements based on biological and psychological factors.

Grief and depression are also closely related phenomena. *Depression* is a generic term that refers to a diverse set of symptoms, such as feelings of helplessness and hopelessness, dejection, apathy, sleep disturbances, anorexia (loss of appetite), and decreased libido, to name but a few. When symptoms such as these become so severe that they interfere with normal functioning, it is common to speak of *clinical depression*. The important point to note about clinical depression is that it represents a classification based on symptomatology and not on etiology. Depressive symptoms represent a "final common path" (Akiskal & McKinney, 1973); that is, they may be elicited by a great variety of conditions, of which bereavement is only one. Depressive symptoms are thus common during grief, but grief is nevertheless a distinct emotional syndrome.[1]

A. The Syndrome of Grief

As explained elsewhere (Averill, 1976), emotions can best be conceptualized as complex syndromes or systems of behavior. A syndrom may be defined as a set of responses that covary in a systematic fashion. Each instance of the syndrome (e.g., any particular emotional episode) is characterized by a subset a variably weighted responses. That is, some responses may be more symptomatic of the emotion than are others; however, there is no single response, or subset of responses, that is *essential* to an emotional syndrome.

---

[1] An analogy might help clarify this point. Paralysis is a common symptom of both polio and muscular dystrophy. Yet, these are two different syndromes, each with its own etiology and prognosis.

Thus, weeping, yearning, depression, etc., may all be symptomatic of grief—even universally so. But no subset of these symptoms, *by itself*, constitutes the emotion of grief. In fact, under appropriate conditions, nearly any response might be taken as a sign of grief. Following the loss of a loved one, for example, the behavior of the bereaved might range from suicide, at one extreme, to the continuance of normal activity "in spite of" the loss, at the other extreme.

Implicit in the concept of a syndrome is the notion of organization; that is, a syndrome is an organized set of responses. However, a set of responses cannot simply be organized; it must be organized with respect to something. In the case of emotional syndromes, that "something" is the object of the emotion. The object of grief is some form of loss (bereavement), as through the death of a loved one. It is such a loss that allows us to identify weeping, say, as a symptom of grief rather than of joy.

With these general observations as background, we may now outline briefly the course of reaction that typically follows bereavement. As described by Bowlby (1961), Gorer (1965), Parkes (1972), and others, grief typically develops in three overlapping stages.

1. Stage 1: Protest and Yearning. The first stage of grief consists of protest over the fact of bereavement and an intense yearning after or urge to recover the lost object.[2] More specifically, Parkes (1970) has identified six types of responses that are particularly common during this period, including motor hyperactivity; preoccupation with memories of the lost person; imagining the presence of the lost person; focusing attention on those parts of the environment that are associated with the person; calling out for the lost person, either symbolically or actually; and an urge to search for the lost person. This stage of "agitated" grief may also be accompanied by considerable psychological distress and heightened physiological arousal (cf. Hofer, Wolff, Stanford, Friedman, & Mason, 1972).

2. Stage 2: Disorganization and Despair. Eventually, the fact of the loss must be accepted and attempts to recover the lost object abandoned. This is generally a slow and painful process. Typical symptoms during this second stage of grief are apathy and withdrawal or, more rarely, compulsive overactivity. A loss of sexual appetite is also common, as is an inability to concentrate on routine tasks or to initiate new activites. A wide variety of somatic complaints may also be observed, including anorexia and other gastrointestinal disorders, loss of weight, and sleep disturbances.

3. Stage 3: Detachment and Reorganization. The symptoms of the preceding stage are ultimately relieved when the person becomes detached from the lost object and establishes new relations. This involves a complex

---

[2] This first stage of grief is not necessarily the initial reaction to bereavement. Immediately following bereavement, there may be a period of "numbing", lasting from a few hours to several days (Parkes, 1970, 1972). But since a kind of numbness or shock is a common first reaction to disaster, and not just to bereavement, we will not consider it further in this chapter.

process of assimilation and accommodation, in a Piagetian sense, and its successful completion requires the establishment of new cognitive structures, that is, new ways of perceiving and thinking about the world and one's place within it. Following such reorganization, detachment may be so complete that return of the lost object may be greeted with indifference, or even rejection.

II. BIOLOGICAL CONTRIBUTIONS TO THE SYNDROME OF GRIEF

Two kinds of evidence suggest that grief is, in part, a product of man's evolutionary past: first, grieflike reactions can be observed in man's nearest biological relatives, the higher primates; and, second, some of the symptoms of grief appear to be universal in the human species. We shall review briefly each kind of evidence and then examine the possible biological functions of grief.

A. The Phylogeny of Grief

When a human infant (after about 6 months of age) is separated from its mother, it displays a pattern of response characterized by protest (yearning), despair, and ultimately detachment (Bowlby, 1960). If separation continues for an extended period, and if substitute attachment figures are not available, severe physiological and psychological impairment may result. This condition, known as *anaclitic depression*, has sometimes been taken as the prototype of human grief. Therefore, let us begin this discussion with a brief review of anaclitic depression in animals.

During the past decade, numerous laboratory studies have been conducted in which young monkeys (ranging from 3 months to several years in age) have been separated from their mothers. Two basic paradigms have been used in this research. In the first paradigm, the infant is separated from its mother and housed alone, except perhaps for brief periods of interaction with other animals; in the second paradigm, the mother is separated from the infant, and the latter remains with an otherwise intact living group. Using the first paradigm, Seay and his colleagues (Seay & Harlow, 1965; Preston, Baker, & Seay, 1970; Schlottmann & Seay, 1972) have investigated reactions to separation in three different species of monkeys, namely, rhesus (*Macaca mulatta*), Java (*Macaca irus*), and patas (*Erythrocebus patas*). In each species, the stage of protest or yearning was clearly evident. Both rhesus and Java infants also showed clear signs of despair following an initial period of protest. However, in none of the species was detachment clearly evident, as postulated by Bowlby (1960). If anything, the infants tended to show increased interaction with, and attachment to, their mothers upon reunion.

Using the second paradigm described above (i.e., removing the mother but leaving the infant in an intact group), Kaufman and Rosenblum (1967, 1969) have compared the responses of pigtail (*Macaca nemestrina*) and bonnet (*Macaca radiata*) monkeys. The pigtail infants showed an especially severe reaction to removal of their mothers; after an initial period of protest, the infants withdrew from social interaction and sat hunched in a ball. When the face could be seen, according to Kaufman and Rosenblum (1969), "it had the same appearance of dejection and sadness that Darwin (1872) described and believed to be 'universally and instantly recognized as that of grief.'" The reaction of bonnet infants was, by contrast, rather mild. This difference between the species is perhaps due to the fact that pigtail monkeys form exclusive and possessive mother–infant relationships, whereas bonnet infants are more free to interact with other adults, both before and after separation. Hence, removal of a bonnet mother is not as socially disruptive for the infant as is removal of a pigtail mother.

Of the species studied, then, both bonnet and patas infants show relatively mild reactions to separation. However, the explanation offered by Kaufman and Rosenblum (1969) for the lack of response in the bonnet would not seem to apply to the patas. It will be recalled that the technique used by Preston *et al.* (1970) resulted in isolation of the patas infants so that substitute attachment figures were not available. Also, the mother–infant relationship is quite different in these two species. While bonnet mothers are rather "permissive" with their infants, patas mothers seem somewhat "overprotective." Preston *et al.* (1970) speculate that separation allows the patas infant to respond in ways that normally would provoke a threat reaction from the mother. But whether the normal relationship of the infant with its mother is permissive or protective, it is apparent that reactions to separation are moderated by other adaptations related to the social organization of the species.

After an extensive review of primate research, much of it conducted in their own laboratory, Harlow and Suomi (1974) concluded that "the consequences of maternal separation in varied species of monkeys correspond closely to the human data and thus provide a feasible model of anaclitic depression" (p. 282). This is a reasonable conclusion, as long as it is kept in mind that there are large—and as yet little understood—differences between species. Moreover, there also are large individual differences *within* species. Lewis, McKinney, Young, and Kraemer (1976) have presented data from five different studies in which infant rhesus monkeys (mostly 6–9 months of age) were separated from their mothers. The variability in these data is, according to Lewis *et al.*, too great to support "any unitary concept of a protest–despair response to mother–infant separation, at least to the extent that such changes are predictable and stable enough to use this experimental paradigm as an induction method for producing animal models for neurobiologic or rehabilitative studies" (p. 704).

Lewis *et al.* do not question the existence of grieflike reactions in rhesus infants, only the reliability of mother–infant separation as a technique for producing such reactions. As an alternative procedure, they suggest infant–infant or peer separation. A study by Suomi, Harlow, and Domek (1970) illustrates this procedure. These investigators removed infant rhesus monkeys from their mothers at birth and reared them together. During the first year, the infants were repeatedly separated from one another for periods of four days each. Definite signs of protest and despair were observed during each separation, with no apparent adaptation over 20 repetition. In fact, the repeated separations resulted in a virtual arrest of normal maturation. These results are clearly suggestive, but until more research has been done using peer separation, it is impossible to say whether it will prove more reliable than mother–infant separation in producing grieflike reactions in infant monkeys.

The studies reviewed thus far have all focused on the reactions of very young animals, typically less than 1 year of age. Grieflike reactions have been more difficult to demostrate in older monkeys, a fact that might raise some question about the generality of the above findings. For example, in studies involving mother–infant separation, the responses of the mother have typically been rather transitory, consisting of a brief period of protest and few signs of despair. This response might, in part, reflect the different biological consequences of separation for the mother as opposed to the infant. But, in part, it might also be a reflection of the laboratory setting. In a field situation, Carpenter (1942) observed two rhesus mothers who carried their dead babies until only skins and skeletons remained. Similarly Schaller (1965) has described a female gorilla who carried her dead infant for four days before discarding it on the trail. And, of course, the loss of an infant can be an extremely potent stimulus for grief in a human mother.

Adults may grieve for other adults as well as for infants. For example, in a study by Suomi, Eisele, Grady, and Harlow (1975), it was found that if strong social bonds exist prior to separation, then grieflike reactions may be observed in older (late adolescent) rhesus monkeys when they are separated from other members of their group. This lends credence to the numerous anecdotal accounts of grieflike reactions among adults of various primate species, including the chimpanzee (Brown, 1879; Garner, 1900; Hebb, 1949; Yerkes & Yerkes, 1929), the orangutan (Zedwitz, 1930), the baboon (Zuckerman, 1932), and the rhesus monkey (Tinkelpaugh, 1928).

It thus appears that the disruption of established social relationships (whether mother–infant, infant–peer, or adult–peer) may produce grief-like reactions in most–if not all–species of higher primates. There is also evidence of grief-like reactions in social species below the primate level. The most extensive and systematic observations in this regard have been made on dogs (Lorenz, 1952; Pollock, 1961; Scott, Steward, & DeGhett, 1973). Of course, descriptions of canine grief must be interpreted with caution, lest loose analogies be drawn to the human condition. Dogs are quite removed from the major branches of primate evolution. Therefore, canine grief—to the extent that it occurs—could be the result of convergent evolution (independent selection due to similar ecological demands), in which case it would not be homologous with human grief. On the other hand, the possibility does exist that at least some features of canine and human grief are based on common physiological mechanisms. Scott *et al.* (1973) report, for example, that the drug imipramine alleviates separation distress in puppies as well as depressive symptoms in humans. They therefore conclude, very tentatively, "that the emotion, or affect, initially experienced by separated pups is the same that is experienced in human depression, although the behavioral symptoms are quite different" (p. 17). If this conclusion is proved valid, then grieflike reactions may be based on physiological systems that are quite ancient and widespread in mammalian species.

B. The Universality of Grief

To the extent that human grief is the product of biological evolution, then similar reactions should be observable across cultures. Unfortunately, good cross-cultural data on this issue are scarce. Anthropologists have been primarily concerned with describing cultural differences in mourning practices rather than with investigating cultural similarities in emotional reactions; on the other hand, psychologists who have entered the field of cross-cultural research have typically been more interested in cognitive than emotional processes. Therefore, most of the detailed observations on grief have been made within Western cultures (cf. Bowlby, 1969; Gorer, 1965; Lindemann, 1944; Marris, 1958; Parkes, 1972; Schoenberg *et al.*, 1975). There is, however, one study that compares directly the symptomatology of grief in a Western and a non-Western culture. Yamamoto, Okonogi, Iwasaki, and Yoshimura (1969) interviewed a group of Japanese widows, using procedures similar to those used by Marris (1958) and Parkes (1965) in their studies of English widows. Significantly, both the Japanese and English women showed similar reactions. The main difference between the groups had to do with experiences of the deceased as somehow still present. While a sense of presence of the deceased was experienced spontaneously by a sizable minority of British widows, it was actively cultivated and hence experienced by the vast majority of Japanese widows. Yamamoto *et al.* attribute this difference to Buddhist and Shinto religious practices, in which the deceased family member becomes an "ancestor" with whom the bereaved may remain in contact (e.g., through offerings of food, water, and incense).

In short, bereavement seems to elicit similar emotional reactions in both Japanese and English widows, even though there are idiosyncracies attributable to differences in mourning practices. Only very gross comparisons can be made among other cultures because of a lack of detailed observations. Rosenblatt, Walsh, and Jackson (1976) have made a content analysis of the ethnographic descriptions of reactions to death in 78 different societies. In the ethnographic records they used, crying was the most frequently mentioned response among bereaved persons (especially women). Of 73 societies that could be rated on this variable, crying was reported in 72—the Balinese were the one exception. Some form of aggression was rated as present in 50 of 66 societies (76%). Other common emotional reactions to bereavement were self-mutilation and fear. Rosenblatt *et al.* conclude that "at least in dim outline, the emotional responses of people in almost any culture resemble those of people in almost any other" (p. 21).

C. Biological Functions of Grief

In an earlier analysis (Averill, 1968), I argued that the biological function of grief is to ensure group cohesiveness in species where a social form of existence is necessary for suvival.[3] A similar suggestion has been made by Bowlby (1961, 1969), among others. Basically, the argument rests on two assumptions: (1) that one way to ensure group cohesion is by making separation from the group, or from specific members of the groups, a painful experience and hence one to be avoided; and (2) that in cases where separation cannot be avoided (e.g., because of death), the relevant reactions may nevertheless run their biological course, often to the distress and even physical detriment of the bereaved. These two assumptions apply primarily to the first (protest and yearning) and second (despair) stages of grief, respectively.

1. Protest and Yearning. Grief is a response to separation or loss. But before there can be separation, there must be attachment, and hence before we can consider the former, we must consider the latter.

Many early psychologists and naturalists noted the tendency among certain species, including man, to congregate in groups, finding comfort in numbers and distress in isolation. McDougall (1936) attributed attachment among members of a species to a "gregarious instinct," and he noted that "its utility to animals liable to the attacks of beasts of prey is obvious" (p. 72). But what seemed obvious to McDougall was not so obvious to other psychologists, most of whom attempted to explain social attachment in terms of more "basic" drives, such as hunger and sex. In part, this reductionist stance reflected an antipathy toward the notion of instinct, with its emphasis on the genetic determinants of behavior; and, in part, it reflected a general cultural bias that favors individuality over group dependence. The latter bias perhaps

---

[3] This proposal does not apply to all social species but only to those whose cohesion depends upon affectional bonds between individual members, or what Eibl-Eibesfeldt (1970) has called "individualized" groups.

accounts for the lack of common terms in Western languages that refer to the need for attachment.

In view of much recent evidence (cf. Eibl-Eibesfeldt, 1970; Harlow, 1971; Hinde 1974; Wilson, 1975), there can be little doubt that group living is a biological adaptation in its own right and that social attachment is not secondary to other needs. The group provides, among other things, protection from predators, efficiency in locating and obtaining food, and the opportunity to learn from the experiences of others. Separations from the group, in turn, greatly diminishes chances for survival.

Because of its adaptive significance, the need for attachment provides the biological anlage for a variety of different emotional syndromes. This can be illustrated by the Japanese response of *amae*. The Japanese consider *amae* to be a very basic emotion, observable even in puppies (Doi, 1962, 1973). Yet there is no equivalent emotion within Western societies. Roughly translated, *amae* can be described as a wish to be loved or a need for dependency. Unlike the English concept of love, however, *amae* does not have a sexual connotation. (In this respect, it might be compared to the notion of Platonic love, except that the latter is considered the antithesis of emotional involvement.) And unlike the English concept of dependency, *amae* has a positive rather than a negative connotation. The Japanese have evidently molded from the need for attachment a positive and pervasive emotional experience; Western cultures, by contrast, have tended to place more emphasis on the opposite, and also biologically important, need for autonomy and independence. Consequently, in the West, the negative aspects of attachment have come to be emphasized, as in the case of dependency, while its positive aspects have been given more circumscribed expression, as in the case of love.

The emotional experiences just described (*amae*, love, dependency) refer primarily to responses that are evoked when the object of attachment is present or potentially available. Other emotional reactions may result when social bonds are broken and the object of attachment is no longer available. Grief is one such emotion.

Among Western psychologists, perhaps no one has done more than Bowlby (1951, 1969, 1973) to focus attention on the importance of attachment and loss to human development. Combining the insights of psychoanalysis with ethological research on animals, Bowlby conceives of attachment as a biologically based system of behavior, comparable in certain respects to a control or "goal-corrected" system in engineering terms. Such control systems (as used, for example, in guided missiles) contain an element of searching, so that a certain relationship can be maintained vis-à-vis the goal–object. In the case of a biological control system, such as attachment, some behaviors (e.g., smiling, clinging, fondling) may be evoked in the presence of the goal–object and thus help prevent separation. Responses of this type enter into emotions such as love and *amae*. Other behaviors (e.g., protest, yearning, searching) are evoked in the absence of the goal–object, and they help effect reunion following separation. Responses of the latter type help comprise the first stage of grief. Under normal conditions, the searching elicited by the absence of the loved one is sufficient to reestablish social bonds, and since social living has survival value, the predisposition toward yearning and searching is maintained within the gene pool of the species through natural selection. During bereavement, however, reunion is no longer possible. The yearning may nevertheless continue, accompanied by great pain and distress, urged on by a deep biological imperative.

2. Despair.   The symptoms of the second stage of grief are not so easily explained from a biological point of view. This is a time not only of intense mental anguish but also of reduced resistance to stress and disease. Moreover, the apathy, the tendency to withdraw, and the inability to initiate new actions tend to hinder any break with the past. And, finally, the loss of sexual desire, a common sympton of the second stage of grief, is hardly conducive to the propagation of the species.

How are such symptoms to be explained? One possibility is contained in a proposal by Engel (1962) that there are two basic, opposing response systems to mounting stress: (1) a mobilizing fight–flight system, which is the biological anlage for anxiety, and (2) a conservation–withdrawal system, which is the biological anlage for depression. Kaufman (1973) has invoked these two systems to explain the grieflike reactions of infant monkeys to separation from their mothers. The initial reactions, based on the fight–flight system are characterized by increased motor and expressive activity and also by increased physiological arousal (as indicated, for example, by changes in heart rate and body temperature—Reite, Kaufman, Pauley, & Stynes, 1974). If separations continues, then further metabolic changes may occur that bring the conservation–withdrawal system into play. The reactions characteristic of this system (in rhesus monkeys, al least) are postural collapse, immobility, withdrawal from the environment, and reduced expressive and visceral activity (Kaufman, 1973; Reite *et al.*, 1974). These reactions supposedly help conserve energy and, through their communicative features, attract sources of comfort.

Schmale (1973) has reviewed a great deal of research relating the conservation–withdrawal system to grief and depression in humans. On the physiological level, according to Schmale, the conservation–withdrawal system is characterized primarily by trophotropic reactions, of which deep (stage 4) sleep is a prototypic example; on the psychological level, the conservation–withdrawal system results in the experience of helplessness and hopelessness. Depressive character disorders and symptom formation are viewed by Schmale as psychic defenses against these psychological reactions.

The views of Kaufman and Schmale are reasonable in that extreme stress, due either to deprivation or to overstimulation, may initiate feedback mechanisms that serve to protect the organism from further excitation. The organism is, in a sense, temporarily shut down.[4] However, this can be only part of the story. It is hard to explain such common symptoms of grief as insomnia and anorexia (loss of appetite) as being part of a conservation–withdrawal system. The same is true of the self-mutilation sometimes observed in animals (cf. Tinkelpaugh, 1928). Symptoms such as these seem to represent a disorganization or breakdown in functioning, and there is no reason to believe that they have any adaptive function in their own right. Rather, they seem to be the natural consequences of an adaptive system (attachment) that cannot achieve its goal. It is not difficult to think of other kinds of biological systems that, if eliciting conditions remain unmitigated, can have unfortunate consequences for the individual. In his analysis of endocrine responses to stress, Selye (1976) has aptly described such conditions as "diseases of adaptation."

Functional explanations are always difficult to prove or disprove. This is especially true in biology, where the relevant (evolutionary) events have typically occurred in the distant past, and where controlled laboratory studies are often impossible. Not every anatomical structure has a function simply because it is there, nor is all behavior adaptive. Yet, natural selection is a very pragmatic mechanism. Most biologically based structures and behaviors do serve a function, or else they are closely correlated with some other system that does have adaptive value. To summarize the present argument with respect to grief, some of its symptoms (e.g., the urge to recover the lost object) may be directly functional in cases where the loss is not irretrievable; other symptoms (e.g., the withdrawal and trophotropic reactions) may be protective responses induced by the unremitted stress of irretrievable loss; and still other symptoms (e.g., anorexia, and insomnia) may represent a breakdown in adaptive functioning. On a broader level of analysis, however, the entire syndrome of grief—even its potentially maladaptive features—makes good sense biologically when viewed in relation to the need for group living and the dangers of separation.

III. PSYCHOLOGICAL CONTRIBUTIONS TO THE SYNDROME OF GRIEF

To say that grief is, in part, a biologically based reaction does not imply that it is an automatic and invariant response. The preceding review of grieflike reactions in animals attests to wide individual as well as species differences. Individual differences in human grief are also widespread. Grief may vary as a function of such *situational* factors as the abruptness and significance

---

[4] Weiss (1971; Weiss, Glazer, & Pohorecky, 1976) has observed that continued responding in the absence of feedback can produce physiological stress reactions, including depletion of norepinephrine in the central nervous system. Depletion of brain norepinephrine has, in turn, been linked to a variety of depressive symptoms, including the inhibition of behavior. We shall have more to say about this issue in a subsequent dissusion of "learned helplessness."

of the precipitating loss, any incidental demands or responsibilities occasioned by the loss, and the availability of a substitute or replacement for the loss. Also important are such *personal* factors as the past experience of the bereaved with other losses, especially during childhood; preferred modes of defensive or coping responses (e.g., denial as opposed to intellectualization); and the amount of ego involvement in the lost object. Space limitations do not allow us to consider in any detail these and other sources of individual differences in grief reactions. Rather, the focus of our attention will be on psychological processes that might account for some of the typical—even universal—symptoms of grief. In particular, we will examine three hypotheses that attempt to account for some of the symptoms of grief in terms of (1) the process of extinction, (2) learned helplessness, and (3) the interruption of behavior. We will then consider briefly some possible psychological functions of grief.

A. Extinction

Let us begin with the commonplace observation that many of our everyday activities are coordinated with the activities of a small number of "significant others" (e.g., a parent, a spouse, or a child). When one party to such an interaction is lost, as through death, then many responses will necessarily fail to elicit their customary rewards. A widow, for example, may continue to set a table for two, even though her spouse will not be there to share the meal. Such behaviors must be extinguished and new ones established. Extinction can be a painful and frustrating process, even for a rat trained in a Skinner box (Amsel, 1972). How much more painful and frustrating it must be for a person to extinguish responses built up through years of common experience with a husband, wife, parent, or other loved one.

Some of the symptoms exhibited during extinction (e.g., an initial intensification and then reduction of goal-seeking behavior) bear resemblance to the first (protest and yearning) and second (disorganization and despair) stages of grief (cf. Davis, 1964). Therefore, it is not surprising that some theorists, especially those of a behaviorist persuasion, have attempted to explain aspects of grief in terms of extinction.

To be completely accurate, most extinction theories refer to depressive symptoms, whatever their source, and not to grief *per se*. Therefore, the present discussion will also focus on the depressive reactions commonly observed during the second stage of grief, and especially on the reduction of voluntary or goal-seeking behavior. When so limited, the extinction hypothesis has considerable intuitive appeal, and undoubtedly it is correct to a limited extent. As just described, bereavement is a time when many customary rewards are no longer available, and extinction must necessarily occur. Having said this, however, we must also add that the extinction hypothesis is not as simple as it might at first appear. Let us consider the matter a little more closely.

Extinction assumes a reduction in reinforcement. This assumption raises two question: First, what accounts for the reduction in reinforcement? And, second, are there qualitative differences among reinforcers, so that a reduction in one kind has different consequences than a reduction in another kind? With regard to the first question, Eastman (1976) has outlined four ways in which reinforcement may be reduced: (1) customary reinforcers may no longer be present in the environment; (2) customary reinforcers, although present, may no longer be effective; (3) the effort required to achieve customary reinforcers may have become too great; and (4) environmental cues may have acquired aversive properties that inhibit previously reinforced responses. Of these four possibilities, the first—the absence of customary reinforcers—is of obvious importance in the case of bereavement. However, each of the other three may also play an important role. For example, following bereavement, many rewards may be *potentially* available in the environment, but some of these may no longer be effective (perhaps because of disturbances in appetite, libido, etc.); also, the individual may lack the initiative to achieve many reinforcers; and/or certain cues (such as old friends and settings) may serve as painful reminders of the loss, thus inhibiting behavior that otherwise could lead to reinforcement.

In short, although a reduction in reinforcement may explain some of the symptoms of grief, the reduction itself must be explained—and that raises a host of biological and psychological issues that we can only point to, but not consider, here.

Turning now to the nature of the reinforcement, some theorists (e.g., Lazarus, 1968) emphasize the reduction of reinforcement *per se*, without regard to kind, while others (e.g., Lewinsohn, Weinstein, & Shaw, 1969) focus on the reduction of social reinforcement. The loss of social reinforcement can, in turn, be of special significance for either of two reasons: (1) social reinforcement is central to many activities, and a reduction in this area may therefore have wide-ranging consequences: it is as though a person suddenly lost his sight—nearly all areas of behavior would ultimately be affected, not just those directly dependent upon vision; (2) social reinforcement may be unique in a biological sense; the absence of social reinforcers might then result in a characteristic pattern of responses, including certain depressive reactions. The former version of the hypothesis (i.e., that social reinforcement is central to a wide range of activities) is that preferred by many behavior therapists. The latter version of the hypothesis (i.e., that social reinforcement is biologically unique) is closely related to the argument presented in the previous section on biological contributions to grief. Therefore, let us consider it in a little more detail.

Staddon (1973) has argued that any explanation of behavior that relies on the notion of reinforcement is essentially incomplete. Reinforcements never operate directly on behavior; rather, they exert their influence through the action of complex mediating mechanisms built up during the course of biological evolution and/or individual development. Since there is a multiplicity of much mechanisms (only a few of which have been studied to date), there is also a multiplicity of ways in which reinforcers can operate. Indeed, Staddon suggests that it might be better not to speak of "reinforcement" at all, for that gives the misleading impression that there is some unitary principle of operation (cf. the controversies between contiguity and drive-reduction theories of reinforcement that so preoccupied the attention of psychologists during the 1940s and 1950s). Although it is more cumbersome, it might also be more accurate to speak of the specific effects of food, sex, pain, separation, etc., on behavior and of the mechanisms that mediate each.

If the above argument has any validity, then its converse must also be considered seriously. That is, there may be no one principle that will explain the effects of a reduction of reinforcement (i.e., extinction). Rather, the effects will depend upon the kinds of reinforcers involved. Applying this line of reasoning to the case of grief, it might be noted that attachment behavior could be considered a "mechanism" in Staddon's sense. Attachment would therefore have its own class of reinforcers, the elimination of which would produce characteristic results, namely, the experience of grief.

B. Learned Helplessness

During extinction, the rewards that customarily follow a response are absent or ineffective. But that is only a special case of a more general condition where outcomes are *independent* of an individual's behavior. Under such conditions, the person (or infrahuman animal) may learn that he is helpless to control the course of events, even though rewards may be plentiful (as in the case of the proverbial "poor" rich kid). According to Seligman (1975; Maier & Seligman, 1976), such "learned helplessness' can lead to deficits in three main areas: (1) motivational—a decline in the initiative or willingness to respond; (2) cognitive—a difficulty in learning new responses; and (3) emotional—an increased susceptibility to stress. These deficits are similar to those observed during the second (despair) stage of grief, as well as to other forms of reactive depression. Moreover, as Seligman (1975) notes, many of the events that trigger depressive reactions (e.g., the death of a loved one, separation from friends, failure at work, physical disease, financial loss, and growing old) have one thing in common, namely, the individual can no longer control those elements of his life that bring satisfaction or relieve suffering.

The theory that Seligman proposes to account for the above-mentioned deficits is as simple as the name *learned helplessness* suggests. The cornerstone of the theory is the proposition that: "When an organism is faced with an outcome that is independent of his responses, he sometimes learns that the outcome is independent of his responses" (Maier & Seligman, 1976, p. 17). But like the extinction hypothesis, the simplicity of the learned-helplessness model can be deceiving. Controversy centers around two main issues: Are the consequences of learned helplessness due solely to learning? And, if so, what kind of learning (e.g., S–R relationships or cognitive expectanices)?

With regard to the first issue, Weiss (see Weiss, Glazer, & Pohorecky 1976) has shown that depletion of brain norepinephrine in the absence of learning (e.g., by means of drugs or by having an animal swim for a brief time in near-freezing water) can produce many of the same deficits attributed by Seligman to learned helplessness. Weiss also reports that repeated exposure to inescapable shock does not produce deficits in rats if the training is conducted over a two-week period; presumably, extended training allows time for the neurochemical systems of the brain to adapt, thus preventing a depletion of norepinephrine. From results such as these, Weiss argues that noncontingent or uncontrollable reinforcement is simply *one* way to influence the biochemical activity of the brain, and that the latter—not learning—is the important mediating variable in the production of depressive reactions following "learned" helplessness.

However, depletion of brain norepinephrine cannot account for all the experimental observations made by Seligman and his colleagues. For example, Hannum, Rosellini, and Seligman (1976) found that rats subjected to uncontrollable shock shortly after weaning had difficulty acquiring an escape response as adults, and, conversely, experience with escapable shock as a weanling protected against the deficits produced by uncontrollable shock received as an adult. Learning, rather than permanent physiological changes, would seem to be the most parsimonious explanation for these results. Moreover, the procedures used by Weiss to produce a depletion of brain norepinephrine have generally been much more severe than those used by Seligman and others to produce learned helplessness. This finding has led Maier and Seligman (1976) to conclude that

> the deficit produced by exposure to extremely traumatic events as used by Weiss *et al.* may be produced by a very different mechanism from the deficits produced by exposure to much less traumatic *uncontrollable* aversive events in the learned helplessness experiments. (p. 37)

Unfortunately, this last conclusion also calls into question the appropriateness of the learned-helplessness model as an explanation for many of the symptoms of grief. Bereavement is certainly a traumatic experience, more severe in its own way than the treatments employed by Weiss *et al.* in their studies on rats. It is therefore an open question whether learned helplessness or a depletion of brain norepinephrine better accounts for the depressive symptoms that often follow bereavement. Of course, this is not an "either/or" question: both mechanisms (and others as well) may be operating.

In fact, not even Seligman attributes all the consequences of helplessness to learning. The learning aspect of the learned-helplessness model applies primarily to the motivational and cognitive deficits described earlier (i.e., decreased incentive to respond and difficulty in learning new responses). But Seligman (1975) also attributes a wide variety of emotional symptoms to helplessness, including loss of libido and appetite, ulceration, increased susceptibility to disease, and even sudden death. Seligman does not suggest that these reactions are learned. Rather, he reasons that having control over rewards and punishments is biologically advantageous (in an evolutionary sense) and hence is accompanied by positive affective experiences, while lack of control is biologically disadvantageous and hence is accompanied by negative affective experiences. The main question that needs to be raised about this line of reasoning is whether all kinds of helplessness have the same biological consequences; for example, whether the loss of control over social reinforcements has the same consequences as loss of control over food, say, or over noxious stimuli. Seligman (1975) implies that helplessness has similar consequences in species "from cockroaches to wild rats, from chickens to chimpanzees, from infant to aged humans" (p. 187), and that the nature of the reinforcement over which control is lost is largely irrelevant (pp. 96–99). Empirical evidence relevant to these broad generalizations is scanty, however, and the same considerations noted earlier in connection with the extinction hypothesis would seem to apply *mutatis mutandis* to the case of learned helplessness also. Specifically, just as there is no unitary mechanism mediating all kinds of reinforcement, so too there may be no unitary mechanism mediating all kinds of helplessness.[5]

This brings us to the second source of controversy surrounding the learned-helpless model, namely, the type of learning involved. Maier and Seligman (1976) suggest that only a "very sophisticated learning theorist" would object to the contention that an organism sometimes learns that outcomes are independent of responses. By "sophisticated," Maier and Seligman apparently mean an S–R theorist, for their own position is cognitively oriented. In particular, they contend that information regarding the independence of outcomes from responses "must be processed and transformed into a cognitive representation of the contingency" (p. 17) before it can produce the deficits ascribed to learned helplessness. We shall not be concerned here with how an S–R theorist might respond to this contention (see Levis, 1976). Rather, suffice it to note that once the door to cognition is opened, a whole new set of challenges may be made with regard to the ability of learned helplessness *per se* to account for many of the symptoms of grief.

---

[5] In a different context, Seligman (1970) has also argued against any unitary process of learning and extinction. In his 1975 book, however, he concludes that since "learned helplessness seems general among species that learn . . . it can be used with some confidence as an explanation of a variety of phenomena" including human depression and even psychosomatic death (pp. 27–28). The extent to which such confidence is warranted is an open question. But at least three factors illustrate the need for caution: (1) there are apparently marked species differences in response to a noncontingency of reinforcement (e.g., dogs are more severely affected than rats); (2) only a few kinds of reinforcement (mostly aversive stimuli such as electric shock) have been investigated to date; and (3) both animals and humans sometimes show less—not greater—stress when confronted with uncontrollable (as opposed to controllable) noxious stimuli (on this last point, see Averill, 1973).

For example, Wortman and Brehm (1975) have suggested that the consequences of learned helplessness might be especially severe if the individual blames himself for the ineffectiveness of his responses. In support of this suggest, Klein, Fencil-Morse, and Seligman (1976) found that failure (or, more specifically, random outcome) on a problem-solving task was not sufficient to induce motivational and cognitive deficits among college students; however, failure that was accompanied by a decreased belief in personal competence did produce depressivelike symptoms.

The findings of Klein *et al.* accord well with clinical observations of depression. As Beck (1976) has noted, the depressed individual "overinterprets" his experiences in terms of defeat or deprivation: "He regards himself as deficient, inadequate, unworthy, and is prone to attribute unpleasant occurrences to a deficiency in himself" (p. 129). Of course, in most cases of grief (e.g., due to the death of a spouse), the bereaved is not at fault for the loss. It is a common observation, however, that bereaved persons often blame themselves "for not having done more." If unduly exaggerated, such self-blame may retard recovery and even transform normal grief into clinical depression.

C. The Interruption of Behavior

Mandler (1975) has presented an analysis of grief and depression that is similar to, but even more cognitively oriented than, that of Seligman.[6] Mandler starts with the assumption that the interruption of ongoing cognitive or behavioral activity leads to a state of nonspecific arousal. Following the lead of Schachter (1964), he further assumes that specific emotions such as anxiety, grief, and anger are a joint product of this nonspecific arousal and the surrounding situational factors. Anxiety is "the emotion of choice" when the onset or offset of the arousal is not under the control of the organism, that is, when there is no alternative to the interrupted activity. Anxiety is characterized by helplessness and disorganization. If activities repeatedly meet failure (noncompletions), helplessness may generalize into hopelessness. This process, Mandler believes, is the basis for depressive symptoms. Such symptoms are likely to be especially severe if the interrupted activities are highly ego-involving and/or if they are important for species survival.

Mandler criticizes the argument (Averill, 1968) that grief is a biological reaction related to group cohesiveness. Instead, he contends that

---

[6] Analyses similar to that of Mandler have been presented by Parkes (1971, 1975) and Marris (1975). Whereas Mandler speaks of cognitive plans and structures, Parkes talks about "assumptive worlds" and Marris about "structures of meaning." But the basic idea is the same, namely, that the individual cognitively structures or imposes meaning on the environment and that when cognitive structures are disrupted, the ensuing loss of meaning is an occasion for grief and/or depression.

the extreme degrees of disruption and interruption occasioned by the loss of a loved member of one's group are adequate to explain the appearance of grief. In particular, it is highly likely that in groups that are socially cohesive and where cohesiveness has become a factor in the survival of the group, increasing numbers of plans and structures exist that incorporate particular individuals. Thus the more elaborate the cognitive structures are that need particular individuals for their execution, the more complex will be the interruptive and disruptive reactions to loss. (p. 226)

As in the case of the extinction and learned-helplessness hypotheses, the basic question is whether all kinds of interruption (as all kinds of nonreinforcement) have the same effect. Mandler does acknowledge that hopelessness and depression are more likely if the interrupted activities are biologically adaptive, and to this extent, his hypothesis is very similar to my own. I would, however, go even further and maintain that not even all biologically adaptive behaviors lead to the same consequences when interrupted, and that at least some of the features of grief are unique to the disruption of interpersonal bonds.

Some light can be shed on this issue by considering briefly the distinction between anxiety and grief. According to Mandler, "the depressive state can easily be subsumed as a further extension of the notion of anxiety and helplessness" (p. 210). Elsewhere (Averill, 1968, 1976; Lazarus & Averill, 1972) I have argued that anxiety and grief are fundamentally different syndromes, although they do bear many similarities. There is no need to repeat that argument here, although it might be worth recounting one line of evidence. Klein (1964) has observed that the disturbance occasioned by real or fantasied separation—what I would call grief—is alleviated by antidepressant drugs, such as imipramine, but not by phenothiazine tranquilizers, such as chlorpromazine. He concludes that the common term *anxiety* many obscure important underlying differences between reactions to separation and other, seemingly similar responses (which he calls "expectant anxiety"). Along similar lines, Scott (1967; Scott *et al.*, 1973) reports that separation distress in puppies is not specifically affected by such tranquilizers as chlorpromazine, meprobamate, and Valium, which are often used in the treatment of anxiety. Imipramine, on the other hand, does alleviate separation distress in puppies, as it alleviates depression in humans. Thus, from a pharmacological point of view, it would seem that the mechanisms mediating anxiety are fundamentally different from those mediating grief and depression.

In short, I would agree with Mandler that anxiety is a state of cognitive and behavioral disorganization that may be induced by the interruption of planned activity (among other things). Moreover, the loss of a loved one, or the disruption of interpersonal relationships, may be an important—even universal—source of anxiety in this sense. But grief is more than anxiety, more than a generalized sense of helplessness and hopelessness. It is a unique emotional syndrome occasioned by the disruption of social bonds.

At this point, it might be helpful to summarize the discussion thus far. In the section on biological contributions, it was suggested that grief is, in part, a biologically based response occasioned by the disruption of established social bonds. But this hypothesis cannot explain all the symptoms of grief, even those that are relatively universal. Bereavement involves more than the disruption of social bonds; it is also a period when old responses must be extinguished, when many rewards and punishments are beyond personal control, and when well-established plans are interrupted. It is therefore reasonable to attribute some of the symptoms of grief to such psychological processes as extinction, learned helplessness, and the interruption of behavior. It must be kept in mind, however, that these processes are themselves quite complex and little understood. It remains to be seen precisely which symptoms can be accounted for in these terms, which are due to biological factors, and which are the product of social custom (as will be discussed shortly).

D. The Psychological Functions of Grief

We may now consider briefly some possible psychological functions of grief. In order to do this, we will have to shift gears, so to speak, and go from the second (despair) to the third (reorganization) stage of grief. That is, we will not be concerned, as in the foregoing discussion, with the depressive reactions that may accompany extinction, learned helplessness, and the interruption of behavior. Rather, we will focus on the reorganization of behavior that these processes necessitate.

At first, it might seem ironical even to speak of the psychological functions of grief. The pain and anguish of grief, as well as the increased susceptibility to a wide range of somatic and psychological disorders, are not something to be glossed over lightly. However, the notion of function is always relative. A response is never functional in and of itself but only within a given context. Therefore, the question is: Can a context be specified or developed in which grief may have some functional significance for the individual and not just for the species?

In a rather selfish way, some persons do turn grief to their own advantages by deriving secondary gains (e.g., undue personal or material support) from their plight. But secondary gains are generally maladaptive in the long run. Not only do they prolong the suffering, but they also block any potential for growth or change that may be present in the situation. And it is in the potential for growth that the positive aspects of grief, if any, may be found.

The relationship between bereavement and growth has been commented upon by many authors. As Carr (1975) has noted, bereavement is a relative experience. Being left alone with a stranger during childhood, altering sex roles during adolescence, leaving home for work or college, advancing in one's profession, moving to a new neighborhood—these and many other common experiences may involve some degree of loss, separation, or disruption of social relationships, and all may elicit some of the symptoms of grief. With time, however, such "losses" are integrated into experience, and a new level of maturity is achieved.[7]

On a more theoretical level, Freud (1923) saw in object-loss a necessary condition for ego development. During the primitive oral phase of development, according to Freud, the child hardly distinguishes between its own self and external objects (e.g., the mother) on which libidinal energy is cathected (attached or concentrated). As object relations are broken or changed during the course of development, the libidinal ties must be decathected. This process may be facilitated by symbolically incorporating the lost object into the ego, thus making it a part of the person's developing self-concept. Freud asserted:

> It may be that this identification is the sole condition under which the id can give up its objects. At any rate the process, especially in the early phases of development, is a very frequent one, and it makes it possible to suppose that the character of the ego is a precipitate of abandoned object-cathexes and that it contains the history of those object-choices. (1923, p. 29)

In recent years, there has been a tendency to view growth or "self-actualization" in a rather Pollyannaish light. If all necessary provisions are met (food, shelter, love, etc.), then the individual will supposedly grow and mature in a healthy fashion, and his human potential will become manifest. Traumatic experiences are to be avoided as unnecessary, at best, and as detrimental to self-actualization, at worst. This point of view may be contrasted with that of Freud, who considered the ego the precipitate of lost objects. Both points of view may, of course, be correct. There is evidence that early bereavement, if not properly managed, can have detrimental effects on later development (e.g., Heinicke, 1973); but at the same time, it must be recognized that as an individual grows and develops, ties with parents, siblings, and even his former self must be altered and rearranged. It is unlikely that such reorganization and growth can be accomplished without experiencing some of the symptoms of grief.

---

[7] A more complete discussion of the psychological determinants of grief would have to consider why so many varied conditions are capable of eliciting grieflike reactions. Simply to say that such events involve some disruption of social relationships is insufficient, for not all the occasions for grief (e.g., the loss of a valued piece of property) are social in a strict sense of the term. Space does not allow a consideration of this issue here, but two points should be made. First, most of the symptoms of grief are common to other syndromes as well, albeit in different combination and degree. Thus, it is not certain that what has sometimes been described as "grief" for the loss of property, say, is comparable to genuine grief reactions—in this area, detailed observations are rare and metaphorical descriptions prevalent. But even when this fact is taken into account, it does seem that ostensibly impersonal events are sometimes the occasion for grief. This brings us to the second point. Human beings live in a symbolic universe. All sorts of inanimate and animate objects—a house, a flag, a keepsake, a pet, etc.—can become the source of strong affectional bonds that, on a symbolic level, are interpersonal in nature. Their loss can thus be an occasion for genuine grief. Similar considerations also apply to events that diminish the self (e.g., the loss of a limb or failure on an examination). In a sense, we are all in love with ourselves, and hence anything that diminishes the self is a potential source of grief, just as anything that enhances the self is a potential source of joy.

The relationship between bereavement and growth can be looked at in still another way. When customary social relationships are disrupted (whether through death, movement, or other forms of social change), new ways of thinking and behaving must be established. The protest and yearning associated with grief may provide a powerful motivation for accomplishing the necessary reorganization, if the individual does not get locked in despair. Therefore, Marris (1975) sees in grief—or at least in some of the occasions for grief—the wellspring for a wide variety of creative activity, including the entrepreneurship of the businessman, the social innovation of the university student, and the intellectual transformations of the scientist. There is, of course, much more involved in these activities than the potential for grief. Nevertheless, the point should be well taken: Grief can be a time for growth and change, as well as for anguish and despair—if it is properly managed.

IV. SOCIAL CONTRIBUTIONS TO THE SYNDROME OF GRIEF

Every society possesses certian mores, beliefs, and customs concerning the appropriate behavior to be displayed upon the death of a significant other. The prescribed behavior, whether sincere or not, must be followed if social censure is to be avoided. Of course, the exact nature of the behavior may vary considerably from one society to the next (Durkheim, 1915; Hocart, 1937; Volkart & Michael, 1957). For example, mourning rites may begin before the expected death of the "deceased" or immediately after his death, or they may be delayed for various periods of time; they may last for days, weeks, or years; they may require abstentions from communication concerning the deceased, or they may enjoin public proclamation. The emotions of the bereaved may be publicly displayed in weeping and wailing, suppressed with stoic resolve, or camouflaged behind the mask of some other affect, for example, with smiling and laughter. The varieties of behavior that society may demand of the individual during bereavement led Durkheim (1915) to state that

> mourning is not a natural movement of private feelings wounded by a cruel loss; it is a duty imposed by the group. One weeps, not simply because he is sad, but because he is forced to weep. It is a ritual attitude which he is forced to adopt out of respect for custom, but which is, in a large measure, independent of his affective state. (p. 397)

The foregoing statement by Durkheim implies that mourning practices do not contribute to the experience of grief *per se*; but, rather, are "duties imposed by the group." This approach, however, underestimates the role of social evolution in determining the inner experience of emotion. Biological evolution has provided us with only a first nature; social evolution has contributed a second. The mechanisms by which this occurs are a matter of dispute that need not concern us here (cf. Campbell, 1975; Berger & Luckmann, 1966). Suffice it to say that any society contains a great number of beliefs and practices that are transmitted from one generation to the next through education and socialization. Some of these practices may prove to be adaptive for the society as a whole and hence are retained within the social system; other practices, which are of little functional significance, die out and are replaced. Of course, the adaptive significance of a custom need not be explicitly recognized by the members of a group, nor need it correspond to the rationale by which the group legitimizes the behavior.

In the case of mourning, many practices may at first appear to be highly disfunctional or detrimental, from the point of view both of society and of the bereaved individual. For example, expensive and elaborate monuments may be erected, nonproductive days of mourning decreed, and even the life of certain individuals sacrificed (as in the custom of suttee, where the wife is immolated on her husband's funeral pyre). In order for such customs to function efficiently in spite of their costs, either they must be forced upon the individual from without (e.g., by a police system or some other form of coercive control), or they must be based on behavioral dispositions that are "second nature." That is, through socialization the individual is encouraged to adopt as his own the relevant attitudes and beliefs of society; then, when the occasion calls for it, he feels an inner compulsion to manifest the prescribed behavior. Such an inner compulsion, although socially constituted, is experienced as emotional.

The foregoing observations would seem to suggest that grief is not a universal emotion, since some of its constituent elements—mourning practices—vary widely from one culture to another. And, to an extent, grief syndromes are culturally specific. However, if the arguments presented in earlier sections have any validity, then some of the symptoms of grief are also biologically determined and/or are the product of such universal psychological processes as extinction, learned helplessness, and the interruption of behavior. Moreover, even mourning practices are not completely free to vary—there are only a limited number of ways a society can cope with such a universal and irreversible phenomenon as death. All these factors impose some universality on the experience of grief.

But that does not settle the issue. As noted earlier, there are no symptoms that are essential to an emotional syndrome, and grief is no exception. Even on a biological level, grief is not "wired into" the organism. Rather, there is a general predisposition to respond in a certain manner; how this predisposition will be expressed—or whether it will be expressed at all—depends upon a host of situational, personal and sociocultural factors. A great deal of latitude is thus possible in the experience of grief, both across individuals and across cultures. The point I wish to emphasize here is that individual and cultural variations are not a mere patina upon a biological substratum; cultural elements are as much a part of grief as are biologically based responses.

There are thus grounds for considering grief a universal experience, while at the same time recognizing that it is subject to a wide range of cultural variations. In this sense, the different expressions of grief might be compared to different languages. Language is a universal human phenomenon that is, in part, biologically based. Yet English is not Russian, and Russian is not Chinese. There is, in short, no basic incompatibility in considering language a universal human experience and yet recognizing that only specific languages are actually spoken. Similarly, when we speak of grief as both a universal phenomenon and a culturally specific emotional syndrome, no contradiction is implied. We are basically speking on two different levels of abstraction.

A. The Social Functions of Grief and Mourning

Although the primary functions of mourning practices are to be found on the level of the group or society, certain aspects of mourning may also benefit the individual. For example, mourning practices help the bereaved to articulate grief in a socially accepted and recognized fashion. This can be extremely important, for grief that is unexpressed may prolong the suffering, while grief that is inappropriately expressed may be so discomforting to others (e.g., friends and relatives) that interpersonal relationships are further disrupted. Mourning practices also may provide support for the bereaved by allowing a recognized period of withdrawal and by setting a time schedule for the reorganization of behavior. And, by formally honoring the dead, mourning practices may help the bereaved to incorporate his or her loss in a meaningful way.

Some of these benefits are well illustrated by the mourning practices of the Kotas, a people of South India (Mandelbaum, 1959). The Kotas observe two funeral ceremonies. The first, or "green funeral," occurs shortly after death. It involves the cremation of the body and is attended by the close friends and relatives of the deceased. This funeral dramatizes the death so that it cannot be denied. There then follows a period of relative quietude for the bereaved, during which time social obligations are rearranged. Yet, the thread of continuity with the past is not completely broken, and the dead person even retains certain prerogatives. Thus, if a Kota widow becomes pregnant during this period, the child is considered that of her late husband. (A faithful wife may actually attempt to become pregnant in order to provide her former mate with an heir.) Finally, the bereaved is aided in the reorganization of his or her life by a second ceremony, called the "dry funeral," which is held every one or two years for all those who have died since the last such ceremony. This second funeral is an elaborate affair that lasts for 11 days. During the first days, the bereaved are encouraged to give full expression to their grief. But as the ceremony progresses, activities become less somber. On the final night, widows and widowers are expected to engage in sexual intercourse, preferably with a sibling of the deceased, thus symbolizing their return as normal members of society.

In Western industrial societies, mourning practices have become increasingly abbreviated. And the trend is continuing. In nineteenth-century England, for example, a widow was expected to mourn for about 2½ years. Among other things, specific clothing was specified for this period, with normal attire being reintroduced only by degrees. Mourning clothes were also worn for various periods of time after the deaths of other members of the family, for example, 12 months for a child, 9 months for a grandparent, and 6 months for a sibling (Lerner, 1975). To the modern reader, such practices would undoubtedly seem anachronistic. Today, little remains of formal mourning customs outside of the funeral ceremony itself. And in the United States, even the funeral has come under much recent criticism as being overcommercialized, ostentatious, and a financial burden on the bereaved. Although some of these criticisms are unfortunately valid, they should not be taken to mean that mourning practices are superfluous or unbecoming of an "enlightened" society. Society's obligation to the bereaved does not stop with the efficient disposal of the body. In fact, with the further breakup of the extended family system and the loosening ties of organized religion, there are indications that the funeral parlor may assume an increasingly important role in American society (cf. Pine *et al.*, 1976).

While mourning practices often aid the bereaved in coping with loss, they serve important social functions as well. Mandelbaum (1959) has suggested that mourning rites can be understood in much the same way as other ceremonies that involve socially important transitions, for example, birth and marriage. Such ceremonies allow the threads of each individual life to be woven into the fabric of society, thus reinforcing the whole. In the case of mourning, this function is perhaps most evident when a prominent figure dies. An entire nation may then mourn together, rekindling mutual allegiance. The nationally televised funeral of President John F. Kennedy, for example, not only elicited sincere mourning in many persons (Sheatsley & Feldman, 1964), but it also reaffirmed the continuity of American society. National mourning was also encouraged in the USSR upon the death of Lenin and in China upon the death of Mao Tse-tung. In these instances (as following Kennedy's assassination), there was threat of civil disturbance, and mourning ceremonies helped to unite the population in grief. In the case of Lenin and Mao Tse-tung, the bodies of the deceased also have been preserved and enshrined for public veneration, so that they may continue to serve as a unifying force long after formal mourning practices have ended.

The preservation of the corpse, as in the case of Lenin and Mao Tse-tung, may be used to illustrate another point, namely, that the public rationale offered for a practice need not reflect its true significance. Thus, religious belief in an afterlife has been the traditional rationale offered for many mourning practices, including preservation of the body or other relics of the deceased. In the USSR and Communist China, there is no question of a religious motive. But not only that, Marxist doctrine minimizes the importance of historical figures, and apparently both Lenin and Mao Tse-Tung expressed wishes to be cremated. Thus, the practice of mummification may survive under special circumstances, not only in the absence of a traditional religious rationale but even in oppostion to official dogma and the personal wishes of the deceased. The social importance of a practice transcends dogma, whether pro or con.

To summarize briefly, mourning practices have evolved to meet the needs of society as well as those of the bereaved individual. When these needs are in conflict, the demands of society generally take precedence, even if they place an increased burden on the individual. In most instances, however, the needs of the bereaved and of society are not incompatible, and mourning practices may help assuage the pain of loss. The relationship between mourning and grief can also be stated somewhat differently, more in line with the present analysis. That is, in the well-socialized individual, mourning practices combine with biologically and psychologically determined responses to form a coherent emotional syndrome: grief. This syndrome may be more or less severe, depending upon prevailing social customs, the past history and present circumstances of the individual, and even genetic predispositions (as reflected, say, in the tendency to form attachment bonds).

V. CONCLUDING OBSERVATIONS

In the introduction to this chapter, it was noted that bereavement may be a period of increased susceptibility to a wide range of somatic and psychological disorders. Although this increased susceptibility to illness can be attributed to a number of different factors, the major determinant seems to be the stress associated with grief (see Epstein, Weitz, Roback, & McKee, 1975, for a recent review of relevant research). But in spite of its potential deleterious effects, it does not seem possible—or even desirable—to eliminate grief completely as a human experience. Engel (1961) has compared grief to a disease. This analogy is in many ways helpful and expedient. But, of course, grief is *not* a disease. The total eradication of a disease, as has almost been accomplished in the case of smallpox, is a major achievement. To total eradication of grief, by contrast, is difficult to imagine—not because it is impossible, but because it would require a fundamental change in human nature. Grief is a natural part of the human condition. It could be eradicated only be denying much of what it means to be human, for example, attachment to, and lives shared with, other human beings. Yet while recognizing the inevitableness of grief, we can and should try to minimize it negative effects, and simple understanding may be a powerful tool in this endeavor. As discussed elsewhere (Averill, 1978), knowledge about a painful event, and about the nature of one's own emotional reactions, can be an important factor in the regulation of stress. The least we can do, therefore, is help the bereaved to understand the reasons for his or her grief and to realize that in some larger perspective, the suffering is not without reason. That realization may not lessen the pain of loss, but it can make the pain more bearable and perhaps lessen the chance of secondary (psycho-pathological) complications.

REFERENCES

Amsel, A. Behavioral habituation, counterconditioning, and a general theory of persistence. In A. Black & W. Prokasy (Eds.), *Classical conditioning. Vol. 2. Current theory and research.* New York: Appleton-Century-Crofts, 1972.

Averill, J. R. Grief: Its nature and significance. *Psychological Bulletin*, 1968, *70*, 721–748.

Averill, J. R. Personal control over aversive stimuli and its relationship to stress. *Psychological Bulletin*, 1973, *80*, 286–303.

Averill, J. R. An analysis of psychophysiological symbolism and its influence on theories of emotion. *Journal for the Theory of Social Behavior*, 1974, *4*, 147–190.

Averill, J. R. Emotion and anxiety: Sociocultural, biological, and psychological determinants. In M. Zuckerman & C. D. Spielberger (Eds.), *Emotion and anxiety: New concepts, methods and applications.* New York: LEA-Wiley, 1976.

Averill, J. R. A selective review of cognitive and behavioral factors involved in the regulation of stress. In R. A. Depue (Ed.), *The psychobiology of the depressive disorders: Implications for the effects of stress.* New York: Academic Press, 1978.

Beck, A. T. *Cognitive therapy and the emotional disorders.* New York: International Universities Press, 1976.

Berger, P. L., & Luckmann, T. *The social construction of reality.* New York: Doubleday, 1966.

Bowlby, J. *Maternal care and mental health.* Geneva: World Health Organization, 1951.

Bowlby, J. Grief and mourning in early infancy and early childhood. *Psychoanalytic Study of the Child*, 1960, *15*, 9–32.

Bowlby, J. Process of mourning. *International Journal of Psychoanalysis*, 1961, *42*, 317–340.

Bowlby, J. Pathological mourning and childhood mourning. *Journal of the American Psychoanalytic Association*, 1963, *11*, 500–541.

Bowlby, J. *Attachment and loss.* Vol. 1. *Attachment.* New York: Basic Books, 1969.

Bowlby, J. *Attachment and loss.* Vol. 2. *Separation.* New York: Basic Books, 1973.

Brown, A. E. Grief in the chimpanzee. *American Naturalist*, 1879, *13*, pp. 173–175.

Campbell, D. T. On the conflicts between biological and social evolution and between psychology and moral tradition. *American Psychologist*, 1975, *30*, pp. 1103–1126.

Cannon, W. B. *Bodily changes in pain, hunger, fear, and rage* (2nd ed.). New York: Appleton, 1929.

Carpenter, C. R. Societies of monkey and apes. *Biological Symposia*, 1942, *8*, 177–204.

Carr, A. C. Bereavement as a relative experience. In B. Schoenberg, I. Gerber, A. Weiner, A. H. Kutscher, D. Peretz, & A. C. Catt (Eds.), *Bereavement: Its psychosocial aspects.* New York: Columbia University Press, 1975.

Clarke, J. The precipitation of juvenile delinquency. *Journal of Mental Science*, 1961, *107*, 1033–1034.

Davis, D. R. The psychological mechanisms of depressions. In E. B. Davies (Ed.), *Depression.* Cambridge: Cambridge University Press, 1964.

Dennehy, C. M. Childhood bereavement and psychiatric illness. *British Journal of Psychiatry*, 1966, *112*, 1049–1069.

Doi, L. T. *Amae:* A key concept for understanding Japanese personality structure. In R. J. Smith & R. K. Beardsley (Eds.), *Japanese culture: Its development and characteristics.* Chicago: Aldine, 1962.

Doi, T. *The anatomy of dependence.* Tokyo: Kodansha International, 1973.

Duffy, E. *Activation and behavior.* New York: Wiley, 1962.

Durkheim, E. *The elementary forms of religious experience.* New York: Macmillan, 1915.

Eastman, C. Behavioral formulations of depression. *Psychological Review,* 1976, *83,* 277–291.

Epstein, G., Weitz, L., Roback, H., & McKee, E. Research on bereavement: A selective and critical review. *Comprehensive Psychiatry,* 1975, 16, 537–546.

Eibl-Eibesfeldt, I. *Ethology: The biology of behavior.* New York: Holt, 1970.

Engel, G. L. Is grief a disease? *Psychosomatic Medicine,* 1961, *23,* 18–22.

Engel, G. L. *Psychological development in health and disease.* Philadelphia: Saunders, 1962.

Freud, S. (1923) the ego and the id. *Standard Edition,* Vol. 19. London: Hogarth, 1961.

Garner, R. L. *Apes and monkeys: Their life and language.* Boston: Ginn, 1900.

Gorer, G. *Death, grief, and mourning.* London: Cressent Press, 1965.

Hannum, R. D., Rosellini, R. A., & Seligman, M. E. Learned-helplessness in the rat: Retention and immunization. *Developmental Psychology,* 1976, *12,* 449–454.

Harlow, H. F. *Learning to love.* San Francisco: Albion, 1971.

Harlow, H., & Suomi, S. J. Induced depression in monkeys. *Behavioral Biology,* 1974, *12,* 273–296.

Hebb, D. O. *The organization of behavior.* New York: Wiley, 1949.

Heinicke, C. M. Parental deprivation in early childhood: A predispostion to later depression ? In J. P. Scott & E. Senay (Eds.), *Separation and depression: Clinical and research aspects.* Washington, D.C.: American Association for the Advancement of Science, 1973.

Hinde, R. A. *The biological basis of human social behavior.* New York: McGraw-Hill, 1974.

Hocart, A. M. Death customs. In E. R. A. Seligman & A. Johnson (Eds.), *Encyclopedia of the Social Sciences,* Vol. 5. New York: Macmillan, 1937.

Hofer, M. A., Wolff, C. T., Friedman, S. B., & Mason, J. W. A psychoendocrine study of bereavement, Part I. 17-Hydroxycorticosteroid excretion rates of parents following death of their children from leukemia; and Part II. Observations on the process of mourning in relation to adrenocortical function. *Psychosomatic Medicine,* 1972, *34,* 481–491, 492–504.

Kaufman, I. C. Mother–infant separation in monkeys: An experimental model. In J. P. Scott & E. C. Senay (Eds.), *Separation and depression: Clinical and research aspects.* Washington, D.C.: American Association for the Advancement of Science, 1973.

Kaufman, I. C., & Rosenblum, L. A. The reaction of separation in infant monkeys: Anaclitic depression and conservation–withdrawal. *Psychosomatic Medicine,* 1967, *29,* 648–676.

Kaufman, I. C., & Rosenblum, L. A. Effects of separation from mother on the emotional behavior of infant monkeys. *Annals of the New York Academy of Science,* 1969, *159,* 681–695.

Klein, D. C., Fencil-Morse, E., & Seligman, M. E. P. Learned helplessness, depression, and the attribution of failure. *Journal of Personality and Social Psychology,* 1976, *33,* 508–516.

Klein, D. F. Delineation of two drug-responsive anxiety syndromes. *Psycho-pharmacologia,* 1964, *5,* 397–408.

Lazarus, A. Learning theory and the treatment of depression. *Behavior Research and Therapy,* 1968, *6,* 83–89.

Lazarus, R. S., & Averill, J. R. Emotion and cognition: With special reference to anxiety. In C. D. Spielberger (Ed.), *Anxiety: Current trends in theory and research.* New York: Academic Press, 1972.

Lerner, J. C. Changes in attitudes toward death: The widow in Great Britain in the early twentieth century. In B. Schoenberg, I. Gerber, A. Weiner, A. H. Kutscher, D. Peretz, & A. C. Carr (Eds.), *Bereavement: Its psychosocial aspects.* New York: Columbia University Press, 1975.

Levis, D. J. Learned helplessness: A reply and an altervative S-R interpretation. *Journal of Experimental Psychology,* 1976, *105,* 47–65.

Lewinsohn, P. M., Weinstein, M. S., & Shaw, D. A. Depression: A clinical-research approach. In R. D. Rubin & C. M. Franks (Eds.), *Advances in behavior therapy.* New York: Academic Press, 1969.

Lewis, J. K., McKinney, W. T., Yong, L. D., & Kraemer, G. W. Mother–infant separation in rhesus monkeys as a model of human depression: A reconsideration. *Archives of General Psychiatry,* 1976, *33,* 699–705.

Lindemann, E. Symptomatology and management of acute grief. *American Journal of Psychiatry*, 1944, 101, 141–148.

Lindsley, D. B. Emotion. In S. S. Stevens (Ed.), *Handbook of experimental psychology*. New York: Wiley, 1951.

Lorenz, K. *King Solomon's ring*. New York: Crowell, 1952.

Maier, S. F., & Seligman, M. E. P. Leanred helplessness: Theory and evidence. *Journal of Experimental Psychology: General*, 1976, *105*, 3–46.

Mandelbaum, D. G. Social uses of funeral rites. In H. Feifel (Ed.), *The meaning of death*. New York: McGraw-Hill, 1959.

Mandler, G. *Mind and emotion*. New York: Wiley, 1975.

Marris, P. *Widows and their families*. London: Routledge & Kegan Paul, 1958.

Marris, P. *Loss and change*. Garden City, N.Y.: Anchor Press/Doubleday, 1975.

McDougall, W. *An introduction to social psychology* (23rd ed.). London: Methuen, 1936.

Parkes, C. M. Bereavement and mental illness, Part I. A clinical study of the grief of bereaved psychiatric patients; and Part II. A classification of bereavement reactions. *British Journal of Medical Psychology*, 1965, *38*, 1–12. 13–26.

Parkes, C. M. "Seeking" and "finding" a lost object: Evidence from recent studies of the reaction to bereavement. *Social Science and Medicine*. 1970, *4*, pp. 187–201.

Parkes, C. M. Psychosocial transitions: A field for study. *Social Science and Medicine*, 1971, *5*, 101–115.

Parkes, C. M. *Bereavement: Studies of grief in adult life*. London: Tavistock Publications, 1972.

Parkes, C. M. What becomes of redundant world models? A contribution to the study of adaptation to change. *British Journal of Medical Psychology*, 1975, *48*, 131–137.

Pine, V. R., Kutscher, A. H., Peretz, D., Slater, R. C., DeBillis, R., Volk, R. J., & Cherico, D. J. *Acute grief and the funeral*. Springfield, Ill.: Charles C Thomas, 1976.

Pollock, G. H. Mourning and adaptation. *International Journal of Psycho-Analysis*, 1961, *43*, 341–361.

Preston, D. G., Baker, R. P., & Seay, B. Mother–infant separation in the patas monkey. *Developmental Psychology*, 1970, *3*, 298–306.

Reite, M., Kaufman, I. C., Pauley, J. D., & Stynes, A. J. Depression in infant monkeys: Physiological correlates. *Psychosomatic Medicine*, 1974, *36*, 363–367.

Rosenblatt, P. C., Walsh, R. P., & Jackson, D. S. *Grief and mourning in cross-cultural perspective*. New Haven: HRAF Press, 1976.

Schaller, G. B. The behavior of the mountain gorilla. In I. DeVore (Ed.), *Primate behavior*. New York: Holt, 1965.

Schmale, A. H. Relationship of separation and depression to disease. *Psychosomatic Medicine*, 1958, *20*, 259–277.

Schmale, A. H. Adaptive role of depression in health and disease. In J. P. Scott & E. C. Senary (Eds.), *Separation and depression: Clinical and research aspects*. Washington, D.C.: American Association for the Advancement of Science, 1973.

Schlottmann, R. S., & Seay, B. Mother–infant separation in the Java monkey (*Macaca irus*). *Journal of Comparative and Physiological Psychology*, 1972, *79*, 334–340.

Schoenberg, B., Gerber, I., Weiner, A., Kutscher, A. H., Peretz, D., & Carr, A. C. (Eds.) *Bereavement: Its psychosocial aspects*. New York: Columbia University Press, 1975.

Scott, J. P. The development of social motivation. In D. Levine (Ed.), *Nebraska symposium on motivation*, Vol. 15. Lincoln: University of Nebraska Press, 1967.

Scott, J. P., Stewart, J. M., & DeGhett, J. J. Separation in infant dogs. In J. P. Scott & E. C. Senay (Eds.), *Separation and depression: Clinical and research aspects*. Washington, D.C.: American Association for the Advancement of Science, 1973.

Seay, B., & Harlow, H. F. Maternal separation in the rhesus monkey. *Journal of Nervous and Mental Disorder*, 1965, *140*, 434–441.

Seligman, M. E. P. On the generality of the laws of learning. *Psychological Review*, 1970, *77*, 406–418.

Seligman, M. E. P. *Helplessness: On depression, development, and death.* San Francisco: W. H. Freeman, 1975.

Selye, H. *The stress of life* (rev. ed.). New York: McGraw-Hill, 1976.

Sheatsley, P. B., & Feldman, J. J. The assassination of President Kennedy: A preliminary report on public reactions and behavior. *Public Opinion Quarterly,* 1964, *28,* 189–215.

Shoor, M., & Speed, M. H. Delinquency as a manifestation of the mourning process. *Psychiatric Quarterly,* 1963, *37,* 540–558.

Spitz, R. A. Anaclitic depression. *Psychoanalytic Study of the Child,* 1946, *2,* 313–347.

Staddon, J. E. R. On the notion of cause, with applications to behaviorism. *Behaviorism,* 1973, *1,* 25–63.

Suomi, S. J., Eiseld, C. D., Grady, S. A., & Harlow, H. F. Depressive behavior in adult monkeys following separation from family environment. *Journal of Abnormal Psychology,* 1975, *84,* 576–578.

Suomi, S. J., Harlow, H. F., & Domek, C. J. Effect of repetitive infant–infant separation of young monkeys. *Journal of Abnormal Psychology,* 1970, *76,* 161–172.

Tinkelpaugh, O. L. The self-mutilation of a male macacus rhesus monkey. *Journal of Mammalogy,* 1928, *9,* 292–300.

Volkart, E. H., & Michael, S. T. Bereavment and mental health. In A. H. Leighton, J. A. Clausen, & R. N. Wilson (Eds.), *Explorations in social psychiatry.* New York: Basic Books, 1957.

Weiss, J. M. Effects of coping behavior with and without a feedback signal on stress pathology in rats. *Journal of Comparative and Physiological Psychology,* 1971, *77,* 22–30.

Weiss, J. M., Glazer, H. L., & Pohorecky, L. A. Coping behavior and neurochemical changes: An alternative explanation for the original "learned helplessness" experiments. In C. Serban & A. Kling (Eds.), *Animal models in human psychobiology.* New York: Plenum Press, 1976.

Wilson, E. O. *Sociobiology: The new synthesis.* Cambridge, Mass.: Harvard Universtiy Press, 1975.

Wortman, C. B., & Brehm, J. W. Responses to uncontrollable outcomes: An integration of reactance theory and the learned helplessness model. In L. E. Berkowitz (Ed.), *Advances in experimental social psychology.* New York: Academic Press, 1975.

Yamamoto, J., Okonogi, K., Iwasaki, T., & Yoshimura, S. Mourning in Japan. *American Journal of Psychiatry,* 1969, *125,* 1660–1665.

Yerkes, R. M., & Yerkes, A. W. *The great apes.* New Haven, Conn.: Yale University Press, 1929.

Zedwitz, F. X., von. Beobachtungen im zoologischen Garten Berlin. *Der Zoologische Garten,* 1930, *2,* 278–286.

Zuckerman, S. *The social life of monkeys and apes.* London: Kegan Paul, 1932.

Editor's Introduction

12

Lewis's work on the role of shame and guilt in personality, psychopathology, and psychotherapy draws from psychoanalytic theory, experimental psychology, and a wealth of personal experience as a practitioner and teacher of psychotherapy. In this chapter, she begins by elucidating the long-standing problems in distinguishing between shame and guilt as separate and important motivational conditions. She shows how the problem began when Freud failed to distinguish between the ego and self and explained the superego solely in terms of instinctual drives (especially the working of the death instinct), emphasizing the role of the affective state of guilt. Within this framework, Freud saw no place for shame in superego functioning, nor did he see a role for shame in depression. Hartman included cognitive and social learning components in his conception of superego functioning, but the impact of his contribution on affect theory was simply to strengthen the role of guilt.

Building on the work of Wertheimer, Witkin and his colleagues developed an experimental procedure for distinguishing between different styles of perceptual–cognitive functioning: field dependence and field independence. It remained for Lewis to develop the relationship between these perceptual-cognitive styles, styles of superego functioning, and the differential relationship of shame and guilt in these processes. Her work demonstrates the usefulness of studying both shame and guilt as the affective states that constitute the superego and determine how it operates.

Lewis points out how reflection on or anticipation of shame functions as a defense against the loss of self-boundaries and as a force fostering the sense of a separate identify. On the other hand, she recognizes that shame as an emotion state temporarily wrecks consciousness and the self and is the opposite of self-autonomy. Her research has shown that shame is strongly associated with self-directed hostility in field-dependent patients.

The individual's field-dependent or field-independent style of perceptual-cognitive functioning is one determinant of the mode of functioning of a superego, with shame being a greater force in the superego of field-dependent patients and guilt a greater force in the field-independent.

Lewis also clarifies the positive functions of shame by showing how it plays a role in maintaining personal dignity and worth and affectional bonds.

Her distinctions between the phenomenology of shame and guilt support her contention that shame as an affective state of the superego leads to depression and hysteria, while guilt leads to obsessive disorders and paranoia. She illustrates her discussion of the phenomenological characteristics of shame and guilt and their effects on the functioning of the self with excerpts from transcripts of psychotherapy.

Her evidence for the role of shame in depression and hysteria comes from both research and clinical experience. She concludes her paper with a discussion of some important sex differences, maintaining that women are more prone to shame and hence to depression and hysteria.

Shame in Depression and Hysteria **12**

HELEN BLOCK LEWIS

Did you feel horribly depressed? I did. I could not write, and all the devils came out—hairy black ones. To be 29 and unmarried—to be a failure—childless—insane too, no writer. I went off to the Museum to try and subdue them, and having an ice afterward, met Rupert Brooke with, presumably, a Miss Olivier. Her beauty was marred by protuberant blemishes; as she wasn't beautiful, only a pretty chit, perhaps she wasn't Miss Olivier.

Letter of Virginia Woolf to her sister, Vanessa Bell
Nicolson and Trautmann (1975, p. 570)

Although psychoanalysis began with Freud's unraveling of the way forbidden sexual longings create neurotic symptoms, close and systematic attention to the actual experience of the psychic censorship have come relatively late in psychoanalytic thinking. When I set out to study the phenomenology of shame and guilt (Lewis, 1971), I found an extensive literature on guilt and comparatively little on shame. For example, in the *Index of Psychoanalytic Writers* (Grinstein, 1966), there are 64 citations under the heading of guilt and only 8 under the heading of shame, Guilt was mainly conceptualized as an indication of a defense mechanism, the superego. This operating force was often "irrational and unconscious" (English & English, 1958). The concept of unconscious guilt itself tended to turn attention away from guilt as a psychic state. The writers also did not distinguish carefully between guilt and shame and except for Tomkins (1963), subsumed shame under the category of guilt. The relatively small literature on shame was also concerned with it as a defense mechanism or an operating force. While I drew heavily on the observations of Piers and Singer (1953) and Lynd (1958), my book was the first attempt to study the phenomenology of shame and guilt, the two affective states that operate as psychic censors and within which "primary-process" neurotic symptoms form.

I. REASONS FOR THE NEGLECT OF THE PHENOMENOLOGY OF SHAME AND GUILT

The reasons for the relative neglect of the phenomenology of shame and guilt are intrinsic both in the history of psychoanalytic thinking and in the

---

HELEN BLOCK LEWIS • Yale University, New Haven, Connecticut.

state of general psychology during the development of psychoanalysis. These historical reasons are interesting in their own right, and they also help to illuminate the problems inherent in understanding both the superego as a defense mechanism and the affective states of shame and guilt. They particularly suggest why shame has been so neglected. At least three major theoretical issues in psychology are connected with the superego concept as it was formulated by Freud. These are (1) the distinction between the self and the ego; (2) a theory of the nature of human nature; and (3) a theory of sex differences in psychological functioning. These three theoretical issues are all embedded in the general theoretical question of whether psychic events may be formulated on their own level of reality and in their own experiential terms, or whether they must always be directly related to the physical basis of reality that is assumed in a materialist conception of nature. Freud was working within the *Zeitgeist* of scientific reductionism and with the relatively limited information from anthropology and psychology available in his time. Perhaps even more important, he was constrained by what we today call a "medical model" of psychological illness. Nothing corresponding to what George Engel (1977) has recently called a "biopsychosocial" model of psychological functioning was available to Freud. This is no small surprise, since both anthropology and sociology, as well as psychology itself, were in embryonic stages of development. Let us examine each of the three areas of theory that are connected with the superego concept to see how limitations of information and theory delayed the phenomenological study of the affective states of shame and guilt.

A. The Distinction between the Self and the Ego

Firmly committed as he was to a materialist conception of nature, Freud at first (1900) formulated psychic conflict as occurring between "ego instincts" and "sexual instincts," each of which had a solid foundation either in the survival of the individual or in the survival of the species. Although he often described in exquisite clinical detail the vicissitudes of the self's experience in relation to beloved or hated others or in relation to self-reproaches, his formal concept of the ego left no room for a separate concept of self. This was in fact a grievous error in conceptualization. It led Freud to the position he took in *Beyond the Pleasure-Principle* (1920), in which he postulated a death instinct. Observing that aggression is "internalized" and directed against the individual, Freud failed to see that it is the *self* that is the target in masochism, not the ego. Even in suicide, which culminates in the ego's total destruction, the main target is the *self*, for which some people sacrifice their lives (cf. Binswanger, 1958). Paradoxically, although it was Freud who described these clinical phenomena in *Mourning and Melancholia* (1915), his failure to distinguish between the self and the ego led him to explain the phenomena of masochism by adopting the notion of a death instinct in human nature. The superego is an expression of the working of the death instinct, directing the internalization of aggression and the formation of an unconscious, "irrational," and very powerful sense of guilt. As Fromm (1951) has observed, Freud's formal notion of human nature was not very different from a concept of original sin.

By the middle 1920s, a correction of Freud's error in confusing self and ego was made by Hartmann (1950) and by Jacobson (1954), both of whom saw little value in the concept of a death instinct. Hartmann, in addition, set out to rectify Freud's concept of behavior as entirely driven by the passions or instincts. In his concept of an "autonomous ego," that is, an ego developing outside the influence of sexual and aggressive "instincts," Hartmann made theoretical room for cognitive and social learning components in superego functioning. As we shall see in a few moments, however, Hartmann's concept of an *autonomous* ego, while a needed correction to one aspect of Freud's thinking, had as one consequence the strengthening of the already established linkage between the superego and a sense of guilt, to the neglect of equally important shame phenomena. We shall return to this point shortly.

During this period of Freud's work, that is, in the early decades of this century, the Gestalt psychologists, operating out of an epistemological tradition that permitted uncertainty about the materialist basis of nature and that fostered close attention to the details of direct experience, were exploring the relationship of the *self* to the field in which it operates and were discovering the modifications in the self that often accompany changing relationships between the self and its surroundings. In these investigations, an explicit and clear distinction between the self and the ego was made, and the phenomenological study of the self was one means of throwing light on the nature of the ego.

A full discussion of the distinction between the self and the ego is beyond the scope of this chapter. Allport (1943) described at least eight meanings of the term *ego*. As Chein (1944) has suggested, the term *ego* refers to an individual's on-going "motivational–cognitive structure built up around the self" (p. 314), while *self* refers to the experiencer of this structure. The self's experience occurs in all perceptual modalities and in at least three parameters: as a registration of identity, as a boundary between the self and others, and as a localization of the self in the field (Lewis, 1958).

Among the problems that Wertheimer (1912) posed was the question whether the ego is "egotistical" or whether it is a product of an interaction between it and the "field." Wertheimer undertook to explore this question by studying the way in which people determine the position of the upright in space. He observed that two sets of experiential factors normally come together to make it possible for us to determine with great accuracy how far "off" our bodies are from the true vertical, and how far objects in space are "off" from the vertical. Under ordinary circumstances, kinesthetic feedback from the pull of gravity on the body combines with the visual perception of the verticals and horizontals that constitute the framework, to give us a large fund of information on which to base our automatic and mostly accurate judgments of the position of objects and of the body in space. If the ego is "egotistical," Wertheimer argued, then postural cues from the body should be more powerful than the influence of the framework. If the ego is not "egotistical," then the influence of the framework should be a more compelling determinant of the perceived position of the self in space.

Wertheimer devised a method of separating "internal" from "external"— that is, postural (body) from visual (framework)—determinants, so that they functioned in opposite directions. This method required people to view objects through a mirror that tilted the reflected scene by as much as 45 degrees. Wertheimer reasoned that if the relationship between the self and the field were of importance in the perception of the upright, the objects reflected in the mirror should appear to right themselves and be undistorted in position because of the changed relationship of the self to the new frame work. If, on the other hand, the self or body alone was the reference point, the objects reflected in the mirror should remain tilted in their appearance.

With Wertheimer's arrival in this country as a refugee from Hitler and with his establishment at the University in Exile of the New School for Social Research, psychologists in this country picked up the problems Wertheimer had raised. Gibson and Mowrer (1938) attempted to replicate Wertheimer's observation that the objects in the tilted mirror righted themselves but found that, at least for their subjects, the objects remained tilted. Asch and Witkin (1948) and Witkin and Asch (1948) attempted to reconcile the discrepancy between Gibson and Mowrer's results and Wertheimer's. They developed new methods of separating the framework and the postural determinants of the upright in space. These included the development of a procedure in which persons in a darkened room assess the position of a luminous stick in a luminous tilted framework. Another method (Witkin, 1949) of separating the postural and framework determinants of the upright in space involved actually tilting the body as the person is seated in a small, lighted room, which also can be tilted. The results of these studies indicated that, on the average, the perception of the upright in space in determined by the relationship of the self to the surrounding framework, as Wertheimer had hypothesized.

In the course of work on these problems, Witkin observed not only that there were wide individual differences in the extent to which a person's judgment about himself or herself is influenced by the surrounding framework but also that there were strong individual consistencies in the extent to which persons were influenced by the framework. Witkin further observed that there were apparently congruent personality differences that accompanied these strong consistencies in the relationship of the self to the surrounding field. These early observations and hypotheses were systematically studied by a team of collaborators and published in *Personality through Perception* (Witkin, Lewis, Hertzman, Machover, Meissner, & Wapner, 1954), in a first statement of the large body of work on field dependence that has since developed.

In the course of my work on field dependence, it became apparent that the relation of the self to a transgression for which it is responsible (guilt) would be very different from the relation of the self to another person in unrequited love (shame). Some clinical observation of field-dependent and field-independent patients confirmed the usefulness of a phenomenological approach to the two affective states that constitute a person's superego: shame and guilt.

Studying neurotic patients with some of the insights gained in my work on field dependence suggested that differences in the way people determine the position of the self in the field reflect not only perceptual and cognitive style but important variables in patients' defensive style and in their relationship to significant others in their lives. In other clinical accounts of psychoanalytic work with neurotic patients (Lewis, 1958, 1959), I used field dependence as a "tracer element" for following characteristic behavior and transference phenomena during treatment. In particular, the patients' perceptual style focused attention on the manner and extent of individuation of the self from significant "others." A field-dependent patient was described as readily merging herself with the surround. She was self-effacing; when she was self-conscious, it was in an awkward and shy way. A field-independent patient, also a woman, was described as having an organized self that took the initiative in vigilantly defending her place in the field. Differences between field-dependent and field-independent patients were also traced in the organization of the self in dreams.

From observations on a child patient who "watched" me vigilantly and continuously, I suggested (Lewis, 1963) that shame functions particularly as a protection against the loss of self-boundaries that is implicit in absorbed sexual fantasy, that is, in states of longing-for-attachment experience. Shame functions as a sharp—in fact, painful—reminder that the fantasy experience of the "other" is vicarious. Shame brings into focal awareness both the self and the "other," with the imagery that the "other" rejects the self. It thus helps to maintain the sense of separate identity, by making the self the focus of experience. This notion about the function of shame is similar to Lynd's (1958 description of how shame can spur the sense of identity. It also parallels Erikson's (1956) observation that shame is the opposite of autonomy, but with the emendation that it is the opposite of the autonomy of the *self* rather than of the ego. This formulation, while recognizing the apparent "narcissism" in shame, regards this narcissism as a phenomenon in which the self is experienced "at the quick," while the person is maintaining affectional ties.

Making a link between characteristics of the self and characteristic functioning of the superego was one step in a line of reasoning that supposed that the superego functioned differently in field-dependent and field-independent patients. A field-dependent mode of superego functioning would be shame, while a field-independent mode would be guilt. Both modes of superego functioning represent an equally developed superego. Both modes could also be associated with an equally severe or malfunctioning superego.

An empirical study undertaken to check these predictions was able to confirm them (Witkin, Lewis, & Weil, 1968).[1] Patients selected on the basis of their perceptual style, and their figure drawings, were placed in individual psychotherapy in "pairs" of matched groups, a field-dependent and a field-independent patient each with the same therapist. Transcripts of their first two psychotherapy sessions were scored (by a "blind" judge) according to the method developed by Louis Gottschalk and his associates (Gottschalk & Gleser, 1969) for affect implied in verbal productions. As predicted, in the transcripts of field-dependent patients, there were significantly more references to anxiety of "shame, humiliation, embarrassment, ridicule and exposure of private details" than references to the anxiety of "guilt, fault, responsibility, being punished, scolded or abused," The converse was true for field-independent patients.

We also made predictions about the direction of hostility that would be found in the "pairs" of transcripts. These predictions were based both upon the nature of shame and guilt and upon what differences might be expected between field-dependent and field-independent patients. Specifically, we found that field-independent patients were more prone to direct their hostility both outward and inward, while field-dependent patients were more prone to self-directed hostility. There was some evidence that, regardless of patient type, shame tended to be found in association with self-directed hostility and that this association was particularly strong in field-dependent patients.

The success in predicting a connection between perceptual style and proneness to shame and guilt encouraged the formulation of the notion of a superego style, which, in turn, practically required a phenomenological analysis of the two states. As self-evident as such an undertaking is (with hindsight), it required both the needed correction of Freud's faulty concept of the ego and the instincts, and the concurrent development of a phenomenological mode of studying psychological and psychoanalytic problems.[2]

B. The Nature of Human Nature

Once attention is drawn to the phenomenology of shame and guilt, it is immediately apparent that shame is an even more neglected affect than guilt. The reasons can be traced to the dominance of an individualistic view of human nature. Hartmann's concept of an autonomous ego deepened psychoanalysis's commitment to an individualistic concept of human nature. The superego, like other psychic institutions, is understood to function in the service of the developing autonomy of the ego, with guilt its prevailing mode.

[1] This study was supported by Grants M–628 and MH 05518 from the National Institutes of Health, U.S. Public Health Service.
[2] Although I differ with existential psychoanalysts—for example, Binswanger (1958), in my adherence to a materialist view of nature, my work has grown out of some of the same roots.

As Tawney (1926) has shown, an emphasis on guilt is congenial to a competitive, individualistic (capitalist) society, which necessarily places a high premium on individualism and personal autonomy. Shame, in contrast, seems to be a more valued sanction in noncompetitive, "primitive" societies, such as the Zuni (Goldman, 1937) or the Arapesh (Mead, 1949), and in close-knit feudal systems, such as in precolonial Japan (Benedict, 1946).

As Turiel (1967) and Schafer (1960) have shown, Freud's early and more clinically derived conception of the superego included some of its "loving" functions. By the time of later metapsychological writings, only the superego's harsh, threatening aspect remained. This difference in emphasis derives from a neglect of the social nature of the species.

The fundamental question—whether the species is social or individualistic by nature—may now be discussed not only speculatively, as it has been throughout the centuries, but with reference to modern evidence both from anthropology and from psychology of infancy. Anthropologists, for example, point out (La Barre, 1954) that the principal evolutionary (genetic) change from lower primate to human life involves the emergence of human culture as our species's unique biological adaptation, with, as a concomitant, an enormous increase in the impact of nurturant social forces on human life.

Psychologists who study infancy are by no means agreed among themselves on the question of innate human sociability, but enough evidence has accumulated so that some of them have adopted the theoretical position that the human infant at birth is a social being. As the editors of *The Competent Infant* (Stone, Smith, & Murphy, 1973) put it, "Love is now an acceptable variable in the design of studies on infant behavior" (p. 6). Rheingold (1969), for example, works from the assumption that the infant is social by biological origin. This is not the place, nor do I have the expertise, to evaluate varying points of view among my colleagues engaged in the study of infancy, but Rheingold's position now has many adherents and can be found in many versions, most notably in the work of Bowlby (1969, 1973) and Ainsworth (1967). Hogan (1975), for example, has recently offered a theoretical paper in which he assembles some of the evidence for the sociocentric nature of human infants.

The way Freud's insights fit into these newer concepts of human infancy is itself a fascinating story, which includes numerous historical paradoxes. Freud had the inspired idea that disturbances in sexuality were at the root of neurotic symptoms. He therefore set out to study the functioning of the sex drive, including its development. In chosing sex as his focus, Freud concentrated on a uniquely social drive, the only drive that directly involves others in the individual's fulfillment. Freud recognized that sex is unlike hunger, thirst, and other tissue needs in that no individual ever dies for lack of sex. He thus recognized that sex was a social drive in the sense that it had to do with species preservation. Even more importantly, Freud recognized that the acculturation or socialization of each individual was embedded in infantile sexuality (the superego is rooted in the id). Freud caught the fact that sexuality and nurturant social behavior are intimately connected, that the origins of adult sexuality lie in the nurturance an infant receives, and reciprocally, that adult nurturant behavior has its origins in infantile sexuality. As Talcott Parsons (1958) points out, Freud's formulation that the ego is formed out of cathexes abandoned by the id assumes a very early "internalization" of others. Out of this earliest matrix of the infant–adult relationship each individual assimilates parental images and cultural values. Freud's theory has thus had enormous implications for the study of human culture in relation to personality.

Freud also recognized the individual assertiveness that sex shares with other more strictly self-preservative drives. [In recent years, for example, it has been suggested (Lichtenstein, 1970) that orgasm emotionally reaffirms the reality of the self.] Individualism was the quality that Freud emphasized in his formal statement of theory. As Holt (1972) has shown, Freud's formal theoretical statements were also modeled after concepts in physics and chemistry, in keeping with the 19th-century *Zeitgeist*.

Whatever his theoretical position with regard to human nature, Freud's hypothesis that neurosis was the result of faulty psychosexual development that began in infancy was a major spur to empirical studies of the mother–infant interaction. The Harlows' (1963) experiments on monkeys and Bowlby's ethological studies (1969, 1973) are only two examples. The Harlows' work required them to postulate the existence of an "affectional system" between mother and infant. Bowlby was also pushed by his observations to formulate the existence of a biologically given goal-corrected system of attachment between mother and infant. Bowlby's theory of infant–mother attachment as an affectional system implies mutual advantage and cooperative functioning between mother and infant. Mutually affectionate feelings of joy and security accompany attachment; sorrowful, angry, and frightened feelings accompany separation and detachment; and these feeling are biologically given to an innately social human being. As Bowlby (1973) has suggested, failure to conceptualize separation anxiety as a "given" concomitant of the attachment system has made it seem that it is "childish, even babyish, to yearn for the presence of a loved figure or to be distressed during her (or his) absence" (p. 80). Similarly, the affect of shame that arises out of "loss of love" is often regarded as an immature or pathological state instead of a normal and universal one.

A social theory of human nature brings with it the corollary assumption that the superego functions as a means of restoring lost affectional bonds. If the context of moral development is a biologically given affectional system, so that the culture's moral precepts are absorbed within an affectional framework, then shame and guilt may be recast as internalized controls not only for the sake of the individual's survival, but for the survival of his or her profoundest attachments. It is this characteristic that makes it possible for some people to sacrifice their lives in acts of principled heroism or martyrdom rather than betray their superego.

A social concept of human nature leaves room for a superego that adheres not only to an abstract sense of distributive justice but to a set of standards of personal dignity or worth that can symbolize a person's existence (Lynd, 1958), and the violation of which evokes shame. In contrast, and individualistic conception of human nature supposes that the superego evolves as a more-or-less painful internalization of the "social contract." The resulting value system has as its apex of development a system of abstract distributive justice (Kohlberg, 1968; Piaget, 1950), in which guilt is a higher-order affect than shame. This inferior status of shame has also tended to discourage phenomenological descriptions of it.

C. Shame and a Theory of Sex Differences

A brief look at Freud's treatment of the two sexes' superego development further clarifies how an individualistic concept of human nature and a male model of superego development, taken together, ignore shame. As is well known, Freud described superego evolution in terms of a male model: The superego arises out of the internalized castration threat, formed out of identification with the father. Freud had, of course, distinguished a second route of identification leading to superego formation: anaclitic identifications. These were thought to precede the defensive identifications formed under the castration threat. Anaclitic identifications also involve threat—but of a complicated punishment known as "loss of love": this loss of parental love becomes loss of "self-love" via loss of esteem in their eyes, that is, shame.

Anaclitic and defensive identifications are by no means mutually exclusive, and they are often difficult to distinguish from one another. Although castration anxiety operates as a threat of personal harm, its potency also derives from the fact that the threatening parent is beloved. Identifications set in motion by the fear of the parents may initiate and be superseded by identifications based upon admiration or love of them. This is, in fact, one of the ways in which masochistic persons remain unaware of the extent to which they fear and exaggerate their own moral failures.

Both males and females develop anaclitic identifications out of which shame arises. And anaclitic identifications—or "loving" identifications, as they are sometimes called—continue to develop throughout the individual's childhood. But because anaclitic identifications begin early in relation to mother, and because males must renounce some of their feminine identifications (while females need not), androcentric thinking automatically assigned shame an inferior place to guilt in a hierarchy of controls. Shame is still conceptualized in modern psychoanalytic writings as a "flooding of the ego with unneutralized exhibitionism" (Kohut, 1971, p. 181), instead of as a complicated superego state in which the self images itself vicariously, that is, in the eyes of the "others."

By assuming that the castration threat and the threat of "loss of love" are equally advanced developmentally, it is possible not only to conceptualize shame and guilt as different modes of the superego but to see how men and women might differ in their prevailing superego mode. Specifically, women, on the basis of their unchanging anaclitic identifications, should be more prone to shame than men. This hypothesis, in turn, calls for a phenomenological description of both shame and guilt.

II. DISTINCTIONS BETWEEN SHAME AND GUILT

I turn now to the phenomenology of shame and guilt and to sequences in which the two superego states lead to different paths of symptom formation. My underlying premise is that symptom formation occurs when *both* shame and guilt cannot be discharged. The state that is to the forefront of the person's experience is one determinant of whether symptoms of depression/hysteria or obsession/paranoia will appear.

Let us first examine the affective states of shame and guilt with respect to the position of the self in the field. Three parameters of the concept of the self are involved in this comparison: the self as registration of identity; the self as comprising the boundaries of experience; and the self as a set of localization experiences.

The self is, first of all, the experiential registration of a "center" by means of which the person's activities are his or her "own." This registration may—in fact, most often does—occur automatically, that is, without the person's awareness of a central registration mechanism. Instances of the failure of automatic registration (such as depersonalization and estrangement) and instances of "inappropriate continued registration (such as occur in "phantom limb" experiences) make clear by contrast how much of the central registration we take for granted. Shame and guilt are automatically registered as one's own experiences (except in the case of psychotic "projection") and in this respect are not intrinsically different from each other.

Shame, however, involves more self-consciousness and more self-imaging than guilt. The experience of shame is directly about the *self*, which is the focus of a negative evaluation. In guilt, the self is not the *direct* object of negative evaluation; rather, the *thing* done (or not done) is the focus of experience. Since the self is the focus of awareness in shame, "identity" imagery is usually evoked. At the same time, however, this identity imagery is also registering as one's own experience, creating a "doubleness of experience" that is characteristic of shame. This "double" experience in shame is a frequent basis for what Freud called the "internal theater" of fantasy that is so characteristic of hysterical patients.

The boundaries of the self describe the extent to which one is engaging in vicarious experience. The self often takes the place of another, especially when the two people are emotionally close. Even when they are not, the self may function vicariously. In experiments involving the Zeignarik effect, it could be demonstrated that when people were working cooperatively, there was no difference in recall between those tasks personally completed and those actually completed by the cooperating partner (Lewis, 1944; Lewis & Franklin, 1944). These results suggested that the person had vicarious closure even when not the sole agent of task completion.

Shame is the self's vicarious experience of the other's negative evaluation. In order for shame to occur, there must be a relationship between the self and the other in which the self "cares" about the other's evaluation. This is a particularly important point since shame is often given its narrowest meaning of either the "fear of getting caught" or else a "narcissistic" reaction.

The self is a perceptual product. It arises out of feedback from all sensory modalities. Kinesthetic and proprioceptive feedback may be regarded as the most primitive and least articulated sources of the self; visual and auditory modalities can be more highly articulated. Specifically, we may compare the "me" concept of the self, which depends on relatively mute and unarticulated feedback, with the "I" concept of self, which may be embellished into a highly verbal and visually articulated concept. The self organizes itself out of a field of "body" and "distance" experiences and ordinarily involves a fusion of the "me" and the "I" concepts of the self. Shame, which involves more self-consciousness and self-imaging, is likely to involve an increase in feedback from all perceptual modalities. It has a special affinity for stirring autonomic reactions, including blushing, sweating, and increased heart rate. Shame usually involves greater body awareness than guilt, as well as visual and verbal imaging of the "me" from the "other's" point of view. A "distancing" activity can also occur, in which the self images itself from the "other's" point of view, without autonomic stirrings. This distancing may be provisionally classified as affectless shame in the sense that it is a relatively disembodied experience. Ordinarily, however, the self is the focus of a variety of noxious stimuli that catch the self "at the quick" and can be experienced as paralyzing the self. This special position of the self as the target of attack makes shame a more acutely painful experience than guilt.

There are intrinsic characteristics of the two superego states that impede their discharge. Difficulties in coping with—that is, discharging—shame and guilt may be grouped under three main headings.

A. Difficulties in Recognizing One's Psychological State: Shame and Guilt Are Often Fused and Therefore Confused

Shame and guilt may both be simultaneously evoked by a moral transgression. The two states then tend to fuse under the heading of guilt. [The dictionary confirms this observation by terming *shame* an acute or "emotional" sense of guilt (Lewis, 1971).] But shame of one*self* is likely to be operating underneath guilt for transgression.

The self-reproaches that are likely to be formed as guilty ideation develops might run as follows: How could I have *done that?* What an injurious *thing* to have done! How I *hurt so-and-so!* What a moral lapse that *act* was! What will become of *that* or of *him* now that I have neglected *to do it* or have injured *him*? How should I be *punished* or *make amends*? Mea culpa! Simultaneously, ashamed ideation says: How could *I* have done that? What an *idiot I am*—how humiliating! What a *fool*, what an *uncontrolled person*—how mortifying, how unlike so-and-so, who does not do such things! *How awful and worthless I am*! Shame! Since, in this kind of instance, the ideation of being ashamed of oneself is the same as that of guilty self-reproach, the shame component, although an acute affect, is buried in the guilty ideation. A current of aggression, however, has been activated against the whole self, in both one's own and the "other's" eyes. This current of shame can keep both guilty ideation and shame affect active even after appropriate amends have been made.

B. The Stimulus to Shame Is Twofold: Moral and "Nonmoral" Shame

Shame may be evoked in connection with guilt, as an acute form of it, or it may be evoked by competitive defeat, a sexual rebuff, a social snub, invasion of personal privacy, or being ridiculed. Ausubel (1955) has drawn attention to the twofold stimulus evoking shame, distinguishing between moral and "nonmoral" shame. When nonmoral shame is evoked, it readily connects with moral shame. For example, under the press of shame for competitive defeat or a sexual rebuff, one can begin an immediate search for moral lapses or transgressions that make sense of the injury one has suffered. Conversely, as we have seen in the preceding example, moral shame is difficult to distinguish from guilty ideation. Thus, shame has a potential for a wide range of associative connections between transgressions and failures of the self and for "stimulus generalizations," so that shame for defeat or a snub evokes guilt for transgression. Shame and guilt states are thus easily confused with one another by the experiencing person, although an observer may have a clearer view of the affects.

One question that arose in our therapy study (Witkin *et al.*, 1968) was whether there would be such great overlap between shame and guilt that the two states would not be distinguishable in our transcripts. This turned out not to be the case: in only a small minority (16.1%) of the "spurts" of shame and guilt did we find them both in the same 500-word unit. It thus appears that the person experiencing shame and guilt is likely to confuse them but that a microscopic analysis of verbal content shows them appearing at different moments.

There are many varieties of shame phenomena. As mentioned earlier, mortification, humiliation, embarrassment, feeling ridiculous, chagrin, shyness, and modesty are all different psychological states, but with the common property of overtly involving the "other" as referent and as being about self. As a beginning of the study of these states, I treated them as variants of the shame family and attempted to understand the variations as differences in the admixtures of pride and of hostility directed against the self, as well as differences in the position of the self vis-à-vis the "other." Mortification, for example, has the element of wounded pride and involves the self in a relatively distant or indirect relationship to the "other." Humiliation is experienced either in one's own or in the "other's" eyes and can involve rapid shifts of position of the self from the active to the passive mode of reaction. Embarrassment, to take another example, involves the self in a feeling of temporary paralysis or "loss of powers" in relation to the "other." Each of these shame variants can be discharged in good-humored laughter if the state is operating without too much underlying guilt.

C. Difficulties in the Functioning of the Self in Shame and Guilt

Shame is about the self; we say, "I am ashamed of myself." Guilt, in contrast is about *things* done or undone. Shame is evoked by failure of the self to live up to an ego ideal (Piers & Singer, 1953). An ego ideal is difficult to spell out rationally; shame can thus be a subjective, "irrational" reaction. Adults particularly regard shame as an "irrational" reaction, which is more appropriate to childhood, especially if it occurs outside the context of moral transgression.

In shame, there is what Laing (1960) calls an implosion of the self. The body gestures and attitudes include head bowed, eyes closed, body curved in on itself, making the person as small as possible. At the same time that it seeks to disappear, the self may be dealing with an excess of autonomic stimulation, blushing, or sweating or diffuse rage, experienced as a "flood" of sensations. Shame is thus regarded by adults as a reaction in which body functions have gone out of control. It is also regarded as an irrational reaction for this reason.

Except for ideation that is often identical with that of guilt, shame is a relatively wordless state. The experience of shame often occurs in the form of imagery, of looking or being looked at. Shame may also be played out in imagery of an internal colloquy, in which the whole self is condemned by the "other." There is, however, a relatively limited vocabulary of scorn. The wordlessness of shame and its imagery of looking, together with the concreteness of autonomic activity, make shame a primitive, "irrational" reaction, to which there is difficulty in applying a rational solution. One is often ashamed of being or having been ashamed. Shame thus compounds itself out of an intrinsic difficulty in finding a "rational" place for itself in the adult's psychic life.

So, for example, a (field-dependent) patient puts her dilemma this way (the patient has entered treatment because she has a facial tic or "twitches"):

P: (laughs): I think I'd be interested in—well, I—think if I could get rid of the twitches, I'd get rid of the feelings that go with it, you know. But uh I guess if I had these things and I didn't care whether I had them or not, I guess it wouldn't matter either. I don't know (slight laugh). But I don't see how I couldn't care . . . you know?

The patient is clearly aware that if she didn't *care* about having tics, that is, if she were not ashamed of them, she would be better off. But she doesn't see how she could manage not to be ashamed of them. Rationally, she is quite aware of the fact that she really need not be ashamed of them but also aware that her feelings are not so easily persuaded. The patient is thus expressing a frequent dilemma in shame reactions: they occur in spite of one's better judgment and compound themselves by making us ashamed that we are ashamed.

Perhaps because it feels like so primitive and "irrational" a state, shame is connected with a specific defense of hiding or running away. It is a state in which the mechanism of denial seems particularly to occur. Denial makes shame difficult for the person experiencing it to identify, even though there is a strong affective reaction. The person often does not know what has hit him or her.

The same patient comments in retrospect on her first session (with a male therapist):

P: (slight laugh): Last time, uh, when I first came in, I was uhm and I started talking to you, I was upset, but I didn't know why, therefore, I really didn't mention it because I felt ridiculous. There was no reason.

The patient clearly is aware that she felt ridiculous (ashamed) because she was on the verge of tears. But she also is trying to say that something about talking to the therapist evoked a threat of tears. This unknown threat might well be the feeling of humiliation that is evoked by being a patient—in this instance, a female patient in treatment with a male therapist.

This excerpt also illustrates the affinity between shame and diffuse anxiety. Since the target of hostility in shame is the self, and the self is not an easily specifiable object, shame is experienced as tension or diffuse anxiety (or being on the verge of tears) but not knowing about what.

Another kind of defense against shame appears to operate before any affective state is evoked. This defense, which is best described as "bypassing" shame feeling, does not obliterate the recognition of shame events but appears to prevent the development of shame feeling. This bypassing of shame is accomplished by a "distancing" maneuver. The self views itself from the standpoint of the "other," but without much affect. The person wonders what he would think of himself if he were in the position of the "other." The content of the ideation in question concerns shame events, but without shame affect. Shame affect is bypassed and replaced by watching the self from a variety of viewpoints, including that of the "other." The following excerpt from the transcript of a (field-independent) male patient who is shortly going to talk about masturbation (to a female therapist) illustrates the phenomenon of by-passing shame. The excerpt begins after a long pause:

T: What are you thinking?

P: I don't know. I have this feeling that there's something (mm, mm) I felt myself almost wince a second ago, and I was trying to think of what it is that I'm, you know. I was also thinking of what I would do if I were the therapist . . . and I had a patient facing me (mm) and uh just what significance I would give to each of his movements and the like. This is something that uh I didn't think about to my knowledge for some time—this is what would I do if I were the other (inaudible).

The patient has clearly shifted the position of the self into the position of the observer in an effort to ward off shame feeling. The primary-process nature of his ideation is subtly expressed in his wondering what significance the observer would give to each of his "movements." Our knowledge that the patient is caught in a state of shame about masturbation makes his use of the term *movements* interpretable as a "concrete" (primary-process) outcome of the conflict in which he is caught. The shift in position of the self into the position of the observer who observes the self also illustrates the "doubleness" of shame experience and its affinity for the development of "scenes in an internal theater" (Breuer & Freud, 1893), in which the self and the other play out their roles.

Guilt, in contrast, is about *things*—acts or failures to act, or thoughts—for which one bears responsibility. It is often difficult, however, to assess the degree of one's responsibility or to assess the extent of the injury that one has caused. It is also difficult to assess what reparation or amends one owes to balance the scales of justice. It is difficult, further, to assess the extent of the punishment that one ought to bear in retribution for one's guilty conduct. An "objective" assessment of the extent of responsibility and of punishment seems to exist and require adherence. Heider (1958) has investigated the phenomenology of guilt and punishment. He describes punishment (p. 27) as "P harming O because O harmed P or acted against the *objective order* as P understands it" (italics added).

When guilt is evoked, it can merge into a "problem" in the rational assignment of motivation, responsibility, and consequences. As the guilty person becomes involved in these problems, it can happen that guilty affect subsides, while ideation about the events continues. Guilt thus has an affinity for "isolation of affect," leaving a residuum of "insoluble dilemma" or worry thoughts, but without the person's being necessarily aware that he or she is in a state of guilt.

The objective character of guilt and the affinity between it and the rational assignment of responsibility can result in the person's becoming very busy in making amends for his guilt or in an insoluble dilemma of thought a-bout his guilt. The self is active in this pursuit. It is intact and self-propelled, in contrast to the self's divided functioning in shame.

The unconscious gratification of being in a morally elevated state also sometimes keeps the state of guilt active beyond the time of expiation. "He who despises himself, "wrote Nietzsche (1937), "thereby esteems himself as the despiser. . . . When we train our conscience, it kisses as it bites." The self, then, may be caught in its own unconscious pride in being guilty, thus prolonging guilt rather than discharging it.

D. Difficulties in Discharging Hostility in Shame and Guilt: Shame–Rage, Which Originates about the Self, Is Discharged upon the Self

Whether it is evoked on the context of moral transgression or outside it, shame involves a *failure* by comparison with an internalized ego-ideal. There is thus an implied framework of negative comparison with others. In the painful experience of being unable to live up to the standards of an admired "image," attention is often focused on the "other," admired figure. Fascination with the "other" and sensitivity to the "other's" treatment of the self can ease the acute feeling of shame, while at the same time it renders the self still more vulnerable to shame. Shame is close to the feeling of awe. It is the feeling state to which one is more susceptible when one has fallen in love. The "other" is a prominent and powerful force in the experience of shame.

In shame, hostility against the self is experienced in the passive mode. The self feels not "in control" but overwhelmed and paralyzed by the hostility directed against it. One could "crawl through a hole" or "sink through the floor" or "die" with shame. The self feels small, helpless, and childish. When, for example, there is unrequited love, the self feels crushed by the rejection. So long as shame is experienced, it is the "other" who is experienced as the source of hostility. Hostility against the rejecting "other" is almost simultaneously evoked. But it is humiliated fury, or shame–rage, and the self is still in part experienced as the object of the "other's" scorn. Hostility aginst the "other" is trapped in this directional bind. To be furious and enraged with someone because one is unloved by him renders one easily and simultaneously guilty for being furious. Evoked hostility is readily redirected back against the vulnerable self.

For shame to occur, there must be an emotional relationship between the person and the "other," so that one cares what the other thinks or feels about oneself. In this affective tie, the self does not feel autonomous or independent but dependent and vulnerable to rejection. Shame is a vicarious experience of the significant other's scorn. A "righting" tendency often evoked by shame is the turning of the tables." Evoked hostility presses toward triumph over humiliation of the "other," that is, toward the vicarious experience of the other's shame. But the "other" may be simultaneously beloved or admired, so that guilt is evoked for aggressive wishes. Or the image of the "other" may be devalued, but in this case, one has lost an admired or beloved object. Shame-based rage is readily turned back against the self, both because the self is in a passive position vis-à-vis the "other" and because the self values the "other."

A prediction that results from this phenomenological analysis is that there should be a particularly strong association between shame and self-directed hostility. This prediction was confirmed in our therapy study (Witkin et al., 1968) and in two recent dissertations (Smith, 1972; Safer, 1975).

The position of the self as the initiator of guilt and the determiner or judge of the extent of responsibility puts the self "in charge" of the hostility directed against the self. It also puts the self in charge of the distribution of hostility, as well as the assessment of the happenings in the field. This active role of the self in guilt opens the possibility that hostility may be directed not only against the self but against the "other" and other forces in the field, thus creating an affinity between guilt and projection of hostility.

The prediction resulting from this phenomenological analysis is that there should be a tendency for guilt to be accompanied by hostility directed out as well as hostility directed against the self. Our therapy study (Witkin et al., 1968) showed a clear association between guilt and hostility going in both directions, in contrast to the close association between shame and self-directed hostility.

III. EVIDENCE FOR A CONNECTION BETWEEN SHAME AND DEPRESSION

A. Phenomenological Similarity between Shame and Depression/Hysterias

Once the phenomenological distinctions between shame and guilt have been made, it becomes apparent that shame and depression have many overlapping characteristics. Since *Mourning and Melancholia* (Freud, 1915), clinical literature has assumed that depression is a product of unconscious guilt. The endless self-reproaches of depressed patients have made this connection eminently plausible. I am suggesting, however, that shame is the superego state that is to the forefront in depression. It is the self that is the focal target of hostility in depression, as it is in shame. A number of established clinical features of depression can be understood as the resultants of shame. Izard (1972) specifically includes shame in his differential emotion theory of depression. He found shame or shyness elevated in the emotion profiles of hospitalized depressed patients and in depressed outpatients in psychotherapy. An empirical comparison of the emotion profiles of depressed patients and high school students recalling and imaging an experience of depression showed that the greatest difference between the two groups was on shyness, with the depressed patients having significantly higher scores. Izard interprets these findings as support for the importance of shame in depression.

This is not to imply that guilt plays no role in depression. Blatt, (1974) for example, has found it necessary to differentiate between "anaclitic" and "introjective" depression, a distinction that has many similarities to the distinction between shame and guilt. It may be that there are different varieties of depressive experience, in which shame and guilt occur in different proportions.

In his classical comparison between depression and actual mourning for a lost person, Freud pinpointed the ambivalent nature of the depressed person's loving feelings. In depression, unconscious hatred of a beloved person has caused the psychic "loss." Out of unconscious guilt for this unconscious hatred, the depressed person "introjects" the "other" (thus reconstituting affectional bonds), but with a resulting experience in which a "shadow" falls upon the self. Hatred unconsciously meant for the introjected other is redirected against the self and appears to come from the "other." In this classical description, the introjection of the "other" into the self is a metaphor for the self's vicarious experience of the "other's" hatred, an experience that is the hallmark of shame.

Beck's (1967) study of the masochistic content of depressed patients' dreams showed the depressed patients as the "recipients of rejection, disappointment, of humiliation, or other similar circumstances" (p. 217), Beck has also called attention to the negative expectations that characterize depressed people's cognitions. Depressed people have a negative self-image that adds up to an image of helplessness. This characteristic self-image is the same as the experience of the self in shame: the self is unable, helpless, powerless.

Of particular interest is the paradox in depression (Abramson & Sackheim, 1977) that depressed people feel helpless to affect their destiny at the same time that their (helpless) self seems to them the appropriate target of hostility. If they are, indeed, as helpless as they feel, logic dictates that they should not feel responsible (guilty) for what they are incapable of. The paradox in depression may be solved if one realizes that depressed people are experiencing two simultaneous characteristics of shame: hatred of the (deficient) self, which is focal in awareness, and the helplessness of the self to change the vicarious experience of the "other's" feeling.

A recent dissertation offers some empirical evidence for the connection between shame and depression (Smith, 1972). Seventy persons, forty men and thirty women, with a mean age of 31 years, all patients at a pastoral counseling center, were studied. Shame and guilt proneness were assessed by using an early-memories test and a shame–guilt test. As predicted, patients who were relatively shame-prone were more likely to be suffering from depression. This result held for both sexes and was stronger for women. In addition, as predicted, shame-prone patients showed significantly more self-directed hostility.

There is only one empirical study that I know of that links shame and the hysterias. But the central phenomenological characteristic of shame—that it involves the image of the self in the eyes of the "other"—makes it seem likely that shame is the spur to the "private theater" that is so often played out in hysterical symptoms. I have traced sequences from shame into "scenes" in microscopic analyses of therapy transcripts (Lewis, 1971). In the classic cases of hysteria reported by Breuer and Freud (1893), the major hidden theme was the shame of unrequited love. Smith (1972) predicted and confirmed that depressed patients high on shame were more likely to be hysterical (while depressed patients high on guilt were more likely to be obsessive). Further empirical studies are needed that will confirm or disconfirm the prediction that hysterical patients are particularly shame-prone.

B. Field Dependence and Depression/Hysterias

Depressives have been described as being "overinvolved" with others (Freud, 1915; Fromm-Reichmann, 1959; Lewis, 1958; Weissman & Paykel, 1974). In addition to this general clinical description, there is empirical evidence of a connection between depression and field dependence (Witkin, 1965; Levenson & Neuringer, 1974). Of particular interest is the finding (Levenson et al., 1974) that male psychiatric patients ($N = 84$) who committed suicide were more field-dependent than a matched group ($N = 84$) of nonsuicidal patients. Scores on the picture-completion, object-assembly, and block-design subtests of the WAIS (which correlate highly with the rod-and-frame and embedded-figures test) were used as the measure of field dependence. The patients who committed suicide had significantly lower scores on the WAIS subtests (although they actually had somewhat higher IQ scores and had achieved a slightly higher level of eduction). Levenson et al. (1974) interpret their finding as indicating that a person who commits suicide has a cognitive style that lacks the "problem-solving processes to reorient his relationship to his environment" (p. 184). This formulation, which is similar to Beck's formulation of the cognitive deficit in depression, is also congruent with the idea that depression reflects the helplessness of shame.

There is also empirical evidence for a connection between field dependence and hysteria (Witkin, 1965). Further evidence on this point is much needed.

IV. SEX DIFFERENCES IN SHAME AND IN DEPRESSION/HYSTERIAS

A network of evidence exists that links depression and the hysterias with field dependence, shame, and sex differences. Pursuing the question of sex differences in psychiatric illness and in cognitive style suggests that sex differences in shame-proneness may be a mediating variable (Lewis, 1976). Let us consider, first, some *a priori* considerations that suggest that women are more prone to shame than men.

A. Sex Differences in Proneness to Shame

That women are more prone to shame than men is a long-standing and widespread observation. Darwin (1872), for example, observed that "women blush much more than men" (p. 311). Two major factors join in fostering women's greater shame-proneness. First, the anaclitic identifications made by girls growing up in the nuclear family remain central in women's personality (Sears, Rau, & Alpert, 1965); these loving identifications continue the threat of "loss of love" or shame into women's adulthood. Women, for example, show more anxiety over "loss of love," while there is a tendency for men to show more "castration anxiety" (Bradford, 1968). Even in their symbolic conceptions of the Deity, as reflected in Rorschach responses, fear of God is more characteristic of men, while more benevolent representations of the Deity are more characteristic of women (Larson & Knapp, 1964).

Second, the widespread exclusion of women from positions of power in work fosters a culturally sanctioned adjustment in women's position of economic dependency and devotion to the family. Men, in contrast, are pressed into aggressive, independent behavior in order to meet their responsibility for a livelihood within a competitive economic system. Women's position of economic and social inferiority provides an objective basis for feelings of inferiority that induce shame; men's greater aggressiveness involves them more in guilt.

Evidence is strong and conclusive that men are more aggressive than women (Maccoby, 1966; Maccoby & Jacklin, 1974). Women's lesser aggressivity alone predicts their greater proneness to self-directed hositlity and shame. The direct evidence for women's greater sociability than men is less clear-cut, but on balance it appears that women are more "nurturant" and "positive" in their attitudes toward "others" than men. In a total of 47 studies (Maccoby, 1966) of "interest in and positive feeling for others," "need for affiliation," and "nurturance," women and girls were reported as showing more positive attitudes than men and boys in all but five studies. (In these five, there was no sex difference.) In their recent survey, Maccoby and Jacklin (1974) have labeled as myth the idea that girls have a greater capacity for social behavior than boys. But the evidence they present that girls and women are more sociable than men and boys is still strong. For example, girls are more motivated by "social goals"; boys are more motivated when the circumstances are competitive; girls' friendships are more intimate, boys' are more gregarious and aggressive, involving gangs; women's ego investment is more affiliative, men's more involved in status and power. Leaving aside the question of whether women's greater sociability is the result of biological role or cultural expectations, positive feelings for "others" find a more significant role in the life experience of women than of men. If women "care more" about "others," the "others" are for this reason alone able to make women ashamed (in their own and "others'" eyes).

Empirical studies that directly approach the question of superego sex differences are pitifully few. Gleser, Gottschalk, and Springer (1961) have evidence that women showed more shame anxiety than men in a five-minute verbal sample. Yale undergraduate women showed more shame than guilt in a Gottschalk and Gleser (1969) five-minute verbal sample; men showed more guilt than shame (Wolf, 1975).

Siebert (1965) compared 100 men and 100 women undergraduates, using a variety of paper-and-pencil tests to assess their experience of the superego and the ego ideal. In response to a question about how they manage when confronting temptation, women were more concerned with the opinions of significant others, while men experienced guilt as a more internalized force. When using metaphors to describe their conscience experiences, men used animal and natural force symbols to express the power of conscience, while women used more human symbolic representations. These findings suggest that women's conscience is a more personalized experience, while men's is more impersonal. In another study of sex difference in proneness to shame and guilt, Binder (1970) found that women are more shame-prone, while men are more guilt-prone, as measured by an assessment of early memories. Smith (1972), however, failed to obtain a significant sex difference in scores on either the shame–guilt test or the early-memories test. The question of women's greater proneness to shame clearly needs empirical work.

B. Sex Differences in Proneness to Depression

The evidence is strong and unequivocal that women are more prone to depression than men (Lewis, 1976, 1977), whether the data are obtained from state hospitals, private hospitals, outpatient clinics, or rural or urban areas, and "whether it is the feeling of depression, neurotic depression, or depressive psychosis" (Silverman, 1968, p. 73). Depression also seems to be more severe in women (Beck, 1967; Blaser, Löw, & Schäublin, 1968; Sedivec, 1969; Davis, Lamberti, & Ajans, 1969).

Depression cuts across class lines (Silverman, 1968), and women's greater proneness to depression than men's also cuts across class lines (Weissman & Paykel, 1974). This finding is in sharp contrast to those for schizophrenia and to the rates for male psychotics, which are strongly associated with poverty and social disorganization (Faris & Dunham, 1939; Hollingshead & Redlich, 1958; Dohrenwend & Dohrenwend, 1969; Levy & Rowitz, 1973). This contrast between depression and schizophrenia can be understood as reflecting men's direct participation in competitive economic struggles, as compared with women's relative exclusion from the world of work (Cohen, 1961).

There is some relationship between depression and high social class; that is, more depression has sometimes (not always) been reported from the more affluent classes (Silverman, 1968). This may be because more affluent women have the leisure in which to cultivate ideals of devotion to others. Ethnic groups among whom women's devotion to the family is an ideal might be expected to show more depression than ethinic groups with a less strong tradition for women. Bart (1971) predicted and confirmed that depression in middle-aged women is more frequent among "Jewish mothers" than among other women, on the basis of a strong Jewish tradition of women's devotion to the family. Along with their exclusion from economic independence, women's biocultural role involves them more directly than men in nurturant roles within the family, at the risk of the shame of "loss of love" when the "nest is empty."

C. Sex Differences in Proneness to the Hysterias

The evidence, although not so plentiful as in the case of depression, is unequivocal that women are more prone both to conversion hysteria and to anxiety hysteria than men (Lewis, 1976). The classical description of hysterical women as suffering from repressed sexual longings and as "histrionic"—that is, overinvolved in the impression they are making on others—can still be found in a modern psychiatric handbook (Abse, 1974). Conversion hysteria, however, is no longer the lot of middle-and upper-class (Viennese) women. In modern times, with the spread of sexual enlightenment, hysteria has become the more frequent lot of poor, uneducated, rural women, who have no other "vocabulary of discomfort" (Bart, 1968). Bart's finding parallels Kinsey, Pomeroy, Martin, and Gebhard's (1973) and Rainwater's (1969) finding that lower-class women report less frequent sexual gratification than their more affluent and better-educated sisters. Overall, the suggested connection between hysterias and shame, like the connection between depression and shame, may help to make sense of the established sex differences in proneness to these two forms of psychiatric illness.

As I have shown in *Shame and Guilt in Neurosis* (Lewis, 1971), reanalysis of Freud's cases from the point of view of undischarged shame and guilt clearly supports the connection between shame and depression/hysteria and between guilt and obsessional neurosis. For example, the Rat-Man opened his analysis by describing his chronic state of guilt. The small fragment of a practically verbatim account of conversation with Lucy R., who was depressed and suffering from rhinitis, was about being hopelessly in love with her employer. It reads as follows (Breuer & Freud, 1893, p. 117):

> "Were you ashamed of loving a man?" Freud asked. "No" came the answer from Lucy. "I'm not unreasonably prudish. We are not responsible for our feelings.

But," she went on, "it was so distressing to me because he is my employer and I am in service and live in his house. I don't feel the same complete independence toward him that I could toward anyone else. I am a poor girl and he is a rich man. People would laugh at me if they had any idea of it."

Lucy says that she is not ashamed and not guilty—as indeed in reason she need not be. She characteristically denies shame as we all automatically do. But she goes on to recite in detail the state of shame that results from an inequality of status. The Gottschalk–Gleser scoring of Lucy's description of her feelings would rate high shame-scores, especially for the last sentence.

Dora, similarly, was in a state that Freud (1905) described as "mortification" at her father's betrayal of her. But neither Freud nor Dora had room in their cognitive systems for the humiliated fury that accompanies mortification at personal betrayal. Both agreed that her rage was "exaggerated," since neither her father nor Herr K. "had made a formal agreement in which she was the object of barter" (Freud, 1905, p. 34). In this system, which Dora and Freud shared, the shame of personal betrayal is, by implication, not of the same status as guilt for breaking a contract. And indeed shame is "subjective" (i.e., only about the self), whereas guilt is "objective" (i.e., about events or things in the world). It is my hope that the microscopic analysis of sequences from shame into depression and hysterical symptoms that occupies a good portion of *Shame and Guilt in Neurosis* (Lewis, 1971) will lead both clinicians and researchers into further, much-needed studies of the role of shame in these two disorders.

REFERENCES

Abramson, L. Y., & Sackheim, H. A. A paradox in depression: Uncontrollability and self-blame. *Psychological Bulletin*, 1977, *84*, 838–851.

Abse, W. Hysterical conversations and dissociative syndromes and the hysterical character. In S. Arieti (Ed.), *American handbook of Psychiatry* (2nd ed.). New York: Basic Books, 1974.

Ainsworth, M. *Infancy in Uganda*. Baltimore: Johns Hopkins Press, 1967.

Allport, G. The ego in contemporary psychology. *Psychological Review*, 1943, *50*, 451–478.

Asch, S., & Witkin, H. Studies in space orientation. I & II. *Journal of Experimental Psychology*, 1948, *38*, 325–337; 455–477.

Ausubel, D. Relationships between shame and guilt in the socializing process. Psychological Review, 1955, *62*, 378–390.

Bart, P. Social structure and the vocabularies of discomfort: What happened to female hysteria? *Journal of Health and Social Behavior*, 1968, *9*, 188–193.

Bart, P. Depression in middle-aged women. In V. Gormick & B. Moran (Eds.), *Women in sexist society*. New York: New American Library, 1971.

Beck, A. *Depression: Clinical, experimental, and theoretical aspects*. New York: Harper & Row, 1967.

Benedict, R. *The chrysanthemum and the sword*. Cambridge, Mass.: Houghton Mifflin, 1946.

Binder, J. The relative proneness to shame or guilt as a dimension of character style. Unpublished dissertation, Universtiy of Michigan, 1970.

Binswanger, L. The case of Ellen West. In R. May, E. Angel, & H. Ellenberger. *Existence—A new dimension in psychiatry*. New York: Basic Books, 1958.

Blaser, P., Löw, D. & Schäublin, A. Die Messung der Depressionstyle mit einem Fragebogen. *Psychiatrica Clinica*, 1968, *1*, 299–319 (Abstract).

Blatt, S. Levels of object representation in anaclitic and introjective depression. *Psychoanalytic Study of the Child*, 1974, *29*, 107–157.

Bowlby, J. *Attachment and loss*, Vols. 1 and 2. New York: Basic Books, 1969, 1973.

Breuer, J., & Freud, S. (1893). *Studies on hysteria*. In J. Strachey (Ed.), *Standard Edition of the Complete Psychological Works of Sigmund Freud*. London: Hogarth, 1955.

Buber, M. Guilt and guilt feelings. *Psychiatry*, 1957, *20*, 114–129.

Chein, I. The awareness of the self and the structure of the ego. *Psychological Review*, 1944, *51*, 304–314.

Cohen, Y. *Social structure and personality*. New York: Holt, Rinehart and Winston, 1961.

Darwin, C. *The expression of the emotions in man and animals*. London: John Murray, 1872.

Davis, D., Lamberti, J., & Ajans, Z. Crying in depression. *British Journal of Psychiatry*, 1969, *115*, 597–598.

Dohrenwend, B., & Dohrenwend, B. *Social status and psychological disorders: A causal inquiry*. New York: Wiley-Interscience, 1969.

Engel, G. the need for a new medical model: A challenge for biomedicine. *Science*, 1977, *196*, 129–136.

English, H. B. & English, A. C. *A comprehensive dictionary of psychological and psychoanalytic terms*. New York: David McKay, 1958.

Erikson, E. Identity and the life cycle. *Journal of the American Psychoanalytic Association*. 1956, *4*, 56–121.

Faris, R., & Dunham, H. *Mental disorders in urban areas*. Chicago: University of Chicago Press, 1939.

Freud, S. The interpretation of dreams (1900). In J. Strachey (Ed.), *Standard edition of the complete psychological works of Sigmund Freud*, Vols. 4 & 5. London: Hogarth Press, 1953.

Freud, S. Fragment of an analysis of a case of hysteria (1905). In J. Strachey (Ed.), *Standard edition of the complete psychological works of Sigmund Freud* Vol. 7. London: Hogarth Press, 1955.

Freud, S. *Beyond the pleasure-principle* (1920). In J. Strachey (Ed.), *Standard edition of the complete psychological works of Sigmund Freud*, Vol. 18. London, Hogarth Press, 1955.

Freud, S. *Mourning and melancholia* (1915). In J. Strachey (Ed.), *Standard edition of the complete psychological works of Sigmund Freud*, Vol. 14. London: Hogarth Press, 1957, pp. 159–204.

Fromm, E. *The forgotten language*. New York: Grove Press, 1951.

Fromm-Reichmann, F. *Personality and psychotherapy*, D. Bullard, (Ed.). Chicago: University of Chicago Press, 1959.

Gibson, J. & Mowrer, O. H. Determinants of the perceived vertical and horizontal. *Psychological Review*, 1938, *45*, 300–323.

Gleser, G., Gottschalk, L., & Springer, K. An anxiety scale applicable to verbal samples. *Archives of General Psychiatry*, 1961, *5*, 593–605.

Grinstein, A. *The index of psychoanalytic writings*, Vol. 9 (Subject Indexes). New York: International Universities Press, 1966.

Harlow, H., Harlow, M., & Hanson, E. The maternal affectional system of rhesus monkeys. In H. Rheingold (Ed.), *Maternal behavior in mammals*. New York: Wiley, 1963.

Hartmann, H. Comments on the psychoanalytic theory of the ego. In *Psychoanalytic Study of the Child*, 1950, *5*, 74–96.

Hartmann, H. *Essays on ego psychology*. New York: International Universities Press, 1964.

Heider, F. *The psychology of interpersonal relations*. New York: Wiley, 1958.

Hill, D., & Price, J. Childhood bereavement and adult depression. *British Journal of Psychiatry*, 1967, *113*, 743–751.

Hogan, R. Theoretical egocentrism and the problem of compliance. *American Psychologist*, 1975, *27*, 533–540.

Hollingshead, A., & Redlich, F. *Social class and mental illness*. New York: Wiley, 1958.

Holt, R. Freud's mechanistic and humanistic images of man. In R. Holt & E. Peterfreund (Eds.), *Psychoanalysis and contemporary science*. New York: Macmillan, 1972.

Izard, C. E. *Patterns of emotions: A new analysis of anxiety and depression*. New York: Academic Press, 1971.

Jacobson, E. The self and the object world. *Psychoanalytic Study of the Child*, 1954, *9*, 75–127.

Kinsey, A., Pomeroy, W., Martin, C., & Gebhard, P. *Sexual behavior in the human female*. Philadelphia: Saunders, 1953.

Kohlberg, L. Moral development. In *International Encyclopedia of the Social Sciences*, Vol. 10. New York: Macmillan, 1968.

Kohut, H. *The analysis of the self*. New York: International Universities Press, 1971.

La Barre, W. *The human animal*. Chicago: University of Chicago Press, 1954.

Laing, R. *The divided self*. Chicago: Quadrangle Books, 1960.

Levenson, M., & Neuringer, C. Suicide and field dependency. *Omega*, *5*, 1974, 181–186.

Levy, R., & Rowitz, R. *The ecology of mental disorder*. New York: Behavioral Publications, 1973.

Lewis, H. An experimental study of the role of the ego in work: I. The role of the ego in cooperative work. *Journal of Experimental Psychology*, 1944, *34*, 113–126. (a)

Lewis, H., & Franklin, M. An experimental study of the role of the ego in work: II. The significance of task orientation in work. *Journal of Experimental Psychology*, 1944, *34*, 195–215. (b)

Lewis, H. Over-differentiation and under-individuation of the self. *Psychoanalysis and the Psychoanalytic Review*, 1958, *45*, 3–24.

Lewis, H. Organization of the self as reflected in manifest dreams. *Psychoanalysis and the Psychoanalytic Review*, 1959, *46*, 21–35.

Lewis, H. A case of watching as a defense against an oral incorporation fantasy. *Psychoanalytic Review*, 1963, *50*, 68–80.

Lewis, H. *Psychic war in men and women*. New York: New York University Press, 1976.

Lewis, H. Sex differences in superego mode as related to sex differences in psychiatric illness. *Social Science and Medicine*, 1978.

Lewis, H. B. *Shame and guilt in neurosis*. New York: International Universities Press, 1971.

Lichtenstein, H. Changing implications of the concept of psychosexual development. *Journal of the American Psychoanalytic Association*, 1970, *18*, 300–317.

Lynd, H. *On shame and the search for identity*. New York: Harcourt, Brace, 1958.

Maccoby, E. (Ed.). *The development of sex differences*. Stanford, Calif.: Stanford University Press, 1966.

Maccoby, E., & Jacklin, C. *The psychology of sex differences*. Stanford, Calif.: Stanford University Press, 1974.

Mead, M. *Male and female*. New York: William Morrow, 1949.

Nicolson, N., & Trautmann, J. *The letters of Virginia Woolf*, Vol. 1. New York: Harcourt Brace Jovanovich, 1975.

Nietzsche, F. *The philosophy of Nietzsche*. New York: Modern Library, 1937.

Parkes, M. C. *Bereavement*. New York: International Universities Press, 1972.

Parsons, T. Social structure and the development of personality: Freud's contribution to the integration of psychology and sociology. *Psychiatry*, 1958, *21*, 321–340.

Piaget, J. *The moral judgment of the child*. Glencoe, Ill.: Free Press, 1950.

Piers, G., & Singer, J. *Shame and guilt*. Springfield, Ill. Charles Thomas, 1953.

Rainwater, L. Sex in the culture of poverty. In C. Broderick and J. Barnard (Eds.), *The individual, sex and society*. Baltimore: Johns Hopkins Press, 1969.

Rheingold, H. The social and socializing infant. In D. Goslin (Ed.), *Handbook of socialization theory and research*. Chicago: Rand McNally, 1969.

Safer, J. The effects of sex and psychological differentiation on responses to a stressful group situation. Unpublished doctoral dissertation. The New School of Social Research, 1975.

Schafer, R. The loving and beloved superego in Freud's structural theory. *The Psychoanalytic Study of the Child*, 1960, *15*, 163–188.

Sedivec, V. Manic phases of mania-melancholgy and its forms during the course of illness. *Czechoslovak Psychiatrica*, 1969, *65*, 85–91 (Abstract).

Sears, R., Rau, L., & Alpert, R. *Identification and childrearing*. Evanston, Ill.: Row-Peterson, 1965.

Siebert, L. Superego sex differences. Unpublished doctoral dissertation. University of Michigan, 1965.

Silverman, C. *The Epidemiology of depression*. Baltimore: The Johns Hopkins Press, 1968.

Smith, R. The relative proneness to shame or guilt as an indicator of defensive style. Unpublished doctoral dissertation. Northwestern University, 1972.

Stone, L., Smith, H., & Murphy, L. (Eds.). *The competent infant*. New York: Basic Books, 1973.

Tawney, R. *Religion and the rise of capitalism*. New York: Harcourt Brace, 1926.

Tomkins, S. *Affect, imagery and consciousness*, Vol. 2. New York: Springer, 1963.

Turiel, E. An historical analysis of the Freudian concept of the superego. *Psychoanalytic Review*, 1967, *54*, 118–140.

Weissman, M., & Paykel, E. *The depressed woman*. Chicago: University of Chicago Press, 1974.

Wertheimer, M. Experimentede Studien Uber das sehen von bewegung. *Zeizschrift für Psychologie*, 1912, *61*, 165–265.

Wolf, Lonn. Personal communication, 1975.

Witkin, H. Perception of body position and the position of the visual field. *Psychological Monographs*, 1949, *63*, 1–46.

Witkin, H. Psychological differentiation and forms of pathology. *Journal of Abnormal Psychology*, 1965, *70*, 317–336.

Witkin, H., & Asch, S. Studies in space orientation: III. & IV. *Journal of Experimental Psychology*, 1948, *38*, 603–614, 762–782.

Witkin, H., Lewis, H., Hertzman, M., Machover, K., Meissner, P., & Wapner, S. *Personality through perception*. New York: Harper & Row, 1954.

Witkin, H., Lewis, H., & Weil, E. Affective reactions and patient–therapist interaction among more differentiated and less differentiated patients early in therapy. *Journal of Nervous and Mental Disease*, 1968, *146*, 193–208.

Editor's Introduction

13

This chapter complements the preceding chapter on shame, yet it shows how the dynamically related emotion of guilt has different evolutionary roots, different effects on consciousness, and different consequences for personal and social adjustment. Lewis holds that it was the shift in the conception of guilt as an essential aspect of one's relationship with God to its conception as a signal of violation of internalized cultural values that brought it within the pale of science. With this secularization of the concept of guilt, social scientists began studying its enculturation and socialization, and psychologists and psychiatrists began studying how its presence in excess produces psychological disorders.

Lewis elaborates the nature and power of guilt with selections from literature and philosophy. This treatment makes it clear that the determinants and consequences of guilt are in large measure a function of the values held by the family, the community, and the culture.

This chapter contains an excellent comparative synopsis of shame and guilt, while contrasting their sources (eliciting stimuli or conditions), their effects on consciousness and self, and ego defenses associated with each of them. She notes that shame results in an apparent deficiency or inability of self, inhibits cognitive processes, renders the self passive, and leads to ego defenses such as denial and repression and to the affective disorder of depression. By contrast, guilt increases cognitive processes, renders the self active, and leads to ego defenses such as isolation and rationalization and to the thought disorders of obsession and paranoia.

Building on her careful delineations of shame and guilt, Lewis uses classical clinical material and excerpts from contemporary psychotherapy in developing the argument that obsessional neurotics are tormented by a pattern of shame and anger (what Lewis calls "humiliated fury"), which cannot be labeled and articulated in consciousness because of a heavy burden of guilt. The guilt then leads to obsessive thinking, a cognitive process that can be seen as an effort to regulate the guilt and the underlying shame/anger. In her analysis of the dynamics of paranoia, Lewis observes that the dominance of guilt is manifested by the paranoid's projections of blame onto others for doing them wrong.

The end of the chapter complements the concluding section of the preceding one. She presents evidence to support her hypothesis that men have greater guilt proneness than women and are thus more susceptible to obsessive-compulsive and paranoid disorders.

Guilt in Obsession and Paranoia   13

HELEN BLOCK LEWIS

> *There's a limit to the guilt you can feel and the forgiveness and pity you can take! You have to begin blaming someone else too. I got so sometimes when she'd kiss me it was like she did it on purpose to humiliate me, as if she'd spat in my face.*
> Hickey's soliloquy in the final scene of Eugene O'Neill's *The Iceman Cometh.*

I. THE ROLE OF GUILT IN MENTAL ILLNESS

With the Enlightenment and the gradual secularization of thought, the role of guilt in a person's life lost its central position as a necessary means of relating to God. Except in religious belief, guilt was no longer an acknowledged, even welcome awareness of basic human sinfulness, carrying with it humility and the striving for redemption through prayer and good works. Guilt became instead the signal of "internalized" cultural values, carrying with it the implication that a person in a state of guilt might be the unconscious dupe of his or her own cultural system. Anthropologists, sociologists, and psychologists now study differences in the way in which guilt is codified in different social systems. Psychologists and psychiatrists study the way in which irrational or excessive guilt deforms individual human functioning, creating neurotic and psychotic symptoms.

Rousseau, Marx, Neitzsche, and Freud are among the enlightened thinkers who have done the most to effect this transformation from the concept of guilt as a human necessity in relation to God into a concept of guilt as a source of psychiatric symptoms. The pathways by which the transformation was effected are in themselves of interest, and they help to illuminate some theoretical issues in psychology that still remain open. All enlightened thinkers specifically denied that our species was predestined to original sin. But, pressed to understand the brutalities that people have inflicted on each other throughout the centuries of recorded civilized history, they each found the fault (the guilt) to lie in the fact of civilization itself. Rousseau lamented the loss of compassion (*pitié*) that civilization inflicts on human nature. Marx saw the fault as lying in the fact that civilization has so far been built on the exploita-

---

HELEN BLOCK LEWIS • Yale University, New Haven, Connecticut.

tion by a few of the majority of humanity. This historical fact was one he accepted without attempting to explain except as the resultant of "blind" social forces that, once understood, would be abolished and replaced by a nonexploitative social system. Nietzsche understood individual guilt as a product of being civilized out of a state of primordial animal instinct for freedom. He (1971) assumed that all guilt was a

> deep-seated malady to which man succumbed under the pressure of the most pro-
> found transformation he ever underwent—the one that made him once and for all a
> sociable and pacific creature [instead of a free, warring] pack of savages, a race of
> conquerors. (pp. 50–51).

Freud agreed that civilized morality is based upon instinctual renunciations, and he added sexuality to the instincts that must be renounced. The point is that each of these influential thinkers specifically exculpated human nature as solely responsible for human brutality. Instead they turned scientific attention not only to the interaction between human beings and the social order in which they develop but to guilt as an inevitable and potentially deforming resultant of becoming an acculturated human being.

The extent to which folk wisdom has understood guilt as the motive force governing the origin of society is itself a fascinating question that I have discussed elsewhere (Lewis, 1976). Lévi-Strauss (1968), for example, has analysed the myth of the Wawilak sisters, a creation myth of the North Australian Murngin people. The story is that the sisters first committed incest with men of their own moiety and then polluted the water hole of the great snake Yurlunggur with menstrual blood. The outraged python rose up and caused a deluge of rain and a general flood. The snake then swallowed the women and their children. When the snake raised himself, the waters covered the entire earth and its vegetation, and when he lay down, the flood receded. But had the Wawilak sisters not committed incest and polluted the water hole of Yurlung-gur, "there would have been neither life nor death, neither copulation nor reproduction on the earth and there would have been no cycle of seasons" (p. 157). Lévi-Strauss's interpretation of the myth shows how its contents help the people make sense of some of the physical conditions of their existence, in this case a cycle of rainy and dry seasons. Lévi-Strauss also interprets the myth and the initiation rites that are based on it as a rationale that helps both to justify and to perpetuate the inferior social position of women and young boys. This inferior position the culture implicitly recognizes as a contradiction, if not an injustice. It is women's guilt that makes their position (and that of the young boys who are their children) *justly* inferior.

The myth of the Wawilak sisters has elements that are amazingly similar to Freud's account of the origin of civilization in *Totem and Taboo* (Freud, 1913). An act of parricide and cannibalism by the young males in a horde who were denied access to the females by their father resulted in a primordial guilt that is carried in the unconscious of succeeding generations of (male) human beings. Apparently even Freud did not take his account seriously (Kardiner, 1977) except as a parable of the origin of civilization. Freud was clearly extending into mythical primitive history what he observed on a small scale in the Viennese nuclear family. The parable implies that the young males revolt against the irrational authority of the father and are thereafter irrationally guilty. More important, it implies that both cultural institutions and individual moral values have irrational and unconscious roots that can remain unsorted from the rational and thereby develop into psychiatric symptoms. From this conception of guilt as inherent in a socialized human existence, it was an easy step (which Freud took) to hypothesize that psychiatric illness is the product of an "archaic" or malfunctioning superego (Freud, 1923). The psychiatrist has thus become the modern "doctor of souls."

But in the course of this development, assumptions about the original nature of human nature as it confronts society tended to become obscured. Both Rousseau and Marx, for example, assumed that human nature in its uncivilized state is still essentially social. Nietzsche and Freud both opted for a darker view of the nature of human nature. As I have shown in Chapter 12, this view of human nature particularly informed Freud's concept of the punitive superego. And since it was Freud whose hypotheses sparked many comprehensive and detailed studies of human social action, an essentially individualistic and aggressive view of human nature easily found its way into modern psychoanalytic psychiatry. Particularly if there is an assumption that human nature is essentially individualistic and aggressive, guilt is readily conceptualized as aggression turned inward. A view of human nature as both social and aggressive permits the concept that guilt is also a striving to maintain intrinsic affectional bonds. This aspect of guilt is most clearly seen when a person experiences both shame and guilt for moral transgression.

Many social aspects of the guilt experience, particularly its frequent shame accompaniment, have been insufficiently studied. For example, there is a quality of guilt that Buber (1971) calls its "ontic character." By *ontic* or *existential guilt*, Buber means that which "occurs when someone injures an order of the human world whose foundations he knows and recognizes as those of his own existence and of all common human existence" (p. 92). Buber believes that "one cannot do evil with his whole soul, one can only do good with the whole soul" (p. 102). Buber's concept of an intrinsic order in human relations and his notion that good involves the whole soul are assumptions that are close to a concept of human nature as intrinsically social. Buber distinguishes "high conscience" from "vulgar conscience": "High conscience" is not only guilt toward oneself but a state in which one will "acknowledge [the other whom one has injured] to his face" and seek reconciliation with him. "Vulgar conscience" is guilt only toward oneself, and it knows only how to "torment and harass." Buber seems to be speaking of shame experience in his description of ontic guilt or high conscience. Using Dostoevski's character of Stravrogin as an example, he suggests that where shame is absent there is a

Table 1. Summary of Working Concept for Shame and Guilt

	Shame	Guilt
Stimulus	1. Disappointment, defeat or moral transgression 2. Deficiency of *self* 3. Involuntary, self unable 4. Encounter with "other" or within the self	1. Moral transgression 2. Event, act, *thing* for which self is responsible 3. Voluntary, self able 4. Within the self
Extent of libidinal component	1. Specific connection to sex	1. Connection to aggression
Conscious content	1. Painful emotion 2. Autonomic reactions 3. Connections to past feeling 4. Many variants of shame feeling 5. Fewer variations of cognitive content (the self) 6. Identity thoughts	1. Affect may or may not be present 2. Autonomic reactions less likely 3. Fewer connections to past feelings 4. Guilt feeling is monotonic 5. More variations of content—things in the world 6. No identity thoughts
Position of self in field	1. Self passive 2. Self focal in awareness 3. Multiple functions of self at the same time 4. Vicarious experience of "other's" view of self	1. Self active 2. Self not focal in awareness 3. Self intact, functioning silently 4. Pity, concern for "other's" suffering
Nature and discharge of	1. Humiliated fury 2. Discharge blocked by guilt and/or love of "other" discharge on self	1. Righteous indignation 2. Discharge on self and "other"
Characteristic defenses	1. Denial 2. Repression of ideas 3. Affirmation of the self 4. Affect disorder: depression	1. Isolation of affect 2. Rationalization 3. Reaction formation: good deeds or thoughts 4. Thought disorder: obsession and paranoia

"false relationship" to guiltiness. Buber describes the psychic healing and spiritual rebirth that come when ontic guilt is expressed and suggests that psychiatry may thus profit from understanding the religious experience of guilt, which implicitly includes shame.

II. THE PHENOMENOLOGY OF GUILT

In Chapter 12, I outlined a fairly extensive phenomenological comparison of the states of shame and guilt. The main features of my account are summarized in a working concept for shame and guilt that is presented in Table 1.

Before turning to clinical material, it is instructive to look at a few examples from literature that clearly represent the phenomenology of guilt. I have chosen illustrations from Sophocles' *Oedipus the King*, Shakespeare's *Hamlet*, and Eugene O'Neill's *The Iceman Cometh*, thus ranging from ancient times to the present. These few examples show that the "objective" quality of guilt and the compulsion to act that guilt evokes have been known to folk wisdom throughout the centuries. The examples also illustrate the presence of convert or unacknowledged shame, which can be traced when guilt cannot be discharged. Guilt then issues in an insoluble dilemma or in a paranoid projection of blame, or both.

A. Oedipus the King[1]

Oedipus' task when the play opens is to "drive out a pollution from our land." Guilt is thus about events in the world. There is also a clear concept of collective guilt resulting from the "objective" circumstance of an unpunished crime. The whole city is therefore being justly punished by the gods, who have unleashed a destroying storm of evils.

Oedipus' first response to the suggestion that he is the guilty person catches exactly the phenomenology of the outraged (humiliated) accused who believes himself innocent. Oedipus forms a paranoid projection. He believes that it is Creon, his humiliating accuser, who is secretly attacking him and is part of a plot to drive Oedipus from the throne. This is the model for guilt that cannot be tolerated because it operates above unacknowledged shame and so issues in a projection onto the accuser. Since guilt is about things or events in the world, this kind of dispute over who is responsible also has an "objective" character. Oedipus' explanation of Creon's attack also has intrinsic plausibility, as do many paranoid ideas.

[1] Translated by David Grene.

As Oedipus' doubt of his own innocence begins to form, he describes a "wandering of the soul—I could run mad". Doubt is indeeed maddeningly insoluble. When Oedipus is in a state of profound guilt, when he sees Jocasta "hanging, the twisted rope around her neck," he *acts:*

> He tore the brooches, the gold-chased brooches fastening her robe—away from her and lifting them up high dashed them on his eyeballs, shrieking out such things as: they will never see the crime I have committed or had done upon me . . . with such imprecations he struck his eyes again and yet again with the brooches.

Again and again the compulsion is to rectify the evil: "dark eyes . . . do not recognize those whom you long for," says Oedipus, preventing himself from ever looking on a beloved face again. Yet even at the moment of making amends for his own guilt, Oedipus is talking about the crime done to him, that is, about others' guilt.

And even after Oedipus has punished himself, there is no peace. When the chorus suggests that Oedipus would be "better dead than blind and living," it is reflecting the insoluble dilemma of action that will not permit guilt to be discharged even by reparation: "What I have done here was best done—don't tell me otherwise, do not give me further counsel." Soon enough, however, Oedipus is begging Creon to let him die on the mountain where his mother and father had wished him to die when he was an infant. Oedipus is here remembering the crime done to him in infancy. But the humiliated fury, the shame of personal betrayal that might have accompanied such a recollection is now expressed only in a masochistic wish to die as his parents had wished. This request Creon coldly refuses, warning Oedipus not to "seek to be master in everything for the things you mastered did not follow you throughout your life."

B. Hamlet

The torturing combination of a compulsion to act to effect justice and an inability to act appropriately is what afflicts Hamlet. Describing his insoluble dilemma—"To be or not to be"—Hamlet reminds us that "conscience does make cowards of us all/And thus the native hue of resolution/Is sicklied o'er with the pale cast of thought. . . . "

Ernest Jones (1949) has interpreted Hamlet's tortured inability to act as the consequence of unconscious guilt for his own incestuous wishes to displace his father. Hamlet's hatred of his uncle is the "jealous detestation of one evildoer toward his successful fellow" (p. 99). It is instructive, however, to realize that Jones does not describe the actual state of humiliated fury, the shame–rage toward both mother and uncle that would be evoked by a successful rival, without any overt transgression whatever on Hamlet's part. The shame of his mother's personal betrayal of himself and of his father is overlooked. It is this state that is never acknowledged by Hamlet himself, except indirectly as an intense disgust of the "reechy kisses" between his mother and Claudius: "O shame! where is thy blush?" I am suggesting, in other words, that unacknowledged humiliated fury is what prevents Hamlet from acting on his own righteous indignation against his father's murderer.

C. The Iceman Cometh

Hickey's soliloquy in *The Iceman Cometh* explaining to his drinking comrades how he came to shoot his wife, Evelyn, illuminates both the phenomenology of guilt, the humiliated rage that being forgiven can evoke, and obsessive thoughts that then arise:

> Christ, can you believe what a guilty skunk she made me feel! It kept piling up, inside her and inside me. God can you picture all I made her suffer, and how I hated myself. If only she hadn't been so damned good—if only she'd been the same kind of wife I was a husband. . . . It was written all over her face, sweetness and love and forgiveness. . . . It kept piling up like I said. I got so I thought of it all the time. . . . I began to be afraid I was going bughouse. . . . And then it came to me—the only way out for her sake. . . . She'd never feel any pain, never wake up from her dreams. So I, I killed her.

A little later on in the same soliloquy Hickey says:

> I felt as though a ton of guilt were lifted off my mind. I remember I stood by the bed and suddenly I had to laugh. I couldn't help it, and I knew Evelyn would forgive me. I remember I heard myself speaking to her, it was always something I wanted to say: Well, you know what you can do with your pipe-dreams now, you damned bitch. Good God, I couldn't have said that. If I had, I'd be insane. Why I loved Evelyn better than anything in life. . . .

Hickey's dilemma is a model for the psychotherapy situation: patients are encouraged to express their aggressions without fear of retaliation from the therapist. As I have shown in *Shame and Guilt in Neurosis* (Lewis, 1971), this guilt-evoking aspect of the patient–therapist relationship needs constant interpretation to prevent the formation of symptoms that are "side effects" of the therapeutic relationship. Hickey's compulsion to kill Evelyn for her sake and the "ton of guilt" that was lifted off his mind when he did kill her also suggest the connection between guilt and the maintenance of affectional bonds.

III. GUILT AND OBSESSIVE-COMPULSIVE DISORDERS

A. Freud's Case of the Rat-Man

Freud's (1909) most famous case of obsessional neurosis, the Rat-Man, was clearly in a chronic state of overt guilt from his earliest childhood. At his first treatment session, the patient spontaneously began his free associations by speaking about a friend to whom the patient used to go when he was tormented by some criminal impulse and ask whether he despised him as a criminal. His friend used to give him (the patient) moral support by assuring him that he (the patient) was a man of irreproachable conduct" (p. 159).

As I have shown (Lewis, 1971), each outbreak of the Rat-Man's obsessional symptoms had as its precipitant an episode in which the patient was coping with some unacknowledged mortification or shame. The patient, however—unlike Dora, who was in an overt state of humiliation over her father's betrayal of her—was much more aware of feelings of guilt than of shame. He was afflicted with obsessional thoughts about what he must do to avoid the responsibility of causing injury to the people he loved. Although he knew that his thoughts were irrational, he was absolutely compelled to act on them, and at the same time, he was unable to decide on appropriate action. His insoluble dilemma at one point reached the stage of an obsessional delirium of indecision.

Freud's account of the case also shows clearly that both he and the patient were aware of the self-initiated and self-propelled character of guilt. The analytic physician, said Freud, understands that "the sense of guilt is not in itself open to further criticism" (p. 175). This very compelling quality of guilt, however, can bring a patient into some hard problems: "How can he admit that his self-reproach of being a criminal toward his father was justified when he must know that as matter of fact he had never committed any crime against him?"

Freud's interpretation of the dynamics of obsessive thinking was that it represents "an act regressively" (p. 246). Freud also had the hypothesis that the specific content of the action was likely to be a tremendous feeling of rage which was inaccessible to the patient's consciousness and directed against someone who had cropped up as an interference with the course of love" (p. 246). This comes close to saying that obsessive thoughts originate in humiliated fury that is inaccessible to awareness. I have suggested, further, that the humiliated fury is rendered inaccessible by the development of a state of guilt that then issues in obsessive thoughts. This sequence will be illustrated in the transcripts of psychotherapy sessions.

B. Excerpts from Psychotherapy Sessions

I turn now to some excerpts from the transcripts of psychotherapy sessions that illustrate the phenomenology of guilt and its affinity to obsessive ideation. The excerpts are from the field-independent patients among whom guilt was a more frequent state than shame (Witkin, Lewis, & Weil, 1968), but there is no implication that these same phenomena do not occur in field-dependent patients as well.

The following excerpts illustrates the "thing" quality of guilt and a frequent phrasing that the patient is "bothered." The excerpt contains the opening sentences of the patient's first psychotherapy session:

> P: I don't know where to begin, uh, even when I had gone to Dr.———a lot of things were really bothering me. Now I don't feel so turbulent. I just think that whatever was bothering me then is still bothering me really. At the time I went to him it was a problem of sexual adjustment with my husband. I was married in June and it's no problem but, it doesn't bother me as much. I think it's taken a different form. I, I used to really resent him very much and I didn't like lovemaking and I still don't, but I don't think it's my fault so much any more. The thing that made me, I don't think I was frigid, uhm, I said "maybe it was me" and now I think maybe it's not. Maybe it's both of us. And maybe it's him just as much and maybe it's not all me.

This excerpt illustrates also the relative lack of affect—the isolation of affect—that occurs in connection with the insoluble dilemma of "Is it my fault or his fault?" Since the "problem" is apparently an objective one and involves the just apportionment of blame, acute affect that catches the self "at the quick" is absent. As the patient puts it, she is not so "turbulent" now, although she is aware that at times she can be. The excerpt also contains references to a shame-provoking circumstances: a failure during sexual intercourse. It thus contains a hint of underlying shame as a contribution to the patient's insoluble dilemma.

The "problems" presented by the patient are so apparently rational that they are not easily identified as obsessive thoughts about guilt. Thus it is easy for both patient and therapist to be caught up in the cognitive content of the patient's "problems" without recognizing the obsessional character of being "bothered."

The following excerpt from a young male patient illustrates the self-propelled and self-contained quality of guilt and its inexorable character even in the face of attempts by the therapist to mitigate it. As in the preceding excerpt, the rationality of the patient's guilty thoughts obscures their "primary-process" character. The specific stimulus to guilt in this excerpt is that the patient went back to bed this morning instead of following his own resolve to get up and look for a job. The guilt that follows from going back to bed cannot be rationally discharged even though the patient himself says he is "really under no pressure to get a job." A bit later in this session, the patient will speak about masturbation, a topic that causes him to "wince" and to "wonder what he would think about himself if he were the therapist." A current of shame is thus operating underneath the patient's state of guilt. The patient's thoughts lead him directly into an insoluble dilemma about his motives: Does he want a job or doesn't he? Does he want reponsibility or not? Does he want to marry his fiancée or not?

On the morning of this session, the patient who had awakened early enough to go job hunting, got out of bed and then said to himself: "What the

408 Helen Block Lewis

hell . . . and then I got right back in bed and couldn't sleep but I refused to get out of bed again." In the wake of this transgression, the patient begins a self-scolding tirade of guilty ideation not only about staying in bed but about widely generalized similar faults:

> P: And uh I think I've grown accustomed to this life of uh, getting up when I please, not working, having no responsibility other than school and perhaps the feeling of responsibility toward home, but I keep destroying all chances of getting a job.

The flow of his guilt cannot be stopped by the therapist's intervention:

> T. Mm, there must be a reason.
> P. Yeah, no doubt. Uh, I don't know, it—I was thinking, it's possible that I don't want additional responsibility—you know that, with having a job, but somehow that just seems like rationalization to me.

When one is in a state of guilt, benign explanations of the reasons for one's conduct seem like rationalizations!

Here is an excerpt from the same session that illustrates the "good feeling" that arises after one has successfully overcome a temptation to transgress. It should be noticed that the patient says he "felt very good about *it*" (italics mine), although he clearly also means that he felt good about himself. But the center of his experience is "winning a small-sized battle" (within himself) about whether or not to get out of bed. The *self* in this instance is not the focus of experience but rather the act or thing done (the patient has entered therapy for a "problem" about dropping out of college):

> P. I won a small-sized battle yesterday.
> T. Yes?
> P. Uh, I told you I had this exam coming up, and uh Wednesday night about midnight I figured well I better start studying. I opened the book and after about three minutes I quit (mm) and went to sleep; and uhm I got up Thursday and was ready to cut, you know—uh to do it over the weekend or something like that and I decided I better not. And I did as much work as I could and I went right and took the exam (mm) and uh I felt very good about it (mm). Funny, today I was here at about 2:30 just to make sure I wouldn't be late, and I was fairly anxious to get here today.

Although the patient was not directly saying so, he was so proud of his obeying his own conscience that he wanted to share with the therapist his good feeling over winning the "small-sized battle." The patient's use of the term *funny* (which would rate a Gottschalk–Gleser shame anxiety score) represents his own registration of what he perceives as incongruous pride in his (and the therapist's) achievement.

The patient's inexorable state of guilt followed upon his telling the therapist his good news about taking the exam and his unacknowledged, "funny" pride in his accomplishment. The sequence in his experience is as follows: he first won a "small-sized battle," but the next morning (the day of his therapy session) he broke his own resolve to get out of bed. This circumstance suggests that the patient is signaling some negative message about therapy as well as pleasure in good news. It should be noted that the *content* of the guilty ideation is the patient's faulty psychological motivation, the main topic of the therapy sessions. It is possible thus to sense a transformation of the patient's bypassed shame vis-à-vis the therapist into a compelling sense of guilt about his faulty motivations.

The following excerpt illustrates the characteristic of guilt that it implies ability to do or to act. This implied ability is a source of pride that often goes unacknowledged because it is registered as incongruous with an adult's autonomous self. When there is a challenge to the ability to act, which guilt implies, the patient remembers (as a joke) his fear of going crazy. In this excerpt, the same patient is trying to ward off a sense of guilt toward his mother. He has just received a long-suffering, self pitying letter from her, accusing him of neglecting her. He had responded by telling his mother that he had just received a "crank letter." He is aware, in other words, that he need not feel guilty toward her, that she is a "master of eliciting guilt feelings." But the feeling of guilt remains:

T: When you say bothered . . .
P: I feel guilty. [Another instance, cf. p. 407 of the equation between "bothered" and "guilty."]
P. That maybe she's right. And um I know I have this fear that she will break down. Uh that perhaps I can prevent it. On the other hand I'm quite sure that if she uh, if she's really determined to make a go, she won't.
T: It must be rather lonely for you having your mother sick, and stepfather sick, father a little distant. Not wanting you around that much.
P: Oh I don't know if it's so lonely as uh as I feel that it's an unfair burden on me. It's not of my making and yet I feel obliged to help out in some way. And uh, of course, as much as I feel obliged to help out. [It should be noted that in this instance, the "burden" of guilt is lighter than the feeling of being lonely and unwanted (shame).]
T: Well, what do you think you can do?
P: I don't know. I don't know if there is; there's probably nothing that I can do. But because if it weren't for my being away—I mean she'd find that there'd always be something. I don't know, it's more or less a standing joke among us that we'll have to reserve a suite of rooms here [mental hospital] for Memorial Day weekend.

Still another excerpt from this same patient illustrates clearly how guilt can temporarily relieve shame. The excerpt occurs a few moments after the patient, "wincing" at the thought, has told the therapist about masturbation:

P: I feel a little shaken by having said this.
T: Why?
P: I think for one, I'm embarrassed he, hem. But actually I set up for myself a situation where, uh, I'm trying to do this thing very diagnostic—you know—unattached. Uh I was bothered by one other thing. She told me that I think that I uh did destroy her dream of being a virgin until she was married, and mm uh I feel very, very guilty about that.

After embarrassment the patient describes an effort to "do this thing very diagnostic, you know unattached." This rather strange phrasing actually refers to the patient's shifting into the position of the therapist watching him (cf. Chapter 12): "I was thinking of what I would do if I were the therapist and I have a patient facing me, just what significance I would give to each of the reactions, each of his movements and the like." This is a state I have labeled *bypassed shame*. The patient progresses abruptly from bypassed shame into a strong sense of being "very, very guilty" of taking his fiancée's virginity.

The patient skipped his next therapy session without notifying the therapist. At their next meeting, he told the therapist that he "couldn't think of anything to say" (shame reaction) and "just panicked" before the session. The patient could not remember the content of the preceding session: "I couldn't tell you what I did last week. The only thing I can remember very clearly is what happened in every class I've been to. And I've been to every class."

When the therapist interpreted that the preceding hour might have given him some pain, the patient replied; "It's funny how that never entered my mind." The patient was, however, feeling very guilty about skipping his hour:

> I really condemned myself very strongly for having absented myself from that one. It's almost as though I'm treating it like a class. You know. I had no right cutting therapy.

On this instance, again, it is apparent that feeling guilty, although an uncomfortable feeling, is less "panicking" (at least for some people) than shame.

A particularly instructive example of a sequence from bypassed shame into guilt and thence into obsessive, paranoid ideation comes from the transcript of a field-independent male patient whose therapist had been interpreting (with some quiet derision) the grandiosity of the patient's ego-ideal. It is easy for an observer to be amused by another person's ego-ideal and also easy to evoke shame in the person whose ego-ideal is under inspection, especially since it is difficult to spell out a rationale for one's own strivings.

The patient had entered treatment for chest pains that had no organic base. He himself connected his symptoms to an "ego-ideal or something that I'm setting up." The patient had a characteristic way of describing his chest pains; he kept saying that he "receives" the pain. The patient had been arguing with the therapist that his ambitions were necessary and inevitable in his life circumstances. In the midst of their dispute about the wisdom of ambition, the therapist called the patient's attention to his peculiar mode of speech about the pains. The patient laughed (most likely with embarrassment, although he did not say so) and several times assured the therapist that he, the patient, *knew* no one was giving him his pains. At the end of this hour, the patient was suddenly moved to ask the therapist about the microphone in the room. This in spite of the fact that the microphone had been discussed at the opening session of the therapy and this was now the third session.

The patient opened his next hour by telling the therapist the following "I was sort of curious last week about that microphone."

It developed, on questioning, that the patient had had a fantasy, which he himself labeled as "weird," "illogical" and "improbable," to the effect that the therapist had sent a copy of the transcript of the therapy session to the school where the patient studies. His exact words are important because they pick up the theme of sending and "receiving" that had been a particular focus of the patient's embarrassment and had evoked the patient's need to reassure the therapist that he, the patient, was not crazy, since he *knew* he was not "receiving" chest pains from anyone. Here is the text of the primary-process transformation that has the patient in "weird" fantasy of the therapist's betrayal made necessary out of "duty":

> P. Well, yeah, I just thought that maybe you were drawing severe conclusions and that someone should *know* about it at school. And some administrative officer should know about me . . . mm. And I was just wondering, 'cause no one's ever *known* that I sort of . . . ah . . . had funny ideas of what (laugh) (inaudible). Just a normal human being . . . and now . . . the picture's changed. I just thought that maybe uh I just thought that maybe you were sending them out of duty or something . . . some way (laugh) (inaudible) some way 'cause what's gonna happen if he does do it though.

The patient's shame and humiliated anger had been evoked by the therapist's interpretation, but it is hostility that has no "rationale" since the therapist is benign. The patient is in a state of guilt vis-à-vis the therapist for the patient's own shame–rage. The outcome is a paranoid fantasy that is very compelling, in spite of the patient's better judgment. And the content of the fantasy concretizes "*receiving*" and "sending" information about the severe conclusions that the therapist must be drawing about the patient's peculiarities and that the therapist is compelled to make *known* on pain of the therapist's being in a state of guilt toward the authorities who should be notified. In this fantasy, both patient and therapist are in an insoluble dilemma of guilt.

Using a computer model to simulate the linguistic behavior of a paranoid patient in a diagnostic interview, Colby (1977) has recently appraised four theories of paranoia. He suggests that a shame–humiliation model is preferable to a homosexual, hostility, or homeostatic model. Although there is an apparent contradiction to my view that guilt is the more frequent state out of which paranoia forms, the discrepancy between Colby and myself is more apparent than real. Colby's suggestion is that the paranoid forestalls the threat of humiliation (detected as a shame signal) by a strategy of "blaming others for wrongdoing" to the self (p. 56). Although Colby does not use the word *guilt*, blaming others for wrongdoing is perceiving them as guilty.

IV. FIELD INDEPENDENCE, SEX, GUILT, AND MENTAL ILLNESS

I turn next briefly to the network of evidence linking cognitive style, sex, and superego mode, which suggests that superego mode may be one factor in predicting sex differences in forms of mental illness. That the two sexes differ in cognitive style is well established (Witkin, Dyk, Faterson, Goodenough, &

Karp, 1962). A linkage between cognitive style and proneness to different forms of pathology also exists (Witkin, 1965). Field-independent perceivers tend to be obsessional rather than hysterical (Witkin, 1965); field-independent perceivers are also more likely to use "isolation of affect" as a defense (Schimek, 1968; Minard & Mooney, 1969; Gleser & Ilihevitch, 1969). There is also a linkage between field independence and paranoia (Witkin, 1965). As I described in Chapter 12, an empirical study predicted and confirmed as association between field dependence and shame and between field independence and guilt (Witkin *et al.*, 1968).

The pattern of known sex differences in proneness to mental illness corresponds to the pattern of sex differences in cognitive stype: women are more field-dependent than men, and they are more prone to depression and the hysterias; men are more field-independent than women, and they are more prone to obsessional neurosis, addictions, sexual deviations (compulsions), and schizophrenia (Lewis, 1976). I am suggesting that men's greater proneness to guilt and women's greater proneness to shame is one underlying factor in this network of connections.

Two major factors join in fostering men's greater proneness to guilt. First, the anaclitic identifications made by boys with an opposite-sex caretaker must be superseded by defensive identifications with the father. This results in what Lynn (1962) has called solving the "problem" of indentification with father (as contrasted to "mother–person emulation" for girls). Defensive identifications remain central in men's personality (Sears, Rau & Alpert, 1965). Renunciation of earliest (feminine) anaclitic identifications involves males in early aggression against female figures and thus in earlier guilt than women (Horney, 1932). This line of reasoning connects with cross-cultural evidence that male initiation rites are more frequent in patrilocal than in matrilocal societies (D'Andrade, 1966) and more severe in father-absent societies, that is, those that segregate women and children from adult men (Burton & Whiting, 1961; Chodorow, 1971).

Second, men, in contrast to women, are pressed into aggressive behavior in order to meet their responsibilities for earning a livelihood within a competitive economic system. Evidence is strong and conclusive that men are more aggressive than women (Maccoby, 1966; Maccoby & Jacklin, 1974). Men's more direct participation in economic struggles has a consequence more opportunities for moral transgression and for resulting guilt. For example, crime rates are higher for men than for women, and they follow the indices of poverty and social disorganization (Dohrenwend & Dohrenwend, 1969). The rates for schizophrenia also follow along class lines (Hollingshead & Redlich, 1958), particularly the rates for young males (Levy & Rowitz, 1973).

What is needed are systematic studies of sex differences in superego mode, both in normal and psychiatric populations. The few studies (cf. Chapter 12) that have differentiated between shame and guilt as superego modes have mostly yielded results in the correct direction (Gleser, Gottschalk, & Springer,

1961; Siebert, 1965; Binder, 1970; Wolf, personal communications, 1975), although Smith (1972) failed to obtain a sex difference in proneness to shame and guilt.

REFERENCES

Burton, R., & Whiting, B. The absent father and cross-sex identity. *Merrill-Palmer Quarterly*, 1961, *7*, 85–95.

Binder, J. The relative proneness to shame or guilt as a dimension of character style. Unpublished dissertation, University of Michigan, 1970.

Buber, M. Guilt and Guilt Feelings. In R. Smith (Ed.), *Guilt: Man and society.* New York: Doubleday/Anchor Books, 1971.

Chodorow, N. Being and doing: A cross-cultural examination of the socialization of males and females. In V. Gornick & B. Moran (Eds.), *Women in sexist society.* New York: New American Library, 1971.

Colby, K. Appraisal of four psychological theories of paranoid phenomena. *Journal of Abnormal Psychology*, 1977, *86*, 54–59.

D'Andrade, R. Sex differences and cultural institutions. In E. Maccoby (Ed.), *The development of sex differences.* Stanford, California: University of California Press, 1966.

Dohrenwend, B., & Dohrenwend, B. *Social status and psychological disorders: A causal inquiry.* New York: Wiley-Interscience, 1969.

Freud, S. Notes upon a case of Obessional Neurosis (1909). In J. Strachey (Ed.), *Standard edition of the complete psychological works of Sigmund Freud*, Vol. 10. London: Hogarth Press, 1955.

Freud, S. *Totem and Taboo* (1913). In J. Strachey (Ed.), *Standard edition of the complete psychological works of Sigmund Freud*, Vol. 13. London: Hogarth Press, 1955.

Freud, S. *The Ego and the Id* (1923). In J. Strachey (Ed.), *Standard edition of the complete psychological works of Sigmund Freud*, Vol. 19. London: Hogarth Press, 1961.

Gleser, G., & Ilihevitch, D. An objective instrument for measuring defense mechanisms. *Journal of Consulting and Clinical Psychology*, 1969, *33*, 51–60.

Gleser, G., Gottschalk, L., & Springer, K. An anxiety scale applicable to verbal samples. *Archives of General Psychiatry*, 1961, *5*, 593–605.

Gottschalk, L. & Gleser, G. *The measurement of psychological states through the content-analysis of verbal behavior.* Berkeley: University of California Press, 1969.

Hollingshead, A., & Redlich, F. *Social class and mental illness.* New York: Wiley, 1958.

Horney, K. The dread of women. *International Journal of Psycho-analysis*, 1932, *13*, 348–361.

Jones, E. *Hamlet and Oedipus.* New York: Doubleday/Anchor Books, 1949.

Kardiner, A. As quoted in the *New York Times*, May 7, 1977.

Lévi-Strauss, C. *The savage mind.* Chicago: University of Chicago Press, 1968.

Levy, R., & Rowitz, R. *The ecology of mental disorder.* New York: Behavioral Publications, 1973.

Lewis, H. B. *Shame and guilt in neurosis* New York: International Universities Press, 1971.

Lewis, H. B. *Psychic war in men and women.* New York: New York University Press, 1976.

Lynn, D. Sex role and parental identification. *Child Development*, 1962, *33*, 555–564.

Maccoby, E. (Ed.). *The development of sex differences.* Stanford, Calif.: Stanford University Press, 1966.

Maccoby, E., & Jacklin, C. *The psychology of sex differences.* Stanford, Calif.: Stanford University Press, 1974.

Minard, J. and Mooney, W. Psychological differentiation and perceptual defense: Studies of the separation of perception from emotion. *Journal of Abnormal Psychology*, 1969, *74*, 131–140.

Nietzsche, F. *"Guilt," "bad conscience," and related matters.* In R. Smith (Ed.), *Guilt: Man and society.* New York: Doubleday/Anchor Books, 1971.

Schimek, J. Cognitive style and defenses: A longitudinal study of intellectualization and field-independence. *Journal of Abnormal Psychology*, 1968, *73*, 575–580.

Sears, R., Rau, L., & Alpert, R. *Identification and child-rearing.* Evanston, Ill.: Row-Peterson, 1965.

Siebert, L. Superego and sex differences. Unpublished doctoral dissertation. University of Michigan, 1965.

Smith, R. The relative proneness to shame or guilt as an indicator of defensive style. Unpublished doctoral dissertation. Northwestern University, 1972.

Witkin, H. Psychological differentiation and forms of pathology. *Journal of Abnormal Psychology*, 1965, *70*, 317–336.

Witkin, H., Dyk, R., Faterson, H., Goodenough, D., & Karp, J. *Psychological differentiation.* New York: Wiley, 1962.

Witkin, H., Lewis, H. & Weil, E. Affective reactions and patient–therapist interaction among more differentiated and less differentiated patients early in therapy. *Journal of Nervous and Neural Disease*, 1968, *146*, 193–208.

Editor's Introduction

14

This chapter presents a good overview of Beck's well-known theory of depression. As most students of depression know, this theory presents an extremely lucid picture of the phenomenology and symptomatology of depression. The depressed may suffer a wide variety of physiological and psychological ailments, but they are characterized most especially as people who have a bleak and despairing view of themselves, their world, and their future and concomitant negative emotions. Kovacs and Beck's paper presents incisive arguments and evidence that suggest that the several diagnostic classifications of depression and the long list of specific symptoms that accompany them may be understood in terms of a general cognitive set or a complex of cognitive-affective structures that determine the thoughts, moods, and behavior of depressive patients.

Kovacs and Beck trace the causes of depression to cognitive processes, but they recognize the importance of emotions and moods once these are activated by negative perceptions and thoughts. Thus, for example, while conception of oneself as a social failure may trigger a depression, the resulting sadness and resentment play a significant role in the individual's phenomenology and sense of well-being.

Like some other emotion theories, Kovacs and Beck describe their position as a kind of continuous feedback loop in which self-deprecatory remarks lead to negative emotions like distress and shame, which in turn are reconstrued negatively, followed by an amplification of the depressed affect and other symptoms.

Kovacs and Beck make an unusually insightful analysis of the characteristics of cognitive processes in depression. They use literary material, clinical interviews, and empirical investigations to show the salience of negative thematic content, distortions of time perspective, and selective recall. They go on to show how these more elemental cognitive processes contribute to the development of cognitive structures that result in the attribution of idiosyncratic meaning to important events in the individual's life. They also show how these cognitive-affective structures lead to characteristic errors in thought, such as arbitrary influence and overgeneralization, making it possible for the depressed person to believe the most morbid of all possible interpretations of an event no matter how improbable it may be.

Finally, they show how quite elemental cognitive processes reflect the underlying depressogenic premises and schemata that characterize the depressive person. The authors conclude by indicating how their analysis of depression leads to a therapeutic approach, cognitive therapy, for which specific treatment procedures have been specified.

Cognitive-Affective Processes in Depression

14

MARIA KOVACS and AARON T. BECK

I. THE PHENOMENOLOGY OF DEPRESSION

The sad, despairing mood and the various behavioral changes that characterize the pathological depressions have been recognized throughout the ages. In the Old Testament, for example, Job and King Saul are described as suffering from depression. The 12th-century letters of Héloise to Peter Abelard vividly convey the milder symptoms of depression subsequent to a traumatic separation. In more recent times, individuals such as Lincoln, Kierkegaard, and Churchill had clear-cut and documented episodes of depression.

In depression, the mood alteration may occur suddenly or insidiously. It may be experienced as sadness, as feeling miserable or "down in the dumps," as feeling bland or irritable, or as a noticeably reduced sense of excitement about life. There may be complaints of tearfulness or of not being able to cry anymore. Depressed people report a loss of interest in themselves and in life, difficulties in carrying out customary tasks and responsibilities, and problems with concentration and memory. Decreased social activity and overt social withdrawal are often noted. Reduced or disturbed sleep and appetite loss are common and so are complaints of fatigue and of bodily aches and pains. Above all, depressed people are characterized by profound self-deprecation and a pervading sense of pessimism and hopelessness. They are preoccupied with their real or imagined flaws or inadequacies and describe themselves as

MARIA KOVACS • School of Medicine, University of Pittsburgh, Pittsburgh, Pennsylvania.
AARON T. BECK • The University of Pennsylvania School of Medicine, Philadelphia, Pennsylvania.

unattractive, stupid, incompetent, and a burden on others. Pessimism and hopelessness are evident in the bleak and despairing description of the future, and suicide is an ever-present danger.

As Beck (1967) noted, in moderate to severe depression, one is struck by the discrepancy between known facts and the patient's evaluation and the apparent obliteration of normal "drives" to survive and procreate. For example, one extremely depressed and suicidal woman was convinced of her impending poverty although her deceased, estranged husband left her over $35,000 and she herself had considerable savings. Another depressed woman with three adolescent children felt that she was useless, "weak," and a burden on her family, she felt that she would be "better off dead."

Although the list of specific symptoms can be extensive, there is general agreement that depression encompasses distinct changes in mood and subjective experience, in thinking and evaluation, and in social, interpersonal, and physiological functioning (Beck, 1967; Becker, 1974; Grinker, Miller, Sabshin, Nunn, & Nunnally, 1961; Mendels, 1970). Nonetheless, there is still controversy as to the causes of these alterations and the most valid diagnostic or classificatory schemata. The heterogeneity of the depressions, in terms of onset, course, duration, specific characteristics, and treatment responsivity, suggests multiple causal agents (Akiskal & McKinney, 1973). Possible diagnostic dimensions have been reviewed and new ones suggested by numerous individuals (e.g., Akiskal & McKinney, 1973, 1975; Becker, 1974; Klein, 1974; Klerman, 1971; Rush, 1975; Secunda, Katz, Friedman, & Schuyler, 1973; Wing, 1976).

Lest the reader despair that diagnostic disagreement makes clinical and empirical work impossible, let us reassure him that work on the depressions continues to flourish. To select individuals for study, clinicians and researchers resort to clinical operational criteria and psychometric tools. In psychiatric research, the most frequently used operational criteria specify a certain number of depressive symptoms of a specified duration for "inclusion" in the study and other symptoms that "exclude" the patient from consideration (Feighner, Robins, Guze, Woodruff, Winokur, & Munoz, 1972). The severity of depression is assessed by means of a self-rated inventory or symptom checklist such as the Beck Depression Inventory (Beck, 1967; Beck & Beamesderfer, 1974), the Zung Depression Rating Scale (Zung, 1965), or the Lubin Adjective Checklist for Depression (Lubin, 1965), each of which is completed by the patient himself. Symptom-rating scales filled out by a clinician on the basis of a detailed interview are also widely employed, for example, the Hamilton Rating Scale for Depression (Hamilton, 1960). Well-designed studies use both psychometric and clinical indices. The reader is referred to Becker (1974) for a comprehensive overview of available reliability and validity data on the various scales.

II. THE COGNITIVE VIEW OF DEPRESSION

As Neisser (1967) pointed out, if asked why you behave in a certain way or do a certain thing, you can answer in dynamic terms, "Because I wanted . . . ," or in cognitive terms, "Because it seemed to me that. . . . " We might add that you could also answer from a behavioristic perspective, "Because in the past whenever I did. . . ." These answers exemplify the dominant current *psychological* perspectives on depression: the dynamic, the cognitive, and the learning-theory orientation. We will discuss primarily the cognitive view of depression, specifically the characteristics of cognitive and affective processes in depression.

The contemporary psychiatric viewpoint is that the depressions are primarily *affective* disorders (Committee on Nomenclature and Statistics of the American Psychiatric Association, 1968). In other words, the disordered mood is the cardinal symptom and is responsible for the patient's impaired functioning. According to Beck (1963, 1967, 1976), however, the most salient psychological symptom of depression is the profoundly altered thinking: the negative view of oneself, the world, and the future.

Through systematic psychotherapeutic observations, Beck (1963) noticed that depressed patients were preoccupied with their alleged negative personal attributes. The unflattering and self-castigating themes, evident in both self-report and dream content, had strong stereotypic qualities. They were frequently inaccurate and were generally inappropriate to a particular situation. Closer examination of the patient's thinking revealed that the inaccurate assessments were not random. Rather, they were systematic errors since the judgment, conclusion, or interpretation *consistently* reflected a negative bias against the depressed person *himself* (Beck, 1963). Such observations led to the hypothesis that the depressed person's cognitions precede the marked dysphoria and the various functional impairments (Beck, 1967, 1971, 1976).

From a clinical point of view, historical antecedents of the cognitive approach may be found in Adler's emphasis that it is not the nature of events but one's subjective evaluation of them that determines adjustment and maladjustment (Ansbacher & Ansbacher, 1964) and in George Kelly's view of man as one who actively construes events and thus shapes his life (Kelly, 1955).

The cognitive viewpoint of depression assumes that the individual selectively attends to and processes certain kinds of data in an idiosyncratic way. It also assumes that one's cognitions, attitudes, values, and the like are accessible to introspection; they can be elucidated, monitored, examined, and altered. The manner in which a person thinks about and evaluates himself, others, and the tasks of life is intimately related to his subjective affective experiences and his concomitant or subsequent observable behaviors. Particular cognitive contents are chained to particular affects. In the depressions, notions of loss or perceived subtractions from one's personal domain are generally linked to feelings of sadness. The personal domain includes the individual himself, significant other people, valued animate or inanimate objects and attributes, and morals or ideals held to be important (Beck, 1971). Withdrawal of affection, for example, will be construed as a major and traumatic loss if the person views continued affection and its correlates as a significant part of his life. Such a construction then leads to sadness and dysphoria.

In clinical depressions, the patient's thinking is dominated by mistaken, erroneous, and exaggerated ways of viewing events. The notions and evaluations are not consensually validated, and the pervasive negative bias against oneself is obviously maladaptive. The self-castigation, the unwarranted negative conclusions, and notions that the future cannot be any different all militate against the patient's active exploration of adaptive problem-solving strategies and the appropriate use of himself and others as resources. The phenomena of passivity, reduced motivation, and despair then clearly follow. The characteristic cognitions not only are causally related to the onset of the depressive syndrome but play a significant role in its maintenance. As in a feedback loop, the negative cognitions lead to depressed affect, which, in turn, is reconstrued in negative terms and intensifies the dysphoria and the severity of other symptoms (Beck, 1967).

The psychological aspects of depression that have been highlighted by the cognitive model are detailed in subsequent sections. But first, we will present a brief introduction to the concepts of cognition and affect.

III. COGNITION AND COGNITIVE PROCESSES

Since *cognition* refers to both the process of knowing and the product of the act of knowing, it subsumes perception, memory, judgment, language, and so forth, as well as beliefs, attitudes, and problem-solving strategies (Mahoney, 1977; Neisser, 1967). Neisser (1967) defines cognition as the processes through which internal or external sensory input is "transformed, reduced, elaborated, stored, recovered, and used" (p. 4). In a similar vein, Broadbent (1971) refers to a "complex of interacting processes, many of which were already in progress" before a particular stimulus arrived. The processes may involve different operations with varied outcomes: transformation, selective attention, partial or complete memory storage, or modification of a preexisting representation of the world.

Unfortunately, cognitive psychology does not have much definitive data on the complex mental activities of remembering, thinking, problem solving, or imagery. Little is known about the nature of the "raw material" being construed in such cognitive phenomena, how it is organized and transformed, and what determines the particular problem or image being attended to (Neisser,

1967, p. 280). Since a satisfactory explanation requires a comprehensive theory of memory and thought (which we do not have at the present time), only suggestions can be made toward an understanding of "higher mental processes."

With respect to memory, Neisser's position is that just as a person does not see objects "because they are there" but as a consequence of an elaborate process of construction, memory involves not a reactivation of intact traces but, rather, a complex process of reconstruction (p. 285). Falmagne (1975) also seems to agree that memory itself is likely to be constructive.

The concepts of *cognitive structures* or *schemata* are frequently used to address questions concerning what is preserved from the past, how it is organized, and how and why a stored experience is recovered. *Schemata* have been defined as nonspecific but organized representations of prior experience that facilitate recall as well as systematically distort new constructions (Neisser, 1967, pp. 286–288). In Piaget's theory, *schema* refers to a basic structure or process that underlies sensorimotor behavior or complex mental activity and explains the organization and regularity of acts. In older children and adults, a schema can transform the character of primary perception (Inhelder & Piaget, 1969).

Problem-solving and reasoning experiments essentially address some aspect of the selective use of prior experience in complex mental activity. However, the tasks investigated or the models of propositional reasoning used tell us little about the psychology of everyday thinking (Johnson-Laird, 1975) and have limited immediate relevance to the problems of disordered thought seen in clinical practice. First of all, many everyday uses of semantic connectives cannot be mapped by traditional logic. Semantic relations that depend on the meaning of verbs, for example, lead to all sorts of interpretations and complexities usually not dealt with or not allowed in logic (Johnson-Laird, 1975; Staudenmeyer, 1975). In other words, logic is constrained to generate only empirically valid conclusions from empirically valid premises (Falmagne, 1975, p. 3).

Consequently, in both everyday and pathological reasoning, the nature of the premise takes on particular importance. Given the range of linguistic meanings, a premise stated in semantic terms is open to varied interpretations. The particular reasoning process will be inherently bound to the nature of the interpretation or content that it operates upon. In sum, there is considerable agreement that the decisions of everyday life are best viewed as intuitive exploitations of knowledge, differences in interpretation, and "emotional decisions to accept or reject premises" (Wason & Johnson-Laird, 1972, p. 2).

Nevertheless, reasoning experiments have yielded observations that are both interesting and relevant to the cognitive approach to psychopathology. As Falmagne's (1975) overview points out, in reasoning tasks, semantic connectives and quantifiers (e.g., *all*, *some*, *always*) are especially involved in errors of interpretation. In semantic problems, the difference between connotative and denotative meanings may be at the root of additional errors (Staudenmeyer, 1975).

Subjects' problem-solving attitudes often interfere with the optimal use of their intellectual resources. For instance, given experiments that required subjects to discover a simple relational rule between a set of elements, Wason and Johnson-Laird noticed that, in spite of instructions, subjects often insisted on announcing the rule prior to having checked its validity. In some cases, subjects refused outright to accept the correct rule around which the experiment was structured. Thus, as Wason (1971) noted, the subjects seemed to want to confirm their own hypotheses "to verify rather than falsify, to believe rather than to doubt." Certain mechanisms alleged to be characteristic of thought-disordered people could also be induced easily in normal subjects, given difficult, abstract reasoning problems. For example, in a number of Wason and Johnson-Laird's (1972) protocols, strong obsessional features could be discerned. In other cases, subjects became so intensely preoccupied with their original hypotheses that they became "blind to the obvious." Impatience, inability to learn from experience, and prejudicial attitudes that rendered the subject "immune from contradictory evidence" were also noted (p. 235). These investigators have concluded that given difficult problem-solving tasks, many subjects systematically deceive themselves and that "every device, ranging from self-contradiction to denial, is brought into the service of self-deception" (p. 237). These observations indicate that given certain demand characteristics of a situation, "normal" subjects exhibit somewhat deviant and unreasonable attitudes and problem-solving approaches. In the depressions, many of these attitudes can be observed to a far more extensive degree and seem to be the norm rather than the exception.

IV. AFFECT AND AFFECTIVE PROCESSES

When we approach the meaning of the word *affect* and the phrase *affective processes* we are in no less difficulty than with the word *cognition*. The words *affect* and *emotion* are used interchangeably (e.g., Plutchik, 1970), and various definitions are available. Some of the approaches to the study of emotion are highlighted by other chapters in this book.

According to Plutchik (1970), all the various approaches to the study of emotions should be incorporated into a general theory or definition. For example, the evolutionary approach exemplified by Darwin's work has focused on the expressive and behavioral aspects of emotions. The James–Cannon approach has emphasized visceral sensations and reportable feelings, while the psychodynamic tradition has been concerned mostly with inferences that can be drawn from the mixture and interplay of the various emotions. More current strategies have highlighted the physiological and neurochemical substrata of emotions and the role of cognitions, evaluations, and labeling in affective experience. Arnold's (1970) book presents a detailed treatment of selected theories while Strongman (1973) briefly summarizes many various approaches to the study of emotions.

Most definitions implicitly or explicity acknowledge the multifaceted nature of affect. Feelings, or more specifically, subjective feelings, constitute one aspect of emotion (Strongman, 1973). Emotion also involves some bodily (physiological) state as well as overt behavior, both of which occur in particular contexts or situations. Some definitions emphasize that emotion is "a state of the organism which effects behavior," while others focus on its qualities as a "response." However, it has been suggested that since theories and empirical research deal with only some aspect of the broad meaning that the term has acquired, at present, *emotion* defies precise definition (Strongman, 1973, pp. 1–2).

Tomkins (1970), for example, stipulates that affects are "sets of muscle, vascular, and glandular responses located in the face and also widely distributed through the body, which generate sensory feedback which is inherently either 'acceptable' or 'unacceptable'" (p. 105). Affects constitute a primary motivational system and are triggered at subcortical centers where innately endowed and genetically inherited programs are stored for each distinct emotion. Distress or anguish—the crying response, for instance—is one of the major negative affects (p. 107).

Izard (1972) distinguishes between the "fundamental emotions" and their various combinations. Fundamental emotions have (1) a specific, innately determined neural substrate; (2) a typical neuromuscular expressive pattern; and (3) a distinct subjective or phenomenological quality. Each of the fundamental emotions (e.g., anger, distress) has a unique motivational property and an inherently adaptive function. In depression, the combination of fundamental emotions is regarded as the principal constituent, in addition to which somatic and cognitive components are also involved. According to Izard's differential emotion theory, "the fundamental emotions of distress, anger, disgust, contempt, fear, guilt and shyness, and the bodily feelings of physical well-being, sexuality and fatigue" constitute the components of depression (p. 281). Other symptoms of depression result from the conflict between the various fundamental emotions, from the pattern in which they combine, or from direct influence of the fundamental emotions on cognition and action.

In contrast to Tomkins (1970), Izard (1972), and others, a number of theorists emphasize the importance of perception, cognition, or appraisal in affective experience. According to Arnold (1970b), emotion is "a felt tendency toward anything appraised as good, and away from anything appraised as bad" (p. 176). Thus, emotion is a two-step process: appraisal of the expected effects of a situation and a felt movement to or away from the object. The direction of the movement is determined by the nature of the appraisal. Arnold also emphasizes the role of "affective memory," which, without our awareness, often predetermines or prejudices current appraisals. Affective memory is a reliving of the original acceptance or rejection of a situation, and is activated by a new but similar situation (p. 176). In a similar vein, Leeper (1970) proposes that emotions are basically "long-sustained perceptions of the more enduring and significant aspects" of situations (p. 156). Leeper regards emotions as motives since they influence the psychological life of the organism by producing the "goal directedness" of behavior and mental activity.

Peters's (1970) definition of emotion is also in the cognitive tradition. He states that emotions are essentially appraisals elicited by conditions "of concern to us" or by "things which we have brought about" (p. 188). Different appraisals involve different emotions. For example, seeing something as threatening brings forth fear, while seeing something as thwarting results in anger. Complex appraisals also involve some "empirical beliefs" (Peters, 1970, p. 196). For instance, jealousy is based on the belief that someone has done or intends to do something that threatens one's claim to someone or something, although this belief can be false. In fact, according to Peters, some forms of neurosis are best characterized by saying that "the patient is a victim of false beliefs" (p. 197).

Lazarus, Averill, and Opton (1970) suggest that from the phylogenetic and physiological points of view, there is little reason to make a sharp distinction between emotion and cognition or to attribute to emotion more primitive functions. Their central thesis is that (1) a person is an "evaluative organism" who searches for and assesses stimuli with respect to their personal significance; (2) emotions are "a function of such cognitive activity," each emotion being ostensibly associated with a different evaluation; (3) since emotional action is a consequence of a particular cognition, the response itself is an "organized syndrome"; and (4) the determining antecedent conditions consist of "situational" factors and "dispositional" factors (beliefs, attitudes, personality traits, etc.) (pp. 217–219). Biological, cultural, and socialization factors all contribute to "disposition" since they shape responses and impose belief systems and rules of conduct. Thus, "disposition" functions as a cognitive filter.

V. COGNITION AND AFFECT IN DEPRESSION

When we talk about cognition in depression, we refer to the depressed patient's characteristic ideas, perceptions, evaluative processes, and beliefs. Our use of the word *affect* is primarily restricted to denote its subjective feeling component. Consistent with the cognitive position (e.g., Arnold, 1970b; Lazarus *et al.*, 1970; Peters, 1970), we propose that depressive affect and dysphoria are a function of characteristic cognitive appraisals of stimuli and situations.

We believe that the phenomenology of depressive thought is relatively easy to illustrate. However, to a "hardheaded" empiricist, such illustrations would hardly constitute evidence that these processes are salient or unique in the psychology of depressions. At the present time, it is not possible to offer conclusive "proof" in matters that relate to complex mental activity for the reasons we cited in a previous section (e.g., Neisser, 1967). As we also noted, studies of reasoning and problem solving give us little assistance. The issues and controversies we deal with in clinical practice and everyday life are not exercises in logic. Rather, they center on the multiple possible interpretations of events, one's willingness to accept or reject premises, and one's openness to new data or facts.

To illustrate the characteristics and salience of cognition in depression, we will present quotations and clinical vignettes, as well as correlational and experimental data. The chapter has been divided into a number of sections or topical subdivisions that are clearly arbitrary. For example, although presented in separate sections, depressive thought content and certain evaluative processes are interrelated. In the same vein, "schemata" and the attribution of idiosyncratic meaning represent different perspectives on the same phenomena. The topical sections are presented in increasing order of complexity, and each section builds on or incorporates previous ones.

A. Thematic Content of the Cognitions

As far back as the 16th century, Burton in his *Anatomy of Melancholia* described the sufferer's constant rumination about the bleakness of his future, his sinfulness, and his worthlessness. Beck (1963), among others, has also noted that the content of depressive thought is negatively self-referential. The depressed person's thoughts revolve around self-derogation, self-castigation, and self-blame. The notion of real, imagined, or anticipated loss is a prominent theme in his thinking. Notions of current loss or deficiency are extrapolated into the future and become manifest as pessimism or hopelessness: the belief that current discomfort will continue forever and that any positive action is doomed to fail. If interaction with others constitutes a significant component of "personal domain," the thought content encompasses presumed lack of importance to other people, anticipated rejection, and an unending series of disappointments and abandonments. Beck (1967) has referred to such thematic content as the "negative cognitive triad": a negative view of the self, the world, and the future.

Kierkegaard, who had fairly distinct episodes of depression, had numerous diary entries that illustrate the negative, self-derogatory, and hopeless cognitive themes in depression, for example, "I was born in 1813, in the year . . . when so many counterfeit notes were put into circulation. I can best be compared with one of them" (Thompson, 1973, p. 8).

Or again, according to Lowrie (1938), he once fell from a sofa at a social gathering, and when his friends hastened to help him, he beseeched them not to pick "it" up: "Leave it there till the morning, when the housemaid will sweep it up" (p. 94). At one point, Kierkegaard also wrote, "The whole of existence is infected for me" (Thompson, 1973, p. 80).

Excerpts from our case files also illustrate the characteristic thematic content in depressive thought. In the dialogue, *T* stands for therapist and *P* for patient:

> T: Why did you want to kill yourself?
> P: I just could not see living without Raymond.
> T: Why do you feel that Raymond is essential for your living?
> P: I guess it's because without Raymond I am *nothing*.

With another patient the following exchange took place:

> P: I am disgusted with myself—I'm lousy.
> T: Why are you disgusted with yourself?
> P: Since New Year's . . . I've been depressed—I hate myself for it. The kids are filthy—and I, I don't care.
> T: Why is that a reason to be disgusted?
> P: *I can't make up my mind about anything*—the cleaning—I think it's gonna take forever and things look unsurmountable (pause) and *I'm not cut out to raise my kids*. You know I don't feel I have ever been a good housekeeper—*I just don't do it right*.

Naturalistic and correlational studies support our contention that the ideational content in depression is negatively self-referential.

Weintraub, Segal, and Beck (1974) devised a set of incomplete stories, each accompanied by four sets of sentences or response options. The response options reflected degrees of (1) expected discomfort and failure; (2) negative interpersonal relationships; (3) low self-concept; and (4) "positive" resolution or attitude. Subjects were instructed to "identify" with the principal character of the stories and complete each story by choosing one response option.

The stories and a self-rated mood checklist were administered to 30 normal male undergraduates five times over a two-month interval. The results indicate that depressed affect was associated with selection of "negative" story completion choices and that the areas of negative cognitive content were highly intercorrelated. In addition, cognitions were more enduring and stable over time than mood.

A similar story-completion task was used in a study of 77 female college students (Hammen & Krantz, 1976). The stories were followed by a number of questions that pertained to the character's thoughts and feelings. Response options reflected low self-concept, pessimism and negative expectations, and negative view of interpersonal experiences. Self-rated symptom checklists were used to classify subjects as depressed or nondepressed. The results indicated that compared to nondepressed women, depressed women selected significantly more responses that reflected negative themes.

Laxer (1964) used a semantic differential test to investigate self-concept changes of hospitalized depressives and paranoid schizophrenics. He reported that compared to the schizophrenic patients, the depressives showed low self-concept at the time of hospital admission, which was much improved by the time of their discharge. Beck (1967, p. 182) found that depressed patients rated themselves low on attributes of personal importance to them, although on "conventional virtues" such as kindness, they generally felt superior to others. In a 1961 study, Beck gave a Focused Fantasy Test to 87 depressed and non-depressed patients. His results indicate that compared to nondepressed patients, depressed patients significantly more often selected story outcomes where the protagonist was hurt or subjected to unpleasant experiences.

An empirical test of depressives' negative view of life experience was facilitated by a scale that operationalized the concepts of pessimism and hopelessness (Beck, Weissman, Lester, & Trexler, 1974). Among psychiatric inpatients, pessimism and levels of depression were found to be significantly correlated, a finding that was subsequently replicated on large samples of hospitalized suicidal patients (Beck, Kovacs, & Weissman, 1975; Minkoff, Bergman, Beck, & Beck, 1973). Melges and Bowlby (1969) similarly observed the predominance of hopelessness in depression. In other words, depressed patients consistently believe that one's plans of action have lost their effectiveness to reach important goals.

Dreams have had a particularly strong fascination for observers of human behavior. The view that dreams represent symbolic expressions of private visions and knowledge is as old as the Old Testament.

However, if we view dream content as a reflection of one's daily conceptualizations, we find additional evidence for negative cognitive themes in depression. Beck and Hurvich (1959) collected the first 20 dreams of six matched pairs of depressed and nondepressed psychotherapy patients. An independent evaluator rated the randomized dreams for thematic content. As predicted, depressed patients had significantly more dreams in which the dreamer was subjected to experiences such as being rejected, abandoned, ill, and punished, and being ugly and undesirable or dysphoric. These findings were replicated in a sample of 218 patients (Beck, 1967, pp. 214–217). Interestingly, a sleep laboratory study by Hauri (1976) indicates that even among remitted depressives there is a preponderance of negative, unpleasant, and "masochistic" dream content compared to that of normal controls.

What are the affective consequences of negatively oriented cognitions? As previously noted, we would expect the affective tone to be congruent with the nature of the thought content. In fact, clinical experience as well as empirical data suggests this association. When asked, depressed patients most commonly label their emotions as feeling sad, miserable, blue, unhappy, lonely, downhearted, useless, guilty (Beck, 1967). In one of the above clinical vignettes, the patient described herself as unable to take care of things and as a bad mother and housekeeper: her expressed feeling was "disgust." The naturalistic, correlational study by Weintraub *et al.* (1974) reported a time-specific correlation between negative cognitions and depressed mood and the relative stability of cognition compared to affect: students who were "thinking depressed" (as defined by their story-completion responses) were feeling more depressed than subjects without such thoughts.

Even more persuasive is the increasing body of literature that indicates that affect can be induced by cognitive means in experimental settings. Velten (1968) examined the effect of self-referent statements on mood in a sample of 100 college students. After reading statements that progressed from neutral to a depressive mood, normal subjects' mood became significantly depressed as defined by a number of self-report and behavioral measures. Coleman's (1975) induction procedure consisted of having the subjects read either positive or negative self-evaluative statements. He reported that the cognitive manipulation produced significant differences in levels of elation or depression, consistent with the content of the cognitive task. The treatments produced criterion performance on self-report, projective, observational, and behavioral measures.

Moore, Underwood, and Rosenhan (1973) induced sadness in children by asking them to think of a sad event. On the other hand, Averill's (1969) mood induction technique involved viewing a movie with sad content whose effect was confirmed by responses on an adjective-rating scale, by self-report, and on physiological measures. In a recent study, Natale (1977) reported successful mood induction through an automatic version of Velten's (1968) cognitive task. Similar success was reported by Hale and Strickland (1976), who investigated cognitive and performance consequences of laboratory mood induction with 60 female college students. Izard (1972) found that a characteristic profile of emotions was reported by subjects instructed to visualize a depressive situation, and Schwartz, Fair, Greenberg, Mandel, and Klerman (1976) obtained expected differences in facial muscle patterning between individuals engaging in sad and happy imagery and between normals and depressives imaging a typical day. All these studies suggest that by focusing subjects' attention on cognitive information, affective tone can be successfully manipulated. Ludwig's (1975) study is probably even more relevant to the cognitive view of depression. Undergraduate women were presented with bogus personality reports designed to induce either elation or depression through altered self-esteem. Reports stating that subjects were immature and uncreative approximate the negative self-referential thinking observed among depressed patients. The technique was successful in the experimental induction of depressed mood.

B. Time Perspective

Both Neisser (1967) and Staudenmeyer (1975) regard cognitive structures that represent temporal succession or arrangement in time as being particularly important. In our society, adults generally construe experiences in a time perspective; personal facts and data are specifically represented in a temporal framework. Existentialist analysts such as Binswanger (May, Angel, & Ellenberger, 1958) emphasize that for man the predominant mode of time is the future and that constriction of that mode represents a disturbance in functioning.

In the depressions, temporal distortion is evident in the patients' often-expressed statements that they have "no future." This conception is clearly tied to the negative personal preoccupation of depressed individuals and their characteristic ruminations that their situation is hopeless. In other words, the futures loses its meaning as a harbinger of prospective solutions (Dilling & Rabin, 1967).

At one point Kierkegaard wrote, "Time passes, life is a stream, men say, &c. It doesn't seem so to me: time stands still, and I with it" (Lowrie, 1938, p. 103). At another time he said about himself, "I was already an old man when I was born. . . . I leapt completely over childhood and youth" (Lowrie, 1938, p. 47). One of our patients wrote in her diary, "The days pass and I don't see them. What is there to look for? Yesterday is tommorow."

Stuart (1962) assessed future time perspective by means of an inventory and semantic-differential ratings of the concept of "the future." She found a highly significant relationship between depressive tendencies and reduced or "constricted" future outlook. Consistent with the observation that the future loses its meaning as a "healer," our work indicates that hopelessness is a very strong correlate of suicidal intent and suicidal risk (Beck *et al.*, 1975; Kovacs, Beck, & Weissman, 1975).

Dilling and Rabin (1967) compared depressives, schizophrenics, and normals on measures of future time perspective, time perception, and time orientation. Their data indicate that compared to both schizophrenics and normals, depressives show a severely limited future time span. On the other hand, both psychopathological groups were inferior to normals in perception of longer time intervals and extent of future orientation. Alteration of time perspective in moderately to severely depressed patients was also reported by Rey, Silber, Savard, and Post (1977). Andreasen and Pfohl's (1976) linguistic analysis of speech in affective disorders indicates that depressives are somewhat more preoccupied with the past than manics. Hauri's (1976) study of remitted depressives and normals reported that the patients' dreams dealt mainly with past events, while normal controls tended to dream about present and future issues. These data may suggest that in depression, some level of cognitive disturbance may be long-term and persist even after symptomatic improvement.

In our clinical experience, the affective consequences of hopelessness and constricted time perspective vary. If the patient is ambivalent about whether or not he does have a future, the reported affective experiences are similar to the ones mentioned in the previous section: sadness, feeling miserable and helpless, feeling hopeless and despondent. However, conviction that the future is completely obliterated usually produces a more devastating affective experience, that of "despair" and "emptiness." In severely depressed patients, the absolute constriction of future time perspective is not uncommonly connected with the utmost in dysphoria—feeling nothing.

C. Selective Recall

Selective recall in depression is most evident when we take the patients' psychiatric/psychological history or ask them to relate events of the past days. Depressed patients have an overwhelming tendency to remember material with unpleasant, self-derogatory content. They emphasize the real or imagined negative implications of past events at the expense of neutral or positively toned material. For example, take the following from our case notes:

> T: And can you tell me how long you have had this depression, feeling this bad and not being able to do things?
> P: All my life!
> T: Was there a time when things were OK—when things went well?
> P: It doesn't seem that way—things *never* were OK for me.

Or let us take another patient who had been asked to keep a diary of her daily activities, which she brought to the therapy session:

> T: I see you brought your diary—and how did things go in the last few days?
> P: (Silence.) Terrible. I didn't get anything done. The house is still filthy and I didn't cook—I don't know—I don't seem to be able to get anything done.
> T: Let's see. (Takes diary.) Well, it says here that on Monday you went to the supermarket and shopped for the week, and you took the kids to a party that evening and in the afternoon you made a number of phone calls and sorted the laundry and. . . .
> P: (Silence.) Well, maybe I did get some things done, but it wasn't much.

A number of studies obtained results consistent with the clinical observation that depressed individuals are more likely to remember negative material than positive material. Lloyd and Lishman (1975) reported that increasing depression is associated with a progressively diminishing ratio between the speed of recall of pleasant and unpleasant memories. Depressed individuals also tend to recall material with higher negative tone than nondepressed patients (Lishman, 1972). In a similar vein, a study by Nelson and Craighead

(1977) indicates that compared to nondepressed controls, depressed subjects significantly underestimated the amount of reinforcement received during an experimental task but overestimated how many times they were punished.

Differential recall of experimental punishment and reward was also reported for depressed male psychiatric patients compared to psychiatric and nonpsychiatric controls (DeMonbreun & Craighead, 1977) and for nonpsychiatric female volunteer subjects divided into a depressed and a nondepressed group (Wener & Rehm, 1975).

Selective recall of negatively toned material is probably tied to and reinforces the depressive's constricted perspective of the future. Since recall of past events provides thematic content for present rumination, it serves as an additional source of unpleasant cognitions that maintain or accentuate the depressed person's dysphoric affective experiences.

D. Idiosyncratic Meaning

Depressed individuals tend to assign global, personalized, idiosyncratic meanings to events and attributes. They view failure experiences in an especially subjective and self-referential manner. Although depressed people are often convinced that they cannot effect positive changes, they consistently assign responsibility to themselves for negative outcomes.

Global, idiosyncratic meaning in depressed cognition is illustrated by another quote from Kierkegaard. After breaking his engagement to Regine Olsen, he noted, "When I left her I chose death" (Thompson, 1973, p. 116). One of our patients wrote in her diary, "The fact that I am single is a shortcoming and it will never change." The following dialogue took place between a therapist and a depressed patient after the patient expressed concern over her lateness to her first session:

P: I thought—"Why did I do this [i.e., being late]?" I thought that you would think that I'm not reliable.
T: How did you know that I would think that?
P: Well, *I* would think that if someone was late.

The same patient later attributed her lateness to her disorganization:

P: I forget things, and—I'm so disorganized—that's a dumb thing!
T: Well, did you ask anyone for directions [when you saw you were lost]?
P: Yeah—when I saw I was lost, I asked this delivery man—but he was disorganized too.
T: And did you think that *he* was dumb—because he seemed disorganized?
P: No! I didn't think bad about him—but for *me*, it's a dumb thing!

Another patient, who, when especially distressed, systematically sought friends' advice and regularly called his therapist, wrote: "I'm despicable for asking opinions. . . . "

In what manner is meaning distorted in depression? To answer a similar question, Stuart (1962) assessed various semantic tendencies: (1) evaluative rather than class associations (e.g., choosing *sweet* rather than *fruit* as an association to the stimulus word *orange*); (2) evaluative rather than denotative associations (e.g., *sweet* rather than *round* for *orange*); and (3) denotative rather than class associations (e.g., *round* rather than *fruit* for *orange*). Two-choice controlled-association items were used to investigate the three semantic habits. Stuart's (1962) data indicate a correlation between depressive tendencies and preference for evaluative rather than class associations. Thus depressed individuals tend to prefer subjective rather than objective semantic meanings.

Recent studies on attribution are also relevant to our topic since causal ascriptions essentially deal with the personal meaning of events. Rizley (1976), for instance, used a novel experimental task to examine depressed and non-depressed subjects' retrospective causal ascriptions for performance outcome. Compared to nondepressed individuals, the depressed ones rated internal factors (effort and ability) as more important determinants of failure but as less important in success. Depressed subjects also self-attributed more interpersonal influence, causality, and responsibility.

Klein, Fencil-Morse, and Seligman (1976) exposed subjects to solvable, unsolvable, or no discrimination problems with experimentally manipulated failure attributions. On a subsequent series of patterned anagrams, depressed individuals (defined by scores on a self-rating scale) were more likely than non-depressed ones to attribute failure (but *not* success) to their own abilities. Calhoun, Cheney, and Dawes (1974) reported that for female subjects, the degree of depressed mood correlated with a tendency to hold oneself responsible for it.

Affective concomitants of personalized meaning are determined by the nature of the attribution or interpretation. In one of the above clinical examples, asking for advice meant to the patient that he was "despicable": the affect he reported was primarily shame and secondarily anxiety. The anxiety arose from the anticipation that people would want nothing to do with him since he was "despicable."

Thus, this patient viewed his opinion-seeking behavior in a highly subjective, negatively evaluative light. Moreover he proceeded to employ his alleged negative characteristic as a proposition that he accepted without questioning. The sequence of his thinking may be mapped as follows:

> I seek out opinions, I call my therapist a lot (objective behavior) →→ therefore, I am despicable (personalized, idiosyncratic meaning) →→ since I am despicable, people may want nothing to do with me (characteristic is used as an unquestioned proposition).

Our clinical observations suggest that in the depressions, characteristic personalized meanings are commonly combined to yield maladaptive conclusions. In the following section, we will describe some of the cognitive processes that are involved in the depressed patients' erroneous conclusions and evaluations .

E. Characteristic Errors in Thought

In everyday life, variation in ideas and acts is the rule rather than the exception. Noticeable repetition in behavior and adaptation that is achieved by narrowing and distorting the environment are generally characteristic of psychopathology (Craig, 1952, p. 91; Neisser, 1967, p. 282).

In the depressions, the patient's stereotypic, maladaptive responses to real or imagined problems result from the interaction of typical ideational content and cognitive interpretative mechanisms. As we have already noted, the depressed person views significant personal interactions and data self-referentially and evaluates them negatively. Positive material is selectively "forgotten." His future time perspective is constricted; meaning is overwhelmingly global, subjective, and connotative. His various cognitive transformations lead to stereotypic conclusions that reflect negatively on himself. Clinical experience indicates that the typical cognitive transformations are evident only in the depressed person's self-related ruminations. In other words, the patients are generally capable of employing more consensually validated interpretations if asked to problem-solve for another person.

Beck (1967, 1976) delineated a number of systematic errors of thought that may be implicated in the depressive's invariant, stereotypic conclusions. *Arbitrary inference*, or drawing a conclusion in the absence of or contrary to evidence, is a commonly observed error, for example, "My boss didn't talk to me for the last few days; he must be thinking about firing me."

Confronted with negative events or attributes, depressed patients typically utilize *magnification*; they exaggerate the significance of the particular incident, for instance, "I was devastated; they asked my opinion at this meeting and I couldn't think of anything to say. My mind went blank. It was disasterous." When it comes to pleasant events, positive attributes, or favorable accomplishments, depressed people resort to *minimization*; they discount the incident's implications. There is also a tendency to ignore salient aspects of a situation and to *abstract selectively* the isolated elements most consistent with their overall negative and pessimistic cosmology. The characteristic and invariant information-processing results in *overgeneralization* and the blurring of discriminations (Beck & Shaw, 1978). The conclusions, no matter how morbid, peculiar, or improbable, are quite believeable to the patient himself.

In one of the above clinical vignettes, the patient minimized the significance of having completed a number of chores and grossly exaggerated or dramatized the fact that some chores were not finished. The patient who concluded that he was "despicable" for asking opinions selectively abstracted this element from his interpersonal interactions and assumed that it warranted a global negative judgment about himself. Overgeneralization is frequently seen when the patient starts out by saying that he is unhappy and miserable because his wife does not love him and concludes that he cannot stand his pain because nobody loves him.

Kierkegaard was forever preoccupied by his sinfulness, which he largely attributed to a youthful visit to a house of prostitution (Lowrie, 1938). As the years went by, he frequently called himself a "leper" and announced to everyone's amazement, "I am a penitent" (Lowrie, 1938, p. 136). Apparently based on this sole incident, he consistently referred to his sinful "lusts and excesses" (Lowrie, 1938, p. 138). Lowrie's comment that no one seemed to agree with Kierkegaard's self-assessment is entirely consistent with our clinical experience that the depressed patient's self-evaluation represents a distortion of reality.

There are a number of systematic studies that support our clinical observations. Hammen and Krantz (1976), whose work we have already mentioned, reported empirical evidence for the presence of cognitive distortions in depression. The response options to their story completion tasks were designed to reflect the following cognitions: depressed-distorted, depressed-nondistorted, nondepressed-distorted, and nondepressed-nondistorted. The depressed-distorted choices encompassed typical depressive cognitive content and the errors of thought, (e.g., selective abstraction, arbitrary inference, minimization) described by Beck (1967). Compared to nondepressed subjects, the depressed ones selected a significantly higher portion of depressed-distorted story-completion responses. Arbitrary interpretations as well as magnification and minimization among moderately to severely depressed patients were also reported by Rey et al. (1977), who analyzed aberrations of language form and content.

Magnification of the negative aspects of experience as well as overgeneralization is reflected in depressed individuals' sensitivity to laboratory failure experiences. As part of their study, Hammen and Krantz (1976) gave depressed and nondepressed subjects a test supposedly designed to assess therapeutic ability. Compared to the rest of the subjects, depressed individuals who received bogus "failure" scores gave the least positive predictions of success on subsequent tasks. In a series of studies, Loeb and his co-workers found that on both a word-completion task and a card-sorting task, depressed patients exposed to negative feedback evidenced lower confidence than those exposed to success (Loeb, Feshbach, Beck, & Wolf, 1964) and also manifested lower aspiration and greater pessimism (Loeb, Beck, & Diggory, 1971). It was also found that while failure feedback impaired depressed patients' subsequent performance, it had the converse effect in the nondepressed group (Loeb et al, 1971).

Characteristic transformation processes, errors of thought, and the apparent impairment in evaluating the soundness or validity of the resultant conclusions produce the impression of some basic thinking disorder in depression. In fact, this impression is partially supported by a number of papers.

A recent study by Braff and Beck (1974) examined the abstraction ability of inpatient depressives and schizophrenics and of normals. Compared to normals, both psychopathological groups manifested a clear abstraction deficit. Moreover, severity of depression correlated with impairment in abstraction. According to Brattemo (1962), depressed patients' responses to a multiple-choice proverbs test were dominated by concrete, although correct, answers.

Ianzito, Cadoret, and Pugh (1974) investigated abnormalities of thought among 47 confirmed unipolar depressed inpatients and comparison groups of random depressives and schizophrenics. While schizophrenics were more likely to show severe cognitive impairment, nearly half of the depressives had moderate to severe thought disorder (e.g., paralogical, unrelated responses), and over three-fourths manifested disordered thought content (e.g., obsessive or repetitive thoughts, notions of worthlessness). These investigators' followup data also suggest that formal thought disorder predicts a more severe episode of depression.

F. Depressogenic Premises and Schemata

Is there a concept that allows us to integrate the thematic content of depressive cognitions and the particular transformations that stimuli are subjected to? How can we explain that when the thought content is self-referential, the depressed patient arrives at distorted and generally erroneous conclusions, while, for another person he can provide far more consensually validated and reasonable interpretations? In clinical practice, the question is "How did this patient come to believe that without her spouse she is 'nothing'?"

As we already noted, we should examine the nature of the premises involved in the depressed patients' interpretations and the subjective decisions that are implicated in their acceptance.

We have used the terms *silent assumptions, formulas,* and *basic equations* to denote the depressed patients' premises that concern self-evaluation and relationship to others (Beck, 1967; Beck, Rush, & Kovacs, 1976; Beck & Shaw, 1978). Premises are implicit or explicit statements of "fact" that form the basis of an argument, a conclusion, an evaluation, or a problem resolution.

Certain clues allow us to infer with some confidence that a depressogenic premise or assumption underlies the patient's evaluations. One clue is the persistent and indiscriminate use of the directive *should* or *must.* The housewife, described previously, preceded most of her self-castigations with the phrase "I should," which encompassed being on time, taking care of the house, being in good spirits, being a good mother, being competent in interpersonal affairs, being charming. Systematic inquiry as to why she "should" be all those things disclosed that one of her basic premises was "I have to be perfect in everything."

Stereotypic conclusions and repeated themes, irrespective of the nature of the stimulus, serve as an additional clue to a depressogenic premise. Consider the following case notes (the numbers refer to the therapy session):

> #6: I'm so dependent—I always need someone else to feel good about myself.
>
> #7: I just can't say "no" to people.
>
> #8: I don't like being single—now—I can admit it to myself—I can only be happy with someone who has money.
>
> #11: P: I'm scared about therapy ending . . . I'm so dependent . . . [cries] . . . How do I overcome this feeling that I need a steady boyfriend? . . . having a need like this is a sign of maladjustment.
>
> T: What do you think would happen to you without a steady boyfriend?
>
> P: I—I'd go to pieces.

It was subsequently revealed that the patient viewed interpersonal situations from the point of view of a "need": her basic premise was "I need the continuous presence of others to survive."

Another woman's depression was related to the return of an adult son who made considerable impositions, a situation many people would have resented. However, the patient became despondent, conceded to the son's demands, and planned to cancel her vocational and academic activities. At one point, the patient had a spontaneous recollection of an allegedly unpleasant childhood experience. The recall was associated with strong anxiety, which mounted to panic and culminated in the patient's becoming suicidal. In conjunction with the anxiety, she had the conviction that she was going out of her mind. A series of inquiries revealed that active negative emotions such as anxiety and anger were construed by the patient in highly unfavorable terms. One of her basic premises was "Feeling and showing strong active negative feelings means that you are insane."

There are also assumptions that employ "either or" connectives that treat two propositions as having equivalent meanings. The middle-aged man who became depressed because he did not make the "big time" consistently used the assumption "Either I am 100% successful or I am a failure." The female patient who assumed that the presence of other people was needed for her survival also had an either–or premise: "Either I am loved by everyone, or I am worthless." It is important to realize that although we can offer a general description of the tone and content of the premises, their specific characteristics vary from person to person.

In our laboratory, Arlene Weissman constructed the Dysfunctional Attitude Scale (DAS) that operationalizes the concept of maladaptive premises and assumptions. The DAS consists of a list of both adaptive and maladaptive attitudes and beliefs that were derived on clinical and empirical grounds. In a pilot study of 35 depressed psychiatric outpatients, we found that the DAS correlated .58 with levels of depression.

The various silent assumptions, premises, and conclusions form a cognitive template or schema. As we have already noted, schemata are nonspecific but organized representations of prior experience that facilitate recall and focus attention (Neisser, 1967). In actuality, schemata are hypothetical constructs that help us to explain characteristic ways of construing events and regularities in problem-solving approaches.

During development and maturation, people probably develop a large number of schemata or cognitive filters that relate to different aspects of experience. The schemata most likely undergo modification and some reorganization as a function of living and the increasing availability of mature cognitive processes. Our clinical experience suggests that certain schemata predispose to depression. Moreover such schemata are apparently relatively stable and invariant. Through years of living, they are not systematically reality-tested or modified. The schemata that predispose to and clearly become hypervalent in depression relate to stimulus conditions that involve a real or potential subtraction from the individual's personal domain. To use Kelly's (1955) phrase, the focus of convenience of these schemata or constructs is most likely those stimulus conditions that resemble the original circumstance within which they were developed. However, their range eventually extends to situations only peripherally similar. Depressogenic schemata encompass premises that contain numerous semantic quantifiers (*all, none, always*), categorical imperatives (*must, have to*), and preemptive class assignments (*nothing–but*). Their formal characteristics including the premises' psychologically simplistic and rather "childish" content, and the categorical imperatives and rules of conduct create the impression that they are relatively intact, developmentally earlier constructions. The work of Hauri (1976) and Weintraub *et al.* (1974) offers partial support of our hypothesis that the depressogenic schemata are stable and enduring. A comprehensive understanding of the development of such schemata must await further studies.

VI. CLINICAL IMPLICATIONS OF THE COGNITIVE VIEW OF DEPRESSION

Although we have attributed a certain stability to the cognitive schemata that become hypervalent in periods of clinical depression, the modification of such schemata is still plausible. In fact, given normal maturation, experience, and growing awareness of oneself and the milieu, modification of one's cognitive structures and modulation of behavior are the norm rather than the exception.

We have developed a specific therapeutic approach, cognitive therapy, to elucidate and alter the depressed patients' maladaptive cognitions. In cognitive therapy, the patient is an active participant in his own treatment and recovery. He and the therapist work together to identify and pinpoint the patient's distorted cognitions, to monitor their content, and to elucidate the processes that he uses to arrive at maladaptive conclusions. As part of the therapy, we question systematically the evidence for and the validity of the patient's interpretations. Ultimately, the treatment focuses on those dysfunctional beliefs and attitudes that form the cornerstone of the patient's depressive schemata. The beliefs and premises are subjected to verbal questioning and actual reality-testing both within the therapy sessions and in the course of the patient's daily life. We use behavioral tasks and homework assignments to assist the depressed patient in the process of correcting his mistaken notions and interpretations. The patient is encouraged to question why he has accepted the premises that form the cornerstone of his depressogenic schemata and to alter or reject premises that have been maladaptive for him.

Cognitive therapy has lent itself to a degree of specification that enabled us to construct a psychotherapy treatment manual (Beck *et al.*, 1976). Its application in the treatment of depression has been reported by Rush, Khatami, and Beck (1975). In a recent study, the efficacy of cognitive therapy was subjected to empirical test. Pharmacotherapy was chosen as a treatment comparison since it is the only form of treatment that has demonstrated effectiveness in reducing depressive symptomatology. In our study (Rush, Beck, Kovacs, & Hollon, 1977), 41 unipolar depressed outpatients were randomly assigned to cognitive therapy ($n = 19$) or pharmacotherapy with imipramine ($n = 22$). The patients were seen over a 12-week period. As a group, they had a long history of depression, with repeated episodes and multiple past attempts at treatment. The severity of depressive symptomatology was assessed at several points in time through self-ratings and clinical evaluations conducted by an independent evaluator. The self-ratings and the clinical ratings showed that while both treatments were highly effective in reducing depressive symptomatology, the cognitive therapy group showed significantly greater improvement than the pharmacotherapy group. These results were essentially replicated at 3- and 6-month follow-up evaluations. Moreover, a significantly larger number of pharmacotherapy patients dropped out during the 12-week treatment phase or reentered treatment for depressive symptomatology in the follow-up phase.

Although at the present time we have no definitive data on exactly *how* cognitive therapy works, the relatively low posttreatment relapse rate may well indicate that some modification of the patients' depressogenic cognitive schemata was accomplished. A more precise understanding of the nature of change due to cogntive therapy will have to await further analyses and detailed inquiry.

REFERENCES

Akiskal, H. S., & McKinney, W. T. Depressive disorders: toward a unified hypothesis. *Science*, 1973, *182*, 20–29.

Akiskal, H. S., & McKinney, W. T. Overview of recent research in depression. *Archives of General Psychiatry*, 1975, *32*, 285–305.

Andreasen, N. J. C., & Pfohl, B. Linguistic analysis of speech in affective disorders. *Archives of General Psychiatry*, 1976, *33*, 1361–1367.

Ansbacher, H. L., & Ansbacher, R. R. *The individual psychology of Alfred Adler.* New York: Harper, 1964.

Arnold, M. B. (Ed.). *Feelings and emotions.* New York: Academic Press, 1970. (a)

Arnold, M. B. Perennial problems in the field of emotion. In M. B. Arnold (Ed.), *Feelings and emotions.* New York: Academic Press, 1970. (b)

Averill, J. R. Autonomic response patterns during sadness and mirth. *Psychophysiology*, 1969, *5*, 399–414.

Beck, A. T. A systematic investigation of depression. *Comprehensive Psychiatry*, 1961, *2*, 163–170.

Beck, A. T. Thinking and depression: I. Idiosyncratic content and cognitive distortions. *Archives of General Psychiatry*, 1963, *9*, 324–333.

Beck, A. T. *Depression: Clinical, experimental and theoretical aspects.* New York: Harper & Row, 1967.

Beck, A. T. Cognition, affect, and psychopathology. *Archives of General Psychiatry*, 1971, *24*, 495–500.

Beck, A. T. *Cognitive therapy and the emotional disorders.* New York: International Universities Press, 1976.

Beck, A. T., & Beamesderfer, A. Assessment of depression: the depression inventory. In P. Pichot (Ed.), *Psychological measurements in psychopharmacology: Modern problems in pharmacopsychiatry*, Vol. 7. Basel, Switzerland: Karger, 1974.

Beck, A. T., & Hurvich, M. S. Psychological correlates of depression: I. Frequency of "masochistic" dream content in a private practice sample. *Psychosomatic Medicine*, 1959, *21*, 50–55.

Beck, A. T., Kovacs, M., & Weissman, A. Hopelessness and suicidal behavior: An overview. *JAMA*, 1975, *234*, 1146–1149.

Beck, A. T., Rush, A. J., & Kovacs, M. *Individual treatment manual for cognitive/behavioral psychotherapy of depression.* Unpublished manuscript, 1976. Available from A. T. Beck, Room 204 Piersol Bldg.—Psychiatry, University of Pennsylvania Hospital, Philadelphia, Pa., 19104.

Beck, A. T., & Shaw, B. F. Cognitive approaches to depression. In A. Ellis & R. Grieger (Eds.), *Handbook of rational emotive theory and practice.* New York: Springer, 1978.

Beck, A. T., Weissman, A., Lester, D., & Trexler, L. The measurement of pessimism: the hopelessness scale. *Journal of Consulting and Clinical Psychology*, 1974, *42*, 861–865.

Becker, J. *Depression: Theory and research.* New York: Wiley, 1974.

Braff, D. L., & Beck, A. T. Thinking disorder in depression. *Archives of General Psychiatry*, 1974, *31*, 456–459.

Broadbent, D. E. Cognitive psychology: introduction. *British Medical Bulletin*, 1971. *27*, 191–194.

Calhoun, L. G., Cheney, T., & Dawes, A. S. Locus of control, self-reported depression, and perceived causes of depression. *Journal of Consulting and Clinical Psychology*, 1974, *42*, 736.

Coleman, R. E. Manipulation of self-esteem as a determinant of mood of elated and depressed women. *Journal of Abnormal Psychology*, 1975, *84*, 693–700.

The Committee on Nomenclature and Statistics of the American Psychiatric Association. *Diag-*

nostic and statistical manual of mental disorders (2nd ed.). Washington, D.C.: American Psychiatric Association, 1968.

Craik, K. J. W. *The nature of explanation.* Cambridge: Cambridge University Press, 1952.

DeMonbreun, B. G., & Craighead, W. E. Distortion of perception and recall of positive and neutral feedback in depression. *Cognitive Therapy and Research,* 1977, *1*, 311–329.

Dilling, C. A., & Rabin, A. I. Temporal experience in depressive states and schizophrenia. *Journal of Consulting Psychology,* 1967, *31*, 604–608.

Falmagne, R. J. (Ed.). *Reasoning: Representation and process.* Hillsdale, N.J.: Erlbaum, 1975.

Feighner, J. P., Robins, E., Guze, S. B., Woodruff, R. A., Winokur, G., & Munoz, R. Dignostic criteria for use in psychiatric research. *Archives of General Psychiatry,* 1972, *26*, 57–63.

Grinker, R. R., Miller, J., Sabshin, M., Nunn, R., & Nunnally, J. C. *The phenomena of depressions.* New York: Hoeber, 1961.

Hale, W. D., & Strickland, B. R. The induction of mood states and their effect on cognitive and social behaviors. *Journal of Consulting and Clinical Psychology,* 1976, *44*, 155.

Hamilton, M. A rating scale for depression. *Journal of Neurology, Neurosurgery, and Psychiatry,* 1960, *23*, 56–61.

Hammen, C. L., & Krantz, S. Effect of success and failure on depressive cognitions. *Journal of Abnormal Psychology,* 1976, *85*, 577–586.

Hauri, P. Dreams in patients remitted from reactive depression. *Journal of Abnormal Psychology,* 1976, *85*, 1–10.

Ianzito, B. M., Cadoret, R. J., & Pugh, D. D. Thought disorder in depression. *American Journal of Psychiatry,* 1974, *131*, 703–707.

Inhelder, B., & Piaget, J. *The early growth of logic in the child.* New York: Norton, 1969.

Izard, C. E. *Patterns of emotions.* New York: Academic Press, 1972.

Johnson-Laird, P. N. Models of deduction. In R. I. Falmagne (Ed.), *Reasoning: Representation and Process.* Hillsdale, N.J.: Erlbaum, 1975.

Kelly, G. A. *The psychology of personal constructs,* Vol. 1. New York: Norton, 1955.

Klein, D. C., Fencil-Morse, E., & Seligman, M. E. P. Learned helplessness, depression, and the attribution of failure. *Journal of Personality and Social Psychology,* 1976, *33*, 508–516.

Klein, D. F. Endogenomorphic depression. *Archives of General Psychiatry,* 1974, *31*, 447–454.

Klerman, G. L. Clinical research in depression. *Archives of General Psychiatry,* 1971, *24*, 305–319.

Kovacs, M., Beck, A. T., & Weissman, A. Hopelessness: An indicator of suicidal risk. *Suicide,* 1975, *5*, 98–103.

Laxer, R. M. Self-concept changes of depressive patients in general hospital treatment. *Journal of Consulting Psychology,* 1964, *28*, 214–219.

Lazarus, R. S., Averill, J. R., & Opton, E. M. Towards a cognitive theory of emotion. In M. B. Arnold (Ed.), *Feelings and emotions.* New York: Academic Press, 1970.

Leeper, R. W. The motivational and perceptual properties of emotions as indicating their fundamental character and role. In M. B. Arnold (Ed.), *Feelings and emotions.* New York: Academic Press, 1970.

Lishman, W. A. Selective factors in memory. Part 2: Affective disorder. *Psychological Medicine,* 1972, *2*, 248–253.

Lloyd, G. G., & Lishman, W. A. Effect of depression on the speed of recall of pleasant and unpleasant experiences. *Psychological Medicine,* 1975, *5*, 173–180.

Loeb, A., Beck, A. T., & Diggory, J. Differential effects of success and failure on depressed and nondepressed patients. *The Journal of Nervous and Mental Disease,* 1971, *152*, 106–114.

Loeb, A., Feshbach, S., Beck, A. T., & Wolf, A. Some effects of reward upon the social perception and motivation of psychiatric patients varying in depression. *Journal of Abnormal and Social Psychology,* 1964, *68*, 609–616.

Lowrie, W. *Kierkegaard.* London: Oxford University Press, 1938.

Lubin, B. Adjective checklists for measurement of depression. *Archives of General Psychiatry*, 1965, *12*, 57–62.

Ludwig, L. D. Elation–depression and skill as determinants of desire for excitement. *Journal of Personality*, 1975, *43*, 1–22.

Mahoney, M. J. Reflections on the cognitive-learning trend in psychotherapy. *American Psychologist*, 1977, *32*, 5–13.

May, R., Angel, E., & Ellenberger, H. F. (Eds.). *Existence*. New York: Simon and Schuster, 1958.

Melges, F. T., & Bowlby, J. Types of hopelessness in psychopathological process. *Archives of General Psychiatry*, 1969, *20*, 690–699.

Mendels, J. *Concepts of Depression*. New York: Wiley, 1970.

Minkoff, K., Bergman, E., Beck, A. T., & Beck, R. Hopelessness, depression and attempted suicide. *American Journal of Psychiatry*, 1973, 130, 455–459.

Moore, B. S., Underwood, B., & Rosenhan, D. L. Affect and altruism. *Developmental Psychology*, 1973, *8*, 99–104.

Natale, M. Effects of induced elation–depression on speech in the initial interview. *Journal of Consulting and Clinical Psychology*, 1977, *45*, 45–52.

Neisser, U. *Cognitive Psychology*. New York: Appleton-Century-Crofts, 1967.

Nelson, R. E., & Craighead, W. E. Selective recall of positive and negative feedback, self-control behaviors, and depression. *Journal of Abnormal Psychology*, 1977, *86*, 379–388.

Peters, R. S. The education of the emotions. In M. B. Arnold (Ed.), *Feelings and emotions*. New York: Academic Press, 1970.

Plutchik, R. Emotions, evolution, and adaptive processes. In M. B. Arnold (Ed.), *Feelings and emotions*. New York: Academic Press, 1970.

Rey, A. C., Silber, E., Savard, R. J., & Post, R. M. Thinking and language in depression. Paper presented at the Meeting of the American Psychiatric Association, Toronto, Canada, May 1977.

Rizley, R. C. *The perception of causality in depression: An attributional analysis of two cognitive theories of depression*. Unpublished doctoral dissertation, Yale University, 1976.

Rush, A. J. The why's and how's of diagnosing the depressions. In J. K. Smith (Ed.), *Biological psychology bulletin*, Vol. 4. Oklahoma City: University of Oklahoma Health Sciences Center, 1975.

Rush, A. J., Beck, A. T., Kovacs, M., & Hollon, S. Comparative efficacy of cognitive therapy and pharmacotherapy in the treatment of depressed outpatients. *Cognitive Therapy and Research*, 1977, *1*, 17–37.

Rush, A. J., Khatami, M., & Beck, A. T. Cognitive therapy and behavioral therapy in chronic depression. *Behavior Therapy*, 1975, *6*, 398–404.

Schwartz, G. E., Fair, P. L., Greenberg, P. S., Mandel, M. R., & Klerman, J. L. Facial muscle patterning to affective imagery in depressed and non-depressed subjects. *Science*, 1976, *192*, 489–491.

Secunda, S. K., Katz, M. M., Friedman, R. J., & Schuyler, D. *The depressive disorders* (DHEW Publication No. [HSM] 73-9157). Washington, D.C.: U.S. Government Printing Office, 1973.

Staudenmeyer, H. Understanding conditional reasoning with meaningful propositions. In R. J. Falmagne (Ed.), *Reasoning: Representation and process*. Hillsdale, N.J.: Erlbaum, 1975.

Strongman, K. T. *The psychology of emotion*. London: Wiley, 1973.

Stuart, J. L. Intercorrelations of depressive tendencies, time perspective, and cognitive style variables. (Doctoral dissertation, Vanderbilt University, 1962). *Dissertation Abstracts International*, 1962, *23*, 696 (University Microfilms No. 62-3419).

Thompson, J. *Kierkegaard*. New York: Knopf, 1973.

Tomkins, S. S. Affect as the primary motivational system. In M. B. Arnold (Ed.), *Feelings and emotions*. New York: Academic Press, 1970.

Velten, E. A laboratory task for induction of mood states. *Behavior Research and Therapy*, 1968, *6*, 473–482.

Wason, P. C. Problem solving and reasoning. *British Medical Bulletin*, 1971, *27*, 206–210.

Wason, P. C., & Johnson-Laird, P. N. *Psychology of reasoning*. Cambridge, Mass.: Harvard University Press, 1972.

Weintraub, M., Segal, R. M., & Beck, A. T. An investigation of cognition and affect in the depressive experiences of normal men. *Journal of Consulting and Clinical Psychology*, 1974, *42*, 911.

Wener, A. E., & Rehm, L. P. Depressive affect: A test of behavioral hypotheses. *Journal of Abnormal Psychology*, 1975, *84*, 221–227.

Wing, J. K. The functional psychoses and neuroses. *Psychiatric Annals*, 1976, *6*, 393–403.

Zung, W. W. K. A self-rating depression scale. *Archives of General Psychiatry*, 1965, *12*, 63–70.

Emotion Awareness, Expression, and Arousal

Editor's Introduction

15

In this chapter, Dr. Buechler and I suggest some new ways of thinking about emotions in infancy. The concept of emotional development is considered too broad to treat as a single topic. The chapter discusses four developmental processes relating to the emotions and to infant development and infant well-being. The expressions of the emotions in infancy are seen as critical in personality integration and the development of infant–parent and other social relationships. The question of the predictive value of emotion response patterns in infancy is placed in perspective, in part by considering the value of studying emotions in infancy apart from the issue of continuity of infant emotion traits.

Emotion Expressions and Personality Integration in Infancy

15

CARROLL E. IZARD and SANDRA BUECHLER

Most people agree that emotions play an important role in human development. Many would also agree on a number of other general statements about relationships between emotions, creative activities, conflict, and coping processes. Agreement would be more difficult to obtain, however, when we begin to make more specific statements about how emotions influence other areas of development. Even more controversy would be generated by statements about how emotions in infancy relate to personality and social behavior in later life.

Regarding this latter issue, we want to emphasize our belief that prediction of later development is by no means the only justification for studying emotions in infancy. Scientifically, emotions and processes of personality integration in infancy are of interest in their own right. Practically, increased understanding of emotions in infancy should facilitate the nurturance of emotionally, socially, and physically healthy infants, and it is desirable to foster well-being at all ages.

We believe that the search for continuities and discontinuities in infancy is very important. We believe that stable individual differences exist, and that those that will be predictive of adaptive and maladaptive personality development will be found in the emotion domain, including emotion–cognition and emotion–behavior relationships. Investigation of these phenomena involves study of infant–environment interactions, a need emphasized by Emde and Robinson (1976). The emotions themselves have a social (expressive, environment-directed, or communicative) aspect and emotion–cognition/behavior

---

CARROLL E. IZARD and SANDRA BUECHLER • University of Delaware, Newark, Delaware.

relationships depend in part on sensory input from the environment, especially from the social surround. The lack of evidence for continuities may be due partly to the infrequency of studies of the emotions and partly to the inadequacy of methods when emotions are investigated.

There have been a number of obstacles to gaining knowledge of the emotion domain and of emotion styles and emotion traits in infancy. First, there is the scarcity of systematic controlled research. Second, there are serious problems of definition and terminology relating to emotion concepts. Third, partly because of the lack of theory and well-defined concepts, methodology often seems weak and not tightly designed for the emotion concept being studied.

Although there is no single solution for all these problems, we shall try to reduce some of the ambiguities in the area by delineating some focal topics in the study of emotions in infancy. Rather than considering the global subject of emotional development in infancy, we propose that research focus on four types of developmental processes that relate to emotions.

Before we discuss these four developmental processes, one other distinction must be made. Since it is generally agreed that emotions have a neurophysiological, subjective, and expressive component, it would avoid confusion if students of emotions designated which of these components they are investigating or discussing. Emotion and emotion expression, for example, are often used interchangeably, even in the literature on the prelingual infant. As a result, it is not always possible to sort out exactly which emotion component an author has in mind when he or she uses the term *emotion*. Attention to these terminological issues is particularly crucial in the study of the preverbal infant, since the infant's subjective experience during moments of emotion expression can only be inferred.

Lacking a mechanism for the study of the subjective component of emotion experience, students of infant emotions must focus on the expressive component. While some people attempt to infer emotion experience from physiological responses, it is always difficult to conclude that by themselves these are reliable indicators of a particular discrete emotion or of an emotion experience at all. For the most part, investigators of emotions in the preverbal infant can design objective studies only of observable emotion expressions and emotion-related behavior.

The first type of developmental process that relates to the emotions is the ontogenesis of emotion expressions. Ontogenesis is concerned with the age of emergence of each emotion-specific expression and the sequence of the emergence of these expressions over time. The basic emotion-expression ontogeny can be thought of as the product of the biological unfolding of the emotion expressions in their natural order—the order in which the capacity for each emotion expression develops. Research on this developmental process involves efforts to determine the age at which the infant is capable of encoding each of the several expressions.

One problem with research on expression ontogeny is that the infant's capacity may be activated at different ages by different events or stimulus situations. For this reason, it will be fruitful to establish the ontogeny of emotion expressions in relation to a limited set of specific, well-defined stimulus situations. These situation-specific expression ontogenies should determine the emergence, peaking, and decline (regulation) of the expressions obtained in the particular situation. Studies designed to establish specific ontogenies should focus on stimulus situations that have been considered either innate releasers or natural clues (Bowlby, 1973) or highly effective stimuli across various cultures. For example, in studying the ontogeny of fear expressions, one might investigate the growing infant's responses to what Bowlby has termed *natural clues to danger* (e.g., strangeness, being left alone, heights). Current evidence suggests that fear is elicited in different situations at different ages. Thus we are not justified in saying that fear emerges at a particular age on the basis of responses to a single stimulus situation. A more complete expression ontogeny for a particular emotion would show the age of its appearance, peaking, and decline in a number of stimulus situations, specially selected for their expected salience at different levels of cognitive and motor development.

There is robust evidence for the innateness and the universality of certain emotion expressions (Izard, 1971; Ekman, Friesen, & Ellsworth, 1972; Emde, Gaensbauer, & Harmon, 1976); however, *innateness* does not mean "present at birth," and both biological and environmental factors can be investigated for their influence on the ontogenesis of expression. Unfortunately, the possibilities for studying brain–expression relationships in human beings are highly limited. One can, however, make some observations on the rate of maturation of the mechanisms underlying the expressions. Evidence on the relative influence of maturational versus environmental variables in directing the ontogenesis of expressions might be obtained by studies of twins or infants exposed to extraordinary environmental conditions, such as severe deprivation or abuse.

The second type of process to be studied is the course of the development of each of the discrete emotion expressions. A number of questions arise in this area. Does each emotion expression appear full-blown at the given age of appearance, or does the expression develop one component at a time? That is, do facial patterns in the eye region develop before those in the mouth region, or does development in different regions of the face vary with different emotions? Does an emotion expression develop along a continuum of intensity or is the infant capable of various intensities of expression as soon as he or she is able to express any degree of the emotion? Does the course of development include predictable changes, over time, in the infant's threshold for expression of a discrete emotion in a particular stimulus situation?

The third major area is the development of the emotion system as a whole. Students of emotions differ in their conceptions of how the emotions are dynamically interrelated. Some think that each emotion has a polar opposite. Others hold that emotion responses are sometimes arranged in hierarchical relationships with respect to certain stimulus situations. Thus certain emotions may have complementary functions in relation to qualitatively similar stimuli that vary only in quantity or intensity. For example, a novel stimulus situation may elicit interest, surprise, or fear, depending on the degree to which it is discrepant from schemata stored in memory. Ontogenetically, the degree of discrepancy and the quality of the resulting emotion may be a function of the amount of stimulus information the infant obtains or processes and the kinds of cognitive comparisons he/she can make with existing schemata. Therefore, a novel stimulus situation, like a strange face suddenly appearing from behind a screen that had just blocked a familiar face from view, may elicit interest in the 2-month-old, surprise in the 6-month-old, and fear in the 10-month-old. The 2-month-old has no schemata stored in memory and can make no comparisons, and only interest (or possibly a smile) results. The 6-month-old has his/her expectations violated, and the misexpectation leads to surprise. The 10-month-old is capable of anticipating distress or harm on being confronted with strangeness and may show fear.

Some theorists hold that it is characteristic of the emotion system that one emotion can influence another by reciprocal amplification, attenuation, or inhibition. Using expressions as emotion indicators, one could study how an ongoing emotion affects the threshold for another emotion that is expected to follow presentation of a new incentive event. Relationships discovered at one stage of development could be tracked longitudinally.

The final process stemming from the emotion domain, and by far the most inclusive, is personality integration: the interrelating of the emotion system with other personality and behavioral systems—perceptual, cognitive, motor, and social. We assume that the emotion system contributes directly to personality integration in two ways. First, the invariance of emotion experiences ensures continuity of consciousness and self-awareness. Second, emotions provide the motivation for integrative processes that engage and interrelate other personality subsystems. The role of emotions as organizing and integrative forces in consciousness has been discussed in more detail elsewhere (Izard, 1977, 1978a). Research at this level should examine developmental sequences of emotion expressions in relation to cognitive and motor responses that are involved in adaptation and coping in various circumstances, especially in natural settings.

More concretely, personality integration involves the development of effective interactions and interrelations between specific emotion processes and particular types of processes in the other systems. For example, it is adaptive to interrelate (and eventually integrate) the emotion of interest with the cognitive processes of attending and comparing and with the motor responses involved in exploration. Studies in this sphere can take a number of directions.

One can study how specific emotion expressions relate to overall cognitive development or to specific cognitive attainments. Similarly, one can study specific emotion expressions as they relate to particular social behaviors, such as empathic or sympathetic responses, or to overall social development. Studies of changes in emotion expressions over time in particular stimulus situations (e.g., separation) can throw light on the development of emotion–cognition processes and affective-cognitive structures and their role in the regulation of emotion. Studies of emotion labeling and emotion recognition of infants' expressions by parents and other caregivers should be included here.

Unfortunately, in reviewing the literature relating to emotion variables in infant development, it will not be possible to maintain clear distinctions among the four types of processes delineated above. Most investigators have not made these distinctions in their writing, and it is sometimes impossible to superimpose them. Most of the published research relates either to some aspect of the ontogenesis of emotions or to personality integration. We consider the latter term to include what Sroufe (1976) has designated as emotional development. Accordingly, these two areas will be emphasized in this review.

The following selected review of studies of emotion expression ontogeny and of factors affecting the development of the emotion system and personality integration will reveal several problems. Different methodologies for studying the same emotion or emotion-related phenomena make it difficult to interpret findings. Differences in criteria for judging the presence of emotion and the use of different terms for what may be the same emotion make comparisons across studies difficult. Finally, most systematic experiments have focused on normal development and it is often necessary for one to draw one's own inferences about emotion dysfunction and maldevelopment.

I. THE ONTOGENESIS OF EMOTION EXPRESSIONS

Knowledge of the ontogenesis of emotion expressions seems critical to progress in research in all spheres relating to emotions and important to the study of personality integration and the infant as an individual, a functioning whole. Systematic studies of emotion expressions in infancy are just beginning (Emde, Gaensbauer, & Harmon, 1976; Hiatt, Campos, & Emde, 1977; Parisi & Izard, 1977; Oster & Ekman, 1977). These investigators acknowledge that what is being measured or studied is expression, not experience. There is strong evidence, however, of one-to-one relationships between certain expressions and certain subjective or felt emotion states in the verbal child and adult (e.g., Izard, 1971; Ekman, Friesen, & Ellsworth, 1972; Schwartz, Fair, Salt, Mandel, & Klerman, 1976). Although there is no such evidence for these relationships in preverbal infants, most students of infancy assume some relationship between expressive behavior and emotion states (e.g., between laughter and joy, Sroufe, 1976; between crying and distress or fear, Bowlby, 1973).

Emotion expressions are worthy of study on their own merit. No one questions the social-signal value of infants' facial expressions, and some researchers have found that they are good indicators of specific cognitive attainments (Charlesworth, 1969, 1974; Ramsay & Campos, 1978).

In spite of the importance of knowledge of the ontogenesis of the emotion expressions, not much of substance has been added to Darwin's (1872, 1877) pioneering work in this area, as has been noted by Charlesworth and Kreutzer (1973). The reasons for this knowledge gap are rooted in the history of psychology and its domination in the first half of this century by theoretical systems unfriendly to the study of emotion constructs. It is also a function of the highly influential work of some early studies of Sherman (1927a,b, 1928) and Landis (1924).

Despite crucial weaknesses in Sherman's work, it had a profound and highly pervasive influence in shaping the conception of emotion responses as environmentally determined or learned responses. The influence of Sherman's work with infants was bolstered by Landis's (1924) study with adults, but the latter research also suffered serious faults. Izard (1971) and Ekman, Friesen, and Ellsworth (1972) have summarized the criticisms of both Landis's and Sherman's studies and have reported strong evidence for the universality of the expressions of a number of basic emotions.

A. The Differentiation Hypothesis

In the decades since Sherman's work, two theoretical conceptions of the ontogenesis of human emotions have been elaborated. The first view holds that by a process of differentiation, the separate emotions derive from a single emotion or arousal state. Strictly speaking, this view holds that there are no emotions in the early weeks of life, unless one considers "excitement" or generalized distress as an emotion.

Bridges (1932) was the first to enunciate the differentiation hypothesis. She maintained that undifferentiated excitement is the only affect or arousal state present at birth. Each of the other separate emotions of human experience, according to Bridges, is derived from general excitement by a differentiation process.

Sroufe (1976) is a contemporary proponent of the differentiation hypothesis of emotion ontogenesis. He noted that Bridges did not link the specific emotions with their precursors nor illustrate the process of differentiation. That is, she did not show how one emotion gives rise to another. He has attempted to shore up some of the weaknesses in Bridges's formulation, especially in relating a given emotion to its precursors and subsequent derivatives.

For example, he sees "early obligatory attention" differentiating into wariness and finally into fear. Early distress gives rise to rage, then anger, angry mood, and defiance. Similarly, the endogenous smile is present at birth and is seen as the precursor of pleasure, laughter, joy, elation, pride, and love.

B. The Discrete Systems Hypothesis

The alternative conceptualization of the ontogenesis of emotions (Izard, 1971, 1972, 1977, 1978b) holds that emotion expressions emerge ontogenetically as they become adaptive in the life of the infant and particularly in infant–caregiver communications and relationships. For example, the distress cry is present from birth to serve the needs of survival, maintain proximity of the caregiver, and guarantee at least minimal social exchange by fostering caregiver–infant interaction. On the other hand, fear, which can be sufficiently toxic to be lethal and which could add little to adaptiveness in early infancy, emerges in the second half year and proves adaptive in facilitating self-protection, self-cognition, and self-control. A detailed theoretical statement of the ontogeny of emotions and their functions in infant development has been presented earlier (Izard, 1978b).

According to this theoretical framework, there are innate neurophysiological substrates for each of certain basic or fundamental emotions that emerge in the normal course of the growth and development of the infant. In effect, each emotion develops as a discrete system and becomes an interactive component of the overall emotion system. The discrete systems view is implicit in Darwin, since he held that the expressive behavioral patterns for various discrete emotions are innate.

The work of a number of other theorists and investigators seems congruent with this position (Goodenough, 1931, 1932–1933; Spitz, 1959, 1965; Tomkins, 1962; Emde & Harmon, 1972; Emde, Gaensbauer, & Harmon, 1976).

C. Research Relating to Expression Ontogeny

In a recent paper Izard (1978b) elaborated his discrete systems theory of the ontogenesis of emotions and discussed the role of each emotion in the development of other behavioral systems and the personality as a whole. His view, like that of others, can currently claim little empirical support, but a cross-sectional study of 5-, 7-, and 9-month-olds (Parisi & Izard, 1977) yielded results consistent with the theory. The study consisted of the administration of 20 brief stimulus situations to 10 infants at each age level in their homes. The infants' facial expressions to the stimuli were videotape-recorded. Judges trained with Izard's Facial Expression Scoring Manual agreed in categorizing 411 of the 600 facial responses into discrete emotion categories. Counting discrete emotion expressions and blends of two emotion expressions, judges agreed on 547 of the 600 facial responses to the stimuli. (Untrained judges agreed on 386 discrete expressions and 437 discrete expressions plus blends.) The expressions of interest, joy, surprise, anger, disgust, and fear were reliably identified at all three age levels, but fear was observed in only one 5- and one 7-month-old.

Oster and Ekman (1977) have shown that the neonate is capable of making all except one of the facial actions they have identified in adults, but they have not published data on identifiable emotion expressions in infants. Hiatt, Campos, and Emde (1977) studied facial expressions of 10- to 12-month-olds in six experimental situations, including the visual cliff, stranger approach, and peek-a-boo. Although the stimulus situations (except for the visual cliff) did not produce the expected emotion very frequently, they showed that the expressions of joy, surprise, and fear could be highly reliably identified by global judgments. In a study of emotion responses to laughter games and acute pain (e.g., inoculations), Izard, Huebner, Risser, and Dougherty (in preparation) have found that infants 2–9 months of age show facial expressions that can be reliably identified as interest, joy, distress, anger, disgust, contempt, and fear.

There have been a number of studies on the ontogenesis of smiling and laughing. (See Sroufe & Wunsch, 1972; Rothbart, 1973; Emde, Gaensbauer, &

Table 1. Age (in Months) Emotion Expressed (0 = Birth)

Emotion expression	Darwin	Bridges	Emde	Sroufe	Izard
Interest					0
Endogenous smile[a]			0	0	0
Social smile	2½	2½	2½	3	1½–3
Laughter	3¾			4	4–5
Startle	0			0	0
Surprise					2–3
Distress	0	3	0	0	0
Disgust		3½			0
Rage				3	3–5
Anger	3¾	3¼/6		7	3–5
Shame				18	4–5
Shyness	27				12–18
Wariness				4½	
Fear	0–5	6	9	9	5–9
Guilt	13			36	12–15
Contempt					15–18

[a] Expressions related to the same emotion experience or subjective feeling are grouped together. Some investigators, however, consider the endogenous smile a special case unrelated to the smile of joy.

Harmon, 1976; and Izard, 1977, for summaries.) These studies generally agree that the neonatal or endogenous smile is present at birth and that the social smile appears at about 2½ months.

Charlesworth (1969) has presented an excellent review of literature on surprise, defining surprise as a function of misexpectation. He concludes that it makes its appearance at around 7 months of age.

Table 1 presents a summary of current evidence and beliefs about the ontogenesis of emotions. Darwin's data, presented in Column 1, is the closest approximation of Bridges's study, but they are based on his observation of a single case—one of his children. As already noted, Bridges's data were based on her own judgments of the expressions observed in 62 infants followed longitudinally from the 1st to the 24th month. The data of Emde *et al.* are based on several of their longitudinal, empirical studies of infants in the first year of life. The data presented in the columns for Sroufe and Izard are based on their own research and that of other investigators.

II. FACTORS AFFECTING THE DEVELOPMENT OF THE EMOTION SYSTEM AND PERSONALITY INTEGRATION

Among the first contemporary scientists to recognize the importance of emotions in the newborn's consciousness and in infant development was Spitz (1959,1965). Spitz's theory and research support the notion that the first structures of consciousness are essentially affective in nature and that it is by means of affective experiences and expressions that the infant first relates to objects and persons in the surrounding world.

In the past decade, a number of developmental psychologists have supported the idea that the emotions play a key role in the growth of the infant and in the organization of the infant's behavioral systems. Stechler and Carpenter (1967) maintain that it is primarily affect by which the infant derives meaning from person–environment interactions. Escalona (1968) suggests that a variety of stimulus conditions differ for 4-week-old infants only in how they make them feel. Sroufe (1976) describes the infant "not as a perceptive being, not as a cognitive being, but as a human being that experiences anxiety, joy, and anger, and that is connected to its world in an emotional way" (p. 1). Taking a position on the importance of the emotions in human motivation very similar to that of Tomkins (1962) and Izard (1971), Sroufe goes on to describe affective life as "the meaning and motivational system which cognition serves" (p. 1). He concludes:

> Studying emotional development, then, is necessary for formulating a total, integrated view of the infant and for engaging central topic areas in social and personality development. (p. 4).

The empirical investigations of Emde, Gaensbauer, and Harmon (1976) support Spitz's position that the emergence of a particular emotion functions as an indicator of the presence of a new "organizer of the psyche" and heralds a "new mode of functioning" (pp. 8–9). A student of delayed development (Zigler, 1973) maintains that the full understanding of mental retardation requires the study of the emotion and social domains together with cognitive factors. Emphasizing the importance of the emotions in normal development, Kagan (1978b) observed "that the child's growth will not be fully understood until we gain greater insight into those aspects of development we call emotional" (p. 49).

There is also increasing support for the idea that emotions are important sources of motivation. Kagan (1971) concluded that "emotions activate motives—thoughts appropriate to certain goals—and maintain our attention to them" (p. 60). Sroufe (1976) observed that while drive reduction, tension reduction, and various energy concepts have proved inadequate in accounting for motivation, "it has not been shown that feeling does not mediate behavior (and there is evidence to the contrary)" (p. 79). The work of Hoffman (1975, 1977) strongly supports the notion that empathic distress is a determinant of altruistic behavior. The motivational effects of emotion experience on children's subsequent behavior have also been demonstrated in a series of studies by Rosenhan and his colleagues (e.g., Rosenhan, Underwood, & Moore, 1974) and Fry (1975).

Investigators focusing on the factors affecting emotion sytem development have been concerned with four broad classes of variables: (1) social class and environment; (2) dimensions of temperament; (3) attentional, perceptual, cognitive processes; and (4) quality of caregiving. Probably the largest group of researchers in infancy have been giving the bulk of their attention to cognitive development, but most of them have made little effort to relate their work to emotion development. Others have expended considerable effort on caregiving, social class, and environmental variables. Dimensions of temperament have probably received the least systematic study, and for the most part, they have been the concern of clinicians, the bulk of the contributions having been made by psychiatrists, pediatricians, and psychoanalytically oriented investigators. As Kagan (1978a) puts it, "Contemporary scientists study the effect of stress, perinatal trauma, or early malnutrition on intellectual functioning, rarely on motivation, temperament, or physical endurance" (pp. 2-12, 2-13). Thus, Kagan continues, we know quite a bit about how infants distribute their attention, especially under controlled conditions, but little about how they are motivated or how they develop maladaptive responses or dispositions. Our review of the four broad domains of variables affecting emotion development—social class and environment, temperament, cognition, and caregiving—tries to focus primarily on the literature most relevant to the study of infants' emotions and their role in development. Unfortunately there is ambiguity as to the specific emotion under discussion in most publications because of failure to specify clearly the criteria by which an emotion, emotion expression, or emotion-specific behavior is identified or measured. Nevertheless, the studies reviewed report findings that have implications for the domain of emotion and the problems of personality integration.

A. Environment and Social Class

Most studies relating to physical environment and social class have been concerned with their effects on cognitive or intellectual development (e.g., Eichenwald & Fry, 1969; Golden & Birns, 1968; Judd & Lewis, 1976; Kagan, 1978a; Lewis & Gallas, 1976; Wachs, Uzgiris, & Hunt, 1971). A general conclusion from these investigations is that environment and social class have little measurable effect on cognitive development in the first two years of life, but a different conclusion was reached by Wachs, Uzgiris, and Hunt, who found significant deficits in disadvantaged groups of 7-, 11-, 15-, 18-, and 22-month-olds.

The investigations of Yarrow, Rubenstein, Pedersen, and Jankowski (1971) and Yarrow, Rubenstein, and Pedersen (1976) are among the few studies of social class and environment that have been concerned with affective and motivational variables. They point to the importance of differentiating among variables within the broad categories of environment and social class. Of fundamental importance is the finding of Yarrow, Rubenstein, and Pedersen that in infants 5–6 months of age, "differential relationships exist between specific dimensions of the environment and specific dimensions of infant development" (p. 157). For example, they concluded that "Visual and auditory stimulation are related only to social responsiveness, while kinesthetic stimulation is related significantly to social and cognitive–motivational characteristics" (pp. 157–158).

Caldwell and Hersher (1964) did a longitudinal study of infants during their first year of life in monomatric (one mothering figure) and polymatric (multiple caretakers) households. At 1 year, infants from monomatric homes were rated as more dependent on their mothers for need gratifications and as showing more proximity-maintaining or attachment behavior and more emotionality, both positive and negative (more smiling and more crying), in interaction with their mothers. They were also seen as more active before and during a medical exam at a well-baby clinic. These findings suggest that the relatively vigorous exercise of emotion functions, including smiling, crying, and attachment behaviors, may be a part of normal, healthy development.

The impact of ethology, behavioral genetics, and biological psychiatry during the past decade may lead to a resurgence of studies designed to assess the relative influence of heredity and environment on certain adaptive and maladaptive behaviors or dispositions. As Emde and Robinson (1976) have noted, however, such studies must allow for individual–environment interaction effects that are not attributable simply to biology or experience. These researchers also added the sobering observation that early environmental influences can even change fundamental brain structures that could influence the behavior being studied.

B. Temperament

The term *temperament* is too broad and ill defined to have precise meaning or to enjoy high status as a scientific construct. Investigators have defined as many as 15 dimensions of temperament, including such diverse phenomena as activity level, attachment, and emotions (fear, anger). Virtually all temperament scales include one or more emotion dimensions, and these have been found to intercorrelate significantly with a number of the other dimensions of temperament (Rothbart, 1977). This finding is in keeping with the traditional conception of temperament as closely related to or substantially overlapping with the affective domain. Consider, for example, Allport's (1961) definition:

> *Temperament refers to the characteristic phenomena of an individual's emotional nature, including his susceptibility to emotional stimulation, his customary strength and speed of response, the quality of his prevailing mood, and all peculiarities of fluctuation and intensity in mood, these phenomena being regarded as dependent upon constitutional make-up, and therefore largely hereditary in origin.* (p. 34)

Allport cautioned readers not to interpret his definition as implying that temperament continues unchanged from birth to death. He thought that it was subject to influence by factors ranging from nutrition to learning and life experiences. Further, as Rutter (1970) has pointed out, several factors inherent in developmental processes and several methodological problems can adversely affect the search for continuities. Nevertheless, it is in the realm of temperament that most (of the still weak) evidence for continuity in personality development and maldevelopment is to be found.

For the most part, researchers obtain data on infant temperament by indirect means: in-depth interviews with mothers or caregivers and objectively scoreable questionnaires for caregivers. Most of the reported long-term longitudinal research has been based on the interview, but the objectively scoreable inventory is coming into more frequent use (Carey, 1970; McDevitt, 1976; Rothbart, 1977; Pedersen, 1977).

Thomas, Chess, and Birch (1968) and Thomas and Chess (1977) show rather convincingly that continuity of specific temperament characteristics (or of mothers' perceptions of such continuity) is clearly evident in some children, although correlations of their temperament scores from year 1 to years 4 or 5 are nonsignificant or quite modest for the sample as a whole. Thomas and Chess also provide some support for the hypothesis of Escalona and Heider (1959) that immature behavioral patterns are most likely to continue among children who experience significant developmental irregularity and maladaptation.

In their integrative analysis of research on the new born, Emde and Robinson (1976) cite very few studies that report stable individual differences in temperament or emotion-related traits during infancy. Schaffer and Emerson (1964) found individual differences in "cuddlability" (preference for being held closely and caressed) during an 18-month longitudinal study. Prechtl (1963) found that infants high in irritability and unpredictability of state changes were much more likely than less irritable, more predictable infants to contribute to rejecting and overanxious attitudes in their mothers. Bell (1971) found that high-intensity reactions to interruption of sucking predicted low-intensity preschool behaviors relating to interest, participation, assertiveness, gregariousness, and communicativeness. This seems like a reversal, but it may not be. It is possible that intense reactions to interruptions of sucking may have reflected irritability and low thresholds for state changes that could interfere with activities indexed by such terms as participation, gregariousness, and communicativeness.

Scarr and Salapatek (1970) did a cross-sectional study of the performance of 91 two- to twenty-three-month-old infants on the object permanence and means–end scales of Uzgiris and Hunt (1966), temperament scales (a questionnaire developed from the data of Thomas, Chess, Birch, Hertzig, & Korn, 1963), and in various "fear situations": stranger approach, visual cliff, jack-in-the-box, mechanical dog, masks and loud noise. Object permanence and means–end scale scores did not correlate with fear responses, but temperament scores did. Infants with a generally negative quality of mood, low response thresholds, poor adaptability, and low rhythmicity were more likely to show fear to the various fear stimuli.

The studies of Scarr and Salapatek (1970) and Birns, Barten, and Bridger (1969) support the feasibility of a direct approach to the study of temperament. Scarr and Salapatek retested 34 of the 6- to 18-month-old infants in their study in the six fear situations to test the stability of their fear measures over a two-month interval. They found that those

> who were most afraid of a particular stimulus situation initially, tended to remain most fearful of that stimulus despite the substantial behavioral changes that occur during any two-month period between 6 and 18 months. (p. 749)

This evidence of stability suggests that the infants' responses in fear (stressful) situations reflect an emotion trait or dimension of temperament.

Birns (1965) found individual differences in arousal of newborns following auditory and tactile stimulation. In a later study, Birns et al. (1969) examined the stability of certain dimensions of temperament from 2 or 3 days of age to 4 months. Their stimuli included a mild stressor: a cold metal disc applied to the infant's abdomen. They found significant coefficients of concordance (.39–.56) among neonatal, 1-month, 3-month, and 4-month ratings for irritability, activity level (1–4 months), sensitivity, and tension. The coefficients for the other dimensions ranged from .23 to .38. They concluded that their data show "trait stability" for certain early-appearing temperament-related behaviors.

Bronson's (1970, 1974) summary of some of the data from the Berkeley Growth study also support the notion of continuity of temperament traits, but in this case continuity was found only for males. For boys, early onset of stranger fear (by 6 months) was significantly associated with greater shyness at 10, 15, 24, and 42 months, and the trend (though nonsignificant) was present at 4 and 8½ years.

One must approach the question of continuities in temperament with caution; general trait measures have been effectively criticized (Mischel, 1968, 1971). Further, outstanding experts on infancy have failed to find much evidence of continuities in the cognitive domain (Kagan, 1971, 1976) and have cautioned against expecting them in any sphere (Emde, Gaensbauer, & Harmon, 1976). Emde and Robinson (1976) suggest that it may be appropriate to conceive of the newborn as having a range of behaviors that oscillate and vary over time. They think that the synchrony of behavior with particular social and physical environments may provide adaptational constants. They concluded that better prediction will emerge from a better grasp of infant–environment interactions.

C. Mother–Infant Interactions and Caregiving

Early studies of the effects of such drastic changes in caregiving as institutionalization with maternal absence led to the conclusion that the withdrawal of maternal care or of positive affective interchanges with a specific caregiver would lead to maladaptive development, depression, and in the worst instances, failure to thrive (Spitz, 1945, 1946; Bowlby, 1951). The findings of these investigators and others (Harlow, 1958, 1964; Werner, 1968; Kaufman & Rosenblum, 1969; Lewis & Goldberg, 1969; Siqueland, 1970) were highly influential in science and in public policy, but they were not without their critics (Pinneau, 1950, 1955; Casler, 1961; Watson, 1972), and the critics succeeded in pointing up the need for specifying the variables ("missing maternal ingredients") involved in maldevelopment.

Rheingold (1956), working with infants 3 months of age, showed that the reduced stimulation of an institution did not decrease infants' visual or manual exploration of social or nonsocial objects. In contrast, Provence and Lipton (1962), working with infants ranging from 4 days to 24 months of age, found a delay in differential response to attendant versus stranger and to face versus mask and a delay in imitation of facial expressions. They also found emotional ties to be tenous and attachment to a particular person absent.

Bowlby (1973) maintains that children who experience a high quality of caregiving ("mothering" that probably protects them from the experience of both intense distress and intense fear) are the ones "least susceptible to respond with fear to situations of all kinds, including separation" (p. 181). Consistent with this, Kagan (1978a) concluded that the quantity of prior mother–child interactions does not predict the age at which an infant will show peak distress on being separated from its mother.

A number of studies of infant–caregiver interactions have focused on the effect of the parent's behavior on the offspring's development (Ainsworth, 1963; Schaefer & Bayley, 1963; Yarrow, 1963) and on the effect of infant variables on caregiver responses (Moss, 1965; Lewis & Rosenblum, 1974; Ling & Ling, 1974). Others have focused attention on the synchrony between caretaker and infant as having a pronounced effect apart from the individual characteristics of either participant (Brazelton et al., 1975; Hinde, 1975). One implication of this line of research is that the infant's ability to emit signals (affect expressions) that are readable by its caretaker is a significant factor in their development of good synchrony. Klaus et al. (1975) have called this system a repertory of "specific interlocking behavior patterns that develop so early between mother and infant and which serve to unite them" (p. 77). The absence of this interlocking pattern may result in failure to thrive (Brazelton et al., 1975; Thoman, 1975).

The work of Lewis and Goldberg (1969), Moss (1967), Sander (1969), Bernal (1974), Thoman (1975), Ainsworth and her colleagues (Bell & Ainsworth, 1972; Stayton & Ainsworth, 1973; Stayton, Ainsworth, & Main, 1973; Ainsworth, Bell, & Stayton, 1974), Brazelton (1974), and Stern (1974) suggests that synchrony and the mother's sensitivity to the baby's signals are important for survival, for integration of the baby into the social world, and for healthy, adaptive development. Sander's research focuses on the role of synchrony in establishing cyclic functions, such as the sleep–wake cycle. In this context, Sander has suggested that the quality of caretaking responses, or the specificity with which they fit the infant's needs, affects infant development more than the quantity of caretaker interventions. The Ainsworth et al. studies of the mother's everyday departures from the baby's room showed that babies who had experienced

> sensitively responsive mothering do not, in the second half of the first year, protest consistently when their mothers leave the room. . . . Babies who had experienced relatively insensitive mothering tended to be more intolerant of everyday separations in the home environment. (Ainsworth, Bell, & Stayton, 1974, p. 121)

Emde, Kligman, Reich, and Wade (1978) have demonstrated the usefulness of both a categorical and a multidimensional approach to analyzing the social signals of 2½- to 4½-month-old infants' facial expressions. One study has shown that infants as young as 4 months old have the ability to discriminate joy, anger, and neutral expressions (LaBarbera, Izard, Vietze, & Parisi, 1976).

III. EMOTIONS, COGNITIVE ATTAINMENTS, AND PERSONALITY INTEGRATION

Relating emotion expressions to the infants' cognitive attainments has been the focus of several studies (e.g., Charlesworth, 1969; Décarie, 1978; Hoffman, 1975, 1978; Sroufe and Wunsch, 1972). In particular, the achievement of object and person permanence concepts, the development of memory, conceptual tempo, and overall mental development have been examined for their relevance to emotions. The evidence suggests that certain cognitive attainments are associated more with the waning or the regulation of some situationally elicited emotion expressions than with their initial appearance or emergence. For example, the decline or regulation of fear, distress, or anger following separation reflects a new level of self-control and personality integration. The control of these stress emotions can be attributed in part to developmental changes in the cognitive system (the emergence of representational memory and anticipation) that enable the infant to comprehend the temporary nature of the separation.

We propose, however, that at a more fundamental level, the gain in personality integration reflected by the regulation of stress emotions in separation is a function of the emotion system. In the first place, the emotion of interest has fostered the cognitive development that now plays a role in emotion regulation. Second, by the end of the second year of life, interest and joy have enhanced attachments to and appreciation of people other than the principal caregiver. These positive emotions motivate exploration of and involvement in the object world, and objects and object play can help regulate (attenuate or inhibit) stress emotions.

A. Emotion Expressions and Specific Cognitive Attainments

The development of the concept of an object (as having permanence) has long been considered a significant landmark in infancy (Piaget, 1954; Piaget & Inhelder, 1969; Kagan, 1978a). Its attainment, requiring some form of memory, has been studied by numerous experimenters (e.g., Bower, 1971; Graft & Landers, 1971; Miller, Cohen & Hill, 1970). More specifically, some investigators have hypothesized that it plays a direct role in emotion expression and emotion-related behavior. Schaffer (1966) suggested that "the establishment of the object concept is therefore a precondition to the onset of fear of strangers" (p. 103). However, empirical studies of the relationship between attainment of the object (or person) concept and the emergence of fear expressions have, on the whole, failed to confirm this hypothesis (Scarr & Salapatek, 1970; Emde, Gaensbauer, & Harman, 1976; Goulet, 1974; Brossard, 1974; Paradise & Curcio, 1974; Jackson, Campos, & Fischer, 1978.)

Emotion responses in particular situations have been found diagnostic of developmental changes in memory. Ramsay and Campos (1978) have shown that the smiling response is perhaps the best single index of the infant's entry into early Stage 6 of object permanence functioning, the stage that is characterized by the capacity for representation and the memory functions associated with this phenomenon. Other investigators have linked the growth of memory skills to the development of attachment (Cohen & Gelber, 1975), differential responses to people (Schaffer, 1971), and other behaviors requiring the ability to make inferences (Flavell, 1977). Discrepancy theorists, such as Bronson (1968, 1972), argue that only when the memory of the familiar is established can the discrepancies presented by novel sights elicit fear.

In his discussion of surprise, Charlesworth (1969) holds that this emotion results from a "misexpected" object or event. Thus it could be argued that surprise, as well as wariness, depends on the development of adequate memory facility for the recognition of expected versus misexpected occurrences. While this might suggest a direct relationship between memory development and the expression of wariness and surprise, recent investigations indicate that one has to consider the type of memory measured and certain intervening experiential variables in accounting for affective–cognitive interactions (Fagan, 1973)

A number of investigators (Sroufe & Wunsch, 1972; Rothbart, 1973; McGhee, 1971, 1974a,b; Zigler, Levine, & Gould, 1967) have suggested that laughter in infancy and humor appreciation in the child may be a useful index of cognitive development. In fact, these authors suggest that laughter results from the mastery of a cognitive challenge. Thus failure to laugh at a given stimulus situation may indicate a lack of comprehension of the event and hence may show that the child has not attained a particular stage of cognitive development or a specific cognitive ability. Failure to show distress or fear in a particular situation (e.g., the visual cliff) may have similar diagnostic significance.

In a forthcoming monograph, Kagan (1978a) presents an excellent integrative summary of the research on infancy, with emphasis on attentional, perceptual, and cognitive processes. In an effort to relate cognitive processes to motivation, he proposes that the key lies in the perception of discrepancy and subsequent uncertainty of response, the uncertainty being considered an affect.

B. Emotion Expressions and Overall Social and Mental Development

Flavell (1977) suggests that attachment—and more generally, the social behavior of the infant—is "at least partly dependent on the developmental level or quality of its mental abilities. The latter is conceived as a necessary but definitely not sufficient condition for the former" (pp. 52–53). However, the few existing experimental efforts to study the relationship between mental development, social development, and temperament or emotion variables in infancy have yielded mixed results (e.g., Lewis & Lee-Painter, 1974; Sostek & Anders, 1977).

The infant's overall mental development has also been investigated as a factor in emotional and social development. Studies in this area are made difficult by the scarcity of reliably identified behavioral continuities related to attentional, perceptual, and cognitive variables (Kagan, 1971, 1976, 1978a) and the notable lack of relationship between measures of intelligence in the first two years of life and later years. It is especially noteworthy, however, that an emotion variable may provide a thread of continuity here. Birns and Golden (1972) found that an index of pleasure or enjoyment in the tasks on the Cattell Infant Intelligence Scale at 18 months was significantly correlated with Binet IQ at 3 years.

Whether or not infants at the more extreme ends of the mental development continuum differ significantly in the development of emotion expressions has recently been investigated in studies of Down's syndrome infants. Emde, Katz, and Thorpe (1978) have shown that the social smile of Down's syndrome infants is a bit delayed and substantially dampened in intensity. The authors observed that the delayed and dampened smile in Down's syndrome infants was frequently a source of distress for the parents. Presumably, if the parental distress is of sufficient intensity and duration, it could influence parent–infant emotion communication and become a complicating factor in the emotional development of the child.

Cicchetti and Sroufe (1978) found that Down's syndrome infants showed significantly less emotion (crying) than younger normals with comparable developmental quotients on perceiving an object looming toward them and on being placed on the visual cliff. The authors found a strong relationship between Bayley Mental Scale scores and emotion expression in this severely retarded group. For example, of the Down's syndrome infants, the 33 who cried on the visual cliff had an average developmental quotient of 72, while the 37 who failed to cry in this situation had an average developmental quotient of 55 ($t = 6.48, 68, p < .01$). They also found a negative correlation of .80 between age of first laughter and Bayley Mental Scale scores.

Results consistent with those of Cicchetti and Sroufe with regard to differential emotion responses of normal and retarded individuals were obtained in a study by Simpson and Izard (1972). In this study, it was found that institutionalized mental retardates matched with normals on the basis of intelligence as measured by the Peabody Picture Vocabulary Test had significantly lower scores on the Emotion Recognition test (Izard, 1971). The findings of Cicchetti and Sroufe coupled with those of Simpson and Izard suggest that there is developmental retardation in both the cognitive and the emotion system of mentally retarded individuals and that there is, in addition, some deficiency in the integration of emotion and cognitive development. The equal intellectual development and unequal emotion responsiveness of different-aged normal and mentally retarded groups suggest some developmental independence of the emotion and cognitive systems.

C. Infant Emotions and Infant Well-Being

Emotion expressions and emotion-related behavior may be studied for their long- and short-term effects on healthy and unhealthy development. Recent investigators have acquired considerable skepticism about long-term predictions on the basis of psychological variables. In a recent essay on human development, Kagan (1976) cited a number of investigations that suggested that human infants have a remarkable capacity to endure unusual and apparently emotionally very unhealthy conditions for extended periods of time and still to function normally in later childhood and adolescence. Most of these articles, however, focused on the recovery (or ultimate development) of normal intellectual functions as measured by standard tests.

While there is not a lot of hard evidence to show clear relationships between emotional life in infancy and personality functioning in later life, we are inclined to agree with Darwin (1872) that the reciprocity of positive emotions between mother and infant help "set the child on the right path." For example, studies of mother–infant "synchrony" provide some evidence of the importance of adequate emotion communication in the early months of life. Aside from the long-term implications of adequate synchrony, its immediate consequences are worthy of exploration. The "readable" (clearly communicative) infant and the infant who can "read" its mother have been found to elicit attachment more easily (Klaus et al., 1975) and to develop a reciprocating, responsive relationship (Brazelton et al., 1975). These effects undoubtedly influence the infant's present experience and sense of well-being and those of the parents. Thus the significance of emotion expression and emotion system development does not rest solely on its long-term effects. Its immediate consequences for the infant's emotional, social, and physical well-being, for parents, and for infant–parent relationships are also worthy of study.

IV. SUMMARY

We have focused on the emergence of the emotions and on some of the factors that influence emotion expressions and personality integration in infancy. Our position is that each emotion serves an important motivational and communicative role in the life of the growing individual.

Alternative theoretical frameworks have conceptualized the emergence of emotion expressions as either a process of differentiation or primarily a function of the maturation of emotion-specific neurophysiological mechanisms.

Despite the theoretical interest surrounding the issue of emotion-expression ontogeny, research effort has been minimal and limited mainly to the study of the expressions of distress, joy, and fear. The emergence of the expressions of interest, surprise, disgust, anger, shame/shyness, guilt, and contempt has received less attention.

To avoid a global, all-inclusive treatment of the topic of emotion development, we propose four developmental processes that relate to the emotions. Study of the first process, ontogenesis of emotion expressions, involves efforts to ascertain the age at which the emotions are first expressed, the stimulus conditions that function as elicitors, and the relative influence of maturational and environmental variables in directing the emergence of emotion expressions.

The second process, the course of development of a particular emotion expression, remains unexplored. Even for those emotions whose emergence has been studied, few data exist to chart the developmental changes in the infant's expressions of these emotions. Expressions may change in complexity (number of components) or in intensity in relation to different stimulus situations. Developmental changes in intensity of expression to a particular event may be related to cognitive development and may reflect an aspect of personality integration. The history of each emotion from its emergence through its peak expressions and regulation in significant stimulus situations is a missing link in our understanding of development.

The third process, the development of the emotion system, has also received sparse attention. Responses to specific stimulus situations, such as the appearance of a stranger, have been studied fairly extensively, but the lack of objective means for differentiating various emotion expressions has been a limiting factor in these studies.

The fourth process is that of personality integration as motivated and guided by the emotion system. This process has not been studied in the conceptual framework outlined here, but a number of studies are generally relevant. Those reviewed include investigations of the relationship of emotion expression to specific cognitive attainments and of the relationships of emotions to overall social and mental development. Directions for future research of this and the other developmental processes relating to the emotions were discussed.

REFERENCES

Ainsworth, M. D. The development of infant–mother interaction among the Ganda. In B. M. Foss (Ed.), *Determinants of infant behavior*, Vol. 2. New York: Wiley, 1963, pp. 76–112.

Ainsworth, M. D., Bell, S. M., & Stayton, D. J. Infant–mother attachment and social development. In M. P. M. Richards (Ed.), *The integration of a child into a social world*. Cambridge: Cambridge University Press, 1974.

Allport, G. W. *Pattern and growth in personality.* New York: Holt, Rinehart, and Winston, 1961.

Bell, R. Q., Weller, G. M., & Waldrop, M. F. "Newborn and pre-schooler: Organization of behavior and relations between periods," *Monograph of the Society for Research in Child Development,* Vol. 132, No. 142, 1971.

Bell, S., & Ainsworth, M. Infant crying and maternal responsiveness. *Child Development,* 1972, *43,* 1171–1190.

Bernal, J. Attachment: Some problems and possibilities. In M. P. M. Richards (Ed.), *The integration of a child into a social world.* London: Cambridge Universities Press, 1974.

Birns, B. Individual differences in human neonates' responses to stimulation. *Child Development,* 1965, *30*(1), 249–256.

Birns, B., Barten, S., & Bridger, W. Individual differences in temperamental characteristics of infants. *Transactions of the New York Academy of Sciences,* 1969, *31,* 1071–1082.

Birns, B., & Golden, M. Prediction of intellectual performance at three years from infant test and personality measures. *Merrill-Palmer Quarterly,* 1972, *18,* 53–58.

Bower, T. G. R. The object in the world of the infant. *Scientific American,* 1971, *225*(4), 30–38.

Bowlby, J. Maternal care and mental health. *Bulletin of the World Health Organization,* 1951, *3,* 355–534.

Bowlby, J. *Attachment and loss: Separation, anxiety, and anger,* Vol. 2. New York: Basic Books, 1973.

Brazelton, T. B. The origins of reciprocity: The early mother–infant interaction. In M. Lewis and L. Rosenblum (Eds.), *The Effect of the Infant on its caregiver.* New York: Wiley, 1974.

Brazelton, T. B., Tronick, E., Adamson, L., Als. H., & Weise, S. Early mother–infant reciprocity. *Parent–Infant interaction.* Amsterdam: CIBA Foundation, Associated Scientific Publishers, 1975.

Bridges, K. M. B. Emotional development in early infancy. *Child Development,* 1932, *3,* 324–341.

Bronson, G. W. The fear of novelty. *Psychological Bulletin,* 1968, *69,* 350–358.

Bronson, G. W. Fear of visual novelty: Developmental patterns in males and females. *Developmental Psychology,* 1970, *2,* 33–40.

Bronson, G. W. *Infant's reactions to unfamiliar persons and novel objects.* Monographs of the Society for Research in Child Development, Vol. 37, No. 3, 1972.

Bronson, G. W. General issues in the study of fear: Section II. In M. Lewis and L. A. Rosenblum (Eds.), *The origins of fear.* New York: Wiley, 1974.

Brossard, M. D. The infant's conception of object permanence and his reactions, 1974. Cited in M. M. Haith and J. J. Campos, Human infancy, *Annual Review of Psychology.* Palo Alto, Califo.: Annual Reviews, Inc., 1977, p. 283.

Caldwell, B. M., & Hersher, L. Mother–infant interaction in the first year of life. *Merrill-Palmer Quarterly,* 1964, *10,* 119–128.

Carey, W. B. A simplified method for measuring infant temperament. *The Journal of Pediatrics* 1970 *77,* 188–194.

Casler, L. Maternal deprivation: A critical reveiw of the literature. *Monographs of the Society for Research in Child Development,* 1961, *26* (2, Serial No. 80).

Charlesworth, W. R. The role of surprise in cognitive development. In D. Elkind & J. Flavell (Ed.), *Studies in cognitive development.* London: Oxford University Press, 1969.

Charlesworth, W. R. General issues in the study of fear: Section IV. In M. Lewis & L. A. Rosenblum (Eds.), *The origins of fear.* New York: Wiley, 1974. pp. 254–258.

Charlesworth, W. R., & Kreutzer, M. A. Facial expressions of infants and children. In Paul Ekman (Ed.), *Darwin and facial expression, a century of research in review.* New York: Academic Press, 1973.

Cicchetti, D., & Sroufe, L. A. An organizational view of affect: Illustration from the study of Down's syndrome infants. In M. Lewis & L. A. Rosenblum (Ed.), *The development of affect.* New York: Plenum Press, 1978.

Cohen, L. B., & Gelber, E. Infant visual memory. In L. B. Cohen and P. Salapatek (Eds.), *Infant perception: From sensation to cognition.* New York: Academic Press, 1975.

Darwin, C. R. *The expression of emotions in man and animal.* London: John Murray, 1872.

Darwin, C. R. A biographical sketch of an infant. *Mind,* 1877, *2,* 286–294.

Décarie, T. G. Affective development and cognition in a Piagetian context. In M. Lewis and L. Rosenblum (Ed.), *The development of affect.* New York: Plenum Press, 1978.

Eichenwald, H. F., & Fry, P. C. Nutrition and learning. *Science,* 1969, *163,* 644–648.

Ekman, P., & Friesen, W. V. *Unmasking the face.* Englewood Cliffs, N.J.: Prentice-Hall, 1975.

Ekman, P., Friesen, W. V., & Ellsworth, P. *Emotion in the human face: Guidelines for research and an integration of findings.* New York: Pergamon Press, 1972.

Emde, R. N., Gaensbauer, T., & Harmon, R. J. *Emotional expression in infancy: A biobehavioral study.* New York: International Universities Press, 1976.

Emde, R. N., & Harmon, R. J. Endogenous and exogenous smiling systems in early infancy. *The Journal of the American Academy of Child Psychiatry,* 1972, *11* (2), 177–200.

Emde, R. N., Katz, E. L., & Thorpe, J. K. Emotional expressions in infancy: II. Early deviations in Down's syndrome. In M. Lewis & L. A. Rosenblum (Eds.), *The development of affect.* New York, Plenum Press, 1978.

Emde, R. N., Kligman, D. H., Reich, J. H., & Wade, T. D. Emotional expression in infancy: I. Initial studies of social signalling and an emergent model. In M. Lewis and L. Rosenblum (Ed.), *The development of affect.* New York: Plenum Press, 1978.

Emde, R. N., & Robinson, J. The first two months: Recent research in developmental psychobiology and the changing view of the newborn. In J. Noshpitz & J. Call (Eds.), *Basic handbook of child psychiatry.* New York: Basic Books, 1976.

Escalona, S. K. *The roots of individuality.* Chicago: Aldine , 1968.

Escalona, S. K., & Heider, G. M. *Prediction and outcome: A study in child development.* New York: Basic Books, 1959.

Fagan, J. Infant's delayed recognition: Memory and forgetting. *Journal of Experimental Child Psychology,* 1973, *16,* 424–450.

Flavell, J. H. *Cognitive development.* Englewood Cliffs, N.J.: Prentice-Hall, 1977.

Fry, P. S. Affect and resistance to temptation. *Developmental Psychology,* 1975, *11,* 466–472.

Golden, M., & Birns, B. Social class and cognitive development in infancy. *Merrill-Palmer Quarterly,* 1968, *14,* 139–149.

Goodenough, F. L. The expression of the emotions in infancy. *Child Development,* 1931, *2,* 96–101.

Goodenough, F. L. Expression of the emotions in a blind–deaf child. *Journal of Abnormal and Social Psychology,* 1932–1933, *27,* 328–333.

Goulet, J. Notion de causalité et réactions à la personne étrangere chez le jeune enfant. In T. Gouin-Décarie (Ed.), *La réaction à la personne etrangere.* Montreal: Presses de l'Université de Montreal, 1974.

Harlow, H. F. The nature of love. *American Psychologist, 1958, 13,* 673–685.

Harlow, H. F. Early social deprivation and later behavior in the monkey. In A. Abrams, H. H. Garner, & J. E. P. Toman (Ed.), *Unfinished tasks in the behavioral sciences.* Baltimore: Williams & Wilkins, 1964.

Hiatt, S., Campos, J. J., & Emde, R. N. Fear, surprise, and happiness: The patterning of facial expression in infants. Paper presented at the meetings of the Society for Research in Child Development, New Orleans, March 1977.

Hinde, R. A. Mothers' and infants' roles: Distinguishing the questions to be asked. In M. O'Conner (Ed.)., *Parent–infant interaction.* Amsterdam: Elsevier, 1975.

Hoffman, M. L. Development synthesis of affect and cognition and its implications for altruistic motivation. *Developmental Psychology,* 1975, *11,* 607–622.

Hoffman, M. L. The arousal and development of empathy. In M. Lewis & L. Rosenblum (Eds.), *The development of affect*. New York: Plenum Press, 1978.

Izard, C. E. *The face of emotion*. New York: Appleton-Century-Crofts, 1971.

Izard, C. E. *Patterns of emotions: A new analysis of anxiety and depression*. New York: Academic Press, 1972.

Izard, C. E. Human emotions. New York: Plenum Press, 1977.

Izard, C. E. The emergence of emotions and development of consciousness in infancy. In J. M. Davidson, & R. J. Davidson, (Eds.), *The psychobiology of consciousness*. New York: Plenum Press, 1978.(a)

Izard, C. E. On the development of emotions and emotion–cognition relationships in infancy. In M. Lewis & L. Rosenblum (Eds.), *The development of affect*. New York: Plenum Press, 1978.(b)

Jackson, E., Campos, J. J., & Fischer, K. W. The question of decalage between object permanence and person permanence. *Developmental Psychology*, 1978,

Judd, E., & Lewis, M. The effects of birth order and spacing on mother–infant relationships. Paper presented at the meeting of the Eastern Psychological Association, New York, April 1976.

Kagan, J. *Change and continuity in infancy*. New York: Wiley, 1971.

Kagan, J. Emergent themes in human development. *American Scientist*, 1976, *64*, pp. 186–196.

Kagan, J. *Infancy: Its place in human development*. Cambridge, Mass.: Harvard University Press, 1978.(a)

Kagan, J. On emotion and its development: A working paper. In M. Lewis & L. Rosenblum (Ed.), *The development of affect*. New York: Plenum Press, 1978.(b)

Kaufman, I. C., & Rosenblum, L. A. The waning of the mother–infant bond in two species of macaque. In B. M. Foss (Ed.), *Determinants of infant behavior*, Vol. 4. London: Methuen, 1969.

Klaus, M. H., Trause, M. A., & Kennell, J. H. "Does human maternal behavior after delivery show a characteristic pattern?" *Parent–Infant Interaction*. Amsterdam: CIBA Foundation, 1975.

LaBarbera, J. D., Izard, C. E., Vietze, P., & Parisi, S. A. Four- and six-month-old infant's visual responses to joy, anger, and neutral expression. *Child Development*, 1976, *47*, 535–538.

Landis, C. Studies of Emotional Reactions: I. A preliminary study of facial expression. *The Journal of Experimental Psychology*, 1924, *7*, 325–341.

Lewis, M., & Gallas, H. Cognitive performance in the 12-week-old infant: The effects of birth order, birth spacing, sex, and social class. Unpublished research bulletin, Educational Testing Service, Princeton, N.J., 1976.

Lewis, M., & Goldberg, S. Perceptual–cognitive development in infancy: A generalized expectancy model as a function of the mother–infant relationship. *Merrill-Palmer Quarterly*, 1969, *15*, 81–100.

Lewis, M., & Lee-Painter, S. An interactional approach to the mother-infant dyad. In M. Lewis and L. A. Rosenblum (Eds.), *The effect of the infant on its caregiver*. New York: Wiley, 1974.

Lewis, M., & Rosenblum, L. A. (Eds.). *The effect of the infant on its caregiver*. New York: Wiley, 1974.

Ling, D., & Ling, A. H. Communication development in the first three years of life. *Journal of Speech Hearing Research*, 1974, *17*, 146–159.

McDevitt, S. C. A longitudinal assessment of continuity and stability in temperamental characteristics from infancy to early childhood. Unpublished thesis, Temple University, 1976.

McGhee, P. E. Cognitive development and children's comprehension of humor. *Child Development*, 1971, *42*, 123–138.

McGhee, P. E. Cognitive mastery and children's humor. *Psychological Bulletin*, 1972, *81*, 721–730. (a)

McGhee, P. E. Development of children's ability to create a joking relationship. *Child Development*, 1974, *45*, 552–556. (b)

Miller, D. J., Cohen, L. B., & HIll, K. T. A methodological investigation of Piaget's theory of object concept development in the sensory-motor period. *Journal of Experimental Child Psychology*, 1970, *9*, 59–85.

Mischel, T. P. Cognitive conflict and the motivation of thought. In T. P. Mischel (Ed.), *Cognitive development and epistomology*. New York: Academic Press, 1971.

Mischel, W. *Personality and assessment*. New York: Wiley, 1968.

Moss, H. A. Methodological issues in studying mother–infant interactions. *American Journal of Orthopsychiatry*, 1965, *35*, 482–486.

Moss, H. A. Sex, age and state as determinants of mother–infant interaction. *Merrill-Palmer Quarterly*, 1967, *13*, 19–36.

Oster, H., & Ekman, P. Facial behavior in child development. In A. Collins (Ed.), *Minnesota Symposium on Child Development*, Vol. 11. New York: Thomas Crowell, 1977.

Paradise, E., & Curcio, F. Relationship of cognitive and affective behavior to fear of strangers in male infants. *Developmental Psychology*, 1974, *10*, 4, 476–484.

Parisi, S., & Izard, C. E. Five-, seven-, and nine-month-old infants' facial responses to twenty stimulus situations. Unpublished manuscript, 1977.

Pedersen, F. A. Personal communication with R. N. Emde, 1977.

Piaget, J. *The construction of reality in the child* (1937). Translated by Margaret Cook. New York: Basic Books, 1954.

Piaget, J., & Inhelder, B. *The psychology of the child*. New York: Basic Books, 1969.

Pinneau, S. R. A critique on the article by Margaret Ribble. *Child Development*, 1950, *21*, 203–228.

Pinneau, S. R. The infantile disorders of hospitalism and anaclitic depression. *Psychological Bulletin*, 1955, *52*,429–452.

Prechtl, H. F. The mother–child interaction in babies with minimal brain damage. In B. M. Foss (Ed.), *Determinants of infant behavior*, Vol. 2. New York: Wiley, 1963.

Provence, S., & Lipton, R. C. *Infants in institutions: A comparison of their development with family-reared infants during the first year of life*. New York: International Universities Press, 1962.

Ramsay, D. S., & Campos, J. J. The Onset of representation and entry into stage 6 of object permanence development. *Developmental Psychology*, 1978, *14*, 79–86.

Rheingold, H. L. The modification of social responsiveness in institutional babies. *Monographs of Soc. Res. Child Development*, 1956, *21*, No. 63 (No. 2).

Rosenhan, D., Underwood, B., & Moore, B. S. Affect moderates self-gratification and altruism. *Journal of Personality and Social Psychology*, 1974, *30*, 546–552.

Rothbart, M. K. Laughter in young children. *Psychological Bulletin*, 1973, *80*, 247–256.

Rothbart, M. K. Development of a caretaker report temperament scale for use with 3-, 6-, 9-, and 12-month-old infants. Paper presented at SRCD meeting. New Orleans, March 1977.

Rutter M. Psychological development—Predictions from infancy. *Journal of Child Psychology and Psychiatry*, 1970, *11*, 49–62.

Sander, L. Regulation and organization in the early infant–caretaker system. In R. J. Robinson (Ed.), *Brain and early behavior*. London: Academic Press, 1969, pp. 311–332.

Scarr, S., & Salapatek, P. Patterns of fear development during infancy. *Merrill Palmer Quarterly*, 1970, *16*, 53–90.

Schaefer, E. S., & Bayley, N. Maternal behavior, child behavior and their intercorrelations from infancy through adolescence. *Monographs of the Society for Research in Child Development*, 1963, *28*.

Schaffer, H. R. The onset of fear of strangers and the incongruity hypothesis. *Journal of Child Psychology and Psychiatry*, 1966,7, 95–106.

Schaffer, H. R. *The growth of sociability*. London: Penguin Books, 1971.

Schaffer, H. R., & Emerson, P. E. The development of social attachments in infancy. *Monographs of the Society for Research in Child Development*, 1964,5 29.

Schwartz, G. E., Fair, P. L., Salt, P. S., Mandel, M. R., & Klerman, J. L. Facial muscle patterning to affective imagery in depressed and non-depressed subjects. *Science*, 1976, *192*, 489–491.

Sherman, M. The ability of observers to judge the emotional characteristics of the crying of infants, and of the voice of an adult. *Journal of Comparative Psychology*, 1927, 7, 335–351. (a)

Sherman, M. The differentiation of emotional responses in infants: I. Judgments of emotional responses from motion picture views and from actual observations. *Journal of Comparative Psychology*, 1927, 7, 265–285. (b)

Sherman, M. The differentiation of emotional responses in infants: III. A proposed theory of the development of emotional responses in infants. *Journal of Comparative Psychology*, 1928, 8, 385–394.

Simpson, R., & Izard, C. E. *Emotion recognition in the severly mentally retarded*. Unpublished manuscript, 1972.

Siqueland, E. R. Biological and experiential determinants of exploration in infancy. Paper presented at the First National Biological Conference, Detroit, Michigan, 1970.

Sostek, A. M., & Anders, T. Relationships among the Brazelton neonatal scale, Bayley infant scales, and early temperament. *Child Development*, 1977, *48*, 320–323.

Spitz, R. A. Hospitalism: An inquiry into the genesis of psychiatric conditions in early childhood. *Psychoanalytic Study of the Child*, 1945, *1*, pp. 53–74.

Spitz, R. A. Hospitalism: A follow-up report. *Psychoanalytic Study of the Child*, 1946, 2, 113–117.

Spitz, R. A. *A genetic field theory of ego formation: Its implications for pathology*. New York: International Universities Press, Inc. 1959.

Spitz, R. A. *The first year of life*. New York: International Universities Press, 1965.

Spitz, R. A., & Wolf, K. M. The smiling response: A contribution to the ontogenesis of social relations. *Genetic Psychology Monographs*, 1946, *34*, 57–125.

Sroufe, L. A. Emotional expression in infancy. Unpublished manuscript, 1976.

Sroufe, L. A., & Wunsch, J. P. The development of laughter in the first year of life. *Child Development*, 1972, *43*, 1326–1344.

Stayton, D. J., & Ainsworth, M. D. Individual differences in infant responses to brief everyday separation as related to other infant and maternal behaviors. *Developmental Psychology*, 1973, *9*, 126–235.

Stayton, D. J., Ainsworth, M. D., & Main, M. B. The development of separation behavior in the first year of life: Protest, following and greeting. *Developmental Psychology*, 1973, *8*, 213–225.

Stechler, G., & Carpenter, G. A viewpoint on early affective development. In J. Hellmuth (Ed.), *The exceptional infant*, Vol. 1. Seattle: Special Child Publications, 1967.

Stern, D. Mother and infant at play: The dyadic interaction involving facial, vocal, and gaze behaviors. In M. Lewis and L. Rosenblum (Eds.), *The effect of the infant on its caregiver*. New York: Wiley, 1974.

Stone, L. J., Smith, H. T., & Murphy, L. B. (Eds.), *The competent infant*. New York: Basic Books, 1973.

Thoman, E. B. How a rejecting baby affects mother–infant synchrony. *Parent–infant interaction*. Amsterdam: CIBA Foundation, Associated Scientific Publishers, 1975.

Thomas, A., & Chess, S. *Temperament and development*. New York: Brunner/Mazel, 1977.

Thomas, A., Chess, S., & Birch, H. G. *Temperament and behavior disorders in children.* New York: New York University Press, 1968.

Thomas, A., Chess, S., Birch, H, G., Hertzig, M. E., & Korn, S. *Behavioral individuality in early childhood.* New York: New York University Press, 1963.

Tomkins, S. S. *Affect, Imagery, consciousness,* Vol. 1. *The positive affects.* New York; Springer, 1962.

Tomkins, S. S. *Affect, imagery, consciousness,* Vol. 2. *The negative affects.* New York: Springer, 1963.

Uzgiris, I. C., & Hunt, J. McV. An instrument for assessing infant psychological development. Mimeographed paper. Psychological Development Laboratory, University of Illinois, 1966.

Wachs, T. D., Uzgiris, I. C., & Hunt, J. Mcv. Cognitive development in infants of different age levels and from different environmental backgrounds: An exploratory investigation. *Merrill-Palmer Quarterly,* 1971, *17,* 283–317.

Watson, J. S. Smiling, cooing, and 'the game.' *Merrill-Palmer Quarterly,* 1972, *18,* 323–340.

Werner, H. Lecture series No. 3: *J. S. Bruner, Processes of Cognitive Growth: Infancy.* Worcester, Mass.: Clark University Press with Barre Publishers, 1968, pp. 35–45, 56–58, 62–64.

Wolff, P. H. Observations on newborn infants. *Psychosomatic Medicine,* 1959, *21,* 110–118.

Wolff, P. H. The natural history of crying and other vocalizations in early infancy. In B, M. Foss (Ed.), *Determinants of Infant Behavior,* Vol. 4. London: Methuen, 1969, pp. 81–109.

Yarrow, L. J. Research in dimensions of early maternal care. *Merrill-Palmer Quarterly,* 1963, *9,* 101–114.

Yarrow, L. J., Rubenstein, J. L., & Pedersen, F. A. *Infant and environment: Early cognitive and motivational development.* Washington, D.C.: Hemisphere Publishing Corp., 1975.

Yarrow, L. J. Rubenstein, J. L., Pedersen, F. A., & Jankowski, J. J. *Dimensions of early stimulation and their differential effects on infant development.* Paper presented at the meeting of the Society for Research in Child Development, April 4, 1971, Minneapolis.

Zigler, E. The retarded child as a whole person. In D. K. Routh (Ed.), *The experimental study of mental retardation.* Chicago: Aldine, 1973, pp. 231–322.

Zigler, E., Levine, J., & Gould, L. Cognitive challenge as a factor in children's humor appreciation. *Journal of Personality and Social Psychology,* 1967, *6,* 332–336.

Zuckerman, M., & Mellstrom, M., Jr. The contribution of persons, situations, modes of responses, and their interactions in self-reported responses to hypothetical and real anxiety-inducing situations. In D. Magnussen and N. S. Endler (Eds.), *Personality at the crossroads: Current issues in interactional psychology.* Hillsdale, N.J.: Erlbaum, 1977.

Editor's Introduction

16

In this chapter Savitsky and Eby extend a line of thinking and research that Savitsky began in his doctoral dissertation. In that study, Savitsky showed that under particular experimental conditions, subjects' punitive attitudes and behaviors were differentially influenced by various emotion-specific facial expressions of the victims. Savitsky and his students have continued to develop evidence for the importance of emotion communication (expressive signals and their interpretation) in various types of interpersonal transactions.

In the present chapter, Savitsky and Eby raise the question as to whether emotion communication may lie at the heart of empathy and empathic behavior. One is reminded of the possibility that the same forces that push us toward anonymity and deindividuation may lead to a general degradation of human empathy and an increase in aggression and social disorder.

In particular, their paper examines the relationship between an individual's awareness of the emotions of others and his/her likelihood of engaging in antisocial behavior.

They define emotion awareness to include sensitivity to emotion signals, sympathy, and empathy, and they maintain that awareness so defined is somehow distorted or deficient in those who persist in antisocial behavior. Clinical observations tend to support their thesis, but the scanty experimental evidence now available is inconsistent. There is the possibility that psychopaths or delinquents may not differ from normals in their response to the emotion signals of others when such responding is adaptive in a self-serving sense. The authors also suggest that chronic exposure to threatening circumstances may lead to a deficit in emotion awareness, and the notion that emotion awareness or some kind of response to the emotion signals of others is essential to empathy and empathic behavior is certainly plausible.

Emotion Awareness and Antisocial Behavior

16

JEFFREY C. SAVITSKY and THOMAS EBY

Perhaps it is a result of the growing complexity of our society, but it appears that many have become fearful that they too will become unwitting victims of nameless and irrational predators. Further, our institutions have seemingly grown larger, only to become less responsive, as they daily reaffirm our beliefs that we are anonymous and that our individual feelings are of little importance. The simultaneous increase in feelings of anonymity and fears about our safety is well founded since the relationship of aggression and anonymity is quite real (Zimbardo, 1969). Studies of aggression have yielded at least one clear generalization: an awareness of our own and of others' humanity lessens the likelihood that aggression will occur. Lorenz (1966) has speculated that at least one reason that aggression can now occur so readily is that we have developed weapons that allow us to harm others over great distances. We have thereby attained the ability to reduce people to unseen, inhuman, emotionless targets. The effectiveness of our weapons precludes an awareness of a victim's feelings.

The present chapter reviews the research evidence for a relationship between the awareness of the emotions of others and antisocial behavior. There is intuitive appeal in relating these interpersonal behaviors. We evaluate as "good" both those whom we see as sensitive or responsive to our feelings and those who we believe are morally righteous. In contrast, we denigrate those who ignore both our feelings and our beliefs in fairness. Perhaps the intuitive appeal of a relationship between emotion awareness and prosocial behavior is most clearly felt when both behaviors are presumed to be absent. It has become a frequent experience to read newspaper accounts of spectacular and

JEFFREY C. SAVITSKY and THOMAS EBY • Purdue University, West Lafayette, Indiana.

wanton acts of violence that follow from slight or apparently nonexistent provocation. Reading these stories yields the confused feeling that such crimes would be impossible unless the attacker was inured to the pain and fear of the victim. If this were not so, how could the crime have occurred?

The commonsense notion that there is a relationship between emotion awareness and prosocial behavior has also found expression in more formalized psychological theory. Hogan (1973) has postulated that moral development is at least partially dependent on five dimensions of character structure. These include moral knowledge, socialization, empathy, autonomy, and moral judgment. Of these postulated dimensions, the one with the greatest relevance to the present chapter is empathy, which Hogan (1969) defines as the "imaginative apprehension of another's state of mind." Later research by Hogan and his associates (Kurtiness & Hogan, 1972) suggests further that empathy can compensate for poor socialization, so that highly empathic people, even if poorly socialized, may still behave in a moral manner.

Aronfreed (1968) has similarly pointed out that empathy is closely related to prosocial behavior. Aronfreed claims that while prosocial behaviors (for example, altruism and sympathy) can be acquired via observation or through contingency-based learning, these behaviors will be maintained only to the extent that a child has a capacity for empathy. It should be noted, however, that Aronfreed employs a more encompassing definition of empathy than Hogan; while the latter regards empathy as a purely cognitive process, Aronfreed defines empathy as the vicarious experience of another's feeling states.

The purpose of the present chapter is to evelute the evidence relating emotion awareness to anti- and prosocial behavior. The beginning of the chapter entails a detailed definition of emotion awareness, which will be broadly viewed as an individual's capacity to utilize nonverbal emotion messages communicated by others. A second portion of the chapter presents a review of research that demonstrates that interpersonal emotion messages are capable of and typically regulate and socialize both anti- and prosocial behavior. Finally, the chapter presents existing research that has both conceptualized emotion awareness as a skill, which varies among people, and examined the relation of varying facets of this skill to anti- or prosocial behavior.

The central thesis of this chapter is that those individuals who habitually and persistently engage in antisocial acts do so partially out of some idiosyncratic use of, or insensitivity to, the emotion communications. It has been demonstrated that emotion messages act as a controlling influence on the behavior of others. Most people, for example, typically avoid behaviors that result in the communication of negative or unpleassnt emotions by others. If, on the other hand, certain individuals were found to be indifferent or insensitive to these negative emotion communications or unable to appreciate their significance, then it would be reasonably expected that these individuals would also violate the guidelines that typically define acceptable behavior.

It should be noted, before continuing, that there is no compelling evidence to support the view that antisocial behavior is an exclusive consequence of aberrations in either the intrapersonal experience or the interpersonal communication of the emotions. Only a portion of criminals, for instance, are reported to suffer emotional disturbance. Furthermore, Hartshorn and May (1928) have shown that nearly every child will transgress social rules if the environment presents contingencies that support such behavior. Antisocial behavior, therefore, must be regarded as a complex phenomenon, the definition of which shifts with changing cultural mores. Further, the antecedent conditions of antisocial behavior may include, but are not necessarily limited to, individual feeling states and the awareness of the feeling states of others. Poverty, inequity, and environmental frustration are undoubtedly the major antecedents of crime. However, these aversive conditions likely act to cause both long- and short- term shifts in how people feel and in how they perceive others. Such shifts in emotional experiencing would seemingly work either to increase or decrease the probability that a given individual will engage in antisocial behavior. Schacter (1971), for example, has speculated that a specific emotion, fear, strongly affects decisions about whether or not one should violate the law. Further, a number of studies (Aderman, 1972; Berkowitz & Connor, 1966; Moore, Underwood, & Rosenhan, 1973; Rosenhan, Underwood, & Moore, 1974; Underwood, Moore, & Rosenhan, 1973) conducted with both children and adults have reported that subjects are more likely to be cooperative, altruistic, and sympathetic when they are happy. In contrast, the experience of sadness leads to avoidance and refusals to cooperate. Experiencing negative emotion has also been found to decrease subjects' willingness to defer immediate gratification and to lower their resistance to temptation (Seeman & Schwarz, 1974), both characteristics that are often attributed to delinquent children. Thus, the intrapersonal experiencing of certain emotion states has been related to a variety of anti- or prosocial behaviors in subjects. This chapter reviews the evidence that relates the interpersonal awareness of emotion states to anti- or prosocial acts.

I. THE NATURE OF EMOTION AWARENESS

Emotion awareness is conceptualized here as a complex set of skills that allows people to gather information about the emotion states of others. The term *emotion awareness*, as used in this chapter, overlaps with several other more frequently used terms, such as *empathy, sympathy,* and *sensitivity.* However, *emotion awareness* is here specifically meant to connote the ability to use a limited source of data, to decode the perceptually available emotion cues that normally accompany virtually all face-to-face interactions. In contrast, some studies of empathy have defined the empathic response as the ability to recognize the consequences of certain situational events for the well-being of others but have left unspecified the method by which subjects gain these beliefs. For instance, Stotland (1969) asked subjects to watch a confederate supposedly receive either aversive or pleasurable stimuli. The subjects' physiological reaction to the confederate's situation was taken as a measure of empathy. Of interest here is the fact that the subjects were partially informed about the nature of the confederate's situation via a verbal explanation given to them by the experimenter. During the supposed administration of the experimental stimuli, the subjects watched the confederate's reaction, but the confederate was seated with his back to them. The subjects were able to observe only the gross motor responses of the confederate (an *emotion cue* as defined here), but they were unable to observe the confederate's facial expressions. These facial expressions would normally communicate much of the information about emotional states, but it is apparent that in this study the subjects gained the bulk of their understanding of the confederate's feelings via the verbal description of the stimulus given to them by the experimenter. The subject could not depend on the confederate's own emotion cues.

Several studies by Baron (1971, 1974) have also informed subjects about the aversive experiences of others via methods that did not call for emotion awareness, as the term is being used here. In these studies, subjects were told to deliver aversive electric shocks to experimental partners, who were actually accomplices of the experimenter. The subjects were then informed of the confederate's supposed experience via a "pain meter." which, subjects were told, measured the autonomic arousal of the confederate. This device clearly communicated the magnitude of a victim's pain and suffering, but it did so via an electronic device, a method that did not permit the utilization of those expressive cues that form the concern of the present chapter.

The expressive cues that deliver information about one's emotional state include nonverbal behaviors such as facial expressions, gestures, and vocal tones. It appears that facial expressions often indicate the quality or specific category of emotional experience, while bodily movements indicate the degree or intensity of that emotional experience (Ekman, 1965). Additional research has shown that vocal cues can also indicate the quality of an emotional state (Mehrabian & Ferris, 1967).

Birdwhistell (1960) contends that in a two-person conversation, verbal components carry less than 35% of the social meaning of the situation. More than 65%, he estimates, is carried by nonverbal bands. Several studies (e.g., Bugental, Kaswan, & Love, 1970) have compared the relative communicative impact of nonverbal cues and verbal content. This has been done by asking subjects to judge the meaning of messages that have incongrous verbal and nonverbal content (e.g., verbal is negative while nonverbal is positive). These studies indicate that the meaning of evaluative-emotion messages is largely contained in facial expressions and vocal tones, while verbal content is relatively less important. The message "I like you" can mean vastly different things depending on whether it is delivered with a smile or a frown.

The communication of emotional experience is a complex process that involves verbal and nonverbal acts. The reception, decoding, or awareness of all emotion messages, but particularly nonverbal cues, is similarly complex and multifaceted. Emotion awareness entails a variety of both intrapersonal and interpersonal skills. These skills will be outlined below. They include perceptual acuity, cognitive classification ability, emotional responsivity or the ability to recognize the importance of emotions, and behavioral or interpersonal responses.

At first thought, there seems little reason to believe that anything beyond gross perceptual skills would be necessary for adequate emotion awareness. However, the physical-configurational properties of emotion cues have been found to be quite complex. Slight changes in facial patterning, which may occur at extremely rapid rates (Haggard & Issacs, 1966) may radically alter the content of an emotion message. One estimate is that the facial musculature is capable of producing some 20,000 recognizably different facial expressions (Knapp, 1972). Vocal messages are similarly complex patterns of stimuli. These considerations alone suggest the importance of perceptual abilities. But in addition, Hogan (1969) has found perceptual skill to correlate with a checklist measure of empathy. Similarly, Izard (1971) found that performance on a test of perceptual-motor ability was significantly correlated with accuracy in classifying facial expressions, and Davitz (1964) reports that several tests of perceptual ability correlate with an ability to classify vocal cues of emotions.

The accurate classification of emotion stimuli, a cognitive skill, is perhaps the most frequently used method of assessing emotion awareness. Early investigators (Feleky, 1914; Ruckmick, 1921; Gates, 1925) had subjects apply verbal labels to posed pictures of facial expressions. These verbal response methods have undergone improvements in more recent studies (Gitter, Mostofsky, & Quincy, 1971; Izard, 1971). In one study, Borke (1971) replaced verbal labels and used situational pictures as a response measure. Dimitrovsky (1964) extended work conducted with facial cues by asking subjects to classify vocal cues as to emotion categories. In general, the findings of these studies show that the ability to classify emotion cues increases with age and can be accomplished by most adult subjects.

Emotion awareness is not limited to cognitive and perceptual skills. It also involves the emotional responsiveness of the observer. The observer of emotion cues often comes to share, or vicariously experience, the observed emotion, but in order to do this, it is nesessary that an observer be able to recognize the importance of emotional expressions. Checklist scales of empathy seem to be one way to assess the importance attributed by a subject to emotions experienced by others. For instance, one empathy scale (Mehrabian & Epstein, 1972) asks subjects to agree or disagree with statements such as "I find it silly for people to cry out of happiness" or "I often find public displays of affection annoying." Responses to these items reflect a subject's attitudes about the importance of the emotions. Additional research (Savitsky & Izard, 1970) has demonstrated that children, with increasing age, attribute greater importance to the emotions of others. In this particular study, children of varying ages were asked to choose the two photographs, from a group of three, that were most similar to each other. Each triad of pictures consisted of three facial photographs of the same person. The pictures were constructed and arranged so that potential pairings could logically be based either on the similarity of objects in two of the three photos or on emotion expressions. The very youngest subjects (4- and 5- year-olds) generally made their pairings on the basis of objects, while older children based their decisions on the facial expressions. This result occurred despite the finding that, on trials where pairing was possible on only a single dimension, the children were equally successful with either response strategy. In other words, all of the subjects were able to use either type of cue as a basis for their choices, but only the older subjects preferred to use the emotion cues.

Emotion awareness also connotes overt interpersonal behaviors. That is, an observer of an emotion will base subsequent actions on those emotion cues. People react when they observe an emotion message. They run or fight, help or ignore, sympathize or ridicule. It is tempting to assume that particular types of observer responses will indicate the degree of the observer's emotion awareness. However, this is not always true. An apparently unsympathetic act, for instance, does not always indicate a lack of emotion awareness. A physician may want to help a distressed child but will instead ignore the child's attempt to avoid an impending vaccination. Cultural norms may also determine varying ways of responding to observed emotion cues. Berger (1962) has pointed out that a vicarious sharing of distress may be quite aversive. If one were unable to curtail the source of this distress, it would be reasonable simply to avoid the person emitting these aversive cues. Thus, paradoxically, a sympathetic person might conceivably avoid the object of his sympathy. The point here, in essence, is that there is not a straightforward relationship between the nature of a person's acts and the quality of that individual's emotion awareness. Instead, situational factors determine the relationship of emotion awareness to behavior. However, while this relationship is complex, the research to be reviewed indicates that emotion cues do have powerful effects on an observer's subsequent behavior.

Thus far, emotion awareness has been conceptualized as a multifaceted skill. Unfortunately, there are few data, other than clinical observations, to support the notion that individuals may possess specific awareness skills but lack others. An example of the effect of deficiencies in specific awareness skills is the child who reacts with terror to a parent's display of playful threat. In this instance, the child is demonstrating high responsivity to emotion cues but low accuracy in classifying them. It is of particular relevance to the present chapter that clinical speculation has frequently characterized the persistently antisocial, amoral, psychopathic individual as affectively insensitive and devoid of affectional ties. Turner (1956), for example, contended that the psychopath can "skillfully identify with the other's state of mind but avoid all emotional involvement with it." In the terminology of the present chapter, the psychopath might be described as exhibiting high accuracy in classifying emotion cues but low emotional responsivity.

II. THE IMPACT OF EMOTION DISPLAYS

A disciplinarian's reaction to another's moral transgression typically involves emotions and their display. These displays are important sources of guidance and information for the recipient of the discipline. Emotion displays by socializing agents serve as rewards, punishments, and guidelines for the recipient's future behavioral decisions. In spite of the important role of emotion messages in the socialization process, there is surprisingly little research on the impact of specific emotion messages on anti- or prosocial behavior, but researchers have only infrequently gone beyond this observation to investigate more preceisely the role of such messages in the socialization process.

Two areas of research are pertinent to this discussion. First, a number of studies have investigated the impact of emotion messages from a target on the subsequent delivery of aversive stimuli, such as aggressive or disciplinary acts, to that target. A second area of relevant research involves the impact of emotion communications on the subsequent modeling of moral transgressions.

Interest in the first area of research, the effect of emotion displays on aggressive behavior, has been stimulated by two sources. First, Sears, Maccoby, Levin (1957) hypothesized that if one goal of aggression is to hurt a victim, then the knowledge that one's victim is indeed being harmed should act to increase subsequent aggression. This hypothesis makes the disturbing prediction that a victim's display of distress and pain should bring about an increase in the aggressor's attacks on that victim.

A second source of interest in the relationship of emotion displays and aggression has been the work of ethologists (e.g., Lorenz, 1966). Observations of animals by ethologists suggest that bodily movements that are seeming indicators of underlying emotion states can have moderating effects on intraspecific aggression. More specifically, submissive appeasement gestures (e.g., a wolf's rolling on its back) seem to inhibit further attack, while threat displays (e.g., the baring of teeth) seem to communicate a willingness or readiness to attack. Often, physical combat among animals is avoided via such threat and appeasement gestures. These observations have stimulated researchers interested in human behavior to explore the possibility that similar appeasement and threat gestures may regulate human antagonistic encounters.

It seems reasonable to expect that there may be analogues to animals' appeasement gestures among human emotion displays. Several studies (Buss, 1966a,b) have shown that emotion cues from a victim that indicate that he is in pain or distress will lessen the subsequent aggressive behavior of a subject, a finding that is contrary to Sears *et al.*'s hypothesis and consistent with ethological observations. Typically, subjects in these studies are asked to administer what they believe to be a painful electric shock to an experimental partner—actually an experimental confederate who receives no shock—whenever the confederate commits a planned error in a learning task. The intensity and duration of the shock determined and administered by the subject serve as a measure of aggression. These studies have often defined victim feedback as vocal cues of distress, but they have not always permitted subjects to see the facial affect of the victim. A study by Tilker (1970) found that adding visual cues to vocal cues, in which subjects could see and hear their victim's pain, served to lower subjects' aggression to a greater extent than vocal cues alone.

One difficulty with studies investigating the effect of vocal distress on subsequent aggression is that they have lacked clear definitions of the vocal stimuli employed. Vocal cues have typically been loosely operationalized, with little regard to identifying the precise emotions portrayed in them. This oversight makes it difficult to specify the precise emotion that helped determine the aggressor's response.

A study conducted by Savitsky, Izard, Kotsch, and Christy (1974) was designed to investigate the effect of facial cues of differing emotions on aggression. Again, using the experimental procedures described above, subjects delivered supposed shock to a confederate for his mistakes in a learning task. During the trails of this learning task, subjects were permitted to watch the confederate's reaction to the shock. These staged reactions consisted of facial displays of fear, joy, anger, or a neutral expression. The results of this study were somewhat surprising, in that fear displays exhibited by the victims had little effect on the intensity of the subjects' aggression. This finding may appear to be somewhat contradictory in light of the results of studies that have reported that a victim's vocal distress lessens subsequent aggression. This apparent contradiction may result from a confusion of distress cues with fear cues. These two emotions differ considerably, both in their manner of expression and in their impact on others, but their verbal labels are often mistakenly interchanged.

A further result obtained in this study by Savitsky *et al.* (1974) was that angry grimaces exhibited by the confederate lessened subjects' aggression. One explanation for this finding is that subjects feared later retaliation by an apparently enraged victim. The results also indicated that displays of joy by victims increased the level of subjects' attacks. This latter finding is consistent with the results of a study by Bramel, Taub, and Blum (1968), who reported that subjects expressed greater dislike for an insulting experimenter who had previously experienced joy. In other words, happiness expressed by an individual who is somehow frustrating (through mistakes or insulting remarks) appears to elicit aggressive responses from others.

Several studies have been conducted (Savitsky & Sim, 1974; Savitsky, Czyzewski, Dubord, & Kaminsky, 1976) to investigate the reaction of subjects, placed in the role of disciplinarians, to the emotion displays of the person they must suggest punishments for. Subjects in these studies were shown videotapes containing children, adolescents, or adults who verbally admitted a minor crime while portraying either distress, anger, joy, or a neutral emotion state. The actors were instructed to portray these emotions nonverbally, so that emotion or feeling words were not verbalized in the tapes. The results indicated that such nonverbal emotion cues changed the subjects' ratings of the severity of the offenses as well as their suggestions of what they considered to be appropriate punishments. Distressed-sad actors, for example, were treated leniently, a finding that is consistent with studies reviewed previously on the impact of vocal cues on aggression. In contrast to the findings of Savitsky et al. (1974), however, angry actors were treated harshly, perhaps because subjects viewing videotapes do not fear retaliation as they might when confronting a live confederate. As found in previous studies, joyful actors were treated harshly. Another interesting result obtained from these studies was that the emotion displays of children had a greater effect on the judgments of adults than did the emotion displays of adults. It is therefore possible that the emotion displays of children may have a large impact on the punitive behaviors of their caretakers.

As noted previously, the effect of emotion displays interacts with situational determinants. This observation was given credence in a study by Savitsky and Sim (1974). Videotapes of the actors in this study were electronically edited so that only visual and vocal cues were preserved. All of the verbal content, which had informed the viewer of the actors' offenses, was eliminated. Subjects were instructed to observe the videotapes and rate how likable each actor was. Joyful actors were rated by the subjects as likable even though these actors had been severely punished by other subjects who had access to the verbal content. Distressed actors were rated as much less likable, even though other subjects had previously been lenient with them. In effect, we may find someone who shows distress to be aversive or someone who is joyful to be likable under one circumstance, but our reactions may be quite different under other circumstances.

Emotion displays are also important in teaching or modeling prosocial behavior. For instance, children observe their parents' emotions while simultaneously receiving instructions on the proper modes of behavior. Bryan (1971) and Midlarsky and Bryan (1972) have demonstrated that a model's smile and positive affect display will increase either sharing or greedy behavior among children if the model's positive affect is contingent on the model's demonstration of the specific altruistic or selfish behavior.

Children also learn about pro- or antisocial behavior by watching their peers react to punishment or reward. A peer's emotion displays can be viewed as vicarious lessons about the consequences of specific behaviors. Slaby and Parke (1971) showed children a film of a child either being punished or rewarded for previously prohibited play. The filmed child then reacted with displays of joy (smile), of distress (crying) or a neutral countenance. The results obtained demonstrated that children imitated the play of a rewarded model to a greater extent when he smiled and least when the model cried. These results indicate that the model's affective display amplified the effects of the reward. Similar results have been reported by Lerner and Weiss (1972) and by Thelen, Dollinger, and Roberts (1975). However, when the filmed child in the Slaby and Parke (1971) study was punished, a smiling model elicited less imitative behavior than did a distressed model. That is, children in this study were more likely to imitate a model who was punished and then cried than a model who was punished and subsequently smiled. This finding was unanticipated by the authors, since they believed that positive affect on the part of a model would act to increase the attractiveness of any behavior. However, this reversal is consistent with research previously cited dealing with reactions to smiling victims. That is, a model who smiles after punishment may be seen as less likable, and subjects may thus either refuse to imitate his behavior or identify more closely with the punishing adult.

In summary, emotion displays have been demonstrated to play a significant role in the socialization and control of behavior. Furthermore, the emotion displays of parents, peers, and victims all can be seen to contribute to forming one's personal definition of behaviors that are to be considered either anti- or prosocial. The question to be raised at this point concerns the behavior of those individuals who show less appreciation or awareness of others' emotion displays. Will their definitions of acceptable behavior differ from those with greater awareness of such cues? The following section reviews studies that have investigated the social behavior of individuals who vary in their awareness of emotion messages.

III. EMOTION AWARENESS AS AN INDIVIDUAL DIFFERENCE

If emotion awareness is in fact a skill, as conceptualized here, then it is reasonable to expect that individuals will exhibit differing levels of awareness. Some people should be highly sensitive to others' emotion displays, while other individuals should be relatively insulated from such cues. Furthermore, if a relationship exists between emotion awareness and anti- or prosocial behavior, then differences in emotion awareness should be reflected in the degree to which individuals conform to social mores and rules.

Studies to be reviewed here have investigated the relationship between emotion awareness and anti- or prosocial behavior by defining emotion awareness as accuracy in classifying stimuli, attitudes toward the importance of emotion cues, or immediate interpersonal reactions to emotion cues. Anti- or prosocial behavior has been operationalized either as membership in groups known to differ in their previous conformity (delinquent versus nondelinquent, socially adjusted versus not adjusted) or as conformity to a widely accepted example of anti- or prosocial activity (sharing or not sharing, aggressive versus not aggressive). Unfortunately, the absolute amount of research has been limited, and any conclusions must be quite tentative. This observation is most apparent in a review of studies examining subjects' immediate interpersonal reactions in social situations. However, studies that have defined emotion awareness as accuracy of classification or as attitudes toward the importance of emotion cues rather consistently show that emotion awareness abilities are related to the frequency with which subjects engage in anti- or prosocial behaviors. On the other hand, studies that have assessed subjects' immediate interpersonal reactions to emotion cues have not found that subjects known to differ in the degree of previous antisocial activity also differ in emotion awareness.

A. Accuracy of Classification

Researchers have assessed accuracy skills among children, adolescents, and adults. Izard (1971) demonstrated, for example, that accuracy in applying emotion labels to photographs of facial expressions is correlated with teachers' ratings of social adjustment among preschoolers. Johnson (1975) similarly found that elementary-school children who are better able to recognize how others are feeling are more likely to be of a cooperative disposition. *Cooperative disposition* was defined in this study as minimizing one's own and a partner's score on an interactional task in which competition was counterproductive. Johnson found that the positive relationship between accuracy and cooperation existed for children from three socioeconomic levels.

Fry (1976) asked school-aged children to view videotapes of adults involved in happy, angry, anxious, and sad interactions. The children were then asked to describe the interactions, and their verbal reports were then scored according to the degree to which they accurately reflected the emotional content of the videotapes. Additionally, the children were given a quantity of pennies and asked to share them. Emotion awareness in this study was found to be correlated with the number of pennies that the subjects altruistically shared.

Several additional studies have compared the accuracy skills of adolescent and adult offender groups with the emotion accuracy skills of nonoffender groups. Hansen (1968) compared a large group of prison inmates with a group of college students on several tasks designed to assess their ability to recognize emotion cues. The groups were equated for age, sex, ethnic background, and intelligence, but despite these controls, the prisoner group was significantly less proficient on three of the four emotion awareness tasks utilized.

Savitsky and Czyzewski (1977) showed 32 short videotapes of actors portraying joy, anger, sadness, or a neutral expression to a group of delinquents (all of whom had been arrested several times) and nondelinquents (none of whom has been arrested). Each videotape segment contained a different actor whose actual words were garbled by electronic filtering devices. The task of the subjects was to select from a short list of such words the emotion word that best described each videotape. The results suggested that the delinquent group of subjects was significantly less accurate. However, further analysis indicated that the delinquent and nondelinquent groups also differed in verbal intelligence, and a covariance analysis, using intelligence test scores as the covariate, revealed that the two groups were not significantly different in their ability to label the emotions.

B. Importance of Emotion Displays

Other researchers have related subjects' scores on checklist measures of empathy with the frequency of anti- or prosocial behaviors. These studies are relevant to the concerns of this chapter in that, as noted previously, empathy measures seem to assess, in part, the likelihood that an individual will attribute importance to the emotion displays of others. Aleksic and Savitsky (1977) administered a revised version of an empathy scale designed by Mehrabian and Epstein (1972) to adolescent delinquents and nondelinquents. The delinquent group was found to be less empathic on this measure. Further, empathy scores were negatively correlated with aggression scores within the delinquent group. That is, delinquents who received low empathy scores were rated more aggressive by institutional caretakers and behaved more aggressively on a laboratory measure of aggression, relative to more empathic delinquents.

A number of studies have attempted to relate subjects' degree of antisocial behavior with their scores on the empathy scale constructed by Hogan (1969). Deardorff, Finch, Kendall, Lira, and Indrisano (1975) reasoned that repeat offenders who more persistently engaged in crime would be less empathic than less involved offenders. They reported that nonoffenders (actually undergraduates and first offenders) did differ significantly from repeat offenders but not from each other on the Hogan empathy scale. Efforts to replicate this finding with adolescents were unsuccessful, however, in that adolescent nonoffenders, first offenders, and repeat offenders did not significantly differ in their obtained empathy scores (Kendall, Deardorff, & Finch, 1977).

Kurtiness and Hogan (1972) also employed the Hogan empathy scale in an effort to compare the empathy scores of adult offenders and nonoffenders. These authors first equated a group of adult prisoners with a group of college students on the socialization scale of the California Psychological Inventory. The results obtained indicated that in spite of the equivalency of socialization scores between the groups, the prisoners obtained lower scores on the measure of empathy. To account for this finding, the authors speculated that high levels of empathy compensated for the poor socialization of the apparently prosocial college student group.

C. Interpersonal Reactions

Thus far, studies have been cited that have related either the ability to classify emotion cues or the realization of the importance of emotion cues to subjects' history of pro- or antisocial behavior. While this relationship is important, of perhaps even greater importance is the question of whether or not individuals who engage in antisocial behavior can base immediate interpersonal decisions on the emotion cues of others. That is, beyond merely assessing the ability of subjects to accurately identify interpersonal emotion cues, do habitually antisocial individuals respond behaviorally to such cues in the same manner as more socialized subjects? Unfortunately, only a few studies have addressed this important question, and the results obtained are far from conclusive. In one study, Hartmann (1969) exposed half of a group of adolescent delinquents to an anger-arousing condition while the remaining subjects were treated in a neutral fashion. The subjects were then shown one of three films: a neutral control film, a film that contained an aggressive fight sequence, or a film that also contained an aggressive sequence but focused on the pain cues emitted by the victim of the fight. After viewing these films, the subjects were given the opportunity to aggress, by means of supposed electric shock, toward an experimental partner. The results indicated that those less frequent offenders who observed the pain cues, regardless of the level of prior anger arousal, were less aggressive than the less frequent offenders who observed the filmed aggression. Similarly, more frequent offenders who had not been angered and who observed the pain-cues film were less aggressive than non-angered frequent offenders who observed the aggressive-content film. These findings are similar to the results of studies previously reviewed that related distress–pain cues to aggression among non-delinquent subjects; that is, the observation of a victim's distress apparently serves to remind subjects of the consequences of their aggressive behavior, with the result that subjects lessen the intensity of their attack. However, this situation was reversed among the frequent offenders who had been angered in that subjects in this group who observed the pain-cues film were subsequently more aggressive than those who had observed the other films. In essence, pain cues served to lessen aggression among all the groups of offenders, just as among nonoffenders, but failed to do this for the angry frequent offenders.

A recent study by Savitsky and Czyzewski (1977) attempted to assess the reaction of adolescent offenders and nonoffenders to a variety of emotion cues. In this study, subjects watched a series of videotapes, each of which contained different actors who admitted committing a variety of crimes. These crimes differed in detail but were equated as to severity. While admitting to the crimes, the actors portrayed anger, joy, sadness, or a neutral emotion in a non-verbal fashion. The subjects' task in this study was to suggest the levels of punishment (via days of recommended incarceration) that each supposed offender should receive. It was expected that, if the delinquent group was in fact less aware of the actors' emotion cues, then either their level of suggested punishment would be more consistent across actors' emotions than would the nonoffenders' suggested levels of punishment or, on the other hand, the pattern of suggested punishments would differ between the groups. However, neither expected results occurred. While the emotion cues caused substantial effects on the punishment decisions, these effects were similar for both groups.

IV. SUMMARY AND CONCLUSIONS

The present chapter has presented evidence to support the claim that emotion displays have important interpersonal effects. Without doubt, these interpersonal cues make a major contribution to socializing and controlling behavior. Research has allowed a somewhat more specific understanding of the impact of specific emotion displays. For example, distress generally serves to lessen the intensity of an aggressor's attack, but available evidence suggests that fear does not. Distress also seems to serve as a warning for children that they should not emulate an activity that caused another to evidence this emotion. People do not like or imitate those who display the distress emotion. An expression of joy seems to increase the likelihood that someone will conform to our wishes. Generally, joyful people are seen as likable, but the expression of joy by a person engaged in frustrating or antisocial behavior seems to cause an observer to experience anger and to become highly punitive. Displays of anger can either provoke or intimidate, depending on such factors as the possibility of retaliation.

Given the importance of emotion displays, the central aim of this chapter was to assess the hypothesis that those less likely to utilize emotion displays would also have suffered some distortion in the socialization process. In part, review of the relevant literature supports this conclusion. That is, subjects who are more likely to attribute value and importance to emotion displays and who are able to label these displays more accurately are also less likely to engage in antisocial behavior. However, a more rigid test of the relationship of emotion awareness and antisocial behavior would seem to be found in studies that have assessed the immediate interpersonal reaction of offenders and nonoffenders to emotion displays. Stated more simply, a few studies have measured the reaction of offenders and nonoffenders to nonverbal emotion cues using measures of behavior that have some resemblance to real-world interpersonal reactions. If, after all, we are interested in generalizing from laboratory to life, the assessment devices, and the circumstances surrounding this assessment, become more valid if we increase their similarity to the situations and behaviors we are trying to predict. While there is some evidence that delinquents, for example, are less accurate in labeling facial expressions of emotion, there is little evidence to suggest that delinquents are less sympathetic than nondelinquents when faced with a crying child or are more aggressive than non-delinquents if an enemy shows distress. While it seems reasonable to expect, given the findings of studies dealing with accuracy and interest in the emotions, that persistently anti-social individuals do react differently to emotion displays, this is an extrapolation, and only studies by Hartmann (1969) and Savitsky and Czyzewski (1977) bear directly on this belief. Hartmann finds that more frequent offenders respond differently to emotion cues than less frequent offenders, but only when the more frequent offenders are angered. Savitsky and Czyzewski found no differences in the reaction of adolescent offenders and nonoffenders to emotion cues.

Taken as a whole, then, there is inconsistency among results, with this inconsistency apparently dependent on the methods used to operationalize emotion awareness. Accuracy and importance measures are related to antisocial behavior, but the studies that may have the greatest external validity find this relationship to be greatly qualified or not present. It may be that some specific feature of the measurement procedures, such as greater reliance on verbal ability or experimenter demands, may account for these inconsistencies, but more research will be needed to clarify this.

For the sake of convenience, the present review has grouped the literature in this area without much regard for the seriousness or intensity of the various types of antisocial behaviors. This is probably a flaw in that there may be considerable difference between antisocial behavior that is simply the transgression of an arbitrary rule stated by an experimenter and antisocial behavior that consists of the continuing attack on a victim whose pain and suffering are evident. Emotion awareness, or lack of it, may have little relevance to one type of behavior but may be a crucial antecedent of another. Similarly, the motivations of those who commit antisocial acts vary widely. For instance, not all delinquents are alike, and any generalization that describes *all* delinquents must be made with caution. It is a popular clinical notion that offenders can be classified into one of three categories: subcultural, psychopathic, and neurotic. The subcultural delinquent engages in anti-social acts that although at odds with the beliefs of the larger culture, are acceptable to subcultural guidelines. We would therefore expect a subcultural delinquent to possess normal emotion awareness skills. In contrast, neurotic and psychopathic delinquents are seen as differing in their emotional reaction to situations. The neurotic delinquent suffers from excesses of guilt and anxiety, and his antisocial acts often represent fearful avoidance or excessive anger and frustration. The psychopathic delinquent is described as suffering from "affective poverty" or an inability to experience emotion states. It is probable that both these latter types of delinquents would experience distortions in emotion awareness abilities. However, it is quite possible that while the psychopathic delinquent is impervious to such cues, the neurotic delinquent may be painfully overreactive to specific subsets of such cues. For instance, the neurotic delinquent may be able to classify another's anger accurately, but he may show an exaggerated interest in the display of this emotion. The important point here, however, is that assuming a linear relationship between emotion awareness and antisocial behavior is probably overly simplified, since this assumption fails to take account of complexities in what antisocial behavior is and in who does it.

It is an interesting, although speculative, effort to hypothesize potential causes of differences in emotion awareness. There are data that suggest that crude forms of emotion awareness exist soon after birth (Sagi & Hoffman, 1976). That is, babies as early as 2 days of age react with distress to the cries of other babies, but they do not react with distress to sounds matched for loudness. This finding brings up the interesting possibility that there may be innate factors that contribute to later differences in emotion awareness abilities. However, environmental and cultural influences are certainly major factors in determining if and how we respond to the emotions of others. Bowlby (1970) has pointed out that disruptions in parent–child relationships will impair the child's abilities to make affectional bonds with others. Rotenberg (1975) has suggested that the emotional insensitivity ostensibly observed among psychopaths is often an adaptive reaction to cultural and environmental demands. If, for instance, an environment provides persistent stress, and perhaps danger, so that victimization is not an unusual occurrence, it becomes a futile and exasperating experience to react to emotion displays; after all, there is little one can do anyway. It becomes instead more adaptive to ignore the emotion displays of others and thereby to reduce the uncomfortable feelings of concern and anxiety that often accompany the observation of distress and pain in others. A lack of emotion awareness would be at least one logical result of the persistent exposure to threatening or adverse circumstances.

REFERENCES

Aderman, D. Elation, depression, and helping behavior. *Journal of Personality and Social Psychology*, 1972, *24*, 91–101.

Aleksic, P., & Savitsky, J. C. Validation of a test of emotional empathy among adolescent offenders. Unpublished manuscript, Purdue University, 1977.

Aronfreed, J. *Conduct and conscience* New York: Academic Press, 1968.

Baron, R. A. Magnitude of victims' pain cues and level of prior arousal as determinants of adult aggressive behavior. *Journal of Personality and Social Psychology*, 1971, *17*, 236–243.

Baron, R. A. Aggression as a function of victims' pain cues, level of prior anger arousal, and exposure to an aggressive model. *Journal of Personality and Social Psychology*, 1974, *29*(1), 117–124.

Berger, S. M. Conditioning through vicarious instigation. *Psychological Review*, 1962, *29*, 450–466.

Berkowitz, L., & Connor, W. H. Success, failure and social responsibility. *Journal of Personality and Social Psychology*, 1966, *4*, 664–669.

Birdwhistell, R. L. Kinesics and communication. In E. Carpenter & M. McLuhan (Eds.), *Explorations in communication*. Boston: Beacon, 1960.

Borke, H. Interpersonal perception of young children; Egocentrism or empathy? *Developmental Psychology*, 1971, *5*, 263–269.

Bowlby, J. Disruption of affectional bonds and its effects on behavior. *Journal of Contemporary Psychotherapy*, 1970, *2*, 75–86.

Bromel, D., Taub, B., & Blum, B. An observer's reaction to the suffering of his enemy. *Journal of Personality and Social Psychology*, 1968, *8*, 384–392.

Bryan, J. H. Model affect and children's imitative altruism. *Child Development*, 1971, *42*, 2061–2065.

Bugental, D. E., Kaswan, J. W., & Love, L. R. Perception of contradictory meanings conveyed by verbal and nonverbal channels. *Journal of Personality and Social Psychology*, 1970, *16*, 647–655.

Buss, A. H. The effect of harm on subsequent aggression. *Journal of Experimental Research in Personality*, 1966, *1*, 249–255. (a)

Buss, A. H. Instrumentality of aggression, feedback, and frustration as determinants of physical aggression. *Journal of Personality and Social Psychology*, 1966, *3*, 153–162. (b)

Davitz, J. R. Personality, perceptual, and cognitive correlates of emotional sensitivity. In J. Davitz (Ed.), *The communication of emotional meaning*. New York: McGraw-Hill, 1964.

Deardorff, P. A., Finch, A. J., Jr., Kendall, P. C., Lira, F., & Indrisano, V. Empathy and socialization in repeat offenders, first offenders, and normals. *Journal of Counseling Psychology*, 1975, *22*, 453–455.

Dimitrovsky, L. The ability to identify the emotional meaning of vocal expressions at successive age levels. In J. Davitz, (Ed.), *The Communication of emotional meaning*. New York: McGraw-Hill, 1964.

Ekman, P. Differential communication of affect by head and body cues. *Journal of Personality and Social Psychology*, 1965, *2*, 726–735.

Feleky, A. M. The expression of the emotions. *Psychological Review*, 1914, *21*, 33–34.

Fry, P. S. Affect and resistance to temptation. *Developmental Psychology*, 1975, *11*, 466–472.

Fry, P. S. Children's social sensitivity, altruism, and self-gratification. *Journal of Social Psychology*, 1976, *98*, 77–88.

Gates, G. S. A test for ability to interpret facial expressions. *Psychological Bulletin*, 1925, *22*, 120.

Gitter, A. G., Mostofsky, D. I., & Quincy, A. J., Jr. Race and sex differences in the child's perception of emotion. *Child Development*, 1971, *42*, 2071–2075.

Haggard, E. A., & Issacs, K. S. Micromomentary facial expressions as indicators of ego mechanisms in psychotherapy. In L. A. Gottschalk & Auerbach, A. H. (Eds.), *Methods of research in psychotherapy*. New York: Appleton-Century-Crofts, 1966.

Hansen, S. B. Expressional cues as related to deviant social behavior. *Dissertation Abstracts*, 1968, *29*,(6a), 1780.

Hartmann, D. P. Influence of symobolically modeled instrumental aggression and pain cues on aggressive behavior. *Journal of Personality and Social Psychology*, 1969, *11*(3), 280.

Hartshorne, H., & May M. S. *Moral studies in the nature of character: Studies in self control*. New York: Macmillan, 1928.

Hogan, R. Development of an empathy scale. *Journal of Consulting and Clinical Psychology*, 1969,*35*, 308–316.

Hogan, R. Moral conduct and moral character: A psychological perspective. *Psychological Bulletin*, 1973, *79*, 217–232.

Izard, C. E. *The face of emotion*. New York: Appleton-Century-Crofts, 1971.

Johnson, J. W. Affective perspective taking and cooperative pre-disposition. *Developmental Psychology*, 1975, *11*, 869–870.

Kendall, P. C., Deardorff, P. A., & Finch, A. J. Empathy and socialization in first and repeat juvenile offenders and normals. *Journal of Abnormal Child Psychology*, 1977, *5*, 93–97.

Knapp, M. L. *Nonverbal communication in human interaction*. New York: Holt, Rinehart and Winston, 1972.

Kurtiness, W., & Hogan, R. Sources of conformity in unsocialized college students. *Journal of Abnormal Psychology*, 1972, *80*(1), 49–51.

Lerner, L., & Weiss, R. L. Role of value of reward and model affective response in vicarious reinforcement. *Journal of Personality and Social Psychology*, 1972, *21*, 93–100.

Lorenz, K. *On aggression*. New York: Harcourt, Brace, World. 1966.

Mehrabian, A., & Epstein, N. A measure of emotional empathy. *Journal of Personality and Social Psychology*, 1972, *40*, 525–543.

Mehrabian, A., & Ferris, S. R. Influence of attitudes from nonverbal communication in two channels. *Journal of Consulting Psychology*, 1967, *31*, 248–252.

Midlarsky, E., & Bryan, J. H. Affect expressions and children's imitative altruism. *Journal of Experimental Research in Personality*, 1972, *6*, 195–203.

Moore, D. S., Underwood, B., & Rosenhan, D. L. Affect and altruism. *Developmental Psychology*, 1973, *8*, 99–104.

Rosenhan, D. L., Underwood, B., & Moore, B. Affect moderates self gratification and altruism. *Journal of Personality and Social Psychology*, 1974, *30*, 546–552.

Rotenberg, M. Psychopathy, insensitivity and sensitization. *Professional Psychology*, 1975, *6*(3), 283.

Ruckmick, C. A. A Preliminary study of emotions. *Psychological Monographs*, 1921, *136*, 30–35.

Sagi, A., & Hoffman, M. L. Empathic distress in the newborn. *Developmental Psychology*, 1976, *12*, 175–176.

Savitsky, J. C., & Czyzewski, D. The reaction of adolescent offenders to nonverbal emotion displays. *Journal of Abnormal Child Psychology*, 1978, *6*, 89–96.

Savitsky, J. C. Czyzewski, D., Dubord, D., & Kaminsky, S. Age and emotion of an offender as determinants of adult punitive reactions. *Journal of Personality and Social Psychology*, 1976, *44*, 311–320.

Savitsky, J. C., & Izard, C. E. Developmental changes in the use of emotion cues in a concept formation task. *Developmental Psychology*, 1970, *3*, 350–357.

Savitsky, J. C., Izard, C. E., Kotsch, W. E., & Christy, L. Aggressor's responses to the victim's facial expression of emotion. *Journal of Research in Personality*, 1974, 346–357.

Savitsky, J. C., & Sim, M. E. Trading emotions: Equity theory of reward and punishment. *Journal of Communication*, 1974, *24*, 140–145.

Schacter, S. *Emotion, obesity, and crime.* New York: Academic Press, 1971.

Sears, R. R., Maccoby, E. E., & Levin, H. *Patterns of child rearing.* Evanston, Ill.: Row-Peterson, 1957.

Seeman, G., & Schwarz, J. C. Affective state and preference for immediate versus delayed reward. *Journal of Research in Personality*, 1974, *7*, 384–394.

Slaby, R. G., & Parke, R. D. Effect on resistance to deviation of observing a model's affective reaction to response consequences. *Developmental Psychology*, 1971, *9*, 40–47.

Stotland, E. Exploratory investigations of empathy. In L. Berkowitz (Ed.), *Advances in experimental social psychology*, Vol. 4. New York: Academic Press, 1969.

Thelen, M. H., Dollinger, S. J., & Roberts, M. C. Model consequences and model affect: Their effects on imitation. *Bulletin of the Psychonomic Society.* 1975, *6*, 478–480.

Tilker, H. A. Socially responsible behavior as a function of observer responsibility and victim feedback. *Journal of Personality and Social Psychology*, 1970, *14*, 95–100.

Turner, R. H. Role-taking, role-standpoint and reference group behavior. *American Journal of Sociology*, 1956, *61*, 316–328.

Underwood, B., Moore, B., & Rosenhan, D. L. Affect and self-gratification. *Developmental Psychology*, 1973, *8*, 209–214.

Zimbardo, P. G. The human's choice: Individuation, reason, and order versus deindividuation, impulse and chaos. Unpublished manuscript, Stanford University, 1969.

Editor's Introduction   17

During the past decade evidence from cross-cultural studies of emotions has provided strong confirmation for Darwin's century-old hypothesis that there is continuity of facial expressions in animals and human beings and that the facial expressions of certain emotions are innate and universal. Scherer's chapter argues that the vocal expressions of certain emotions also show evolutionary continuity and universality. The adaptive advantages of vocal expression over facial expression are obvious in situations where darkness or distance would prevent social communication by way of the facial–visual system.

Studies of vocal expression fall into two broad classes: those concerned with the classification of vocal sounds by means of global judgment and those concerned with the differentiation of vocal expressions on the basis of the physical characteristics of the vocalization. A number of studies have shown that vocal expressions can be reliably classified into emotion categories by global judgment. Fewer studies have been done on the physical or acoustic characteristics of vocalizations, but the work of Scherer and his colleagues provides some good examples.

Scherer focuses on a single acoustic characteristic of vocalization, fundamental frequency, to show how emotional arousal can influence speech production. For example, one simple way in which emotional arousal affects speech production is through its influence on the general tonus of muscles of the voice box.

In his analysis of vocal indicators of nonspecific arousal, Scherer concludes that fundamental frequency is a reliable indicator for most people and that further research may provide other reliable indexes. He also notes that further research on the large individual differences in vocal reaction and arousal may show relationships between characteristics of vocalization and types of coping or defense mechanisms. He also suggests that differences in the vocal indicators of nonspecific arousal may be associated with certain personality traits.

Although global judgements of vocal expressions are rather successful for certain emotions, the research on the acoustic characteristics of specific emotions is still rather scarce. There is rather good agreement, however, on the acoustic differences between anger and sadness, the two most frequently studied emotions in vocal research.

Scherer observes that skillful clinicians make effective use of voice and speech disturbances in assessing and treating human problems. There are not many careful experimental analyses of the acoustic characteristics associated with different psychological disorders, but there are enough positive findings to show the potential fruitfulness of further research in this area. Scherer reviews the work done with manic-depressives and schizophrenics. There are some good leads for identifying acoustic characteristics associated with depression, and Scherer suggests that research on the acoustic characteristics of schizophrenics may become more productive with the careful classification of schizophrenics into homogeneous groups. Finally, Scherer points to the potential efficacy of the joint analysis of vocal, facial, and verbal phenomena in social communication.

Nonlinguistic Vocal Indicators of Emotion and Psychopathology

17

KLAUS R. SCHERER

I. EVOLUTIONARY CONTINUITIES IN THE VOCAL EXPRESSION OF EMOTION

While it is still a matter of hot debate whether a qualitative dichotomy or merely a large quantitative difference in complexity separates animal communication and human language, consensus on the evolutionary continuity of affect displays, particularly with respect to facial expression, seems to be on the increase (cf. Chevalier-Skolnikoff, 1973). Even though the vocal mode of affect expression has received less attention in research there seems to be reason to assume evolutionary continuity for affect vocalizations as well as for visual affect displays. Although parallels in the semantic labeling of human and primate vocalizations do not constitute evidence, it is interesting to note that both apes and men are said to scream in terror, to growl in antagonistic encounters, and to grunt in maintaining contact with each other. At least in comics, people also pant, bark, screech, squeak, roar, and even hoot.

Charles Darwin, whose monumental work *The Expression of the Emotions in Man and Animals* (1872) laid the foundations for current theorizing and research in this field (cf. Izard, 1971; Ekman, 1973), pointed out that many vocalizations have evolved from by-products of the organism's adapative functional responses to environmental stimuli, such as deep inhalation in surprise (to prepare for prolonged exertion) or blowing air out of the mouth or

KLAUS R. SCHERER • University of Giessen, West Germany. Our own research reported herein has been supported by grants from the NIMH (MH 19-569-01) and the Deutsche Forschungsgemeinschaft (DFG Sche 156/1–4).

nostrils in contempt or disgust (to expell noxious matter or smell). Given the important role of the respiratory system in emotional arousal, this explanation might be expected to account for a large variety of vocalizations, such as panting, sighing, and moaning, which are determined both by a particular pattern of expulsion or inhalation of air and by the setting of the supraglottal vocal tract (especially the way in which teeth and lips modify the airflow).

Affect vocalizations, in addition to being residuals of functional behavior patterns or concomitants of physiological adjustments, may also be the result of selective pressures for acoustic signals suited to inter- and intraspecies communication (especially in the case of vocalizations involving phonation). The origin of phonation has been attributed to adaptive physiological responses such as protective closure or narrowing of the glottis (Andrew, 1972). However, as Lieberman (1975) has convincingly argued, the primate larynx is selectively adapted for phonation to serve communicative purposes—at the expense of optimal protection of the lungs or respiratory efficiency.

If affect vocalizations are used for communication, selective pressure will obviously operate on those acoustic characteristics relevant to the effectiveness of the transmission of the signal in the auditory channel. It was again Darwin who pointed out, based on Helmholtz's theory of hearing, that distress calls should by necessity be "loud, prolonged and high, so as to penetrate to a distance" (1965, pp. 90–91). Recent work on vocal communication in animals supports the notion that the acoustic characteristics of certain calls are optimally suited to travel large or small distances, to prevent or to allow fast localization of the sender in space, or to resist masking by noise, depending on amplitude, signal shape, and spectral composition (Marler, 1965, pp. 567–569; Tembrock, 1971, pp. 163–173). Consequently, in discussing affect vocalizations, one has always to consider the possible role of communicative functions in addition to the externalization of emotional states.

While most species communicate via a restricted, closed system of fairly invariant, discrete calls, some of the higher monkeys and apes have a vocal system that allows gradation of signals in various dimensions, such as intensity, spectral composition, rate, and temporal pattern of delivery (Marler, 1965, pp. 563–564). The capacity for independent variation of such dimensions of vocal production, depending on system state or communicative function, may well have developed along with the evolution of a more complex nervous system and a larynx more optimally suited for phonation. It allows the combination of a "closed signal system" consisting of a finite number of vocalization types with an "analogue qualifier system" allowing continuous variations of signal parameters in correspondence to variations of internal states or environmental situations.

The vocalizations of rhesus monkeys, for example, are characterized by an almost infinite variety of potential blends and transitions between the major types of calls with multiple variations of various acoustic elements. Tembrock (1971) concludes that the spectral composition of various types of these rhesus calls depends on the animal's position on a dominance–submission continuum, with lower frequencies more characteristic for the dominant, higher frequencies for the submissive or defeated animal. While systematic comparative investigations of the vocal communication in primate species that utilize modern acoustic analysis techniques are still missing, observational evidence does not rule out the possibility of identifying specific acoustic characteristics for state of arousal, dominance–submission relationships, distance regulation, etc., across different primate species. The ability to vary several dimensions of the signal structure by rapid succession of modulations according to different aspects of the sender state has obvious advantages since it frees behavior from stereotypic reaction patterns and allows more flexible responses to fast-changing environmental situations as well as finer discrimination of message types by the receiver.

The evolution of increasingly complex social structures required communication systems that provide a potential for flexible and finely discriminated responses. Ploog (1974, pp. 41–42) points out that the feature of independent variation of several vocalization characteristics is found only in some Old World monkeys and in anthropoid apes and may well be one of the prerequisites for the development of human language. It certainly seems reasonable to assume that it has played a major role in the development of prosodic features in human speech. The evolution of the human language has provided *Homo sapiens* with an instrument for communication that is enormously more flexible and efficient than any animal communication system. This symbolic signal system has been superimposed on a more primitive earlier system without altogether replacing it. The human neocortex, with its associational areas providing the cognitive capacity for language use, has overgrown phylogenetically older brain structures that seem to mediate emotion and emotional expression in a manner largely homologous to the mechanism found in primates (Chevalier-Skolnikoff, 1973). Magoun (cited in Whitaker, 1976, p. 125) points out that a "deep-lying mesencephalic system for emotional vocalization" is already functional at birth in human infants, whereas the cortical mechanism for speech processing develops only between one and two years after birth. Considering the possible evolutionary continuity of the phylogenetically old neurophysiological mechanisms for affect vocalization and the intricate interrelationships between the neocortex and the subcortical structures, one would expect to find remnants of a primitive discrete call system as well as evidence of a more highly developed version of the analogue qualifier system for emotional vocalizations found in nonhuman primates. The nature of the physiological processes that mediate the effects of emotional arousal on human vocalization will be discussed in the next section.

II. EFFECTS OF EMOTION ON THE PROCESSES OF VOICE PRODUCTION

As there are culturally determined display rules i.e., conventions regarding control of emotional expression for vocalization, just as for facial expression (cf. Ekman, 1973, pp. 176–179), full-blown discrete affect vocalizations reminiscent of primitive call systems tend to occur only in situations of extreme emotional arousal, such as strong surprise or terror, where the intensity of the neuronal firing in the subcortical areas may overpower the controlling and inhibiting influence of the cerebral cortex. However, many of these primitive vocalizations have been ritualized and conventionalized to such an extent that they have almost attained the status of linguistic elements. While affect vocalizations have rarely been studied by either linguists or social psychologists in recent times, such "interjections" in the speech flow fascinated early psychologists interested in the evolution of language. Kleinpaul (1888) assumed that reflexlike affect sounds (e.g., "aah," "ooh") are similiar across cultures and language groups. Wundt (1900) made a distinction between primary interjections ("isolated fragments of a prelinguistic stage"), which interrupt the continuity of speech, and secondary interjections, which are assimilated to linguistic form (e.g., "o," "gee") and tend to replace primary interjections with the progress of civilization in a linguistic community. Some of the communicative properties of these types of affect vocalizations are discused elsewhere (Scherer, 1977a).

A more important system for the vocal expression of emotion in humans is equivalent to the analogue qualifier system and is superimposed on continuous speech vocalizations rather than on discrete calls. Since variations of certain acoustic parameters such as pitch and loudness also function linguistically as semantic or syntactic markers, with much debate among linguists as to the continuity or discreteness of such prosodic features, one cannot hope to do justice to the complexity of this signal system (cf. Lieberman, 1967, 1974; Crystal, 1969) within the confines of this chapter. Here, the emphasis is placed on the way in which the physiological structures involved in speech production may be affected by emotional states and on the effects of such influences on the acoustic characteristics of the resulting vocalizations.

In producing a voiced speech segment, such as a vowel, an air column is set into vibration by air flowing from the lungs through the glottis and by a particular setting of the articulators (pharynx, palate, tongue, teeth, lips), so that the resonance characteristics of the resulting shape of the vocal tract differentially emphasize particular harmonics of the fundamental frequency of the periodic sound wave (corresponding to the formant structure for this particular vowel). Although speech does not consist of isolated vowels, it is best to start, for the sake of simplicity, by discussing the possible effects of emotional arousal on the production and the resulting acoustic characteristics of a sustained vowel.

The respiratory, phonatory, and articulatory processes involved in the production of a vowel are largely dependent on muscular activity in the respiratory organs, the intrinsic and extrinsic laryngeal muscles, and a large number of articulators. While our knowledge about the details of muscle innervation in speech production is still limited (cf. Harris, 1974; Sawashima, 1974; MacNeilage & Ladefoged, 1976), we can be reasonably certain about the action of certain muscle groups in regulating the fundamental frequency and the intensity of the glottal wave and in producing the articulatory setting required for particular phonemic segments.

Unfortunately, most of the electromyographic research in acoustic–phonetic studies has been concerned with the physiological substratum in linguistically relevant changes in intensity or fundamental frequency, such as stress patterns or terminal contours (cf. Lieberman, 1967, 1974; MacNeilage & Ladgefoged, 1976). Except for a few very speculative discussions by clinically oriented researchers (Moses, 1954; Trojan, 1975), there are no published reports on the effect of emotional arousal on the physiology of speech production. Fundamental frequency (F_ϕ hereafter) will be used as an example to demonstrate how one could try to piece together evidence from different areas of research in attempting to predict the possible effects of emotional arousal on speech production.

The fundamental frequency (F_ϕ) of the human voice is determined by the periodicity of the pulses produced by the opening and closing of the glottis (caused by airflow from the lungs). The frequency and the spectral quality of the glottal pulses are primarily determined by the mass and tension of the vocal folds and the subglottal pressure, which determine the frequency of vibration and the characteristics of the opening and closing phases. There is fair agreement in the recent literature (Zemlin, 1968; Harris, 1974; Sawashima, 1974; MacNeilage & Ladefoged, 1976) that the tension of the vocal folds is mainly regulated by the antagonistic action of two tensor muscles (the cricothyroid and the thyroarytenoid vocalis) and the most important abductor muscle (the cricoarytenoid posterior, which increases the distance between the vocal folds and thus relaxes them). A number of extrinsic laryngeal muscles can also increase the tension of the folds by changing the relative positions of the cricoid and thyroid cartilages.

The effect of sympathetic or ergotropic arousal, characteristic of many emotional states, in increasing the tonus of the striate muscles has been documented repeatedly (Gellhorn, 1967; Malmo, 1975). How does increased general muscle tone affect the phonatory processes regulating fundamental frequency? This problem has not yet been empirically investigated, but there is reason to assume that the effect of general tonus increase is not canceled out by the antagonistic action of tensor and relaxor muscles. Even if there were an equal amount of tonus change in both, structural differences may result in stronger action of the tensor muscles. Sawashima (1974) reports that the mass of the abductor muscles is four times that of the abductor muscles. Also, the extrinsic laryngeal tensor muscles may add to the effect of the intrinsic laryngeal muscles in increasing fold tension, and there may be differences in the phasic or tonic muscle fiber structures of tensor and relaxor muscles. One may hypothesize, then, that an increase in general muscle tone will tend to increase F_ϕ unless a given level of F_ϕ is maintained via proprioceptive feedback or with the aid of the auditory monitoring system. However, research in the area of the laryngeal processes in phonation has not progressed beyond a preliminary stage, and further evidence is urgently needed if the effects of emotional arousal on speech production are to be understood in physiological terms.

Emotional arousal may affect not only the general tonus of the muscles involved in speech production but also the intricate coordination of the many agonistic and antagonistic muscle groups and the rhythms of reciprocal inhibition and excitation. For example, Wyke (1967) postulates a complex reflex servomechanism, organized at the level of the brain stem, that regulates the complex coordinated patterns of contraction and relaxation of the laryngeal musculature to maintain a level of F_ϕ voluntarily preset by the speaker. This complex servomechanism further interacts with the voluntary adjustments that the speaker may make in response to the acoustic monitoring of his own vocal performance.

This complex coordination of muscle group action must be regulated by a hierarchically organized set of rhythms to allow smoothly integrated sequences of excitation and inhibition. Apparently, the modulation of finely tuned coordinated movements is physiologically mediated by the cerebellum, which, like a sculptor who selectively "chisels away stone from an initial amorphous block," seems to operate by selectively inhibiting the superfluous innervation potentials provided by the relatively rough tonic state of readiness of the entire neuromuscular apparatus (Eccles, Ito, & Szentagothai, cited after Pribram, 1971, pp. 225–237).

Since the cerebellum is strongly interconnected with the "emotional brain" in the limbic system, there is little doubt that affective arousal will affect this structure. Some theories of emotion (e.g., Arnold, 1960) explicitly include the cerebellum in their description of the physiological substratum of emotion. While we can readily observe how motor coordination is affected by states of strong arousal (e.g., the trembling of hands or limbs and/or rigor), the exact nature of the neuromuscular processes is not at all well known. Possibly the tonic innervation produced by strong sympathetic arousal cannot be completely controlled by the inhibitory potential of the cerebellum, or the functions of this structure are affected by input from the limbic system or other brain structures.

Disturbances in the smoothness of the coordination of the muscles involved in phonation could lead to changes in F_ϕ (due to a dominance of either tensor or relaxor muscles), to irregularities in the lengths of the period of the glottal pulses (jitter, possibly due to lack of smooth coordination of agonistic and antagonistic muscle action), to increases or decreases of intensity or loudness as well as intensity modulations (due to inefficient laryngeal control of the air flow through the glottis), and/or to changes in subglottal air pressure due to irregularities in the action of the respiratory muscles.

Increased muscle tone and disturbance of coordination may not only affect respiration and phonation but articulation as well. Excessive muscle tension in the buccopharyngeal and labioglossal musculature may produce general tenseness or constriction in the articulatory structures. Laver (1975, pp. 251) provides an excellent survey of the literature on effects of overall muscular tension throughout the vocal system. While there seems to be some agrreement that "tense voices" sound metallic, strident, or sharp and that "lax voices" sound mellow or muffled, opinions as to the importance of various physiological parameters in producing tense or lax voices diverge. Acoustically, tense voices seem to have relatively higher energy in the upper harmonics than lax voices, although there are strong sex differences concerning the range of these harmonics, maybe due to higher F_ϕ for females. Laver (1975, p. 254) suggests that tense voices might generally have an energy concentration in the area between 500 and 1000 Hz. In addition, tense voices are likely to have a higher pitch range and a greater loudness range than lax voices, although tense voices may often appear louder and higher pitched than they really are due to the spectral distribution of energy (Laver, 1975, pp. 258–259).

Up to now, only a relatively simple, static case—namely, the production of a sustained vowel—has been considered. Such vowels have sometimes been used to obtain voice samples in the research to be summarized below. The complexity of the physiological processes involved in the utterance of a continuous segment of articulated speech, such as a sentence, is staggering. As adjoining phonemes are not isolated units but show continuous transitions (particularly in vowel–consonant transitions), the neuromuscular control of articulatory movements must be very finely tuned to ensure the smoothness of the dynamic adjustment from one articulatory setting to another (cf. MacNeilage & Ladefoged, 1976). In addition, the laryngeal musculature is involved in the continuous adjustment of linguistically relevant changes of F_ϕ and intensity for prosodic phenomena (linguistic stress or accentuation, intonation), which must be intermeshed with the control of the articulatory movements.

The physiological details of the effects of emotional states on the complex regulatory mechanisms are almost completely unknown. It is to be expected that disruption of neuromuscular coordination will affect pitch and loudness variability, stress patterns and intonation contours, speech rate (in terms of

Table 1. Survey of Studies on Vocal Indicators of Nonspecific Arousal

Number	Study	Subjects	Induction	Voice sample	Instrument	Data analysis
1.	Bonner (1943)	(a) 24 female, 28 male students (b) 3 students (c) 10 students	(a) Presenting radio speech (b) Simulating fear (c) Stressful stimuli	(a) Standard sentence (b) Standard sentence (c) "Ah"	Oscillograph Amplitude level recorder	Percentages
2.	Ostwald (1963, pp. 96–102)	9 male, 11 female subjects (hospital staff)	Vile smell	Standard sentence	Filter bank analyzer	Signed rank test
3.	Friedhoff, Alpert, & Kurtzberg (1964a)	(a) 10 students (b) 10 students (c) 7 students	Lying about occurrence of a given number in a series	"No" answers	Filter bank analyzer	(a) t tests (b) t tests (c) Mann–Whitney U
4.	Friedhoff, Alpert, & Kurtzberg (1964b)	Case studies	Various types of aversive stimulation	Numbers	Filter bank analyzer	Descriptive
5.	Rubenstein (1965)	(a) 15 student nurses (b) 9 student nurses	(a) Sensory isolation (b) Electric shock	Yes–no answers	Frequency meter Filter bank analyzer	ANOVA Chi-square

Study	Subjects	Situation	Material	Analysis	Statistics
6. Olechowski (1967)	20 male, 20 female Austrian high school students	Interrogation on cheating	Selected answers in interrogation	Ratings by 3 groups of judges	Unspecified Significance tests
7. Hecker et al. (1968)	10 adult subjects	Reading off meters under time pressure	Standard sentences Meter readings	Spectrograph Amplitude level recorder	Qualitative
8. Williams & Stevens (1969)	Aircraft pilots	Serious flight difficulties	Radio transmissions	Spectrograph	Qualitative
9. Ciofu (1974)	16 Rumanian students	Lying	Standard sentences	Filter bank analyzer	t tests
10. Streeter et al. (1977)	32 male students	Lying to a fellow student	Interview responses	Digital computer analysis	ANOVA
11. Scherer (1977b)	31 student nurses	Lying about reaction to stress movie to an interviewer	Interview responses	Digital computer analysis	ANOVA, t tests Pearson rs

length of phonemes as well as number and length of pauses), the onset and decay of phonations, the precision of articulation, rhythms of speech, and many other speech parameters. Since speech production is centrally regulated by cortical areas, one has to take the effects of emotional arousal on cortical functioning into account. It has been shown that quite a number of speech disruptions and speech disturbances may be mediated by cognitive processes (cf. Goldmann-Eisler, 1968).

Because of space limitations, the following review is limited to studies investigating the effects of affective arousal on vocal parameters related to phonation and resonance. Thus, the vocal indicators to be reviewed are restricted to the energy and frequency dimensions of the voice (F_ϕ and intensity as well as their variation) and energy distribution in the voice spectrum (timbre or voice quality). Temporal or continuity aspects of speech, such as pauses or speech disruptions (cf. Mahl & Schulze, 1964; Rochester, 1973), are not included except, in some instances, for speech rate. Results on articulatory parameters are also reported for some studies.

III. VOCAL INDICATORS OF NONSPECIFIC AROUSAL

In this section a number of studies which have investigated the effect of unspecific arousal or "stress" on voice will be reviewed.[1] It seems reasonable to assume that in all of these cases the researchers attempted to produce sympathetic (or ergotropic) arousal by exposing subjects to noxious or aversive stimulation and/or to induce them to deceive someone about the occurence of an event or about their feelings. A systematic overview of some important procedural details in those studies the reports of which could be obtained for the preparation of this chapter is given in Table 1. The numbers in Column 1 are used to identify the respective study in the text.

Stress induction is accomplished in three major forms: by exposing subjects to aversive stimulation (Table 1:1c, 2, 3, 5), by asking subjects to cope with a difficult task (Table 1:1a, 7, 8); or by requesting subjects to lie to the experimenter (or an accomplice) about the occurrence of some event, the truth of some statement, or their feelings (Table 1:3, 6, 9, 10, 11). In almost all of these studies, the intensity of the stress induced must be considered rather slight. In the deception studies particularly, lying was mostly demanded and thus sanctioned by the experimenter; there were rarely any consequences, nor was the situation in which the deception took place and the material about which the subjects had to lie of much significance for them. Independent

---

[1] No mention will be made of the commercially marketed Psychological Stress Evaluator (PSE), since the author has not yet seen any serious, scientifically valid research reports using this gadget. Judging from reviews (Jones, 1974; Holden, 1975), there may be both scientific and ethical reservations about the use of the device.

checks on the degree of arousal created by the experimental situation are lacking in most studies. Study 11 in Table 1 is a special case since several strong stressors and independent checks were used. The present author analyzed records collected in two experiments by Ekman and Friesen (1974a; Ekman, Friesen, & Scherer, 1976) in the following manner. Student nurses saw a pleasant nature film and had to give truthful reports about it and their feelings toward it to an interviewer (baseline situation), while in the stress situation, they saw an extremely unpleasant medical film and had to deceive the interviewer about their feelings. The situation was made highly ego-involving by pointing out to the subjects that their career would require a well-developed ability to hide their feelings from patients. Paper-and-pencil checks of arousal showed that the manipulation had reliably produced stress for the subjects; in other experiments, similar films had been found to produce reliable changes in psychophysiological arousal (Ekman, 1973, pp. 216–218). Even though the study does not allow us to separate arousal due to aversive stimulation (the medical film) and arousal due to deception induction (which is equally true for many natural situations in which negative affect has to be concealed), it clearly produced a fairly elevated level of arousal in a meaningful and involving situation.

Table 2 shows the patterns of results in those studies reporting quantitative data on changes in F_ϕ from baseline to a state of arousal. For most subjects, F_ϕ does seem to increase under stress, vindicating earlier views on the matter, for example, "If your voice rises in pitch you thereby loudly proclaim your emotional tension" (Morgan, cited after Bonner, 1943, p. 269). However, about a third of the subjects studied did not change or actually decreased F_ϕ under stress. Strong individual differences in vocal reaction have been found in virtually every study in this area, a fact that will be taken up again later.

The extent of pitch increase under stress is difficult to gauge since the presumed levels of arousal are not at all comparable across studies. Speculating on the probable degree of arousal from the descriptions of the induction, one might almost be tempted to assume a linear relationship between extent of F_ϕ change and arousal potential of the experimental situations listed in Table

Table 2. Mean F_ϕ Increase and Percentage of Reversals in 5 Studies

Number	Study	N	Mean F_ϕ Increase in Hz	p	% of Reversals
1.	Bonner (1943)	(a) 52	(a) 2.1	—	(a) 30.8
		(c) 10	(c) ?	—	(c) 20.0
5.	Rubenstein (1966)	(b) 9	(b) 3.0	—	(b) ?
8.	Hecker et al. (1968)	5	0.2	—	60.0
10.	Streeter et al. (1977)	32	3.3	<.05	31.3
11.	Scherer (1977b)	31	9.0	<.01	25.8

2. Details of the results in Study 10 in Table 2 support this speculation: the investigators ran two groups of subjects, one with an additional arousal condition (increased ego involvement) and one without, finding a mean increase of 0.6 Hz in the less-aroused and 6.0 Hz in the more-aroused condition. It is not surprising that the F_ϕ increase is highest in Study 11 in Table 2, since it seems reasonable to assume that the medical films plus the deception induction resulted in the highest degree of arousal.

In studies 1 and 11 in Table 2 that analyzed F_ϕ variability, no systematic effect of stress on these parameters was found. Also, in the studies measuring total intensity of the speech signal (Table 1:2, 3, 5, 7, 9) no unequivocal, systematic effects of stress were found. Studies 2, 3, and 4 in Table 1 are frequently cited in the literature as showing that emotional arousal manifests itself by changes in the energy distribution in the lower frequencies of the voice. These assumptions seem to be based on findings presumably showing (there are some questions on the choice of significance tests and on the significance levels) that changes in the energy in a low-frequency band (100–250 Hz in Studies 3 and 4; 150–212 Hz in Study 2) from an individual baseline are valid indicators of stress for an individual (energy in this band increasing or decreasing depending on the individual in Studies 3 and 4, generally increasing in Study 2).

These investigators do not consider the possibility that their results may be artifacts of F_ϕ changes (even though Friedhoff and his co-workers take F_ϕ range into account in Study 3). Since both male and female subjects were used in these studies, it is possible that F_ϕ increases for male subjects with habitual pitch lower than the *low* cutoff point of the frequency band will add the energy at F_ϕ to this band, yielding an increase in energy, while F_ϕ increases for female subjects may take their F_ϕ beyond the *high* cutoff point, thereby reducing the energy in the band. Since the data are not differentially analyzed for male and female subjects, the significance of such artifacts cannot be assessed. Ostwald (Study 2) also finds significant energy increases in the 425–600 Hz band. This seems consistent with the acoustic characteristics postulated for tense female voices but not for male voices (cf. p. 501 above; Laver, 1975). Again, the lack of separate analyses for male and female subjects renders an interpretation of these results virtually impossible. Recently, Simonov and Frolov (1973) have suggested somewhat more complex parameters for the energy distribution in the frequency spectrum of the voice, using illustrative case studies.

The following additional effects of stress may occur for some speakers: lengthened and irregular glottal periods at the end of a breath group, change in the amounts of high-frequency energy in the glottal pulses, and other irregularities possibly due to inadequate control of the laryngeal musculature. For some subjects, there was also a decrease in precision of articulation (Study 7). Since these are mostly qualitative interpretations from spectrograms, further study of these parameters using more objective digital analysis procedures and quantitative data analysis is clearly needed.

Two major conclusions can be drawn from these results: (1) F_ϕ is at present the only vocal parameter that can be regarded as a reliable vocal indicator of nonspecific arousal for a majority of subjects, although there are also other potentially important parameters that deserve further investigation; and (2) individual differences in vocal reaction are of such magnitude and importance that the study of the causes for such differences should be one of the major issues in further research.

Before starting to speculate on possible psychological explanations for individual differences in vocal indicators of stress, one has to consider the possibility of methodological artifacts. For example, while there might be a decrease of F_ϕ under stress for some subjects, the size of this difference might still be negligible and fall well within the normal sampling variation of F_ϕ. In none of the studies has the significance of decreases in F_ϕ been established. It is quite possible that less affect had been aroused in those subjects whose F_ϕ decreased: a reanalysis of Bonner's (Study 1) data shows that only 19% of the subjects indicating (on a questionnaire) high or at least some arousal showed F_ϕ decrease, compared to 38% of those indicating little or no arousal (Fisher's exact probability .11; $N = 52$). Given the rather mild stress induction procedures in most studies, one can hardly expect that the situational pressures were strong enough to ensure high uniformity of reaction or response in the subjects.

Apart from such methodological problems, however, individual differences in reactivity might well be an important factor in studies of vocal indicators of arousal, just as there seem to be strong individual differences in autonomic reactivity in physiological stress experiments (cf. Lacey, 1967; Oken, 1967; Lang, Rice & Sternbach, 1972). Such differences in vocal reaction may be caused by three types of differences in coping or defense mechanisms that may all be operative to different degrees for certain individuals in particular situations: arousal differences, vocalization differences, and self-presentation differences.

Differences in arousal mechanisms may be due to differential mediation of external sensory input (cf. repressors versus sensitizers; Eriksen & Pierce, 1968) or differential involvement of different excitation or inhibition systems, for example, ergotrophic or trophotropic reaction (cf. Gellhorn and Kiely, 1972) or dysthymic versus hysteric reaction (Claridge, 1967). Differences in vocalization mechanisms may be based on differential excitation or inhibition of the peripheral neuromuscular systems involved in the regulation and control of various structures responsible for respiration, phonation, or articulation. There may be a differential preference for certain kinds of servomechanisms, given that not all vocal parameters can be optimally regulated under high arousal; for example, preference might be given to the coordination of the intrinsic laryngeal musculature to maintain a certain level of F_ϕ at the expense of the regulation of rhythmic or articulatory features. Self-presentation strategies in terms of expressive vocal behavior imply acoustic monitoring of one's vocalizations and centrally initiated regulation attempts to make one's vocal behavior conform to cultural or situational norms or to adopt a "stance" that is deemed advantageous in covering up or externalizing stress, depending on the individual's strategic decisions in the interaction.

This is not the place to discuss to what extent these mechanisms may be learned coping activities or to what extent they are consciously and voluntarily employed. Clearly, a much higher level of theoretical sophistication is necessary before detailed hypotheses suitable for empirical analysis can be formulated. One would expect, however, that these coping mechanisms are not independent of personality. We have found some interesting first leads in Study 11 by correlating F_ϕ change scores with California Psychological Inventory (CPI) scores collected in the original experiment. For example, the partial correlation of F_ϕ change (stress minus baseline) with achievement via independence (keeping achievement via conformance constant) is $r = .66$, $p < .01$, $N = 31$). A median split on achievement via independence shows that there is virtually no change at all for low scorers, but a very significant increase of about 20 Hz for high scorers. The overall picture that emerges from the correlations between the CPI scales and F_ϕ change is that subjects whose F_ϕ rises strongly under stress tend to be nonconforming, independent, active, dominant, demanding and flexible (Scherer, 1977b).

Unfortunately these results cannot be cross-validated against other research findings since none of the other studies have assessed personality traits of their subjects. Our results do show, however, that an assessment of personality traits, in spite of the rather unsatisfactory measurement instruments, may be of considerable help in trying to understand patterns of individual differences in vocal indicators of nonspecific arousal. This is particularly relevant for the type of studies conducted in this area so far, since generally strong situational demand characteristics force subjects to suppress, hide, or mask their arousal, which may be accomplished by widely different coping strategies. Therefore, another major advance in the state of the art could be expected if vocal indicators of stress could be studied in situations where there is no demand or need to dissimulate the felt arousal.

IV. VOCAL INDICATORS OF DISCRETE EMOTIONS

The convergence of the results of a number of large-scale studies on the facial expression of emotion (Ekman & Friesen, 1969; Ekman, 1973; Izard, 1971) seems to leave little doubt that most discrete emotions are expressed by a specific set of facial cues produced by differential patterns of innervation of the facial musculature. Since the recognition of facial expressions of emotion seems to be independent of culture, both Ekman and Izard, following Tomkins

(1962), postulate emotion-specific innate neural programs for the innervation of the facial muscles. Various attempts to provide detailed descriptions of the activity of the facial musculature and the resulting facial features for a number of primary or fundamental emotions have been reported and reviewed by Ekman and Friesen (1976).

One might ask whether there are sets or patterns of vocal cues comparable to facial displays that characterize discrete primary emotions and whether it is reasonable to assume that they are elicited by innate neural programs. One could argue that in terms of allowing recognition of a sender's emotion in a content- and context-free judgment situation, vocal cues have, if anything, fared at least as well as facial cues—at least for some emotions (cf. surveys by Kramer, 1963; Davitz, 1964)—since even rather extreme speech distortions, such as playing the tape backwards, whispering, or low-pass filtering the signal with a cutoff frequency around 500 Hz, have not prevented listener–judges to identify emotional portrayals with better than chance accuracy. Even if sequential speech cues are removed by random splicing (Scherer, 1971) in addition to low-pass filtering and distortion of the speech signal (Rogers, Scherer, & Rosenthal, 1971), judges can still identify the differential positions of various emotional expressions in a multidimensional space of emotional meaning (Scherer, Koivumaki, & Rosenthal, 1972). One could argue that the results of these recognition studies imply the existence of emotion-specific patterns of vocal cues. However, until now there has been no attempt to provide a definitive compilation of the vocal cues that characterize the expression of the primary discrete emotions, based on empirical research results.

Does our present knowledge justify the assumption that there are specific patterns of vocal cues for discrete emotions? This section summarizes the relevant studies on vocal indicators of emotion that were available to the author. Since the number of studies using stringent experimental methodology and quantitative measurement is exceedingly small, "empirical" studies in the widest sense are included in this survey. Since many of these studies are either fairly old and/or were conducted by nonpsychologists, mostly speech researchers, the available reports often lack sufficient detail on procedure and data analysis to evaluate the soundness of the interpretation of the results. Table 3 lists the studies that have been reviewed for this section.

As in the area of facial expression the large majority of the studies to be summarized (13 out of 16) use actors or simulating subjects to portray emotional expressions. Simulated portrayals may serve useful functions in studying emotional expression and, given the constraints on legitimately recording full-fledged emotional reactions in real-life settings, may be the only realistic possibility for this research. However, one should keep the manifold sources for artifacts in mind when reviewing the results of such studies. This is particularly salient when emotional expressions are to be simulated by the recitation of

Table 3. Survey of Studies on Vocal Indicators of Discrete Emotions

Number	Study	Encoders	Induction	Voice sample	Instrument	Data analysis
1.	Skinner (1935)	9 male, 10 female drama students	Mood induction	"Ah"	Oscillograph	Significance tests
2.	(a) Fairbanks & Pronovost (1939) (b) Fairbanks & Hoaglin (1941)	6 male actors	Simulation	Standard sentences	Oscillograph	Descriptive
3.	Eldred & Price (1958)	1 female depressive	Interview topics	Interview responses poem	Ratings by 4 M.D.s	Qualitative
4.	Zuberbier (1957)	20 German students	Mood induction		Amplitude level recorder	Chi-square
5.	Sedláček & Sychra (1963)	23 Czech actresses	Mood induction	Standard sentences	Pitch and amplitude level recorder	Qualitative
6.	Davitz (1964, Ch. 5)	3 male, 2 female speakers	Simulation	Standard sentences	Ratings by 5 judges	Qualitative
7.	Davitz (1964, Ch. 8)	3 male, 4 female speakers	Simulation	Standard sentences	Ratings by 20 judges	Pearson *r*

8. Bortz (1966)	5 male German speakers	Simulation	Nonsense word	Filter bank analyzer	ANOVA
9. Huttar (1968)	1 male speaker	Spontaneous	Selected utterances from natural speech	Spectrograph; Ratings by 12 judges	Pearson *r*
10. Costanzo, Markel, & Costanzo (1969)	12 males, 11 female speakers	Simulation	Standard sentences	Ratings by 7 trained judges	Chi-square
11. Scherer, Koivumaki, & Rosenthal (1972)	1 male, 1 female actor	Playacting	Excerpts from play	Ratings by 61 judges	Pearson *r*
12. Williams & Stevens (1972)	3 male actors	Playacting	Standard sentences	Spectrograph, amplitude level recorder	Qualitative
13. Markel, Bein, & Phillis (1973)	50 male students	TAT cards	TAT responses	Ratings by 15 trained judges	Chi-square
14. Scherer, London, & Wolf (1973)	1 male actor	Simulation	Standard text	Digital analysis Amplitude level recorder	ANOVA
15. Green & Cliff (1975)	1 male drama student	Simulation	Letters of alphabet	Ratings by 17 judges	Canonical analysis
16. Levin & Lord (1975)	1 male, 3 female drama students	Simulation	Freely chosen words	Digital analysis	*t* tests

nonsense material such as numbers, letters of the alphabet, nonsense syllables, or isolated words (Table 3:1, 8, 15, 16), where the unusual and meaningless stimulus material could lead to stereotypical exaggerations or other artifacts on the part of the encoders. Similarly, reading habits or stereotypes concerning recitation may have influenced the emotional expression in studies where subjects had to recite parts of poems or similar material (Table 3:4, 5) particularly when "mood induction" via music or poetry is used. The most frequently used technique, originally developed by Fairbanks and his collaborators, is the insertion of a standard sentence into text passages with varying emotional context (Table 3:2, 6, 10). Kramer (1963) found that a typescript of the passage, "There is no other answer. You have asked me that question a thousand times, and my reply has always been the same. It always will be the same," is significantly more often identified as anger than as any other emotion. Thus, emotional reading style rather than natural emotional expression may have been studied.

However, even if professional actors are used to portray emotional scenes in scenarios allowing identification with the affective experiences of the characters in more realistic situations (Table 3:11, 12), there may still be marked differences in naturally occurring spontaneous emotional expressions (cf. Ekman, Friesen, & Ellsworth, 1972, pp. 35–38). In addition, strong individual differences in encoding ability for naive subjects or drama students and effects of different schools of thought on acting style for professional actors might be expected. Frequently, only one or two actors were used in this research, and encoder variability was rarely systematically studied. Also, there may have been large encoding differences with regard to the intensity of emotion or possible subtypes of discrete emotions, for example, "subdued anger" versus "explosive anger."

If the speech samples used in simulation studies are not natural enough, the samples consisting of spontaneous speech are not emotional enough: utterances by one adult speaker from a series of classroom lectures and discussions (Table 3:9), segments from interviews with one female depressive patient clinically judged as indicative of angry or depressive mood (Study 3), and responses to TAT cards classified as indicative of "depression" by content analysis procedures (Study 13). In each of these studies, both the intensity and the specificity of the emotional states of the speakers probably fall far below the levels attained in real life or in simulation studies.

Apart from the differences in elicitation procedures, the studies to be reviewed differ markedly with respect to the techniques that have been used to measure the vocal parameters of the speech samples. In the majority of studies, objective analyses of pitch, intonation, loudness, and tempo (using filmed oscillograms, filter bank analyzers, spectrograms, or digital computer analysis, depending on the state of the technology available) were performed (Studies 1, 2, 4, 5, 8, 9, 12, 14, 16). Others used trained or untrained listener–judges and scales with various degrees of specificity to assess these vocal parameters (Studies 3, 6, 7, 10, 11, 13, 15). A comparison of the results is complicated by the fact that some studies contrast emotionally expressive speech with neutral, baseline situations, whereas others contrast various emotional portrayals. In most studies, independent groups of decoders were used to check the adequacy of the emotion portrayal.

The summary of the major results from these studies is shown in Table 4. Only vocal indicators that were measured in at least two or more studies and for two or more emotions are included in the listing. Some research reports, particularly Fairbanks and Pronovost (Study 2a) and Williams and Stevens (Study 12), contain interesting and suggestive leads for further vocal indicators, which deserve to be followed up in future research. Table 4 also lists only those emotional states that were investigated in more than one study (happiness/joy and grief/sadness/sorrow are each treated as one emotion, independent of the specific label used in a particular study). In addition to the discrete emotions, the basic three dimensions of emotional meaning that one finds repeatedly in theories of emotion as well as in studies on emotional

Table 4. *Summary of Results on Vocal Indicators of Emotional States*

Emotion	Pitch level	Pitch range	Pitch variability	Loudness	Tempo
Happiness/joy	High 1,5,6,9	?	Large 5	Loud 6,9	Fast 6
Confidence	High 9,14	?	?	Loud 9,14	Fast 9,14
Anger	High 2a,3,6,9,12,16	Wide 2a,12	Large 2a	Loud 3,6,8,10,12	Fast 2b,3,6,8,13
Fear	High 2a,12	Wide 2a	Large 2a	?	Fast 2b
Indifference	Low 2a	Narrow 2a	Small 2a	?	Fast 10
Contempt	Low 2a	Wide 2a	?	Loud 10	Slow 2b
Boredom	Low 6,9	Narrow 9	?	Soft 6,8,9	Slow 6,8,9
Grief/sadness	Low 2a,3,5,6,9,12	Narrow 2a,12	Small 2a	Soft 3,6,9	Slow 2b,3,6,12,13
Evaluation	?	?	?	Loud 11	?
Activation	High 7,9,15	Wide 9	?	Loud 4,7,9,11	Fast 4,7,9.11
Potency	?	?	?	Loud 11	?

expression (cf. Davitz, 1964; 1969) are listed. In each cell of the matrix, the characteristic level or value of a particular vocal indicator for the respective emotional state (compared to an imaginary standard for neutral voice) as reflected in the research results is given. Below each of these, the identification numbers of those studies (from Table 3) are listed that found roughly the same effect or a result in the same direction.

Given the enormous differences in design, methodology, and analysis techniques in the studies reviewed here, the degree of convergence of the results on the patterns of vocal parameters characteristic for particular emotions is quite impressive. Even though the problem of individual differences was not investigated systematically in these studies, particularly as often only one actor or very few subjects were used, there seems to be greater uniformity of the characteristics of vocal indicators of simulated emotions as compared to nonspecific arousal. The present evidence does not allow us to decide to what extent this finding is due to the lack of demands for dissimulation of affect or self-presentation, inviting differential coping strategies, or to shared cultural stereotypes about vocal indicators of affect and/or personality (cf. Kramer, 1963; Scherer, 1972). It is also possible that a specific emotional reaction has definite vocal behavior correlates, just as there are definite innervations of the facial musculature, which are reproduced in simulation and which, because of the specificity experienced by actors or subjects, do not allow for much individual variation. Unfortunately, these questions cannot be answered until we have data for many subjects in nonsimulation settings.

We still find many white spots marked by question marks in Table 4, indicating that certain vocal parameters were rarely studied in connection with some emotions or did not yield definitive results. In addition, for some emotions and/or vocal cues results are based on only one or two studies, a problem that is aggravated by the fact that those results that are not supported by many independent studies tend to stem from the early, more qualitative or descriptive reports (e.g., Fairbanks & Pronovost, 1939, for the pitch range and pitch variability results). Therefore, many entries in Table 4 can claim little more status than that of promising leads for further empirical work.

From the present evidence, then, we can be reasonably certain only about the vocal indicators of the two emotions studied most frequently: anger and grief/sadness. Anger seems to be characterized by high pitch level and wide pitch range, loud voice, and fast tempo, whereas the opposite ends of these vocal dimensions characterize grief/sadness: low pitch and narrow pitch range, downward pitch contour, soft voice, and slow tempo. As the results in Table 4 show, these vocal parameters are also closely identified with the opposite poles of the activation dimension, inviting the conjecture that only the activation differences between simulations of highly agitated anger (as compared to the suppressed kind) and quiet grief/sadness (as compared to desperate mourning) have been measured by these parameters.

The pattern of results in Table 4, as well as theoretical considerations based on the relevant literature, support a notion expressed earlier (Davitz, 1964; Scherer, 1971; Scherer et al., 1972), namely, that the major dimensions of emotional experience may be differentially expressed by patterns of vocal cues and that discrete emotions are characterized by their position in this dimensional space. Although it is reassuring that the same three or four dimensions (with somewhat different labels, depending on the auther) tend to reappear again and again in the literature, this is not a substitute for theoretically based predictions (Izard, 1971). In order to obtain a solid foundation for further studies on the vocal indicators of emotional dimensions, one might attempt to link theories of emotion concerned with the organism's evaluation of external stimulation (Arnold, 1960; Tomkins, 1962; Lazarus, 1968) in terms of expectedness of a stimulus, evaluation of its goal relevance, and competence in coping with it, to the physiological theories concerning the nature and interrelationships of the arousal and organizing systems that mediate stimulus processing and response organization (Claridge, 1967; Routtenberg, 1971; Gellhorn & Kiely, 1972; Pribram & McGuinness, 1975). If, in addition, we were able to link the predictions of the latter theories to the neuromuscular processes in speech and voice production, the theoretical status of the field would be less desolate than it appears now. Until such theoretical integrations across several disciplines as well as several subareas of psychology are achieved, there is little choice but to continue working with the conceptual and technical tools available at the present time. It seems quite feasible to design studies to test some specific hypotheses about the relationship between emotional dimensions and vocal parameters that have been proposed, albeit somewhat vaguely and rather speculatively, by some writers in the field. Thus Trojan (1975) makes specific predictions about voice types associated with ergotropic and trophotropic arousal and the articulatory characteristics of speech in pleasure–displeasure situations (constriction of the faucal pillars). It is surprising that there have not yet been any systematic attempts to jointly assess peripheral physiological indicators (particularly EMG) and acoustic parameters of voice and speech.

A different, yet complementary approach to the study of the vocal correlates of emotion uses systematic experimental manipulations of various acoustic parameters to determine the nature of vocal cues and cue combinations that are perceived as indicative of a certain emotion by listener–judges. Using MOOG-synthesized stimuli, we were able to show in two studies that judges agree to a surprising degree in differentially labeling particular combinations of vocal cues as expressing certain emotions (Scherer, 1974; Scherer & Oshinsky, 1977). The results from these studies show a high degree of agreement with the pattern of results in Table 4. This convergence invites the utilization of a research design, based on Brunswik's lens model, utilizing both encoding and decoding strategies and path-analysis–based evaluation procedures, which seem to be most useful in assessing expressive and communicative functions of voice quality in relation to personality (Scherer, in press a).

V. VOCAL INDICATORS OF AFFECTIVE DISTURBANCES IN PSYCHOPATHOLOGY

It is a matter of common knowledge that psychopathological affect disturbances may have strong effects on the patient's voice and speech. Not infrequently these are used as major symptoms in diagnosing the syndrome presumably underlying a person's abnormal behavior or feeling state. Unfortunately, the description of voice and speech disturbances and the weight they receive in the diagnostic process seem to depend on personal skill and experience as well as on the idiosyncratic predilections of the respective clinician. Psychiatrists and clinical psychologists cannot be blamed for using these important behavioral cues of their patients' state somewhat loosely and individualistically, since there is neither an accepted terminology and a concise description for many of these vocal parameters nor a body of systematic research on their relation to clinical states or syndromes. Linguistic (and some paralinguistic) aspects of psychopathological speech disturbances have received attention both in clinical psychology and in psycholinguistics, particularly in relation to underlying cognitive processes. For example, there has been intensive work on the language of schizophrenia (Maher, 1972). Nonlinguistic vocal phenomena, however, are on the whole sadly neglected. While there is a research tradition in terms of the temporal and continuity aspects of speech (Goldmann-Eisler, 1968; Mahl & Schulze, 1964; Dittman, 1972), only a few scattered studies on voice quality can be found.

Even though some early investigators attempted to use electroacoustic equipment in trying to analyze objectively particular phonatory and articulatory parameters of speech in clinical populations (e.g. Scripture, 1925; Isserlin, 1925; Zwirner, 1930), most published work in this area consists of nonempirical, qualitative reports based on general clinical experience or isolated case studies (Brody, 1943; Rousey & Moriarty, 1965; Edelheit, 1969), often with psychodynamic explanations for the vocal phenomena described. One of the most comprehensive and systematic clinical discussions of voice correlates of affective disturbances is Moses's *The Voice of Neurosis* (1954). This book is a valuable source of hypotheses, derived from clinical experience, on the physiological mechanisms in affective disturbances that may be responsible for particular types of voice changes or disorders. Another major contribution to the field is the work of Ostwald (1963), who was one of the first psychiatrists to advocate and consistently use spectrographic methods of voice analysis for diagnostic purposes.

In this section, studies attempting to use "objective methods"—that is, not relying solely on the clinical expertise and experience of the author—and quantitative analyses to determine vocal indicators of psychopathological states will be reviewed. Because of the small number of studies meeting these criteria, some case studies that do not use strictly quantitative procedures are included as well. The coverage of this review is restricted to depressive and schizophrenic patient populations, since only isolated studies are available on other clinical syndromes. A review of voice and speech correlates of nonpathological personality traits can be found in Scherer (in press b). Table 5 shows a summary of the procedures used in these studies according to the clinical group studied. The column "Purpose" in this table indicates whether the authors attempted "comparison" of the vocal parameters between clinical groups or between a group of psychiatric patients and a group of normal speakers, or "description" in terms of implied standards or levels of the vocal parameters considered by the authors "normal" for the respective speech community.

Of the seven studies on vocal indicators of depression only the study by Zuberbier (Table 5:4) meets some of the criteria for quantitative research, the remainder being mostly qualitative. Consequently, most of the results summarized below must be treated as hypotheses rather than established findings. Contrary to stereotypical expectations and some claims in the literature concerning flaccidity of the laryngeal musculature in depressed states (cf. Kainz, 1954, p. 246), none of the studies report abnormally low F_ϕ for the speech of depressives. On the contrary, Zuberbier (Study 4) finds similar mean F_ϕ values for depressives and normals. She interprets this as indicative of comparatively higher tension of the vocal cords in depressives since their level of voice intensity is significantly reduced (she assumes apparently that decreased subglottal pressure must be offset by higher tension of the vocal folds to keep a "normal" level of F_ϕ). Moses's observations (Study 3, p. 124) that decreases in pitch seem to be accompanied by proportionately decreasing intensity may imply that the elevated tonus of the laryngeal musculature requires depressive speakers to make heavier use of subglottal pressure to regulate F_ϕ If this observation should prove correct, one would expect depressives to show higher F_ϕ than normals in speech situations where a standard level of intensity is required by the situation.

There is some indication that pitch range is reduced in depressives (Studies 2, 3, 4, 7) and that they tend to show stepwise rather than gliding pitch changes (Studies 2, 4). Some authors claim that the well-known monotony of depressive speech is due to frequent repetitions of stereotypic downward pitch contours (Studies 1, 2, 3). The empirical results in Study 4, however, show significantly more level or linear contours in depressive speech, which appear particularly incongruent at the end of sentences, where inflection normally drops.

Table 5. *Survey of Studies on Vocal Indicators of Affective Disturbances*

Number Study	Subjects	Purpose	Voice sample	Instrument	Data analysis
1. Zwirner (1930)	1 female depressive patient (German)	Description	Interview responses	F_ϕ analyzer	Qualitative
2. Newman & Mather (1938)	40 patients with depressive symptoms	Description	Interview responses	Rater judgments	
3. Moses (1954)	1 male patient	Description	Interview responses	Expert judgments	Qualitative
4. Zuberbier (1957)	20 female depressive patients 20 matched normals (all German)	Comparison	Reading standard passage, series of "la-la"	Amplitude level recorder	Significance tests
5. Ostwald (1963)	1 female, 7 male patients with depressive symptoms	Description	Interview responses Standard passages	Filter bank analyzer	Qualitative
6. Ostwald (1964)	1 female depressive patient	Description	Interview responses	Filter bank analyzer	Qualitative
7. Hargreaves *et al.* (1965)	23 female, 9 male depressive patients	(a) Predicting mood ratings (b) Description	Interview responses	Filter bank analyzer	(a) Regression analysis (b) Qualitative

Study	Subjects	Type	Task	Method	Significance tests
8. Moskowitz (1952)	40 schizophrenics, 40 normals	Comparison	TAT responses, MMPI responses	Expert judgments	Significance tests
9. Ostwald (1963)	1 female schizophrenic	Description	Interview responses	Filter bank analyzer	Qualitative
10. Ostwald & Skolnikoff (1966)	1 male schizophrenic	Description	Interview responses	Filter bank analyzer	Qualitative
11. Spoerri (1966)	Case studies of 350 schizophrenics (Swiss)	Description	Interview responses	Spectrograph, Clinical judgments	Qualitative
12. Saxman & Burk (1968)	37 schizophrenic females, 22 normal females	Comparison	Standard passage, Impromptu speaking	F_ϕ analyzer	t test, ANOVA
13. Rice et al. (1969)	2 male, 7 female patients, matched normals	Comparison	Standard passage, Storytelling	Oscillograph	t test
14. Chevrie-Muller et al. (1971)	26 female, 27 male adolescent schizophrenics, 22 female, 15 male normals (all French)	Comparison	Standard passage, Storytelling	Oscillograph, Glottograph	Various significance tests
15. Goldfarb et al. (1972)	25 schizophrenic, 25 matched normal children	Comparison	Directed speech, Conversation	Ratings by speech pathologist	Fisher's exact probability test

Zuberbier (Study 4) reports significantly lower intensity, reduced dynamic range, and lack of emphatic accents (also found in Study 2) for depressive speech, a pattern that, on the whole, seems to be supported by clinical observation. One also finds some agreement on the slow and halting quality of depressive speech, apparently due to both a slowing of articulatory processes and an increase in number and length of pauses (Studies 2, 4). Articulation appears lax (Studies 2, 4) which Zuberbier (Study 4) ascribes to lack of ability to differentially tense and relax different parts of the articulatory musculature. Thus, lax articulation in depressives may also correspond to an abnormally high level of muscle tension rather than general flaccidity, as is often assumed.

Statements on voice quality or timbre are difficult to evaluate since authors use rather different descriptive labels. Thus, the voices of depressives have been described as nasal and throaty (Study 2), flat and hollow (Studies 5, 6), and dull (Study 7). It is one of the most pressing tasks in this field to identify possible acoustic concomitants of these impressionistic labels.

Studies 8–15 in Table 5 summarize studies on schizophrenic patients. Because of the greater variability of symptoms in various subcategories of schizophrenia, the results of these studies are even more difficult to review, particularly since in two studies children (Study 15) or adolescents (Study 14) were used as subjects. In addition, contrary to the research on depressive speech, quite a few contradictions appear in results and observations; thus both reduced (Study 14) and increased (Study 12) F_ϕ variability have been found. The general impression generated by these studies is that there are very pronounced individual differences in the vocal parameters shown by schizophrenic patients. Most agreement can be found on the "inadequacy" of the paralinguistic features of schizophrenic speech, in relation to either verbal content or situational constraints (Studies 3, 11, 15). Obviously the present state of the evidence does not allow us to attempt even a preliminary survey of vocal indicators of schizophrenia.

Considering the large variability of vocal behavior in schizophrenics, it is not surprising that naive judges as well as clinicians seem unable to identify psychotic states (Sharp, 1963) or severity of disturbances (Cohen, 1961) on the basis of vocal cues alone. Clearly, attempts to determine vocal correlates of particular types of affective disturbances empirically are beset by an unusually large number of methodological problems in addition to many of those already mentioned above for vocal analyses. The most damaging impediment to progress in this research area, as for many other clinical research problems, is the lack of a valid and reliable taxonomic system of nosological entities with definitive and well-operationalized criteria for the diagnosis and classification of affect or "mood" disorders. Current debates on "types" of schizophrenia and depression show that the present psychopathological categories contain cases with widely different etiology and physiological, psychological, and behavioral symptomatology. It is not surprising, then, that one cannot expect clear-cut patterns of vocal indicators for heterogeneous groups of patients lumped together by fiat on the basis of traditionally valued, but possibly meaningless, labels. Chevrie-Muller, Dodart, Seguier-Dermer, and Salmon (Study 14) have argued on the basis of their inconclusive results for male schizophrenics that certain symptoms or groups of symptoms rather than clinical syndromes ought to provide the basis for the study of acoustic correlates. However, even if one could agree on reliably identifiable clusters of symptoms, there are still the ever-present problems of phases in mood and drug effects (even on admission) and of matching or providing for adequate control groups.

Hargreaves and Starkweather (1964, 1965) have attempted to use depressive patients as their own control by regressing mood states (as assessed by psychiatric ratings) on spectral characteristics of patients' voices in these states. Although they claim good success in predicting mood states from voice spectra, it is hard to evaluate the significance of these results since the authors do not reveal the number of predictors compared to units in the analysis and since no information on the weights of the predictors or their significance is given. In the earlier study (1964), the authors interpret spectral changes in the voice for *one* patient recovering from severe depression as showing an increase in overall intensity of the voice and greater relative amplitude in the upper frequencies, particularly between 200 and 1000 Hz (judging from their Figure 1, p. 87).

Surprisingly, there are almost no systematic studies on the vocal changes due to therapy or treatment effects, even though one would expect vocal parameters to be likely candidates for easily, unobtrusively, and continuously obtainable monitoring variables for patient improvement. Ostwald (1963, pp. 103–113) reports a study on spectral changes in the voices of 17 female and 13 male psychiatric patients following psychiatric treatment. Both diagnoses and treatments varied over patients. He found that total energy and the energy in the half-octave band from 425 to 600 Hz increased significantly for 9 patients (7 males, 2 females) who received electroconvulsant treatment, but not for patients receiving other forms of treatment. However, Darby and Hollien (1977) did not find any significant changes in F_ϕ, long-term speech spectra, vocal intensity, speaking-time ratio, and speech rate following electroconvulsant therapy for two male and four female depressive patients. This failure to replicate is not surprising if one considers that one of Ostwald's two female patients (1963, Table 5, p. 108) also showed a reversal. Allowing for possible sex differences, the two male patients in the Darby *et al.* study do not constitute a large enough sample to replicate Ostwald's findings.

Using the computer-based voice analysis system developed in our laboratory, we obtained data on F_ϕ and F_ϕ variability as well as amplitude levels in third-octave bands for 9 depressive and 11 schizophrenic female patients between 20 and 59 years of age (with fairly heterogeneous etiological and symptomatological subclassifications) who had been subjected to a standard interview shortly after admission and shortly before discharge from a psychiatric clinic. These records were made available to us by Ekman and Friesen, who had filmed and audiotaped these interviews earlier (cf. Ekman & Friesen, 1974b, pp. 215–217). These patients were hospitalized for an average of approximately two months; different types of therapy were used both on the same and on different patients. All interview responses of the patients in the first four minutes of the interview were digitalized, the silent pauses eliminated and F_ϕ extracted (using autocorrelation methods). In addition, long-term spectra were obtained using hardware FFT processing.[2]

The results show a mean decrease of 9.5 Hz ($t = 2.75$, $df = 8$, $p = .025$, two-tailed) for the fundamental frequency of the voices of the depressive patients. A 5.4-Hz decrease in F_ϕ for the schizophrenic patients is not significant ($t = .89$, $df = 10$), nor are the changes in F_ϕ variability for either group or differences between groups on any of these parameters. The results for the depressive patients support Zuberbier's (Study 4) claim of abnormally (compared to the patients' habitual level) high tension of the laryngeal musculature, which could lead to abnormally high F_ϕ at normal intensity levels.

The long-term power spectra were analyzed in terms of the mean energy level in third-octave bands between 200 and 9040 Hz, controlling for changes in the overall loudness of speech by dividing all values for individual bands by the total energy in this frequency region. The purpose of this analysis was to obtain a measure of the *relative* distribution of energy in the frequency range. As shown above (cf. p. 501), one would expect a relatively greater proportion of the total energy in the range below 500 Hz for lax voices and between 500 and 1000 Hz for tense voices. Apart from the effect of differential vocal tract resonances as in the tense–lax voice distinction, the relative amount of energy in the higher harmonics of F_ϕ, which depends on the frequency spectra of the glottal pulses, also determines the energy distribution observable in the long-term spectrum of the speech signal. One might expect that excessive tension or lack of coordination in the laryngeal musculature can lead to deviations from the normal pattern of opening and closing of the vocal folds. Thus the folds may not close completely, or the relation between the opening or closing phase may change (Zemlin, 1968), in which case less energy concentration at the frequencies of the higher harmonics seems to result. Consequently, the relationship between the energy concentrations in different frequency regions of the spectrum may be of diagnostic significance.

Disregarding the first third-octave band (200–260 Hz), which still contains F_ϕ energy for most patients, we computed the proportion between the second and third bands (260–440 Hz) and the remaining bands (440–9040 Hz), following Laver's (1975) suggestion of 500 Hz as a possible cutoff point. We found that 6 out of 9 depressive patients showed an *increase* of energy in the low

[2] Much of the software for these analyses has been developed by Reiner Standke and Hede Helfrich with the collaboration of Harald Wallbott. A joint publication of this study is in preparation.

region relative to the high region (mean change for 9 patients: + 10.2%, t = 1.66, df = 8, p = .13, two-tailed), whereas 7 out of 11 schizophrenic patients showed a relative *decrease* of energy in the low band (mean change of −7.5%, t = 1.30, df = 10, p = .22, two-tailed). The difference between the two diagnostic groups is significant with t = 2.06, df = 18, p = .027 (one-tailed).

While the results for the schizophrenics are difficult to interpret because of the weakness of the relationship and the heterogeneity of the patient group, the strong changes for two-thirds of the depressives do suggest that in these cases, stabilization of affect following therapy resulted in marked changes of voice quality. The auditory impression obtained from listening to the speaking voice before and after therapy supports this notion. However, most voices for which an increase in energy in the lower frequency region has been found do not sound more muffled, as one would expect if the vocal tract settings had changed from tense to lax. Rather, these voices often sound more "full" or resonant, which suggests that a more flexible control of the laryngeal musculature (possibly due to a decrease of overall muscle tone) may have led to vocal fold activity resulting in strong harmonic partials. Since the first harmonic partial above F_ϕ would be expected in the range between 360 and 440 Hz, our results seem to support this interpretation.

These considerations, and the results on which they are based (decrease in F_ϕ, increase of energy in the region of the first harmonic), even though preliminary, suggest that the depressive patients investigated in this study may have been characterized by an abnormally high level of muscular tension at admission and that a normalization took place during therapy. The assumption of a generally increased level of muscle tonus in depressed patients is in accord with physiological studies showing increased EMG potentials for psychoneurotic, particularly depressive, patients in reaction to stress (Malmo, Shagass, & Davis, 1951; Goldstein, 1965) and theoretical assumptions about ergotropic system dominance in cases with strong components of anxiety and states of tension (Gellhorn & Kiely, 1972, p. 249; Malmo, 1975).

VI. EPILOGUE

Even though the present knowledge about vocal indicators of psychopathology consists mostly of hunches derived from clinical observation, and even though both the quantity and the quality of research leave much to be desired, there can be little doubt that this area should no longer be neglected. Vocal behavior is a powerful index of emotional state—both normal and pathological—and it is constantly used in diagnostic decisions by practitioners in a very impressionistic and possibly unreliable manner. Further research is urgently needed to assess both the predictive validity of vocal indicators of emotional states and the clinician's ability to put it to good use in diagnosing affective disturbances and outcomes of therapy.

Contrary to earlier statements about the primary diagnostic significance of changes of intensity, particularly in the lower frequencies of the voice (Ostwald, 1963; Friedhoff, Alpert, & Kurtzberg, 1964), this review has established a clear lead for fundamental frequency (F_ϕ) or voice pitch as a fairly reliable vocal indicator of emotional states—for nonspecific arousal, for the activation dimension of discrete emotions, and for anxiety or tension states in psychopathological disturbance, particularly in cases of depression. It is quite probable that the phonation processes and resonance characteristics of the vocal tract also produce important acoustic indicators in the form of particular voice qualities that may be assessed objectively by sophisticated analyses in the time and frequency domains. However, the present work in our laboratory suggests that the relevant voice quality parameters are likely to be much more complex than straightforward intensity levels in half-octave bands. Unfortunately, the search for relevant parameters cannot benefit much from the highly sophisticated acoustic–phonetic work on automatic speech decoding, since the very variability of interest to psychologists is by necessity treated as error variance in speech-understanding systems.

One of the most important tasks of future research is to try to disentangle the respiratory, phonatory, and articulatory contributions to the speech signal. In addition, the complex interdependence between phonemic, prosodic, and nonlinguistic vocal phenomena requires careful analyses, which can be fruitfully carried out only by interdisciplinary teams of linguists, phoneticians, and psychologists. The intricate relationship between expression as a physiologically mediated externalization mechanism and expression as strategically used, communicative behavior in social interaction demands the incorporation of social-psychological and microsociological approaches into a comprehensive investigation of vocal indicators of affect. Finally, although nonlinguistic nonvocal behavior had to be excluded from this review, there can be no question that only the joint analysis of vocal and nonvocal, verbal and nonverbal phenomena in human communication can ultimately further our understanding of the complex phenomenon of the expression of human affect.

ACKNOWLEDGMENTS

The author gratefully acknowledges helpful comments and suggestions by Howard Giles, Hede Helfrich, Paul Ekman, and Ursula Scherer. Of course, none of them is to blame for any errors remaining.

REFERENCES

Andrew, R. J. The information potentially available in mammal displays. In R. A. Hinde (Ed.), *Non-verbal communication*. London: Cambridge University Press, 1972.

Arnold, M. B. (Ed.). *Emotion and personality* (2 vols.). New York: Columbia University Press, 1960.

Bonner, R. Changes in the speech pattern under emotional tension. *American Journal of Psychology*, 1943, *56*, 262–273.

Bortz, J. Physikalisch-akustische Korrelate der vokalen Kommunikation. *Arbeiten des Psychologischen Instituts der Universität Hamburg*. Nr. 9, 1966.

Brody, M. W. Neurotic manifestations of the voice. *Psychoanalytic Quarterly*, 1943, *12*, 371–380.

Chevalier-Skolnikoff, S. Facial expression of emotion in nonhuman primates. In P. Ekman (Ed.), *Darwin and facial expression: A century of research in review*. New York: Academic Press, 1973, pp. 11–89.

Chevrie-Muller, C., Dodart, F., Seguier-Dermer, N., & Salmon, D. Étude des paramètres acoustiques de la parole au cours de la schizophrénie de l'adolescent. *Folia Phoniatrica*, 1971, *23*, 401–428.

Ciofu, I. Audiospectral analysis in lie detection. *Archiv für Psychologie*, 1974, *126*, 170–180.

Claridge, G. S. *Personality and arousal: A psychophysiological study of psychiatric disorder*. Oxford: Pergamon Press, 1967.

Cohen, A. Estimating the degree of schizophrenic pathology from recorded interview samples. *Journal of Clinical Psychology*, 1961, *17*, 403–408.

Costanzo, F. S., Markel, N. N., & Costanzo, P. R. Voice quality profile and perceived emotion. *Journal of Counseling Psychology*, 1969, *16*, 267–270.

Crystal, D. *Prosodic systems and intonation in English*. Cambridge: Cambridge University Press, 1969.

Darby, J. K., Hollien, H. Vocal and speech patterns of depressive patients. *Folia Phoniatrica*, 1977, *29*, 279–291.

Darwin, C. *The expression of the emotions in man and animals*. Chicago: University of Chicago Press, 1965. (Originally published 1872.)

Davitz, J. R. *The communication of emotional meaning*. New York: McGraw-Hill, 1964.

Davitz, J. R. *The language of emotion*. New York: Academic Press, 1969.

DeVore, I. *Primate behavior: Field studies of monkeys and apes*. New York: Holt, Rinehart and Winston, 1965.

Dittmann, A. T. *Interpersonal messages of emotion*. New York: Springer, 1972.

Edelheit, H. Speech and psychic structure. The vocal–auditory organization of the ego. *Journal of the American Psychoanalytic Association*, 1969, *17*, 381–412.

Ekman, P. (Ed.). *Darwin and facial expression: A century of research in review*. New York: Academic Press, 1973.

Ekman, P., Ellsworth, P., & Friesen, W. V. *Emotion in the human face: Guidelines for research and an integration of findings*. New York: Pergamon Press, 1971.

Ekman, P., & Friesen, W. V. Detecting deception from the body or face. *Journal of Personality and Social Psychology*, 1974, *29*, 288–298. (a)

Ekman, P., & Friesen, W. V. Nonverbal behavior and psychopathology. In R. J. Friedman and M. M. Katz (Eds.), *The psychology of depression: Contemporary theory and research*. Washington, D.C.: Winston and Sons, 1974. (b)

Ekman, P., & Friesen, W. V. Measuring facial movement. *Environmental Psychology and Nonverbal Behavior*, 1976, *1*, 56–75.

Ekman, P., Friesen, W. V., & Scherer, K. R. Body movement and voice pitch in deceptive interaction. *Semiotica*, 1976, *16*, 23–27.

Ekman, P., Sorenson, E. R., & Friesen, W. V. Pan-cultural elements in facial displays of emotion. *Science*, 1969, *164*, 86–88.

Eldred, S. H., & Price, D. B. The linguistic evaluation of feeling states in psychotherapy. *Psychiatry*, 1958, *21*, 115–121.

Eriksen, C. W., & Pierce, J. Defense mechanisms. In E. F. Borgatta and W. W. Lambert (Eds.), *Handbook of personality theory and research*. Chicago: Rand McNally, 1968.

Fairbanks, G., & Hoaglin, L. W. An experimental study of the durational characteristics of the voice during the expression of emotion. *Speech Monographs*, 1941, *8*, 85–90.

Fairbanks, G., & Pronovost, W. An experimental study of the pitch characteristics of the voice during the expression of emotion. *Speech Monographs*, 1939, *6*, 87–104.

Friedhoff, A. J., Alpert, M., & Kurtzberg, R. L. Infracontent channels of vocal communication. *Association for Research of Nervous and Mental Disease*, 1964, *42*, 414–423. (a)

Friedhoff, A. J., Alpert, M., & Kurtzberg, R. L. An electro-acoustic analysis of the effects of stress on voice. *Journal of Neuropsychiatry*, 1964, *5*, 266–272. (b)

Gellhorn, E. *Principles of autonomic–somatic integrations: Physiological basis and psychological and clinical implications*. Minneapolis: University of Minnesota Press, 1967.

Gellhorn, E., & Kiely, W. F. Autonomic nervous system in psychiatric disorder. In J. Mendels (Ed.), *Biological psychiatry*. New York: Wiley, 1972, pp. 235–261.

Goldfarb, W., Goldfarb, N., Braunstein, P., & Scholl, H. Speech and language faults of schizophrenic children. *Journal of Autism and Childhood Schizophrenia*, 1972, *2*, 219–233.

Goldman-Eisler, F. *Psycholinguistics: Experiments in spontaneous speech*. New York: Academic Press, 1968.

Goldstein, I. B. The relationship of muscle tension and autonomic activity to psychiatric disorders. *Psychosomatic Medicine*, 1965, *27*, 39–52.

Green, R., & Cliff, N. Multidimensional comparisons of structures of vocally and facially expressed emotion. *Perception and Psychophysics*, 1975, *17*, 429–438.

Hargreaves, W. A., & Starkweather, J. A. Voice quality changes in depression. *Language and Speech*, 1964, *7*, 84–88.

Hargreaves, W. A., Starkweather, J. A., & Blacker, K. H. Voice quality in depression. *Journal of Abnormal Psychology*, 1965, *70*, 218–220.

Harris, K. S. Physiological aspects of articulatory behavior. In T. A. Sebeok (Ed.), *Current trends in linguistics*. Vol. 12. *Linguistics and adjacent arts and sciences*. The Hague: Mouton, 1974, pp. 2282–2302.

Hecker, M. H. L., Stevens, K. N., von Bismarck, G., & Williams, C. E. Manifestations of task-induced stress in the acoustic speech signal. *Journal of the Acoustical Society of America*, 1968, *44*, 993–1001.

Holden, C. Lie detectors: PSE gains audience despite critics' doubts. *Science*, 1975, *190*, 359–362.

Hooff, J. A. R. A. M. van. A structural analysis of the social behaviour of a semi-captive group of chimpanzees. In M. von Cranach and I. Vine (Eds.), *Social communication and movement: Studies of interaction and expression in man and chimpanzee*. London: Academic Press, 1973, pp. 75–162.

Huttar, G. L. Relations between prosodic variables and emotions in normal American-English utterances. *Journal of Speech and Hearing Research*, 1968, *11*, 481–487.

Isserlin, M. Psychologisch-phonetische Untersuchungen: II. Mitteilung. *Zeitschrift für die gesamte Neurologie and Psychiatrie*, 1925, *94*, 437–448.

Izard, C. E. *The face of emotion*. New York: Appleton-Century-Crofts, 1971.

Jones, W. R. Evidence vel non: The non-sense of voiceprint identification. *Kentucky Law Journal*, 1974, *62*, 301–326.

Kainz, F. *Psychologie der Sprache*, Vol. 3: *Physiologische Psychologie der Sprachvorgänge*. Stuttgart: Ferdinand Enke, 1954.

Kleinpaul, R. *Sprache ohne Worte: Idee einer allgemeinen Wissenschaft der Sprache*. Leipzig: W. Friedrich, 1888. (Reprint: The Hague, Mouton, 1972.)

Kramer, E. Judgment of personal characteristics and emotions from nonverbal properties of speech. *Psychological Bulletin*, 1963, *60*, 408–420.

Lacey, J. I. Somatic response patterning and stress: Some revisions of activation theory. In M. H. Appley and R. Trumbull (Eds.), *Psychological stress: Issues in research*. New York: Appleton-Century-Crofts, 1967.

Lang, P. J., Rice, D. G., & Sternbach, R. A. The psychophysiology of emotion. In N. S. Greenfield & R. A. Sternbach (Eds.), *Handbook of psychophysiology*. New York: Holt, Rinehart, and Winston, 1972.

Laver, J. D. M. H. Individual features in voice quality. Ph.D. thesis, University of Edinburgh, 1975.

Lazarus, R. S. Emotions and adaptation: Conceptual and empirical relations. In W. J. Arnold (Ed.), *Nebraska Symposium on Motivation*. Lincoln: University of Nebraska Press, 1968.

Levin, H., & Lord, W. Speech pitch frequency as an emotional state indicator. *IEEE Trans. Systems, Man, Cybernetics SMC-5*, 1975, *2*, 259-272.

Lieberman, P. *Intonation, perception, and language*. Cambridge, Mass.: MIT Press, 1967.

Lieberman, P. A study of prosodic features. In T. A. Sebeok (Ed.), *Current trends in linguistics*, Vol. 12. The Hague: Mouton, 1974, pp. 2419-2450.

Lieberman, P. *On the origins of language: An introduction to the evolution of human speech*. New York: Macmillan, 1975.

MacNeilage, P., & Ladefoged, P. The production of speech and language. In E. C. Carterette and M. P. Friedman (Eds.), *Handbook of perception*. Vol. 7: *Language and speech*. New York: Academic Press, 1976, pp. 75-120.

Maher, B. The language of schizophrenia: A review and interpretation. *British Journal of Psychiatry*, 1972, *120*, 3-17.

Mahl, G. F., & Schulze, G. Psychological research in the extralinguistic area. In T. A. Sebeok, A. S. Hayes, & M. C. Bateson (Eds.), *Approaches to semiotics*. The Hague: Mouton, 1964, pp. 51-124.

Malmo, R. B., *On emotions, needs, and our archaic brain*. New York: Holt, Rinehart and Winston, 1975.

Malmo, R. B., Shagass, C., & Davis, J. F. Electromyographic studies of muscular tension in psychiatric patients under stress. *Journal of Clinical and Experimental Psychopathology*, 1951, *12*, 45-66.

Markel, N. N., Bein, M. F., & Phillis, J. A. The relationship between words and tone-of-voice. *Language and Speech*, 1973, *16*, 15-21.

Marler, P. Communication in monkeys and apes. In I. DeVore (Ed.), *Primate behavior: Field studies of monkeys and apes*. New York: Holt, Rinehart and Winston, 1965.

Moses, P. *The voice of neurosis*. New York: Grune and Stratton, 1954.

Moskowitz, E. W. Voice quality in the schizophrenic reaction type. *Speech Monographs*, 1952, *19*, 118-119.

Newman, S. S., & Mather, V. G. Analysis of spoken language of patients with affective disorders. *American Journal of Psychiatry*, 1938, *94*, 913-942.

Oken, D. The psychophysiology and psychoendocrinology of stress and emotion. In M. H. Appley & R. Trumbull (Eds.), *Psychological stress: Issues in research*. New York: Appleton-Century-Crofts, 1967.

Olechowski, R. Experimente über den Stimm- und Sprechausdruck beim Lügen. *Zeitschrift für experimentelle und angewandte Psychologie*, 1967, *14*, 474-482.

Ostwald, P. F. *Soundmaking: The acoustic communication of emotion*. Springfield, Ill.: Charles C Thomas, 1963.

Ostwald, P. F. Acoustic manifestations of emotional disturbance. In *Disorders of communication XLII: Research publications*. A.R.N.M.D., 1964, pp. 450-465. (Reprinted in P. F. Ostwald, Ed., *The semiotics of human sound*. The Hague: Mouton, 1973.)

Ostwald, P. F., & Skolnikoff, A. Z. Speech disturbances in a schizophrenic adolescent. *Postgraduate Medicine*, 1966, *40*, 40-49.

Ploog, D. *Die Sprache der Affen und ihre Bedeutung für die Verständigungsweisen des Menschen*. München: Kindler, 1974.

Pribram, K. H. *Languages of the brain: Experimental paradoxes and principles in neuropsychology*. Englewood Cliffs, N.J.: Prentice-Hall, 1971.

Pribram, K. H., & McGuinness, D. Arousal, activation, and effort in the control of attention. *Psychological Review*, 1975, *82*, 116–149.

Rice, D. G., Abroms, G. M., & Saxman, J. H. Speech and physiological correlates of "flat" affect. *Archives of General Psychiatry*, 1969, *20*, 566–572.

Rochester, S. R. The significance of pauses in spontaneous speech. *Journal of Psycholinguistic Research*, 1973, *2*, 51–81.

Rogers, P. L., Scherer, K. R., Rosenthal, R. Content-filtering human speech: A simple electronic system. *Behavioral Research Methodology and Instrumentation*, 1971, *3*, 16–18.

Rousey, C. L., & Moriarty, A. E. *Diagnostic implications of speech sounds*. Springfield, Ill.: Charles C Thomas, 1965.

Routtenberg, A. Stimulus processing and response execution: A neurobehavioral theory. *Physiology and Behavior*, 1971, *6*, 589–596.

Rubenstein, L. Electro-acoustical measurement of vocal responses to limited stress. *Behavior Research and Therapy*, 1966, *4*, 135–141.

Sawashima, M. Laryngeal research in experimental phonetics. In T. A. Sebeok (Ed.), *Current trends in linguistics*, Vol. 12: *Linguistics and adjacent arts and sciences*. The Hague: Mouton, 1974, pp. 2303–2348.

Saxman, J. H., & Burk, K. W. Speaking fundamental frequency and rate characteristics of adult female schizophrenics. *Journal of Speech and Hearing Research*, 1968, *11*, 194–203.

Scherer, K. R. Randomized splicing: A note on a simple technique for masking speech content. *Journal of Experimental Research in Personality*, 1971, *5*, 155–159.

Scherer, K. R. Judging personality from voice: A cross-cultural approach to an old issue in interpersonal perception. *Journal of Personality*, 1972, *40*, 191–210.

Scherer, K. R. Acoustic concomitants of emotional dimensions: Judging affect from synthesized tone sequences. In S. Weitz (Ed.), *Nonverbal communication*. New York: Oxford University Press, 1974. pp. 105–111.

Scherer, K. R. Affektlaute und vokale Embleme. In R. Posner & H. P. Reinecke (Eds.), *Zeichenprozesse—Semiotische Forschung in den Einzelwissenschaften*. Wiesbaden: Athenaion, 1977. (a)

Scherer, K. R. Effect of stress on fundamental frequency of the voice. Paper delivered at the 94th Meeting of the Acoustical Society of America, Miami Beach, December 1977. (Abstract in *Journal of the Acoustical Society of America*, 1977, *62*, Suppl. No. 1, p. S25-S26.) (b)

Scherer, K. R. Voice and speech changes following stress induction in a deceptive interaction. Unpublished manuscript. University of Giessen, 1977. (c)

Scherer, K. R. Personality inference from voice quality: The loud voice of extraversion. *European Journal of Social Psychology*, in press. (a)

Scherer, K. R. Personality markers in speech. In K. R. Scherer & H. Giles (Eds.), *Social markers in speech*. Cambridge: Cambridge University Press, in press. (b)

Scherer, K. R., Koivumaki, J., & Rosenthal, R. Minimal cues in the vocal communication of affect: Judging emotions from content-masked speech. *Journal of Psycholinguistic Research*, 1972, *1*, 269–285.

Scherer, K. R., London, H., & Wolf, J. The voice of confidence: Paralinguistic cues and audience evaluation. *Journal of Research in Personality*, 1973, *7*, 31–44.

Scherer, K. R., & Oshinsky, J. S. Cue utilization in emotion attribution from auditory stimuli. *Motivation and Emotion*, 1977, *1*, 331–346.

Scripture, E. W. Die epileptische Sprachmelodie. *Archiv für Psychiatrie und Nervenkrankheiten*, 1925, *72*, 323–325.

Sedláček, K., & Sychra, A. Die Melodie als Faktor des emotionellen Ausdrucks. *Folia Phoniatrica*, 1963, *15*, 89–98.

Sharp, F. A. Judgments of psychosis from vocal cues. *Journal of Speech and Hearing Disorders*, 1963, *28*, 371–374.

Simonov, P. V., & Frolov, M. V. Utilization of human voice for estimation of man's emotional stress and state of attention. *Aerospace Medicine*, 1973, *44*, 256–258.

Skinner, E. R. A calibrated recording and analysis of the pitch, force and quality of vocal tones expressing happiness and sadness, and a determination of the pitch and force of the subjective concepts of ordinary, soft, and loud tones, *Speech Mongraphs*, 1935, *2*, 81–137.

Spoerri, T. H. Speaking voice of the schizophrenic patient. *Archives of General Psychiatry*, 1966, *14*, 581–585.

Streeter, L. A., Krauss, R. M., Geller, V., Olson, C., & Apple, W. Pitch changes during attempted deception. *Journal of Personality and Social Psychology*, 1977, *35*, 345–350.

Tembrock, G. *Biokommunikation: Informationsübertragung im biologischen Bereich*, Teil II. Berlin (GDR): Akademie-Verlag, 1971.

Tomkins, S. S. *Affect, imagery, consciousness* (2 vols.). New York: Springer, 1962.

Trojan, F. *Biophonetik*. Zurich: Bibliographisches Institut, 1975.

Whitaker, H. A. Neurobiology of language. In E. C. Carterette, and M. P. Friedman (Eds.), *Handbook of perception*. Vol. 3. *Language and speech*. New York: Academic Press, 1976, pp. 121–144.

Williams, C. E., & Stevens, K. N. On determining the emotional state of pilots during flight: An exploratory study. *Aerospace Medicine*, 1969, *40*, 1369–1372.

Williams, C. E., & Stevens K. N. Emotions and speech: Some acoustical correlates. *The Journal of the Acoustical Society of America*, 1972, *52*, 1238–1250.

Wundt, W. *Völkerspychologie. Eine Untersuchung der Entwicklungsgesetze von Sprache, Mythos und Sitte*, Vol. 1: *Die Sprache*. Leipzig: Engelmann, 1900.

Wyke, B. Recent advances in the neurology of phonation: Phonatory reflex mechanisms in the larynx. *British Journal of Disorders of Communication*, 1967, *2*, 2–14.

Zemlin, W. R. *Speech and hearing science: Anatomy and physiology*. Englewood Cliffs, N.J.: Prentice-Hall, 1968.

Zuberbier, E. Zur Schreib- und Sprechmotorik der Depression. *Zeitschrift für Psychotherapie und Medizinische Psychologie*, 1957, *7*, 239–249.

Zwirner, E. Beitrag zur Sprache der Depressiven. *Journal für Psychologie und Neurologie*, 1930, *41*, 43–49.

Editor's Introduction

18

Exline and his colleagues' ingenious and pioneering studies of eye contact and gaze patterns in interpersonal interactions constituted a significant force in making nonverbal communication an important domain of research in contemporary psychology. Their work has always had the attraction of focusing on variables and conditions that easily translate into life outside the laboratory. The studies reported in this chapter represent three important innovations: (1) the introduction of a dynamic model that analyzes gaze directions in real-time sequences; (2) the study of relationships among different gaze directions in affectively different interactions; and (3) the application of the new model to a psychiatric (schizophrenic) group.

In Study 1, they show that behavioral indicators of closeness, visual attention to the other's face, and postural inclination toward the other can be used by observers in making judgments of the quality of emotion expressed in the retelling of a story that is seen but not heard. The accuracy of such judgments is a direct function of the consistency of these two types of behavioral indicators of closeness. While these indicators were significantly related to accuracy of observers' judgments of the quality of the emotion experiences described in the stories, scores on Jourard's Self-Disclosure Scale, purportedly reflecting an attitudinal or cognitive disposition to closeness, were not.

In Study 2, Exline and his colleagues developed a model of gaze patterns that predicts judgments of emotion-related behavior. Central to the model is the Gaze Direction Index, the difference in the frequency with which a stimulus person casts his gaze toward the eyes of the other compared to the frequency with which the gaze is cast downward. The model predicts a different Gaze Direction Index for the retelling of qualitatively different emotional stories. For example, it predicts a relatively high percentage of direct gazes during the retelling of a happy story and a relatively high percentage of downward gazes in the retelling of a sad story. This prediction was confirmed. They also found significant differences in Gaze Direction Indexes attributable to the intensity of the affective involvement of stimulus persons (as judged by the verbal content of their stories) and to diagnosis (normal versus schizophrenia).

In a *post hoc* analysis of a subsample of the stimulus persons, the investigators found some evidence that gives indirect support to a long-standing clinical observation: the dullness or flatness of affect in schizophrenia. They found that normals telling bland stories (with little affective involvement) tended to show a pattern of gazes similar to schizophrenics telling stories whose verbal content indicated intensive involvement.

Gaze Patterns of Normals and Schizophrenics Retelling Happy, Sad, and Angry Experiences

18

RALPH V. EXLINE, ALFONSO PAREDES,
EDWARD G. GOTTHEIL, and RICHARD WINKELMAYER

I. INTRODUCTION

One factor in the recent growth of interest in research on the nonverbal behavior of humans is the belief that human emotion in face-to-face encounters can be revealed through expressive displays and that such displays are, by definition, nonverbal in nature. Thus, Ekman (1972), Izard (1971), and their colleagues have intensively studied facial expression; Birdwhistell has studied kinesic movement (1970); others have investigated postural arrangements—both individually (Hewes, 1957; Mehrabian, 1969) and in concert (Scheflen, 1973)—and Mehrabian (1970) has developed data to indicate that accuracy of judgment of emotions is more influenced by nonverbal than by verbal expression.

While the greater proportion of the studies of nonverbal aspects of emotion have utilized normals as both stimulus persons and judges, a number of investigators have focused on mentally and emotionally disturbed persons. An interesting variety of problems have been studied. Some investigators focused

RALPH V. EXLINE • University of Delaware, Newark, Delaware. ALFONSO PAREDES • University of Oklahoma, Norman, Oklahoma. EDWARD G. GOTTHEIL • Thomas Jefferson University, Philadelphia, Pennsylvania. RICHARD WINKELMAYER • Delaware State Hospital, Wilmington, Delaware. Studies reported in this chapter were supported by funds from the Office of Naval Research, Contract No. NR 2285, PHS Grant 1T. 1MH11473, and the Delaware State Hospital.

upon comparisons of specific nonverbal encoder behaviors of both normal persons and psychiatric patients (Gottheil, Thornton, & Exline, 1976; Hinchliffe, Lancashire, & Roberts, 1971; Williams, 1974; Rutter & Stephenson, 1972), others on comparisons of the accuracy with which normal and abnormal persons judged emotional expressions of others (Gottheil, Paredes, Exline, & Winkelmayer, 1970). McGhie (1973) and Dougherty, Bartlett, and Izard (1974) concentrated on a single dimension of nonverbal behavior—that is, facial expressions—while Duncan (1969), Ekman and Friesen (1969a,b), Mehrabian (1972), Dittman (1972), and particularly Rosenthal, Hall, DiMatteo, Rogers, and Archer (1978) concerned themselves with multidimensional studies. Rosenthal's PONS test, for example, purports to establish one's profile of nonverbal sensitivity over 11 separate dimensions, that is, face, torso, entire figure, two vocal dimensions and six first-order combinations of the five "pure" dimensions.

In this chapter, we shall report results of two studies that follow the more complex line suggested above. In the first study, we investigated the interrelationships among verbal and nonverbal measures of affective behaviors of normal stimulus persons. In addition, we investigated the effects of such behaviors upon the accuracy with which a panel of psychiatrists were able to discriminate among the nonverbal expressions of stimulus persons relating experiences of anger, sorrow, and joy.

A second study utilized both normal and abnormal individuals as stimulus persons and presents a model of affective gaze direction used to predict the discriminative judgments made by untrained observers who watched silent films of stimulus persons retelling happy, sad, and angry personal experiences.

II. STUDY 1: INTERRELATIONS AMONG BEHAVIORAL AND COGNITIVE INDICATORS OF CLOSENESS AND THEIR EFFECT UPON ACCURATE DISCRIMINATION OF ANGER, SORROW, AND JOY

Assessment of "closeness" or intimacy in dyadic relationships is a continuing problem in studies of human interaction. This problem is particularly relevant to the very special variety of interaction that characterizes psychotherapy. What cues does the therapist use to assess the feeling of openness or alienation of the patient? Are there signals that reliably signify moment-to-moment fluctuations in such orientations? If such signs exist, can they be summed over time within one interview or across several interviews to provide indices of behavior that are relevant to specifiable outcomes of the relationships?

If we are to investigate these broad questions pertaining to the long-range aspects and outcomes of a relationship, we must first establish that behavioral manifestations of intimacy can be identified and meaningfully encoded and decoded. Does, for example, a feeling of closeness to or intimacy with another manifest itself in behavior that can be judged as representing such a feeling? Are there a variety of behaviors that serve this purpose? Are they more likely to be verbal or nonverbal? Are they correlated with one another? Do feelings of intimacy toward others result in more readily decodable affective expressions? Finally, are intimacy feelings situation-specific, or do they result in decodable congruent behaviors over many situations and a variety of affects?

The purpose of this study is thus to investigate interrelationships among behavioral and cognitive indicators of "closeness" or "immediacy" (Weiner & Mehrabian, 1968) (i.e., an orientation toward interpersonal intimacy) and the extent to which these indicators are related to the ease with which observers can evaluate affective communications.

The rationale underlying this study is that generalized feelings of "closeness" to others should, in the absence of factors strongly inhibiting the expression of intimacy, result in the more open expression of affective behavior. More cues would then be provided that sensitive judges could use in making accurate discriminations among a variety of affective expressions.

In the 19th century, Sir Francis Galton (1884) noted that

when two persons have an "inclination" to (liking for) one another, they visibly incline or slope together when sitting side by side, as at a dinner table, and they throw the stress of their weight on the near legs of their chairs.

More recently, Little (1965) attempted to coordinate conceptions of geographical and personal space. His subjects placed models of human figures on a background closer together when they were described by the experimenter as close friends than when they were described as acquaintances. Gottheil, Corey, and Paredes (1968) found that psychological distance as measured by a projective technique was positively related to overt behavior in a real interaction. When subjects felt "close" to an interviewer, they maintained less physical distance from that interviewer during an interview. In addition, Exline and Winters (1965) have shown that preference for one of two other codiscussants is directly related to the amount that the chooser looks into the other's line of regard. Thus, the behavioral orienting measures used in this study will be concerned with eye contact and the use of interpersonal space as indicators of the psychological distance between interviewer and interviewee.

Among the various cognitive measures of orientation toward others—for example, measures of n affiliation (Shipley & Verhoff, 1952; French & Chadwick, 1956), of affection, control, and inclusion orientation (Schutz, 1958), and of liking and love (Rubin, 1970)—Jourard's measure of self-disclosure, designed for the express purpose of measuring "the process of making the self known to other persons" (Jourard & Lasakow, 1958, p. 91) seems to be particularly applicable to the purpose of this study. Taylor and Altman

(1966), for example, using an adaptation of Jourard's scale, showed that the amount that college roommates disclosed to each other varied inversely as a function of item intimacy levels and directly as a function of time and compatibility.

In order to obtain data relevant to the interrelationships described above, we first obtained measures of self-disclosure, then asked subjects to relate experiences reflecting three different kinds of affective experience. Postural inclination toward and eye contact with the interviewer were measured from videotapes of the stories projected without sound in an attempt to judge the affective theme underlying each of the three stories from nonverbal cues.

We are concerned, then with two sets of operational hypotheses. The first deals with the interrelations among cognitive and behavioral measures of closeness to others. We predict significant positive intercorrelations among self-disclosure scores, close physical positioning vis-à-vis another, and degree of eye contact with the listener. If there is a feeling of "closeness" and a willingness to disclose personal information, then these various expressions of intimacy with the interviewer should be congruent. The second set of hypotheses bears on the orienting tendencies of the performers and the accuracy with which the judges label the affective stories. In this case, we predict positive correlations between the accuracy measure and measures of eye contact, self-disclosure, and postural orientation.

A. Method

1. Subjects. Subjects consisted of 22 white female volunteers employed by a state mental hospital. All but one had at least a high school education, and the median age of the sample was in the mid-thirties. Subjects were videotaped as they related three personal emotional experiences to a male experimenter in his late twenties. In order to ensure that the participants' displays were not dominated by cognitive work, the subjects were asked to relate recent experiences and were given ample time to think about the experiences they would be willing to talk about.

2. Procedures. All subjects knew and accepted the fact that their stories were being videotaped from a camera outside the studio. They were shown the arrangements and appeared to pay little attention to the window behind which the camera was located. The camera shot gave a clear view of the subjects from the waist up, and the resolution was clear enough to see facial expressions and the direction in which they gazed. Numbered lights mounted behind and out of the view of the subject identified the order of stories for later analyses—the elicitation of the specific affective themes was randomly arranged across subjects.

3. Postural Inclination. Inclination during each story was recorded by using a fixed camera to photograph the subject immediately after the interviewer asked the subject to recount the disignated emotional experience. Inclination was determined by a procedure that utilized fixed reference points within the picture to obtain a measure of subtle inclination toward or away from the listener. Observation (later supported by data) indicated that subjects moved very little, if at all, once they had settled themselves in the firm but comfortable chair used in the study.

4. Visual Attention. Gaze directions were recorded from replays of the videotaped interviews by observers trained to record such behavior. The amount of time spent in direct visual attention to the listener over the total story time was computed for each story and was averaged over the three stories to obtain an overall percentage of direct gaze time. The listener (experimenter) was instructed to attend steadily to the speaker, thus the percentage of direct gaze represents the exchange of mutual glances.

5. Self-Disclosure. Disclosure was measured by means of the Jourard Self-Disclosure Scale (Jourard & Lasakow, 1958), weighted as recommended by Jourard but corrected to take misrepresentations or lies into account. This was done on the assumption that misrepresenting or lying deserves to be treated as less revealing than if one said nothing.

6. Affect Judgment. Three psychiatrists independently judged the affective theme of each story told by each subject. They were informed that they would see videotaped recordings presented without sound of a number of persons, each of whom would tell one happy, one sad, and one angry story. They were advised that the three stories would not always be in the same order, that they would be shown twice, and that they should not attempt to identify the order of the stories until after the second presentation. The rationale and reliability of this rating procedure has been described previously (Gottheil *et al.*, 1970). The score used was the number of correct discriminations on each stimulus person summed over the three judges.

In addition to the determination of the accuracy with which the stories were judged, a measure of the time taken to tell each story was obtained. Time data were collected in order to explore possible relationships with overall accuracy and with the various cognitive and behavioral measures of closeness.

B. Results

Intercorrelations among the measures used in this study are presented in Table 1. Examination of the scatter plots showed a linear relationship to hold for all correlations with the exception of the correlation between percentage of direct gaze on the happy story and the mean weighted Jourard score. An eta

Table 1. *Intercorrelations among Cognitive and Behavioral Measures of Closeness to Others over Three Affect Stories, and Their Correlation with a Discrimination Measure of Total Accuracy*

Measures	Stories	Direct gaze				Postural inclination				Accuracy of discrimination
		Happy	Angry	Sad	Total	Happy	Angry	Sad	Total	Combined stories
Jourard SD		$.01^a$	.15	.07	.10	.22	.05	−.27	−.13	.10
Percent direct gaze	Happy	—	$.79^b$	$.73^b$	$.91^b$	−.07	.04	.16	.29	.39
	Angry		—	$.75^b$	$.93^b$	.28	.29	.28	.31	$.43^c$
	Sad			—	$.88^b$	.11	.08	.13	.08	.31
	Total				—	.17	.17	.17	.17	$.46^c$
Postural inclination	Happy					—	.28	.26	.31	.06
	Angry						—	$.88^b$	$.97^b$	−.10
	Sad							—	$.96^b$	.00
	Total								—	−.01

^{a} Eta = .72 $.025 > p > .01$.
^{b} $p < .01$.
^{c} $p < .05$.

coefficient of .72, $p < .025$, computed to determine the correlation between the latter two variables, showed a significant curvilinear relationship between direct gaze and self-disclosure as measured by the Jourard technique.

Data in Table 1 show significant, high intercorrelations among direct gaze behavior across the three affect stories, significant positive correlations only between angry and sad postural inclination toward the listener, and significant positive correlations between the stimulus persons' percentage of angry and total direct gazes and the accuracy with which the panel of judges discriminated among the three affect stories.

Thus, we find that individuals who gave relatively high, moderate, or low direct visual attention to a listener while telling a happy personal experience also maintained, relative to each other, such proportions of direct gaze while relating angry and sad personal experiences. In addition, the mean percentages of direct gaze recorded for happy and angry stories are both significantly greater than that recorded during the sad story. Finally, though the mean inclination toward the listener did not differ across stories, those persons who inclined toward (or away from) the listener on the happy story were not necessarily those who did so on angry and sad stories.

Contrary to expectations, then, we find no positive general relationships between cognitive measures of closeness as defined by Jourard Self-Disclosure scores and either the amount of visual attention or the bodily inclination toward a strange listener. Neither do we find a significant correlation between two behavioral indicators of immediacy orientations toward a listener.

We also hypothesized that there exist positive relationships between the presenters' cognitive or behavioral indications of immediacy with a stranger and the accuracy with which a set of judges discriminate among the affective displays of the presenters. We found a significant positive relationship only for the amount of visual attention (direct gaze) directed toward a listener and the accuracy with which the affects of their stories were judged. Those stimulus persons whose average visual attention to a listener was relatively high over all three stories were judged significantly better than those directing moderate and low amounts of visual attention to the listener. Congruency among indicators of closeness was not found, and immediacy measures whether verbal or non-verbal were not generally related to accuracy in decoding affective expression from nonverbal displays. Only the angry and total visual behavior of the stimulus persons appeared to be significantly related to success in decoding affects from nonverbal displays.

It was earlier noted that cognitive self-disclosure was curvilinearly related to direct gaze when telling a happy story (see Figure 1). This finding suggests that a number of the stimulus persons could be designated as false positives, that is, persons who describe themselves as high in self-disclosure (verbal immediacy) to others but who manifest little immediacy in their nonverbal behavior. Identification of such false positives may help to explain the low correlation between self-disclosure scores and the accuracy with which their affect stories were judged. Moreover, since the only cues available to judges were nonverbal behavioral cues, the extent to which these cues were consistent with one another could be predicted to be more directly related to the judges'

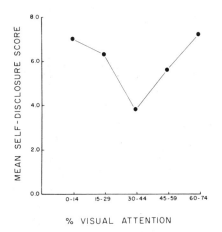

Figure 1. Jourard Self-Disclosure score in relation to percentage of visual attention.

accuracy than the verbal self-disclosure score would be. To summarize: those persons whose visual and postural behavior implied either closeness or distance should, regardless of their verbal self-disclosure score, be easier to judge than those whose behaviors on one dimension implied an immediacy orientation that was contradicted by their behavior on the other.

Accordingly, the results of an *ad hoc* analysis of the effect of the internal consistency of stimulus persons' visual and postural immediacy behaviors upon judges' accuracy are graphically illustrated in Figure 2. The data show mean accuracy scores made by judges on stimulus persons categorized by above- and below-median performances with respect to direct gaze and postural inclinations on the happy story, the story type on which a judge might well expect consistency in the display of positive immediacy cues. Results of a 2×2 analysis of variance showed that the only significant differences were those for the main effect of direct gaze ($F = 5.50$; $p < .05$, $df = 1$ & 18) and for the interaction of gaze and postural inclination ($F = 11.69$; $p < .01$, $df = 1$ & 18). Stimulus persons are judged more accurately when they look much at the listener and lean toward him and when they both look and lean relatively little toward him. They are judged less well when they look at but lean little toward him and are judged *least* well when they lean toward but do not look at the listener.

The data graphically portrayed in Figure 2 indicate that the consistency

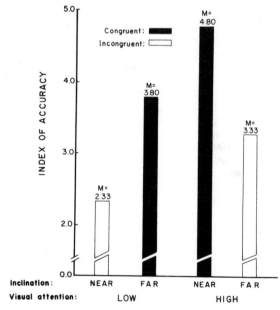

Figure 2. Mean judgment accuracy elicited by stimulus persons categorized by postural inclination and visual attention.

with which the behavioral cues provided by the storyteller suggest either openness or withdrawal is significantly associated with the ease with which the judges assess the stimulus persons' nonverbal expression of affect. Stimulus people who send mixed behavioral messages are judged significantly less well than those who send consistent behavioral messages, regardless of whether the message is one of approach or avoidance (t congruent versus incongruent = 2.43, $p < .05$, $df = 21$).

We have suggested that congruent, as compared to incongruent, performance on two nonverbal dimensions of behavior will facilitate the accuracy with which judges can estimate the affective state of the performers. We have not yet considered the effect on accuracy of another possibly important factor, namely, the length of time that judges took to view the performances on which they based their judgments. Would greater exposure alone be sufficient to improve accuracy? If for some reason the amount of time taken by stimulus persons to tell their stories was associated with behavioral congruency–incongruency, the relationship, while interesting in itself, would confound the relationship between congruency and accuracy of judgment.

To test for the above-mentioned possibility, the time used to recount personal experiences was correlated with accuracy of judgment. The correlation of $-.34$ not only did not reach significance at the .10 level but was in the negative direction—accuracy tends to be associated with shorter stories. Sheer amount of time on display is most certainly not a major contributor to the accuracy with which the presenter's affect is judged.

Finally, there was no evidence that cognitive self-disclosure combined with either or both of the nonverbal measures of immediacy to render stimulus persons easier to judge. Within the behaviorally consistent set of stimulus persons, those whose self-disclosure scores (high or low) were congruent with both of the nonverbal immediacy measures (total congruence) were no more accurately judged than those who were congruent only with respect to the nonverbal dimensions. While there was a tendency for the presenters to be more accurately judged if their self-disclosure scores matched their visual as compared to their postural behavior, the difference was not significant.

III. STUDY 2: GAZE DIRECTION AS A FACTOR IN THE JUDGMENT OF NORMAL AND SCHIZOPHRENIC NONVERBAL EXPRESSIONS OF AFFECT[1]

The preceding study demonstrated that the visual attention (direct gaze) a speaker gives to one who listens to the retelling of an emotional experience is potentially useful to the accurate judgment of the nature of the speaker's

[1] This study is an extension and elaboration, with additional data, of work reported in the proceedings of the 76th meetings of the American Psychological Association (Exline *et al.*, 1968).

experience. In particular, this is true if the gaze behavior of the speaker is congruent with other nonverbal cues concerning the presence or absence of immediacy in the speaker's orientation to the listener. Thus the study supports the implicit suggestion of other investigators (e.g., Argyle & Dean, 1965) that the interpretation of gaze behavior is, for certain purposes, facilitated by comparing and contrasting the direct gaze with other nonverbal orientation cues.

This study is an extension of that position in that we treated different aspects of gaze behavior as providing different nonverbal orientation cues. In other words, we compared and contrasted different directions of gaze to create a model of affective gaze direction that we assumed to be systematically related to the normal encoding and decoding of specified affective states. With the exception of the studies of conjugate lateral eye movement (Day, 1964; Duke, 1968; Bakan, 1971; Kinsbourne, 1974; Libby & Yaklevich, 1973), previous studies have treated the direct gaze only in terms of its presence, duration, and/or absence. We suggest that it is fruitful to investigate the role played by different patterns of gaze direction in both expressing and judging the manifestations of different affects.

This study reflects an extension of a position first expressed by Theodore Piderit, a German contemporary of Charles Darwin. In *Mimik and Physiognomik*, published over a century ago, Piderit (1867) suggested that to think of an object or event brings about similar facial responses as would occur in the presence of the object or event itself. Thus, the thought of a bitter, unpleasant food would be accompanied by a wry mouth, while the recollection of an unpleasant scene would affect the expressive movements of the eyes.

Piderit, while referring to the total facial display, specifically suggested that a pleasant thought opens the eyes and that pleasant emotions are accompanied by receptive movements, while unpleasant emotions are accompanied by movement designed to impede the reception of stimuli. Our interest is not directed to the total display, which interest is well represented in the work of Ekman, Friesen, and Ellsworth (1972), Izard (1971), Frijda (1969), and others, but is restricted to a consideration of patterns of gaze direction within the affective display, and particularly how such patterns are related to the accuracy with which such displays are interpreted or judged. It is not clear whether or not Piderit intended his propositions to hold independent of culture, but we suggest that in the United States, at least, receptivity is directly associated with the amount of time in a given period during which one person gives his visual attention to another, particularly if the other returns the glance (Exline, 1963; Exline, Gray, & Schuette, 1965; Rubin, 1970; Argyle & Cook, 1976).

If the mutual or direct glance is interpreted as a sign of receptivity, or pleasant affect, what of the averted glance? We suggest that it is likely to be associated with low receptivity, inattention (Exline, 1972), and avoidance (Exline & Winters, 1965), or in other words, with behavior related to unpleasant affect. Connotations of avoidant glances, moreover, could well differ according to the directions in which they depart from the direct line of regard. We believe that a consistently downcast gaze would carry a different meaning to an observer than would a consistently upward or sideward gaze. Folk sayings would seem to reflect this bit of conventional wisdom. Consider, for example, "He cast down his gaze in sorrow" as compared to "He looked fearfully about" or "the averted gaze of shame." The first statement evokes the image of bowed head with eyes directed vertically downward from a point in space that would be directly in front of the nose of the upright head. The second statement suggests eyes shifting from side to side, as if seeking a means of escape, while the third intuitively brings to mind a glance directed obliquely down and to the side.

We suggest, then, that in the United States, speakers when describing a joyful, pleasant event will accompany their words with a relatively more direct visual display than when they are describing less joyful, less pleasant events. Furthermore, we suggest that, if others are denied the verbal content but are permitted to view the behavioral display that accompanies the spoken message, their judgments of affective meaning will be influenced by patterned combinations of receptive (direct) and unreceptive (avoidant) glances. Finally, according to our preceding argument in regard to gaze aversion, we suggest that the nature of the avoidant glance will differ with the nature of the unpleasant affect and that the nonreceptivity of persons relating an experience of sorrow will be manifested by a different pattern of gaze aversion than will be the nonreceptivity of persons relating experiences of fear or anger. Specifically, we suggest that recounting of sorrow, relative to joy and anger, is more likely to be characterized by a directly downcast glance.

Our model, primitive though it is, permits us to test hypotheses concerning the visual aspects of the nonverbal display accompanying affective communications, as well as hypotheses concerning the expectations that judges hold concerning the affective theme of a conversation when it is judged from the total nonverbal display alone. Finally, if the model satisfactorily explains both the performance and the judges' expectations of the performance, accuracy of judgment should follow automatically; that is, it should be highly correlated with the nature of the patterned visual display as postulated by the model.

Before specifying the hypotheses to be tested, however, we shall consider the generality of the model. We have already indicated that we shall limit ourselves to North Americans in general. In this preliminary investigation we shall also limit ourselves to adult Caucasian women of predominantly middle-class origins, asked to express the three affects of sorrow, joy, and anger. In part, this limitation is due to practical considerations relevant to the availability of subjects and complexity of affective display behavior, but also it is due to our interest in exploring further an earlier finding that nonschizophrenic judges, using only nonverbal cues, were better able to discriminate among the affective themes of stories told by nonschizophrenic than by schizophrenic women (Gottheil *et al.*, 1970). This finding suggested that the nonverbal displays of nonschizophrenic women more closely match the expectations that normal judges have of the behavioral concomitants of affective verbalization than do those of schizophrenic women.

Since our model is concerned with one component of behavioral displays, it seems reasonable to suggest that it should better describe the affect-related gaze patterns of normal than of schizophrenic women. Thus, if the receptive direct gaze is more characteristic of joy than of anger or sorrow, and the avoidant downcast gaze is more characteristic of sorrow than of joy or anger, our model suggests that the difference between the time spent in direct as compared to downcast looking should be largest when associated with a happy affective state; smallest or even negative when associated with sadness; and intermediate when linked with anger. Furthermore, we suggest that the above pattern of direct-to-down gaze differences should be more salient the more intensely the communicator feels and thus, we assume, expresses affect. Limiting ourselves, then, to the investigation of the three affects of sorrow, joy, and anger, as communicated by normal and schizophrenic women, we present the following hypotheses:

I: For nonschizophrenic more than for schizophrenic women, the relative amount of direct as compared to downward avoidant glances of a speaker will be greatest during happy communication, least during sorrowful communication, and intermediate during communication pertaining to anger.

The model predicts that the salience of the pattern of gaze direction stated in Hypothesis I will increase as the intensity of the affective involvement in the verbal communication increases. Accordingly, we present the following corollary to the hypothesis stated above:

II: For nonschizophrenic more than for schizophrenic women, the relative differences between direct and downward glances predicted in Hypothesis I will occur in the gaze behavior of those women who tell more intensely happy, sorrowful, and angry stories.

The above hypotheses are concerned with the validity with which the model represents gaze direction patterns that make up the actual nonverbal display coordinate with the affective theme of spoken thoughts; that is, it predicts encoding. From the standpoint of judges asked to use only the total nonverbal display to discriminate among the various affective themes, the closer the predicted gaze-direction patterns are to judges' expectations of display cues representing the affective themes,[2] the more likely will the judges be

---

[2] This is not to say that judges need to be consciously aware of their expectations concerning the use of gaze direction and other cues. Indeed, it is likely that the average judge is but dimly aware of the others' gaze-direction patterns. He is more likely to be consciously aware of the other aspects of the nonverbal display, for example, facial expressions, gestures, head and body movements, and the like.

to label the affective presentations as predicted by the model; that is, it predicts decoding also. Decoding will be facilitated by the ease with which the direct-down gaze pattern can be differentially discriminated across the three stories. Representing such inter-story discriminability by an index of affective gaze direction developed for that purpose, we hypothesize:

> III: Stimulus persons characterized by a high index of discriminability of affective gaze direction will be more "accurately" judged than stimulus persons with a low index of discriminability.

In Hypothesis III, *accuracy* refers not to the intended but to the expected affective value of the story, that is, to accuracy in terms of an expected judgment model. Thus, from the point of view of the judge, our model states that a story that is accompanied by the greatest positive difference in direct minus downward gaze will, regardless of the intended affect it may represent, be expected (and hence judged) to be happy. In addition, the story that is accompanied by the least positive differences in direct minus down gazes will be expected (and hence judged) to be sad, and the story that is intermediate in direct-downward gaze differences would be expected (and judged) to be angry. The least positive difference in direct minus down gaze could of course be negative; that is, more time would be spent in looking down than in looking directly at the listener. According to our model, if this occurs, it will occur on the sad but not on the happy story. If it occurs on the angry story, the negative difference will be less than on the sad story. Hypothesis III, then, is concerned with how closely the judges' expectations (and judgments) follow the gaze-direction model presented above.

If our model is valid for the sender and subjects do in fact show the greatest positive direct-down difference on happy, intermediate differences on angry, and the least positive direct-to-down difference on sad, then the discriminability index will be an index of appropriate affective gaze direction. In this case, the expected judgment will by definition be a truly accurate judgment. A corollary of Hypothesis III, then, would be:

> III A: Stimulus persons characterized by a high discriminability index of appropriate affective gaze direction will be more accurately judged than those whose behavior is characterized by a high degree of inappropriate affective gaze direction.

A. Method

1. Subjects. Twenty Caucasian women volunteers were used in making a 16mm black-and-white stimulus film. Of the stimulus persons, 10 were staff members of a state mental hospital, and 10 were resident schizophrenic patients. Normals and schizophrenics were paired as to age, education, and birthplace. All women wore street clothes for the filmmaking sessions.

2. Procedures. Procedures used to collect the data and create the stimulus film were the same as described in the first study. It should be noted that, as in the first study, segments of a duplicate film were spliced to the original copy in such fashion that the three-story sequence of a given stimulus person was shown twice in succession before viewers judged that person and saw the next one. Schizophrenic and nonschizophrenic stimulus persons were randomly ordered over two reels of 10 persons each.

3. Intensity of Affective Involvement. The intensity of each stimulus person's involvement with the affective theme of her stories was measured as follows: (a) each story of each person was coded and typed on a separate sheet; and (b) stories representing each type of affect were grouped and randomly arranged within the set. Two judges, unaware of the identity of the stimulus person, rated the 20 stories in each set (happy, angry, or sad) on a 5-point scale to indicate the extent to which the story reflected the affective theme of the set. Ratings correlated .81, .62, and .75 for happy, angry, and sad sets, respectively, and agreement was judged to be sufficiently reliable to obtain an intensity score for each stimulus person on each story.

4. Gaze Direction. Direct gazes were coded as described earlier, and, in addition, coders reran the films to record downward, sideways, and angled glances. Upward glances were so few as to be negligible and were not recorded. In addition to recording gaze directions, an index of discernible affective gaze direction was developed to test our hypotheses. This index (hereafter to be referred to as the Discriminable Gaze Direction Index) took into account both the absolute value of the difference between the largest and the least direct minus down gaze differences and the relationship of the intermediate difference to the other two. Thus a set of stories in which the range between the extreme differences is large while the intermediate-sized difference is balanced between the two extremes would result in a higher discriminability index score than would a set of stories in which the range between extremes is great but the intermediate difference close to the size of one or the other of the extremes. Similarly, a set of stories in which the range between extremes is small should result in a lower index score than would a set of stories for which the range is great and the distribution is balanced. Finally, a set of stories in which the range is small and the distribution is unbalanced would result in the lowest discriminability index score. See Figure 3 for a representation of the model described above.

5. Judgment of Affects. The stimulus film was shown to 32 male college students and 53 female college students. Male students were undergraduate and graduate psychology majors from the University of Delaware and first-year medical students at Thomas Jefferson University in Philadelphia. Female students were undergraduate and graduate psychology majors at the University of Delaware and nurses in training from Methodist Hospital in Philadelphia.

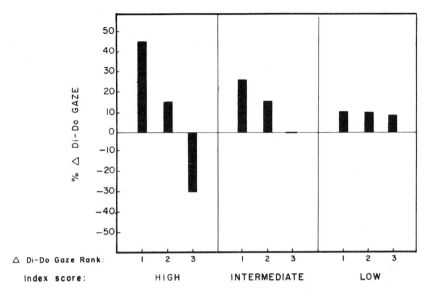

Figure 3. Hypothetical examples of discriminable gaze pattern index scores (1 to 3 = rank order of stories by greatest direct minus down gaze).

The film was shown silently to the judges, who were given a 15-minute rest priod between viewing two reels of 10 stimulus persons each. Judges knew that they would see a number of women each describe one happy, one sad, and one angry personal experience. They were unaware that half of the stimulus persons were schizophenic. They were instructed that each person' stories were arranged in a random order and that they would be shown two successive sequences of that order before viewing the next person. They were asked to observe the range of each woman's expressive behavior in the first sequence, then use the second showing to judge the affective theme of each story. Judges recorded their decisions by printing *happy, sad,* or *angry* for each story for each stimulus person on a form labeled and provided for that purpose. Judges were permitted to change their judgments any time prior to the exposure of the next stimulus person. The projector was shut down between the showing of each stimulus person's double sequence in order to permit all observers to complete their judgments prior to the presentation of the stories of the next stimulus person.

A score on "expected value" of judgment was obtained for each stimulus person by summing over all three stories the number of affective judgments that were consistent with the judgments predicted by the model presented earlier. Thus, if the direct minus downward gaze difference was greatest on the first story, intermediate on the second, and *least* (or even negative) on the third story, judgments that specified the first story as happy, the second as angry, and the third as sad would be counted as hits (successful predictions by the model). The hits summed over all judges provide the "expected value judgment" score for each stimulus person. The maximum number of expected value hits for each stimulus person would be three times the numer of judges, or 255.

B. Results

Our hypotheses concerning the pattern of differences between direct and downward gazes across the three affect experiences are based on certain implicit assumptions concerning normal, but nonschizophrenic, visual attention in affective communications. First, a person's happy story is assumed to be accompanied by more direct (i.e., potentially shared) glances at a listener than are angry and sad stories. Conversely, a sad story is characterized by a great percentage of downward gazes than are happy and angry stories. Finally, the gaze behaviors described above are expected to be pronounced as the affect inherent in a given story is more intense.

Table 2 lists the mean percentage of time spent in direct gaze and in directly downward gazes and the difference between the two for normal and schizophrenic stimulus persons grouped by the judged intensity of their affect stories. Not only are the mean percentage data in Table 2 consistent with the above-stated assumptions concerning direct gazes and down gazes across the

Table 2. Mean % Direct Gaze, Downward Gaze, and Difference Recorded for Normal and Schizophrenic Women Describing Intense or Superficial Affective Experiences of Joy, Anger, and Sorrow

Affect theme	Affect intensity	Normal stimulus persons			Schizophrenic stimulus persons		
		Gaze direction			Gaze direction		
		Direct	Down	ΔDi–Do	Direct	Down	ΔDi–Do
Happy	High[a]	51.6	9.0	42.6	43.6	7.8	35.6
	Low[a]	36.3	10.8	25.5	65.7	4.7	61.0
	Total[b]	44.0	9.9	34.1	54.6	6.2	48.4
Angry	High	26.7	11.7	15.0	29.5	11.8	17.7
	Low	49.9	7.4	42.4	64.3	7.6	56.8
	Total	38.3	9.6	28.7	46.9	9.7	37.8
Sad	High	30.6	28.3	2.4	67.8	1.3	66.5
	Low	45.1	8.6	29.4	40.3	7.4	33.0
	Total	37.9	18.4	15.9	54.0	4.4	49.7
Combined	High	36.3	16.3	20.0	46.9	7.0	40.0
	Low	43.8	8.9	32.4	56.8	6.6	50.6
	Total	40.0	12.6	26.2	51.9	6.8	45.3

[a] $N = 5$.
[b] $N = 10$.

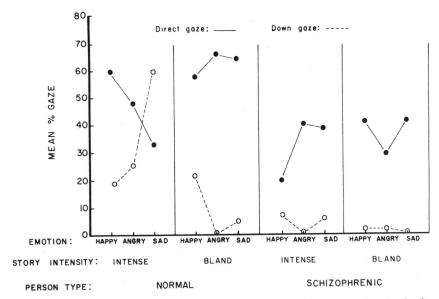

Figure 4. Mean percentage of direct and down gazes of normal and schizophrenic stimulus persons when telling consistently intense or bland personal experiences.

three stories, but within-stimulus-person comparisons for each gaze direction showed that the appropriate pattern was significantly more characteristic of normal than of schizophrenic stimulus persons. (Direct gaze pattern: $t = 2.236$, $p < .025$. Down pattern: $t = 4.270$, $p < .001$.) In other words, for normals, but not for schizophrenics, direct gaze was greatest on the happy story and downward gazes were greatest on the sad story.

The mean percentage of direct and downward gazes listed in Table 2 suggest that strong emotion affects the gaze as assumed. In other words, for normals the previously remarked differences are intensified and in the appropriate direction. In fact, the assumed pattern—direct gaze greatest on the happy story, down gaze greatest on the sad story—occurred only in the stories of the most intense normals. The percentage data, however, do not most appropriately demonstrate the effect of intensity upon gaze direction. The data represent the behavior of somewhat different persons on each story, and our model is concerned with gaze differences across the emotions portrayed *by each individual stimulus person*. Thus, the effect of intensity is best determined by examining the comparisons provided by those persons who were consistently much or little involved when retelling each affective experience. Only two normals and one schizophrenic met the cross-story consistency requirement for each intensity level (high or low). The data for these persons are graphed in Figure 4, and the differences, while based on small *n*s, are both internally consistent and dramatic. Indeed the graphed data for the intense normals provides an ideal pictorial representation of the direct-to-down gaze patterns that, story by story, constitute our model.

To summarize: we suggest that the data reported above are consistent with the assumptions underlying our hypotheses and permit us to use the direct minus down gaze differences to test the hypothesized pattern across the three affects.

1. Encoding Results. Verification of the implicit assumptions concerning direct and down gazes, separately, anticipated the results of the tests of the first two hypotheses. Data listed in Table 3 under the column heading "ΔDi–Do" follow the predicted pattern for all normals (happy = 34.1%, angry = 28.7%, sad = 15.9%) but not for schizophrenics, for whom the difference was greatest on sad (49.7%) and least on angry experiences (37.8%).

The above data represent averages for all normal and schizophrenic stimulus persons. A more appropriate test of the first hypothesis is to compare each stimulus person's pattern across the three stories. Assignig a score of 4, 3, 2, or 1 to each stimulus person to indicate whether three, two, one, or none of the possible comparisons across stories fit the model (ΔDi–Do happy greater than angry, which is greater than sad), we obtain a mean pattern score of 2.90 for normals, which is significantly greater than the mean score of 2.00 for schizophrenics ($t = 2.211, p < .025, df = 18$). The data thus provide support for the first hypothesis. The predicted excoding pattern is more likely to characterize the affect-specific gaze behavior of normals than of schizophrenics.

Examination of Figure 4, specifically the pattern of difference between the direct and down gaze points plotted for each affect, clearly shows that striking differences in gaze pattern are associated with consistently strong and weak verbal expressions of affect. Normal persons in each intensity category showed the pattern of gaze behavior represented by the combined curve for that category. Although the number was small, we are encouraged to suggest that normals, but not schizophrenics, most clearly show the theoretical pattern when, as predicted by the second hypothesis, the affect is intense.

Our model is concerned with patterns of gaze direction rather than with the direct gaze only. Thus, we made no predictions concerning the absolute amounts of direct gaze given by normal as compared to schizophrenic speakers. Nevertheless, our study provides data relevant to the question of whether or not schizophrenics show more gaze avoidance than do normals (Argyle & Cook, 1976). The percentage of direct gaze combined across stories and intensity categories is listed in Table 2. The data show no evidence of schizophrenic gaze avoidance. Their direct gaze behavior is in the normal range and tends, though the difference is not significant, to be greater than that of normals (52% to 40%).

2. Decoding Results. Thus far, we have focused only on the gaze behavior of the stimulus persons: the encoders. If the model is valid, it should also influence the judgments made by observers (decoders) who watch the stimulus persons retell (without sound) the three specific emotional experiences. Thus, the third hypothesis is concerned with the effect upon observers' judgments of the discriminability across all three stories of a stimulus person's direct-to-downward gaze differences within each story. If, for example, these differences are similar across all three stories, the pattern is not discriminable. On the other hand, if the direct minus down gaze of a stimulus person is positive and very large on one story. intermediate on another, and either very small or reversed on a third, the overall pattern is potentially quite discriminable.

Hypothesis III stated that when observing the three stories told by a single stimulus person, the observers will judge the story accompanied by the greatest direct minus down gaze as "happy," judge the story accompanied by the least difference (or a reversed direction of difference) as "sad," and judge the remaining story as "angry" when the differences between the direct minus down differences in gaze are more discriminable from story to story. this hypothesis is derived from our postulate that decoders expect, whether consciously or unconsciously, that gaze patterns are linked to the encoders' specific affects as prescribed for intense normals by our general model (see Figure 3). Thus, whether or not the theme of the story being told is happy, the observer, unable to hear the person's words, will judge it to be happy if the amount of the stimulus person's direct gaze minus down gaze is greater on that story than on the other two. Coversely, the story accompanied by the least positive difference in direct minus down gaze (ideally by a relatively greater amount of downward gaze) will be judged "sad" no matter what the intended verbal theme.

We tested the third hypothesis by comparing each stimulus person's index of discriminable gaze direction to the total number of observer judgments that matched the postulated expectations described above. These matching judgments are termed *expected-value hits*, and an example of how they were computed follows. Assume that a stimulus person's pattern of direct minus down differences was greatest on the first experience of the three described, least on the second, and intermediate on the third. According to our model, an observer should judge the first experience "happy," the second "sad," and the third "angry." If the observer should so judge, the result would be three expected-value hits. If all 85 observers were to make the identical judgments, the "hits" associated with the gaze pattern of the stimulus person would number 255. On the other hand, if an observer were to label (judge) the first story "happy," the second "angry," and the third "sad," the expected value score would amount to only 1, summing to 85 if all observers were to follow suit.

The expected-value hits elicited from male judges did not differ from those elicited from female judges concerning each stimulus–person category. The judgments from both sexes were combined to obtain a single score for each stimulus person for use in further analyses.

The observers who provided the judgments used to test our third hypothesis were unaware that the stimulus persons consisted of both normal and schizophrenic women. Thus our decoding model provides no basis for differential predictions concerning differences between normal or schizophrenic stimulus persons on either the discriminability of gaze direction or the expected value hit scores. For exploratory purposes, however, both the Discriminable Gaze Index and the expected-value hit scores for each stimulus person are categorized by type (normal-schizophrenic) in Table 3 and graphed in Figure 5.

Given the ordinal nature of the data listed in Table 3, the Mann–Whitney U test was used to compare normals to schizophrenics on both the Gaze Discriminability Index and the expected-value hit score. The difference did not reach acceptable levels of significance ($p < .05$), and the data from both categories were combined to test the hypotheses.

The data suggest that the model has considerable predictive power. The rho correlation between the gaze index and the expected-value hit score for the combined stimulus person sample amounts to .52, significant beyond the .01 level (one-tailed test). In addition, 15 of the 19 stimulus persons elicited expected-value hits in excess of 85, the number that would be expected by chance. We conclude that the data provide evidence to support our third hypothesis, namely, that the more discriminable is the direct minus down gaze pattern assumed to differentiate among the affective expression of happiness, anger, and sorrow, the more likely will it elicit the appropriate affective judgments from observers.

Though the rho correlation described above was significant for the combined sample of subjects, the separate rho's for normal and schizophrenic

Table 3. *Gaze-Direction Index and Expected-Value Hit Scores Recorded for 10 Normal and 10 Schizophrenic Women Stimulus Persons*

Normal			Schizophrenic		
Stimulus person no.	Gaze[a] index	Expected-value hits	Stimulus person no.	Gaze[a] index	Expected-value hits
9	311	213	8	508	186
1	264	201	10	396	104
12	115	149	3	213	91
17	112	123	15	137	74
4	98	104	14	135	135
20	70	115	18	111	168
6	64	111	7	38	151
13	63	102	16	34	41
5	58	65	19	29	97
2	48	42	11	00	—[b]

[a] Index scores ranked in terms of theoretical ease of discrimination of gaze-direction differences across stories.
[b] No discriminable differences in gaze direction across stories; therefore not possible to predict expected guesses.

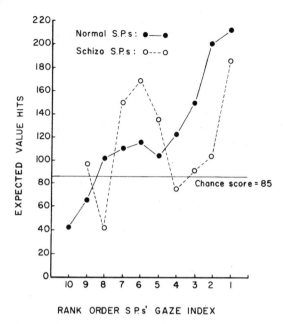

Figure 5. Discriminable Gaze Index ranks plotted against number of expected judgments.

subjects showed a striking difference. The correlation for normals was almost perfect (rho = .96, $p < .01$), while that for schizophrenics is reduced to .30 and did not reach significance. This striking difference between normals and schizophrenics will be discussed in a later section.

3. Gaze Pattern Discriminability and Judges' Accuracy. The corollary to our third hypothesis was supported by the extent to which observers' judgments were correct in terms of the affective theme of the story told by the stimulus person; that is, a happy story was judged happy, etc. Of the four stimulus persons with the highest discriminability index in each normal-schizophrenic category, two either perfectly displayed (normals) or tended to show (schizophrenic) our ideal encoder pattern (direct minus down gaze difference greatest when telling the happy experience, least when telling the sad). Two others in each category clearly failed to match the model (i.e., accompanied an angry or sad story with the greatest difference in direct as compared to downward gazes). Correct judgments of the four who fit the model well were far greater in comparison to those made by observers when judging the four persons who fit it poorly. This was true for judgments of both the normal (213 and 201 to 56 and 67) and the schizophrenic (141 and 136 to 96 and 89) stimulus persons.

Accuracy in decoding another's affective display would, especially in the absence of information carried by speech, seem to be facilitated by the extent to which an encoder's gaze pattern fit our model. Since the gaze pattern predicted by the encoder model appears to be positively related to the strength of affect expressed in words, it would seem that those who feel intensely about an emotional experience will be more likely to communicate it nonverbally when recalling it for another.

IV. DISCUSSION

There are both similarities and differences in the foci of interest represented in the two studies reported in this chapter. Both studies were concerned with the communicative properties of nonverbal behaviors that accompanied the retelling of personal emotional experiences to another in face-to-face conversation, and both used the same technique to produce the material that observers used to judge the emotion-related behavior of the stimulus woman. Gaze behavior was a central variable of interest in both studies but was investigated in conjunction with other cognitive and nonverbal immediacy cues in the first study, while in the second study, it was differentiated into two directions of gaze (direct and downward) and studied in conjunction with the intensity of verbal expressions of emotion. The first study employed only normal women as stimulus persons and used a panel of psychiatrists as observers and judges of emotion. The second study used male and female college-age students as observers and judges and employed both normal and schizphrenic women as stimulus persons.

A final comparison points up a major difference in focus. The first study explored interrelations between and among cognitive and noncognitive immediacy cues and their relationships to accurate emotional judgment. The second study investigated the utility of a model of affect-related gaze-direction patterns to predict the gaze behavior in the nonverbal display accompanying each verbal expression of emotion by encoders (stimulus persons) as well as the decoders' labeling (whether accurate or not) of encoders' displays.

The results of the two studies are summarized below:

Study 1: Normal Stimulus Persons—Psychiatric Judges

1. No significant linear correlations were found when interrelating the stimulus persons' Jourard Self-Disclosure Scores, direct gaze, and postural inclination toward another.

2. A significant curvilinear relationship was discovered between Jourard Self-Disclosure scores and the amount of direct gaze recorded on the happy story.

3. Direct gaze was significantly intercorrelated across all three stories, postural inclination only between angry and sad stories.

4. Judges' accuracy in discriminating among the nonverbal expression of happy, sad, and angry experiences was significantly and positively correlated with gaze behavior. Further analysis showed that stimulus persons whose nonverbal behavior (gaze, postural inclination) was congruent on the happy story (i.e., "look at" associated with "lean toward" and "no look"

associated with "lean away") were more accurately judged over all stories than incongruently behaving stimulus persons regardless of self-disclosure scores.

5. Time taken to tell the three stories was unrelated to accuracy in judgment of the emotional themes of the stories.

Study 2: Normal and Schizophrenic Stimulus Persons—Student Judges

1. Normals, but not schizophrenics, showed greatest direct gaze on the happy story and least direct gaze on the sad story. The pattern was reversed for downward gazes for normals but not for schizophrenics. Thus, normals, but not schizophrenics, showed the greatest direct minus gaze differences on the happy story, least on the sad.

2. The gaze pattern described above was more discriminable in the behavior of those normal stimulus persons whose verbal stories were independently judged to express consistently intense emotion across all three experiences. This was not found for schizophrenics.

3. Where silent films of stimulus persons telling the three affective experiences were shown to both male and female observers, the observers' labeling of the affects correlated positively and significantly with ease of discriminating within-story direct minus down gaze differences *across the three stories*. That is, the story accompanied by the greatest direct minus down difference would be cailed "happy," the least, "sad" (regardless of the verbal theme) if the pattern difference were clearly different from story to story. No sex differences between observers' judgments were found.

4. While the correlation cited above was positive and significant for the combined sample of normal and schizophrenic stimulus persons (rho = .52), further analysis showed the correlation to be strikingly higher for normal as compared to schizophrenic stimulus persons (rhos were .96 and .30, respectively).

5. High discriminability of the direct minus down gaze pattern is associated with very inaccurate judgment of the affects (normal and schizophrenic) if the pattern deviates markedly from the postulated affective gaze-direction model.

6. Direct gaze of normal stimulus persons combined over all stories tended to be less, though not significantly less, than that recorded overall for schizophrenics.

7. The stimulus persons' direct gaze did not correlate significantly with the accuracy of observers' judgments of normal, schizophrenic, or combined normal and schizophrenic stimulus persons.

8. Time taken to tell stories did not correlate significantly with accuracy in judgment of the emotional theme of the stories of normals, schizophrenics, or of both together.

The results of both studies strongly suggest that gaze behavior is an important component in the nonverbal expressive displays that accompany the emotion-relevant speech of normal women. There is also the suggestion that observers trained to be alert to the nuances of nonverbal concomitants of emotion may be more affected by variations in the amount of direct gaze. The overall amount of direct gaze that the stimulus persons displayed as they retold their three emotional experiences was directly and positively associated with accurate judgment of the stories by our small panel of psychiatrists in the first study, but not by our much larger panel of college-age students in the second.

Similarly, the generality of the effect of congruence of direct gaze and postural inclination upon accuracy of judgment of the three emotions studied remains open to question. Postural inclination was not compared to either direct gaze or the gaze-direction difference pattern in the second study. Thus we do not know whether or not congruence–incongruence would have affected the judgments of students in ways similar to the effect on psychiatrists.

Though the data from the second study provide no evidence for or against the hypothesis that congruent gaze and postural cues are concomitant features of the emotional displays of more easily judged stimulus persons, the data in the first study provide a reasonable rationale for the hypothesis. The curvilinear relationship between happy visual attention and cognitive self-disclosure graphed in Figure 1 suggests that persons differ in the extent to which they act out their stated willingness to relate closely to others. we speculate that the instruction to disclose affectively loaded thoughts to another aroused conflict in some persons but not in others. We are reminded of the "intimacy equilibrium" posited by Argyle and Dean (1965) as an explanation of why some people may be quite forthcoming on one dimension of closeness but inhibited with respect to disclosing such cues on other dimensions of behavior. Perhaps the revelation of personal information required by this technique motivates some persons more than others to achieve and intimacy equilibrium by nonverbal behaviors characteristic of withdrawal or distance (reduced eye contact, minimal forward lean).

In any event, the *ad hoc* analysis of congruency of two categories of nonverbal behaviors of stimulus persons in the first study showed that the affect stories of consistently close or distant persons were more easily judged than were the stories of inconsistent persons. Ekman and Friesen (1969b) have described differences in the extent to which different parts of the body "leak" nonverbal cues when individuals attempt to withhold information from another. Perhaps when one has conflicting tendencies to express and to withhold information, the resulting ambivalence would be reflected in inconsistency between gaze and postural orientation. When there is no conflict with respect to either expressing or withholding affective information, such cues, whether indications of psychological closeness or distance, would be consistent.

While further research is necessary to delineate unambiguous and reliable sets of cues for the assessment of intimacy in a variety of relationships and cultural settings, our findings suggest that there are behavioral manifestations of closeness that can be identified and meaningfully encoded and decoded. when these cues are congruent, affective messages are more effectively received.

It is of interest to note that a cognitive self-report measure of general openness to others (Jourard's Self-Disclosure Scale) was unrelated to either of the concrete behavior cues (physical distance from or visual attention to an interviewer), and appears to have no bearing on how readily the affect of the presenter can be judged. This is not to say that there are no systematic interrelationships between and among verbal and nonverbal indicators of immediacy that will facilitate effective encoding and decoding of affective displays. We do, however, suggest that the results of the two studies reported in this chapter showed that a cognitive self-report measure of traits or attitudes (e.g., Jourard's Self-Disclosure instrument) was less likely to be positively related to nonverbal cues of immediacy (Study 1) than was an indication of cognitive self-disclosure elicited in the immediate situation—a measure such as the intensity rating of the verbal expression of personal emotional experiences (Study 2).

In our second study, we attempted to go beyond the use of a single gaze direction, whether direct or avoidant, to study both encoding and decoding of emotion-related behavior. We suggested that specific combinations of gaze directions, differing according to the salient emotion, are characteristic of the emotional displays of normal stimulus persons. The stress on combinations of gaze directions inevitably requires that such behaviors be studied over time, for two directions of gaze cannot occur simultaneously. The point emphasized by the present findings is that a gaze-direction model requires a dynamic methodology—that is, the use of films or videotape—to study the encoding and decoding of affective behavior. Since time is a central feature of our methodology, it is appropriate to question whether time alone can explain our results more efficiently than our model. This is not the case, since time was not related to accuracy of judgment. Neither was it related to the size of the Discriminable Gaze Index (Study 2) nor to the judgments predicted by that index. All correlations, whether for normals, schizophrenics or the combined sample, were low and insignificant. Rhos ranged from .37 to −.10.

While our results encourage us to accept the validity of the model with reference to both encoding and decoding of the three affects studied, certain limitations on the generality of the model must be noted. To establish the model's relevance to the encoding of affects, the gaze behavior of many more stimulus persons must be recorded. Especially needed are more persons who would be consistently and intensely involved in relating their three affective experiences as well as more who would be consistently bland. While consistently high and consistently low involvement was very strongly associated with the extent to which the direct minus down gaze differences did or did not fit the ideal rank-order across stories (happy, angry, sad), reaffirmation of this relationship with a larger sample of stimulus persons is desirable.

How general is the model with respect to its use in both encoding and decoding? The data of this study were provided only by white middle-class women. Many more varieties of stimulus persons in different national cultures must be tested before its general relevance to encoding behavior can be ascertained. The first author once watched films in which a male member of the Fore cultural group in the southeast highlands of New Guinea was asked to represent joy and sorrow. Ekman (1972) describes the Fore as a preliterate, isolated, Neolithic cultural group, and the stimulus person in question was one who had had little, if any, contact with Western culture. When showing how he felt when representing "watching children play" (happy), the native looked directly at the camera for several seconds while smiling. The representation of the "death of a child" (sad) involved a directly downcast gaze, among other display features. While it is encouraging that a male person from a cultural group greatly different from that of our female stimulus persons showed gaze-direction behavior consistent with our affect model, such limited evidence of cross-cultural generality must be more systematically investigated both within and across several national cultures.

Tomkins (1962,1963), Izard (1971), and Ekman's (1972) theory of facial expressions of emotions posits the operation of cultural display rules that interfere with pure manifestations of the universal facial affect program. While the facial affect program appears to refer to the firing of a particular pattern of facial muscles (expression) rather than to gaze attention and avoidance *per se*, it is highly probable that display rules exist for the latter as well. The general test of our model requires that we use stimulus persons from a variety of cultural and national groups.

Before turning to a consideration of our model's relevance to decoding the affects, we note that the mean overall percentage of direct visual behavior of our schizophrenic sample is approximately 48%, some 8% higher than the mean recorded for our normal controls, and that mean differences are consistent across affect stories. While this is not a significant difference, it is the reverse of what has been found in previous studies summarized by Argyle and Cook (1976), namely, that while some investigations show that schizophrenics look at others significantly less (Lefcourt, Rotenberg, Buck-span, & Steffy, 1967) and others show them to be in the normal range (Rutter & Stephenson, 1972), none shows schizophrenics even tending to look more than normals. Ours is a puzzling finding and adds another to the many contradictions reported in Argyle and Cook's thorough discussion of schizophrenic gaze behavior. We will not attempt to suggest a definitive solution but suggest only that our results support the need to refine and test the hypothesis that schizophrenics indicate an aversion to social contact by means of gaze avoidance.

The data graphed in Figure 5 are relevant to the decoding aspect of our model. Though the data indicate that observers' judgments of stimulus persons' affects are highly correlated with those predicted by our model, we do not claim that these guesses are based only, or even primarily, upon differences in gaze direction across the stories. Gaze-direction differences are only part of the total display—facial expression, gestures, postures, and (in real life) verbal and paravocal material form the complex information pool that the observer integrates to form an impression of the affect. Our findings may be best interpreted only as indicating that the discriminability across stories of the relative differences of direct minus down gazes is an important concomitant of normals' total display. Yet, it is interesting to note that where the pattern was clear, and consistent with the ideal encoder pattern for the three affects, the judgments made were very much more related to the theme of the story than when the discriminable pattern was clear and at variance with the theme. Similarly, where the pattern was consistent with the encoder model but not discriminably clear, the observer was less likely to judge correctly the true theme of the experience. We speculate that the discriminability of the pattern calls attention to the congrunce or incongruence of the gaze to other affect-relevant cues—improving the observer's judgment accuracy in the former case, diminishing it in the latter.

The above suggestions are not applicable to the schizophrenic stimulus persons, for in no case did the direct-to-down gaze differences follow the pattern happy greater than angry, angry greater than sad. We suggest that the schizophrenic data provide another example of the manifestation of inappropriate emotion and emotion-related behavior in schizophrenia.

We introduced the second study with Theodore Piderit's suggestion that to think of an event subtly brings about facial responses similar to those that would occur in the presence of the event. He also suggested that a pleasant thought opens the eyes, that pleasant emotions are accompanied by receptive movements, and that unpleasant emotions are accompanied by movements designed to impede the reception of stimuli. He specifically mentioned the expressive movements of the eyes and implied an interest in gaze direction when he wrote that a person who "habitually looks quickly and lively . . . is mentally lively and flexible," and "A person with a fixating, firm look disposes of energy in thinking and activity" (quoted in Izard, 1971, p. 24). However, his own work was based on a set of still photographs with interchangeable features.

We believe that our results concerning the encoding behavior of consistently intense normals indirectly support his position. To retell an emotional event certainly requires thinking about it, and to look more directly when retelling a happy event than a sad event can be argued to indicate receptivity at least as well as does "opening the eyes." The same can be said for the down gaze that accompanies a sad story. Clearly it involves a movement that can be said to impede the reception of stimuli. Piderit's ideas would seem to be relevant to the direction of gaze as well as to the operation of other aspects of the facial display.

Taken together, the results of both studies provide further evidence that although the direct glance alone is no simple indicator of one's affective state, visual attention indexed as patterns of gaze direction is an integral part of expressive emotional displays. These studies suggest that the investigation of gaze and patterns of gaze in terms of their congruence or incongruence with other indicators of immediacy is a fruitful research direction for both intra- and intercultural research.

REFERENCES

Argyle, M., & Cook, M. *Gaze and mutual gaze* New York: Cambridge University Press, 1976.
Argyle, M., & Dean, J. Eye contact, distance and affiliation. *Sociometry*, 1965, *28*, 289–304.

Bakan, P. The eyes have it. *Psychology Today*, 1971, *4*, 64–67.

Birdwhistell, R. L. *Kinesics and context*. Philadelphia: University of Pennsylvania Press, 1970.

Day, M. E. An eye-movement phenomenon relating to attention, thought and anxiety. *Perceptual and Motor Skills*, 1964, *19*, 443–446.

Dittman, A. T. *Interpersonal messages of emotion*. New York:Springer, 1972.

Dougherty, F. E., Bartlett, E. S., & Izard, C. E. Responses of schizophrenics to expressions of the fundamental emotions. *Journal of Clinical Psychology*, 1974, *30*, 243–246.

Duke, J. D. Lateral eye movement behavior. *Journal of General Psychology*, 1968, *78*, 189–195.

Duncan, S. Nonverbal communication. *Psychological Bulletin*, 1969, *72*, 118–137.

Ekman, P. Universals and cultural differences in facial expression of emotion. In J. K. Cole (Ed.), *Nebraska Symposium on Motivation*, Vol. 19. Lincoln: University of Nebraska Press, 1972.

Ekman, P., & Friesen, W. V. Nonverbal leakage and clues to deception. *Psychiatry*, 1969, *32*, 88–105. (a)

Ekman, P., & Friesen, W. V. The repertoire of nonverbal behavior: Categories, origins, usage, and coding. *Semiotica*, 1969, *1*(1), 49–98. (b)

Ekman, P., Friesen, W. V., & Wellsworth, P. *Emotion in the human face: Guidelines for research and an integration of findings*. New York: Pergamon Press, 1972.

Exline, R. V. Explorations in the process of person perception: Visual interaction in relation to competition, sex, and need for affiliation.*Journal of Personality*, 1963, *31*, 1–20.

Exline, R. V. The glances of power and preference. In J. K. Cole (Ed.), *Nebraska Symposium on Motivation*, Vol. 19. Lincoln: University of Nebraska Press, 1972.

Exline, R. V., Gottheil, E., Paredes, A., & Winkelmayer, R. Gaze direction as a factor in the accurate judgment of nonverbal expressions of affect. *Proceedings of the 76th Annual Convention of the American Psychological Association*, 1968, *3*, 415 (summary).

Exline, R., Gray, D., & Schuette, D. Visual behavior in a dyad as affected by interview content and sex of respondent. *Journal of Personality and Social Psychology*, 1965, *1*, 201–208.

Exline, R. V., & Winters, L. C. Affective relations and mutual glances in dyads. In A. Tomkins & C. Izard (Eds.), *Affect, cognition and personality*. New York: Springer, 1965.

French, E., & Chadwick. I. Some characteristics of affiliation motivation. *Journal of Abnormal Social Psychology*, 1956, *52*, 296–300.

Frijda, N. H. Recognition of emotion. In L. Berkowitz (Ed.), *Advances in Experimental Social Psychology*, Vol. 5. New York: Academic Press, 1969.

Galton, Sir Francis. Measurement of character. *Fortnightly Review*, 1884, *42*, 179–185.

Gottheil, E., Corey, J., & Paredes, A. Psychological and physical dimensions of personal space. *Journal of Psychology*, 1968, *69*, 7–9.

Gottheil, E., Paredes, A., Exline, R. V., & Winkelmayer, R. Communication of affect in schizophrenia. *Archives of General Psychiatry*, 1970, *22*, 439–444.

Gottheil, E., Thorton, C. C., & Exline, R. V. Appropriate and background affect in facial displays of emotion. *Archives of General Psychiatry*, 1976, *33*, 565–568.

Hewes, G. W. The anthropology of posture. *Scientific American*, 1957, *196*, 122–132.

Hinchliffe, M., Lancashire, M., & Roberts, F. J. A Study of eye-contact changes in depressed and recovered psychiatric patients. *British Journal of Psychiatry*, 1971, *119*,(549), 213–215.

Izard, C. E. *The face of emotion*. New York:Appleton-Century-Crofts, 1971.

Jourard, S. M., & Lasakow, P. Some factors in self-disclosure. *Journal of Abnormal Social Psychology*, 1958, *56*, 91–98.

Kinsbourne, M. Eye and head turning indicates cerebral lateralization. *Science*, 1974, *176*, 529–541.

Lefcourt, H. M., Rotenberg, F., Buckspan, R., & Steffy, R. A. Visual interaction and performance of process and reactive schizophrenics as a function of examiner's sex. *Journal of Personality*, 1967, *35*, 535–546.

Libby, W. L., Jr., & Yaklevich, D. Personality determinants of eye contact and direction of gaze aversion. *Journal of Personality and Social Psychology*, 1973, *27*(3), 197–206.

Little, K. B. Personal space. *Journal of Experimental and Social Psychology*, 1965, *1*, 237–247.

McGhie, A. Psychological studies of schizophrenia. In B. A. Maher (Ed.), *Contemporary abnormal psychology*. Harmondsworth, England: Penguin, 1973.

Mehrabian, A. Significance of posture and position in the communication of attitude and status relationships. *Psychological Bulletin*, 1969, *71*, 359–372.

Mehrabian, A. A semantic space for nonverbal behavior. *Journal of Consulting and Clinical Psychology*, 1970, *35*, 248–257.

Mehrabian, A. *Nonverbal communication*. Chicago: Aldine-Atherton, 1972.

Piderit, T. *Wissenschaftliches System der Mimik und Physiognomik*. Detmold, Klingenberg, 1867.

Rosenthal, R., Hall, J. A., DiMatteo, M. R., Rogers, P. L., & Archer, D. *Sensitivity to nonverbal communication: The PONS test*. Unpublished manuscript, Harvard University.

Rubin, Z. Measurement of romantic love. *Journal of Personality and Social Psychology*, 1970, *16*, 265–273.

Rutter, D. R., & Stephenson, G. M. Visual interaction in a group of schizophrenic and depressive patients. *British Journal of Social and Clinical Psychology*, 1972, *11*, 57–65.

Scheflen, A. E. *Communicational structure: Analyses of a psychotherapy transaction*. Bloomington: University of Indiana Press, 1973.

Schutz, W. C. *FIRO: A three-dimensional theory of interpersonal behavior*. New York: Rinehart, 1958.

Shipley, T. E., & Verhoff, J. A. A projective measure of need for affiliation. *Journal of Experimental Psychology*, 1952, *43*, 349–356.

Taylor, D., & Altman, I. Intimacy-scaled stimuli for use in studies of interpersonal relations. *Psychological Reports*, 1966, *19*, 729–730.

Tomkins, S. S. *Affect, imagery, consciousness*. Vol. 1. *The positive affects*. New York: Springer, 1962.

Tomkins, S. S. *Affect, imagery, consciousness*. Vol. 2. *The negative affects*. New York: Springer, 1963.

Wiener, M., & Mehrabian, A. *Language within language: Immediacy, a channel in verbal communication*. New York: Appleton-Century-Crofts, 1968.

Williams, E. An analysis of gaze in schizophrenia. *British Journal of Social and Clinical Psychology*, 1974, *13*, 1–8.

Editor's Introduction

19

This chapter addresses an exceptionally important issue that has significant implications for emotion theory and research as well as for methods of clinical intervention. The issue has achieved its status largely on the basis of a single experiment reported by Schachter and Singer in 1962. We are probably still too close to the action to see this experiment in historical perspective and to determine whether it falls in the camp with those that significantly advance knowledge or with those that discover phlogiston or the N-ray. Put another way, was the Schachter–Singer study and the emotion model it supported a significant factor in the cognitive psychology boom of the past two decades, or did it merely gravitate to an unearned place on the crest of the wave made by such works as Miller, Galanter, and Pribram's *Plans and the Structure of Behavior* and Neisser's *Cognition and Reality*? If one were judging merely by the frequency with which the Schachter–Singer study is cited, one would have to conclude that it is a study of the first rank.

The present chapter provides the most elegant and detailed critique of the Schachter–Singer study that has ever been written. This critique, along with the empirical data from Maslach's modified replication and those from an exact replication by a colleague, show that the Schachter–Singer study was seriously flawed and that the model it proposed is erroneous.

The Schachter–Singer design, results, and conclusions are reviewed in Maslach's chapter, along with those of her own well-controlled experiment. The familiarity of the original study makes a precis unnecessary, but it might be helpful to examine one or two of the issues briefly. It is important to remember that the Schachter–Singer study was concerned with a rare event: mysterious, undifferentiated arousal and exposure to the somewhat unusual emotional behavior of a stranger. The conditions required for the experiment were (1) strong physiological arousal (heart palpitations, tremors, rapid breathing); (2) lack of explanation of the arousal; and (3) varied situational or contextual cues provided by a confederate of the experimenter. These conditions hardly describe the occasions for emotion in daily life. This is not necessarily a fault in a scientific experiment, if attention is called to the limitations on the generalizability of findings. Schachter and Singer did not make clear the rareness of the event they studied. It is so rare as to be strange, and strangeness has been considered by some a natural clue to danger under certain circumstances.

Maslach's chapter and the companion study she summarizes demonstrate that unexplained, undifferentiated physiological arousal is not a necessary and neutral component of emotion that can serve equally well as the physiological basis for anger or joy (or any discrete emotion), depending upon the kind of normative data provided in the situation. It shows that subjects with unexplained, undifferentiated physiological arousal are subsequently more likely to report negative emotion, regardless of whether they were exposed to a happy or an angry confederate. One important question could not be answered either by the Schachter–Singer study or by the replications discussed by Maslach. Was the unexplained, undifferentiated arousal actually a component of the subsequently reported emotion, or was it merely a set of cues or conditions that triggered cognitions that in turn activated one or another specific negative emotion, which then may have been amplified or otherwise influenced by the arousal?

The Emotional Consequences of Arousal without Reason

19

CHRISTINA MASLACH

The study of emotion has had a rather erratic history in psychology. Although initially considered an important subject for scientific inquiry (James, 1884), it was often excluded from psychological theorizing, largely because of controversies over its definition. More recently, several models of emotion have been developed and are being subjected to empirical test. However, there continue to be major differences in the conceptualization of emotion, with various researchers defining it in terms of motives, behavioral responses, the sensations of bodily changes, subjective feelings, and cognitive processes.

Within the more cognitive models of emotion, the most influential work has been the classic experiment by Schachter and Singer (1962). Two dimensions of emotion were independently manipulated in the study: physiological arousal and cognitive cues. Male subjects either were made to feel physiologically aroused, via an injection of epinephrine, or were not (they received a placebo injection). Some of the aroused subjects were correctly informed as to the source of their arousal, while the others were either uninformed or were given an erroneous explanation. Cross-cutting this manipulation of arousal was the manipulation of the emotional cues presented in the immediate situation. Subjects interacted with someone who was acting either euphoric and exuberant or angry and upset. According to the authors, the results showed that subjects who were experiencing arousal but had no prior appropriate explanation for it used the available situational cues to label their emotion. If they were with a euphoric person, they labeled their own arousal as "euphoria," but if they were with an angry person, the same physiological arousal was labeled

---

CHRISTINA MASLACH • University of California, Berkeley, California. This research was financially supported by the Office of Naval Research Contract NOOO 14-67-A-0112-0041 to Philip Zimbardo.

as "anger." Subjects who were unaroused or who already had an appropriate explanation for their arousal were reported to be uninfluenced by the emotional cues provided by the other person.

This experiment represented an important conceptual change from previous theoretical positions, all of which postulated a direct causal relationship between physiological arousal and cognitions about emotional states. In contrast, Schachter and Singer proposed that the factors of physiological arousal and emotional cognition were independent. According to their theory, which seems to have been inspired by the work of Marañon (1924), these two factors interacted with each other to produce an emotional state. Either factor alone was not sufficient to produce a true emotion. In addition to this interactionist model, Schachter and Singer made a second significant contribution by demonstrating the importance of situational determinants of emotion.

The theoretical impact of this study cannot be overestimated, foreshadowing as it did the rise of cognitive analysis in social psychology. This general line of thinking played an important role in the current development of attribution theory, as a result of its emphasis on the role of cognitions in defining reality (see Jones, Kanouse, Kelley, Nisbett, Valins, & Weiner, 1971). Furthermore, it has inspired several new lines of theory and research about a variety of internal feeling states, including fear, hunger, passion, and pain (see Schachter, 1971; Walster, 1971; London & Nisbett, 1974; Mandler, 1975).

I. CRITIQUE OF THE SCHACHTER AND SINGER STUDY

Despite its ingenious paradigm and its theoretical contributions, the Schachter and Singer study cannot be accepted uncritically. Indeed, a close analysis of the methodology and the results seriously questions the authors' conclusions and interpretations (see also the critiques by Plutchik & Ax, 1967; Lazarus, 1968; Leventhal, 1974).

A. Empirical Issues

Although Schachter and Singer's conclusion is a provocative one, is it in fact supported by the evidence? A careful inspection of the reported findings suggests that the most reasonable answer is "no." The initial data analysis reveals *no* significant difference in self-reported emotion between any of the unexplained arousal groups and the placebo control groups. Although the authors point to the predicted overall pattern of means within each emotion condition, this pattern is not very dramatic in size since the difference in emotion between any of the groups amounts to less than one single scale unit on a 9-point scale. The theory also requires absolute differences in emotion ratings between the experimental groups of the euphoria and anger conditions.

However, *all* subjects reported feeling slightly happy, regardless of the emotional cues provided by the euphoric and angry confederates.

The behavioral data are not much more convincing. The comparison between unexplained arousal groups and placebo controls reaches statistical significance only in the anger condition, not in the euphoria one. Even though this pattern of "anger units" is in line with the authors' theory, the size of this response is certainly not. The low mean score for subjects with unexplained arousal could conceivably represent merely one instance of verbal agreement with the angry confederate's position over nearly 20 minutes of interaction. Somewhat stronger behavioral differences emerged after a sizable number of subjects was discarded in an internal analysis.

B. Methodological Issues

There are a number of flaws in the design of the Schachter and Singer study, which further preclude an uncritical acceptance of their conclusions. One of the major difficulties centers on the use of epinephrine to produce physiological arousal, since this drug has different effects for different people. As a result, there was no experimental control of the onset, intensity, or duration of the arousal. An additional problem involves the probability of subjects' attributing their arousal to the injection, in spite of the experimenter's statement that it was only a vitamin supplement without side effects. Receiving an injection and suddenly experiencing arousal are two rather unusual experiences (especially in a psychology laboratory experiment). When they occur in close proximity, it is quite likely that people will assume that one caused the other or that they are somehow related. Indeed 26% of the subjects in the euphoria condition reported being "self-informed" about the injection, in addition to 13% of the anger subjects. More subjects may have also made this association but failed to tell the experimenters for one reason or another.

The euphoria and anger conditions varied in activity level, as well as in the mood of the confederate. In the euphoria condition, the confederate was physically active, while in the anger condition, he sat quietly for most of the time. If the subject joined in the "euphoric" activity, he might then have had an alternative, nonemotional explanation for his physiological state ("I'm feeling aroused because I've been running around"). No such "activity" explanation existed in the anger condition.

Further methodological difficulties involve the dependent measures, which were either confounded, ambiguous, or absent. Because there was no assessment of the emotional cognition factor, it is not known how subjects actually perceived the confederate's mood—as "euphoria" or "anger" or some other emotion. For the factor of physiological arousal, two measures were used—one direct (pulse rate) and one indirect (self-report of physiological symptoms). However, neither of these measures provides an accurate assessment of the ongoing course of the arousal. They were taken at the end of the session and are thus confounded with any physical activity on the part of the subject.

The measures of the subject's emotional response included a self-report of emotional feeling and a series of behavioral ratings made by hidden observers. For the first measure, subjects were asked how "good or happy" they felt and also how "irritated, angry, or annoyed" they were. Rather than presenting these scores separately, the experimenters subtracted each subject's "anger" rating from his "happiness" rating to yield an index of emotional feeling. The meaning of such scores is unclear, since the same score could result from totally different emotional states. For example, a person with a "happy" rating of 2 and an "angry" rating of 0 (no anger) would have a total emotion score of 2, but so would someone with a "happy" rating of 4 and an "angry" (or annoyed or irritated) rating of 2. The compound phrasing of the emotion statements could mean that subjects were responding "good" and "irritated," which are not justifiably translated into the more extreme polarities of "euphoria" versus "anger." Furthermore, these two self-report ratings were the only dimensions of emotion that were measured. If subjects labeled their arousal in terms of other emotions, there was no way of assessing it.

For the behavioral measure, different ratings were used for the euphoria and anger conditions, and so no direct comparison of the two is possible. Secondly, various behaviors were arbitrarily assigned different weights (e.g., flying paper airplanes was +3; disagreeing with the angry confederate was −2). In the euphoria condition, each weight was then multiplied by an estimate of the amount of time spent by the subject in that activity (although, inexplicably, this was not done in the anger condition). For both conditions, these weights were then summed into a single, overall index whose meaning is not at all clear.

II. FAILURE OF AN EXACT REPLICATION

Given the theoretical significance of the Schachter and Singer study, one would expect that more methodologically rigorous replications had already been done in the decade since it appeared. Surprisingly, only one attempt has been made to replicate the study. Marshall (1976) tested 80 male subjects in an exact replication of the basic Schachter and Singer procedure for the euphoria condition. Epinephrine injections were used to create a state of physiological arousal, and the confederate followed the euphoria routine outlined in the original study (throwing paper basketballs, twirling a hula hoop, etc.). Marshall added some slight modifications to improve the basic paradigm, such as conducting the experiment in a physical therapy room of the student health center. This provided an appropriate setting for the drug injections and the vision tests and made the presence of hula hoops and other equipment seem reasonable. Marshall also included a variety of new dependent measures, such as pre- and post-self-reports of emotion and continuous physiological recording via telemetry.

Even with this ideal procedural replication, Marshall found *no* empirical support for Schachter and Singer's conclusions. Subjects who had received the standard (.5 cc) epinephrine injection, along with an "inadequate" explanation of its side effects, did not differ from placebo controls in either emotional affect or behavior. Although not statistically significant, whatever differences did exist were in the direction of *less* positive affect for the experimental group. To see if significant differences would emerge if the arousal were stronger, Marshall increased the epinephrine dosage level for some of the subjects. These subjects did experience a significant change in intensity of physiological arousal. However, they reported a *negative* emotional state, rather than the positive "euphoria" predicted by Schachter and Singer. This self-report of negative affect occurred even when subjects behaved in a positive, sociable manner with the euphoric confederate.

III. ALTERNATIVE VIEWS

The lack of supportive evidence in both the Schachter and Singer (1962) and the Marshall (1976) experiments leads one to consider some alternative hypotheses. One possibility is that the Schachter and Singer theory is incorrect. The qualitative differentiation of emotions may have some basis other than situational cues. Furthermore, an undifferentiated autonomic arousal may not be the physiological basis for emotion. For example, theorists such as Tomkins (1962) and Izard (1971) have argued that emotions are a function of the somatic system and that the autonomic system is involved subsequently to the initial occurrence of emotion. While the Schachter and Singer and the Marshall studies do not address this theory directly, their findings support it in an oblique way by their failure to show any systematic relationship between undifferentiated arousal and any particular discrete emotions. The Schachter and Singer model may also be incorrect in its assumption that autonomic arousal is a neutral activator. Marshall's findings suggest that such arousal may have a negative quality that will overshadow any positive emotional cognitions. If so, this would argue for the importance of physiological feedback in determining the quality (and not just the quantity) of the emotion.

An alternative interpretation is that the Schachter and Singer theory is correct but that the particular paradigm did not provide a good test of it. Schachter and Singer present their model as an explanation of emotion in everyday situations, in which the physiological and cognitive factors are completely entwined. However, they test their model by separating the two factors and creating a situation of unexplained autonomic arousal. Such a situation is rather rare and unusual in everyday life, and it may be erroneous to generalize from this special case to more common emotional experiences. Because of its strangeness, the situation of unexplained arousal may not be affectively neutral, as Schachter and Singer assume, but may instead produce a bias in the search for an emotional cognition.

A. Negative Biasing

The idea that unexplained arousal is an affectively neutral state seems intuitively correct only for someone who is experiencing such arousal for the first time (such as a child) and who must look to other people and/or the situation to make sense of this strange and puzzling experience. The concept does not apply as well to people who have had numerous experiences pairing arousal with emotional labels and with appropriate arousal instigators. If they were to feel aroused without knowing why, it would be not only an unusual experience but also a disturbing or even frightening one, since this uncertainty would be felt as a loss of personal control over their own internal states. Indeed, the concept of unexplained arousal is very close to the clinical definition of "free-floating anxiety," which is always characterized by negative emotional affect. Therefore, unexplained arousal may generate a *biased*, rather than an unbiased, scanning of evidence and alternative hypotheses. That is, the search for an appropriate cognitive label for the arousal could be biased by a retrieval algorithm that selects primarily from available negative instances. A negative bias also seems more probable because noticeable physical arousal is a far more common concomitant of negative emotional experiences than of positive ones. With the exception of sexual excitement, positive affects are typically lacking in the arousal symptoms of palpitations, tremor, and rapid breathing.

This proposed alternative view suggests that unexplained arousal in adults leads to an initial negative emotional biasing. The resulting affective state may in turn generate a cognitive search for its causal antecedents (the "why" behind the emotion). Without such causal knowledge, behavioral–situational control strategies cannot be activated; with such knowledge comes at least a sense of cognitive control. As Dostoevski (1876) reminds us, "the greatest happiness is to know the source of unhappiness." But is unexplained arousal as likely to be a source of happiness as of unhappiness? According to the present argument, the answer would be "no." In contrast to the Schachter and Singer hypothesis, it predicts that people will not label their unexplained arousal as euphoria or happiness but instead will use negative emotional cognitions.

B. An Expanded Search

This alternative view still accepts the Schachter and Singer notion of a cognitive search for an emotional explanation. However, their experimental test of the search process was a narrow one that did not consider the full range of information that a person might have used. Basically, they looked only at the impact of the confederate's mood on the subject and ignored any other information in the immediate situation or in the subject's life experiences. For example, they did not consider the possibility that a person will search his or her memory for past events or prior comparable situations that would provide an appropriate explanation for the current state of arousal. Subjects might have tried to recall similar situations in which they had felt aroused (such as being in a testing situation or visiting a doctor). They might have then used these memories to derive an appropriate emotional cognition ("I must be getting upset about the tests they are going to do, since I always worry about failing" or "I've never liked getting stuck with needles by doctors, so that's why this injection bothers me"). In other words, subjects may have indeed searched for an appropriate cognition, as the theory predicts, but they may have relied on sources of information other than those limited to the confederate's behavior in the immediate social situation. To the extent that subjects' explanations were based on their past history, their health, or nonsocial aspects of the environment, it might explain the relatively weak impact of the confederate's mood or the within-condition variance that attenuates treatment effects.

Although Schachter and Singer postulate that the relevant emotional cognitions arise from the immediate *situation*, they operationalize this concept in terms of a *person* who serves as a social comparison referent for the subjects. They predict that it is the emotion displayed by this comparison person that will be the "appropriate cognition" that the subjects use to label their own arousal. However, such a prediction must rest on the assumptions that subjects will view the other person as (1) being someone similar and comparable to them; (2) responding to a set of situational demands that are also impinging on the subjects; and (3) behaving in an appropriate way to these demands.

The first assumption may be justified in the experiment, since the comparison person was the same sex and age as the subject and had a similar educational background (however, there are considerable differences even within this common population). There is less evidence to support the other two assumptions. A close examination of the experimental procedure reveals that the comparison person was not always responding to the same situation as confronted the subject. For example, there is nothing inherent in a messy room that should cause people to experience euphoria. Given this lack of situational inducements,[1] the confederate's playful behavior says more about his

---

[1] In a personal communication, Bibb Latané (who was the confederate in the euphoria condition) pointed out that the confederate exerted a great deal of pressure on the subject to join him in the "euphoric" behavior and that this constituted a relevant situational inducement. However, this raises even more problems in interpreting the data, since the subject's behavior would then reflect social conformity rather than an experienced emotion. One could also argue that once subjects had been induced to imitate the confederate, they would make judgments of their emotional state on the basis of observing their own behavior (Bem, 1972; Walters & Amoroso, 1967). According to this self-perception interpretation, the "appropriate cognition" is not the mood of the confederate but the behavior of oneself (which has been induced by the confederate).

particular personality than it does about the appropriate way to respond to a situation. This *dispositional* interpretation is made especially salient by the confederate's own statement that "this is one of my good days" (Schachter & Singer, 1962, p. 384). From the subject's point of view, whatever is causing the confederate to feel euphoric is something unique to him and not something that they share in common. In contrast, the anger condition does provide some relevant situational demands, since the confederate's anger is directed at a long and insulting questionnaire that the subject is also completing.

Finally, there is not much evidence to suggest that subjects would view the confederate's behavior as appropriate to the situation. In both experimental conditions, the confederate behaved in unusual ways (agitated, manic, and assertive), especially compared to the norm of quiet compliance that is generally characteristic of research subjects. Spontaneously playing with paper airplanes and hula hoops is not a typical thing to do in a scientific laboratory, nor is abruptly walking out of the experiment. To the extent that subjects perceive the confederate as acting in idiosyncratic, unusual, or inappropriate ways, he loses his social-comparison reference power, and subjects would not be likely to label their own arousal in terms of their cognition of his mood. Instead, as argued earlier, they would probably turn to other aspects of the immediate situation and use those cognitions to arrive at an emotional explanation.

IV. CURRENT STUDY

The current research was designed to investigate further the process of a cognitive search for the causal antecedents of unexplained arousal. Since an exact replication of the Schachter and Singer experiment has been done by Marshall (1976), the present study involved a modified replication in which procedural elements were designed to correct some of the original methodological problems. These improvements are described in the following sections.

A. Unexplained Physiological Arousal

An arousal state was produced by a hypnotic induction rather than a drug injection. Previous research has demonstrated that marked physiological changes can be produced hypnotically (see the review by Sarbin & Slagle, 1972). In addition, the use of hypnosis instead of epinephrine allowed for a better degree of experimental control over the onset and the maintenance of the physiological arousal. The arousal symptoms were hypnotically conditioned to a specific cue and were introduced at the appropriate time during the procedure.

In the Schachter and Singer study, the lack of an explanation for the arousal was created by giving subjects the erroneous expectation that either there would be no side effects of the injection or that the effects would be different from those actually experienced. In the present experiment, the lack of an explanation was produced by a posthypnotic suggestion for amnesia of the true cause of the arousal. Subjects experienced physiological arousal but did not know why the arousal was occurring and did not remember that it was due to the hypnotic suggestion. Posthypnotic amnesia is a phenomenon that has been demonstrated in numerous studies (see Cooper's review, 1972) and is believed to involve a temporary disruption of the normal retrieval process (Evans & Kihlstrom, 1973). Cues that normally aid the process of recall are not utilized as they would be in normal waking memory.

B. Cognitive Factors

The scenarios of emotional behavior enacted by the confederate were purposely different from those employed by Schachter and Singer. First of all, the behaviors of the two emotion conditions were directly comparable—the nature, level, and timing of the activity were equivalent in both conditions, and only the confederate's obvious emotional state (happy or angry) was varied. The types of reasons given for the confederate's emotion were the same in both conditions and were also ones that the subject could readily share. Furthermore, the confederate's behavior appeared believable and appropriate in the laboratory setting.

C. Dependent Measures

Several measures were added to the study, both to assess the validity of the experimental manipulations and to reflect more precisely the differences in emotional behavior. The occurrence of the arousal state was measured directly by the physiological recording of heart rate and galvanic skin response. In addition, two indirect measures of arousal were used: self-report of physical symptoms and learning performance. The latter was suggested by the work of Easterbrook (1959), which demonstrated that high emotional arousal reduces cue utilization. The subject's perception of the confederate's mood and personal reaction to the confederate were assessed by questionnaire items. The subject's emotional state was assessed by a battery of scales (including the two used by Schachter and Singer), as well as by open-ended questions. Also, the subject's behavior with the confederate was monitored and scored by hidden observers who used common behavioral rating scales for both emotion conditions.

D. Hypotheses

The proposed modification and extension of the concept of cognitive search leads to some different predictions than those made by Schachter and Singer. These competing hypotheses center on the questions of (1) whether the search is limited to, or goes beyond, the immediate situation; and (2) whether the search is unbiased or biased. On the first question, Schachter and Singer imply that subjects will rely primarily upon the information provided by the confederate to label their own unexplained arousal. In contrast, the current study predicts that subjects will also utilize information from both their past and their present life. Thus, their emotional response will be more independent of the confederate's mood and less constrained by the immediate situation.

On the second question, Schachter and Singer argue that subjects with inadequately explained arousal will engage in an unbiased search for a cognitive label—it would be equally easy to label the arousal as "happiness" or as "anger," depending solely on the cognitive aspects of the situation. In contrast to this "plasticity" hypothesis, the current study proposes that the cognitive search will be biased toward labels for negative emotions, since a state of unexplained arousal is initially anxiety-provoking for adult subjects. Thus, both theories agree that in the presence of a confederate who is behaving in an angry manner, subjects experiencing unexplained arousal will use negative emotional labels to define their state. However, the two approaches differ in the anticipated emotional consequences in the euphoria condition. As opposed to the Schachter and Singer predictions, a biased scanning model hypothesizes that subjects experiencing unexplained arousal in the presence of a confederate who is behaving in a happy manner will be more likely to use negative than positive emotional labels. This is because their search for an explanation is biased by the learned associations of unexplained arousal with negative antecedents or consequences. Since overt behavior is controlled to a large extent by social contingencies, there should be public conformity to the confederate's standardized routines, but not necessarily a corresponding positive emotional state. For those not experiencing arousal or those given an appropriate explanation for their arousal, both theories agree on the absence of a search for cognitive labels of emotion.

V. METHOD[2]

The study consisted of two experiments that followed the same procedural format. The testing session was divided into two parts. The purpose of Part I was to establish a verbally conditioned arousal response to a specific cue. Sub-

---

[2] Only a summary overview of the methodology is presented in this chapter. For details of the procedure, see Maslach (1979).

jects were given the hypnotic suggestion that they would experience four physiological symptoms (increased breathing, increased heart rate, moist palms, sinking feeling in stomach) when they saw the word *start*. In addition, posthypnotic amnesia for the source of this arousal was suggested. To determine if this arousal response involved substantial physiological changes, continuous recordings were made of the subjects' heart rate (HR) and galvanic skin response (GSR). Subjects were also asked to describe their mood state both before and after the arousal response, using the Nowlis Mood-Adjective Checklist (1963). In Part II of the experiment, this arousal response was either elicited or not in the presence of a same-sex confederate who was behaving happily or angrily. While doing a learning task, subjects saw either the arousal cue word (*start*) or a neutral one. The confederate went through a prearranged series of behaviors (e.g., talking to the subject, working with various test materials) while expressing either happy or angry emotions. Hidden observers recorded the subject's verbal and nonverbal responses, as well as the amount of time that the subject looked at the confederate. At the end of this emotional modeling period, the confederate left the room and the subject completed two questionnaires that assessed the efficacy of the experimental manipulations and the extent to which the subject's arousal was interpreted in terms of the emotion displayed by the confederate.

The first experiment consisted of a 2 × 2 factorial design with the addition of two unhypnotized control groups. There were two levels of arousal: aroused (hypnotized + arousal cue) and unaroused (hypnotized + no arousal cue). There were two levels of confederate emotion: happy and angry. Subjects who were trained in hypnosis were randomly assigned to these four conditions, with six subjects per cell. Subjects who were not trained in hypnosis were randomly assigned to the two unhypnotized groups (not hypnotized + arousal cue)—six were in the happy condition and six in the angry condition. The experimental conditions of most interest are the two aroused groups, in which the subjects were both physiologically aroused and exposed to a happy or an angry model. The arousal was produced by a combination of two factors: training in hypnosis and a conditioned arousal stimulus. The unaroused and unhypnotized conditions lacked either one or the other of these two factors and thus represent two different types of control groups.

Because the results of the first experiment did not replicate those found by Schachter and Singer for the "euphoria" treatment, two additional experimental conditions were tested to discover the basis for these differing outcomes. In both conditions, additional subjects were given the arousal treatment (hypnotized + arousal cue) and were exposed only to the display of happy emotion by the confederate. One of these additional groups (informed arousal) remained aware of the basis for their arousal since they were not given any suggestion for posthypnotic amnesia. In fact, they were told that they would remember having been informed of the causal relationship between their arousal and the prior conditioning experience. This group parallels that of the informed treatment in the Schachter and Singer study. The other group (simplified arousal) was given only two physiological symptoms for the hypnotically induced arousal state (heart beating faster, respiration increasing), rather than the four symptoms used in the first experiment. It was conceivable that the other two symptoms (sinking feeling in the stomach, moist hands), although found in reactions to epinephrine, too strongly suggested a negative arousal state. This may have been the reason for the negative emotions experienced by aroused subjects in the happy condition, rather than the predicted biasing effect of unexplained arousal. The simplified-arousal condition was designed to ensure a more purely neutral arousal than may have existed in the first study. As before, subjects trained in hypnosis were randomly assigned to these two conditions, with six subjects per group.

A. Subjects

From the introductory psychology course subject pool at Stanford University, 48 undergraduate subjects (25 males and 23 females)[3] were selected and were paid for their participation in this experiment. All subjects had received scores of high hypnotic susceptibility on the Harvard Group Scale of Hypnotic Susceptibility (Shor & Orne, 1962). Of these subjects, 36 were randomly assigned to training in hypnosis prior to the experiment, while 12 subjects were randomly assigned to control groups that did not receive such training. The hypnotic training, which averaged about 10 hours per subject, was conducted in small groups and utilized a relaxed and permissive approach (see Zimbardo, Maslach, & Marshall, 1972). The training program sampled a wide variety of hypnotic experiences and included as criterion tests: (1) the successful completion of posthypnotic suggestions with accompanying amnesia, and (2) increased tolerance of ischemic pain (a measure developed by Lenox, 1970).

Throughout the experimental session, trained and untrained subjects were treated identically except, of course, for a brief hypnotic induction for the trained subjects. At the end of the session, the hypnotic suggestions for the arousal response and the amnesia were removed, and subjects were interviewed about their reactions to the study. All subjects promised not to talk about the experiment until it was completed. Experimental silence was maintained, and all subjects later participated in an elaborate debriefing session conducted in a series of informal small-group sessions. There was no evidence of any emotional carry-over beyond the immediate experimental setting.

---

[3] There were no significant differences between the responses of male and female subjects, so their data were combined.

VI. RESULTS[4]

Presentation of the results will be organized around six issues: (1) effectiveness of the physiological arousal manipulation; (2) evaluation of the confederate's mood; (3) behavioral differences between treatments; (4) experienced emotional differences between treatments; (5) attribution of arousal and emotions; and (6) comparison of the informed and the simplified-arousal control groups with the arousal groups of the first experiment.

A. Physiological Arousal

The use of hypnotic training and the conditioning procedure in Part I of the testing session did indeed produce a strong, persistent level of physiological arousal. Trained hypnotic subjects displayed a substantial increase in heart rate and a greater number of GSRs when they saw the arousal cue word (as compared to neutral cues), while untrained subjects did not. This difference in arousal response is even more striking given the fact that both trained and untrained subjects showed a more rapid recognition of the cue word (as evidenced by the shorter latency and higher amplitude of the first GSR).

A comparison of the Mood-Adjective Checklists that were completed before and after the arousal response reveals that a marked shift in emotions occurred for the trained hypnotic subjects. Once they were experiencing a state of unexplained arousal, they checked more negative emotional terms and fewer terms that represented positive emotions or passive responses. In contrast, the untrained subjects did not display a change in reported mood. These findings suggest that a state of unexplained arousal is not as affectively neutral as Schachter and Singer had assumed.

Because hypnotic subjects responded physiologically to the arousal cue in Part I, it was assumed that they would respond similarly when they again saw this stimulus during Part II of the testing session. Unfortunately, we could not directly assess the validity of this assumption because the lack of telemetry equipment made it impossible to record the subjects' physiological responses while they were freely interacting with the confederate. However, two indirect measures of arousal provide support for this reasoning.

The first of these measures was the subject's recall performance on the learning task. Since the word list either did or did not contain the arousal cue, it was thought that differences in subsequent arousal states might interfere with the recall process. Although there was no between-group difference in

---

[4] Only a summary overview of the major results is presented in this chapter. All reported findings achieve at least a .05 level of significance (two-tailed). For detailed statistical analyses, see Maslach (1979).

overall recall accuracy, subjects in the arousal groups made significantly fewer errors of commission than did the unaroused and unhypnotized groups. It appears that subjects performing under the distracting influence of intense arousal were less likely to search their memory for words that might have been on the list and thus were less likely to produce commission errors by recalling "new" words. Rather, they seemed to write down only the words they had stored in readily accessible memory and then to stop—leading to relatively more errors of omission than of commission.

The second indirect measure of arousal was part of the final questionnaire. Subjects were given a list of eight physiological symptoms and asked to indicate which (if any) they were now experiencing. The percentage of subjects who checked each symptom was calculated for each of the experimental conditions. From 92 to 100% of the subjects in the aroused conditions reported experiencing each of the four suggested symptoms, while only 26 to 52% of the unaroused and unhypnotized subjects reported having even a single one of the symptoms.

As indicated earlier, all of the hypnotic subjects had to pass a criterion test of responding to posthypnotic suggestions with accompanying amnesia. Thus there was prior evidence that the amnesia suggestion would be effective for the aroused subjects. Further assessment of the success of the posthypnotic suggestion was provided by questions on the final questionnaire, as well as by an in-depth post-experimental interview conducted by a clinical psychologist who was not affiliated with the experimenters. Both sources of data clearly support the conclusion that the trained hypnotic subjects who were given an amnesia suggestion were unaware of the true cause of their arousal.

B. Perception of Confederate

Three bipolar scale items of seven alternatives focused on the confederate's emotional behavior (sad-happy, angry-peaceful, friendly-unfriendly); the mean score for these items served as a check on the confederate manipulation. On this index, the data were, without any exception, in opposite directions for subjects exposed to the happy versus the angry confederate. Subjects in the happy condition evaluated the confederate's mood as significantly more positive than the neutral midpoint of zero, while subjects in the angry condition reported it as significantly more negative than zero.

Five bipolar scales dealt with the subject's more general personal reaction to the confederate (intelligent-unintelligent, irritating-nice, pleasant-unpleasant, rude-polite, someone I want to know better–do not want to know better), and a mean score of these scales was computed for each subject. Subjects had more negative reactions in the angry condition than in the happy one. While the personal reaction of the angry subjects was significantly more negative than zero, the reaction of the happy subjects was neutral and did not differ from the zero midpoint.

C. Overt Emotional Behavior

Differences in the behavior of the confederate were reflected in systematic differences in the subjects' overt behavior. Subjects in the presence of a happy confederate exhibited a significantly higher amount of positive social behaviors than did subjects who were with the angry confederate. This was true for both verbal behaviors (such as agreeing with the confederate) and nonverbal behaviors (such as smiling and nodding). All of these behaviors had been independently coded by two hidden observers (interrater reliability was at least +.80). The amount of time spent looking at the confederate was a function of both the confederate's behavior and the arousal conditions. Basically, subjects in the angry aroused group did not look as much at the confederate as did those in all the other groups (which did not differ from each other).

D. Reported Emotional Experience

Although the confederate's mood had a demonstrable effect on the subjects' overt behavior, it did not influence their reported emotional state. Regardless of whether they had been exposed to the angry or the happy confederate, aroused subjects reacted negatively across a range of self-reported items of emotion. Control subjects, who were not experiencing a comparable state of unexplained arousal, either did not react emotionally or reacted with a more positive emotional tone.

This basic pattern of results was found for the two questionnaire items used by Schachter and Singer, whether analyzed separately or in a combined score. In addition, subjects completed eight bipolar scale items on emotional response (tense-relaxed, confident-apprehensive, anxious-calm, open-closed, happy-sad, irritated-not irritated, serene-annoyed, angry-peaceful). Each of these items was analyzed separately, and when it was found that they each showed the same pattern of results, they were combined into a single index of emotional response (see Figure 1). Again, on this overall index, there was a significant main effect of arousal condition, and a comparison of means revealed that the aroused groups reported a significantly more negative emotional state than both the unaroused and the unhypnotized groups (which did not differ from each other). The negative emotions reported by the aroused conditions were significantly different from the neutral midpoint of zero. While the unhypnotized subjects were neutral in their emotions, the unaroused subjects often rated themselves as feeling a positive emotional state. Apparently,

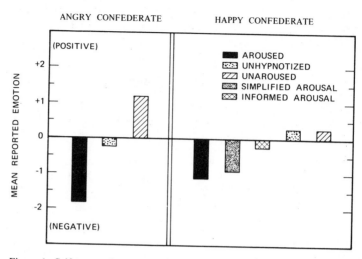

Figure 1. Self-reported emotion (mean self-ratings on an eight-scale index of emotion).

the unaroused subjects were responding appropriately to the posthypnotic suggestion that they would feel relaxed and good when they came out of hypnosis, while the unhypnotized subjects were unable to respond similarly to that same suggestion. The positive feelings of the unaroused group offer a dramatic comparison level for the negative reaction reported by the aroused subjects (despite the same posthypnotic suggestion to feel good).

E. Attribution of Causality

On the final questionnaire, subjects were asked if they knew why they felt as they did and, if so, to state the reason. These responses were scored by judges who were blind to both the purpose of the experiment and the condition of the subject. The aroused subjects always reported reasons for a *negative* emotional state, regardless of the mood expressed by the confederate. Some subjects said they were worried about performing well on the experimental tests, others said they were feeling upset about upcoming final exams, while still others labeled their arousal as irritation generated by the confederate's "talkativeness." In only one case did a subject explicitly state that the confederate's mood determined his own: "The other guy was really hassled—it rubbed off."

It is possible that the posthypnotic suggestion had the effect of blocking any search for an explanation of the experienced arousal, rather than merely preventing the "correct" explanation. This does not seem to be the case, since the number of aroused subjects (67%) who said they knew the cause of their current feelings was just as high as that of the unaroused and unhypnotized groups. However, in not a single instance did the aroused subjects state that the reason was related to the experimentally induced cause of posthypnotic suggestions.

Subjects were also asked to describe previous situations in which they had felt as they now did, and these open-ended responses were also rated by the judges. Aroused subjects described situations that were rated as more negative (e.g., waiting to take an exam, waiting to see the dentist, hearing bad news) than those described by subjects in both the unaroused and the unhypnotized conditions.

F. Comparison of Arousal Control Groups

To clarify alternative interpretations of these findings, two additional control groups (informed arousal and simplified arousal) were tested in the happy confederate condition. The former group was not given the suggestion of amnesia for the cause of their arousal, while the latter was given an arousal suggestion limited to only two general physiological symptoms, rather than the four given originally.

Both of the control groups displayed basically the same pattern of physiological arousal as the happy-aroused subjects in the first experiment. They showed the same increase in HR, similar changes on the Mood-Adjective Checklist, the same pattern of recall errors, but not a similar change in GSR.[5] On the self-report of physiological symptoms, all of the informed-arousal subjects reported experiencing the four suggested arousal symptoms. The simplified arousal subjects reported increased breathing and heart rate, as expected. Surprisingly, however, all of them also reported sweaty palms, and two-thirds reported a sinking feeling in the stomach. Even though they had not received any suggestion for these last two symptoms, they spontaneously generated them as correlates of changes in respiration and heart rate.

The perception of the confederate by the two control groups was the same as that of the happy-aroused group: they rated the confederate's mood as positive and their personal reaction to him or her as neutral. They showed the same pattern of positive social behaviors (both verbal and nonverbal) in their interaction with the confederate and also the same pattern of looking behavior.

Overall, then, the two arousal control groups were similar to the happy-aroused group in terms of physiological arousal, veridical perception of the confederate, and overt behavior. However, they differed from each other in

---

[5] While this may reflect a lower level of physiological arousal, this interpretation is weakened by the fact that these subjects did show the same pattern and degree of change in HR and reported awareness of physiological symptoms. A more probable explanation is that since these two groups were run several months after the original conditions, the source of invalidity may be instrument variation, through unmonitored changes in the electrodes or the GSR coupler.

experienced emotional state. The informed-arousal subjects reported a neutral set of feelings and stated that the reason for their arousal was the hypnotic suggestion. In contrast, the simplified-arousal group reported the same negative emotion as the happy-aroused group and gave the same type of causal explanations. Their emotion rating was significantly more negative than the neutral midpoint on the eight-item index of emotion (see Figure 1). In other words, despite a posthypnotic suggestion of only the two most basic physiological concomitants of arousal, these subjects who were unaware of the "appropriate" explanation for their arousal did *not* label their emotion as "happy" in accordance with the cognitions provided by the confederate's behavior. Rather, they experienced a negative emotional state.

VII. DISCUSSION

The current study was designed as a modified replication of Schachter and Singer's experiment and an extension of their two-factor theory of emotion. The necessary conditions of strong physiological arousal, lack of an explanation for that arousal, and varied emotional-situational cognitions were all achieved within an experimental setting that controlled for many of the methodological problems of the original study. However, the results reveal a remarkably consistent and coherent pattern of emotional response (especially noteworthy given the small sample size) that is at variance with the interaction pattern predicted by Schachter and Singer. In all cases, subjects with unexplained arousal reported negative emotions, irrespective of the confederate's mood. This finding seems to contradict Schachter and Singer's assumption that unexplained physiological arousal is a neutral, energizing variable that does not contribute directly to the qualitative labeling of the emotion. Whereas Schachter and Singer postulated that the lack of explanation for arousal would motivate people to search in an unbiased way for an appropriate cognition, the present study suggests that it both motivates and biases the search, since it tints perception of that arousal with negative affect. The fact that Marshall (1976) also found self-reports of negative affect among people who lacked an explanation for their strong physiological arousal lends additional support to this alternative view.[6]

[6] It is important to note that Marshall's research provides a connecting link between the current study (which found a significant negative emotional bias) and the Schachter and Singer study (which found no systematic biases from the baseline of the placebo control condition). In the conditions that were an exact replication of Schachter and Singer's experiment, Marshall "replicated" their finding of no difference between epinephrine and placebo subjects. Some of his physiological data suggested that the experienced arousal was not very strong or salient for the subjects, and this may explain why their responses did not differ from those of the unaroused placebo controls. However, when Marshall did make the physiological arousal more salient for the subjects, they reported a negative emotional state. The hypnotic manipulation used in the current study also made the arousal state salient for the subjects, and their consistently negative emotional responses replicate those found by Marshall in his "salient arousal" conditions.

What might account for this negative emotional bias? One possibility is that since there are more terms referring to negative emotions than to positive ones (e.g., Izard, 1971), people might report negative emotions more often on a purely statistical basis alone. Secondly, if noticeable physical arousal is indeed a more frequent correlate of negative emotional experiences in everyday life, then the negative affect reported by subjects in the arousal conditions could be regarded as a logical learned response based on prior experiences. Thirdly, as proposed earlier, it may be that unexplained arousal is always characterized by negative affect because it is, by definition, a state of free-floating anxiety.

The results of the current study suggest that a negative emotional bias will have implications for the person's search for causal information. Subjects who reported negative feelings almost always provided an explanation for them, such as "I'm upset because I don't do well on tests" or "I'm annoyed because this guy keeps joking all the time." In contrast, subjects reporting positive or neutral emotions rarely indicated their cause and gave, instead, such nonexplanatory statements as "I don't know, it's just the way I normally feel."[7] In line with the proposition by Jones and Davis (1965), it seems as if negative experiences are more likely to motivate a search for causal information. People want to know why they feel upset, frightened, or angry, perhaps because they want to control (and thus reduce) the future occurrence of such experiences. On the other hand, they are less motivated to know why they feel happy, pleased, or content, perhaps because they consider such feelings to be their normal baseline condition as opposed to a "deviant" response that demands explanation. Thus people may be more likely to search for explanations of their emotional state when it is a negative or aversive one than when it is positive—a hypothesis that was more elegantly stated by Ralph Waldo Emerson:

> The sun shines and warms and lights us and we have no curiosity to know why this is so; but we ask the reason of all evil, of pain, and hunger, and mosquitoes and silly people. (*Journals*, 1830)

A. Social Influences on Emotion

An important conclusion to be derived from the current research and that of Marshall (1976) is that experienced and expressed emotion are not perfectly correlated. In both studies, subjects with unexplained arousal expressed positive, sociable behaviors while in the presence of the happy confederate but reported that they were not experiencing a corresponding positive mood. According to their postexperimental comments, their behavior was more influenced by social contingencies (i.e., norms of social appropriateness) than

---

[7] In a personal communication, Gerald Blum reported that subjects in his research on affective arousal (Blum, 1972) showed a similar pattern of response, giving more causal statements about their negative feelings and fewer about their positive feelings.

was their more private, experienced feeling. Such deliberate "management" of one's emotional expression is a fairly common experience for people—as when, for example, one laughs and acts happy at a party even though feeling depressed or hurt by some remark. To assume, as Schachter and Singer did, that one's behavior and one's self-reported mood are equivalent indices of emotion is to ignore functional differences between these two responses.

This issue is relevant for interpreting the results of Schachter's followup study on the effects of variations in unexplained arousal on amusement (Schachter & Wheeler, 1962). In this experiment, subjects received an injection of either epinephrine, a placebo, or chlorpromazine (a depressant drug) and were led to believe that there would be no side effects. They then watched an excerpt from a slapstick movie. Whether or not subjects labeled their arousal state in terms of the available cognition of "amusement" was measured by self-reported evaluations of the film and observation of their amusement behavior. Even with large numbers of subjects, there were *no* significant differences between the three conditions on the self-report measures. As for the behavioral measures, the epinephrine subjects and the unaroused placebo controls did not differ on the overall index (although there was a significant difference on the behavior of laughs, as opposed to smiles and grins); the major finding was the depressed behavioral response of the chlorpromazine subjects. This lack of correspondence between amusement behaviors and self-reported evaluations of amusement, combined with the lack of variation in self-report, makes it difficult to assess whether or not there were real differences in experienced emotion. To rely on the expressed behavior alone as an indicator of experienced emotion could be misleading, as both Marshall (1976) and the current research would agree. Furthermore, the rather weak differences between the epinephrine subjects and the placebo controls in the Schachter and Wheeler study not only "replicate" the lack of difference in the Schachter and Singer experiment but fail to provide a serious challenge to the results, the line of reasoning, or the implications of the present study.

A second important conclusion to be drawn from the current research is that people utilize far more sources of information in generating their emotional explanations than was initially suggested by Schachter and Singer's analysis. Schachter and Singer postulated that the emotional label attached to a person's arousal state is primarily a function of the emotion being expressed by another person in the immediate situation. However, while the aroused subjects in the current study perceived correctly the emotion being expressed by the confederate, they did not necessarily use this emotion to label or explain their own state. Their emotional explanations appeared to be a complex function of their past experience, their current life situation, and the immediate situational circumstances rather than just the mood of the confederate. Not only does this finding extend the notion of "cognitive search," but it points to the necessity of reconceptualizing the type of information that is presented by the confederate.

Schachter and Singer's model is based on a theory of social comparison (Festinger, 1954) that argues that self-evaluation is often accomplished by comparing onself with other people. This is particularly true when one has doubts about the appropriateness or correctness of one's feelings, beliefs, or behavior. According to this viewpoint, what is provided by the confederate (the social comparison referent) is *normative* information. The confederate models the "appropriate" way to label the arousal, and the subject adopts a similar response in order to appear normal (both to self and others).

While normative information indicates *how* one should feel and act, it does not necessarily indicate *why* one should feel that way. In other words, normative information is not always *causal* information as well. Although the importance of causal information is recognized by Schachter and Singer, the distinction between causal and normative information is sometimes blurred in their theoretical analysis (e.g., their examples of "cognitions" involve causal explanations in some cases and normative information in others). Basically, they argue that the lack of causal information about one's aroused state is what motivates the search for an emotional cognition. However, in postulating that this cognition is obtained via social comparison processes, they are suggesting that the ultimate solution to the search is normative information. The search is initiated by "why" but terminated by "how." If only normative information is needed, then the subject has to look only at the confederate's reaction and no further in order to evaluate his or her emotion (in a sense, the confederate is a partial cause of the subject's emotional response). However, if the subject wants information as to why the response is occurring, then the confederate's reaction becomes a possible clue to the cause but is not the cause itself. The subject will look beyond the confederate's reaction for such causal information and may arrive at an emotional cognition that differs from the emotion being expressed by the confederate.

B. Unexplained Arousal and Emotional Pathology

As mentioned earlier, a state of unexplained physiological arousal may be a rather rare occurrence in everyday life and thus may not be appropriate paradigm for studying common emotional experiences. However, the negative emotional bias associated with unexplained arousal suggests that it may be a useful paradigm for studying emotional pathology and madness, particularly if it is viewed as just one of a class of anomalous personal and social experiences. Such anomalous reactions are anxiety-provoking because they represent a threat to self-control. Events without causes do not make sense; internal events without apparent, immediate explanations are irrational. People are sometimes willing to employ rather tenuous causal relationships to account for such occurrences, even to the point of limiting such explanations to labels or nominal antecedents, as in "It's my nerves." But for most people, on most occasions, the experience of an anomalous event generates some search for suitable causal linkages.

One might assume that people engage in a scientific (unbiased) search, in which they seek out and consider all possible evidence in an objective way. However, it may be more correct to assume that they are biased toward certain types of explanations as a result of their past history of reinforcement for classes of explanation or ways of thinking about new experiences. Thus, some people may learn to seek explanations in the physical environment (e.g., "It's probably due to a virus going around"). Others may bias their search toward social sources of explanations (e.g., "My boss must be upsetting me"). Once acceptable causal links are established to account for a particular internal reaction, it may be assumed that the generic properties of the linkage will, in the future, make some types of explanation more available. For example, where reaction X is effectively linked to bodily processes or health issues, future comparable reactions are also more likely to be explained by reference to other specific instances of biological functioning, such as flu, fatigue, tension, and metabolic deficiencies. An extreme bias toward locating causes within bodily processes may be an underlying basis for such pathological responses as hypochondria or psychosomatic symptoms.

Future research on this process of searching for causal explanations would provide a clearer (if more complex) picture of how people come to understand their internal responses. Furthermore, following from an earlier argument, the study of this process would benefit from an experimental analysis that focused on children's reactions to novel or anomalous events. This line of research might also illuminate the process by which particular forms of emotional pathology develop as a consequence of biased explanations for unexplained arousal. We are currently conducting exploratory research on this biasing process, again using hypnosis as a methodological tool to create unexplained arousal in subjects who are programmed to search for a likely cause within only one class of explanations: body, people, environment, the past, or spiritual forces. The various explanations generated by these subjects are indeed limited to the suggested generic category and, in some cases, result in reactions that observers judge to be "irrational" (Zimbardo & Maslach, 1978).

1. A Model of Madness. It is possible that delusional systems can be understood as the individual's attempt to explain or make sense of some unusual or novel experience. Zimbardo (1977) has begun to develop a model of madness that is based on this notion of cognitive search. He proposes that madness begins with the perception of some intolerable discontinuity, either in oneself or in one's relations with the environment. Unexplained arousal would be one example of a discontinuity, as would sudden anxiety, a violation of an expectancy, a change in physical or social status, a loss of someone or something loved, an inability to perform a customary function, a sensory experience without apparent sensory stimuli, etc. Since people assume that there is continuity, lawfulness, and regularity in the world, they try to impose a cognitive structure upon the experienced discontinuity in order to make it familiar, under-standable, more predictable, and, ideally, controllable. Thus, when a discon-tinuity is perceived, a cognitive search for a causal explanation is instigated. For some discontinuities, there are ready explanations provided by the culture in the form of truisms, homilies, common sense, folklore, tradition, etc., and therefore the search process is limited. However, for other discontinuities, there are not immediately available explanations because the real cause of the discontinuity may be unknown, nonsalient, unacceptable, or overlooked. In these cases, a more extensive search process is required.

Critical to the individual's search for an explanation is the early determi-nation of whether a potential cause is located inside the person (mind or body) or is in the external environment. This determination is often made by a social comparison analysis of the behavior of others in the same situation. To the extent that others are perceived as reacting in ways comparable to one's own, it is probable that there is a common, external cause. If the comparison persons are not reacting similarly to the situation, then the cause is more likely to be internal and specific to the individual. For example, if all the people sit-ting in a room begin to feel hot and sweaty, they will look for an external cause (e.g., the heat's been turned up) to explain this discontinuity. However, if one person begins to feel hot and sweaty, while everyone else complains of being chilly, then that person will look for a specific, internal explanation (e.g., I'm getting sick, I'm nervous about being with these people).

According to Zimbardo, two different search processes are involved. One is a search for *rationality*, in which the individual looks for causal explanations that will account for the perceived discontinuity. In addition, there is a search for *normality*, in which the individual looks for normative information that will establish that he or she is just like everyone else. Either search is intensified and will engender more anxiety if the other proves negative. An experience that cannot be explained by the individual and is thus considered irrational (e.g., a nightmare) will produce less anxiety if it is seen as "normal" (i.e., everyone has them). On the other hand, an experience that is abnormal (i.e., it's happening only to me) will be less upsetting for the individual if there is a rational explanation for it.

Zimbardo postulates that these search processes are often biased ones. They can be biased by selectively attending to some probable causes and excluding others, as was suggested earlier. Such selective attention may result from a history of reinforcement, from childhood on, for certain classes of explanation. These search processes can also be biased in the ways one processes information, stores it in memory, and retrieves and analyzes it. Biases can also exist in the way one finally presents such causal evidence to other people. According to Zimbardo, when certain biases are present in the search process, it increases the probability that the individual will be labeled as "mad." In this "Catch-22" model, the process by which one tries to prove to oneself and others that one is either rational or normal or both is often the basis by which others judge one to be crazy. For example, a man who cannot hear people talking (perhaps because of a growing deafness of which he is unaware) may develop a paranoid delusion that people are whispering behind his back and plotting to harm him. This is a rational explanation of the apparent change in their behavior and their denial to him of their whispering, but it is also the evidence to others that the man is psychologically disturbed.

Zimbardo's model suggests that mental illness is not an impairment of one's cognitive abilities, as is often assumed, but is a normal cognitive process used to explain an unusual state or event. It extends and expands Maher's (1974) hypothesis about the perceptual genesis of delusional thinking and provides a unique social psychological perspective on the dynamics of abnormal behavior and on its treatment.

VIII. CONCLUSION

The theory and research presented in this chapter began with questions about emotion but have ended with a consideration of emotional pathology. Although it is possible that the Schachter and Singer model holds for the development of emotional explanations, the evidence presented here suggests that it is not an appropriate model for everyday emotional experience. However, the idea that the concept of unexplained arousal may be a key to understanding emotional pathology is an exciting one that we intend to pursue in future research. The importance of emotion for understanding fundamental psychological processes is becoming more and more evident, and once again it is being accorded a central position within the field of psychology.

ACKNOWLEDGMENTS

I wish to thank my colleagues, Philip Zimbardo and Gary Marshall, for their advice and assistance with the experiment, as well as for their help in training the hypnosis subjects. I am also very grateful to the following people who served as confederates, observers, and interviewers: Virginia Dupraw, Nancy Green, Jocelyn Gunnar, Craig Haney, John Manzolati, Neil Morse, Nancy Perry, and John Rhead. Requests for reprints should be sent to Christina Maslach, Department of Psychology, University of California, Berkeley, California 94720.

REFERENCES

Bem, D. J. Self-perception theory. In L. Berkowitz (Ed), *Advances in experimental social psychology*, Vol. 6. New York: Academic Press, 1972.

Blum, G. S. Hypnotic programming techniques in psychological experiments. In E. Fromm & R. E. Shor (Eds.), *Hypnosis: Research developments and perspectives*. Chicago: Aldine-Atherton, 1972.

Cooper, L. M. Hypnotic amnesia. In E. Fromm & R. E. Shor (Eds.) *Hypnosis: Research developments and perspectives*. Chicago: Aldine-Atherton, 1972.

Dostoevski, F. M. *A diary of a writer* (1876), *4*, July–August.

Easterbrook, J. A. The effect of emotion on cue utilization and the organization of behavior. *Psychological Review*, 1959, *66*, 183–201.

Evans, F. J., & Kihlstrom, J. F. Posthypnotic amnesia as disrupted retrieval. *Journal of Abnormal Psychology*, 1973, *82*, 317–323.

Festinger, L. A theory of social comparison processes. *Human Relations*, 1954, *7*, 114–140.

Izard, C. E. *The face of emotion*. New York: Appleton-Century-Crofts, 1971.

James, W. What is an emotion? *Mind*, 1884, *9*, 188–205.

Jones, E. E., & Davis, K. E. From acts to dispositions: The attribution process in person perception. In L. Berkowitz (Ed.), *Advances in experimental social psychology*, Vol. 2. New York: Academic Press, 1965.

Jones, E. E., Kanouse, D. E., Kelley, H. H., Nisbett, R. E., Valins, S., & Weiner, B. (Eds.). *Attribution: Perceiving the causes of behavior*. Morristown. N.J.: General Learning Press, 1971.

Lazarus, R. S. Emotions and adaptation: Conceptual and empirical relations. In W. J. Arnold (Ed.), *Nebraska symposium on motivation*. Lincoln: University of Nebraska Press, 1968.

Lenox, J. R. Effect of hypnotic analgesia on verbal report and cardiovascular responses to ischemic pain. *Journal of Abnormal Psychology*, 1970, *75*, 199–206.

Leventhal, H. Emotions: A basic problem for social psychology. In C. Nemeth (Ed.), *Social psychology: Classic and contemporary integrations*. Chicago: Rand McNally, 1974.

London, H., & Nisbett, R. E. (Eds.). *Thought and feeling: Cognitive alteration of feeling states*. Chicago: Aldine, 1974.

Maher, B. Delusional thinking and cognitive disorder. In H. London & R. E. Nisbett (Eds.), *Thought and feeling: Cognitive alteration of feeling states*. Chicago: Aldine, 1974.

Mandler, G. *Mind and emotion*. New York: John Wiley, 1975.

Marañon, G. Contribution à l'étude de l'action émotive de l'adrénaline. *Revue Française d'Endocrinologie*, 1924, *2*, 301–325.

Marshall, G. The affective consequences of "inadequately explained" physiological arousal. Unpublished doctoral dissertation, Stanford University, 1976.

Maslach, C. Negative emotional biasing of unexplained arousal. *Journal of Personality and Social Psychology*, 1979, in press.

Nowlis, V. The concept of mood. In S. M. Farber & R. H. L. Wilson (Eds.), *Conflict and creativity*. New York: McGraw-Hill, 1963.

Plutchik, R., & Ax, A. F. A critique of "determinants of emotional state" by Schachter and Singer (1962). *Psychophysiology*, 1967, *4*, 79–82.

Sarbin, T. R., & Slagle, R. W. Hypnosis and psychophysiological outcomes. In E. Fromm & R. E. Shor (Eds.), *Hypnosis: Research developments and perspectives*. Chicago: Aldine-Atherton, 1972.

Schachter, S. *Emotion, obesity, and crime*. New York: Academic Press, 1971.

Schachter, S, & Singer, J. E. Cognitive, social, and physiological determinants of emotional state. *Psychological Review*, 1962, *69*, 379–399.

Schachter, S., & Wheeler, L. Epinephrine, chlorpromazine, and amusement. *Journal of Abnormal and Social Psychology*, 1962, *65*, 121–128.

Shor, R. E., & Orne, E. C. *The Harvard Group Scale of Hypnotic Susceptibility, Form A*. Palo Alto, Calif.: Consulting Psychologists Press, 1962.

Tomkins, S. S. *Affect, imagery, consciousness*. New York: Springer, 1962.

Walster, E. Passionate love. In B. I. Murstein (Ed.), *Theories of attraction and love*. New York: Springer Press, 1971.

Walters, R. H., & Amoroso, D. M. Cognitive and emotional determinants of the occurrence of imitative behaviour. *British Journal of Social and Clinical Psychology*, 1967, 6, 174–185.

Zimbardo, P. G. Understanding madness: A cognitive–social model of psychopathology. Invited address at the annual meeting of the Canadian Psychological Association, Vancouver, June 1977.

Zimbardo, P. G., & Maslach, C. Biased searches for causal explanations of experienced discontinuities. Unpublished paper, 1978.

Zimbardo, P. G., Maslach, C., & Marshall, G. Hypnosis and the psychology of cognitive and behavioral control. In E. Fromm & R. E. Shor (Eds.), *Hypnosis: Research developments and perspectives*. Chicago: Aldine-Atherton, 1972.

Index